John C. T[...]
Edin[...]
1978

ITALY:
AN HISTORICAL SURVEY

ITALY:
AN HISTORICAL SURVEY

JACK F. BERNARD

DAVID & CHARLES : NEWTON ABBOT

To my mother and father, in gratitude

ISBN 0 7153 5405 1

First published in 1970 in the United States of America by Doubleday & Company Inc

First published in Great Britain in 1971 by David & Charles (Publishers) Limited
South Devon House Newton Abbot Devon

Copyright © Doubleday & Company Inc

Printed in Great Britain by
Clarke Doble & Brendon Limited Plymouth

CONTENTS

FOREWORD   IX

I   THE FALL OF THE ROMAN EMPIRE AND THE
    INVASION OF THE BARBARIANS (397–731 A.D.)   1

II THE EMERGENCE OF SUCCESSORS TO CAESAR
    (731–962)   54

III ITALY IN THE MIDDLE AGES: The Clash Between
    Empire and Papacy (962–1418)   100

    1. The Holy Roman Church and the Holy Roman
       Empire   100
    2. The Rise of the Italian Cities   122
    3. The Triumph of the Popes   139
    4. The Fall of the Medieval Empire   151
    5. The Collapse of the Medieval Papacy   170
    6. The Final Gasp of Empire   180
    7. Italy at the Close of the Middle Ages   186

	8.	The Transition from the Middle Ages to the Renaissance	195
IV		AN AGE OF RENEWAL: The Renaissance (1400–1580)	230
	1.	The Early Renaissance (1400–1464)	233
	2.	The Golden Age of the Florentine Renaissance (1464–1492)	244
	3.	The Barbarian Invasions (1494–1537)	253
	4.	The High Renaissance (1499–1521)	272
	5.	The *Cinquecento:* Italy in the Sixteenth Century	286
V		ITALY IN THE MODERN WORLD (1580–1814)	298
	1.	The End of the *Cinquecento*	298
	2.	The Age of Stagnation: Politics (1580–1789)	310
	3.	The Age of Stagnation: The Arts (1580–1789)	318
	4.	The Napoleonic Era (1789–1815)	326
VI		FROM ABSOLUTISM TO INDEPENDENCE (1814–1870)	340
	1.	A Time for Conspiracy (1814–1848)	340
	2.	A Time for Diplomacy (1848–1859)	357
	3.	A Time for Violence (1859–1870)	370
VII		THE NEW ITALY (1871–1920)	385
	1.	The Opening Years (1871–1896)	385
	2.	The New Italy and the New Nationalism (1896–1915)	397
	3.	The War and the Peace (1915–1920)	413
VIII		THE AGE OF FASCISM: Benito Mussolini (1920–1945)	425
	1.	The Rise and Triumph of Fascism (1920–1922)	425

Contents

2.	Il Duce (1922–1939)	442
3.	The End of a Dream (1939–1945)	459

APPENDIX I — Chronological Tables of Popes and Emperors — 485

APPENDIX II — Genealogy of the Medici — 494

APPENDIX III — Skeleton Table of the Kings of the Two Sicilies — 495

APPENDIX IV — The Visconti and Sforza Houses of Milan — 497

BIBLIOGRAPHY — 498

INDEX — 510

MAPS

1.	The Barbarian Kingdoms of Europe c. 500 A.D.	2–3
2.	The Empire of Charles the Great	55
3.	Italy c. 1300 A.D.	142–143
4.	Italy in the 15th and 16th centuries	254
5.	The Napoleonic Empire (1810)	328–329
6.	The Unification of Italy (1859–1870)	371
7.	The Italian Empire (1939)	444

FOREWORD

No one knows better than one who has attempted it that it is impossible to write a one-volume history of Italy which is satisfactory in all aspects. The chronological span of Italian history is so vast, the number of political entities involved so great, and the complex of pertinent social and intellectual factors so massive, that volumes rather than chapters are required for a merely adequate treatment of the subject. This book, therefore, is, of necessity, only a sketch in outline. It makes little pretense to original investigation, and none at all to a complete examination of the voluminous literature which deals with every aspect of Italian history.

The purpose of the work is to convey to the general reader an overall impression of the history of Italy by describing the themes which have dominated the period between the fall of the Roman Empire and the end of World War II: the barbarian invasions, the rise and fall of the medieval papacy, the foundation and collapse of the Holy Roman Empire, the intellectual revolution of the Renaissance, the *Risorgimento,* and the birth and death of Fascism. So limited an objective presupposes a work of selection; and perhaps no two persons would agree upon what to put in and what to leave out. Certainly, many readers will find that some personality or some event of special interest to them has not been mentioned, or has been treated in a cursory fashion. The author, while regretting that circumstance, hopes that such readers will refer to the list, given at the end of the book, for works which treat of various aspects of Italian history in more detail.

No account of Italian history would be complete, of course, or even intelligible, without a comprehensive treatment of the one great supranational, and for that reason most consistently unifying and civilizing, influence in the peninsula, the Roman Catholic Church. In this respect, the author has made a particular effort to maintain an academic objectivity. If there are, occasionally, words which seem harsh to the reader, he is asked to remember that an ideal is not to be judged by way of the means adopted for its attainment. The ideal, once conceived, exists independently of human foolishness; the means, however, may be judged as objectively as any other product of man's fallibility.

As a setting for these more important developments, the author has attempted to give only what is necessary concerning the growth and decay of dynasties, the territorial changes, the wars, and the involved relations between principalities and nations which accompanied the developments which it is the purpose of this work to relate. The reader will see that those are the circumstances, and not the ultimate reality, of history.

Finally, the author must apologize in advance for any ideas which appear in this book for which proper acknowledgment has not been made. Such acknowledgment would entail an apparatus which would be excessively cumbersome in a general work of this kind. Moreover, as every student knows, it is not always easy, when working extensively in a particular field for a long period of time, to determine precisely whether a thought is one's own, or whether, having been taken from another, it has slipped into the subconscious mind only to emerge later as one's own contribution. In the final analysis, the author claims for himself only such errors and inadequacies as a careful reading of the book may uncover.

I
THE FALL OF THE ROMAN EMPIRE AND THE INVASION OF THE BARBARIANS
(397-731 A.D.)

In the year A.D. 475, a handsome and wealthy young man named Romulus was proclaimed Emperor of Rome. In the year A.D. 476, Romulus, now mockingly called Augustulus, "the little Augustus," was deposed from the throne of the Caesars by a barbarian general.* With that event, the Roman

---

* For our purposes, it is sufficient merely to record the fact of Rome's progressive disintegration without delving into the almost limitless number of causes which have been adduced to explain it. The classic (but by no means the standard) explanation is, of course, that of Gibbon, who attributes Rome's fall to the rise of Christianity. More recent literature on the subject is vast and, indeed, there are almost as many opinions as there are historians. This wealth of speculation, all of it presented logically and argued persuasively, may well serve to convince the reader that the decline and fall of the Empire was the result, not of any single one of the causes advanced, but of the interplay of all of them and of many more besides. The problem which faces the historian is to determine the role to be assigned to each one in its just proportion—a task which awaits the appearance of a genius of analysis and synthesis of Aquinas' caliber. Until then, the field remains one of fascinating, and sometimes brilliant, speculation. The reader will note that the present author seeks, albeit briefly, such causes in economic and social factors—a tendency which is strengthened by observing, in mid-twentieth century, the progress of another empire, one analogous to that of Rome, as it totters toward dissolution under the weight of those same factors.

For a thorough discussion of the various probable causes of the fall of the Roman Empire, one may refer particularly to the following: Sinkhovitch, Vladimir G., *Toward the Understanding of Jesus*, New York, 1937, pp. 84-139, where it is argued that the Empire collapsed because of the exhaustion of its soil. Huntington, Ellsworth, "Climatic Change and Agricultural Exhaustion of Elements in the Fall of Rome," in *Quarterly Journal of Economics*, Vol. XXXI, 1917, pp. 173-208, which offers in evidence a change in climate. Seeck, Otto, *Geschichte des Untervangs der antiken*, Vol. I, 4th ed., Berlin, 1921, pp. 269-307, finds an intriguing factor in what the author calls *Die Ausrottung der Besten*—"The extermination of the most capable men" by the

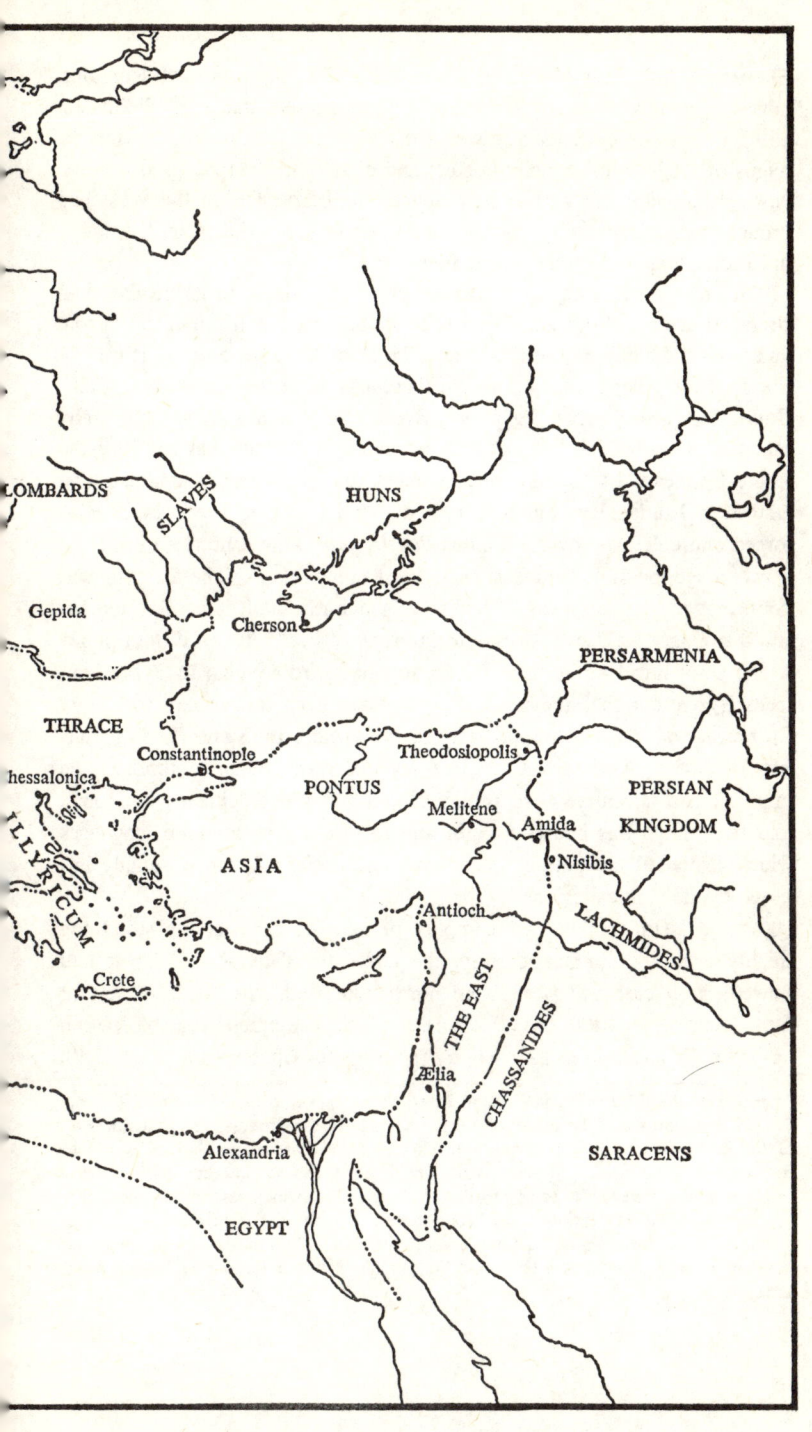

Empire in Italy formally came to an end. The deposition of Romulus, however, merely served to formalize a situation that had existed for decades. The reality of Roman power had long since disappeared, during the reigns of Augustulus' equally august, and equally ineffectual, predecessors. Now, in principle as well as in practice, the barbarians in the West had brought to victory their centuries-old struggle against Roman hegemony in Europe, and the Empire was no more.

The state which they thus destroyed was one which, in its heyday, had stretched from remote and barbarous Britain to the frontiers of Persia, and from the banks of the Rhine and the Danube to the Sahara. It was an Empire comprising many races—Etruscans, Ligurians, Iberians, Celts, Gauls, Basques, Greeks, Egyptians, Syrians, Armenians, Jews, and many others—but one which had been able to impose a functional unity on the whole by means of an unparalleled talent for military and administrative efficiency. Roman law and Roman order had prevailed everywhere, reinforced and enhanced by the famous *Pax Romana*—the centuries of internal peace made possible and sustained by Roman might. The Empire was bound together by a system of highways which ran in all directions and ensured comparatively swift communication and travel between distant points of the sprawling Empire, from Cadiz to Milan, from Milan to Byzantium, from Byzantium to Palmyra, and, of course, from everywhere to Rome. Currency, weights, and measures were everywhere the same. The inhabitants of Africa, Asia Minor and Europe, like their Italian brethren in the imperial confraternity, were proud to call themselves citizens of Rome; and they made this boast in Latin and in Greek, the common languages which cemented the political, economic and social coherence initially imposed by the Roman legions.

At the head of this vast complex of peoples and nations stood the mighty arbiter of human destiny, the *Urbs,* the City, Rome. To it had flowed, from east and west, from north and south, the spoils of war at first; then, taxes, tribute, and gifts. Even after the official seat of Roman government had been transferred, by the Emperor Constantine, in A.D. 330,

---

emperors of the third century. Nillson, Martin P., *Imperial Rome,* London, 1926, pp. 317–67, maintains that the decay of Rome was due to the progressive mongrelization of the Latin race by intermarriage with ex-slaves and barbarians. A further jolt to democratic sensibilities is given by Rostovtzeff, M. I., *Social and Economic History of the Roman Empire,* rev. ed., Oxford, 1957, pp. 535 ff., which asserts that the blame lay with the social revolution which brought about the absorption of the upper classes by the lower and thus caused a fatal lowering of standards. For the gist of these and many more such theories, see Haywood, R. M., *The Myth of Rome's Fall,* New York, 1958.

from Rome to Constantinople, visitors to the ancient capital were astonished at the incredible wealth everywhere on display, at the temples, amphitheaters, forums, circuses and palaces, all glittering with precious marbles and bronzes, and at the ancient aristocracy, equally ablaze with the jewels and silks of the Orient.

These riches, however, acquired directly or indirectly by conquest, were the manifestations of an economic situation which, more than the machinations of hostile barbarians, contained the seeds of Roman destruction. In the latter days of the Empire, society was divided into two classes: there were the very rich and there were the unspeakably poor; and there was hardly anyone in between. The relatively simple life of the free man of ancient Rome, of the time of Caesar, had disappeared and been forgotten. The trades and the arts had been abandoned, for the most part, to slaves and serfs. The great Roman middle class, which had been of enormous economic strength and importance during the Roman Republic and the early Empire, had sunk to the level of the plebs. Outside the City, small farmers had been reduced to a position little better than that of the serfs, and the great landowners gathered, by means as often foul as fair, vast tracts of land into their own hands. By the beginning of the fifth century, half of the Roman population were slaves.

Taxes, that classic destroyer of the health and wealth of nations, increased and finally became unbearable as the demands of the Empire grew. The imperial government, which was controlled by the rich, gradually succeeded in shifting this enormous burden from their own shoulders to those of the poor; and thus, the rich grew even richer, while those who had been merely poor were now made destitute. Such taxation was necessary, the people were told, in order to meet the exigencies of the imperial treasury: there were wars to be fought, mercenaries to be engaged for the Roman legions, barbarian chiefs to be bribed, doles to be paid out.

A few emperors were perceptive enough to foresee the disaster that lay at the end of this road, but even these, too Roman to admit even to themselves that the Empire had reached the stage where her commitments, both domestic and foreign, exceeded her means, were unable to do more than offer meaningless alternatives. Diocletian, for example, decreed that farmers could pay their taxes in farm produce, and laborers could pay in labor. But this arrangement, though it provided some small relief to the poor, ignored the fact that, while it relieved them of the necessity for finding the hard cash with which to pay taxes, it also deprived them of their means of livelihood—the farmer of his vegetables, and the workman of his time.

Rome's system of crushing taxation had been designed to be applied intermittently, in time of crisis when supplementary funds were required to meet a national emergency. But, in the usual way of taxes, once imposed they had remained; then, at the appearance of the next crisis, they were again increased. Had the system been applied according to its original concept, it is possible that the Roman taxpayer could have found the means, and the courage, to meet these emergencies on an *ad hoc* basis; but with a method of exorbitant taxation maintained over a period of two centuries, the citizens were not only deprived of the means, but also drained of the will, to support an omnivorous state. As one historian has put it, "The emperors did not merely fleece their flock; they skinned it."

The sheep, once skinned, began to take on the characteristics of wolves. In the cities of the Empire, an enormous and unruly class sprang up, composed of the disenfranchised, the unemployed and the unemployable, the *nouveaux pauvres* and the perennially poverty-stricken. It was a vicious, disorderly mob, given to rioting and looting and, potentially, if a competent leader had appeared on the scene, perhaps to revolution. The government, since it could neither disperse this new class nor control it, was forced to bribe it, and a new form of popular opiate was introduced: the famous *panem et circenses,* the "bread and circuses" by means of which the emperors hoped to feed and amuse the mobs and to keep their minds off more serious, and more dangerous, things. This form of public dole—welfare "in kind," as it were—was paid, of course, out of public funds, which in turn necessitated newer and higher taxes and therefore drove more and more of the poor into the ranks of the recipients of this ignominious tribute. It was not the first time in history, nor the last, that an empire set about the task of demoralizing its citizenry and of taxing itself into dissolution, all under the pretext of maintaining public order.

As poverty increased, the population declined while the expenses of government did not. Finally, in order to prevent the population from becoming irreversibly divided into an enormous mass of the utterly destitute and a tiny group of the fantastically rich, the government had recourse to an extreme measure. It was decreed that, in order to preserve the means of production and of services, and to maintain the flow of state revenue, Romans could no longer change their occupations or their economic status. Farmers were obliged to remain on their farms, workmen were bound to their labor, mechanics to their trades, civic officials to their responsibilities. This system of bondage was not entirely new to the Empire. It had long existed in certain of the Eastern provinces. The innovation consisted in its application to the Empire as a whole. With this enactment, tens of millions of men were reduced to the level of bondsmen and serfs. "The Empire," Mikhail Rostovtzeff has concluded, "was one vast prison."

By the end of the fourth century, therefore, the Empire as a whole, and the West in particular, lay prostrate and virtually bankrupt. Its restless and politically indifferent population was presided over by a series of shadowy emperors, created at the whim of the military, whose subjects had, through taxation, lost all property and incentive for the maintenance of the state, and who had, through subsistence on public funds, abandoned any pretense of individual independence and self-respect. It is small wonder that the barbarians, when they finally came, had little trouble in overturning the Empire. The Romans, through a century of political, social and economic corruption, of blundering reforms which only exacerbated an already hopeless situation, had already subverted themselves.

The barbarian tribes themselves lived a very different sort of life on their lands beyond the Danube and the Rhine. They were bound together by a common Teutonic blood into a simple, and essentially democratic, form of society. They lived in small communities which were banded together into tribes; the latter, in turn, were united in a loose confederation which acted in concert only when required to take unified military action. At that point, the entire male population of the tribes were expected to take up arms. In time of peace, the barbarians supported themselves by hunting, by cultivating their lands, and by tending their flocks. Their needs—as reflected by their buildings, which were rude and temporary constructions, and by their clothing, which was designed for warmth and freedom of movement rather than for style—were simple and their lives uncomplicated. Their arts were functionally primitive, and the vast majority of the people could neither read nor write; and it was not among their ambitions to learn to do so. Only war and hunting interested them, and they excelled in these activities by dint of constant exercise. But, for all their lack of polish and their devotion to violent pursuits, these barbarians were a free, self-respecting, self-governing, and moralistic people, who freely elected their leaders and who met periodically in one great assembly to enact their laws.

Their religion, as might be expected, was a primitive one. Their gods, of which there were many, were the personifications of the natural forces and human virtues most feared and admired by the tribes. Many of the barbarians who lived on the frontiers of the Empire had embraced Christianity, but, since they invariably chose to become Arians rather than Catholics, they were regarded by the Romans more as barbarians who were heretics into the bargain rather than as fellow Christians. Such conversions therefore did little to smooth relations between the barbarians and the now almost wholly Catholic Empire.

Nonetheless, it would be a mistake to imagine that an unbridgeable chasm existed between the German tribes and the Latins. Many of the barbarians had been trained in the armies of Rome and had lived in Rome, or in Constantinople, or in Trier or Milan, and they were familiar with the military arts of Rome and with Roman civilization as a whole. In addition, Roman merchants traded regularly with the barbarian tribes. In one way or another, most of the leaders of the barbarians had come into contact with—and therefore, to a certain extent, under the influence of—Roman civilization, and they regarded that civilization with a superstitious amazement and respect which, at times, bordered on religious awe. Athanarich, a Gothic chief, doubtlessly reflected accurately the sentiments of his fellow barbarians when he caught his first glimpse of imperial Constantinople. "Without doubt," he exclaimed, "the Emperor is a god on earth!"

Despite such exchanges and attitudes, however, it cannot be denied that the Romans and the barbarians were basically unsympathetic to one another. It was unlikely that two societies of such divergent ideals and ways of life could exist peaceably side by side and, in fact, the struggle between the Empire and the Teutons was almost continuous since the days of the first Caesar. For several centuries, the might, the diplomacy, and the money of Rome had prevailed. But then, as deterioration set in and the imperial system began visibly to disintegrate, the tide changed. By the opening years of the fifth century, the doom of the Empire had been sealed, and the City, the Head of the World, Rome herself, lay open to any takers.

The takers were not long in coming. In the year 376, a rumor had spread throughout the Empire that an enormous mass of barbarians was in motion beyond the Danube. Such reports were easy to ignore, for they were nothing new. The Romans shrugged and went back to their bread and their circuses. Then, refugees began streaming southward, across the imperial frontiers. They brought with them news of a hitherto unheard-of and terrible force, a horde of bloodthirsty savages whom they called Huns. These Huns, they reported, had come sweeping out of the East, driving all before them, and they were now heading toward the borders of the Empire. As it turned out, however, it was not the Huns whom the Empire had cause to fear, but the Germanic tribes. The latter, fleeing before the Hunnic invaders, crossed the Empire's frontiers by the tens of thousands, seeking protection within the confines of Roman territory. Now the Roman government had not infrequently been willing and able, in the past, to absorb entire tribes within the Empire, either as settlers or as paid military mercenaries. But suddenly to be called upon to provide for this horde of landless, penniless, and starving immigrants was another matter. The tottering economy of the Empire—even in the East, which was considerably better off than Italy—was clearly unequal to the task. Since the Empire could not provide for the barbarians, the sole alternative was to fight them, and thereby either to destroy them or to drive them back into the arms of the Huns. The battle took place in 378, not far from Constantinople. The Teutons, driven by desperation, completely routed the Roman legions, and the Emperor himself, Valens, was killed. Thereafter, the provinces of the East were the prey of the Goths, the Huns, and of sundry small tribes egged on by famine. It was all that splendid Constantinople could do to keep the conquerors outside her walls.

The significance of these events was not lost upon the West. There, all possible measures were taken to protect the Empire from the imminent danger of foreign, whether Gothic or Hunnic, invasion. The cost was high: the Roman armies were filled with barbarian mercenaries, and the emperors surrendered all effective military authority into the hands of the barbarian chieftains who were the new commanders of the legions of Rome. The greatest and most famous of these barbarians, who were paid to fight Rome's battles against their fellow barbarians, was Stilicho, a Vandal. This Stilicho secured his paramount position in Italy by audaciously seeking, and winning, in marriage the niece of the reigning emperor, Theodosius I. When Theodosius died in 395, the Empire was divided between his two sons, Honorius (who took the West), and Arcadius (who got the East). Stilicho was designated, by the will of Theodosius, as guardian to the new Emperor of the West. Not content with being Honorius' guardian and cousin (by marriage), Stilicho aspired to become also his father-in-law; and in 398 he arranged the marriage of his daughter, Maria, to the fourteen-year-old Caesar. Honorius, however, seemed as little suited to the responsibilities of the marital bed as he was to those of the imperial throne. According to Zosimus, a contemporary observer, Maria was still a virgin when she died ten years later. It is perhaps a more apt commentary on Honorius' abilities that his reign of twenty-eight years was characterized by Edward Gibbon in one sentence: "In the eventful history of a reign of twenty-eight years, it will seldom be necessary to mention the name of the Emperor Honorius." The young emperor was perfectly content to allow the courageous and skillful barbarian Stilicho to manage the affairs of the Empire. He himself, for his part, was largely content to confine his activities to the barnyard, and his most serious concern was the care and feeding of the imperial chicken flock at Ravenna.

Stilicho, capable though he was, was destined to become the victim of policies over which he had no control. The Emperor Theodosius had kept the Goths more or less at peace by making use of them in war, and by paying a large annual bribe—thinly disguised as a subsidy—to them in peace. The new emperor at Constantinople, Arcadius—a young man as weak as his Western brother, but without the good fortune to have acquired a talented father-in-law—refused to continue these payments, and the Empire found itself now full of Gothic warriors who had suddenly become idle, quarrelsome, and hungry. The barbarians had lived, under Theodosius, for war and plunder; and now they were arbitrarily deprived of both. But they found that they had something better: a new leader, Alaric, who knew how to make the most of the situation. The Empire obviously was dying, Alaric pointed out to the Goths; why not take advantage of this circumstance and found a Gothic kingdom for themselves? In the same year as the ascension of Honorius and Arcadius, therefore, Alaric led a vast Gothic army into Greece, where the barbarians were allowed to fight, plunder, and rape to their hearts' content. Glorious Athens herself escaped destruction only by surrendering to the invaders every item of value that could be moved from the city. Stilicho attempted to come to the rescue of Greece, and he had just managed to force the Goths into an indefensible position when he was recalled to the West to put down a revolution in Africa. Arcadius by now had come to his senses, and he took time out from his study of religious dogma to offer a new alliance to Alaric. The Goth, with an eye toward the future, accepted, and he was allowed to settle with his followers at Epirus.

For the next four years, the Empire was at peace. At Ravenna, Honorius fed his chickens. At Constantinople, Arcadius caviled with his theologians. At Epirus, Alaric drove the armorers to outfit his army with new weapons in record time.

By 401, the Goths were ready for their next move. Alaric had already pillaged the moderately prosperous European provinces of the Eastern Empire; those of Asia were inaccessible; Constantinople had already proved impervious to his armies. There now remained the wealth of Italy and of fabled Rome herself, and it was in that direction that Alaric turned his eyes and his armies. The Goth's cupidity was perhaps fortified by superstition. Claudian, a contemporary historian, tells us that a mysterious voice had predicted to Alaric that he would one day be master in Italy and in Rome: "The Alps of Italy will flatten at your approach, and unto the

City herself will you penetrate." Whatever Alaric's motivation, it is certain that to Italy he came like a whirlwind out of the Balkans and across the Alps. Refugees by the thousands streamed before him into Milan and Ravenna. The country dwellers forsook their open farms for the putative safety of the city walls, while the more fortunate rich gathered up their portable wealth and embarked for the islands of the Mediterranean.

Meanwhile, Stilicho, the barbarian protector of the Roman way, had not been idle. Gathering together a hastily collected army from the provinces, he marched out to meet the conquering Goths. The latter, good Christians all, were at Pollentia when Stilicho found them, at prayer—for it was Easter morning, 402, and their religious sensibilities would not permit robbery or rape on so holy a day. Though the Goths were caught at a disadvantage, they fought courageously, and the battle was indecisive. Alaric and his men were able to retreat in good order—toward the now unprotected city of Rome. Before they reached the City, however, Honorius offered a stupendous bribe to the Goths, and thus persuaded them to leave Italy.

The shaken Emperor, who had been residing at Milan, decided that he needed a safer capital and, after considering first the transfer of the throne to Gaul, decided upon Ravenna, a city protected from sea attack by its shoals and from land by its impassable marshes and swamps. He was surprised and disappointed when, shortly after Alaric's withdrawal and the translation of the imperial capital, all Italy—and Ravenna as well—trembled once more to the tread of a new barbarian invader, Radagaisus, who came at the head of some 200,000 Ostrogoths, Vandals, Quadi, and Alani. Once more Stilicho marched out, and this time he saved the day, and the Empire, by defeating, with a relatively small force, his fellow barbarians. Moreover, he restored honor to the throne, at least partially, by throwing Radagaisus in chains at the feet of Honorius. The imperial court, from emperor through patricians and bishops down to the most humble slave, now felt themselves safe at last.

So safe, in fact, did they feel that Honorius consented to the execution of the man who had saved him and his throne. Persuaded by the imperial chancellor Olympius that Stilicho was plotting to put his son on the throne in Honorius' place, the Emperor allowed the jealous chancellor to order Stilicho's execution. The Goth, as proof of his innocence, did not resist, but offered his neck to the sword. Olympius then commanded the slaughter of thousands of Stilicho's supporters, including the leaders of the barbarian legions, which were Italy's sole defense against invaders.

Alaric, who had been watching events closely, now crossed the Alps with an army more mighty and savage than ever, complaining loudly that the four thousand pounds of gold promised to him by Honorius had not been forthcoming. When Honorius refused to pay, the Goths sacked Aquileia and Cremona. Then, their ranks swelled by the recruitment of the survivors from among Stilicho's followers, they marched down the Via Flaminia to the walls of Rome. For the first time in six centuries, an enemy was encamped around the City. The Senate, in a panic, could think of nothing more rational than to order the execution of Stilicho's widow. Alaric, unimpressed, surrounded the City and would allow no food to enter, and no Romans to leave. The population was reduced to eating cats, dogs, and rats. When those had been exhausted, the Romans had recourse to what St. Jerome, with care for the niceties of classical rhetoric, described as "impious food." "Men tore one another's limbs," he recorded, "while mothers did not spare their infants and received again into their bodies that which they had only recently brought forth."

Honorius promised relief, in the form of soldiers, and this hope sustained Rome for a time. But no reinforcements arrived. Since escape by natural means no longer seemed possible, the Romans determined to invoke the supernatural, and a plan of attack was drawn up according to which, through magic, lightning from the sky was to be directed against the barbarian camp. There was some talk that the plan had been approved by Innocent, Bishop of Rome; but eventually the Senate, fearful of the vengeance of the Christian God, and certain of that of the Christian Emperor, decided against it on the grounds that it would be tantamount to the reinstitution of paganism.

There was nothing left but to ask Alaric to state his terms, and an embassy was dispatched from the Senate for that purpose. The terms were straightforward enough: all the gold and silver in Rome; everything of value that could be moved; all the slaves who could prove that they were barbarians. The Roman ambassadors—one of whom was an erstwhile friend of Alaric—asked, thunderstruck, "If such are your terms, O King, then what will you leave to us?" "Your lives," replied Alaric. And the ambassadors, says Gibbon, "trembled and retired."

Having demanded the impossible, Alaric then proceeded to the possible. He would accept, he said, instead of everything that the City possessed, merely most of what it possessed. The new price was five thousand pounds of gold, thirty thousand pounds of silver, four thousand silken robes, three thousand bolts of fine cloth and an equal number of pounds of pepper—an enormously expensive delicacy for which the barbarians had developed a taste in the banquet halls of Rome. With some difficulty, the citizens were pried loose from their valuables, and these terms were met.

The Fall of the Roman Empire

Thereupon, food began once more to flow into the City from the countryside, and some measure of public order was restored. For a while, it seemed that the proverbial luck of Rome had, to some degree, held. Luck, however, did not take into account the duplicity of one Sarus, one of Alaric's subordinate chieftains, who unexpectedly changed sides and, now in the pay of Honorius, attacked Alaric with a large force of renegade Goths. The attack was put down and Sarus' forces dispersed, but Alaric was not to be satisfied with this easy victory. Shouting that Sarus' revolt had been a violation of the truce—as indeed it was—he led his armies into the City through a gate opened by a disgruntled slave, and, for the first time in eight centuries, eternal Rome was occupied by an enemy (410). For three days, the City was given over to looting. The rich were slaughtered, and their wives and daughters raped and then, if they were ugly, killed, or, if comely, taken to be sold as slaves. Everything that contained gold or silver was melted down for their precious metals. Thousands of Romans were made prisoners, to be held for ransom—among whom was Gallia Placidia, the Emperor Honorius' half sister. In the whole city, only the churches of St. Peter and St. Paul, and those who found sanctuary in them, were spared.

At the end of the third day, Alaric regained control of his troops; but the harm had already been done, not only to Rome herself but also to the spirit of the Roman world. The news of the City's fall resounded throughout the Empire like the clap of doom. St. Jerome, in faraway Bethlehem, heard the news, and wept:

> My voice is choked, and my sobs interrupt the words that I write. The City which took the whole world is herself taken. Who could have believed that Rome, which was built upon the spoils of the earth, would fall? That the City could be simultaneously the cradle and the grave of her people? That the coasts of Asia, Egypt and Africa should be filled with the slaves and maidens of Rome? That holy Bethlehem itself should receive, daily, as beggars, men and women who formerly were famous for their wealth and luxury?

Next to the elaborate rhetorical devices of his time, Jerome loved Virgil best; and he could not resist flinging in the face of Alaric, from a safe distance, an appropriate verse or two from the *Aeneid:*

> Who can tell that night of havoc, who can shed enough of tears
> For those deaths? The ancient city that for many a hundred years

Ruled the world comes down in ruin; corpses lie in every street
And men's eyes in every household death in countless phases meet.

Alaric, perhaps not knowing, and certainly not caring, what effect his act was having upon the sensibilities of the civilized world, then led his troops southward toward the rich cities and fields of Sicily; but, on the way, he was stricken with a fever, and shortly died at Cozensa. He was buried in a secret grave in the bed of the river Busento, and, Jordanes tells us, the slaves who prepared the grave were slain so that the secret of the location might be kept forever.

The brother of Alaric, Athaulf, was chosen to succeed the dead king. Almost immediately, he offered to withdraw from Italy, on two conditions: first, that he be given Honorius' half sister, Gallia Placidia, as his wife; second, that he be given southern Gaul as his fief. As to the first, Placidia was willing enough, but Honorius was not, and Athaulf was required to utter some mighty threats before the nuptials could be celebrated. As to the second condition, Honorius was willing, and it mattered little to anyone what the Gauls themselves thought of being ruled by a foreign barbarian. Athaulf therefore decamped with his new wife and his army for Gaul, where he established, in 414, a Visigothic kingdom with its capital at Toulouse. A contemporary writer, Orosius, explains, in what he claims to be the words of Athaulf, the reasons for the new king's decision to abandon his brother's conquests and, with them, his own chance for the richest prize in the world:

> It was at first my wish to destroy the very name of Rome, and to erect in its place a Gothic empire and to take for myself the place and the powers of Augustus. But experience taught me that the invincible barbarism of the Goths would not allow them to accept the yoke of the law, and that to abolish the laws, which are the foundation of the state, is to destroy the state itself. I therefore chose the glory of renewing and maintaining, by Gothic strength, the fame of Rome, desiring to be known to posterity as the restorer of that Roman power which I would not have been able to replace. Wherefore, I strive for peace and avoid war.

Athaulf was as good as his word, and so long as he lived he maintained the peace and was, at least in principle, subject to the Empire. He did not, however, live for long. The year after the establishment of his kingdom, he was assassinated. Placidia, who truly loved her husband, vowed that she would never marry again; but statecraft has reasons of which the heart knows not, and shortly afterward she was again a bride—this time, that of the general Constantius, whom she wed at Honorius' command. Constantius soon followed Athaulf to the grave, and after the death of the forgettable Honorius in 423, Placidia became Regent of the Empire for her son, Valentinian III. For the next quarter century, she was to rule the West with that measure of justice, discretion and firmness of which her half brother had been so conspicuously innocent.

During the span of Placidia's authority, Italy enjoyed a period of relative peace and prosperity. The barbarians, one and all, were once more safely beyond the Alps, where they contented themselves with destroying the trans-Alpine provinces and, occasionally, for diversion, one another. Of particular rapacity were the Vandals who, inspired by the successes of Alaric, ravaged Gaul and invaded Spain, then crossed over into Africa where, under the capable but brutal leadership of Gaiseric, they established a Vandal kingdom, seized Carthage, and built a pirate fleet with which they terrorized the coasts of Italy. Placidia eventually, in the name of Valentinian III, secured peace by placing an imperial princess in Gaiseric's marital bed, while the Vandal king agreed to pour African corn into the kitchens of Italy.

The Vandals were thus, for the moment, pacified. But soon a much greater threat appeared on the imperial horizon. The Huns had disappeared from the Roman purview after the great barbarian migrations of some seventy-five years before. Now, they reappeared with a suddenness and a ferocity that threatened to ring down the curtain on the civilization that Italy had managed so precariously to preserve. Their reputation as devils in battle had preceded them, and when they appeared in Italy in 451, after sacking and burning Trier and Metz and slaughtering their inhabitants, the very name of Hun was sufficient to make Romans quake. If we can believe Jordanes (and sometimes we cannot), the Huns were fearsome indeed. "By the terror of their very features they inspired great fear in those whom they did not really excel in combat. They caused their enemies to flee in terror because of the fearfulness of their faces, for they had shapeless lumps instead of heads, with pinholes rather than eyes . . . . They grow old beardless, and with faces scarred by the sword." The King of the Huns, the famous Attila, was a leader worthy of this legion of demons. "He was a man born to shake the world, the scourge of all nations, who somehow terrified all the earth by the rumors concerning him." This personification of terror, however, was not without certain virtues that even the Romans could respect: "Although he was a lover of war, he was yet restrained in action, mighty in counsel, gracious to petitioners, and kindly to those who sought his protection."

In 451, Attila, having milked dry the provinces of the East and pillaged the trans-Alpine territories of the West with a ferocity that won for him the title of "Scourge of God," turned his attention to Italy. Aquileia fell to him first, and it was destroyed utterly, as were Altinum, Concordia, and Padua. Vicenza, Verona, and Bergamo were treated more leniently, which is to say that they were sacked and many of their inhabitants sold into slavery. Pavia and Milan offered tribute: all of their movable wealth; Attila accepted, and the astute Pavians and Milanese were allowed to escape with their lives and their cities intact. At this point, the Huns were too close to Ravenna for comfort, and the Emperor, Valentinian III, timid son of valorous Placidia, now deprived of his mother's protection, fled with his court to Rome. There, he hid behind the skirts of the Roman Senate and the Roman pontiff. The Senate, hoping perhaps to emulate the Milanese and the Pavians, proposed sending an embassy to the Hunnic king. Leo the Great, Bishop of Rome, agreed to head this delegation, and he met with Attila on the banks of the Po. What happened there, in Attila's tent, is one of the mysteries of history. Legend has it that, as a result of Pope Leo's prayers, the Apostles Peter and Paul, in an apparition, threatened Attila with instant death if he dared defile with his presence the mother-city of Christianity, and this account gained wide credence among historians during the Middle Ages and even later. It is more likely, however, that a combination of circumstances, coupled with Leo's undoubted persuasiveness and majestic presence, accomplished a task for which the armed might of the Empire would probably have proved inadequate. Disease had broken out in Attila's horde; food was running low, and the farmlands of central Italy, repeatedly devastated by waves of barbarian invaders, was incapable of supporting a half million hungry Huns; rumors circulated to the effect that the Eastern Emperor Marcian was sending strong reinforcements. All that is known for certain is that, after meeting with Leo, Attila retreated from Italy and disappeared from its history. Shortly afterward he died while celebrating his marriage to the young Ildico (whose importance is not as the occasion of Attila's death, but as the historic basis for the Kriemhild figure in the *Niebelungenlied* cycle), and his empire disintegrated in the hands of his imbecilic heirs.

If the people of Italy thought that Attila's retreat marked the end of their troubles, then they had not reckoned with the madness of Valentinian, the imperial incumbent. Since Placidia's death in 450, there had been no one to restrain Valentinian, and he had become the plaything of a succession of astute politicians. The last of these, Petronius Maximus, persuaded the Emperor to execute Aëtius, the only surviving Roman general worthy of that title, for no reason other than that the general had had the temerity to propose that his son marry Valentinian's daughter. The wily Petronius then advised two of Aëtius' devoted followers to avenge the general's death by assassinating the Emperor. When this had been done, Petronius' aims became clear. He had himself declared Emperor and, to establish his claim beyond dispute, he forced Eudoxia, Valentinian's widow, to marry him. Eudoxia was a woman of no mean character. During the reign of Valentinian, she had become known as "the only man of the imperial court." Moreover, she was something of an expert in the Latinate art of exquisite revenge. The only possible source of aid in ridding herself of her new and unwanted husband was at Carthage, in the person of the Vandal king, Gaiseric. It was to this latter that the outraged Empress now turned, pleading that he come to her rescue in the name, or at least in the guise, of justice, honor, and mercy.*

Gaiseric was too astute a man not to know a good thing when he saw it, and he had already seen Italy at first hand. In 455, the Vandal fleet landed at the mouth of the Tiber, and Rome trembled anew. Petronius Maximus, being a man of action, tried to persuade the Senate to flee, and failed. He then tried himself to flee, and failed at that also, for the exasperated Romans stoned him to death as soon as he showed himself in the streets, and then gaily threw his mangled body into the Tiber. Three days later, Gaiseric was at the gates of the City. He found no army steeled to resist, no Senate girded for diplomacy. There was only an old man, at the head of a few clerics. It was again Leo, first pope of that name, who had come to plead the cause of the Romans; the same Leo who had been the occasion of Attila's retreat from Italy. But Gaiseric was no superstitious Hun. He was a Vandal and an Arian Christian; it was a combination that would brook no nonsense from a Roman pope. The most that Leo could do was to exact a promise, which was to be little honored, that the Vandals would spare the lives of those Romans who offered no resistance, that there would be no fires set in the City, and that captives would not be tortured. The Vandals were then turned loose on the capital of the world, and for fourteen days and fourteen nights they pillaged and plundered. At the end of that time, they returned to their ships with everything that they could carry, including even the gilt bronze tiles from the roof of the Temple of Jupiter

* The story is given by many of the ancient historians—Procopius, Evagrius, Idatius, Marcellinus, etc.—though there is some controversy about it among modern scholars. On the whole, however, it seems that the weight of evidence is in favor of the ancients. Their account, in the words of J. B. Bury, is "credible, though it is not certainly true."

and many thousands of prisoners—among whom, ironically, were the Empress Eudoxia and her daughters, Eudocia and Placidia. Eudoxia and Placidia were eventually sent to Constantinople, at the request of the Emperor Leo I, while Eudocia remained at Carthage as the wife of Gaiseric's son, Huneric.

The two decades following the Vandal invasion were a time of utter chaos in Italy. Repeated invasions, with their resultant famines and plagues, had left the country on the verge of starvation. Thousands of farms lay deserted, and tens of thousands of acres lay untilled. Vast stretches of countryside were, as St. Ambrose and Pope Gelasius noted, "empty of mankind." Rome herself, between the middle of the fourth century and the middle of the fifth, had lost four fifths of her population. The exactions of the barbarians, the wastefulness of the emperors, and the demands of those on the public dole, had, in that time, stripped Italy bare of the wealth that, to earlier generations, had seemed literally inexhaustible. As in all times of national disaster, the birth rate declined, and the Latins, once a race of conquerors, sank into a cynical sensuality that seemed the only possible escape from the ruin that surrounded them.

The despair of the citizens was reflected in the leaders whom they tolerated, and the final years of the Empire saw a line of mediocrities on the throne of the Caesars. After the death of Petronius Maximus, the Gothic legions of Gaul proclaimed one of their leaders, Avitus, emperor. Constantinople approved the election, but the Roman Senate, not knowing quite what to do, first confirmed Avitus' ascension and then, sensing the new emperor's unpopularity among the Romans, withdrew their confirmation. The grave Senators then mollified the deposed emperor by naming him to the episcopal throne of Placentia. The next emperor, Majorian (456–461), was a man of parts, and he strove to re-establish public order in Italy; but eventually he was deposed by his *Patricius,* or prime minister, Ricimer, a Visigoth who was to be the most powerful man in the West for the next fifteen years. Severus (461–465) was a nonentity, a puppet of Ricimer. Anthemius, his successor, was a wise man, a philosopher, who nevertheless was foolish enough to be a virtual pagan on a Christian throne. He therefore was as unacceptable to the politicians as he was to the papacy, and he was deposed and killed by Ricimer in 472. The next emperor, Olybrius, ruled for two months in the same year and shocked all Italy by dying a natural death. Glycerius sat on the throne for a while in 473, until he was deposed and replaced by Julius Nepos, who had the wit to survive for two years.

In 475, a new force of barbarians—the Heruli, Rugii, Sciri, and others, all of whom had already sampled the wealth of Italy as allies of Attila—swept down over the Alps into the broad valley of the Po. At the same moment, a barbarian general in the service of Rome, Orestes, deposed Julius Nepos and put his own son, Romulus—he who was derisively called Augustulus—on the throne. The invading barbarians demanded from Orestes an exorbitant tribute: one third of the land of Italy. When he refused, Orestes was captured and killed (476). At the same time, Romulus was deposed, but the leader of the barbarians, Odoacer, "granted him his life, pitying his youth and because he was handsome, and gave him an income of six thousand *solidi* and sent him to live in Campania, with his relatives."

Odoacer, in deposing Romulus, had no intention of separating Italy from the Empire, and he had the foresight and the diplomatic wit to observe the formalities necessary to reassure the restless Italians. It is true that he did not relish the idea of having a puppet emperor in Italy, as had Ricimer; but, like the latter, he wanted his position to be regularized by recognition from the Emperor of the East at Constantinople. Accordingly, he persuaded the Roman Senate to send an embassy to the Emperor Zeno. In their luggage, the delegated Senators carried the imperial regalia of the West which, upon arrival at the Bosphorous, they presented to Zeno, with a lengthy oration declaring that there was no need for an emperor in the West, since Zeno's wisdom was more than sufficient for both parts of the Empire. They then requested that the Emperor, who by now was in a receptive mood, confer the rank of *Patricius,* or Patrician, on Odoacer, who was, they swore, well suited to the office.

Unfortunately for the embassy, there also arrived in Constantinople at this time a delegation from Julius Nepos, the deposed predecessor of the now equally deposed Romulus, asking for money and troops to enable Nepos to recover his throne from Odoacer. The Emperor Zeno, caught in the middle between these two factions, could not have cared less about the West, and it was a matter of consummate indifference to him whether Italy was ruled by Odoacer or Nepos. It was recalled to him, however, that he himself had crowned Nepos, and that he could not afford to undermine his imperial authority by repudiating him now. Accordingly, he played the game of half-truths and half-measures at which the Byzantines already excelled. He told Odoacer's representatives that their only course was to take back the legitimate emperor, Nepos. And he told Nepos' representatives that, while he respected the legitimacy of Nepos' claim to the throne, he could provide neither men nor money to support that claim. Then he wrote a letter to Odoacer, praising him for "preserving the authority of Rome" and addressing him as "Patrician"—but carefully refraining from conferring that title on him formally. Odoacer therefore contented himself with this ambiguous confirmation of his position and ignored the claims and the existence of Nepos. In lieu of the grandiloquent *Patricius,* he used the barbarian title of *rex,* king, like his barbarian counterparts in other provinces of the West.

As bizarre as this arrangement between Rome and Constantinople may seem, it must be remembered that neither Odoacer nor his followers thought of themselves as subverters of the Western empire, let alone as "conquerors of Rome." To the barbarians as well as to the Romans themselves, the Roman world had always been a single political entity, undivided and indivisible. The separation into eastern and western components had been effected merely for reasons of administrative convenience. Thus it was that no one seems quite to have realized that in the West the Empire was no more. The barbarian conquest of Italy was regarded—thanks to Odoacer's machinations with respect to Constantinople's approval—as a change in administration rather than in government, and even as a reunification of the West with East. In fact, the Roman Senate (not particularly noted, at this time, for its perspicacity), went so far as to erect a statue to Zeno, in celebration of this happy, but wholly fictional, re-establishment of Rome's ancient unity.

The truth of the matter, however, was quite otherwise. Odoacer ruled Italy, in practice if not in principle, with an authority so absolute as to leave no doubt in anyone's mind—his own, or the Senate's, or the Emperor's—that he was wholly his own man, and that he and his Germans had conquered Italy in the same way that Gaiseric had conquered Africa, as the Visigoths had recently seized Spain, as the Angles and the Saxons were taking over Britain, and as the Franks were overrunning Gaul.

As may be expected, the results of this barbarian take-over in Italy were striking. The Empire had been a largely urban, or at least a municipal, culture; but the barbarians lived by farming, herding, hunting, and war. Therefore, Italy became once more a decentralized, non-municipal community. Politically, the conquest established a comparatively primitive form of monarchy in which, as in all primitive societies, power and authority were regarded as being vested in persons rather than as emanating from laws. Consequently, the arbitrary exercise of power, and the concomitant incidence of violence, increased. Economically, Italy had been progressively exhausted by the repeated barbarian invasions, and now the final conquest by Odoacer completed the process; the habit of luxury was perforce replaced by a mode of life that was comparatively austere and simple. In-

The Fall of the Roman Empire

tellectually, the Empire had, for three centuries, been on the decline, and, by the middle of the fifth century, originality of thought and expression had been completely displaced by a reverence for form, for tradition, and for the works of the ancient masters. Now, even exercises in imitation almost ceased, and intellectual activity was concentrated simply on preserving as much as possible of the intellectual heritage of Greco-Roman civilization.

On the more immediate level, the period of Italian history following the Germanic conquest is the story of the mingling, or rather of the attempted mingling, of the old Latin population of Italy with the barbarian conquerors. It was a process, of course, that had been initiated long before the fall of the Empire. For generations, Germans had been received by the Empire as civilian colonists, as military recruits, and even as emperors. Whole tribes of them had been permitted to settle within the boundaries of the Empire, and, as earlier events have illustrated, they had risen to command the armies of Rome against other barbarians. The government of Rome had realized that the Empire, if it could be upheld at all, would survive only through an infusion of barbarian virility, and therefore it had favored the process. But the hoped-for assimilation had not taken place, and the mixture of barbarian with Latin blood had not notably invigorated the Italian people. Now that power had changed hands, there were two distinct and very real social strata: at the top were the barbarian conquerors, and at the bottom was the feeble conquered race, ten times as numerous, and ten times as civilized, as their new rulers.

The barbarians were well aware, trained as they were in the ways of Rome, of certain points of inferiority to the Latins. It was obvious to them, for example, that if they were to achieve a stable working government they would have to abandon their own unsophisticated governmental structures and adopt the complex machinery of the old Empire. They also realized that they themselves were untrained in and generally unsuited for the working of that machinery. At the same time, they were forced to concede that a state which had an all-barbarian military service and an all-Latin civil service could not stand firm.

To these problems was added a third, of even greater magnitude. There was, in the Italian peninsula, a power as independent of Odoacer as it had been of his predecessors and of Constantinople; and that power was the Roman Church. It was a power which constituted the single most important element in the barbarians' attempt to found a permanent government in Italy.

The Church, at the time of Odoacer's reign, was not only the one vigorous institution in Italy, but it had already begun to foreshadow its future greatness and almost limitless power. The origins of that authority and vigor are obscure enough. There is no sound historical evidence that, in the time of Constantine the Great (323-337)—the first Christian emperor and the founder of Christianity as the state religion—the Bishop of Rome exercised any primacy of authority over the other bishops of the Christian Church. It is significant, however, that he claimed such primacy, and that he did exercise a certain claim to precedence—a sort of primacy of honor, according to which the Roman pontiff was *primus inter pares,* the first among equals. The source of this primacy of honor was the fact that Rome was at the same time the source and cradle of Roman dominion and also, in a real sense, the source and cradle of the institutional Church. St. Paul, the great propagator—indeed, according to some, the great formulator—of the Christian faith, had died there. Above all, it was universally acknowledged at that early date that the Apostle Peter, chief of the apostles of Jesus, had founded the Roman bishopric. It was to the Church of Rome, therefore, in a very special way, that Christ was thought to have referred when he said to Peter, "Thou are Peter, and upon this rock I will build my Church; and the gates of hell shall not prevail against it." Hence, logically, an ancient axiom (and one still heard occasionally at Rome) has it that *ubi Petrus, ibi ecclesia*—"Where Peter is, there is the Church."*

To these theological considerations may be added those of a more historical and practical nature. Rome, at the time of Odoacer's establishment, and for long periods before, was a city without a temporal ruler. The removal of the great agencies of government to Constantinople, under Constantine, and the consequent absence of any real civic life, had made of Rome a predominantly ecclesiastical city. Consequently, the head of the ecclesiastical community there, the pope, became the most important and influential personage of the City. The great rivals of the Roman pontiff, on the other hand, the Patriarchs of Constantinople, were hamstrung by the presence of an emperor who claimed to be not only the divinely appointed ruler of the whole earth, but also *isos apostolōn,* "the equal of the Apostles," a title which no mere bishop could hope to equal. In just a few years, the imperial presence had so eclipsed the Constantinopolitan patriarch, and the imperial absence in Italy had so liberated the Roman Bishop,

---

* The popes have never ceased their search for historical evidence to support the Petrine tradition. In 1969, Pope Paul VI, the 236th Bishop of Rome, declared certain bones found under the Basilica of St. Peter to be those of the Apostle himself. In 1948, Pius XII, with more piety than perceptiveness, had declared another set of bones to be those of St. Peter, only to have it discovered later that they were, beyond a doubt, those of a woman.

that, by the middle of the fourth century, we find general acknowledgment that the Bishop of Rome ranked above all other bishops. He is referred to as "head [*caput*] of the Church," and we find a Dacian council of bishops asking Rome to settle jurisdictional conflicts. A century later, there was no longer room for doubt or discussion on the subject. Leo I, the man who had persuaded Attila and bargained with the Vandals, was merely expressing a universally held opinion when he declared that "St. Peter and St. Paul are the Romulus and Remus of the new Rome, as much superior to the old as truth is to error. If ancient Rome was at the head of the pagan world, then St. Peter, prince of the Apostles, came to teach in the new Rome, so that from her the light of Christianity should be shed over the whole world."

Along with theoretical jurisdiction over the Christian Church, the Roman Church had gathered to herself whatever remained of the administrative ability of ancient Rome, both in personnel and in policy. With acute diplomacy and practical sense, she condemned those subtle doctrines of the East, those late flashes of Greek metaphysics, which kept springing up in Africa and Asia Minor and which, if they had been triumphant, would have made of Christianity something less than a religion of universal appeal. Moreover, though she may thus have cut herself off from the perhaps invigorating influence of neo-Platonic thought, and though she may have, by the necessity for survival, set her heart too much on domination, still, by her insistence upon uniform law and obedience, by steadfastly maintaining the unity of the Christian faith, by her adherence to immutable dogma at a time when all else was in flux, she succeeded in becoming the great cohesive force in the West. She became, indeed, the "Rock" which she had always claimed to be, the sole bastion of stability and order.

Partly by good fortune and partly by her success in making her cause prevail through political means, Rome was always orthodox. She fought the Arians, who believed that Christ, having been created by the Father, was inferior to him. She fought the Nestorians, who alleged that the Virgin was the mother of Christ only insofar as Christ was man. She fought the Monophysites, who denied that Christ had two natures, human and divine. She fought plundering barbarians, theologizing emperors, dissident bishops, and overenthusiastic reformers. She fought vigorously, sometimes gallantly, and always triumphantly. And as she fought she drew to herself, as the champion of orthodoxy and as the sole effective force within the framework of the Western Empire, the loyalty and trust of the people of Italy. For in those days ecclesiastical affairs were inseparable, at every level, from political affairs. No man of the era, no matter how radical politically or heretical theologically, would have dreamed of separating the two. The state and the Church were simply two aspects of the same reality, corresponding to the two aspects of human life: body and soul. The idea of a state apart from the Church, or of a Church separate from the state, would have seemed an abomination, a monstrous invention of Satan, like a body living without a soul.

To gain the confidence and approval, and then the co-operation, of this potent Church was the first task that faced Odoacer and his barbarians in their attempt to establish a permanent kingdom in Italy. That done, they might hope to succeed in the second and third tasks: to establish friendly relations with the Empire, and to blend the barbarian conquerors with the subject Latins. In all the long period of barbarian domination in Italy, each chief in turn had to face the always imminent danger that these three powers—the Church, the Empire, and the Latin people—would make common cause against him. And the barbarians were, in fact, always unsuccessful in their efforts to woo these powers; not one of them managed to achieve more than an ephemeral *modus vivendi* with respect to any of the three of them. Consequently, they were never able to make of Italy a kingdom.

Odoacer himself had too brief a reign for him really to come to grips with these problems. After adding Sicily to his Italian domain and occupying Dalmatia, he was attacked—at the instigation of the Emperor Zeno—by Felitheus, King of the Rugians. After a bitter campaign (487–488), Felitheus was crushed, but the victory left Odoacer's army exhausted. It had not yet recovered in the following year, when Theodoric, King of the Ostrogoths, marched with his armies into Venetia.

The Ostrogoths, or East Goths, were one branch of the great Gothic nation, of which the Visigoths (or West Goths) were the other. Immediately prior to their invasion of Italy, the Ostrogoths had inhabited Pannonia, on the south side of the Danube. They were a vigorous and warlike people who had given much trouble to the Eastern emperors—so much so that Constantinople had been obliged not only to cede the Pannonian territory to them, but also to pay them tribute. Finally, the redoubtable Zeno, sensing a final chance to rid himself of Odoacer and, at the same time, to dispose of the troublesome Ostrogoths, suggested to Theodoric that he lead his people into Italy, conquer Odoacer, and rule there as imperial lieutenant. Theodoric did not hesitate for a minute. Pannonia was gray and damp, while Italy was sunny and warm; Pannonia was a bleak wilderness, while Italy, even in its current state, was comparatively rich and filled with the good things in life. In 488, almost a hundred thousand Ostrogoths began their tedious emigration to the tempting land in the south. In the next year, after two bloody encounters, Odoacer was forced to retire to Ravenna. The following year he tried again to contest Theodoric's superiority, and again he was beaten and obliged to take shelter in Ravenna. Finally, in the spring of 493, Theodoric offered to share the rule of Italy with Odoacer in exchange for the surrender of Ravenna. Odoacer took the bait. What he had in mind probably was a territorial division of Italy with the Ostrogothic chief. What Theodoric had in mind is entirely academic, for it is clear that he had no intention of honoring his arrangement with Odoacer. A fragment from the history of John of Antioch tells the story:

> Theodoric invited Odoacer, who was now sixty years of age, to a feast at the palace of the Consul at Ravenna on March 5, 493. As they sat at table, two men knelt before Odoacer with a petition, and they clasped his hands. Then soldiers, who had been concealed in alcoves on either side of the room, rushed out, but for some reason they could not bring themselves to strike the King [Odoacer]. Then Theodoric himself stepped forward with his sword raised. Odoacer cried, "Where is God?" And Theodoric answered, "Thus did you to my friends." And he struck him and split him in one stroke from collarbone to loin, so that he was astonished at his own stroke, and cried out, "This wretch has no bones in his body!" . . . On the same day were slain all of Odoacer's soldiers who could be found, and all of his family.

Theodoric was now master of all Italy, by right of conquest as well as by imperial commission. In addition, ambassadors came from the Vandal kingdom in Africa to surrender to him the island of Sicily (which the Vandals had seized as soon as they heard of Odoacer's troubles) as an integral part of his kingdom. He was accepted and hailed by the Senate and people of Rome as the savior of the City. Nothing was lacking to complete his glory but the imperial purple itself; but, much to the Ostrogoth's chagrin, when he had requested that honor from Constantinople in 490, Zeno had died, and his successor, Anastasius I, replied that he had decided to reserve the imperial color to himself alone. Theodoric therefore had to content himself, like Odoacer before him, with the barbarian appelation of king, though he also held, and continued to use, the title of Patrician, which had been conferred by Zeno at an earlier stage of the Ostrogothic chieftain's checkered career.

Theodoric's reign in Italy lasted for thirty-three years (dating it, as is customary, from his second victory over Odoacer in 490). After Odoacer's death, Theodoric seems to have undergone an almost miraculous transformation. He was no longer the man whose rampages in Thrace and Illyria had made Constantinople tremble, no longer the avenger who slew Odoacer to secure his own rule. Now he bent his formidable energies to two tasks: the conciliation of his Italian subjects, and the maintenance of peace with his neighbors. His reign, in fact, was largely a continuation of the political and administrative policies of Odoacer. Like that unfortunate predecessor, he set himself to the task of blending barbarians and Italians into one people and uniting them under a stable government. But his problems were even more difficult than those of Odoacer. For one thing, the immigrating peoples whom he had led into Italy, though mainly of the Gothic family, were an amalgam of several mutually suspicious tribes who, once in Italy, constituted an alien army of occupation in the midst of a numerically and culturally superior, as well as a hostile, population.

This Roman, or Latin, population of Italy, which had forgone completely the use of military arms and now never took part in any battle more formidable than a street riot, was largely urban and inhabited almost the same cities that exist today. To the north were Turin, Pavia, Ferrara, Milan, Bergamo, Verona, Aquileia; on the eastern coast, Ravenna, Rimini, Ancona; on the western coast and in the center, Genoa, Pisa, Lucca, Perugia, Spoleto, Rome, Benevento, Naples, Salerno, Amalfi; and, to the south, the old Greek cities. In these urban centers, all the day-to-day business of life was in the hands of the Latins; all of the lawyers, physicians, weavers, spinners, carpenters, masons and cobblers were Romans, as were most of the workmen on the great *latifundia,* or estates. The Ostrogoths, on the other hand, were primarily, and almost exclusively, men-at-arms, and they exercised only those primitive crafts that had been necessary in their Pannonian villages. Naturally, therefore, the Goths and the Latins looked upon each other at first with suspicion, then with dislike, and finally with contempt. To the Romans, the invaders were filthy, ignorant savages. To the Goths, the Latins were weaklings, the degenerate offspring of warlike ancestors, a herd of neutered clerks and bookkeepers. It was obvious to Theodoric that both time and statesmanship would be required before the two peoples would understand each other, share occupations, intermarry, and feel themselves to be citizens of the same community.

The internal problems of assimilation that Theodoric faced were, to a large extent, controlled by the necessity to satisfy and placate the three powers that Odoacer also had faced: the Latins, the Emperor in Constantinople, and the Church. With the Latin people, Theodoric was, for the most part, just. Rather than seize any and all worth-while land, in the classic fashion of the conquering barbarian, he limited the division of real property among his warriors to those lands which the massacre of Odoacer's followers had made available. The civil administration of Italy, he was wise enough to leave in the experienced hands of the Romans. While he retained the Gothic law for his own people, he allowed the Latins to continue to live under the Roman law to which they were accustomed. As his chief counselor, he had the famous Cassiodorus, a noble Roman of great wealth and learning. He compiled a legal code based upon the imperial codes. And finally—a sure step toward popularity—he lightened the burden of taxation. In order to conform to the custom of the Romans, he made his residence at Ravenna, where the churches of S. Apollinare Nuovo and Santo Spirito, as well as a baptistry and a mausoleum, still testify to his presence as well as to his piety and tact.

By the year 500, Italy had achieved a semblance of public order, and Theodoric journeyed to Rome, where he was received with imperial honors. He vowed publicly to uphold faithfully all the institutions established by the emperors of Rome, and he showed himself as interested in the welfare of the City as though he himself had been a Roman. He spoke of Rome as the city "which is indifferent to none, since she is foreign to none; the fruitful mother of eloquence, the spacious temple of every virtue, comprising within herself all the cherished marvels of the universe, so that it may in truth be said, Rome herself is one great marvel." So successfully did he flatter the Romans, and so careful was he in all his relations with the people of Italy, that his reputation became a legend throughout the Empire. Procopius, a Byzantine historian of the following generation, recorded the universal opinion of Theodoric:

> Theodoric was careful to be always just . . . and he attained the highest degree of wisdom and manliness. Although he was, at least in name, a usurper, yet in practice he was as truly an emperor as any who bore that title from the beginning of history. Both the Goths and the Romans loved him greatly. When he died . . . he left to his subjects a keen sense of bereavement and loss.

Theodoric was considerably less successful in conciliating the emperors at Constantinople than he was in winning the affection of the people of Italy. The Empire had recognized Theodoric's authority in Italy, and Theodoric was at pains to register his respect for the imperial authority in every way—so long as it did not interfere with his own prerogatives. For example, while he minted his own coins—which were, one authority assures us, "singularly neat, and even elegant"—he made sure that it was always the image of the reigning emperor, and not his own, that was superinscribed. Nor did he date his proclamations according to the first year of his own reign, as was customary among autonomous potentates, but according to that of the emperor. Similarly, when Theodoric legislated, he designated his enactments as *edicta* (edicts) rather than as *leges* (laws), since only the Emperor, or, in certain circumstances, the Roman Senate, could formulate *leges*. To these reassuring observances, Theodoric added soft words. "We have everything that is required for us to be a part of your empire," he wrote to Zeno. And to the difficult Anastasius I he asserted that "our kingdom is but a reflection of your own," and "be assured that we do not believe that, between these two nations, which, as is declared by ancient traditions, form but one body, there can ever be permanent discord." But Theodoric, while publicly acknowledging, by word and deed, that his position was merely that of ruler of one of the imperial provinces, within the confines of Italy always acted as an independent monarch. The emperors at Constantinople, since Theodoric's tactics enabled them to save face, were compelled to swallow the bitter with the sweet. They smiled and nodded benignly in the direction of Italy, while in their hearts they wished the ingenious barbarian all possible evil and watched for an opportunity to make their wishes come true. For almost three decades, and through the reigns of four emperors, the true state of affairs was concealed beneath fair words, and Theodoric's relations with the Empire were ostensibly amicable enough to deceive everyone but Theodoric and the emperors.

Theodoric's relations with the Church were even more complex. They were not a matter of private conscience, nor were they dictated by spiritual considerations. They were purely political, and they were viewed by Theodoric within the framework of public policy. The situation was considerably complicated for him by the fact that he was often caught in the perennial crossfire between pope and emperor; there were misunderstandings aplenty, religious and otherwise, between the Roman and the Greek minds, and constant friction between papal and imperial authority. The Byzantine emperors, as "the equal of the Apostles," had a fervent interest in matters theological, and they liked nothing better than tinkering with the complicated formulas and subtle dogmas of the faith—a tinkering that was not infrequently inspired by political motives.

The subjects of the Empire were divided into the orthodox and the heterodox, and this division was a constant menace to the security of a state in which the emperor's authority was based upon his recognition as the representative of Christ on earth. In the early part of Theodoric's reign, the emperor had devised a scheme of compromise designed to heal the breach between the two parties, a *via media* which he hoped would unite all his subjects in one common faith. Rome, however, was outraged by this imperial trifling with orthodoxy and by the imperial assumption of a right to interfere in matters theological, and she denounced the compromise in bitter terms. The consequence was a schism between Rome and Constantinople, which lasted until the reign of the Emperor Justin (518–527), when an imperial nephew who had the emperor's ear effected a reconciliation. This nephew was the famous Justinian, himself a future emperor, and a man of no small ambition. He had already formulated a plan to regain Italy for the Empire, and he realized that the support of the papacy would be necessary to the success of his project. He therefore persuaded the feeble Justin to capitulate on Rome's terms, and, in 519, a Roman embassy bearing the olive branch was warmly received at Constantinople. Both emperor and imperial nephew publicly repudiated the compromise of their meddling predecessor and accepted orthodoxy as defined by Rome. Thus, the schism was healed.

During the period of this rupture between East and West, Theodoric had managed his relations with the Church very prudently. Although, like all barbarians except the Franks, he was an Arian, rather than a Roman Catholic (and therefore, in the eyes of Rome, a heretic), he regarded himself as the guardian of public worship in Italy, and he was scrupulously benevolent toward the established Church. Indeed, he was the protector of all forms of worship in Italy, and he often quoted a maxim of admirable impartiality: "We cannot impose a religion, for no one can be forced to believe if he is unwilling to do so." Among his friends and advisers he counted bishops and saints, and he made not the slightest objection when some of his favorite Goths, and even his mother, abandoned Arianism for the faith of Rome. He followed the ancient custom of making an offering at the Basilica of St. Peter, says a contemporary, and he did so "very devoutly, as though he were a Catholic," but apparently without inquiring too closely into the creed of the Apostle. He refrained from interfering in the internal affairs of the Church unless he was compelled to do so in the interest of public order, and, while in Rome, he maintained an exaggeratedly correct attitude toward the Bishop on whom the tranquillity or the revolt of Italy might depend.

Nonetheless, though Theodoric acted with great moderation and only followed well-established precedent where the Church was concerned, he failed to win the friendship, or even the confidence, of the papacy. What was resented was not so much his interference as his very existence. The Church felt instinctively, and quite correctly, that Italy was too small for both king and pope, and that a barbarian king would overshadow a Roman pontiff just as surely as, at Constantinople, the emperor eclipsed totally the patriarch. The Church was aware, also, that it could gain its full stature only in the vacuum of authority created by the absence of a strong civil government. The ecclesiastical power was, therefore, almost of necessity, always inimical to the civil authority. Nevertheless, during the period of schism between emperor and pope, the papacy dared not offend Theodoric, who was, after all, the defender of orthodox Italy against the armies of heterodox Constantinople, and during that time relations between the barbarians and the papacy were, if not cordial, at least smooth.

In 524, there occurred that correlation between the resentment of the Church, the ambitions of the Empire, and the emotions of the Latins, that Theodoric, and Odoacer before him, had always feared and tried to prevent. The wily Justinian, strong now in his reconciliation with the papacy, felt that the time was ripe to set about the recovery of the lost provinces of the West, and he made his first hostile move. An imperial command was issued to the effect that all Arian churches throughout the Empire were to be handed over to the Catholics. This action, predictably, won the approval of the pope. Its effect in Italy, just as predictably, was to alienate the Arian Goths from the Catholic Latins. Theodoric was furious. He not only refused to honor the imperial edict but threatened to suppress the Catholic ritual throughout Italy if the command were obeyed elsewhere in the Empire. The threat served to complete the union of pope, emperor, and people, for it drove the Catholic Italians into the camp of Theodoric's enemies. Thus, the three natural enemies of barbarian rule closed ranks: the Empire, from the desire to recover Italy; the Church, so as to rid herself of a competing and heretical ruler; the Latins, out of national and religious pride.

In this climate, it was inevitable that there should spring up various intrigues between Rome and Constantinople. And, in fact, a conspiracy, involving some of Rome's noblest names, was uncovered by Theodoric's agents. The king was in no mood to play the civilized representative of Roman law. Several Roman Senators were arrested on the charge of high treason, tried before improper tribunals, and summarily executed. Among them was the illustrious Boëthius, whose *Consolations of Philosophy* was to have immense vogue during the following centuries. Despite these sacrifices on the altar of Theodoric's suspicions, his anger was not appeased. He finally compelled the pope himself, John I, to go to Constantinople to ask that the Arians be treated justly and the Arian churches restored. The pope went, and he was magnificently welcomed and entertained. But when he returned to Italy it was discovered that he had spent his time obtaining new favors for the Catholics, and nothing at all for the Arians. Theodoric thereupon threw Pope John into prison and kept him there until the latter's death in 526. The king then nominated a papal successor, who was promptly elected, according to the custom of the time, by the now thoroughly frightened people of Rome. This highhanded act of Theodoric's stimulated such discontent throughout Italy that it seemed the time for a Byzantine invasion had come. But Justinian, not having fully spun his web, delayed still. Perhaps he feared Theodoric's armies and wished to wait for his death. If so, he did not have long to wait. In the summer of that same year, Theodoric expired, after having divided his treasures and his provinces between his two grandsons. The vengeance of an outraged Church pursued him even beyond the grave, and Pope Gregory I related approvingly the story of a hermit who, in a vision, saw Theodoric burning in the flames of hell for his sins against the Church.

Theodoric's death ended once and for all the possibility of a unified Gothic kingdom of Italy. Even during his reign, a process of deterioration had set in among the younger generation. The civilization of Italy had exercised a detrimental influence upon the unsophisticated Goths, and the luxurious ways, the idle habits, and even the culture of the Romans had served to rob them of their natural vigor and independence of character. The conquerors became divided among themselves, some adhering to the old Gothic traditions and others adopting the "new ways" of the Latins. Theodoric's own family affords a conspicuous example of this process of deterioration. The new king, Athalaric, a boy of eighteen, succumbed to debauchery. His successor, Theodatus, a cousin and the last of the royal line, a student of philosophy and literature, was wholly incapable of vigorous action—indeed, of any action at all—and was deposed by his soldiers.

Justinian, who by now had succeeded his uncle on the throne, had been awaiting his opportunity. Surely the time had come. The Goths were divided and weakened; the papacy and the Italian people were hostile to the barbarians; and Justinian's most successful general, Belisarius, fresh from his conquest of the Vandal kingdom of Africa, was ready for the task. In 535, the war for the reconquest of Italy began.

The invading armies found the Goths confused and leaderless, whereas Belisarius was a man of military genius, with an army composed of veteran Huns, Isaurians, and other mercenaries. The issue could not remain long in doubt. Sicily, Naples, Rome, and Ravenna fell in turn. The reconquest would have been complete, but Justinian, conscious of the peril represented by a too popular general, recalled Belisarius to Constantinople. The Goths then, under their new king, Totila, a formidable and valiant warrior, managed to regain for a time a part of the territory that had been lost, including Sicily, Naples, and Rome itself. Justinian, however, had a remarkable knowledge of men. To replace Belisarius he appointed an extraordinary little old man named Narses—a eunuch, by which title he is known to history—who, though innocent of any military experience, handled the emperor's legions as though he had been born and bred in battle. After a comparatively brief campaign, in which Totila was killed, Narses compelled the last remnant of the Gothic army to surrender (553). The following year, groups of barbarian Franks and Alemanni, called in by the Goths, marched across Italy fighting friends and enemies alike, until they were crushed by imperial troops near Capua. The last Gothic strongholds, Brescia and Verona, held out until 563, when they too were destroyed. Thus, the Goths disappeared from Italy, leaving behind no racial or linguistic relic in the history of the country, and Narses the Eunuch was immemorialized as "the restorer of happiness to Rome and to the whole of Italy" by a contemporary observer, Prosper of Aquitaine.

Prosper apparently had not visited Italy when he wrote that phrase. Under Odoacer and Theodoric, the peninsula had enjoyed a period of comparative prosperity. The lengthy wars of the Reconquest, as it is called, now left it once more drained of men, money, and the means of producing food. By the time of Narses' final victory, the country was exhausted. The unfortunate natives, regardless of which side had been winning, were required to house and feed a foreign army, Gothic or Byzantine, and to endure the insolence and insults of a brutal soldiery. Plague, pestilence, and famine followed in the wake of the armies. The ordinary business of life came to a stop in the face of an even greater need, that of simple survival. Houses, churches, public buildings, and aqueducts fell into ruin. Roads were left unrepaired, and communication almost ceased between different parts of Italy. Rivers were left undiked and flooded the fields. Immense tracts of hitherto fertile land were abandoned. The herds roamed loose, without shepherds; harvests rotted for want of reapers; grapes shriveled on the vine for want of pickers. With lack of nutrition came disease, and mothers abandoned their sick babies while sons left their mothers unburied. On top of it all came the "happiness" promised by Prosper: imperial taxes.

Rome herself fared no better than the rest of Italy. Under Theodoric, the City had had a population of several hundred thousand—an immense drop from its palmy days as the center of empire, but still sufficient to make it the largest city of the West; under Justinian, it was reduced to perhaps forty thousand inhabitants. The temples, baths, palaces, and public buildings that had been the wonder of the world became ruins, for there was neither the means nor the incentive for their upkeep. The aqueducts leading into the City had been cut, and there was little uncontaminated water. The countryside around Rome had been devastated to the extent that it took on that aspect of Hadean desolation which it retained into the twentieth century. Now the citizens of Rome lived solely on the money which they were able to extort from pilgrims—and thus established a tradition which apparently is to endure so long as the City itself—and on the charity of the pope, whom circumstances required to establish a Christian version of *panem et circenses*.

The people of Rome had to choose, therefore, between a pope who fed them, and an emperor who fleeced them. There was little hesitation. The authority of the papacy replaced that of the throne. There was, it is true, an imperial Exarch, or viceroy. But his residence was at Ravenna, and impassable roads and lack of funds confined his effective jurisdiction to the north of Italy. There was still a Prefect of the City, but that official now reported to the pope. The office of Consul disappeared, and the Senate itself vanished somewhat mysteriously—probably by the indifferent method of attrition.

The truth of the matter was that Italy, exhausted, starving, sunk in misery and ignorance, little cared now whether its master was a Roman pope, a Constantinopolitan emperor, or a trans-Alpine barbarian. The Latins had not the spirit left to fight against any one of them. They meekly bowed their heads and submitted to the most convenient yoke.

It is ironic that Justinian, whose sole purpose was to reunite Italy to the Empire, not only destroyed the country by the Reconquest and the reimposition of imperial taxes, but also lost it forever for the "new Rome" on the Bosphorous. In eradicating completely the Goths, he deprived Italy of the one force which might have saved it from the Lombards and Avars who threatened from beyond the Danube. By re-establishing the shadow of imperial authority in Italy, in the person of his Exarch at Ravenna, he seemed to reduce the importance of the papacy; the popes were therefore forced to consider the possibility of subtracting themselves altogether from the East and turning toward the West in a search for more tractable protectors. In the aftermath of the great war which left Italy in ruins, it may have been Justinian who was the conqueror, but it was the Church who was the winner. Ferdinand Gregorovius, the great historian of medieval Rome, summed up the situation perfectly: "In the tempest of the Gothic war, the old life had disappeared forever. In the towns, burnt and deserted, only the ruins recalled a vanished prosperity. The Sibyl's prophecy was fulfilled, and a deep night spread over the Latin world. In the darkness, there shone no light except the candles of the churches and the solitary lamp of a monk within his monastery."

The rule of Constantinople in Italy, for all its historic effects, lasted only a few years. In 565, Justinian died, and with him passed away the strength to hold together the East and the West. He was succeeded by a nephew, known as Justin II, who had no particular claim to the throne other than that he was in Constantinople when the throne became vacant, and that he had had the foresight to insinuate himself into the good graces of various palace officials. On the basis of those qualifications, he was promptly proclaimed emperor by the Senate.

Justin had an exaggerated opinion either of the dignity of his throne or of the strength of his armies. Almost his first official act was to offend the Avars, a powerful barbarian tribe who lived along the eastern Danube and whom Justinian had pacified by payment of an annual tribute. The ambassadors of the Avars had presented themselves at Justin's throne and requested the payment of the customary tribute. Justin was beside himself with rage at their temerity. "The Empire," he rebuked them, "abounds with men and horses, and with arms sufficient both to defend our frontiers and to punish the barbarians. You come offering aid and threatening war; but we despise your enmity as well as your aid. . . . The tribute was paid by our uncle because of your misery and in answer to your humble prayers. But from us you will receive a more precious gift: the knowledge of your own weakness. Be gone from our presence; the lives of ambassadors are sacred. If you return to ask our pardon, then perhaps you may even taste of our benevolence." The Avars withdrew, publicly chastened but secretly angry. Justin puffed himself up and strutted about. But he was not heard to suggest a more effective way of keeping peace with the barbarians than by bribing them.

The fierce Avars were now placed in the difficult position of having somehow to earn a living. An opportunity for them to do so was not long in coming. Another barbarian tribe, the Lombards, settled by Justinian in Illyricum, invited the idle Avars to join them in a war against the Gepids, a tribe who had the misfortune to inhabit a stretch of land between those of the Lombards and the Avars. The Avars agreed, on condition that they be given immediately one tenth of the Lombards' cattle, and, upon a successful completion of the war, one half of the booty and of the land to be conquered. The hapless Gepids did not long survive the Lombards' acceptance of this bargain. Once the Lombards and the Avars were comfortably settled in their new lands, however, the former took a close look

The Fall of the Roman Empire

at the latter and decided that, as neighbors, they left much to be desired. Since the Avars were stronger than the Lombards, however, they could not be destroyed in combat. The Lombards therefore did the next best thing: they moved away from the Avars. Their destination was Italy, the Mecca of restless barbarians. Many of the Lombards had seen that land as allies of Narses the Eunuch, and, stricken though Italy may have been at the time, it seemed infinitely preferable to the lands previously inhabited by them. In 568, under the leadership of their king, Albion, the Lombards, accompanied by thousands of Saxons and other Teutonic tribesmen, marched into Venetia. The Emperor Justin, with that genius for misjudgment which characterized his reign, had just dismissed Narses from his command, and Italy was virtually defenseless. In a short time, the northern part of the peninsula was in the hands of the Lombardic invaders.

Albion, the Lombard king, was murdered in 573, and Cleph, his successor, was murdered in 574. For a while thereafter, the Lombards elected no king—perhaps none could be found to accept the title—and instead divided themselves into approximately thirty groups, each led by a *dux*, or duke. Under this regime they continued their advance and gained first Spoletum, to the east of Rome, and then Beneventum, to the south. By 578, Rome was begging the new emperor, Tiberius (Justin's precarious sanity had at last vanished entirely, and he had been deposed), for aid; but Tiberius advised Rome either to bribe the Lombards to leave Italy, or to bribe the Franks to come and drive them out. The pope, however, was unable to raise sufficient gold for either, and there matters rested until Tiberius' demise in 579.

The new emperor, Maurice, proved to be a man of action. He offered a price of fifty thousand *solidi* to the Frankish king, Childebert II—a great-grandson of that Clovis who had converted the Franks to Catholicism, and the last of the Merovingian line—in exchange for an invasion of Italy by the Franks. Childebert did indeed invade the northern part of the country, and he was able to force the local dukes to acknowledge him as their master. His success, however, had the unexpected effect of bringing home to the Lombards their need for a unified command, and they forthwith elected Authari, son of the murdered Cleph, to the throne. Authari immediately negotiated a three-year truce with the Frankish king, so that he might devote his full strength to the imperial forces. It is not recorded what the emperor thought of this arrangement. When the truce expired in 588, Childebert again attacked the Lombards, but he was overwhelmingly defeated. In the following year, he tried again; but this time Authari, taking a page from the imperial book, bribed him to withdraw. In 590, the indefatigable Franks again invaded Italy, but the Lombards shut themselves up in fortified cities, and their foes could only plunder the countryside. Childebert was by now thoroughly bored with Italy, and when Authari died in that same year he took the opportunity to grant peace to his successor, Agilulf, in exchange for an annual tribute.

By the end of the sixth century, the condition of Italy was one of comparative stability, at least so far as geographic divisions were concerned. The Lombard conquest was at no time a conquest of the entire peninsula; part of the land was won by the Lombards, and part was retained by the Empire. The imperial and the Lombard possessions, moreover, intersected one another in a way that prevented the growth of any kind of national unity, either under the Lombards or under the imperial Exarchate of Ravenna. The Lombards founded a kingdom in the north of Italy—an area known thereafter as Lombardy—and the smaller duchies of Spoletum and Beneventum. To the Empire remained Ravenna itself, Rome, Naples, and Venice, as well as the southern tips of the peninsula and, for the moment, Sicily, Corsica, and Sardinia. The Lombards, it is true, never succeeded in mastering their lust for the entire peninsula. Sporadically they attacked Rome or Ravenna. Rome always withstood them, but Ravenna eventually fell (758). Ironically, the fall of that city, which marked the apogee of Lombard power in Italy, was the remote cause of the fall of the Lombards, for it set in motion a chain of events which was to lose for them their kingdom.

The period of Lombard domination in Italy lasted over two hundred years (568–774), and during that time was played out the drama which was to foreshadow the history of the country for almost a thousand years. The Lombards, like a chorus of spear carriers, occupy the greater part of the stage, but the *prima donna* of the piece is the papacy, with the Empire playing a supporting role.

The Roman Empire, or, as it was known in its Greek incarnation, the Byzantine Empire, was an anomalous thing after the fifth century. The most marvelous thing about it was that it existed at all, and its prolonged life—it was to endure for almost a thousand years yet—was a tribute to the almost miraculous nature of Byzantine political genius. The countries which comprised the Empire at this time—Thrace, Illyria, Greece, Asia Minor, Syria, Palestine, Egypt, and, for the time being, parts of Italy—had no visible bond except submission to the emperor. Even that common link of the old empire, the universal languages of Latin and Greek, had disappeared, and only Greek was spoken at Constantinople. Yet, this

Greek empire was still regarded as the Roman Empire of Augustus and Trajan, and as such was still held in esteem by the infant barbarian kingdoms of Europe. A king of the Franks did not think it beneath him to address the Byzantine emperor as "glorious, pious, eternal, renowned and triumphant lord, ever Augustus, my father Maurice, emperor"; and he was honored to be called in return, "Childebert, glorious man, King of the Franks."

The emperor who ruled over this kaleidescopic collection of nations was an autocrat; in fact, one of his proudest titles was that of *autokrator Romaiōn*, Autocrat of the Romans. Into the imperial hands were gathered all the reins of government, civil, military, and ecclesiastical. The foreign policy of the Empire was simplicity itself: to defend its frontiers against the Persians to the east, the Avars to the north, and the Arabs (in the seventh century and afterward, the Saracens) to the south. Its domestic aims were equally uncomplicated: first, to hold together its component parts; second, to extort money from them. The reigning emperor, when he could spare the time from these pursuits, usually devoted himself to the study of theology, for in Byzantium the problems of government were, to a great extent, religious in nature. The greatest interest of the people, after the reproduction and sustenance of life, was religion. It had always been so in Constantinople, and it was to remain so until the crescent standard of Mohammed was raised over Santa Sophia many centuries later. Already, in the fourth century, this obsession had been the object of astonishment to foreigners. Gregory of Nyssa recorded his amazement that "everywhere, in humble homes, in the streets, in the marketplace, at street corners, one finds people talking about the most extraordinary things. If I ask for my bill, the reply is a comment about the Virgin Birth. If I ask the price of bread, the baker tells me that the Father is greater than the Son. If I ask whether or not my bath is ready, I am informed that the Son was created from nothing."

The authority of the emperor himself had a uniquely religious basis. Next to the imperial throne, there was another, empty, on which the Gospels were displayed; it was "the throne of Christ, our true sovereign." Monuments were inscribed and dedicated to *Christos Basileus,* "Christ, the emperor." The famous gold coins of Byzantium, called bezants, bore the head of Christ crowned with the imperial diadem. The laws of the emperor were promulgated not in his name but in that of "The Lord Jesus Christ, Our Master." The emperor, or *Basileus* as he was now called, was essentially Christ's representative on earth—a sacred representative, to be sure, but still only a vicar who ruled by divine sufferance. Because the emperor was sacred, any attempt on his life was, of course, a horrible sacrilege if it failed; if, on the other hand, it was successful, it was obviously God's will that a new emperor be chosen. In this climate, it was clear that an emperor who wished to preserve the Empire intact could do so only by means of enforcing religious unity. This basically political need explains the ever-expanding stream of theological decrees and enactments that emanated from the Sacred Palace in Constantinople throughout the history of the Empire, for heresies were as numerous as the peoples of the Empire were diverse. Justinian had had only the Manicheans, Monophysites and Nestorians to deal with. The Emperor Heraclius, in the seventh century, had, in addition to those, the Syrian Monophysites and the Neo-Severianists. Later emperors had to deal with the Paulicians, the Bogomiles, the Sabellians, the Adoptionists, the Massalians, the Marcionites, the Montanists—and a dozen or so lesser heresies. This necessary preoccupation with the subtleties of theology explains also, among other things, the wariness of the Roman pontiffs with respect to "the Equal of the Apostles" at Constantinople.

In Italy, the emperor governed through the Exarch of Ravenna. This exarch was, in effect, a military rather than a civil governor, since the constant incursions of the Lombards kept the imperial forces in Italy on a wartime footing. The imperial domains there were divided into dukedoms, ruled by dukes, and counties, governed by generals. These officials were Greeks, born and trained in the Byzantine Empire, who regarded themselves as exiles in a foreign and barbarous land. Their official responsibilities were to raise money for the Empire and to repulse the Lombards. Their private occupations were to raise money for themselves and to seduce the women of Italy. Despite such oppressions, both official and personal, the Latins preferred the rule of the Greeks to that of the Lombards, partly because of their common heritage and culture, and partly because, after all, the Empire was still the Empire.

Such a preference is understandable, for the Lombards were not a people whom the tradition-proud people of Italy could easily find attractive. Unlike their barbarian predecessors in Italy, the Lombards had had little to do with the old Empire, and they were both less civilized than the Goths and inferior to them as soldiers and as administrators. Moreover, the Goths had come, at least nominally, at the invitation of the emperor, and they made a pretense of subservience to the Empire. The Lombards had the sword as their only title, and they invariably regarded the Empire as an enemy. They came as barbarian conquerors, and they remained barbarian conquerors for a long time afterward, for they did not make rapid progress in civilization. For generations, they held onto the old ways, spending their time in hunting and brawling and leaving the arts and crafts and industry to the Latins. Still, it was impossible to avoid forever the consequence of contact with the civilized Italians; and, with the passing of time, the manners and mores of the Lombards acquired at least a superficial polish. Desiderius, the last Lombard king of Italy, sought out the company of scholars, and his daughter was encouraged to learn by heart "the golden maxims of philosophy and the gems of poetry." Each advance of the Lombards in civilization was a boon for the Latins, whose lives became easier as the two nations grew closer. The conversion of the Lombards from Arian to Roman Catholicism in the seventh century did much to bridge the gap.

The one national characteristic that contact with the Italians was not able to eradicate among the Lombards was their political incompetence. The time they spent in Italy failed to teach them even the rudiments of Roman statecraft and polity, and the Italy of the Lombards remained a loose collection of some three dozen semiautonomous duchies. There was indeed a central government at Ticinum (Pavia), but it was too weak to impose a unity of purpose on the jealously independent dukes. As a result, the Lombards were never able to weld Italy into a single, strong kingdom. Each city, with the territory immediately surrounding it, came to regard itself as an independent quantity, different and distinct from its neighbors. There was no sense of unity with the remainder of Italy, no sense of duty or loyalty toward a mother country. The virtues esteemed by the Lombard dukes were those of individuality, independence, and jealousy of neighboring dukes; and those virtues made of Italy a nation composed not of Italians, but of Milanese, Romans, Neapolitans, Florentines, Pavians, Beneventese, etc.

This fragmentation of Italy had a second, equally important, effect. It gave to the papacy the opportunity to grow strong and independent of civil authority. Had the Lombards been united, they surely would have overrun the imperial provinces of Italy and the pope would have become a Lombard appointee. Had Italy remained a province of the Empire, the pope would have become merely a provincial metropolitan, perhaps taking an honorific precedence over his fellow Italian bishops. But with the Lombards weakened by disunity, constantly at the throats of the Byzantines, and with each side needing papal support and sometimes bidding for it, the pope was enabled to make himself master of Rome and the real leader of the Latin clergy and people.

If the weakness of the Lombards and of the imperial Exarch furnished the popes with the opportunity to grow strong and independent, the power and the ability to take advantage of that opportunity came from within the papacy. It was a power that found its source in factors material as well as spiritual. Every upheaval in the history of the West has resulted in a revival, sometimes lasting and sometimes transitory, of religious faith, in which religion appears as a haven from the evils and powers over which the individual has no control. So it was in fifth-century Italy, a country at the nadir of its political, economic, and social life. With Latin impulsiveness, the Italians sought comfort, refuge, order, and security in the Church. The Church had no competitor at the secular level, for the state was either barbarous and oppressive, as in the case of the Lombards, or ineffectual and oppressive, as in the case of the Byzantines. Nor was there an alternative to Christianity on the spiritual or intellectual planes; the whimsical gods of the Roman pantheon had been vanquished by the new dispensation, and the philosophies that had enabled the ancients to bear the vicissitudes of fate had been shattered by the hammer blows of Christian theology. Literature, art, and science—all had vanished; or rather, they had been converted and now lived only within the walls of the Church. In the midst of the general ruin of Roman civilization, the Church stood stable and secure, offering peace to the timid, rest to the weary, comfort to the afflicted, sanctuary to the oppressed, culture to the intelligent, a career to the ambitious, and power to the strong. In a dozen ways, the Church drew Italy to herself; and in a hundred ways she sowed the fruitful seeds of an ecclesiastical patriotism which propagated anew the sense of a single people, bound together not by geography but by faith, not by the title of Roman but by that of Christian. To be a Roman was to be a Christian; and to be a Christian was to be a Roman. For the Christian Church in the West was essentially Roman, and she took for herself what remained of life and vigor in the ancient capital of the Empire. With a structure and an organization modeled on the imperial paradigm, she slowly assumed in men's minds an imperial image. Rome, though now but a provincial city, once again began to inspire men with a strange confidence in a new imperial power.

In addition to the strength which the Church derived as the result of her moral and practical resources, there was another strength, this one more sinister, which supported her: the force of superstition and ignorance. The general dissolution of the old order had lowered the common level of knowledge. Almost everyone was ignorant; and, consequently, almost everyone was superstitious. The laws of nature were even more obscure than the laws of theology, and the latter—at least in the popular interpretation of them—soon came to replace the former. Every evil, from the death of a cow to the swelling of a thumb, was the work of the Devil, Satan, an evil spirit of immense power against whom an ordinary man was helpless. His only source of aid was the local priest, who was transformed by public imagination into a sort of wizard. With amulets, bones, relics, incense, and incantations he could protect afflicted mankind from Satan who "like a roaring lion, goes about seeking whom he may devour."

It should be noted that fear and ignorance were not propagated by the Church for her own selfish ends. Indeed, the papacy, even though it occasionally nibbled at the edge of superstition itself, managed in the main to preserve a relative purity of doctrine and practice. The lower levels of the clergy, however, were hardly superior to their flocks in education and sophistication, and their co-operation in the superstitions of the faithful gave to such practices a veneer of ecclesiastical approbation from which the Church, willy-nilly, profited.

To these resources the Church added others, of a more tangible kind. For centuries, men of piety, as they saw death approaching, had made great gifts of land to the Bishops of Rome, as a sort of eternal fire-insurance policy, until the popes had become the greatest landowners in all of Italy. In Sicily, on the mainland, in Corsica and Sardinia, the papacy was undisputed lord of almost two thousand square miles of prime farmland. The income from this enormous estate enabled the popes to establish and maintain churches and monasteries, schools and missionaries, to bribe marauding barbarians, and, as necessity demanded, to equip armies of her own. During the Gothic occupation, and shortly after the Reconquest, the Church had ruled these lands merely as landlord. Later, however, during the period of war between the Lombards and the Byzantines, we find the popes exercising absolute sovereignty over their estates as well as over Rome.

The cornerstone of papal power on the imperial scale was laid by two men. The first of these was Benedict of Nursia (480-544), who founded, and put at the service of the papacy, Western monasticism. The second was Pope Gregory I (540-604), who had the wisdom to reap the fruit of Benedict's work. There had been monks in Italy long before Benedict's time, but they were monks in the Eastern manner; that is, they were hermits, who lived alone in caves or in forests, and shunned the society of other men. Benedict himself, at the age of fifteen, had abandoned Rome for a cave near Subiaco, in the Sabine hills. He knew the solitary life well enough to conclude that the vast majority of men were not suited to it. As civil society disintegrated and great numbers of men sought refuge in monasticism, he founded twelve small monasteries near his cave. In 529, he took the most devoted of his followers to Monte Cassino, and there founded a monastery and formulated the *Regula Suncta,* the famous "Holy Rule" which was to be the inspiration of monasticism throughout the West. Inside the walls of the monastic enclosure, a simple law obtained: *ora et labora*—"work and pray." The Rule was but a commentary on this injunction. The monks were bound by a vow of absolute obedience to their elected superior, the abbot, and by additional vows of poverty, chastity, stability—that is, they were not to leave the monastery without the abbot's permission—and conversion of morals. Once a man entered the monastery, he was dead to the world, and the world to him. Previous honors or rank meant nothing; there was to be "no distinction of persons in the monastery. A free-born man shall not be preferred to one who was a slave, unless there is some other reasonable cause; for whether we are slave or free we are all one in Christ." Alms and hospitality were to be given to the extent that the means of the monastery permitted, and the monks were required "to receive all guests who come, as though they were Christ."

In the spirit of the Holy Rule, the monasteries became oases of quiet and contemplation in a tumultuous age. Some monks quietly tilled their fields, and when the barbarians or the Byzantines devastated the fields of the peasants there was always food to be had for the asking from the good Benedictines. Other monks were set to work copying manuscripts in the monastic libraries, and thus—even though the pious monks often erased a gem of antiquity so as to have room for some fantastic tale of miracles—were preserved works of the Romans and Greeks that otherwise would have been lost forever. Through their sanctity, industry, and generosity, the monks soon won the loyalty of the people of Italy as well as their respect; and with the support and encouragement of the populace, the monasteries of the Holy Rule multiplied and spread throughout Italy and, soon, beyond the Alps.

It is not without significance that the monasteries of St. Benedict of Nursia were bound by a special loyalty to the Bishop of Rome, for, three years before Benedict's death in 543, a man was born in Rome who would know how to take advantage of that loyalty for the greater glory of the Church and, sometimes, of God. Gregory, whom history would call "the Great," was the son of an ancient patrician family whose wealth and position assured him of the highest honors that the decrepit state of his era could offer. Indeed, at the age of thirty-three he was already Prefect of Rome. He soon tired, however, of the honors of the world, and, renouncing his rank, he distributed most of his fortune to the poor of the City and used the rest to found seven monasteries. He turned his own palace into a cloister and inhabited it no longer as Prefect but as a monk. But the Church was not content to leave her gifted son in peace. One pope ordained him as one of the seven deacons of Rome, and another made him ambassador to the imperial court of Constantinople. In 586, he returned to Rome and was elected abbot of St. Andrew's monastery, where he was allowed to live quietly for a time. Then, in 590, a terrible plague swept Rome. So terrible was its contagion that, during a religious procession that was formed to implore heaven's mercy, no less than eighty people died. A contemporary chronicler, as though reality were not horrible enough, adds that there was present in the City a monstrous dragon, and a horde of venomous serpents. The reigning pope, Pelagius II, was one of the plague's first victims, and the clergy and people of Rome at once chose Gregory to succeed him. The humble monk wanted nothing more than to be left to his prayers, and he tried to escape the honor by fleeing from the City; but he was seized, conducted by force to St. Peter's, and there, all unwilling, he was acclaimed the successor to St. Peter. Once enthroned, however, Gregory knew how to make the best of a bad bargain. Though he often complained of the burdens he was forced to bear, he had seen enough of the world to know that the hope of civilization, and the future of religion, lay in the papacy. He therefore applied himself with energy, ability, and devotion to his new task.

Rome, at that time, was in a pitiable state. Its nominal ruler, the Exarch of Ravenna, was unable to defend it, and it was preyed upon by the Lombards of Spoletum who raided under its very walls and carried off Romans as slaves. Gregory, of necessity, had to take complete charge of the civil and military, as well as of the ecclesiastical, administration of the city. "I do not know any more whether I am a priest or a temporal prince," he moaned. "I must take care of the defense of the City and of everything else. I am become only a paymaster to the soldiers."

To the people of Rome, he was considerably more than a paymaster. Instead of spending the revenues of the Church in the construction of new churches, he used the money for charity, for gifts to monasteries, and in ransoming captives. To every poor family in the City he gave a monthly ration of corn, wine, cheese and milk, oil, meat, fish, and clothing. Daily, the Church of Rome delivered meals, already prepared, to the sick and the infirm. He was as gentle and fatherly to the poor, the distressed, and the weak as he was tyrannical and overbearing to the clergy and bishops who would not follow his example of pastoral benevolence. For the sake of these latter, Gregory composed his *Liber Pastoralis Curae,* a book of advice for bishops, which was to become one of the classics of the Middle Ages.

It was manifestly impossible for a man of Gregory's time to discern the seeds of a new empire germinating underneath the ruins of the old; yet, Gregory acted as though he saw them. And, although he repeatedly warned the faithful of the imminent end of the world, he organized the Church and the clergy as though he were certain that they were to endure for a thousand years in the form that he gave them. He had the true imperial instinct, and under his guidance Christianity spread beyond the confines of the ancient Empire. Among the events of his pontificate are the conversion of England by St. Augustine (597), and that of the Franks, Alemanni, and Lombards by Irish missionaries. In the same vein, he encouraged the clergy of trans-Alpine Europe to visit Rome, and to apply to him for advice and help. The respect and esteem which he inspired throughout Christendom may be inferred by the way in which he was addressed by Columbanus, an Irish monk: "Holy lord and father in Christ; most beautiful ornament of the Roman Church; the most illustrious flower, so to speak, of languishing Europe; to him who is sufficiently learned to inquire into the theory of the divine causality, I, a mean dove [Columbanus' name was derived from the Latin word for dove], send greetings in Christ." Gregory also established and maintained close relations with the clergy of Africa and of Spain, which had recently been won over from Arianism. He was in frequent correspondence with the barbarian kings and queens of Europe, and with the Byzantine emperors and empresses.

Gregory's administration of the internal affairs of the Church was marked by the spirit of reform. He struggled successfully to suppress the practice of offering ecclesiastical offices to the highest bidder, and unsuccessfully first to coax, and then to wean forcibly, the clergy of Italy from the practice of concubinage. He reformed the already relaxed practices of the monasteries, and bound those institutions to himself with chains of tempered canonical steel. He administered the estates of the Church wisely and firmly, but he was generous in loans and gifts to his tenant farmers—though he somewhat marred his record by offering reduced rents to Jewish tenants in return for their conversion to Christianity.

He met the rulers of his day not only in the confessional and in the churches, but also on the battlefield of diplomacy. Some of these battles he lost; but he won more often than not, and in the end he left the power and prestige of the papacy enormously enlarged and almost universally recognized. Theoretically, he acknowledged the authority of the Byzantine emperor over the Church, and that of the Exarch of Ravenna. When the

Emperor Maurice, in 593, issued a decree prohibiting the reception of soldiers as monks, Gregory felt the blow acutely, but his timid remonstrance on that occasion showed how implicit was his acceptance of the facts of political life. "What am I," he wrote, "but a worm, and dust, thus to address my Masters? I have done my duty in every respect; I have obeyed the emperor, and still have not been silent about what I felt to be due to God." It was a subordination which Gregory had already recognized in 590, when he had vainly begged the same Maurice to refuse his confirmation to the election which placed Gregory upon the papal throne. But though he was willing to subscribe to the theory of imperial authority over the Church, in practice he was equally willing to ignore it—particularly when it was a question of civil authority. Thus, when the Lombards of Spoletum threatened Rome, Gregory signed a treaty with them without bothering to consult either Constantinople or Ravenna. He was careful, however, to keep the peace, both civil and religious, with Constantinople, mostly by acquiescing on those rare occasions when the emperor did intervene in the affairs of the Church, and occasionally by addressing adulatory letters to the imperial, and reverent ones to the patriarchal, throne.

For all his wisdom, experience, and sanctity, Gregory was a man of his time. He was not particularly learned, nor especially sophisticated theologically. As he ruled a disintegrating empire with one hand and struggled with the other to organize a new empire, his mind was filled with thought of devils, miracles, and the approaching end of the world. He accepted without question all the wonders of popular legend, and he lived in a world darkened by the intrigues of ghosts, devils, witches, and evil spirits of all kinds. His books—the *Dialogues,* the *Magna Moralia,* and the *Homilies,* particularly—recorded and passed on to succeeding generations the concept of a universe of evil against which man was to feel himself powerless for many centuries. It is difficult to believe that this is the same man who built the temporal power of the papacy, freed it from imperial domination, and administered it with a sagacity that ensured its endurance. It is possible to wonder, with Will Durant, "whether the great administrator believed what he wrote, or merely wrote what he thought it well for simple souls to believe."

Gregory was also a man of this time in the sense that he shared the opposition of many Church Fathers to any idea, any culture, any creation, that was not specifically Christian in origin. Perhaps he felt that, with ignorance and superstition rampant among both clergy and laity, any reversion, or even any allusion, to the values of the old pagan days would inevitably confuse the old gods with the new. Whatever the cause, Gregory condemned, several times, the works of the great minds of antiquity as wholly unfit for Christian eyes. The most famous incident of this kind was a letter of reprimand to Desiderius, Bishop of Vienne:

> It has reached our ears, dear brother, that you are occupying yourself with the teaching of grammar to certain of your friends. We are much disturbed at this report, and outraged at such behavior on your part. It ill becomes the mouth that is ordained to sing the glory of the Christ to befoul itself with the praises of Jove. Moreover, consider how serious, and indeed how scandalous, it is that you, a bishop, should find delight in something that is fit not even for a dutiful layman. . . . If, on the other hand, it should happen that what we have heard is untrue, and you are able to prove to our satisfaction that you are not in fact idling away your hours in the empty vanities of secular learning, then we shall give thanks to God.

There is no record of the consequence of this reprimand, but it is safe to assume that any irregularity, which came to Gregory's notice once, seldom came twice.

Gregory and Benedict were the great figures of their age, and the edifice that they had built was to endure virtually unchanged for a thousand years. That fact is even more remarkable in view of the caliber of some of Gregory's successors, who found it as difficult to emulate their predecessor's virtues as they did to equal his power and authority. Pope Honorius I (626–638), for example, so far forgot himself as to agree to a proposal of the Emperor Heraclius (designed to unite the Monophysite East, which believed that there was but one nature in Christ, with the orthodox West, which distinguished two) to the effect that there was but one will in Christ. To everyone's embarrassment, it turned out that the proposal was heretical, and it was roundly condemned by the Sixth Ecumenical Council, at Constantinople, in 681, as "foreign to the Apostolic dogmas, to the definitions of the Councils, and to the opinions of the Fathers. It follows the false doctrines of the heretics, wherefore we totally reject it as harmful to souls. . . . Moreover, we eject from the Holy Catholic Church of God, and we anathematize, Honorius, the former Pope of Rome . . . for having approved of such impious dogmas." This incident, born of the tension between pope and emperor, was to plague for centuries the proponents of the dogma of papal infallibility.

Pope Martin I (649–653), on the other hand, was determinedly orthodox; but he had to pay a high price for it. When he refused to ratify a proclamation of the Emperor Constans I which promulgated the Monothelite heresy, he was summarily arrested by the Exarch and hustled off to Constantinople to answer for his impudence. Apparently that answer was not satisfactory, for he was exiled to the Crimea, where he died. Yet, at the other end of the scale, we see this same Martin exercising the immense extension of papal prerogatives which had accrued to Rome as the result of Gregory's policies and Constantinople's weakness. In 649, we read that he appointed John, Bishop of Philadelphia, as apostolic vicar in the dioceses of Antioch and Jerusalem, with the power to ordain priests and bishops in those large and important areas.

The struggle against the heresy of the Monophysites, though it is a dreary tale of theological hatred, was not without some importance for the history of Italy. The battle ended when the Mohammedans took over Syria and Egypt in the seventh century, and thus rid the Empire of the two strongholds of heresy. Under the impulse of the same Council of Constantinople that had condemned Pope Honorius, the East then joined the West in orthodoxy, and, for the moment, peace reigned between Rome and Constantinople. But it was an uneasy peace. Constantinople had gone too far in its humiliation of Gregory's successors, and both the emperors and the popes knew it. Such treatment might have been accepted, as it often had been in pre-Gregorian days, if the Empire had been in a position to give the papacy its *quid pro quo*. The emperors had fallen upon hard days. The Empire had been almost fatally weakened by the rise of Moslem power and its expansion into Spain, northern Africa, and Asia Minor. The Mediterranean, which as recently as the time of Justinian had been a Roman lake, was now the exclusive domain of the sons of Mohammed, whose bravery on the battlefield was matched only by their success as pirates. In the face of these difficulties, Constantinople was less than ever in a position to fulfill its responsibilities and protect Rome from the incursions of the Lombards.

It might be supposed that the papacy, under the threat of a Lombard conquest of the City, would have clung to the Empire in the hope, if not of immediate aid, then at least of the rise of another Justinian who would deliver it once again from the barbarians. Things, however, had changed in Italy. The Lombards, once savage Arians, had been converted to Roman Catholicism and had finally begun to blend with the Latins. Relations between the papacy and its newly found spiritual sons were comparatively simple. They vacillated between war and friendship, sometimes simulated and sometimes real. It was an understandable, a human relationship, uncomplicated by anything as difficult as a conflict of jurisdiction. The Lombards, as Catholics, were perfectly willing to acknowledge the pope as their spiritual father—an acknowledgment which was quite distinct from, but not contrary to, their repeated efforts to add the pope's city to their Italian domains. It was the kind of relationship that the papacy could understand. As the spiritual head of the Church, the pope was content to shower blessings on the heads of the Lombards. As temporal ruler of Rome, he was just as ready to make that shower one of arrows, spears, and boiling oil. Both parties understood the arrangement, and the Lombard king, in the act of assaulting Rome, could salute the pope as "Most Holy Father in Christ," and the pope could answer, "My most beloved son."

With respect to the Empire, however, the situation was different. By the beginning of the eighth century, and in the aftermath of the Monophysite unrest, the gap between Romans and Byzantines was as wide, and considerably more unbridgeable because of bitterness, as that between Lombards and Romans. There seemed to be an essential difference between the Greek mind, adrift in a sea of vague speculative theology and even vaguer metaphysics, and the Roman mind, bound as the latter was by necessity to political expediency and immediate ends. A theology capable of ravishing a congregation in Sancta Sophia could leave unmoved the worshipers in St. Peter's. The Empire, obliged by its military weakness to adapt theological niceties to the requirements of unity, consistently favored a creed of compromise. Rome, with the imperial instinct bequeathed to it by Gregory the Great, and with the means of enforcing it created by St. Benedict of Nursia, maintained that its strength lay in orthodoxy, and it defended an inflexible credo. Empire and papacy, in short, had become impossible bedfellows, and it was inevitable that their ancient cohabitation should now come to its term.

The end, when it came, was sudden in its execution and simple in its conception. The Empire, pressed by the Mohammedans, tried once more to find unity and political strength in theological legislation. The effect of this legislation was to cause rebellion against the emperor's authority in the imperial provinces of Italy. The papacy broke its ties to the Empire, and then, finding itself open once more to the attacks of the Lombards, made an alliance with the Franks, who invaded Italy and overthrew the Lombard kingdom.

The elaboration of this chain of events begins with a great religious movement of the seventh century, for it was that movement, basically, which acted as a wedge between the Empire and the papacy. Out of one of the obscure tribes of Arabia, there suddenly appeared a man who has had few equals in the history of the world. At the age of forty, he declared himself a prophet, and, in the fire of genius, he forged and disseminated one of the great religions of the world. The religion of Mohammed—for such was the

The Fall of the Roman Empire 49

prophet's name—worked almost magically upon the ambitions and the temperament of the Arabs. It engendered, among other things, a fierce passion for conquest and for the conversion of the infidels who worshiped Christ, one of the prophets of Allah, rather than Allah himself. With incredible rapidity, nomadic Arab tribes joined together both as a sect and as a nation, and then erupted out of their deserts to spread quickly over western Asia and northern Africa. The armies of Byzantium were powerless to stop them, and the natives of the imperial provinces, mercilessly taxed and always at theological odds with Constantinople, were not unhappy to accept a new and unknown master in place of one whom they had learned to know too well.

Mohammed died in 632, but his successors, the Caliphs, carried on his work with undiminished enthusiasm. Under them, the Mohammedan armies advanced from conquest to conquest, driven by the promise of Paradise if they fell in battle and by the threat of hell if they failed in their duty to Allah. "Behind you is the Devil and the everlasting fires of hell," urged the Caliphs. "Before you there is only Paradise." Cities and provinces were torn from the Empire. Syria, the Holy City of Jerusalem, Damascus, Mesopotamia, Armenia, Egypt, and Rhodes succumbed in rapid succession. All of the imperial dominions in Africa, and many places of which the emperor had never heard, were consumed bit by bit. Mighty Persia was beaten to a standstill, and then pounded to her knees. Sicily was raided by roving Moslem pirates. On two occasions, the armies of the Caliphs were at the very walls of Constantinople, crises to which the Byzantines responded each time, first by a series of colossal religious processions, and then, in a burst of good sense, by complete mobilization. On both occasions, the invaders withdrew, and it is left to the bias of the individual to determine whether the orations of the Byzantines, or their arms, prevented the substitution of the crescent for the cross over the towers of the city.

In the extremity of the situation, the statesmen of Byzantium perceived that if something drastic were not done, then the whole of the Empire would be forced to assume the sweet yoke of Allah. As often happens, a man arose to meet the challenge of his time, in the person of a vigorous emperor, Leo the Isaurian (717–741). Leo was a man not only capable of radical action but actually prone to it. The solution he conceived hinged, as always at Constantinople, on theological considerations. The Empire had been weakened, and the nobility and people divided by the great religious schism which gave its name to the period from 717 to 867: The Iconoclastic Epoch. The Iconoclasts (image breakers) were those who, as their appellation implies, maintained that the use of images—that is, of paintings and statues of holy subjects—should not be allowed in Christian worship. The case for the Iconoclasts had been stated as early as the fourth century by Epiphanius of Cyprus, who preached that the use of images reduced the divine to the level of the material, and that their worship was a revival of the gods of the pagans. "A Christian," he thundered, "should have no need to find his soul through the medium of his eyes or the straying of his senses." This not illogical position had had a long history in the East, and its adherents were a political as well as a religious power in the Empire by the time of Leo's ascension. It is not impossible, as some authorities have maintained, that Iconoclasm was Jewish in inspiration; and, indeed, the Mosaic injunction against "graven images" was well known. It seems more likely, however, that a more important stimulus after the second half of the seventh century was provided by the Moslems, with whom, between wars, the Byzantines were in constant contact, and whose sacred book, the Koran, was unequivocal on the subject: "Images are an abomination and the work of Satan."

To the Iconoclasts were opposed the Iconodules (image worshipers) who, since they represented the *status quo,* were less controversial and, consequently, less famous. Their stand was summed up, with brevity and good sense, by that model of both qualities, Gregory the Great. Gregory wrote to the Bishop of Marseilles praising him for ordering that nothing made by human hands should be adored, but at the same time censuring him for the destruction of the images which were, after all, the only means of educating an illiterate populace "who can at least read, by looking at the walls, those things that they cannot read in books." In another letter to the same bishop, Gregory wrote that "it is one thing to adore a picture; but another thing entirely to learn, through the picture, about that which is to be adored."

Over the centuries, the struggle between the Iconoclasts and the Iconodules took on the proportions of a major internal upheaval and on several occasions, as was customary in Constantinople, controversies between opposing theologians were settled in the streets, and not without the effusion of blood. Such intervals of tragedy were punctuated by moments of high comedy. On one occasion, the Iconodules repaired for Mass to their favorite Church of the Holy Apostles, to find that the walls, which the day before had been painted with the effigies of saints, were now covered from ceiling to floor with crude sketches of carrots, cauliflowers, cabbages, and other ignoble vegetables.

Leo the Isaurian was an Iconoclast by conviction. Moreover, he was irritated because the saints invariably got credit for whatever victories the

The Fall of the Roman Empire

Byzantines were able to wring out of their struggle with the Moslems; and there were not enough victories to satisfy the vanity of both saints and emperors. And finally, it did not please Leo that a large part of the spoils of war had to be handed over to the churches to enrich the altars of the saints. Emperors are, after all, men, even before they are Christians; their motives are seldom simple, and almost never pure. In 725, therefore, Leo officially endorsed the iconoclastic movement and issued an edict denouncing the use of images as a form of idolatry.

The reaction in the West was immediate and violent. The pope, Gregory II (715-731), refused categorically to acquiesce in this blasphemy and, perforce, to order that the images be removed from the churches of the West. Writing to Leo to inform him of this decision, Pope Gregory did not bother to conceal his disgust with the emperor's position:

> During ten peaceful and happy years, we have known the comfort of your royal letters, signed in purple in your own hand, attesting to your attachment to the orthodox creed of your predecessors. How deplorable is the change! How universal the scandal of it! You now accuse the Catholics of idolatry, but by this accusation you betray your own impiety and ignorance. To such ignorance, we are compelled to make our own arguments conform in grossness of style. For even the first elements of Holy Writ are sufficient to confound you. Indeed, were you to enter a grammar school and declare yourself to be opposed to our form of worship, the very children, pious as they are, would throw their books at your head.

After these pleasantries, Gregory got down to business:

> Tyrannically, you persecute us with the sword and the secular arm. But we, naked and unarmed as we are, and protected by no earthly power, we invoke the Lord of Hosts, Christ on high, commander of the powers of heaven, to send to you a devil, as says the Apostle "To deliver such a one unto Satan for the destruction of the flesh, so that the spirit may be saved." . . . You declare, with your foolish pride, "I will show my might in Rome. I will break in pieces the image of St. Peter, and Gregory will be brought in chains to the foot of our imperial throne." . . . It is our duty to live for the edification and support of the faithful, and we are not reduced to risking our safety on the hazards of combat. Although you have been incapable even of defending your Roman subjects in the past, still, the proximity of the City to the sea may perhaps expose us to your depredation. In that event, we shall remove to the first fortress of the Lombards, and you will be left to pursue the winds. . . . The barbarians themselves have submitted to the yoke of the Gospels, while you alone remain deaf to the voice of the Shepherd. These

pious barbarians are inflamed with rage, and they thirst to avenge the persecution by the East. Abandon, O Emperor, your rash and fatal enterprise. Reflect; and then tremble, and repent. If you persist, we will be innocent of the blood that will be spilled. On your head be it!

In the face of such defiance, Leo had no recourse but to try to enforce his decree. No one, not even a pope, could be allowed to insult the emperor with impunity. Gregory, learning of Leo's determination, forgot his resolution to rely solely upon the Lord of Hosts, and he lost no time in writing to the churches of Europe, warning them both of the emperor's impiety and of his designs upon the life of the Vicar of Christ. "And there was a great disturbance," says a contemporary chronicler, "and the Five [Greek] Cities and the armies of the Venetians resisted the order of the Emperor, declaring that they would never permit the murder of the pontiff, but that they would fight manfully in his defense." Even Ravenna and the cities of the Exarchate declared for the pope, and they were prepared to fight side by side with their hereditary enemies, the Lombards, for the sake of orthodoxy. Gregory also appealed to the Franks, but Charles Martel, Mayor of the Palace of the Frankish king and the real ruler of the Franks, listened respectfully, and then called upon heaven to witness his filial devotion to Rome. But he could not send troops, he said, since he was engaged in repelling the Saracens from his own lands.

All Italy was indeed, as Gregory had boasted, inflamed against the impiety of the East, and the passions of Italy found relief in two ways. First, images were destroyed throughout the peninsula—but they were not the images of the saints; they were those of Leo and his predecessors. Second, and more effectively, the imperial cities of Italy refused to remit their taxes to the emperor. Now Leo felt that he could exist well enough without the statues, but taxes were another matter. Shortly, he dispatched a fleet and an army to Italy, by way of the Adriatic Sea. The papal allies met the imperial forces in the vicinity of Ravenna, and a fierce battle raged throughout the day, with one side winning now, and now the other. In the fashion, or at least in the legends, of the time, the issue finally was decided by a frightening apparition in the sky and by a mysterious voice from heaven. The Byzantines retreated in disorder to their ships, where they were trapped and massacred until the Po ran red with their blood. The pope, by now Gregory III, successor to the second pontiff of that name, had the satisfaction of unleashing the thunders of excommunication against the heretical Isaurian and the obsequious hierarchy of the Greek Church (731).

The break between the East and the West was now, for all practical purposes, complete, and, except for a few brief intervals it was to endure. Italy no longer had need of Constantinople and her emperor. She now had a new master, one of her own choosing.

II
THE EMERGENCE OF SUCCESSORS TO CAESAR
(731–962)

With the disappearance of effective Byzantine power in Italy, the whole of the peninsula—with the exception of the south and Naples, which were to remain formally part of the Empire for another three and one-half centuries—fell, as were, into the hands of the Roman pontiffs. That is not to say that the popes were, in effect, kings of Italy, or that the rule of Constantinople was rejected in principle or that of Rome acknowledged. The laws of Byzantium, and those of the Lombards, continued to be enforced, and the nominal suzerainty of the emperor was still recognized. It was to the throne of St. Peter, however, that the peoples of Italy, Byzantines as well as Lombards and Latins, now looked for leadership and guidance. It was a shadowy crown that the popes wore; and, to their credit, they wore it uneasily, at least at first.

Since the time of Gregory the Great, the papacy had aspired to independence, and even to a certain temporal sovereignty which would guarantee that independence. But they had not bargained for, nor did they particularly want, a temporal sovereignty whose responsibilities were clearly without the ambit of the spiritual Vicars of Christ, and one the burdens of which might deprive them of that very independence of action for which they had fought.

Pope Gregory II (715–731) would have been the first to acknowledge that an independent Church in a virtually independent Italy was a practical impossibility, no matter how attractive that proposition might seem in theory. An independent Italy meant, at that time, an Italy free from the domination of a strong secular ruler; it also meant, therefore, an Italy at

the mercy of the first ambitious barbarian who happened on the scene. And the Church had had too much contact with barbarian conquerors by now to imagine that she would be able to function freely in such a situation. Gregory, therefore, contrived a solution to the dilemma. In casting about for allies against Constantinople, he had perceived a new star ascending in the West, and from that time forward his basic policy was directed toward the forging of a bond between the popes and the kings of the Franks.

Still, the habits of centuries die hard, and the popes were reluctant to flaunt their newly found independence in the faces of the emperors—at least, not until they were able to bind the fortunes of the Franks to those of Rome. As late as 772, for example, we find papal documents bearing the name and dates of the detested Emperor Constantine Copronymus, the most vigorous partisan of Iconoclasm. But no one, unless it was the emperor himself, was more aware than the papacy that the threads that had linked together Church and Empire since the time of the great Constantine I were now unraveled, and that the popes would never again submit to the whims of the amateur theologians on the Bosphorous. The claims of the Bishops of Rome to universal primacy had always irritated Constantinople, and there was always the danger that a heretical emperor might set up his own tame pope in the imperial city. It was, therefore, in that most important respect, expedient that Peter now break away from Caesar. And what could be more plausible than that the bastion of orthodoxy in the West should wish to dissociate itself from the stronghold of heresy in the East? There were other reasons, too, of more practical, and sometimes of more emotional, significance. The language of the papacy, and of the entire West, was Latin, while that of the Empire was Greek. As a result, the theologians of East and West could not discuss freely the differences that had been a source of constant friction between pope and emperor. Moreover, there were liturgical differences, cultural differences, and economic differences which made Italians and the Greeks mutually suspicious and suspect, while, on the other hand, liturgical, cultural, and economic similarities between the Italians and the barbarian kingdoms of the West increased with each new generation. Finally, the popes were now fully aware that the Empire was too weak to wield the sword that was necessary if the Church was not to be victimized by the barbarians. This was, in the final analysis, the effective reason for the decision of the popes to look henceforth to the Franks for that support which they had been so long unable to obtain from the Byzantines.

By the middle of the eighth century, the Kingdom of the Franks had been established in what is now Belgium, Holland, and large parts of France and

Germany. It was by far the greatest power in Europe, and therefore the one on which would most naturally devolve the duty of protecting the Vicar of Christ. The Franks alone of the barbarians had, from the beginning, embraced Catholicism. Moreover, in their efforts to extend their domains, they had been greatly assisted by Roman missionaries who had first prepared the way for conquest, and then helped consolidate the authority of the conquerors by preaching submission in every corner of the conquered lands. These missionaries, of course, were absolutely loyal to the Roman see, and they spread this loyalty wherever they went. St. Boniface, for example, the Apostle of the Germans, assures us that "as often as God sends me an audience and followers in this mission of mine, I never cease to preach and to urge submission to the Holy See." Thus was forged an enduring bond between the Franks and Rome, and a firm basis for a political alliance. The papacy required only an opportunity to build upon that foundation.

The opportunity presented itself soon enough. Once it became clear that the popes had irrevocably disavowed their effective allegiance to the emperors, the Lombards, those long-time occupiers of much of Italy, judged that the moment of glory had come. As soon as the Byzantines had disappeared across the Adriatic, the Lombards acted. But they acted foolishly. Instead of launching one bold and sudden campaign against Rome and the south of Italy, they expended their resources and their enthusiasm in assaulting and subduing a few unimportant cities. Papal Rome had time to cry for help; and every time the Lombards made a hostile move—and there were many such times—the popes appealed frantically to the Franks for aid.

Now the Franks, good Catholics and barbarians though they were, were not unskilled in the art of political advantage. On more than one occasion, they considered, quite rightly, that the disadvantages of intervention in Italy outweighed the advantages; and each time that the Holy Father in Rome appealed to them, they would express pious horror at the temerity of the Lombards and then go back to their own affairs. Charles Martel, as we have seen, was unwilling to help Gregory I even when it seemed likely that the latter would be submerged by the armies of Byzantium. Charles's son and successor, however, Pepin le Bref ("the Short"), came to take a different view. Pepin, like his father, held the office of Mayor of the Palace under the ancient line of Merovingian kings established by Clovis in the early sixth century. Unlike his father, however, he was not content with the reality of power; it was his ambition to acquire the trappings of absolutism that only formal and unquestioned investiture can confer. He proposed, therefore, to depose the Merovingians, in the person of the regnant Childeric III, and to establish his own family, in the person of himself, upon the throne. But as the Merovingians had reigned for many generations, and as the Franks, like other barbarians, attached great importance to the concept of legitimacy, Pepin realized that the revolutionary course which he wished to adopt could be successful only if his projected kingship were ornamented, as it were, with heaven's cachet. He therefore dispatched ambassadors, in 751, to Pope Zacharias, asking whether or not it would be sinful to depose Childeric and himself ascend the Frankish throne. Zacharias saw his chance. "In the exercise of his Apostolic authority," the chronicler tells us, "he replied that it seemed to him better, and indeed necessary, that he who held and wielded power in the kingdom should be called king, and be king, rather than he who falsely bore that title. And the pope therefore commanded the King of the Franks and his people that Pepin, who held the power of a king, be seated on the throne and be called king." Childeric III was therefore deposed and hidden away within the secure and convenient walls of a monastery, and Pepin, with the approval of the assembly of Frankish nobles and bishops, and after an anointing by St. Boniface, sat upon the throne and was thenceforth called King of the Franks.

Pepin was not allowed to forget, however, that he owed throne and title to the Vicar of Christ. In 753, the Lombards, with renewed vigor, began once more their struggle to subdue the whole of Italy. In a surprising display of military competence, they captured Ravenna and then turned toward Rome. On October 14, the new pope, Stephen II (752–757) left Rome for Pavia to negotiate, as he thought, terms of an armistice with Aistulf, the Lombard king. In the Lombard capital, he was entertained magnificently, complimented generously, listened to reverently, and then dismissed empty-handed. But Stephen was a man of imagination. Instead of returning to Rome, on November 15 he set out across the already frozen Alps toward Pepin's winter camp. In his hands, he carried the destiny of Italy, for, from that date, the fate of the peninsula was to be fixed for a thousand years. Italy was no longer to be attached, however loosely, to the Empire of the Greeks; she was not to be unified, as were Gaul and Spain, under the authority of barbarian kings; instead, she was to bow for centuries beneath the heavy scepters of monarchs from beyond the Alps. For Stephen lost no time in striking a bargain with Pepin. He anointed (again) and crowned Pepin *rex gratia Dei*, "king by the grace of God," anointed and blessed Pepin's son and heir, Charles, and, in a perhaps excessive act of legitimation, forbade the Franks, under pain of excommunication, ever to

The Emergence of Successors to Caesar

elect a king from a family other than that of Pepin. In return for such munificence, Pepin engaged himself to render such military assistance to Pope Stephen as circumstances might require.

Stephen then returned to Rome, and almost immediately summoned King Pepin to discharge his obligation. Twice the Lombards assaulted Rome, and twice did Stephen beseech his new ally to come to the rescue—the second time by means of a letter which, in a flight of rhetorical fancy, declared itself to be written by St. Peter himself and proclaimed the Franks to be "among all peoples the most congenial to me, Peter, the Apostle of God, and therefore I give into your care, through the hands of my Vicar, the Church which the Lord entrusted to me." The newly crowned king was not remiss in his new duties. He stormed across the Alps, handily defeated the Lombards and forced them to cede to the Pope the Exarchate of Ravenna and the five coastal cities to the south of it (the Pentapolis). It was a pious donation, and one by virtue of which the pope became a sovereign prince in title as well as in fact.* The not ungrateful pontiff responded in kind by conferring on his benefactor and deliverer the title—one hitherto reserved to the approval of the Byzantine emperor—of *Patricius Romanorum,* "Patrician of the Romans."

The founding of the papal monarchy in Italy by force of Frankish arms is of such importance for the future history of the country that it would be helpful to explore briefly the theoretical basis for this gift of sovereignty. There was a legend, universally accepted at the time of Pope Stephen and King Pepin, that an early pope, Silvester (314–335), had cured the Emperor Constantine I of leprosy. The emperor had given tangible expression to his gratitude, the legend went on, by making a grant of territory to the pope. Over the centuries, and in the retelling of the story, this grant had grown until it was said that the popes had received, as an inalienable gift, almost the whole of central Italy—including, of course, Rome. The purpose of the legend is clear enough. As papal authority waxed and that of the emperor waned, it was necessary to give a semblance of legitimacy to papal domination in matters temporal. No good Latin of the era would have been satisfied by a title derived from barbarians, be they Lombards or Franks; for the barbarians, having never had a legitimate title to the land of Italy, obviously could not convey legitimate title to it. The only indisputable, the only possible, source of legitimacy was the Empire; and

---

* The exact extent of the donation of Pepin cannot be ascertained from any reliable document in existence today, and the matter has been much disputed. It is generally accepted, however, that the territory involved was that described above.

it was to the Empire that the storytellers of the age betook themselves and found their source in the person of Constantine.

Eventually, the myth of the "Donation of Constantine" was embodied in a document, which itself became known as the "Donation of Constantine," and which was universally regarded as being the actual instrument by means of which the emperor had transferred the sovereignty of Italy from himself to the Roman pontiff. This document was probably composed at about the time of Pepin's Donation, very likely by someone in the papal chancery, and it presented the facts as the writer thought them to be, or else as he thought they should be. Although this "Donation" is, beyond a doubt, an utter falsification, it is not a "forgery" in the modern sense—a distinction which, as difficult as it may seem to later generations, was perfectly obvious to the falsifier's contemporaries. The author had no intention of fabricating claims on behalf of the papacy. He wished only to provide an irrefutable legal basis for prerogatives which the popes not only exercised in practice, but the origins of which were believed to be wholly authentic. The proof of the author's skill, and perhaps of his convictions, lies in the fact that, despite the contradictions and anachronisms inherent in the document, the "Donation of Constantine" was accepted without question for almost seven centuries—that is, until it had served its purpose well.*

This magnificent fabrication reads as follows:

> In the name of the holy and undivided Trinity, Father, Son, and Holy Ghost, the Emperor Caesar Flavius Constantine . . . to the most holy and blessed Father of fathers, Silvester, Bishop of Rome, and Pope, and to all his successors in the seat of Peter, so long as the earth shall endure.

Here follows a rambling account of the cure of Constantine's disease, of his conversion and his realization that St. Peter and his successors had been given "all power both on earth and in heaven." Then comes the substance of the document, the grant:

> We, together with all our Satraps and the whole Senate, Nobles and People . . . have deemed it fitting that, even as St. Peter is on earth the appointed Vicar of Christ, so also the Pontiffs, his vice-regents, should receive from us and from our Empire a power and a sovereignty greater than that which belongs to us. And thus we have commanded, according to the extent of our terrestrial Empire, that the Holy Roman Church be honored and venerated,

---

* It was finally exposed for what it was, in the fifteenth century, by Laurentius Valla and Cardinal Nicholas Cusa.

The Emergence of Successors to Caesar

and that the throne of St. Peter, above our own earthly domain, shall be gloriously exalted. . . .

Let him who shall be pontiff of the Holy Roman Church be sovereign of all the priests of the world, and by his judgment let all things be ordered which pertain to the worship of God or to the faith of Christians. . . .

To holy Silvester, our father, the supreme pontiff and universal Bishop of Rome, and to all his successors who shall sit, until the end of time, on the seat of Peter, we hand over and relinquish our palace of the Lateran, our diadem, which is the crown of our brow, together with all the insignia of our imperial office, including even the purple leggings and the tunic, and the imperial sceptre. . . . And, as the imperial household is clothed, so also shall the clergy of the Holy Roman Church be clothed. . . .

And in order that the supreme priesthood shall not be held in contempt by men but rather be lifted up above the power and the glory of the terrestrial Empire, we give to the most holy Pope Silvester not only our palace, but the city of Rome and all the provinces, places and cities of the West; and we ordain by this, our pragmatic sanction, that they shall be governed by him and his successors, and we command that they shall remain forever under the authority of the Holy Roman Church. . . . For where the principality of the priesthood and the head of the Christian religion has been established by the Heavenly Emperor, it is not fitting that an earthly ruler should have authority.

In the face of such splendid pretensions, one hardly knows whether to admire more the audacity of the author of the "Donation" (which, naively enough, was couched in the terminology of an eighth-century legal instrument, complete with Latin neologisms and crude barbarisms) or the faith even of the most erudite medieval scholars who, for almost eight centuries, were to accept this massive fraud as an authentic document. One should not make the mistake, however, of applying twentieth-century standards (either of criticism or of morality) to the Middle Ages. In the latter epoch, fictions were everywhere accepted as truth, and they were used constantly to explain accomplished facts. It was a practice that gained such wide acceptance, indeed, that writers did not blush to admit, in the prologues of their works, that they had made use of this technique. One bishop, Agnellus of Ravenna, for example, wrote in the ninth century that, in composing the biographies of his predecessors on the episcopal throne, when he was "not able to obtain information concerning them from any authentic source, then, in order that there might be continuity, I have made up the life myself."

A fraud of the proportions of the "Donation of Constantine" differs from the efforts of Bishop Agnellus only in the matter of degree. The purpose of both documents was the same: to provide a written basis for what all good Christians believed anyhow.

In the case of the Donation, as might be expected, the commendable desire of the popes to secure the political independence of the Church was mingled with, and degraded by, the wish to add temporal wealth to spiritual domination. Even that motive was not without some basis in justice. Ever since the authority of the emperor had been extinguished in central Italy, it had become the responsibility of the papacy to provide for the safety and welfare of the citizens. The popes were obliged to raise armies, to defend the City, to negotiate treaties, and to care for the poor. Even in Theodoric's day, no one—least of all the pope himself—had been surprised when Cassiodorus remarked to the pontiff that "the security of the people is your responsibility, since it has been placed in your hands by divine providence." Such responsibilities could not be fulfilled by drawing on heavenly capital; they required temporal resources.

Justifications, moral or otherwise, are beyond the purview of history, and one must confine oneself, however intriguing the alternative, to the consideration of what was, rather than what could have, or should have, been. In the harsh light of that fact, one thing stands out with respect to the Donation of Constantine: the theory embodied in the Donation was filled to overflowing with the seeds of future strife. For the moment, however, the situation was as promising as it was tranquil between the Franks and the papacy. The former was recognized as the strongest power in the West, and the latter as the most prestigious. Between them, they were in a position to dominate Europe. There was only one question left to be settled: which of the two would succeed in dominating the other?

By the latter half of the eighth century, the papacy had good reason to believe, first, that it had secured the moral and political leadership of the West, and, second, that that hegemony would be supported by a powerful, but deferential, Frankish state. This new self-confidence was soon demonstrated by the papal resolve to rid itself once and for all of the troublesome Lombards, or at least finally to subject them to Roman authority. On the death of Aistulf, the Lombard king, destiny turned up two claimants to the vacant throne. One of the pair, Desiderius, asked for the support of the pope, Paul I (757–767), and received it in exchange for several cities. Strengthened by papal approbation, Desiderius was crowned. The pope, pleased by this new recognition of the power of the Church to dispose of thrones, informed his Frankish ally of Desiderius' accession: "Now that Aistulf, that disciple of the devil, that devourer of Christian blood, is dead; and since by your aid and that of the Franks [a bit of flattery, for Pepin and his Franks had done nothing to aid Desiderius' cause], he has been succeeded by Desiderius, a most gentle and good man, we pray you to urge him to continue in the way of righteousness."

The honeymoon between Desiderius and Paul was not of long duration. The "most gentle and good" Lombard king, now secure upon his throne, refused to cede the promised cities to the pope, and the latter once more called upon Pepin to secure the rights of Holy Mother Church. Pepin, however, was now also secure; moreover, he felt that he had already more than fulfilled his obligation to Rome. He refused to cross the Alps for the sake of Pope Paul's cities.

The moral of Pepin's posture was not lost upon Paul, who, after all, was the successor of a line of popes who had experienced, not infrequently, the fickleness of secular princes. It was clear to him that the West was not being shaped in the pattern intended by the Donation of Constantine. The prestige of Christendom might well be centered in Rome, in the hands of the popes; but the power of Christendom lay across the Alps, in the arms of an undependable Frankish chieftain. The papacy, once again, after a brief respite, seemed subject not only to the clumsy ambitions of the Lombards, but also to the moods of a desultory protector. For the moment, therefore, Pope Paul was forced to swallow his pride, and he contented himself with a few sharp words to King Desiderius on the subject of ingratitude toward one's benefactors.

King Pepin died in 768, and all Rome was outraged to learn soon afterward that his wife, now the dowager Queen of the Franks, was negotiating with the Lombards. The subject of these exchanges was Charles, better known to history as Charlemagne, the son and heir of Pepin. Through his mother's machinations, Charles was betrothed to a daughter of Desiderius. The pope wrote in horror, or perhaps in terror, to Charles, declaring that the proposed marriage had been conceived in hell and forbidding it under pain of everlasting damnation. But Charles, even at the age of twenty-eight, had a mind of his own, and he married the Lombard princess in 770. As it turned out, the pope's fears for the safety of the Church were not justified, but his predictions of catastrophe for the marriage were. The union between the King of the Franks and the Lombard dynasty came to an end in 772, when Charles divorced the princess—"without any crime on her part," a contemporary observer tells us—and sent her home to King Desiderius. The Lombard monarch was livid with rage at the insult thus inflicted upon his house, and, driven by fury, he embarked on a course which was to make of him the last Lombard King of Italy. First, he attempted to stir up internal dissension among the Franks, and then, the intricacies of successful intrigue being, as always, beyond the abilities of the Lombards, he began to attack and seize, one after the other, the cities guaranteed to the popes by the Donation of Pepin.

Finally, and inevitably, Desiderius turned his armies toward Rome. The pope, now Adrian I (772–795), feverishly set about fortifying the city once more against the barbarians. He also sent messengers to Charles (by sea, since the Lombards held all the land routes), but without much hope of rescue since the Lombards would reach the City long before the Franks could send aid. Adrian, in the final analysis, had to rely, like his predecessors, on his spiritual authority rather than on military prowess. Surprisingly, it once more turned out to be an effective defense. Adrian solemnly and publicly declared that an attack upon Rome could call down upon the heads of the Lombards the curse of Heaven, and an irrevocable and eternal damnation. Desiderius, the wolf whom the papacy had once mistaken for a sheep, undoubtedly would have shrugged off the terrors of excommunication, but his followers were of a more superstitious nature, and they refused to advance to within more than fifty miles of the City of the Apostles. The papal anathemas did not, however, extend to the cities already taken by the Lombards, and Aaenza, Ferrara, and Commacchio remained in the hands of the pious barbarians.

Charles, meanwhile, had received Adrian's ambassadors at his palace, and he listened with sympathy to their tales of Lombard depredations in Italy. Despite the pro-Lombard sentiments of some of his nobles, he decided on a declaration of war. It was a question, he pointed out, not only of papal territory, but also of Frankish honor; his own father, Pepin, had guaranteed the cities of the Exarchate of Ravenna to the late Pope Stephen. Still, since the Lombards had by now integrated the captured cities into their domains, Charles decided to attempt to negotiate with them before crossing the Alps. Accordingly, he sent an embassy to Desiderius, offering fourteen thousand gold coins in exchange for the disputed cities. It was a move designed more to placate pro-Lombard sentiment at the Frankish court than to forestall the necessity of military operations in Italy. Charles probably suspected, and he certainly hoped, that Desiderius was in search of glory, not gold. He did not miscalculate. The Lombard king rejected the gold with such scorn and such angry words that the Frankish emissaries were able to report to their master that the honor of the Franks could not tolerate the insult of Lombard contempt. Charles breathed a sigh of relief and crossed the Alps with a vast army.

It had been Desiderius' plan to engage the Franks at the Alpine pass of Mt. Cenis; but the sight of the enemy hordes was too much for him, and he immediately retreated to his capital at Pavia. Charles was therefore able to march into Italy without opposition, and, as Einhard, his friend and biographer says, "with the aid of the Lord and the intercession of Saint Peter the Apostle" to advance to the walls of Pavia. There, this aid and intervention apparently ceased, for the Franks were unable to take the city by assault, and they were forced to settle down around the walls to spend the winter in siege. Charles, leaving the major part of his army encamped there, marched down the valley of the Po toward Verona, subduing on the way a number of Lombard cities. Verona herself surrendered without a struggle.

Pope Adrian, in the meantime, had taken advantage of the disorders in the north of Italy to expand his dominions. Having persuaded the Lombards of Spoleto to desert the cause of Desiderius and place themselves under his protection, he proceeded to appoint one of his own nobles as Duke of Spoleto. This highhanded act, made possible only by Charles's intervention in the north, was not well received by the Franks. Charles felt that, as the conqueror of Lombardy, Spoleto was his by right as well as by the customs of war. Moreover, Adrian was giving signs of an independence of action in other ways that was not fitting in one who was, after all, Charles's protégé and not his master, or even, in the eyes of the Franks, his equal. It therefore seemed expedient to Charles to open discussions with the pope even before the fall of Pavia since, in view of the still undecided fate of the Lombards, he could avoid making any definite commitments. In that frame of mind, he journeyed southward to Rome in the spring of 774.

The City was, for Charles, considerably more than the capital of Christendom. It was the Imperial City, which, even though it had fallen upon hard times, was still hallowed by the shadow of an imperial presence, a shadow which could not fail to inspire and to impress a king whose aspirations were at least equal to those of the most ambitious Caesar. To set the note for his visit, Charles did not bother to inform Pope Adrian of his intentions. Adrian, himself a master of diplomatic innuendo, could not fail to grasp the implications of this omission: Charles was master in Italy; he could come and go as he liked, without or with the approval of the pope. "When Pope Adrian learned that the Frankish king was coming, he was almost overcome by astonishment," records a contemporary papal clerk. It is likely that Adrian was equally affected by chagrin, for he had hoped that Charles would treat him as the ruler of a sovereign state rather than merely as a local lord. Still, he did his best to put a good face on the situation, and he mounted a reception calculated to impress upon the Franks the importance of his double crown as pope and prince. The entire papal court was sent to meet Charles on the road, and when the king arrived at the walls of the City he found crowds of people singing hymns and waving palm leaves in greeting. The clergy of Rome met him with the pope's official cross, as was the custom in greeting an Exarch or a Patrician of the Romans. At the Basilica of St. Peter's—which was, at that time, outside the walls of Rome—the piece continued to be played out. Charles, in an excess of devotion at the sight of Christendom's most venerable and hallowed temple, fell upon his knees and kissed each step as he mounted toward Adrian, who was waiting for him at the door of the church. Then, lest his devotion to the Apostle be mistaken for subservience to the pope, he seized Adrian by the hand and roughly pulled him inside the Basilica, thereby demonstrating to the gaping crowd that it was his church, and not Adrian's.

During Charles's stay in Rome he discussed with Adrian the political and religious questions of the day. It is likely, in view of the results of these meetings, that the pope was more than able to hold his own with the rather rough Charles. The two men were, other than in their ambitions, the antitheses of each other. Charles, though he was a patron of learning and had great respect for scholars, was himself barely literate. He was, in effect, a barbarian who had, by military might and native ability, risen above his station. Einhard wrote that Charles "tried to write, and usually placed tablets and sheets of parchment under his pillows so that, at odd moments, while he was resting, he could practise by tracing letters. But he had begun too late in life, and the results were not very happy." His usually genial disposition was tempered by occasional bursts of violent temper, and his marital adventures—he had nine wives, whom he divorced one after another either through boredom or political expediency—bear witness to a barbaric license in his private life. Though he was not by nature a cruel man, he was unsparing of blood when it suited his needs, and, on one occasion, he caused some four thousand Saxons to be beheaded in a single day. It was an act of wanton butchery compared to which the punishments that he ordinarily imposed, such as the death penalty for refusing baptism or for eating meat during Lent, pale into insignificance. Adrian, on the other hand, was a Roman noble from the peak of his tiara to the toes of his pontifical slippers, supremely elegant and personable, the scion of Rome's proudest and most aristocratic family. He had risen rapidly in the Church, propelled, as was the custom of the time, by his family's influence, but equally by the learning, charity, and devoutness for which he was famous. He was at the same time gentle and forceful, kind to his subjects but relentless in the defense of orthodoxy, subtle in diplomacy, and skillful in the pursuit of his goals. As so often happens between men of dissimilar backgrounds and temperaments, Adrian and Charles took an immediate liking to one another, and their discussions laid the foundations for a friendship which, as durable as it was unexpected, was to survive innumerable crises in Franco-Roman relations.

Most of their conversations concerned the extent of the pope's authority in Italy, and the delineation of Frankish authority with respect to it. Adrian's ambition, like that of his predecessors as far back as Gregory the Great, was to form an independent and viable state, capable, in case of need, of defending itself. Charles, for his part, was not inclined to allow the temporal expansion of the papacy. He had sincere doubts about the wisdom of joining in the same hand the swords both secular and spiritual. Moreover, any Italian territories that might be ceded to the Roman pontiff would have to come, as it were, out of Charles's own pocket. And finally, at this time, Charles's own vision of the relationship between his throne and that of the pope was beginning to emerge as one in which the Church was to be the spiritual arm of the Frankish kingdom, rather than, as Adrian thought, the Franks being the temporal arm of the Church. This concept was one to which Charles adhered all his life, and which he enunciated, some years later, for the edification of one of Adrian's successors:

> It is our duty outwardly to defend everywhere, with divine aid, the holy Church of Christ from the incursions of the pagans and the depredations of the infidels, and inwardly to fortify the acceptance of the Catholic faith. It is your duty, Most Holy Father, with your hands raised in prayer to God, like Moses, to aid our arms, since by your intercession God himself will lead us and give to his Christian people, in his name, constant and universal victory, so that the name of Our Lord Jesus Christ will be glorified throughout the world.

Despite these convictions, Charles wanted to help Adrian. He liked the pope, and he was generous, albeit sporadically, with those whom he liked. Furthermore, he was a genuinely pious man, according to his own lights, who felt a deep reverence for the Holy Roman Church. The combination of these factors, added to Charles's natural tendency to overenthusiasm, culminated in a brilliant and dramatic ceremony in St. Peter's on Easter Sunday. On that occasion, Charles presented Adrian with a document attesting to a new donation and confirming the earlier one of Pepin. Although no text of the Donation of Charlemagne exists today, it is certain that there was, in fact, a donation, and that the episode was not, as in the case of the Donation of Constantine, merely the fabrication of some well-intentioned cleric. It is equally certain that the terminology of the donation was highly and intentionally ambivalent. According to Adrian's contemporary biographer, from whose work we have the most reliable information concerning the gift, Charles granted to the papacy the whole of the Exarchate of Ravenna, the provinces of Venetia and Istria, the troublesome duchies of Benevento and Spoleto, and Corsica. If that is so, then Charles gave away everything in Italy except the imperial provinces in the south and his own newly acquired possessions in Lombardy. But it appears, from Adrian's many letters to Charles in later years, that the Donation was substantially more circumscribed than the biographer would have us believe; for Adrian himself, as quick as he was to defend what was legally his, never once referred to so extensive a gift. All that is known for certain is that the gift was made, and that it was of considerable extent.

When Charles left shortly afterward to return to the siege of Pavia, he quit the City with the cheers of the Romans ringing in his ears and the blessing of the pope upon his head. Neither, however, could obscure the fact that he had done himself a disservice by allowing Adrian's soft words and aristocratic demeanor to wring concessions from him. Already Charles had begun to covet at leisure what he had distributed in haste. Such second thoughts were not based so much on selfishness as they were on strategy. Some of the lands that he had so lavishly donated to the Patrimony of St. Peter—the Duchy of Spoleto, for example—were necessary to the defense of his hard-won Italian possessions. For the rest, he did not begrudge the pope a certain amount of territorial expansion so long as it was clear to everyone, and especially to the pope, that such acquisitions were the gift of the King of the Franks and not the result of a legitimate papal right. The situation, Charles resolved as he rode northward, was one that he would correct at the first opportunity.

Once at Pavia, Charles received the surrender of the city and of Desiderius himself. He took possession of the former as undisputed master, and he dispatched the latter to a Frankish monastery where the last native King of the Lombards was to remain immured for the remainder of his life. Thus, after two hundred years was extinguished Lombard rule in Italy. But the Kingdom of the Lombards was destined to live on, at least in name, for Charles had determined to add it to his own dominions. He accomplished this by a sophisticated expedient hitherto unknown to the barbarians: by annexation, a solution which resolved, to a certain extent, the difficulties inherent in governing two dissimilar kingdoms separated by the Alps. The alternative would have been to appoint a new king, either a Lombard or a Frank, in which case the natural frontiers of Lombardy would have invited eventual treachery. Charles therefore proclaimed himself King of Lombardy, and henceforth he desired to be known as "Charles, by the grace of God, King of the Franks and of the Lombards, Patrician of the Romans." It was a resounding title, but not one destined to fall happily upon the papal ears, for it announced to the whole world that Charles regarded his Roman patriciate as secondary in importance to his Lombard crown. The King of the Franks was no longer a mere protector of the popes, to be summoned across the Alps at the pontifical whim and then dismissed with a nod. He was now an Italian potentate and, from this time, Italy and the papacy were to swing in his orbit.

In the months that followed the fall of Pavia, Charles successfully exercised his primacy in Italy—so much so that Adrian, moved almost to despair, complained that the subjection of the Lombards had profited him not at all. None of Charles's promises had been kept and, indeed, Adrian had even lost some of the cities given to the papacy by Pepin. The rival Archbishop of Ravenna had seized large parts of the Exarchate, and he claimed that he was doing so on Charles's authority. "It is said," Adrian wrote, "that the King no longer loves the Holy Father."

The fact of the matter was not that Charles loved the Holy Father less, but that he loved his rich Italian cities more. Where Adrian and his predecessors had miscalculated in their plans for an alliance with the Franks was in not taking into account the possibility that a masterful personality might appear on the throne of that nation. To their amazement, one such had come forth in the son of Pepin; to their chagrin, he did not hesitate to demonstrate his mastery of the Church as well as of Italy. Charles not only had no intention of allowing Adrian to exercise sovereignty in the peninsula, but he doubtless planned to extend his own rule throughout the land. The north of Italy was already his, and the papacy held, at his pleasure, the central portions of the country. All that remained for him to do was to march into the Byzantine domains in the south and in Sicily. It was an ambition in which Pope Adrian, always at odds with the imperial Iconoclasts, wholeheartedly acquiesced, although such an acquisition would place his already precarious domains between two segments of Charles's kingdom—an awkward bit of geography in the book of any prince. Already, in fact, the king was beginning to nibble away at the papal possessions. For instance, when he returned to Rome for the second time, in 780, he informed Adrian that he had changed his mind about the gift of Spoleto, and he forbade the pope to exercise any authority, or to interfere in any way, in the affairs of that duchy. With respect to the Byzantine possessions, however, circumstances conspired to prevent Charles from attaining his objectives. The Empress Irene had, after the death of the heretical Emperor Leo IV, renounced the Iconoclastic heresy, and she was now making overtures to the West. In 781, an embassy arrived from Constantinople asking for the hand of Charles's daughter, Rothrude, on behalf of the Empress' son. The king could not find it in his heart to refuse such an honor, or to spurn the imperial approbation that such an alliance would imply, and the couple were formally betrothed. It was not, therefore, a time for war with the Empire.

By the end of 786, Charles was again in Rome, from where he put down a minor rebellion by Arachis, Duke of the Lombard duchy of Benevento. No sooner had he turned his back, however, than the Duke was again conspiring, this time more dangerously, with Byzantium. According to the terms arranged, Arachis was to receive the title of Patrician, and he was to represent the Emperor in Italy and even in Rome itself. Thus, both king and pope were suddenly threatened by an attack which was to be supported, if not actually reinforced, from Constantinople. It was not entirely a vain threat, for Arachis' duchy of Benevento was a large and relatively wealthy one, encompassing as it did the major portion of southern Italy.

Once again Charles appeared at Rome, and once again Adrian welcomed him warmly—all the more so because of a rumor that had spread rapidly throughout Italy, to the effect that the Franks intended to subdue the entire south of Italy and to incorporate into their kingdom the lands of the perfidious Byzantines as well as those of the perennially troublesome Lombards. Arachis had, of course, heard the same report, and he was in a panic. For all his brave words, the Lombard knew that his military forces were inadequate and ill prepared, and worse, that the double-dealing Byzantines, while they might be prepared to rattle their swords, were unwilling to draw them in defense of a mere barbarian princeling. The Duke of Benevento could, in his mind's eye, envision himself joining his father-in-law, ex-King Desiderius, in some dreary monastery of Frankland. Hoping that, since words had created this desperate situation, words might be able to resolve it, Arachis sent his eldest son, Romuald, to Rome, to plead with the king for peace, or that failing, for mercy.

Romuald was a personable young man, princely in bearing and pleasing in appearance, more cultivated than was the wont of the scions of barbarian dynasties, and he enjoyed a reputation for valor that was substantiated by his willingness to plead a cause that, in view of Charles's reputation for exacting terms that amounted to unconditional surrender, appeared hopeless. But Charles, while he could not be moved by threats of force, was peculiarly susceptible to personal charm, and to idealism and courage. Almost did Romuald persuade the mighty Frank to accept the terms that Arachis offered: the Duke of Benevento would take an oath of fealty to the Frankish king and would regard himself as Charles's vassal and his kingdom as an appendage of the Frankish crown. Clearly, this was almost as much as Charles would have been able to obtain by outright war, and he was mightily tempted to accept the offer. But Pope Adrian was altogether opposed to peace by negotiation. He pointed out to Charles that the Lombards, as their history demonstrated amply, were an untrustworthy, aggressive, mendacious, and degenerate race, to whom the ordinances of earthly overlords meant even less than the laws of God. Adrian's position was strongly sustained by Charles's nobles and commanders, for to them the south of Italy represented a rich prize and a potential treasure chest of booty. Moreover, they argued, the very fact that Arachis offered to capitulate before battle had even been joined indicated that a campaign against Benevento would meet with little resistance. Thus opposed on every side, Charles acquiesced in the ambitions of his nobles and his Church, and he marched toward Benevento (788).

Arachis fled to Salerno, a city strongly fortified and difficult of access, from where he sent another offer of peace. This time his terms were agreement in advance to any requirements that Charles might state, an unconditional oath of loyalty to the King of the Franks, and the surrender of his second son, Grimoald, as hostage for the fulfillment of his promises. These terms were tantamount to unconditional surrender, and Charles, to the disappointment of everyone but the Lombards, accepted them. Peace was proclaimed, and Charles announced publicly that his actions had been dictated by a desire to spare southern Italy the horrors of war.

Pope Adrian remonstrated both publicly and privately with the king, pointing out, with odd theology and even odder logic, that the ways of peace were hardly becoming to the secular arm of the Prince of Peace. But Charles, though he claimed to be neither theologian nor logician, was more than sufficiently acute as a ruler to perceive the advantages of winning a war without striking a blow, and Adrian was forced to accede with as much grace as he could muster. It was a bitter pill, sweetened slightly by Charles's promise to enlarge his original donation to the papacy to include several cities in Benevento and Tuscany as well as Capua. Then trouble broke out in Charles's domain of Bavaria, and, before he had had the opportunity to effect the transfer of those cities, he was called northward. Behind him, he left Italy virtually united, for the first time in centuries, and, with the exception of the imperial provinces in the south and on the Venetian littoral, bound to one king and held together by a common oath of allegiance. He also left behind him a smiling, but unhappy, Adrian.

For the years of Charles's domination in Italy, the peninsula enjoyed a tranquillity and a relative prosperity such as she had not known for centuries. Farms were reclaimed and made productive once more. Monastic schools flourished under Charles's encouragement and learning once more became respectable. Lombards and Italians, no longer conquerors and conquered, but subjects all of a trans-Alpine lord, forgot what differences still remained between them and lived peaceably side by side, intermarrying and breeding a race of northern Italians whose appearance and demeanor, to this day, attest to its mixed origins. Charles, in his absence, dominated the Roman Church as thoroughly as he had while in Rome. Indeed, like the Byzantine emperors, he was not above dictating to the pope in matters of dogma. In 787, the Council of Nicaea, representing both the Eastern and Western branches of Christianity, had condemned Iconoclasm and had, at least from the doctrinal standpoint, reconciled Rome and Constantinople. Charles, however, refused to accept several of the conciliar decrees, and he sent an ambassador to Rome armed with a document listing, in eighty-five points, the king's objections. In 794, Charles adverted to the matter again and convoked a council of his own at Frankfurt, to which he summoned all the bishops of the West. Adrian was peremptorily ordered either to attend in person or to send representatives. This new council, in obedience to Charles's dictation, condemned the doctrines of the image worshipers, along with several other resolutions of the Nicaean Council. In several of the documents of the Frankfurt synod, Charles was acclaimed, significantly, as *rex et sacerdos*—"king and priest."

In many additional respects, Charles was moving slowly, and perhaps unconsciously, toward the revival of the Empire of the West. As king, he was the protector of Christianity, and, apart from the minor princes of Spain and Britain, he was the only true sovereign in the West. As "priest," in a metaphorical sense, he exercised a control over the affairs, both internal and external, of the Church to an extent that might have awakened the envy of the Emperor of the East. It was a situation the implications of which did not escape Charles's more perceptive intimates. Alcuin, his friend and teacher, would write to the king, with the assurance of being understood perfectly, about certain matters "pertaining to the administration of your imperial domains." Charles was, in fact, regarded as something more than a barbarian king by both pope and emperor. In 796, after the death of Adrian, his successor, Leo III (795–816), sent to Charles the standard of the City and the keys to the Tomb of St. Peter, in recognition of the Frankish king's supremacy in Rome. In the same year, Leo began the practice of dating his edicts, not from the beginning of his own reign or from that of the Byzantine emperor, but from that of Charles. In 798, an important embassy reached Charles's court at Aachen from Constantinople. The Empress Irene—who had, in the previous year, deposed and blinded her son, and who now claimed to rule in her own right—had sent a letter expressing a wish for "peace"; that is, for the stabilization of the situation in Italy. The implications of this *démarche* from Constantinople were obvious: the ruler of Byzantium, still universally regarded as the dispenser *par excellence* of legitimacy, was willing to recognize Charles's presence in the peninsula and to treat him as an equal.

Charles's current position in Italy, in the former provinces of the Empire that stretched across the peninsula diagonally, from the mouth of the Tiber to the Po and the Adige, was vague, at least from the standpoint of constitutionality and legitimacy. In the past, he had promised to the popes, and sometimes allowed them to exercise, temporal authority over the duchies of Rome, Perugia, and Spoleto, as well as over the former imperial territories across the Apennines which he had taken from the Lombards. There is no mistaking the fact that Charles regarded himself, and that first Pope Adrian I and then Pope Leo III regarded him, as the papacy's temporal overlord. An indication of this was not only the remittal to Charles of the Roman standard as the symbol of secular authority, and of the keys of the Tomb of the Apostle as the symbol of spiritual protection, but also that, during this period, Charles's name began to appear regularly in the liturgy of the Roman Church—a prerogative hitherto reserved solely to the emperor. On the basis of these tenuous privileges, Charles was quite willing to accept not only the honors entailed by his unique position, but also the responsibilities. And he was soon called upon to exercise those responsibilities in a way that was to confer the ultimate legitimation of his reign and to open the door to one of the crucial events of European history.

In 798, Charles sent to Rome one Arno of Salzburg, a Frankish cleric, to receive the *pallium,* a symbol of archiepiscopal authority which only the pope could bestow. Arno, after some months in Rome and Tuscany, returned to Frankish soil ornamented with the *pallium,* wearing a head full of gossip concerning Pope Leo's conduct of affairs in Rome, and carrying an account of grave internal difficulties in the City as a consequence of the pope's highhanded ways. The causes of these difficulties are obscure, and there is little information about them in contemporary documents.

From what is known, however, it appears that Leo's reign was being opposed by a faction led by relatives of the defunct Adrian. Leo's fault—and it was regarded as such at the time—was that he was a man of the people, sprung not from Rome's ancient nobility but from the great unlettered and unmoneyed masses of the City. It was a defect that Adrian's splendid relatives could hardly overlook, and from it they spun a web of intrigue and opposition in which they hoped the parvenu pope would entangle himself fatally. Charles's reaction to these reports was to send an observer, the Abbot of Stablo, to Rome. He hoped that the presence of a royal legate would quell the disorderly nobles and, if need be, keep the feet of the new pope on the narrow paths of righteousness.

It was a vain hope. In the spring of 799, Leo, while celebrating the mysteries of the Greater and Lesser Litanies, was taken prisoner in the sight of a great multitude of the faithful and shut up in a monastery. He languished there for a few days, and then escaped and placed himself under the protection of Charles's troops at Spoleto. It was reported to Charles that Adrian's rascally family had first blinded Leo and then cut out his tongue, but that these organs had immediately been restored, by divine intervention, to the unhappy pope's head. Leo lost no time in claiming that his miraculous cure demonstrated God to be on his side. Nonetheless, Charles's representatives thought it wise to remove Leo from the neighborhood, and they conducted him across the Alps to the royal summer camp at Paderborn, in Saxony. For two months there, Charles and Leo discussed the situation at Rome. In the midst of these discussions, letters arrived from Leo's enemies accusing the pope of various crimes, among them those of adultery and perjury. There is no evidence that Leo was either an adulterer or a perjurer. Indeed, his reputation generally was that of a saintly man. One may conclude that the obstreperous Roman nobles had simply chosen those accusations that would be the hardest for Leo to disprove. For example, it is clearly impossible to prove that one has not committed adultery.

The charges made against the Vicar of Christ, however, were so serious, and the situation had become so public and so scandalous, that Charles felt obliged to settle the affair publicly. He sent Leo back to the papal city in October 799, with a large entourage, and probably with the understanding that it would be necessary for the pope to submit to a judicial inquiry as soon as Charles's affairs permitted his presence in Rome.

By October of the year 800, Charles had set out for the City with a large and splendid escort. Pope Leo met him at Mentana, at the twelfth milestone from Rome—an honor that would have been unprecedented in the case of an emperor and that was unheard of in that of a mere king. Pope and king feasted together, and the following day Charles made his ceremonial entry and was officially received by Leo at St. Peter's with a display that recalled an Augustan triumph in the old days of Empire.

Leo's lavish hospitality was undoubtedly designed, at least partly, to mollify Charles, in view of the forthcoming inquiry into the pope's conduct. For almost a year now, Charles's emissaries in Rome had been investigating the charges against Leo. According to the custom of the Franks, they had proceeded by trying to uncover evidence in support of the charges. When no such evidence was forthcoming, or, if found, when it had proved too flimsy to be convincing, the accusers of the pope were forthwith arrested and sent to Frankland—a primitive sort of justice, but one not without some merit. The pope was not officially exonerated, however, until the convening of a court of inquiry over which Charles himself presided. Contemporary accounts of this trial differ. According to the Frankish chronicles, no one was there to accuse the pope—small wonder, in view of the previous action of the investigators. According to the *Liber Pontificalis,* the papal annals, the bishops and abbots who had been summoned to judge the pope declared that they were unwilling, and indeed unable, to pass judgment on their superior. A third account, that of the German author of the *Lorsch Annals,* records that King Charles, unable to find any evidence of wrongdoing on Leo's part, invited the pope to swear to his innocence so that the charges might be dismissed as groundless and spiteful. Whatever the truth of the matter, on December 23, Pope Leo mounted the pulpit of St. Peter's and addressed the nobles, clergy and people of Rome in the presence of Charles:

> It is well known to everyone, dear brothers, that wicked men have risen up against me and attempted to mutilate me, and that they have made most serious charges against me. Now, Charles, our most gracious and illustrious king, has come to the City, with his bishops and nobles, to investigate this matter. Therefore I, Leo, Pope of the Holy Roman Church, acting not under duress but of my own volition, do declare before God, who knows my conscience, and before St. Peter, Prince of the Apostles, in whose temple we are assembled, that I have neither committed, nor caused to be committed, the heinous crimes of which I am accused. I do this of my own free will, so that all suspicion may be removed, even though the canons of the Church do not require it. I do not wish, however, to establish a precedent in this respect, nor to impose this practice upon the bishops, my brothers in the episcopacy.

Thereupon, Charles embraced the vindicated pope. The assembled nobles, clergy and people burst into a loud *Te Deum,* and the City congratulated itself upon the preservation of the virtue of its Shepherd. The anti-Leonine troublemakers, however, remained in their dank Frankish prisons to meditate the folly of calumny, and never more did they cast a shadow over the conscience of Christendom or over the tranquillity of Charles's Italian realm.

By a curious coincidence, on the day that Leo publicly was restored to grace, there arrived in Rome certain ambassadors from the Holy City of Jerusalem. These emissaries carried with them the symbols of authority of that city, which they ceremoniously presented to Charles, with the entreaty that, as Protector of the Church of Christ, he would extend his sword to cover the Holy City and shield it from the infidel Mohammedans. The embassy may well have appeared at the instigation of the diplomatic Leo, but its significance was far more than that of a mere courtesy. By it, notice was served that Charles, King of the Franks and of the Lombards, Patrician of Rome, was the protector not only of the Church in the West, but of the universal Church. It was a calculated affront to Constantinople, and a grievous one which, in the days of Byzantine power, would have brought swift retribution upon the heads of those who dared so to insult the Equal of the Apostles. Now, however, there was no emperor in Constantinople. There was only an empress, Irene, who was too occupied with palace intrigue to take notice of the affront, and too weak to avenge it in any case.

Still, for all of Byzantium's weakness and for all of Charles's strength, the Empire remained, in the eyes of Christendom, the sole proper source of authority. In the office of emperor was vested, as everyone knew, the *imperium,* the rule of the world by divine mandate, by virtue of which an emperor became the secular arm of God on earth. Charles, though his authority might be imperial in extent, was still only a king, and a barbarian king at that. It was obviously time for the imperial dignity to be added to imperial power—perhaps on the precedent established for the benefit of Charles's own father, to the effect that "he who held and wielded power in the kingdom should be called king, and be king, rather than he who falsely bore that title." Moreover, Charles was already widely regarded, at least by his own people, as the equal of Constantinople's emperor. Alcuin, an illustrious scholar whose reputation for probity preserves him from the accusation of sycophancy, had written to Charles, in 799, that:

> Hitherto, there have been three exalted persons in the world. One is the Apostolic and sublime being who rules the see of Saint Peter in his [Peter's] place. . . . The second is the emperor, the secular possessor of the second

The Emergence of Successors to Caesar

Rome [i.e., of Constantinople]; even though the whole world is scandalized by reports of the ruler of that Empire who has been deposed, not by aliens but by his own subjects. The third is the possessor of that royal dignity which the Lord Jesus Christ has bestowed upon you as the ruler of a Christian people, a dignity more complete in power than others, more eminent in wisdom, more sublime in the power of the kingdom. You are the avenger of injustices, the shepherd of those who have wandered astray, the consoler of the afflicted. Power is given to you to exalt the good.

The stage was thus set for the enactment of one of history's great dramas. On Christmas morning, the day after Pope Leo's exculpation, in the year 800, Charles, accompanied by a great crowd of Frankish and Roman nobles, made his way through the streets of Rome to the Basilica of St. Peter. There, at the top of the broad marble steps, Leo and the entire papal court greeted him, and then pope and king passed through the great atrium, past the fir-cone fountain and the papal tombs, through the great central doors, and then, with the measured pace of a religious procession, to the Tomb of the Apostle. Thirteen hundred and seventy candles in a single great candelabrum glowed on the silver floor of the shrine and reflected from the gold and precious stones of the statues which lined the walls. Charles knelt at the tomb and prayed for a time. Then, a chronicler of the time records, "when the king was rising for the Mass, after praying before the Tomb of the Blessed Apostle, Pope Leo, with the consent of all the bishops and priests and also of the Senate of the Franks and of that of the Romans, set upon his head a crown of gold, and the people of Rome shouted aloud. And when the people had finished chanting Lauds, he was adored by the pope, as were the emperors of olden times. And this, also, was done by the will of God." Another observer, this one an Italian, saw the proceedings through a Roman, or at least through a Latin, eye, and added that ". . . all the faithful of Rome, seeing the defense that he [Charles] provided and the love that he bore to the Holy Roman Church and to her Vicar, by the will of God and of St. Peter did cry, with one voice and in a great shout, 'Charles, the most pious Augustus, crowned by God, great and peace-giving Emperor; to him be life and victory forever'. . . . And the most holy pontiff anointed Charles with holy oil, and likewise his most excellent son [also named Charles] to be king. . . . And when the Mass was finished, then did the most serene Lord Emperor offer gifts." Another chronicler, Theophanes, adds an irreverent detail, to the effect that Pope Leo, in ignorance of the ceremonial of coronation, "smeared Charles with oil from head to toe," as though he were administering Extreme Unction—the sacrament of the dying. But since Theophanes was a Byzantine, we may ascribe his barb to pique rather than to a passion for detail.

Einhard, Charles's biographer, remarks that his master was taken completely by surprise at the coronation, and that he had such an aversion to the titles of Emperor and Augustus "that he declared he would not have set foot in the church on the day they were conferred, even though it was a great Holy Day, had he known of the pope's intention beforehand." It is generally agreed, however, that Charles not only knew in advance exactly what would happen at St. Peter's, but that he and the pope had planned the whole drama together—perhaps as long ahead of time as the preceding year, during their meeting at Paderborn.

There are as many opinions as there are historians regarding the motives of Charles and Leo. Two facts stand out, however, which are—or should be—incontrovertible. The first is that Charles's coronation was an event of immeasureable importance for the history of Europe and particularly for that of Italy. For over a thousand years, Italy would be ruled, or at least dominated, from beyond the Alps, and it was to be the battleground on which emperors, popes and princes were to contend for the control of the continent. "The coronation of Charles," wrote James Bryce, "is not only the central event of the Middle Ages, it is also one of those very few events of which, taking them singly, it may be said that, if they had not happened, the history of the world would have been different."

The second thing to be noted is that the proclamation of Charles as Emperor of the West constitutes one of the great fictions of the Middle Ages, one on a par with the "Donation of Constantine." Under this aspect, the coronation is known as the "Translation of the Empire"—that is, its transferral from the East to the West. The problem for Leo and Charles was to explain how Charles legally could lay claim to the imperial dignity; how, in other words, the Empire had been translated from the Greeks to the Romans. The Empire established on Christmas Day, 800, was no mere revival of the extinct Western Empire of the unfortunate Romulus Augustus, for authority over that empire had reverted, as had been acknowledged for centuries, to Constantinople. Nor was it a new Empire, separate and distinct from that of Constantinople; two Roman empires and two Roman emperors were as unthinkable as two Gods in heaven. The fact is that both Charles and Leo believed that, in reviving the title of emperor, they had reclaimed from Constantinople the right of electing the ruler of the Roman Empire, and that Charles, as emperor, became the ruler and continuator of a single Roman Empire—one which embraced the East as well as the West. They had been furnished a pretext for this by events in Constantinople.

In 797, the Empress Irene had dethroned the legal emperor, her son Constantine VI, and had announced herself as sole and single ruler of the Empire, taking upon herself the style and prerogatives of Basileus, or emperor. Empresses had ruled the Empire before; but they had done so through their persuasiveness and their control over weakling husband-emperors; or they had done so as regents, during the minority of a child-emperor, and then only with the advice of wise and aged councilors. But never, in the centuries of Empire, had a woman claimed to exercise the fullness of imperial authority in her own right. It was unthinkable. In Byzantium, where custom was all, and change was the work of the devil, it was worse than unthinkable; it was anti-traditional. Rome, naturally, took an even dimmer view of the situation. So far as she was concerned, the imperial throne was vacant, and Charles, in accepting the crown, became heir to the throne of Irene's legitimate predecessor. One German chronicler tells us that "because the name of emperor had now ceased among the Greeks, and their Empire was possessed by a woman, it seemed both to Leo the Pope and to all the holy fathers who were present . . . as well as to the rest of the Christian people, that they ought to take as their emperor Charles, King of the Franks, who held Rome herself, where the Caesars had always ruled, and all the other regions he ruled throughout Italy and Gaul and Germany." Another explains that it was necessary that Charles become Emperor "lest the heathen mock the Christians, saying that the title of emperor had ceased among them."

As might have been expected, the events at Rome did not fill the hearts of the Byzantines with joy. Irene may have been a female, but she was, after all, a Byzantine, and, as such, she was infinitely preferable to a barbarian male. Constantinople, therefore, and the Greeks as a whole, regarded Charles's accession to the imperial dignity as an attempt at revolt, by some of the lapsed provinces of the West, against the legitimate and sole ruler of the Empire. Their indignation was seasoned by the not irrational fear that Charles might, with the blessing of Leo, try to assert his claim to the throne by seizing Constantinople. It had happened before in Byzantine history, and it would happen again. But it would not happen now, for, despite the elaborate theory of the "Translation," Charles was well aware of the precarious nature of his claim to the throne of the Caesars. He realized, for one thing, that the Greeks could simply elect a male emperor in place of Irene, and that the new emperor's title would be unassailable. But Charles was a practical man. In his long career, he had been required to find solutions to many delicate problems. And this was a surpassingly delicate one. There could be only one Empire, and only one Emperor; but there were now two of each. How to join them together, indissolubly, in the sight of God and man, so that the two might become, as it were, two in one flesh? The answer came quickly, and Charles forthwith dispatched a grand embassy to Constantinople to ask for the hand of the Basileus in marriage.

For a time, it seemed that the Empire might indeed be revived in all its strength and glory. Irene—at fifty, reputed still to be one of the most beautiful women in the world—was sorely tempted by Charles's proposal. She was beset from within by the intrigues of her courtiers, and her Empire was assailed from without by the Slavs and the Moslems. The armies of Charles would solve her problems in the field, and his strong presence might exercise a moderating influence on her nobles. The very advantages of the match, however, were to be the occasion of Irene's downfall. The courtiers, alarmed by the prospect of a strong master in the house, brought to fruition one of their innumerable plots against the throne. In a classic palace revolution, Irene was deposed and exiled, perhaps ironically, to the Isle of Lesbos. Her successor was a general named Nicephorus, in whose person the male line of emperors was restored to the throne of Constantinople and of the Empire.

Charles immediately opened negotiations with Nicephorus, probably hoping to be recognized by him as co-Emperor in the West, but their correspondence came to naught. It was not until 812, during the reign of the Emperor Michael I, that Charles was addressed by Byzantine ambassadors as "Emperor and Augustus." Thus, finally, was legitimated the coronation of 800. From that time onward, there were to be two Roman emperors, one in the East and one in the West, despite the theory of one single and indivisible Empire.

If the failure of the Byzantine line of male emperors had been the pretext for Charles's coronation as emperor, it was not necessarily the reason for it. Both the papacy and the Franks had much to gain by the event, and the benefits to both of them were more in the realm of practical politics than of theoretical legitimacy. Charles, after having subjected most of Italy to his rule, had continued his triumphs elsewhere. Across the Pyrenees, he annexed the Spanish March. In northern Germany, he subdued the Saxons and pushed his frontiers to the Elbe. To the southeast, he subjugated the country as far as the upper Danube. His domain now contained barbarians and Romans, Christians and pagans, Franks, Celts, Visigoths, Burgundians, Saxons, Lombards, Italians. It was a motley group of peoples without a common language, or a common religion, or a common culture, or common aspirations, held together only by Charles's strength. How could such widespread territories and such disparate peoples be united permanently? The papacy, with its wisdom and experience of centuries, propounded, at an opportune moment, the restoration of the Empire of the Caesars. There were more than a sufficient number of justifications at hand. The Kingdom of the Franks, with its power and its conquests, was not unworthy to succeed to Imperial Rome. Moreover, the vast expanse of Charles's dominions was already united, to some extent, by the presence of the Church itself; everywhere, the liturgy was celebrated in the Latin tongue and according to the Roman ritual; bishops, priests and monks, working among the pagans, all acknowledged the Roman pontiff as their lord and master, and they had conscientiously preached that acknowledgment to all who would listen. To such spiritual unity, a complementary political unity might easily be grafted.

Then, too, there still existed in Europe a strong Roman tradition. The idea of nationality was still undeveloped, if not wholly unknown, for Europe had experienced no political system other than subjection to the Roman Empire. The concepts of civilization, or order, of peace and plenty were still tied in, in the minds of the Franks as well as of the Latins, with that of a civilization on the Roman pattern. The Church, when the Empire had decayed, had adopted the imperial organization and had kept the memory of the old system alive in the minds of men, so that now the evils of that system were forgotten and the Age of the Caesars was remembered as a golden era.

The papacy had good reason for suggesting these views to Charles. Christianity had been born and had matured under the Empire. Under the Caesars it had acquired power and authority and had become the religion of state. The Church might quarrel with the emperors and, occasionally, she might excommunicate them; but she never ceased to regard the Empire as her joint tenant in the world. Leo III, in addition, had other reasons, less large but no less cogent. Before Charles's conquest of the Lombards, the lack of a strong secular arm had been deplorably apparent. One usurper after another had forced his way onto the papal throne over the corpses of his competitors and enemies. It was plain that the papacy alone could not maintain order, or for that matter, its own dignity, without a potent secular government. The papacy, in short, could not endure without the Empire. And it was for that reason, more than any other, that Charles and Leo accomplished their restoration of the Empire in the West.

The internal history of Italy during the fourteen years between

Charles's coronation and his death was a continuation of the relative peace and prosperity of the earlier years of his reign. Now that, as emperor, he ruled Italy officially as well as factually, he lost no time in transferring to that disorderly realm the institutions that had worked so well in the land of the Franks. He sent *missi dominici,* royal legates, the length and breadth of Italy, organizing local governments, listening to the complaints of the citizens, deposing corrupt officials and judges, and establishing the rule of law. He did not hesitate to subject the Patrimony of St. Peter itself to the same measures as his kingdom of Lombardy—a sure indication that, as Emperor of the Romans, he regarded his new office as more than an honorific distinction. In the cities and provinces in which the popes claimed sovereignty, Charles himself, at first, and later his legates, sat in judgment, deposed and appointed papal vicars, and collected taxes. In fact, the royal *missi* exercised their functions with such alacrity that Leo felt compelled to register a complaint, asserting that, once the Franks had finished with the flock, there was nothing left for his own tax collectors to shear. Charles, however, was not to be moved. He had borne the expense of freeing Italy from the yoke of the Lombards; now, it was only fair that the Italians compensate him for his expenditures.

Charles's intention during this time was to leave no doubt in anyone's mind as to who was master in Italy. In addition to the exercise of judicial and fiscal authority, he set about the task of making his sovereignty felt at every level. He issued new imperial coins bearing his image and superscription. He required that legal documents, papal and otherwise, bear his name and the date of his reign. He exacted from the pope himself, and from the people of Rome and other papal cities, an oath of allegiance and loyalty to himself as emperor. And he assured respect for his authority and prerogatives by commanding that, thenceforth, approval of papal elections be reserved to himself. All of this, to a certain extent, Pope Leo had brought upon himself. So preoccupied had he been with the grand designs of the papacy that he had had no time for the day-to-day problems of government in which the mettle of the true statesman is proved. Consequently, the internal economic, social and political affairs of the papal domains were, to say the least of it, in grave disorder. And disorder was a condition that Charles would tolerate nowhere in his Empire, for it was a danger not only to the state but an offense to Him whose representative Charles was. To the new Emperor of the Romans, the fine line between the medieval state and the medieval Church was virtually non-existent; a crime against one was a crime against the other, and the criminal was liable to penalties spiritual as well as temporal:

With all the strength we possess, we command that men cease and shun slaying one another, a practice through which many of the faithful perish. If God forbids us to hate, how much more does he forbid us to kill . . . And where can one flee God, to whom all secrets are known? By what audacity can one hope to escape His anger? We, therefore, have taken care to forbid, by every kind of law, that those committed to our care perish by this means of evil. For he who fears not God's anger will hardly find us gentle and merciful.

Almost all of Charles's legislation, particularly after his imperial coronation, bears the same stamp. It is the legislation of a man who regarded himself as having united Church and state into a virtual theocracy, with himself interpreting and serving the divine Master who was, in almost Byzantine fashion, the true Emperor of the Romans. It was perhaps for this reason that Charles, when he began to make arrangements for the disposition of the Empire after his death, stipulated that the imperial dignity and title were to die with him, and that his three sons must be content to reign as equals and kings, "in the unity of the Trinity." Or perhaps it was because an ancient Frankish tradition ordained that a monarch might, according to his pleasure, divide his kingdom among his surviving sons. Or, more likely, Charles's main concern was to obviate the possibility of discord among his heirs. According to Charles's wishes, as expressed in the "Disposition of Aachen" of 806, his three sons—Pepin, Charles, and Louis—were to reign equally, but independently, after his death, all three being jointly responsible for the defense of the Holy Roman Church. But Pepin died in 810, and Charles (the younger) in 811. Only Louis was left, and he was the weakest and most unworldly of the three, being so taken with the study of theology and of the lives of the saints as to be utterly helpless in more mundane affairs. Nonetheless, Charles, with a father's blindness—or perhaps with a father's fond hope—designated Louis as his sole heir, and as emperor into the bargain. He was careful to specify, however, that Bernhard, son of the dead Charles, should be King of Italy, but subject to Louis' authority. In 813, at a most solemn ceremony, Louis was invested with the imperial insignia, and the Emperor Charles, as the head of Church and state, crowned his son. "Blessed be thou, O Lord God," he cried, "who has allowed me to see my son seated upon my throne!"

Charles did not long survive the event. On the twenty-first day of January 814, he was stricken with a high fever, complicated, Einhard says, "by a pain in his side, which among the Greeks is known as the pleurisy." The emperor prepared for death, confessing his sins and receiving the

Eucharist from his chaplain. Early the next morning, he was heard to sing, in a weak voice, the psalmodic verse, "Into thy hands, O Lord, I commend my spirit." A few moments later, he was dead.

With Charles was interred any hope for the survival of the vast Empire he had built and of the emperor-ruled fusion of Church and state he had wrought. His dynasty in the male line was to endure for another one hundred and seventy-five years, but his decendants grew progressively worse until the last of them, Louis the Sluggard, made himself so obnoxious that he was deposed. The names by which the rest of his heirs are known to history virtually tell the story: Louis the Pious, Charles the Bald, Louis the Stammerer, Charles the Fat, Charles the Simple. Such were the posterity of Charles the Great.

Louis the Pious was a good man, unassuming, kind, generous, and forgiving to a fault. He had the misfortune to rule, however, in an age that respected force rather than piety. In a fit of bad judgment—or simply to escape a burden that he knew himself to be incapable of bearing—Louis decided (817) to crown his eldest son, Lothair, as co-emperor, and to hand over to Pepin and Louis, his younger sons, the kingdoms of Aquitaine and Bavaria, respectively. As might be expected, the division pleased no one, and the unhappy emperor's lot was further aggravated when his wife bore him still another son, Charles. Now the claims of four sons had to be satisfied. The story of Louis' reign, until his death in 840, is one of struggle between himself and his sons for domination. As so often happens, none of the chief participants in the struggle won. The only winners were the nobles of Frankland, Germany, and Italy, who sold their services and their loyalties to the highest bidder.

When Louis died in 840, the star of Lothair was in the ascendancy. Two years later, calling together his brother Louis and his nephew Charles (Pepin, his elder brother, had died in 838), he persuaded them to swear to be his allies, an arrangement which they formalized by taking public oaths (the famous "Strasbourg Oaths") to that effect. For a time, peace was maintained, and the following year the Frankish bishops persuaded the contestants to agree to a permanent arrangement. According to the Treaty of Verdun, as this settlement is known, central and northern Italy were to be ruled by Lothair, along with Frisia (the Low Countries), Alsace, Burgundy, Provence, and the western Rhineland. The western portion of the empire of Charles the Great (roughly, modern France) went to Charles, known as "the Bald." To Louis, called "the German," went Saxony, Swabia, Bavaria, and Franconia.

The effects of the Treaty of Verdun were to be far-reaching and enduring. By that agreement were born France and Germany, the kingdoms of Charles the Bald and Louis the German, and also a third element—Lotharingia, named after King Lothair—a strip of land a thousand miles long, reaching from the North Sea to the south of Rome, over which Germany and France were to quarrel and war for the next ten centuries. None of the new kingdoms, in fact, was particularly viable at birth. None of them had sufficient resources to carry on the work of government on a scale even approximating that of their imperial predecessor. Moreover, each of the three was ruled by a feeble and incompetent king. Obviously, it could be only a matter of time before Lothair, Louis, and Charles were overtaken by their folly.

Lothair's kingdom, half of which was Italian and half German, was the first to collapse. When he died in 855, his brother and his nephew pounced upon his portion like wolves, fighting and intriguing constantly and ineffectually. When Louis died in 875, and Charles in 877, the empire that Charles the Great and Pope Leo had so painstakingly put together followed its natural tendency to disintegrate into its component parts. Dozens of smaller states were formed, each wholly independent, for purposes of government, from the degenerate successors of Charles. And so ended the first revival of the Roman Empire in the West.

This empire had been a power for civilization. It had been conceived and, in a sense, founded by the papacy. And when it fell, it inevitably pulled the papacy down with it. Without the support which a strong central government could provide, the popes were again at the mercy of circumstance. Unfortunately, they also picked this moment to attempt to assert their independence. So long as Charles had lived and ruled with a strong hand, the Church had been content to accept peace and prosperity in place of independence and authority. With the great emperor's passing, however, the urge first to be one's own master, and then to be master in one's own house—and the house, in this case, was Italy—began to make itself felt. To this impulse was coupled the realization that, though Church and state might in principle be equal partners, in practice one of them had to be the master and one the servant. And, of course, each of them wanted to be the master. It is on the axis of this ambition and this conflict that the history of Italy—and of much of Europe—began to revolve during the decline of the Carolingian monarchy.

The seeds of the contest had been sown shortly after Charles's coronation. Immediately the two authorities had begun jockeying for position. Charles the Great, infinitely the stronger, invaded the traditional competence of Rome by dabbling in dogma and by highhandedly dictating to the clergy in matters great and small. In 813, as we have seen, he conferred the imperial dignity on his son Louis the Pious, without so much as a glance at Rome. This did not sit well with the popes, who regarded the Empire as a plum to be bestowed or withheld according to whether or not their terms were met. And finally, Charles's decision to reserve to himself approval of papal elections had been a master stroke in this rather primitive game of political one-upmanship. But Charles was at a disadvantage. He was an individual, a mortal; his competitor was an institution, and one operating "under the light of eternity." Rome could well afford to bide its time, and it did so until after Charles's death. Then, in 816, Pope Stephen IV (816–817) seized the opportunity of an interview with Louis the Pious, at Rheims, to crown him anew, with a diadem that he had brought for that purpose, and to anoint him. It is likely that Louis himself was persuaded that the imperial title could be conferred only by the Bishop of Rome. Thegan, Louis' devoted biographer, is careful not to style his master "imperator" until after the coronation at Rheims; and Ebbo, the Archbishop of Rheims who was Louis' brother-in-law, noted in an inscription at the time that "Louis became Caesar by Stephen's coronation." Thus, the first two emperors had been crowned by popes—Charles at Rome and now Louis at Rheims—and a precedent had been set to which Louis' successors bowed. The prerogative of crowning the emperors had been secured, beyond dispute, by Rome. That advantage was, to a certain extent, counterbalanced by the right of the emperors to supervise and approve papal elections, a right which was also beyond dispute.

Since Pope Leo III had survived Charles the Great, no papal election had occurred during the first emperor's reign. During the reign of Louis the Pious, however, the latter's representative in Rome required the Romans to swear that no pope would be enthroned without the emperor's consent. It is not known what was done at the election of Stephen IV in 816, but the next pope, Paschal I (817–824), was not consecrated until Louis had had the opportunity to investigate and ratify the election. Thereafter, the right of the emperors to confirm a new pope was conceded, somewhat grudgingly, in theory, although in practice the elected pontiffs did not always wait for confirmation before assuming office.

During the twilight of the Carolingian Empire, there appeared a great pope who, despite the corresponding decadence of papal prestige, was able to snatch the two great victories from the feeble grasp of Charles's descendants. Nicholas I (858–867) brought to the papal throne a combative spirit, an unconquerable will, limitless energy, daring tempered by prudence, and a rare knowledge of men and of the spirit of his times. It was a combination of qualities that enabled him to establish as absolute rights the principles that had hitherto remained in the realm of speculation. The churchmen of the age, when not aghast at Nicholas' imperious audacity, recount his exploits with something approaching professional pride: "He lorded it over kings and princes," one of them wrote, "and superseded their authority with his own as though he were lord of the world."

It was with such a man that a Carolingian prince, Lothair, King of Lotharingia and son of the emperor of the same name, thought to cross swords. Lothair had been married to a woman named Teutberga in 856. In the following year, however, Teutberga was confined to a convent on a trumped-up charge of incest, and Lothair married one of his concubines. Teutberga, a woman of some spirit, escaped from her convent and fled to the domains of Charles the Bald, from where she appealed to Pope Nicholas for justice. Nicholas sent delegates to investigate the affair, but Lothair bribed them and succeeded in obtaining a favorable verdict, even though the matter had now taken on the proportions of a national scandal. The exonerated then dispatched two great prelates, the archbishops of Cologne and Trier, to Rome, to announce the verdict to Nicholas. The pontiff, who had had informants of his own at the proceedings, was beside himself with rage. He forthwith annulled the fraudulent sentence and, to make his point, then and there deposed and excommunicated the two archbishops. King Lothair then appealed to the emperor, Louis II, for aid, and the emperor accommodatingly voyaged to Rome in his behalf. But Nicholas stood like a rock, threatening to excommunicate not only the adulterous Lothair and all his sycophantic bishops, but the interfering emperor as well. "Never in the memory of man has a pope spoken thus," says Hincmar, a contemporary chronicler, "not with the apostolic gentleness and smoothness that one is accustomed to hear from the Roman bishops, but with open threats . . . and terrible, unheard-of curses." There was nothing that either emperor or king could do. Lothair was obliged to submit, or face both eternal damnation and temporal revolution. Teutberga returned to the royal palace with honor—and Nicholas sent a papal legate to accompany her, to make sure that all went well. In a later development, Lothair traveled to Rome to attempt to justify his conduct to Adrian II, Nicholas' successor. There, he perjured himself with respect to his relations with his mistress. No sooner had he left the Eternal City than he was stricken, in the flush of youth, with a mysterious disease and died almost immediately in great agony. The effect was prodigious. God, it seemed, had directly vindicated the acts of Nicholas and had loosed his vengeance on the adulterer who had sought, by the further crime of perjury, to escape the punishment of his sins.

It would be difficult to overestimate the importance of this victory of the papacy, for it not only established the primacy of the spiritual over the temporal power, but it also exalted the popes as the champions of the weak and as the defenders of justice. It may well be that the papacy stood forth as the champion of innocence when policy coincided with righteousness. But it was righteousness, and not policy, that gave strength to the papacy in the eyes of Europe.

The second papal victory was one over the spirit of nationalism in the Church. When the nascent nations of France and Germany began to emerge as recognizable entities after the dissolution of the Carolingian empire, the spirit of nationalism began to manifest itself in ecclesiastical as well as in political affairs. It was a logical, almost an inevitable, development, since the Church presided over by the Bishop of Rome, once it was removed from the context of the Empire, seemed, to the newly self-conscious French and Germans, a specifically Italian, and therefore a foreign, institution. There was an obvious tendency for the churches of the new nations to identify with local interests and ambitions rather than with those of a minor potentate across the Alps, and, consequently, an equally obvious tendency for them to govern themselves. Should they succeed in doing so, however, the now universally accepted supremacy of the papacy would collapse, just as the Empire had collapsed. Moreover, such a development would remove from the field the last unifying, civilizing, supranational element capable of uniting Europe under one rule. Here, undoubtedly, was a great danger, to civilization as well as to Christianity, and it was not likely to escape the notice of the astute Nicholas I. He met the challenge, as he met all challenges, boldly.

Nicholas' opportunity to act came when a French—that is, a West Frankish—bishop appealed to Rome against an action of his local archbishop. The archbishop objected that there was no precedent for papal intervention in the case. He did not deny that the pope had a certain appellate authority —indeed, to do so would have been heresy—but he maintained that if Rome interfered directly in the functioning of the dioceses, then the powers of the archbishops would be seriously impaired. Now there was nothing of more importance in the eyes of Rome than that the papacy should be free to exercise its authority everywhere within the Church, and particularly that every bishop should be immediately dependent upon the pope. That, after all, was the basis of papal supremacy. It was clear, therefore, that upon the issue of this case depended the future of the papacy: whether the pope was to be a truly universal and absolute monarch over the whole Church, or merely a limited court of appeal, with a certain honorific primacy over the other bishops.

The significant factor in this incident is not that Nicholas, taking advantage of the troubled political situation and the lack of a strong temporal government, was able to impose his will upon the troublesome archbishop, but that he did so by arguing from a document that, after the Donation of Constantine and the Translation of the Empire, constitutes the third and final fiction upon which medieval civilization was based. By means of it, the pristine authority of Caesar's Rome, now in clerical dress, managed to reimpose itself upon Europe.

The document—or rather, the collection of documents—in question, which had been in existence for some years before the time of Nicholas, is known today as the "False Decretals" or the "Pseudo-Isidoran Decretals" —though obviously they were called by a more respectful title during the period in which they were accepted as authentic. A decretal, in ecclesiastical parlance, is the authoritative rescript of a pope in reply to a question asked on a matter of doctrine or morals. The False Decretals consisted of a collection of spurious letters ascribed to the popes of the first three centuries, opening with a preface attributed to one "Isidorus Mercator" (Isidore the Merchant) or "Isidorus Peccator" (Isidore the Sinner); and since the original copy was said to have been brought to Rome from Spain, this Isidore, mercenary or sinful, was easily confused, in the general ignorance of the age, with St. Isidore of Seville, an eminent canonist and very learned bishop who had died in 636. The collection, of course, gained additional authority from the mistake.

The letters were probably fabricated sometime between 829 and 845, and they were first made public in a collection in Germany, at Mainz. Until that time, Church law had consisted almost exclusively of precepts taken from the Bible, from the writings of the early Fathers such as Augustine and Ambrose, from the proceedings of the ecumenical councils, and from the decretals of the Bishops of Rome—although none of the latter were dated earlier than the middle of the fourth century. The fact that there were no papal decretals until after the reign of Constantine I might have suggested to the skeptical that papal authority had really been inaugurated in the fourth century and not at the time of St. Peter; but to the believer such an idea was blasphemous. What nature had not preserved, according to the mentality of the age, it seemed right to create anew. And therefore Pope Nicholas suffered no qualms in producing a newly minted batch of documents to support his claim to universal supremacy. The subjects of these decretals were found to correspond, as if by magic, to the very problems that had engaged the attention of the Church under Nicholas and his immediate predecessors. They established papal jurisdiction over all bishops and over all the clergy and laity by demonstrating that such authority had been exercised as far back as the time of St. Peter. By the same means, they secured all clerical offices and positions against lay interference, they erected the clergy into a community with an absolute right to legislate in all church affairs without the interference of the secular government, and they conferred immunity on the clergy from all complaints by the laity. Such immense prerogatives, which placed the popes not only above bishops and archbishops, but also above kings and emperors as well, justified Nicholas in his bout with the West Frankish archbishop. But more significant was the importance which this stupendous forgery was to have for the future. During the next seven hundred years, they served the papacy well in the struggle with secular authority by ranging on her side the legal sentiment of Europe.*

These two triumphs of the papacy over secular and episcopal government were the victories of a strong pope rather than of a strong papacy. They were important victories, particularly with respect to the foundations which they laid. For the present, however, Nicholas' successors were unable to reap the fruits of them, for the Holy See, and Italy with it, now fell into a state of degradation unequaled in its long history. As always, once the imperial authority was no longer perceptible in the peninsula, the papal throne tended to become the plaything and the prize of the political factions of Rome. The populace of the city, even under the Caesars, had always been turbulent and unmanageable; and now, the popes, with no weapons save the majesty of their office, found themselves at the mercy of the bellicose aristocracy and the fickle mobs. The Romans lived too much in the shadow of St. Peter to be awed by his successor; and they, whose putative ancestors had ruled the world, were too proud to be impressed by barbarian kings or even barbarian emperors—particularly so long as they remained on the other side of the Alps. The Roman view of the Holy See was essentially a pragmatic one: the papacy was a feature of the City designed to facilitate, as of old, the flow of the world's gold into the coffers of its citizens.

Now that there was no emperor, the election of the popes rested solely in the hands of the "Senate and the People of Rome"—that is, of the nobil-

* The authenticity of the *Decretals* was not effectively assailed until the last half of the sixteenth century, with the publication of the first great Protestant work of church history, the *Centuriae Magdeburgenses*. Their spuriousness was thereafter conceded by Roman Catholic historians, following the lead of St. Robert Bellarmine and of Cardinal Baronius.

ity, clergy, and laity, or their representatives, assembled for that purpose. "The Senate and the People" were generally divided into two parties, according to their view of the papacy and the Empire. One party centered its interests on purely local matters and, wholly indifferent to the essentially supranational character of the papacy, wished the pope to be a mere provincial prince. Its efforts, therefore, were aimed at ridding Rome, and all of Italy, of imperial or foreign control. The opposite party constituted a sort of imperial faction and intrigued for the re-establishment of imperial control and of papal—i.e., Roman—hegemony over Christendom. The rulers of the neighboring states (Tuscany, Spoleto, Naples, Benevento) lent their support now to one party and now to the other, depending upon which was, for the moment, in the ascendancy. Strife between the two factions was the order of the day, and their enmity more than once erupted into riot and civil war. The immediate aim of each party was to elect one of their own men to the Chair of St. Peter, for whoever controlled that throne controlled the City and, by extension, Italy.

Under Adrian II (867–872), Pope Nicholas' successor, the papacy lost control almost completely of the City and of its own destiny. His successor, John VIII (872–882), was ignominiously captured and imprisoned by the Duke of Spoleto who then, by starving the pope, tried to persuade him to name the duke to the imperial dignity. The next pope, Formosus, a member of the imperial faction, invited the German king, Arnulf, an illegitimate sprig of the Carolingian tree, to come to Rome and receive the imperial crown. Arnulf came and was crowned in 896. But Germany was as torn by internal strife as was Italy, and the new emperor was in no position to exert any authority in the peninsula; indeed, he disappeared across the Alps immediately after his coronation and was never heard from again. Italy, having seen the last of this shadowy emperor, lapsed into a state of fractional independence, or of license, for the next sixty years. In the following year (897), there was a new pope, Stephen VI, a man of the opposite party, who decided to punish Formosus for this treason. He called a synod of cardinals and bishops, and before it he convoked, under pain of violating the laws of the Church, the defunct Formosus. The body was exhumed, dressed in full pontificals, and propped up on a throne. Counsel was assigned to it. The charges were read, and Stephen himself questioned the corpse which, being silent, was pronounced guilty. Formosus was then formally deposed from the papal dignity, the pontifical robes were torn off, the fingers of the right hand were hacked off, and, as a final insult, the body was dragged through the streets of the City and, to the cheers of the Roman mob, was thrown into the Tiber.

Pope Stephen himself did not long survive this triumph of justice. In the same year, he was overthrown by a revolution, imprisoned, and strangled. The leader of this uprising was a certain Theophylact, an official of the papal court. For the next half century, popes were to be made and unmade by himself and his family. In 904, Theophylact's daughter, Marozia, obtained from her father the election of her paramour as Pope Sergius III (904–911). Theophylact's wife, not to be outdone, required, and obtained, the election of *her* lover as John X (914–928). This John had the misfortune to reign too long. In 928, Marozia, becoming impatient, conspired with her complacent husband, Guido, Duke of Tuscany, to overthrow Pope John. John fell victim to this intrigue, was thrown into prison, and died or was killed shortly afterward. In 931, Marozia raised her son, reputed to be her bastard by Pope Sergius III, to the throne under the name of John XI (931–935). In the following year, another son, Alberic, imprisoned John in the Castel Sant'Angelo and ruled Rome as dictator for the next twenty-two years. Before he died, he made the nobles and people of Rome promise to elect his son, Octavian, pope. It was done as he ordered, and Octavian ascended the papal throne as John XII (955–964), at the age of nineteen years. His reign of eight years was a scandal besides which the many scandals of ecclesiastical history are reduced to insignificance. Liutprand, a contemporary, gives us a catalogue of John's indecencies. He refused to wear the papal vestments, preferring the garb of a soldier. He drank constantly, swore magnificently, fought with the sword "even to the spilling of blood," gambled, hunted, and wenched unceasingly. He scandalized even the stoic Romans by publicly invoking the blessings of Jupiter and Venus. He openly sold ecclesiastical offices to the highest bidder—but the Romans regarded that as perfectly understandable. He turned his Palace of the Lateran into a very brothel—"a house of prostitutes," says Liutprand candidly—and amused himself by seducing the wives, and deflowering the daughters of the Romans with a surprising disregard for rank and condition. So insatiable was his lust, according to rumor, that women ceased making pilgrimages to the Tomb of St. Peter, "for they had heard that, only a few days before, some matrons, widows, and virgins had been taken by force and ravished."

This litany of vice sheds light not only on the papacy of the time, but also on medieval Rome, and on the people with whom the popes had to live and whom they had to rule. Chaos reigned in the City, and all of the popes, the good, the bad, and the indifferent, whether they were locked in battle with the nobles or simply struggling to survive from day to day, had always to have one eye open and one hand free to deal with the brutal mob of Romans, who were always poised to rob, burn, riot, plunder, and murder.

The Emergence of Successors to Caesar

The situation of Rome was a microcosm of that of Italy as a whole. The Italian world was out of joint, politically, intellectually, and morally. Lawless barons ruled everywhere. The imperial title, which now represented nothing and conveyed no power, seemed, however, to have some will to exist, some ghostly strength. At least, sundry kings and princes thought so, and they fought for it. But, for a while yet, it was to remain a shadow. While, to the north of the Alps, in France and Germany, duchies and principalities united into kingdoms, the Italian peninsula remained fragmented. The Po Valley was divided into numerous duchies, peopled by a mixed race of Latins and Lombards, whom the pressure of the conquering Franks had welded together. South of the Po lay the marquisate of Tuscany, nominally an imperial appanage. Across the middle of the peninsula stretched an artificial strip, from Ravenna to Rome, inhabited by a people of comparatively pure Latin blood. This domain, included in the donations of Pepin and of Charles and nominally subject to the pope under the suzerainty of the emperor, was actually controlled by petty nobles who knew no law other than that of guile and intrigue. South of this papal territory was the duchy of Spoleto, the Lombard duchy of Benevento, and such principalities as Naples, Amalfi, and Salerno. Finally, in the toe and heel of Italy, were the remnants of the Greek Empire. To the northeast, on its Adriatic islands, lay a small city of fishermen and shopkeepers, which was called Venice.

The Italians, if they may now be so called, lived in a deplorable state. Those who inhabited the countryside were only slightly better off than slaves. Most of them worked the soil as serfs, and they were attached to the land in such a way that, when it was sold, they were sold along with it. Some, however, were bound only to render a certain kind of service on certain days—usually harvesting with their own hands, or lending their beasts for it—and such men were regarded as among the fortunate ones. Below the serfs were the slaves, who had no personal rights at all; they were simply property, to be bought and sold like household items. The number of slaves in Italy, however, was diminishing under the benign influence of the Church and particularly of the monasteries. It became very common for a man, on his deathbed, to free all of his slaves as a last act of Christian virtue.

In the cities, the people were slightly better off, for the artisans and mechanics and tradesmen were all free. By banding themselves into guilds (which had existed since the days of ancient Rome), they were able to bargain for and obtain a more comfortable existence. The only thriving places, however, were the coastal cities—Venice, Genoa, Pisa, Amalfi—

where trade was beginning already to lay the foundation of future wealth and greatness.

These glimmerings of mercantile prosperity were the only lights in a general darkness. Everything else seemed to have been infected by the decline which characterized the papacy and the Empire at this time. The clergy, whose duty it was to preserve and disseminate learning, failed utterly in the task. Even in the palmy days of the Carolingian Empire, Charles had found it necessary to legislate for their guidance, exhorting his monks to learn their Latin to perfection, since "it is fitting that men of God should not only live in accordance with their Rule and dwell in holy conversation with one another, but that they should devote themselves to literary pursuits, each one according to his talents, in order to prepare themselves to teach others." (Einhard adds that few things caused Charles to lose his temper so readily as to receive letters from churchmen which were "correct in their sentiments, but incorrect in their grammar.") After Charles, however, his successors were too busy fighting among themselves to be concerned with the state of learning in their domains. In almost every church council and synod of the period, the assembled fathers spoke with horror of the invincible ignorance of their clergy. At one such convocation, it was stated without contradiction that hardly a single cleric in all of Rome had even the rudiments of an education. At another, it was pointed out that hardly one priest in a hundred could carry on even the simplest correspondence. If this was the state of the clergy, it can well be imagined to what condition the laity had been reduced. Yet, in Italy, conditions were not as bad as in the barbarian lands beyond the Alps. There is evidence during this period that schools, either public or private, existed in every important Italian town. What is even more remarkable, there were schools for the education of the laity as well as of the clergy, and they were conducted, in most cases, by laymen. They had no religious instruction as such, but followed, as well as they were able, the ancient *trivium* and *quadrivium* of the liberal arts, with perhaps increased emphasis on the art of drawing up legal instruments and of letter writing—lucrative skills at a time when so much of the population was illiterate. Wipa, a German writer of the period, was much impressed by the Italian schools, and he contrasted the ignorance of the Germans with the comparatively flourishing schools of Italy where "all the young people are sent to sweat over their books."

The clerical schools—that is, those maintained by the Church for the education of aspirants to the clerical state—were also of importance in Italy. They were, however, common to all of western Europe at this time, and they continued the ecclesiastical tradition of a minimal cultivation of the liberal arts so as not to distract the mind from "the more important pursuits." These schools were usually established in the cathedral town of a diocese. In towns of less importance, the parish priest sometimes attempted to share his meager store of knowledge with promising local youths. In both cathedral and parish schools, however, only aspirants to the priesthood were received as students; there, they were taught the essentials of Latin and given some instruction in doctrine. The monastic schools, although of greater repute—Monte Cassino, for instance—generally fulfilled the same function as their lesser brethren. It was not until the end of the ninth century—and then only in Italy—that the monasteries began to admit lay students to a limited participation in their academic curricula.

The reason for Italy's superiority to the rest of Europe in the preservation and transmittal of learning was not hard to find. There had been no break in Italy between Greco-Roman civilization and her medieval development. Despite the peninsula's transition from paganism to Christianity, and from Roman civilization to barbarian domination, the Latins always remained in the majority, and they always maintained a cultural continuity with antiquity. When the Goths, Germans, and Lombards invaded Italy, the Italians did not become Gothicized or Lombardized or Germanized; rather, Italy worked its ancient magic and the invaders became Latinized. Theodoric, for example, had cared sufficiently for Latin culture to order that schools be founded for its preservation—though he was still barbarian enough to forbid his own people to attend such schools. The other invaders disturbed the schools, of course, but they invariably succumbed in turn to the gentling influence of the country, and learned to admire, and even to cultivate, the pursuits which their abrupt coming had disrupted. Thus, in Italy as in no other land, the general current of education, though often disturbed violently, was sufficiently strong to remain at least partially intact through the frequent political catastrophes. Though successive waves of barbarians might hammer at the gates of Rome, still the schools in the towns and provinces had teachers who, when their funds from Rome were cut off, supported themselves by taking pupils from families who were able to pay for such instruction. Yet, despite the persistent presence of schools throughout Italy from the seventh through the tenth centuries, it would be misleading to suppose that the people, as a whole, were much above the level of absolute illiteracy. Few people, even among the clergy and the nobility, had either the means or the inclination to follow the call of the Muses, and those who had, received only the rudiments of culture. If one could do simple sums, read, and write a not utterly corrupt Latin, then one had pretty well mastered the curriculum of the ordinary school.

The necessary concomitants of ignorance followed ineluctably: immorality and superstition. Even under the comparatively strict supervision of Charles the Great, the clergy's high spirits and worldly inclinations had not been tamed. "Let the clergy," he had had occasion to command, "according to the commands of the Apostle, refrain from carousing and drunkenness; for some have the habit of sitting up until midnight, or even later, drinking with their friends. And then these men, who are supposed to comport themselves with holiness and the spirit of religion, some of them go to their churches too drunk and gorged with food to be able to perform their priestly offices, while others then sink down to the floor in a drunken stupor." Without the strong hand of either emperor or pope, things were worse in the following century. We find a bishop of Verona begging his clergy, if they could not live chastely, then at least not to bring up their children as clerics. Another, Bishop of Vercelli, despairing of ever being able to force his clergy to give up their concubines, asked them to cease dividing up church property among their sons and daughters. The Council of Spalatro (925), so well understood the situation that the bishops found themselves forced to forbid the clergy of their dioceses to have more than one wife at a time. Even darker crimes were laid to the clerics, as attested by the commands of one bishop, to the effect that his clergy were not to allow even their mothers, nieces, or sisters to live in the same house with them, "because, at the instigation of the devil, crimes are frequently committed even with those women." Instances of promiscuity and of homosexuality in monasteries and convents were too frequent to be worth noting—so much so that one council directed that convents be built in such a way that there would be no closets or dark corners "where scandals can be perpetrated out of sight." The canon in which this measure is ordered is entitled, revealingly enough, "Concerning those convents of women which, in certain places, seem to be whorehouses rather than monasteries."

Such was the moral condition of the clergy during the century following the death of Charles the Great. It follows that that of the laity was hardly better, though less well documented. The good that the clergy was able to do was more than counterbalanced by the horror of the example they set and by the encouragement of superstition that they, in their own ignorance, gave. They first frightened laymen out of their wits by portraying the terrors of hell, and then preached the magical powers of the sacraments and of relics, until their victims either abandoned all self-confidence and surrendered themselves entirely to priestly control, or else abandoned all hope and gave themselves up to the enjoyment of all that the world could offer. Johan Huizinga, one of the great historians of the Middle Ages, has expressed the situation well: "So violent and motley was life, that it bore the mixed smell of blood and roses. The men of that time always oscillate between the fear of hell and the most naive joy, between cruelty and tenderness, between harsh asceticism and insane attachment to the delights of the world, between hatred and goodness, always running to extremes."

Italy, thus oppressed by political anarchy, by division, by a degenerate papacy and an ignorant and immoral clergy, might seem to have its full cup of evil. Only one thing was still lacking to complete the picture of despair: a new barbarian invasion. It came in the middle of the ninth century.

The triumphant followers of Mohammed, having overrun Spain and raided France in the West, and having encircled and contained Byzantium in the East, now threatened to plant their standard in the heart of Christendom. As early as the last years of Charles the Great, they had descended upon and sacked a town only forty miles from Rome. In 827, they had invaded Sicily, and by 837 they were masters of the whole island with the exception of a few strongly fortified places which were able to hold out until the end of the century. The Byzantines retired to their possessions on the mainland, but they were still not beyond the reach of Saracen pirates who, from their Sicilian bases, raided the coast of Italy up to the Tiber. In 846, one band of troops disembarked in the vicinity of Rome and, after pillaging the countryside, advanced to the very gates of the City and sacked St. Peter's and St. Paul's, both of which were outside the walls. All of the southern provinces and duchies were overrun, and many of them became Saracen strongholds. For a while, it seemed that Italy must undergo the fate of Spain and become a Moslem emirate.

The danger to Rome, however, roused the Italians. A league of Christian princes was formed among the Byzantine forces in Italy, the pope, and the coastal cities of the south. The pope blessed the fleet hastily assembled by the league, and when the Moslems next ventured within reach, the Christians trounced them soundly in a great battle not far from the mouth of the Tiber (849). Some of the prisoners taken were put to work building new walls around the Vatican Hill, to protect St. Peter's from future attacks. The fighting continued all over the south, and the immediate danger of Moslem conquest was averted. Throughout the ninth and tenth centuries, however, the Christians were never strong enough to prevent raids on the south, and the tales told of Moslem cruelty and ferocity almost defy belief. Isolated villages and remote monasteries suffered most; but perhaps in the latter case some good was extracted from evil, for it is recorded that the abbots and the terrified monks often "spent days and nights fasting and in prayer" so as to ward off the terrible infidels.

These conditions, once the Carolingian Empire had run its course and petered out in petty interfamilial squabbles—the pervasiveness of anarchy everywhere, politically, morally, socially, economically, and intellectually —argued the need to recall an age of law and order by restoring the Empire. But the papacy, the sole agency capable of effecting that restoration, did not know how to go about the job. Various claimants came forward, and Italian dukes and princelings fought tooth and nail for the imperial diadem, but none of them had sufficient power to take the prize, or, having taken it, to establish their authority beyond the bounds of their own small domains. One such, Berengar, Marquis of Friuli, or the March of Treviso, held the title of emperor for thirty-six years (915-951), but he was powerless, ineffectual, and unrecognized by most of Italy.

In the midst of this confusion, only one real effort was made, as we have seen, to re-establish the Empire in any real sense, and that was when Arnulf, King of the Germans, at the invitation of the ill-fated Pope Formosus, assumed the crown. The event was without importance in itself, other than for the understanding which it provides of the nature of the papacy and of the different views of it on the two sides of the Alps. Arnulf wished to become emperor, and he was convinced that coronation by the pope was essential to the legitimacy of the title. When he reached Rome, however, the very citadel of papal power, he found the gates of the City barred, the walls guarded by jeering citizens, and the pope locked in prison. The local nobility was again in revolt. Arnulf liberated the pope easily enough and doubtless enjoyed a splendid coronation, but the incident serves to illustrate the contrast between trans-Alpine reverence and Roman pragmatism, which was to plague the papacy throughout the Middle Ages. The popes, viewed with supernatural awe by the simple Franks and Germans, in their own City of Rome were constantly being robbed, insulted, imprisoned, deposed, and even killed by their own subjects. This local love of anarchy was often the seemingly insignificant occasion of papal actions which were to have far-reaching effects for Italy as a whole. Since the popes were never strong enough by themselves to deal with their frivolous subjects, they required support from some power, Italian or foreign. And as they would hardly consider the idea of an Italian—and therefore directly competitive—power of any consequence other than themselves, they now, necessarily and consistently, began casting about for foreign aid when all possible domestic remedies seemed to have failed.

By the middle of the tenth century, the situation in Italy was again so desperate as to require that the papacy once more seek a strong right arm from beyond the Alps. That part of the country that had acknowledged the supremacy of Charles the Great now lay in the power of a dozen noble families, each devoted only to the ruin of its neighbors and its own aggrandizement. The once great Lombard duchy of Benevento, which had withstood the might even of Charles, had fallen into decay and now was harassed by the Greeks of Apulia, and by the principalities of Capua and Salerno which had been carved from its territory. The Saracens infested the coasts and were a constant menace from the south. From the north, marauding hordes of Magyars (Hungarians) burst across the Alps and raided as far south as Rome. The papacy was tossed back and forth, like a ball, among the great families of Rome, and the City had begun to accept chaos as its natural state. There was only one way out: the pope must call in a strong, docile, and satisfactorily pious, foreign prince.

III
ITALY IN THE MIDDLE AGES:
The Clash Between Empire and Papacy
(962–1418)

1. *The Holy Roman Church and the Holy Roman Empire*

If the solution to Italy's problems seemed to lie in help from beyond the Alps, it was necessary first to determine who might safely be called in to provide that assistance. Pope Formosus and King Arnulf had already come up with the only possible answer: the Kingdom of Germany. Germany, since the division of the Carolingian Empire, had attained the blessings of comparative unity, and it now comprised the extensive and populous duchies of Bavaria, Swabia, Franconia, Saxony, and Lorraine. It was strong at home and, in the manner of nations only recently redeemed from barbarism, eager for new horizons abroad. The King of Germany, Otto I, reflected the ambitions of his people. His primary concern—after the securing of his own position—now became the search for new lands for his armies to conquer. And, as always, the eyes of the Germans turned southward.

In the year 951, Otto found his first pretext for crossing the Alps into Italy. And, as it happened, that pretext was a highly romantic one. A lady famous for her beauty, Adelaide, the widow of an Italian magnate, had refused the attentions of a pretender to the throne of Italy, and her disgruntled suitor had shut her up in a dungeon. She managed to escape, and then began to send piteous and continuous appeals for help to Otto who, fortuitously, was then a widower. The pope, Agapitus II (946–955), also sent messengers asking for Otto's help against his own enemies. Moved, undoubtedly, more by Adelaide's appeals than by the pope's plight, Otto finally came. He met no serious resistance and, on September 23, he entered

Pavia, the capital of the Lombard kings. Adelaide, no mean judge of opportunities, appeared in Pavia at the same time, and Otto almost immediately married her and assumed the title of King of Italy. He also approached Rome with the suggestion that he be crowned emperor, but the pope was a perceptive man who, seeing that Italy could not compete with Adelaide for Otto's devotion, politely but firmly declined to listen. Otto, it seemed to Pope Agapitus, had the strength required of a protector of the Holy Roman Church, but his ambitions exceeded the required limits set by papal prudence. Otto then withdrew to Germany, leaving one of his generals to complete the conquest of northern Italy.

Nine years elapsed before Otto again appeared in the peninsula. The new pope, John XII—that descendant of Marozia who distinguished himself by ravishing lady pilgrims at the Tomb of the Apostle—was on the papal throne. John's great political ambition was to establish the dominance of his family in central Italy. To this project he found opposition in the person of Berengar, sometime "emperor" and now Otto's vassal King of Italy, who, now that his new master was safely in Germany, had designs of his own upon these lands. In 957, Pope John appealed to Otto for aid against Berengar, and the king dispatched his son, Ludolf of Swabia, to put down the rebellious Italian. After an initial success, however, Ludolf was carried off by a fever, and Berengar became more independent and bellicose than ever. Finally, in 960, Pope John once more appealed most urgently to Otto for assistance. As it happened, Otto had long felt the need of papal support in carrying out certain schemes of his own for the reform of the German Church. Now the long-awaited opportunity for effecting an alliance with the head of the Church seemed at hand. Moreover, Otto was being urged by his own clerics to restore peace and order to the Italian Church. In August 961, therefore, he marched through the Brenner Pass at the head of an imposing army. In January 962, he entered Rome, and two days later, the papal annalist records, "he was acclaimed by all the people of Rome and was named and consecrated Emperor and Augustus by Pope John." Pope and emperor exchanged the customary ceremonial embraces, and Otto swore loyalty to the Holy Roman Church and to the Supreme Pontiff. The new emperor, however, was cautious as well as pious, and he knew too well the nets of intrigue in which an absent prince might ensnare himself. He, therefore, like his predecessors on the imperial throne, did all that he could to impress upon Pope John and the Romans that he, and not they, was ruler of the city and of the peninsula. To that end, he required that John publicly acknowledge himself to be a subject of the emperor, and that the citizens of Rome swear to elect no future pontiff without Otto's consent.

The coronation of Otto, as portentous as it will become in the light of later events, was not viewed by his contemporaries as an event of extraordinary importance. Since the fall of the Carolingians, there had been too many impotent and obscure "emperors" for the title to add much to Otto's prestige. Neither was the assumption of that dignity the starting point, so much as the result, of Otto's intervention in Italy. Its importance was that the title of Emperor of the Romans, when assumed by a strong and capable prince such as Otto, gave unity and legitimacy to his power over both Italy and Germany. Still, the *imperium* made very little difference in the character and policy of the new emperor. He never attempted, as did Charles, to build up a unified administrative system or an imperial legal code. In Germany, there were no laws other than those of the five great duchies, and the German king had to content himself, outside of his own duchy, with being recognized as the greatest of the dukes and the one to whom the others deferred in matters of policy and war. Moreover, Otto made no effort to extend into Italy the primitive system on which his power in Germany was based. Despite these factors, the combination of his own strength with the legitimacy of his new title was gradually to work a great change, more under Otto's successors than under Otto himself, in Italy and Germany. For the new emperor became the founder of that peculiarly medieval entity which was to be known as the Holy Roman Empire; and therefore he was the originator of that close connection of Italy with Germany which was to shape the life of Italy for centuries to come.

Otto's empire was by no means "universal," but its supremacy was acknowledged, at least in principle, by Bohemia, Moravia, Poland, Denmark, and sometimes by Hungary and by France, as well as by Germany and Italy. It was, however, to be an Empire of the Germans rather than of the Romans, and the theory of imperial election was now centered, at least initially, in the hands of the Germans. The electors of Germany (i.e., the greater lords, spiritual and temporal) chose a King of the Germans, who was crowned with a silver crown at Aachen and who, by virtue of that investiture, received also the title of King of the Romans. This king then took the iron crown of the Lombards at Pavia and was proclaimed King of Italy. And finally, he might hope to receive the golden imperial crown from the pope at Rome, and thus become emperor. The election of the son of the emperor as his father's successor was not mandatory, but in time it became customary. The emperor's authority, since it rested essentially on the military might of the Germans, and as this depended on the good will and obedience of the jealous and rebellious dukes, was intermittent and, at best, uncertain.

Italy in the Middle Ages

The papacy, which contributed legality and the cachet of divine approbation to the imperial title, was basically more stable, for it was a moral, rather than a military power, and it derived its authority not from the swords of men, but from their consciences. Moreover, it was far better organized and infinitely more closely knit than the Empire. The Roman ecclesiastical system had spread over all Europe, and countries that only reluctantly and sporadically acknowledged the suzerainty of the Empire would have been scandalized at the very idea of contesting papal authority in matters spiritual. The papacy also enjoyed, in addition to spiritual weapons such as the formidable bans of excommunication and interdict, more subtle ones, such as its ability to raise up, under its universal banner, enemies against its enemy, and then to spread the cloak of pious duty over war and rebellion. Against such weapons, as the history of Italy will show, the brute force of the Germans was to prove of little use.

The Emperor Otto, having laid, unwittingly, the groundwork for the future of Europe, now left Rome to carry on his campaign against Berengar. John XII, however, once he had been saved from his nobles, regretted the coronation of Otto; or perhaps he regretted only the vows of obedience and loyalty that had been exacted from himself. In any case, he lost no time in forming an alliance with his old enemy, Berengar, and in complaining publicly that Otto had reneged on a promise to restore the territory of the old Exarchate of Ravenna to Rome. It was a foolish move. Otto immediately, and predictably, marched back to Rome. There he summoned a synod of Italian bishops to try John XII for perjury, murder, sacrilege, adultery, and such other crimes, both public and private, for which the pope was conspicuous. Luitprand of Cremona gives an interesting account of the process by which the emperor exercised his claim to make and break popes:

> At the request of the bishops and people of Rome, there was summoned a great assembly in St. Peter's Church, and with the Emperor sat the archbishops of Aquileia, Milan, and Ravenna, the archbishop of the Saxons. . . . When they were seated and silence established, the holy Emperor arose and spoke thus: "How fitting it would be that our lord, Pope John, be here present. But since he has refused to join us here, we ask your advice and counsel, holy fathers, for you have the same interest as he." Then the prelates, cardinals, priests, deacons, and all the people of Rome, cried out: "We are astonished that you should require us to investigate matters that are known even to the Iberians, the Babylonians, and the Indians. He [Pope John] is no longer even one of those who trouble to come in sheep's clothing, while inwardly they are ravening wolves. Now he rages so openly and works his diabolical crimes so publicly that we have no need to be prudent." The

Emperor answered, saying, "We think it just that the accusations be stated one by one, and then we will take counsel together concerning what must be done."

The prelates and priests then stated their charges: that John had celebrated Mass sacriligeously; that he had ordained bishops for money (including a ten-year-old boy); that he had murdered one cardinal and mutilated another; that he had drunk a toast to Satan; that he had invoked the guidance of Venus and Jupiter—and so forth, including, of course, the charges of adultery and rape.

> When the Emperor had heard all this . . . he got up and said: "It often happens, and we know it from our own experience, that men in high places are slandered by the envious; for a good man is as easily disliked by bad men as a bad man is by the good. And for this reason, we have some doubts concerning these accusations . . . being uncertain as we are whether they spring from zeal for justice or from envy and impiety. I beseech you, therefore, let no accusation be cast at our lord the Pope for faults that he has not committed and that have not been witnessed by trustworthy men." The accusers then reaffirmed their charges under oath, and the Holy Synod said, "If it please the Emperor, let letters be sent to our lord the Pope, bidding him come and answer these charges." The wary John, however, did not come, but wrote: "I, John, bishop, servant of the servants of God, to all the bishops. We have heard that you propose to elect another pope. If you do so, then I shall excommunicate you in the name of Almighty God, so that you shall not have the right to ordain whomsoever, nor to celebrate Mass."

The cardinals and bishops, however, were not to be put off by the threats of a pope whom the emperor was determined to replace. John was deposed, and a new pope was set up, who took the name of Leo VIII and who openly acted as the creature of Otto.* John, refusing to accept the sentence of deposition, Luitprand says, escaped and "hid in the woods and hills, like a wild beast." Otto then withdrew from Rome to continue the battle against Berengar. The Roman nobles soon tired of a pope who was not pope at all but the servant of a foreign prince, and they invited John to resume his pontifical office. John did so with alacrity, but hardly was he seated anew on the Chair of the Fisherman than he died, suddenly but apparently from natural causes (964). Before Otto could intervene, the dead pope's partisans chose a successor, Benedict V (964–966).

* The Roman Catholic Church today regards Leo as an anti-pope and usurper and attaches no validity whatever to his decrees and edicts.

Otto, understandably exasperated, once more hurried to Rome, where he convoked a synod which, at his orders, deposed Benedict and reaffirmed the claims of Leo VIII. There was no point in opposing Otto, and the deposed Benedict made a humiliating submission, kneeling before the emperor and crying, "If I have sinned in any way, have mercy upon me." Otto had mercy according to his lights, and the ex-pope was banished beyond the Alps. His fall made obvious to all the now complete dependency of the papacy upon the emperor. A last revolt of the contentious Romans was sternly repressed, and when Pope Leo died, his successor, John XIII, humbly followed in Otto's train. The emperor's son, also named Otto, crossed the Alps at his father's bidding and, on Christmas Day, 967, Pope John crowned the youth as co-emperor with his father. Otto had done his very best to make the Empire not only supreme, but also hereditary.

In Otto's last years, secure in the obedience of the Church and in the succession of his son, he ruled Italy with ever-increasing authority. Most of the Lombard dukes and princes subjected themselves to his government, and the citizens of their cities were happy with a change that seemed to insure order and tranquillity. Along with peace, there came, for the first time in many years, a measure of prosperity, and trade and agriculture began to flourish anew. Otto wished to extend these benefits to the southern portions of Italy, and, having won over to his side Pandulf, ruler of Benevento and Capua, he enlarged and strengthened the latter's domains so that they might serve as a bulwark against the Moslems and the Greeks. But circumstances intervened to give to the Germans what it would have been costly for them to attempt to take by force of arms. The Greek emperor, John Zimisces, offered the hand of Theophano, his predecessor's daughter, to young Otto II, with the Greek provinces of Italy as her dowry. Early in 972, Theophano was crowned by John XIII at Rome, and immediately afterward married to the young co-emperor. The union demonstrated clearly the reality of Otto's power to anyone who may have still doubted it.

Otto died in 973. His long and busy life had not only brought peace and prosperity to a hitherto distracted Italy, but his policies had initiated a new development in history that was to last nearly three centuries and that was to determine the general direction of European civilization up to the time of the Reformation. He had welded together a mighty state. He had made Germany the leading power of the continent, and to it he had subjected the Church and Italy. Under him, the Roman Empire had once more acquired, in a real sense, the domination of the West. The situation, however, is not without an aspect of irony. Otto and his successors entertained no doubt that the popes were their servants, and that they were responsible for the election of worthy servants. They were therefore at pains to remove the papacy from the hands of the Roman nobility, to purify it, and to appoint honest, capable, and upright men as popes. It was the Empire, then, that lifted the papacy to the position in which it eventually would be able to turn upon the emperors, defy them, fight them, and finally destroy them. The emperors' popes rose so high that, as a matter of course, they became the heads of the great movement of ecclesiastical reform that swept over Europe in the eleventh century; and it was from that movement that the papacy drew such force and energy that it was to become the greatest power in Europe.

The tide of reform first arose at Cluny, a small place in Burgundy, and it began simply as a monastic reform. All over Christendom, monasteries had grown rich. Many monks had forsaken their Holy Rule and, corrupted by luxury, had forgotten their vows, married, and raised families upon Church revenues. Other monks burned with indignation at such sinfulness and, in order to halt it, started a countermovement of reform. The first such monks gathered at the monastery of Cluny at the opening of the tenth century and, from there, they sent disciples far and wide, purging old monasteries and founding new ones. Their reforms were at first ascetic in character, but, after a time, the reformers passed beyond the stage of a moral revolt against immorality. They formulated a creed which epitomized antagonism to the material world and pitted saints against sinners and the Church against the state. This credo had three main tenets. First, no ecclesiastic should marry, and men who were married should, upon ordination, put away their wives. Second, ecclesiastical offices should not be bought and sold, either directly or through simony (the payment of money before an office or benefice could be conferred), or indirectly through bribery of the one who had the power to appoint to office. Third, no layman should interfere with the appointment of bishops.

As reasonable, and even as laudable, as these principles may seem, they aroused bitter antagonism and opposition among both clergy and laity. Celibacy of the clergy, although it had been a rule of the Church since time immemorial, had fallen into general disregard. Quite naturally, the married clergy, and those who hoped to be married, were violent in their denunciations of this proposed reform. Nonetheless, it was obvious that a celibate clergy, with no ties or affections other than to the Church, would be a formidable force in Europe, and the popes supported the reformers in this respect. The practice of trading in church offices was one that everyone admitted to be reprehensible; yet, many bishops and abbots had obtained those dignities by such means, and many nobles looked forward to high places for themselves and their children in the Church. They therefore surreptitiously opposed a reform in this direction. The third article, against the lay investiture of bishops, was one which was to be particularly vexing to both Church and Empire. The principle which it formulated was a logical conclusion of the article against simony, for it was not to be supposed that kings and bishops, in the appointment of bishops, would disregard political considerations and appoint men solely for the good of souls. This was particularly true, and even justifiable, in the light of the fact that the great bishoprics and abbacies of Germany were among the most important fiefs in a king's gift, and they carried with them not only the prestige of the highest nobility, but also the very real powers of feudal sovereignty, such as the rights of coinage, of toll, of the holding of courts, etc. Such spiritual benefices were, in fact, secular fiefs, with ecclesiastical prerogatives superadded. It therefore seemed natural that the German emperors should claim the right to appoint these spiritual lords, and to invest them with the symbols of their rank, and that they should insist that such bishops and abbots be subject to the same feudal obligations and duties as their lay counterparts. Perhaps more important, it seemed inescapable that, if imperial jurisdiction over the bishops was eliminated, then vast territories—estimated to be nearly half the Empire—would be withdrawn from civic obligation and military service, and the pope therefore would become monarch of half the imperial domain.

The trouble lay, as it so often does, not in the theory of lay investiture, but in its application. According to the ancient canons of the Church, the clergy and people of a diocese elected their own bishop, and the Roman Church then bestowed the ring and staff upon the bishop-elect. But princes soon discovered that there were advantages to be gained from endowing bishops with great fiefs. First, the bishops were generally loyal to the sovereign, and they served to balance the insubordination of the secular lords. And secondly, since the bishops were required to be celibate, even when the lower clergy were not, the fiefs could not become hereditary and they reverted to the crown when the bishop died. When the reformers looked into the matter, they were shocked to discover that, in practice, the crown did not wait for a proper election, but appointed their own men to the office—usually in return for money and the promise of military service. The office of bishop, St. Peter Damien complained, was obtained "by flattering the king, studying his preferences, obeying his every whim, applauding every word that fell from his mouth, and generally by playing the buffoon." The real source of the difficulty, of course, lay in the attempt to combine in the episcopal office the functions of both spiritual and temporal lords. And the problem of these divided loyalties would not yield to a peaceable solution until there had been a dramatic trial of strength between the two contestants, the Empire and the Church.

The immediate consequence of the reforming spirit of the tenth century was to prepare the Church for the struggle by ennobling the papacy, by purifying her members, and by animating them with a common zeal. The conflict over lay investitures was recognized by both parties as one of exhaustive proportions, and at first they were content with lesser reforms. The papacy was still a dependent bishopric which the emperors could fill or vacate at will, and the emperors in fact continued to depose bad Roman popes and appoint upright Germans. The latter worked hand in hand with the emperors to enforce celibacy and to eradicate simony.

It was not apparent to these emperors that the spirit of reform would inevitably take full possession of a purified papacy, and that the popes would be content no longer to be glorified German bishops; that the papacy, in obedience to the inexorable law that links political vigor to political ambition, would soon feel itself strong enough to attempt to reduce the Empire itself to the status of a papal fief. This spirit did, however, soon take possession of the papacy, in the person of a man of genius. And the great battle was joined.

Among the thousands that flocked to Cluny, eager for a new life, was a young Italian, a Tuscan of plebian origins, named Hildebrand. This Hildebrand was small of stature, vehement of character, passionate of feeling, and convinced of his own righteousness. An eager and brilliant scholar, fond of solitude, tranquillity and study, he was nonetheless a man of action and a natural leader of men. He believed absolutely in the tenets of the reformers and in the authority of the Holy See. He could not endure the idea of secular governments meddling in the affairs of the Church, which was the work of God. And he devoted his whole life to the exaltation of the Church and its authority over that of the temporal governments of Europe.

Hildebrand has been called the Julius Caesar of the papacy. The analogy is not far from exact. From the time (1048) that he returned to Rome under Leo IX and was appointed cardinal and administrator of the Patrimony of St. Peter, papal policy began to be characterized by vigor and definitiveness of purpose, and marked by the ancient Roman stamp of authoritarianism and imperialism. The rule, though not the reign, of Hildebrand had begun when he was but twenty-five years of age. His first project was to protect the papal throne from Roman factionalism; to that end, he supported papal candidates of high character in whom, above all, ecclesiastical

Italy in the Middle Ages

devotion would be stronger than national patriotism. These popes, Victor II (1055–1057) and Stephen IX (1057–1058), put Hildebrand's views into practice.

Now that the papacy had been rescued from the vagaries of Roman politics, the next step was to liberate it from the Empire. Hildebrand watched for an opportunity to strike a blow. It came when the Emperor Henry III, died, leaving his infant son, Henry IV, as successor to the German and imperial thrones. There was to be a long minority, and Hildebrand took advantage of the occasion to act. It had long been obvious that a principal cause of papal subjection to the Roman factions and to the imperial throne lay in the uncertainty of the electoral process. The emperors, the Roman clergy and nobles, and the Roman rabble all enjoyed certain electoral rights. Hildebrand, now papal chancellor, resolved not to unravel this Gordian knot of political opportunism, but to cut it apart in one stroke. Under the new pope, Nicholas II (1058–1061), a council was called, and it was declared and defined that the right of election of the popes lay exclusively in the hands of the Sacred College of Cardinals. Some right of approval was left to the clergy and people of Rome, and some right of confirmation to the emperor; but the election itself was vested in the cardinals, and, in time, it was to become an exclusive right.

This was nothing less than an act of rebellion toward the Empire, and it was not expected that the Empire would acquiesce tamely. For the time being, however, the papacy was too strong, and the imperial power too weak in the hands of a child, for matters to come to a head. The height of the conflict was not to be reached until Hildebrand himself became pope in 1073, under the name of Gregory VII. Burning with the fire of his convictions, he now took the offensive and appealed to all Christendom for justice in the cause of God, denouncing simony and proclaiming principles of papal supremacy that were as universal as they were absolute:

> The Roman Church was founded by God alone. She has never erred and never will err, and no man can call himself a Catholic unless he is at peace with her. The Roman Bishop alone is universal. He may depose bishops and reinstate them, and he may transfer them from one diocese to another. He may depose emperors and he may release the subjects of unjust princes from their allegiance. Without his consent, no council is ecumenical. Without his authority, no cathedral chapter and no book is canonical. No man may sit in judgment over him, but he himself is the judge of all men.

Here indeed was a Caesar, and more. Gregory claimed feudal supremacy over Bohemia, Russia, Hungary, Spain, Corsica, Sardinia, Dalmatia,

Croatia, Poland, Scandinavia, and England—that is, he maintained that the princes of those lands were not merely the spiritual subordinates, but the temporal subjects as well, of the popes, and that they held their realms at the pleasure of the Vicars of Christ. Such claims were, at best, tenuous, to be advanced or held in abeyance according to the needs of the moment. But the right, which Gregory claimed, to interfere between the German kings and the German bishops was definite and direct, for it declared, in precise terms, that the papacy was supreme in the Empire, and that the emperor had but one duty with respect to Rome: absolute obedience. As pope, Gregory enjoyed enormous moral prestige. Yet, this would not have sufficed to protect him from the wrath of the Germans if he had not had support in other quarters. Indeed, he was too wise in the ways of the world to venture on so drastic a course without substantial friends. These allies were four in number, and they require some description.

First in importance came the Normans. The southern provinces of Italy in the tenth century were divided among the Byzantines, who had their capital at Bari, in Apulia, on the heel of Italy. On the Mediterranean coast, there were three duchies: Naples, Gaeta, and Amalfi—which, although they were autonomous, had preserved some connection, however tenuous, with the Greek Empire. The rest of the area was divided among the Lombards of Benevento, Capua, and Salerno. This collection of principalities, duchies, and provinces had one thing in common: they were weak. They were therefore an easy prey for any prince with a strong army and a loose conscience. The Normans, it happened, were blessed with such princes in abundance. They had settled originally in France, in the duchy of Normandy, and had only recently been converted to Christianity. Yet, they were a pious folk, given particularly to the custom of making pilgrimages to the Holy Land, a voyage which satisfied both their devotional aspirations and their love of adventure. Well armed on account of the lawlessness of the times, bands of Norman warriors had for years passed through southern Italy in the course of these pious peregrinations. Once, so the story goes, a handful of them had helped a Prince of Salerno to repel a Saracen attack. They fought with such ferocity and courage on that occasion that the prince had invited them and their compatriots to settle in the neighborhood. The invitation was readily accepted, and these first settlers were followed by bands of Norman adventurers who occupied themselves in fighting against Saracens, Greeks, or against the princes and dukes of southern Italy, depending upon who was paying their wages at the time.

In time, the Normans founded a small city of their own, Aversa, near

Italy in the Middle Ages

Capua. This, however, was not adequate to their appetite for land, and they were soon looking around for a place more splendid and more worthy of their talents. They had their chance in 1042, when, unhappy at their payment from the Greek emperor for a war against the Saracens, the Normans invaded the province of Apulia, easily subdued it, and divided it among twelve brothers. One of the twelve, Robert Guiscard (Robert "the Fox"), soon took the sovereignty of Apulia for himself and, by invading the remaining Greek province of Calabria, put an end to the long reign of Constantinople in southern Italy (1057). Robert then overran the principalities of Salerno and Benevento—in the latter instance sharing the spoils with the pope, who received the city while Guiscard kept the surrounding countryside. Meanwhile, a younger brother, Roger, undertook the conquest of Sicily where, with a small band of followers, he found the Saracens disunited and demoralized. After several years of war, Roger became sole master of the island and took the title of Count of Sicily. Roger's son, upon the extinction of the line of his uncle, Robert Guiscard, united Sicily with the Norman possessions on the mainland, and conquered the cities of Naples and Amalfi and the principality of Capua (1127). Thus, all of southern Italy below the Patrimony of St. Peter, along with Sicily, formed a new kingdom, that of the Normans, which was known as the Kingdom of Naples.

The first successes of the Normans in Italy were viewed in a dim light at Rome, particularly since, in their enthusiasm for loot, they had trespassed upon papal territory. Pope Leo IX himself had marched, at the head of an army of German mercenaries, against Robert Guiscard, but he was beaten and taken prisoner. Leo was relieved to discover that he had fallen into the hands of a people as devout in religion as they were terrible in war. The first thing that the Normans did was calculated favorably to dispose their papal prisoner: they implored his absolution for making war against the Vicar of Christ. Then, they treated Leo with a deference and an awe which the pope, accustomed to the rough-and-tumble of life in Rome, found touching. The Normans' devotion to the Holy See, however, did not prevent them from keeping Leo prisoner for several months. At the end of that time, the two parties were able to arrive at an agreement. The Normans were in possession of Sicily and southern Italy, but merely by right of arms—which, at that time, was hardly the same as a legitimate title. The pope, on the other hand, was too weak to hold these lands himself, although he did have a certain legal title to them (thanks to the Donation of Constantine) and Nicholas II conferred the south of Italy and Sicily on the Normans, which they received from him as his vassals. They then took an oath of fealty to the Holy See and agreed to pay an annual tribute to the pope. In this way, no one lost anything, and everyone gained.

It is true that the Normans, as vassals, left something to be desired, and in any choice between their devotion to St. Peter and the pursuit of gold there was little doubt in anyone's mind which would win out. Still, they knew that the Empire regarded them still as bandits and usurpers, and they could be counted on, in any contest between the papacy and the Empire, to support the popes.

The second ally of the papacy and of Pope Gregory VII was Mathilda, Countess of Tuscany (1046–1115). If the Normans were a fortress to the south, then Mathilda was a bulwark to the north of Rome, and as such she rendered invaluable service to the papacy during this period. Her devotion to Gregory, particularly, was famous: "Like a second Martha, she ministered unto him; and just as Mary hearkened unto Christ, so too did she, attentive and diligent, hearken to the words of the Holy Father." One particular act of devotion has fixed Mathilda in the memory of history. Her vast estate, which stretched from the northern boundary of the papal territories across the Po into Lombardy, consisted of lands of two kinds. First, there were those which she held as fiefs of the Empire, and of which she had no right to dispose; second, those which she held as private possessions, and which she was free to donate or bequeath according to her pleasure. All of them, imperial lands as well as private domains, she gave, or rather she attempted to give, to the Church. This donation, the largest since that of Charles the Great, was a cause of further strife between popes and emperors. The former attempted to make good their claim, and the latter, unable to distinguish one kind of territory from another, claimed the whole.

A third ally of the papacy was the cities of Lombardy, which had now become rich and important: Pisa, Genoa, Venice, and Milan. In these cities—in Milan, particularly, which was by far the dominant commercial power—trade had created a burgher, or middle, class, which already gave strong evidence of a desire to participate in the political destinies of their communities. In Milan herself, for example, there obtained an extreme instance of political instability, which had been brought about by the abuse of ecclesiastical offices. The Milanese clergy were very numerous and exceedingly wealthy. The sons of the highest nobility held the most exalted church offices, and when they died they were succeeded by their nephews, brothers, or cousins. One and all, they had obtained their dignities by way of bribery, simony, or intimidation. Being nothing more than princelets in prelatial garb, they led lives in which public scandal was an everyday occurrence and in which celibacy was virtually unknown. In the time of Gregory VII, the lower classes of the city, horrified at the lives led by their spiritual lords, and perhaps frustrated at the impossibility for their own sons to advance into the ranks of the higher clergy, were inflamed with the passion for religious reform. A new sect, the *Patarini* ("ragged ones"), appeared, who were, ascetically and spiritually, the forebears of the later Puritans. They took up the cry against clerical laxity, immorality, simony, concubinage, and marriage. Religious discontent gave birth to social and economic unrest. The citizens and the nobility flew at each other's throats. There were riots in the streets and civil upheavals. Several eminent men—friends of Pope Gregory, all—set themselves up as leaders of the people, and the battle between the people and the *Patarini* against the nobles and the higher clergy became a factor in the more encompassing struggle between the papal and the imperial partisans. Similar eruptions, equally rooted in the passion for religious reform and in class enmity, took place in other cities of the north, in Pavia, Padua, Piacenza, and Cremona. All over Lombardy there were two parties. One was the party of aristocratic privilege that looked to the emperor for support. The other was the party of the people and of the religious reformers, which regarded the pope as their protector and ally against the German Empire.

The pope's fourth and last ally was, paradoxically, the nobility of Germany. The German nation was disloyal and divided in its allegiance to the emperor; had it been otherwise, the Empire would easily have been able to assert its power in Italy. As it was, however, the reigning king or emperor hardly dared turn his back on his nobles long enough to undertake an Italian campaign. The prince-bishops of the great sees, the powerful dukes, counts, and minor lords, were intensely envious of one another's position and possessions. They were united only in an all-consuming jealousy of the power of the German king. The internal history of Germany in this era is largely the story of attempts by the nobles and spiritual lords to encroach upon the royal prerogatives, and of the efforts of the kings and emperors to defend their rights against the rebellious barons. These nobles found a natural ally in the popes, whose design it was to destroy the imperial power in Italy just as it was that of the German barons to circumscribe it in their own country. There were, therefore, many lords who were grateful to have the pope's name, and sometimes his material aid, in their rebellions. It was a situation which the papacy, through the agency of its thousand eyes and hands in Germany, was not reluctant to aggravate.

Ranged against Pope Gregory and on the side of the Empire were the loyal German nobles and clergy, the imperial party in Italy, the married and simoniac clergy everywhere, and all those, both clerical and lay, whom Gregory's energetic reforms had angered, estranged, and sometimes dispossessed. At their head was Henry IV of Germany, a dissipated young man, gifted with high intelligence and spirit, but headstrong, untutored, and superstitious, who entertained exaggerated opinions of his royal and imperial prerogatives. The characters of Gregory and Henry probably would have brought them into collision even if the irreconcilable claims of Empire and papacy had not intervened.

In February 1075, Pope Gregory assembled a council at Rome which, at his direction, formulated a canon forbidding any cleric to receive an ecclesiastical office from the hands of a layman. Going still further, Gregory declared that all investitures thus conferred in the past were now null and void, that the recipient was excommunicated, and that the donor—whether emperor, king, or other potentate—shared in the same punishment. Gregory, by this one daring stroke, hoped to secure that independence of action of the clergy and the Church which he regarded as essential to its unity and purity. His defiance of the temporal power, however, came at a bad time. In that same year, Henry had managed to unite a sufficient number of his unruly nobles to put down one of the innumerable Saxon revolts against the royal authority. For the first time he rode at the head of an army, and a victorious one at that. His most dangerous enemies at home, the Saxon princes, were safely buried in the royal dungeons. Now, and for almost the last time, he was able to feel himself to be truly a king. In the exaltation of his success, the friendship of Pope Gregory no longer seemed indispensable to his security, and he was not disposed to accept Gregory's legislation despoiling him of the rights enjoyed by his predecessors. Still, it would have been foolhardy to defy the pope openly, and Henry was satisfied simply to disregard the papal edict and to go on appointing bishops and archbishops at his pleasure.

Matters might have rested there indefinitely, with neither party willing to precipitate an open breach, if Henry had confined himself to the sees north of the Alps. But when he ventured, without even consulting Rome, to fill the vacant Italian bishoprics of Spoleto and Fermo, and particularly when he deposed the papal appointee, Azzo, from the Milanese archbishopric and appointed one of his own men in his stead, he passed beyond the point that Gregory was willing to endure for the sake of peace. There is nothing that Henry could have done, in fact, that was better designed to offend papal pride or to prejudice Gregory's political and religious aspirations. The pontiff was not slow to remonstrate, even though he realized

Italy in the Middle Ages 115

that, in so doing, he was provoking a conflict that must end in the downfall either of the Empire or of the papacy. At the end of 1075, he addressed a letter to Henry which, under the pretext of paternal admonition, lay the papal cards on the table for all the world to see. Henry was informed that he had incurred the penalty of excommunication for not removing simoniac prelates from his court, but that Gregory would absolve him if he proved obedient and if he performed the public penance which Rome would prescribe. His actions in filling the episcopal thrones of Spoleto, Fermo, and Milan were declared null and void. The edict of the recent council with regard to lay investiture was pronounced final and unalterable, but Henry was asked to send envoys to Rome to attempt to find some way in which the enforcement of the decree might be made less burdensome to him. Finally, he was warned to compare his earthly and passing glory with the infinite power of heaven as represented by the papacy, and cautioned not to allow his vanity to blind him to the duty he owed to God and to the Holy Roman Church. If he did not keep these things in his mind, Gregory closed ominously, then Henry might find that his forgetfulness would cost him his throne.

Henry, as may be imagined, was furious. When the papal legates, following receipt of this missive, attempted to convoke him to a trial at Rome and threatened that, if he failed to appear, he would be cut off from the communion of the faithful, he could no longer contain himself. The legates narrowly escaped from the royal presence with their lives. Henry then hastily summoned all the prelates of Germany to a synod at Worms. This council charged Gregory with every manner of offense, moral as well as political, absolved Henry and his bishops from their allegiance to Gregory, and, in a stroke of ill-timed audacity bordering on genius, declared Gregory deposed from the Throne of the Apostle. Henry himself wrote Gregory as follows:

> Henry, king, not by usurpation but by God's will, to Hildebrand, no longer pope but false monk:
> You have deserved this greeting because of the turmoil you have caused, for everywhere in the Church you have sown confusion instead of honor, a curse instead of a blessing. I will say only a little of the much that could be said. . . . You have trampled under your feet the rulers of the Holy Church, the archbishops, bishops, priests, God's anointed, as though they were slaves. And by doing so you have won the support of the rabble. You have decided that they know nothing, and that you alone know all; and you have used this knowledge not to build up, but to destroy. All these things have we borne, and we have striven to uphold the honor of the Apostolic See. But you have

interpreted our humility as weakness, and for that reason you have dared to raise yourself up against our royal power and even to threaten to take it from us—as if we had received our kingdom from you, and as if kingdom and empire were not in God's hands but in yours. Our Lord Jesus Christ has called us to the throne; but he has not called you to the priesthood. You have climbed up by other means. By intrigue you gained money—hateful in a monk. By money, you came to favor. By favor, to the sword. By the sword, to the throne of peace. But from that seat you have overturned peace. You have turned subjects against those set over them. You, the non-elect, have held our bishops, the elect of God, up to contempt. . . . Even I, who, though unworthy, am the anointed king, have not been safe from you, although the holy fathers have taught that a king may be judged by God alone; and this for no offense other than an alleged deviation from the faith—which God forbid. You have asserted that I am to be deposed, when even Julian the Apostate was left, in the wisdom of the holy fathers, to be judged by God alone. St. Peter, the true pope, said, "Fear God, and honor the king." But you do not fear God, and you dishonor me, who was appointed by him. And blessed Paul, who would not spare an angel from heaven who preached other doctrines, did not except you who, here on earth, now teach other doctrines. For he says, "But though we, or an angel from heaven, preach any other gospel unto you than that which we have preached unto you, let him be accursed."

You, therefore, are anathematized by Paul, and condemned by the judgment of all our bishops and by mine. Come down from the apostolic throne which you have usurped. Let another mount the throne of Blessed Peter, one who shall not cloak violence with religion but who shall teach the sound doctrines of Blessed Peter. I, Henry, by God's grace King, and all our bishops, say to you, "Come down, come down, you who are damned forever!"

While Henry, in the imagined security of his kingdom, was attempting to dispose of the pontifical throne, Gregory was as calm as any man who is sure of his game. Far better than Henry, he knew the ambitions and hatreds which consumed Henry's nobles—emotions which a word from Gregory could translate into activity. The word was spoken. The Roman synod, again at Gregory's behest, called upon the pope not only to cut off the blasphemous king from the Holy Church, but also to depose him from his German throne. Gregory immediately pronounced the sentence which began a new era in the relations between Church and state and between Italy and the Empire:

> O Blessed Peter, prince of the Apostles, hear me now, the servant whom you have sustained from infancy and kept safe from the wicked who hate me

because of my fidelity to you. You are my witness, as is the Mother of God, Blessed Paul your brother, and all the Saints, that you did give into my unwilling hands the rule of the Holy Roman Church, and that I did not force myself upon the throne, but that I wished only to spend my days in pilgrimage rather than in usurping your place. I believe, therefore, that it has pleased you, through your grace and not by any act of mine, that the Christian people committed to my care should obey me in your place; and by your grace is granted to me, by God, the power of binding and loosing in heaven and on earth.

Fortified by this belief, and for the honor and defense of your holy Church, in the name of the all-powerful God, the Father, the Son, and the Holy Spirit, and your own power and authority, I do hereby remove the government of all Germany and Italy from Henry, the king, son of Henry the emperor, who, with incredible pride, has risen up against the holy Church. And I do absolve all Christians from any oath they have taken or may take to him, and I prohibit them from obeying him as king. For it is fitting that one who wishes to diminish the honor of your Church should himself lose the honor which he seems to possess.

And since he, as a Christian, has refused to obey the Lord and return to Him whom he has abandoned by communing with excommunicates and by holding in contempt the admonitions which, as you know, I have addressed to him for his own good, and since he has separated himself from your Church in a vain attempt to divide it, in your name I bind him with the bonds of the anathema, that all the world may know and learn that you are Peter, the cornerstone on which the Son of the living God has built his Church, and that the gates of Hell shall not prevail against you!

The power of dethroning a king was now assumed and exercised for the first time. In Italy, the effect of Gregory's sentence was hardly noticeable. Perhaps the Italians were too familiar with spiritual penalties to hold them much in awe. Indeed, many Italian prelates and nobles spent much of their time, during Gregory's reign, under some form or another of the papal ban, for resisting the reforming spirit of the papacy. In Germany, however, the excommunication and deposition of Henry came as a thunderbolt. The country, as always, was ripe for revolt, and Gregory's edict supplied the necessary pretext. Rudolph, Duke of Swabia, had long had designs on the crown, and now it seemed that at last his chance had come. The Saxons, too, rose once again in revolt. Henry's fair-weather friends, the princes of southern Germany, far from coming to the monarch's aid, as he had expected, were spinning conspiritorial webs of their own. One of the king's most powerful nobles, Udo of Treves, declared that, as a good Christian, he could not contaminate himself by associating with an excommunicate*; and, one by one, the other nobles followed Udo's example, declaring that they could not risk their immortal souls for Henry's benefit.

Henry summoned his princes and prelates to meet with him in council, but no one came. He tried to convoke them by threats, and then by entreaties. Still no one came. He then marched against the Saxons, and met with a humiliating defeat. Meanwhile, the princes arranged for a council to be held at Tribur, under the presidency of the papal representatives, to arrange for Henry's formal deposition and for the election of a successor. When this diet met, the papal legates made a profound impression by refusing all contact with those who had had anything to do with Henry since the excommunication, until they had purged themselves by public penance and had received absolution. At this point, Henry, who was at Oppenheim just across the Rhine, began sending one proposal after another, each one more degrading and mortifying than the other, to the council; and the prelates and nobles rejected all of them, replying that, since Henry was an excommunicate, and no longer their king, they could not treat with him on any matter whatsoever.

Henry was in despair by the time that the council deigned to offer him terms. He was to retire to the city of Speyer, where he was to live as a private citizen, abstaining from the sacraments, until another assembly, to be held at Augsburg in 1077, could try him for his offenses. He was warned, however, that he would be obliged to obtain absolution from the sentence of excommunication before that time; otherwise, according to custom, he would be regarded as a criminal under civil law. As harsh as these conditions may seem, they would doubtless have been even more severe had it not been for the intercession of Pope Gregory, who had commanded the Germans to show mercy rather than strict justice to Henry. Gregory wished the king to be humbled, but he really had no intention of replacing a powerless Henry by a monarch who might be more able to maintain the prerogatives of the Empire.

Henry eagerly accepted the terms offered. In doing so, he realized that it would be of the utmost importance for him to be absolved of the sentence of excommunication; otherwise, he would be declared an outlaw—which, at the time, meant that he would be deprived of all legal rights, and that he would be completely at the mercy of any noble who might choose to

---

* The excommunication imposed by Gregory was of the species known to canon lawyers as *vitandus;* that is, the faithful were forbidden, under pain of excommunication, to have any contact, social or otherwise, with the king. Henry therefore was cut off from human society and solace as well as from the spiritual communion of the Church.

rob or kill him. He therefore decided to go at once to Italy where, face to face with Pope Gregory, he might hope to extricate himself from his impossible situation. Accompanied by one noble—and one of obscure family at that—he crossed the Alps in the dead of the most severe winter that Europe could remember. Gregory, meanwhile, had set out from Rome for Augsburg, but, hearing that Henry was in Italy, he halted in Tuscany, at the Countess Mathilda's stronghold of Canossa. To him there came, in advance of Henry, a flock of excommunicated bishops and nobles of Henry's party, whom Gregory, being convinced of their sincere repentance, absolved one and all.

Henry, hearing of this act of magnanimity, was mightily encouraged. But he still had much to learn of Gregory. When he dispatched mediators to Canossa, Gregory replied that he would judge Henry's offenses only at Augsburg, as had been agreed. After much persuasion, however, he allowed himself to relent to the extent of agreeing to receive the king at Canossa, and of promising that, if Henry showed evidence of sincere contrition, he might be allowed to expiate his sins by vowing implicit and eternal obedience to the Church. Henry came, and for three days and three nights he stood outside the castle, in the snow and freezing cold, until Gregory, yielding to the entreaties of the Countess Mathilda, signaled that the king be allowed to enter the pontifical presence. Henry threw himself on the ground before the pope, who then proceeded to dictate the terms of Henry's absolution. Gregory was to convene an assembly of German princes, where the charges against Henry, and Henry's defense, were to be heard. Gregory would then declare that Henry was to be restored to the throne, or formally deposed, according to the laws of the Church. Meanwhile, he was not to wear the royal insignia or to exercise any of the powers of government. Finally, it was understood that the absolution from excommunication was provisional, and that the ban would automatically revive if Henry failed to meet any of the conditions imposed. Henry accepted without demur, even gratefully, and, as Gregory recorded, "at length we removed the excommunication from him, and received him again into the bosom of Holy Mother Church."

The event was a triumph of the first magnitude for Gregory and the papacy. In one fell swoop, the pope had gained recognition of himself and his successors as the overlords of all Christendom, at whose nod thrones were bestowed and at whose pleasure they were taken away. The principles on which he had operated, and in which Henry had now acquiesced, were those which Gregory himself, basing himself upon the forged *Decretals,* had enunciated earlier:

... The Roman Church is governed by God alone. She has never erred, and never will err, and no man may call himself a Catholic unless he is at peace with her. The Roman bishop alone is universal. He alone . . . may depose emperors and he may release the subjects of unjust princes from their allegiance. . . . No man may sit in judgment over him; but he himself is the judge of all men.

Despite Gregory's stunning victory, however, these principles were too radical to be accepted without further resistance. Henry returned to Germany where he almost immediately attempted to regain his throne; but the German princes resisted him and proclaimed Henry's arch-rival, Rudolph of Swabia, as King of Germany (1077). For two years, the contesting kings embroiled Germany in civil war without attaining a definite result. In 1080, Pope Gregory, after some hesitation, threw his support to Rudolph and, after again excommunicating Henry, offered absolution from their sins to all Christians who would assist Rudolph in defeating Henry. Henry, for his part, acted as before, calling a council of nobles and bishops and deposing Gregory. Another subservient council declared Guibert, Archbishop of Ravenna, to be pope, and Guibert then empowered Henry to enforce the decrees of the new pope. When Henry finally was defeated by Rudolph in Germany, dissension among his opponents allowed him to escape into Italy with his army, where he marched unopposed through Lombardy, collecting men, money, and supplies. Very shortly, his forces were encamped around the walls of Rome. Gregory appealed to his faithful Norman prince, Robert Guiscard, for help, but Robert was away on one of his chronic wars against Byzantium. The pope then appealed to William the Conqueror, whose project against Britain (1066) the papacy had supported; but it seemed to William that Henry's defeat would bode ill for all the temporal princes of Europe, and, protesting his love for Gregory, he pleaded urgent business elsewhere. Notwithstanding a courageous defense of their City by the Romans, Hènry seized a large part of Rome, and Gregory fled to the fortified Castel Sant'Angelo. At Henry's command, a Roman synod deposed Gregory, excommunicated him, and consecrated Guibert of Ravenna as Pope Clement III (1084). A week later, Clement paid his debt and crowned Henry Emperor of the Romans.

While Henry was amusing himself by making popes in Rome, Guiscard and his Normans had heard of the Holy Father's predicament. Leaving the spoils of Byzantium for another time, they hastened back to Italy and, without pausing even to visit their families, they marched on Rome with an army of thirty-six thousand men. Henry's little comedy was finished and, without offering resistance, he fled back across the Alps as fast as he could. The Normans entered the City, freed Gregory from Sant 'Angelo, and then, either in frustration at being deprived of their German prey or in a rage at having had to forsake their Byzantine loot, they sacked Rome thoroughly. Leaving the City half in ruins, they took Gregory with them, for the Romans were so indignant at the depredations of the Normans that their ally, rightful pope though he was, could not remain there in safety. Gregory went to Salerno, where he again hurled defiance at Henry, excommunicating and deposing him. Then, broken in body and spirit, he expired, saying, "I have loved righteousness and hated iniquity, and therefore I die in exile" (1085). Henry, back in Germany, was not to enjoy a happier fate. After a lifetime of revolts and rebellions, he was finally deposed, in 1105, by his younger son, Henry V, who was blessed with the support of the papacy.

Despite the circumstances of Pope Gregory's death, the policies which he advocated had triumphed in the end, and his successors would realize, to a great extent, Gregory's dream of a Christian world united under the scepter of the successor of Saint Peter. The insistence of Gregory VII (or Hildebrand, as he was still called by some), upon clerical celibacy gave to those successors a clergy and a hierarchy whose undivided loyalties were to be a source of immeasurable strength and wealth. His campaign against simony and lay investiture would bear fruit, so that the bishops of Christendom would shortly become the willing servants of an exalted papacy. By Gregory's wise legislation, papal elections were now free from imperial control and popular pressure, and the cardinalatial conclaves would give to the Church a remarkable line of strong popes. Eventually, even the thorny question of the lay investiture of bishops and abbots would be settled amicably, by the Concordat of Worms (1122), with the Emperor Henry V renouncing the right to invest prelates with ring and staff and recognizing the freedom of election and of ordination of the clergy. The pope (Callixtus II, at that time), in return, agreed that the elections of bishops should take place in the presence of the emperor's representatives, and that bishops should receive their secular fiefs in a separate ceremony. It was a workable compromise, and one that seemed, in retrospect, absurdly simple. But it settled only the immediate quarrel between Empire and papacy. The larger issue, that of who was to be master in Italy and in Europe, was still to be fought out.

2. The Rise of the Italian Cities

Before the eleventh century, as has been apparent, there were only two powers in Italy: the Empire and the papacy. It was upon these two forces that the destiny of the peninsula turned. From the beginning of that century, however, a third power began to make itself felt. It was a power which, at least in its early stages, did not seem to be a match for either of the giant contestants, but which, even initially, was nonetheless sufficient to shift the balance in favor of either emperor or pope, and which was later to prove the equal of either of them. This third force was that represented by the city-republics of Italy. It embodied a new social mover, the spirit of commerce, which was opposed to the old force of aristocratic privilege and prerogative as represented by the Empire. It was a power with which henceforth the emperors, its natural enemy, and even the popes, its natural ally, would have to contend.

The chief figure in Europe during the rise of the Italian city-republics was that of the Emperor Frederick I (1152–1190), of the German house of Hohenstaufen. Frederick was a handsome man by the standards of the time, with an intelligent and candid countenance, fair and slightly curly hair, and a red beard—hence the name by which he is commonly known, "Barbarossa"—which, for some reason, inflamed the imagination of the Italians. Brave to a fault, determined, full of energy, generous, devout in the observance of religious practices, Frederick was a wholehearted friend, and an implacable enemy. In another age, he would have been acknowledged as the paradigm of chivalric accomplishment. He was born to rule, however, in an age which had begun to esteem buying and selling and the accumulation of money more than chivalry. Indeed, Frederick's conception of his own place in the world was more suited to an earlier time than to his own. As emperor, he failed to recognize that the Europe of the twelfth century was the Europe of the popes and not of the emperors, and he thought himself entitled to all the rights enjoyed by Charles the Great and by Otto. He measured his prerogatives by those standards, and he resolved to exercise the authority which his immediate predecessors, for reasons which he could not fathom, had let slip from their grasp. "During all his reign," noted one chronicler, "nothing was dearer to his heart than the re-establishment of the Empire of Rome on its ancient basis."

Opposed to these old-fashioned, even romantic views, was the hard-headed commercial spirit of Italy; and the cities in which this spirit was

Italy in the Middle Ages

most manifest were Barbarossa's natural foes, and he, theirs. The Lombard cities, particularly, were hostile to him, but that was probably because they were the ones nearest and most accessible to him, for the same respect for mercantile accomplishment pervaded all the cities of the peninsula. In fact, it had sprung up in the maritime cities before reaching Lombardy.

The southern cities had flourished earlier than those of the north. In the eleventh century, Amalfi, for instance, was a thriving republic of some fifty thousand citizens who prospered from a brisk trade with Sicily, Egypt, Syria, and Arabia. The wives and daughters of the merchants were decked out like imperial princesses, in the silks and jewels of the East. The republic built monasteries and a hospital in the Holy City of Jerusalem for the benefit of pilgrims, and her coins were circulated and respected throughout the Levant. Salerno, Amalfi's nearest neighbor, had become famous for her school of medicine, from which medical knowledge, acquired from the Arabs, was diffused throughout Europe. Salerno was also famous as a city of beauty, and vineyards and orchards flourished round her walls. Within, handsome palaces abounded, inhabited by an attractive and wealthy people. "The women did not lack beauty," one traveler notes, "nor the men honesty." Naples, Gaeta, and the Greek cities of Apulia, were also populous and thriving.

The cities of the south, however, were soon equaled, and then surpassed, by those of the north, particularly by Pisa, Genoa, and Venice. Pisa is said to have been a free commune before the beginning of the tenth century. She had extensive commercial relations both to the east and to the west, and was strong enough to drive the Saracens from Sardinia, capture the Balearic Islands, and even to carry the war into the Moslem home territory of Africa. Swollen by the spoils of war and the profit of commerce, she erected, according to one traveler's (perhaps hyperbolic) report, ten thousand towers within her walls, built her splendid cathedral, and completed the wondrous baptistry. Even though she nominally recognized the German emperor as her overlord, Pisa enacted her own laws and judged her own citizens. No imperial governor was allowed to enter Tuscany until he had been approved by the Twelve Men of Pisa, who were popularly elected officials. Her power spread in the Levant; and Jaffa, Acre, Tripoli, and Antioch were largely under control, while Pisan factories dotted the coasts of Syria and Asia Minor.

Genoa, further to the north, was, for a time, Pisa's ally against the Saracens, and then became her bitter rival, and finally her enemy. Genoa, like Pisa, was almost wholly devoted to commerce, and she had settlements in Constantinople, the Crimea, in Cyprus, Syria, Majorca, and Tunis. She had been granted a municipal charter by the Empire, and was a self-governing republic, free in all but name.

The greatest commercial power of the time, however, was neither Pisa nor Genoa, but Venice. The city traced its origins to a band of men who, fleeing from the ravages of Attila's Huns, left the mainland and found refuge on the marshy islands off the Adriatic Coast (452). Later, others fled before the Lombards and joined the descendants of the earlier settlers. Under the feeble control of the Eastern Empire, the Venetians gradually grew strong. With strength came independence, and as early as the end of the seventh century the Venetians were electing their own Doge, or duke. The city of Rivo Alto, modern Venice, was begun about 800. Some years later, the body of St. Mark the Evangelist was brought to the city from Alexandria, and work was begun on the Basilica of St. Mark as a fitting repository for the relic of the saint. Politically, Venice maintained her allegiance, more or less steadily, to Constantinople; not through sentiment or praiseworthy loyalty, but because Constantinople was the first city of the world, and therefore the largest market of the world, the center of art, luxury, and commerce. Her arrangement with Constantinople was to set the pattern for her relations with the papacy and with the rest of Europe. During the crusades, for example, Venice succeeded in mixing war, commerce, and religion into one profitable whole; she sold supplies and rented vessels to the Christian armies—strictly on a cash-and-carry basis.

The maritime cities often shared the same markets, and, consequently, they were often at war with one another. In the course of these conflicts, commercial as well as military, Pisa destroyed Amalfi, Genoa ruined Pisa, and Venice crippled Genoa. The advantages and the profit that each city won in these wars was the result of an individual, isolated effort. In this, they differed from the cities of Lombardy, whose glory it was that they were able to arrive at a certain unity of action, however imperfect it was, in the face of imperial oppression.

These Lombardic cities were, in effect, small republics, comprising not only the city itself but the surrounding countryside, which enjoyed a certain amount of independence. It has been a matter of dispute, among historians and among modern inhabitants of those cities, whether these little republics dated from old Roman days. Whatever their origins, it is certain that they virtually began with trade, lived by trade, and grew rich through trade. Their commerce began with neighboring cities and gradually extended itself northward over the Alps. It was greatly influenced by the maritime cities, whose ships, to turn a profit, had to have cargoes, and the call for goods by the shipowners of Venice, Genoa, and Pisa was a powerful stimulus to the manufacturers in the Lombard cities. The Venetians, for instance, were eager to carry an ever wider and more profitable range of merchandise to Alexandria and Jaffa, and for that purpose they held expositions, or fairs, in the inland cities, where they exhibited the wares that they had fetched home from far-off lands and thereby stirred mercantile interest and industry. Merchants from many cities met in the market places of the Lombard towns, exchanged information, discussed the ways and means of expanding profits, considered the conditions of production and exchange, and became a shrewd, wealthy, and capable class. It was, however, a frustrated class, for the moment that commerce ventured beyond the walls of the city it ran into trouble with the feudal rights of the nobility, and at every crossroads, bridge, or ford it found itself enmeshed in the sticky web of feudal privilege. Commerce, obviously, could not survive in a system devised for, and only tolerable in, a purely agricultural society—and the increasingly wealthy burghers were not prepared to resign themselves to the limitations which that system imposed.

As the merchant class grew in prosperity, it grew also in influence, for it began to have both the leisure and the means for politics. And politics in those days frequently meant civil strife. The citizens of Milan and Pavia, the two wealthiest and the largest of the Lombard cities, were particularly well suited to insinuate themselves into the government of their communes. They had certain civil rights to use as an opening wedge, for they had long had a voice in the election of their bishops, and they had their guilds, which, collectively, represented an economic and social force which the nobles were hard put to equal. The burghers enlarged those basic rights at every opportunity, sometimes by legal means and often by violence, but more often than both by means of economic pressures. Such opportunities presented themselves frequently in the constant quarrels between Empire and papacy, between the emperor and the local bishops, between the local bishops and the papacy, and between factions in the local nobility. Both sides in every quarrel courted the favor of the mercantile class, and the merchants were sufficiently astute to sell their support to the highest bidder, in exchange for civic and economic privileges. They took a little here, and a little there, until, in the aggregate, they had obtained, for practical purposes, an equal share in the government of their cities.

As the importance of commercial interests grew in local government and the merchants began to be recognized as a power, the petty nobility, who often had more in common with the merchants than with the great nobles, began to make common cause with them. Eventually, the great nobles were left standing alone, until, under pressure from the other nobles and the merchants, they combined with their former adversaries to form a single civic union. These latecomers, who had heretofore been small tyrants, and often little better than ennobled bandits, in the countryside, were now compelled by law to live within the city walls for several months of the year. During that time they were, in effect, hostages for their own good conduct. Thus, with the passage of years, they were converted from enemies into leading citizens of the republics. The overall effect of this union was that the government of the cities by local bishops—which, in the course of time, had replaced the Carolingian system of government by an imperial count—was, in its turn, supplanted by a more popular form of government. The bishops' authority in civil matters was now narrowly limited, and the executive power was usually entrusted to men, two or more, who bore the ancient title of Consuls and were elected annually. The legislative power was vested in a general council of citizens (in Milan, the council was composed of as many as fifteen hundred burghers), and in a smaller inner council which represented the aristocratic element. In Barbarossa's time, therefore, the government of the cities had ceased to be aristocratic and had become communal, or republican. There was, of course, a basic antagonism between the cities of Lombardy and the Holy Roman Empire. The complex of Lombard towns personified the revolt of trade against the feudal system, of businessmen against arbitrary and excessive taxation, of citizens against foreign princes—in short, it embodied an intense discontent with a political system which its component cities had long outgrown.

With this community of interests among the people of the Lombard plain, there was involved the necessity for a certain unity of action; and from the first half of the twelfth century the larger cities began to impose, whether by force, trickery, or diplomacy, that unity. The long wars of the investitures had shown the necessity for that step, demonstrating as it did the necessity for a system of interurban alliances by virtue of which the cities could present a common front to intruders, whether papal or imperial. Thus, two leagues were formed, one of the cities that adhered to the papacy, and the other of those who favored the Empire. At the head of the papal party was powerful Milan, whose league included the cities of Tortona, Crema, Bergamo, Brescia, Placentia, and Parma. Within Milan's ambit also fell the towns of Lodi and Como, but these had opposed the alliance, and the Milanese had destroyed the former and dispersed its inhabitants, while the latter was compelled to dismantle its fortifications. The imperial league, much smaller and weaker than the Milanese consortium, was headed by Pavia, and comprised Cremona and Novara.

Elsewhere in Italy, things were not very different. In Piedmont, Turin took the lead and set herself in opposition to the counts of Savoy, who regarded themselves as the emperor's viceroys and who, with the marquises of Monferrat, were among the few great feudal lords to have survived the civic revolutions of the eleventh and twelfth centuries. The cities of Verona, Padua, Vicenza, Treviso, and Mantua maintained their respective independence, since they were all practically equal in population, wealth, and arms. To the south of the Po, Bologna was supreme among the cities and equaled in strength Modena and Reggio to the west, and Ferrara, Ravenna, Imola, Faenza, Forlì, and Rimini to the east. In Tuscany, the Countess Mathilda was the last representative of her ancient and powerful feudatory line, and, after the extinction of her dynasty, Florence had risen to power by destroying Fiesole, her chief competitor. Thereafter, Florence dominated the whole of Tuscany, without, however, exercising direct control over the other cities of the vicinity: Pistoia, Arezzo, San Minato, Volterra, Lucca, Cortona, Perugia, and Sienna. Pisa, the only city of sufficient strength to contest Florence's primacy, was too preoccupied by her maritime interests to pay much attention to what was happening on land. To the south, the line of the dukes of Spoleto had died out, and the towns of that duchy had regained their ancient independence; but their comparative isolation in the mountains of central Italy prevented their rise to political or mercantile importance.

Rome herself did not escape infection by the spirit of independence and popular government. In 1139, a young monk by the name of Arnold of Brescia preached to the Romans a doctrine of political and religious reform, calling upon them to find again that "antique liberty that was their right." This, however, was more than even a reformed papacy could endure, and Arnold, having been driven from Italy and captured by the Emperor Frederick I, was delivered up to the Church to be burned alive, for heresy, before the gate of the Castel Sant'Angelo. "His ashes," wrote Otto of Freising, "were thrown into the Tiber, lest his relics be worshiped by the obstinate populace."

The Normans, in their papal fiefs of Naples and Sicily, had even less understanding than the papacy of such things as "antique liberty" and republicanism, and they sternly put down all revolutionary manifestations. The only city that was able to retain some semblance of civic autonomy in their domain was that of Aquila, in the Abruzzi.

Such was the state of Italy when, in 1152, the Germanic diet bestowed their nation's crown on Frederick I, Barbarossa. The story of that monarch's reign is chiefly to be that of his wars in Italy, for he considered the Italian cities, with their newfangled notions of liberty, to be in revolt against the imperial throne and against the German nation. Hence, he regarded it as his primary duty to subdue them and to render them once more docile to the laws, and to the taxes, of the Empire. By 1154, Frederick had had more than ample pretext for intervening in the peninsula. Como and Lodi were complaining of Milan, who, in her enthusiasm for unity among the towns surrounding her, had committed cruel acts of aggression against them. The popes were complaining of the insubordinate Romans who, at the instigation of Arnold of Brescia, had so far forgotten themselves as to attempt to throw off the benevolent yoke of papal rule and set up a republic. The lord of the city of Capua, an imperial vassal, was complaining of the incursions of the Normans. Barbarossa, therefore, gathered together an army and descended into Italy to settle all these troubles at once.

Entering Italy by the Brenner Pass, he proposed first to reduce Milan to obedience, and he began by commanding her to render justice to Como and Lodi. Milan responded by slamming shut the city's gates in the face of the king. The proud city and the even prouder monarch were at sword's point. But since Milan was invulnerable, Frederick had to content himself with wreaking vengeance on the city's allies. In a letter written at this time, Frederick himself describes the situation:

> The Milanese, deceitful and proud, met us with a thousand excuses and reasons, and offered us immense sums of money if only we would allow them to dominate Como and Lodi. We refused to be influenced one whit by their entreaties or their gold, and for that reason, when we marched into their territory, they kept us away from the fertile areas and made us spend three whole days in the middle of a desert, until, ignoring their protests, we pitched our camp one mile from Milan itself. Once we were there, they refused to sell us provisions, and so we seized one of their finest castles, which was defended by five hundred horsemen, and burned it to the ground, and our own horsemen advanced to the very gates of Milan and killed many citizens and took many prisoners. Thus, open war broke out between us. We then crossed the river Ticino on the way to Novara, and captured two fortified bridges which, after we had crossed, we destroyed. We later captured and dismantled three of their fortresses. And after we had celebrated Christmas with great merrymaking, we marched through Vercelli and Turin to the Po, which we crossed, and then destroyed the fortified city of Chieri and burned that of Asti. This done, we then laid siege to Tortona, which had been made virtually impregnable, both by art and by nature. But on the third day we captured the environs, and we would easily have taken the city itself if we had not been prevented by the darkness and by a violent storm. Finally, however, after many assaults and many deaths, and a pitiful slaughter of the

citizens of the town, we forced the citadel to surrender; and we accomplished this without a great loss to ourselves.

The chivalrous Frederick allowed the citizens of Tortona to withdraw to Milan with as many possessions as they could carry. Then the city was burned to the ground. Milan herself this time escaped intact; but she had learned that Frederick was not a man to be trifled with.

King Frederick, now content that he had taught the city-republics a lesson, marched to Pavia, where he crowned himself with the iron crown of the Lombards and was proclaimed King of Italy. Then he turned southward, for it was only in Rome that he could receive the most splendid crown of all, that of Emperor of the Romans. There he found an Englishman on the Apostle's Chair, Pope Adrian IV (1154-1159), a man of pious and kindly disposition, high character, great learning, and sound judgment, who felt so keenly the responsibilities of the pontifical role that he was able to declare that "the papal tiara is splendid only because it burns like fire."* Adrian was also, so far as papal supremacy was concerned, a veritable Hildebrand. As the feudal superior of the Norman kings of Naples and Sicily, as protector of the cities of northern Italy, and as claimant of the vast lands which the Countess Mathilda of Tuscany had bequeathed to the Holy See, he had the air and dignity of a sovereign prince. It was a posture for which King Frederick had little liking; no man was less willing than he to submit to the slightest encroachment on his own prerogatives.

Frederick's visit to Rome (1055) began inauspiciously enough. Determined that the ruler of the Empire was not to be suborned by the pretensions of the Vicar of Christ, he refused to hold the pope's stirrup or to assist him to dismount—traditional acts of courtesy to which great symbolic importance was attached both by the Romans and the Germans. Adrian, however, was no less stubborn than Frederick, and he swore to withhold the imperial crown unless Frederick followed the custom in these matters. The king therefore submitted, but ungracefully, and Adrian, not without misgivings, crowned him in St. Peter's on June 18.

As this domestic drama was being enacted at Rome, the new Norman king of Sicily, William, was devastating the Campagna and threatening to march on Rome. The Romans, sensing trouble in the air, had taken to riot-

* The Irish, above all, have little cause to remember this saintly man with affection. It was he who gave to the English their original title to Ireland, by conferring the latter, as a papal fief, on King Henry II. The papacy had derived its own title from the Donation of Constantine, according to which "all islands" fell under the temporal jurisdiction of the pope.

ing in the streets and, being as little disposed as ever to accept a German monarch, tried unsuccessfully by force of arms to prevent the coronation. But the new emperor had hardly sufficient troops with him to check the Roman mobs, let alone to risk an open battle with the Normans, and he was forced to flee the City. Pope Adrian was invited to accompany him, but the invitation was couched in such terms as to leave little room for doubt that the pope, if he refused the imperial hospitality, would be dragged from his palace by force. The determined emperor and the frightened pope therefore set out northward. It was observed by some in Frederick's train, however, that the presence of the pontiff seemed to draw down the curse of heaven upon their progress. The heat of the summer grew intolerable, and the emperor's mercenaries deserted their responsibilities to seek out the cool of the Italian lakes. Fever then invaded the imperial camp and quickly decimated what was left of Frederick's forces. The emperor did the only thing left to do. He released Adrian and, gathering the remnants of his Germans, he hurried back to his own country. There, the imperial chronicler recorded, "there now reigned such an unwonted peace that men seemed changed, the land a different one, the very skies milder and softer . . . and all the earth, filled with admiration for the clemency and justice of the Emperor, and moved both by love and by fear, strove to overwhelm him with novel praises and new honors." After Italy, with its unruly cities, rampaging Normans, insubordinate pontiffs, and mortal fevers, this Germany seemed to Frederick a very heaven.

Pope Adrian, meanwhile, left to his own devices, found the courage not only to turn and confront his enemies, but even to use them for his own ends. He formed an alliance with the feudal barons of Apulia, who resented King William's highhanded ways and who were ripe for revolt. He opened negotiations with the Byzantines, who declared themselves eager to fight William if the pope would grant them three seaports in the south of Italy. William, frightened at this coalition, offered to become the pope's vassal, and Adrian, in return for an oath of fealty and a vow of peace, invested with Apulia and Sicily. The pope then strengthened his position in Rome by granting certain liberties to the citizens, whereupon he was respectfully invited by the Romans to take up his residence among them once more. Without the least help from Frederick, Pope Adrian had turned the deadliest enemies of the Holy See into its stanch allies.

None of this, of course, sat well with the emperor, who regarded this new alliance as a breach of faith on the pope's part. But Adrian had a few complaints of his own, among them that Frederick had recently deposed and imprisoned an archbishop. On the occasion of the Diet of Besancon in 1157, he therefore sent legates to remonstrate with Frederick. The appearance of the Cardinal of Siena, the chief legate, created a stir, and the Diet erupted into a near riot. Siena waited patiently for order to be restored. Then he spoke. "The Pope," he said, "greets you as a father, and the cardinals greet you as brothers." A murmur ran through the emperor's party. The pope might indeed claim spiritual paternity of them all; but who were these cardinals, that they could claim to rank as the equals of Caesar? But that was not all. The cardinal now read a letter from the pope to the Diet, in which Adrian stated that he had "conferred many benefices" on the emperor. The phrase used was *beneficia conferens*—which, to the medieval mind, could mean only that the pope, as feudal overlord, had granted fiefs to the emperor, as his vassal. Shouts of indignation were heard, to which Siena replied icily, "From whom, then, does your Emperor hold the Empire, if not from the lord Pope?" The question, to which there was no answer possible, so outraged the nobles that Siena was forced to retire from the hall and, that night, to escape from the city. Frederick, for his part, was moved to draw up and circulate throughout the Empire a declaration of his rights: "The Empire is held by us, through the election of the princes, from God alone, who has ordained that the world be ruled by two swords, and who taught through St. Peter that men should fear God and honor the king. Whosoever says that we have received the imperial crown as a benefice from the lord Pope goes against the divine command and the teaching of St. Peter, and is therefore guilty of falsehood." The matter was resolved, to no one's satisfaction, early the next year, when Adrian explained that he had intended *beneficia* to mean "benefits" and not "benefices."

In July of the same year (1158), Frederick, at the head of a great army, again crossed the Alps. He made no secret of his purpose: "The arrogance of the Milanese has long caused them to raise themselves up against the Roman Empire, and it has now created turmoil in all of Italy. We have therefore resolved to proceed against them with all the might of the Empire." Brescia, the first Milanese ally in Frederick's path, was so terrified that it renounced the Milanese alliance and paid the Germans an enormous sum of money in exchange for peace. The Milanese, however, were made of stouter stuff. When Frederick's army, with contingents from the imperial cities of Pavia and Cremona, arrived before the walls of the city, they found the gates barred and the ramparts manned. Frederick's forces were not sufficient to breach the walls, and he settled down to starve out the defenders, ordering that their graineries be seized, their corn burned, and their harvests destroyed. He then made a public vow that he would not raise the siege until the Milanese had, once and for all time, been reduced to obedience. It seemed that the siege would endure for years. There was, however, a third factor in the situation, in the persons of several powerful Lombard nobles who had, up to the present, studiously maintained their independence from both the emperor and the city-republics, and who could therefore claim to be free of self-interest in the quarrel. One of these, whom the Milanese had had occasion to trust in the past, now presented himself to Frederick as mediator between the city and the imperial camp. Frederick, under the benign influence of this nobleman, a certain Count Blandrate, offered surprisingly generous terms to the Milanese. They were to pay a large amount of silver as reparation, to recognize the emperor as their suzerain, to restore the towns of Lodi and Como to independence, and to ask the emperor's approval in the election of their consul. In exchange, Frederick and his army were not to enter the city, the Milanese were to retain their right to elect their officials, and the Milanese allies of Crema and Tortona were to be granted the same terms as Milan herself.

The Milanese accepted, and it appeared that the age-old enmity between the city and the Empire was about to be resolved amicably. Frederick, however, heartened by an easy and bloodless triumph, decided, after reflection, that he had been too lenient. But he could not repudiate the treaty before the whole world without sufficient cause. He therefore convoked a diet on the plain of Roncaglia, not far from Piacenza, to which he summoned bishops, dukes, marquesses, counts, and other nobles of the realm, two representatives from each of the Lombard cities, and four distinguished jurists from the famous school of law at Bologna. The emperor, it was heralded, was a just man, and he wished to establish the nature of his legal rights in Italy. The determination of those rights was left to the lawyers, whose decision came as no surprise to anyone. The spokesman for the Lombard nobility, the Archbishop of Milan, was required, by Frederick's sense of irony, to announce their verdict: "Let all men know that every right of the people to make laws has been granted to you. Your will is law, in accordance with the principle that 'What pleases the prince has the force of law,' since the people have vested in you all authority and sovereignty." In substance, these words meant that the imperial rights were restored as they had been under Otto I, before the rise of the city-republics. In accordance with that decision, all tolls, taxes, forfeits, and exactions of various kinds were placed in the hands of the emperor, and it was declared, moreover, that he alone had the right to appoint the supreme magistrates of the cities. Henceforth, it became Frederick's policy to establish a governor of his own choosing, called a *podestà,* in each town, to replace the heretofore popularly elected consuls. Immediately upon the dissolution of the diet, Frederick dispatched a group of his nobles to the cities of Lombardy in order to establish a *podestà* in each. The noblemen were received courteously in Milan, but when they stated their business they were told quite clearly that the presence of an imperial governor in the city would constitute a violation of the recent treaty with the emperor. The imperial ambassadors attempted to use threats to make the Milanese submit, but the church bells were rung, the burghers poured into the streets with their arms, gates were slammed shut, and Milan declared itself once more in open revolt against the Empire. Other cities immediately followed Milan's example, and Frederick's terrified representatives, happy to escape with their lives, were forced to carry this unhappy news back to the imperial camp.

Frederick once more laid siege to Milan, and once more he used starvation as his chief weapon. After three years, famine succeeded where German arms had failed, and Milan opened her gates to the emperor. The terms which Frederick dictated were not unduly severe, considering the nature and duration of Milan's offense, for Frederick, while terrible in war, was famous for his generosity in peace. The lives of the Milanese were to be spared, and their city was to be allowed to stand. But the consuls and the chief magistrates of the city would have to deliver themselves into Frederick's hands as hostages, and the walls and fortifications of the city were to be razed. Milan, on the verge of starvation and utterly exhausted, could do nothing but accept. It seemed, in effect, that the independence of the cities of northern Italy was now extinct, and that Frederick Barbarossa was to rule, as well as reign, in Italy.

At least, so it seemed to Frederick. But if the emperor had thought that Adrian was a difficult pope, he had not reckoned with the next one, who took the name of Alexander III (1159–1181). Alexander, interestingly enough, before his election had been known as Roland, Cardinal of Siena—that same Cardinal of Siena who had dealt so imperiously with Frederick and his nobles at the Diet of Besancon. Frederick, of course, protested the election of his enemy, and a rival consistory of German cardinals went so far as to elect an anti-pope (Victor IV) and, when he died, still another (Paschal III). But all of Europe, except Frederick Barbarossa, recognized and obeyed only Pope Alexander III; and not even Frederick's authority could keep his own German and Italian bishops from acknowledging the legality of Alexander's election. The anti-popes, however, held Rome, and Alexander took refuge in France, under the protection of Henry of Anjou, where he summoned a council which excommunicated his rival at Rome. Then, sensing the hostility of the Lombard municipalities to Frederick, Alexander ventured back into Italy, and, by November of 1159, he was enthroned under the golden canopy of St. Peter's at Rome. From there, he solemnly pronounced the sentence of excommunication against the Emperor Frederick.

The dread papal anathema served to revive the Lombard cities. In 1164, Verona, Vicenza, Padua, and Treviso rose against their imperial governors and drove them from Italy, and then founded a league for the defense of their restored liberties. Venice, always the open enemy of Frederick, supported the Veronese league. Milan once again rebelled, ejected its *podestà* and its archbishop (who had recognized Frederick's anti-pope), rebuilt its walls, and armed itself.

It was time for Frederick to come again to Italy. Come he did; but not daring to face the Lombard leagues in the open field, he marched straight for Rome. The cities, on their side, could not find the courage to draw the emperor's attention to themselves by attempting to interfere with his progress. After a fierce siege, Rome capitulated, Alexander III fled to his faithful Normans at Gaeta, and the anti-Pope Paschal was again installed. Once more heaven frowned on Frederick. A terrible plague fell like a thunderbolt upon his camp and almost destroyed his army. The Lombard cities, proclaiming that God was on their side, were now emboldened to fall upon what remained of the German troops with such vigor that it was only with the greatest difficulty that the emperor himself managed to escape to his city of Pavia. The papal party took advantage of the situation to proclaim that God had destroyed the army of Frederick "as of old He struck the host of Sennacherib before the walls of Jerusalem."

As Frederick rested and attempted to regroup his forces at Pavia, in 1168, the league of Lombard cities began to take on its definitive form. The members swore to aid each other against anyone who would make war against them, or who would try to exact anything more than had been customary before the accession of Barbarossa. Hatred and fear of the emperor destroyed, temporarily, lesser hatreds and fears, and the league now included all the cities and towns of the northern plain, from Milan to Venice, and from Bergamo to Bologna. Even Lodi allied itself with its ancient enemy, Milan. Pavia itself, the imperial city, was restless, and seemed to begrudge Frederick the safety that her walls afforded.

The emperor knew when he was beaten. Gathering together his troops, he made his weary way, under the watchful eyes of the cities, through Mt. Cenis and over the Alps. His departure from the scene was the signal for new members to join the Lombard league, and Pope Alexander sent the papal blessing to the cities who had saved themselves, and the papacy, from the terrible Barbarossa.

For the next six years, the Lombard league was left in peace, and Italy was virtually free of foreign rule. Even Pavia, the last stronghold of imperial power, now adhered openly to the league. But Frederick, by nature, was incapable ever of conceding permanently. In 1174, he again invaded Italy, capturing Asti and Susa. The league gathered its forces, and both armies prepared for a great confrontation at Montebello; but, on the day that the engagement was to begin, the Lombards offered terms to Frederick: he was to recognize and guarantee their liberties, and he was to recognize Alexander III as lawful pope. These were not terms, however, that a Holy Roman Emperor could accept. Accordingly, the armies again prepared themselves for battle at another time and in another place. In the meantime, Frederick managed cleverly to immobilize those formidable papal allies, the Normans, by sending his warrior-Archbishop of Mainz, at the head of a small army, to invade their province of Apulia. The contest, therefore, was to be between Frederick and the Lombard league of cities. On May 29, 1176, the forces of the league encountered the imperial army at Legnano, a few miles northeast of Milan. At first, it seemed certain that Frederick's mail-clad knights would carry the day; but the Italians, at the prospect of defeat, began to fight with such suicidal courage that panic gripped the ranks of the imperialists. By nightfall, the Germans were in full flight, and the armies of the Lombards were celebrating a great victory.

In the face of the battle of Legnano, Frederick could do little other than submit to the inevitable. In 1177, he journeyed to Venice, where he humbly begged Pope Alexander to remove the penalty of excommunication. Once absolved, says the papal chronicler, "he was touched by the grace of God, and, abandoning his imperial dignity, he threw himself most abjectly at the feet of the lord Pope." Alexander, with tears in his eyes, raised up his valiant but foolhardy enemy and gave him the kiss of peace. It was exactly one hundred years since another emperor, Henry IV, had thrown himself on his knees before the great Hildebrand at Canossa.

In August of that year, the Peace of Venice settled the details of Frederick's reconciliation with the papacy. A truce was then secured for the Lombards and the Normans, and made final by the Peace of Constance in 1183, according to the terms of which the cities of the Lombard league were confirmed in all their rights. They were allowed to fortify themselves, to perpetuate their league, to levy troops, to coin money, and to exercise complete jurisdiction over their own members. The imperial *podestàs* were dismissed, and the consuls were restored.* The only imperial rights retained were those of the emperor to confirm the elected consuls, to hear appeals from the courts of the cities, and to exact a certain contribution to his military expenses. For all practical purposes, the Treaty of Constance made the Lombard republics into self-governing city-states. The mercantile spirit of Italy, in conjunction with the papacy, had conquered the spirit of feudalism represented by Frederick. It was a great blow to the Empire, but not a mortal one. It assured, however, that henceforth Italy and Germany would develop along independent lines.

Frederick Barbarossa had yet seven years to reign, but after the Peace of Constance he virtually disappeared from the history of Italy. One of his actions during this period, nonetheless, deserves to be mentioned. Frederick had always hoped to unite the Norman crown of the Two Sicilies, or Naples, with that of the Empire. The Empire indeed had always maintained a claim to southern Italy, but it had never been in a position to enforce that pretension. Particularly since the establishment of the Normans there, the south not only seemed lost to the Empire, but it also had become the chief ally of the Empire's archenemy, the papacy. But if the Empire could somehow acquire that territory, it would then surround the papacy and, perhaps, be able to crush it into submission. Frederick therefore considered it a brilliant stroke of diplomacy—as indeed it was—when he was able to arrange for the marriage, in 1186, of his son, Henry, to Constance of Sicily, heiress of the Norman kingdom. Then, happy at the prospect of the power that was to be his son's—but happier still that he could not foresee what the future truly held for that son—he took the cross of the crusaders and departed with his army for the Holy Land. He died on the way, in 1190, leaving behind him a legend, and a reputation for chivalry, that have endured from that day to this.

Barbarossa's son and heir, Henry, was a rather puny young man, and during his father's lifetime he had suffered by comparison to the strong and vigorous Frederick. His intellectual gifts, however, and his strength of character, were not inferior to those of his sire. He was as good a general and as capable a diplomat and politician; his policies showed him to be daringly original—a characteristic to which Frederick made no claim. Henry also shared Frederick's grandiose ambitions; but, unlike him, the young king was cold-blooded, selfish, ruthless, cruel, greedy, and treacherous in

* The title of *podestà* lingered on in Italy, but henceforth it was used to designate a foreign governor summoned by the citizens to rule them in the hope that his allegiance to another city would make him impartial in judging the affairs of their own.

Italy in the Middle Ages

the pursuit of an empire in which magnificent Italy, rather than bleak Germany, would be the center of power and authority.

Henry was first brought to Italy in 1191 by a threat to his wife's—i.e., to Constance of Sicily's—kingdom. William the Good, the ruler of Sicily, had died in 1189, and his throne, according to the custom of the Normans, should have descended to the husband of his aunt, Constance—that is, to Henry, who, by virtue of his father's death, had also become King of the Romans. The Sicilian nobility, however, was never eager for the rule of northerners, and they were determined to crown as king, Tancred, Count of Leece, who was young, vigorous, warlike, popular, and an illegitimate descendant of the Norman royal dynasty. When Henry crossed the Alps in the spring of 1191, he found the Lombard cities once more squabbling among themselves. Several years of security had made them forget the benefits of unity, and they were in no position to resist the young German king. Henry, however, needed their support more than he desired their submission, and so, concealing his imperial ambitions for the moment, he prudently cultivated the friendship of the cities. He won the support of both Pisa and Genoa, who together had fleets sufficient to convey his army to Sicily. He next turned his attention to Rome, where a pacific pope, Clement III (1187), declared that if Henry came seeking the imperial crown, then that dignity would not be withheld. But Pope Clement died almost immediately, and his successor, Celestine III (1187–1191), an old man, feared the union of Sicily to the Empire even more than he feared a breach with Henry. When, therefore, Henry demanded a coronation, Celestine put him off by postponing his own installation on the papal throne. Henry resolved the dilemma by offering to the people of Rome the destruction of the city of Tusculum, an ancient and detested enemy, in return for their support. The Romans succumbed to the temptation for an easy revenge, Tusculum was destroyed, Celestine was forced to put on the triple tiara, and Henry received the imperial crown on April 14, 1191.

With the northern cities content to stand aside, and with the papacy subdued, Henry was now able to march against the Sicilian usurper, Tancred. At first it seemed too easy. All the south succumbed, and only Naples held fast against Henry. But that resistance was the signal for a series of incidents that were to defeat Henry. An admiral of Sicily, named Margarito, drove away Henry's Genoan and Pisan ships and reopened the lines of communication between Naples and Sicily. Then, the Italian summer, as usual, brought a plague into the German camp. No sooner had it become apparent that Henry was in trouble than a fierce reaction against the Germans swept through southern Italy and the people rose against the invaders. Baffled by the temperament of the southerners and bested by their climate and their determination, Henry raised the siege of Naples and returned to Germany, where a revolt was brewing among the nobles of the Rhineland.

During Henry's absence from Italy, the imperial party there declined. He attempted, nonetheless, to keep in contact with his Italian partisans, for he had every intention of returning to claim his southern kingdom as soon as circumstances allowed. He saw that the cities of Lombardy had fallen back into their ancient enmities and feuds, and that the two leagues, one headed by Cremona and the other by Milan, were both indifferent to the Empire and to the papacy, and that both were willing to invoke the one to crush the other. Henry therefore worked to establish treaties with both leagues, while happily filling his pockets from the treasuries of both Milan and Cremona. Then, in 1194, he again appeared on the Italian plains, determined that this time the south would find its master in him. Genoa and Pisa again provided him with ships.

Tancred, meanwhile, had foreseen what would come, and he had done his best to prepare for the struggle. In 1192, he had requested and obtained the formal investiture of Apulia and Naples from the compliant Celestine III, and he had obtained the coronation of his son, Roger, as joint king. Thus provided with credentials, he had negotiated a marriage for Roger with Irene, daughter of the Greek emperor. All these preparations were frustrated, however, by the untimely death of Roger. Soon afterward, Tancred himself died, and although his nobles recognized a surviving son, William, as their king, the Norman cause had become hopeless. When Henry invaded the south, there was virtually no resistance, and, by November 1194, Palermo was in the hands of the Germans, and Henry was crowned King of Sicily. Young King William was blinded and mutilated, and then sent to spend the remainder of his days in a German monastery, while his supporters were left to languish in the dungeons of Sicily. When Henry returned to Germany in 1195, his position was secure enough to enable him to leave Constance as Regent of the kingdom.

Never since the days of Charlemagne had an emperor been so powerful in Italy. Henry was King of Germany, King of Italy, Holy Roman Emperor, and King of the Two Sicilies. He had forced the imperial crown from the hands of a reluctant pope, and that pontiff was now Henry's obedient servant. The fleets of Genoa and Pisa, at his command and in his name, had added the islands of Corsica and Sardinia to his list of conquests. To complete his triumph, Constance now bore him the long-desired heir, a son, the future Frederick II. Henry, at the apex of earthly glory, was overcome by a triple ambition. He would unite forever the thrones of Germany and the Two Sicilies. He would rule Europe from Italy—a true Roman Emperor. He would make himself master of the East and reunite the two halves of the antique Empire by undertaking a crusade that would conquer the schismatic Greeks and establish Latin—that is, German—power at Constantinople. In the light of Henry's earlier achievements, his visionary ambitions did not seem wholly unrealistic, and he had no difficulty in winning most of the German nobility to his plans. Before the end of 1196, he had assembled a great army and was again in Italy, on the first stage of his eastward march. With the support of Pope Celestine, who was delighted at the prospect of a crusade against the schismatic Greeks, Henry demanded that the Byzantine emperor, Alexius III, surrender to him all the provinces east of Thessalonica as part of the Sicilian inheritance. Alexius demurred, but wisely agreed to pay a heavy tribute to Henry in order to avoid an attack on his domains. Thus enriched, Henry now had funds for a complementary project, a crusade against the Moslems. In September, the first ships set sail from Messina to Acre, with the blessing of Celestine—who was almost as eager for this crusade as he had been for that against the Christian Byzantines. But, on the verge of his final triumph, Henry died. He was cut down by a sudden fever on September 28, and his ambitions were interred with him alongside his Sicilian predecessor-kings in the cathedral of Palermo.

3. The Triumph of the Popes

If Pope Gregory VII, Hildebrand, had been the Julius Caesar of the papacy, then Europe was now to see the man who was to be its Augustus. After the death of Alexander III, there had been a succession of popes of small strength and less ability, and there had been a strong and capable emperor. Consequently, a reaction had set in, and the papal party—the Guelfs, as they had come to be called—seemed on the point of being overwhelmed by the Ghibellines, or the imperial party. Now, within four months after the death of Henry, the papal authority was to be put into the hands of a man most capable of wielding it effectively, Pope Innocent III. At last, the dreams of Gregory VII and of Alexander III were to become accomplished facts. Europe was to be ruled from the Chair of St. Peter, while the Empire was to be reduced to a position of total dependence upon the whims of the popes.

Before his election to the papal throne, the new pope was known as

Lothair dei Segni, a Roman noble who had won for himself a reputation as a jurist, diplomat, and writer. The favor of his uncle, Pope Clement III, had obtained for him a cardinal's hat before he was thirty; but Celestine III had mistrusted the former papal nephew and relegated him to an obscure position. Upon Celestine's death, however, Lothair was universally reputed to be the man most able to defend the papacy against the encroachments of the Empire, and he was elected and acclaimed as Innocent III (1198).

This new pope was a handsome man, majestic and noble in appearance, polished in manners, eloquent and imperious, endowed with an indomitable will, but afflicted with a temper of unparalleled ferocity and subject to fits of melancholy. He brought to the throne a full-blown theory of papal supremacy more ambitious and universal than that even of Hildebrand, as well as the courage, the intelligence, the perseverance, and the energy to promulgate these theories boldly. "The Roman Pontiff," he wrote, "is the vicar, not of man but of God himself. . . . The Lord gave to Peter the rule not only of the universal Church but also that of the whole world. . . . The Lord Jesus Christ has set up one ruler over all things as his universal vicar; and as all things in heaven, on earth, and in hell bow to the name of Christ, so should all obey Christ's vicar, so that there may be but one flock and one shepherd. . . . No king can reign happily unless he devoutly serve Christ's vicar. . . . Princes have power on earth, but priests have power also in heaven. Princes reign over the body, but priests also over the soul. Just as the soul is more noble than the body, so too is the priesthood more noble than the monarchy. . . . The priesthood is the sun, the temporal power the moon. Kings rule, each over his own kingdom; but Peter rules the world. The priesthood is of divine foundation; the temporal power is but the result of human cunning."

The mind of Innocent III, filled with these visions of universal monarchy, took in the smallest as well as the greatest of European affairs. Primarily, his work was that of the ecclesiastical statesman, but in his understanding of that work he ventured far into the field of temporal government. We shall see him restoring the papal authority in Rome and in the Patrimony of St. Peter, cherishing the municipal freedom of Italy, and castigating the kings of Portugal, Leon, Castile, and Navarre. Under him, the King of Hungary was threatened; the nobles of Iceland, warned; the King of Bohemia, rebuked; the King of France, reduced to servile obedience; the King of England, made happy to "yield up to our lord, the Pope Innocent, and his successors, all our kingdom of England and all our kingdom of Ireland, to be held as a fief of the Holy Roman Church."

Italy in the Middle Ages

Nevertheless, Pope Innocent, a complex man, was as eager for the spiritual and intellectual rejuvenation of the Church as he was for the political correction of the universe, and he exhibited the utmost zeal for the extension of Christ's kingdom of the spirit. The most bitter pill of his life was to be his failure to rouse Europe to undertake a crusade for the recovery of Jerusalem. He was unyielding in his defense of doctrinal orthodoxy against the heretics of southern France. He foresaw in the work of the great religious teachers of his time, such as Francis of Assisi and Dominic, the revival of the inner life of the Church, and he was quick to offer them his friendship and support. As many-faceted as he was strong, and as strong as he was successful, Innocent III represented the embodiment of the medieval papal ideal, and he represented it worthily and gloriously.

By the time that Innocent was crowned pope, the worst dangers to Italy from the Empire had already run their course. After the death of Henry VI, the crowns of Sicily and Germany were once more separated. The antiimperial reaction that had erupted all over the south during the ultimate years of Henry's reign had been allowed to continue unimpeded, so that, finally, it seemed that anarchy would replace despotism in the land. Queen Constance, Henry's widow, observing which way the wind was blowing, and doubtless repelled by the cruelty of her husband's German soldiers and ministers to her own people, judged it wise to secure her son's succession in Naples and Sicily by doing homage to the pope, renouncing the ecclesiastical privileges granted to her ancestors, and promising a yearly tribute to Innocent. Having thus secured the succession of her son Frederick, and the continuance of her own regency, she drove away the German oppressors—a policy which she could have not dared follow without the support of Rome. Thereafter, she proved a loyal daughter of the Church. At her death, in 1198, Constance appointed Pope Innocent as guardian of the young Frederick.

Pope Innocent was nothing if not honorable. He took his position as guardian very seriously indeed, and he struggled mightily, and for many years, to protect the Two Sicilies against its many enemies. No sooner was Constance buried than the Germans tried once more to claim the kingdom, and Innocent, desperate for allies, finally invited Walter, Count of Brienne and husband of Tancred's daughter, to drive out the invaders. For several years the contest continued without decisive results. Then, Innocent, conscience-stricken by the thought that he was not fulfilling his obligations toward Frederick, pleaded with his own brother, Richard, Count of Segni, to fight the Germans. Richard, a man not unlike his pon-

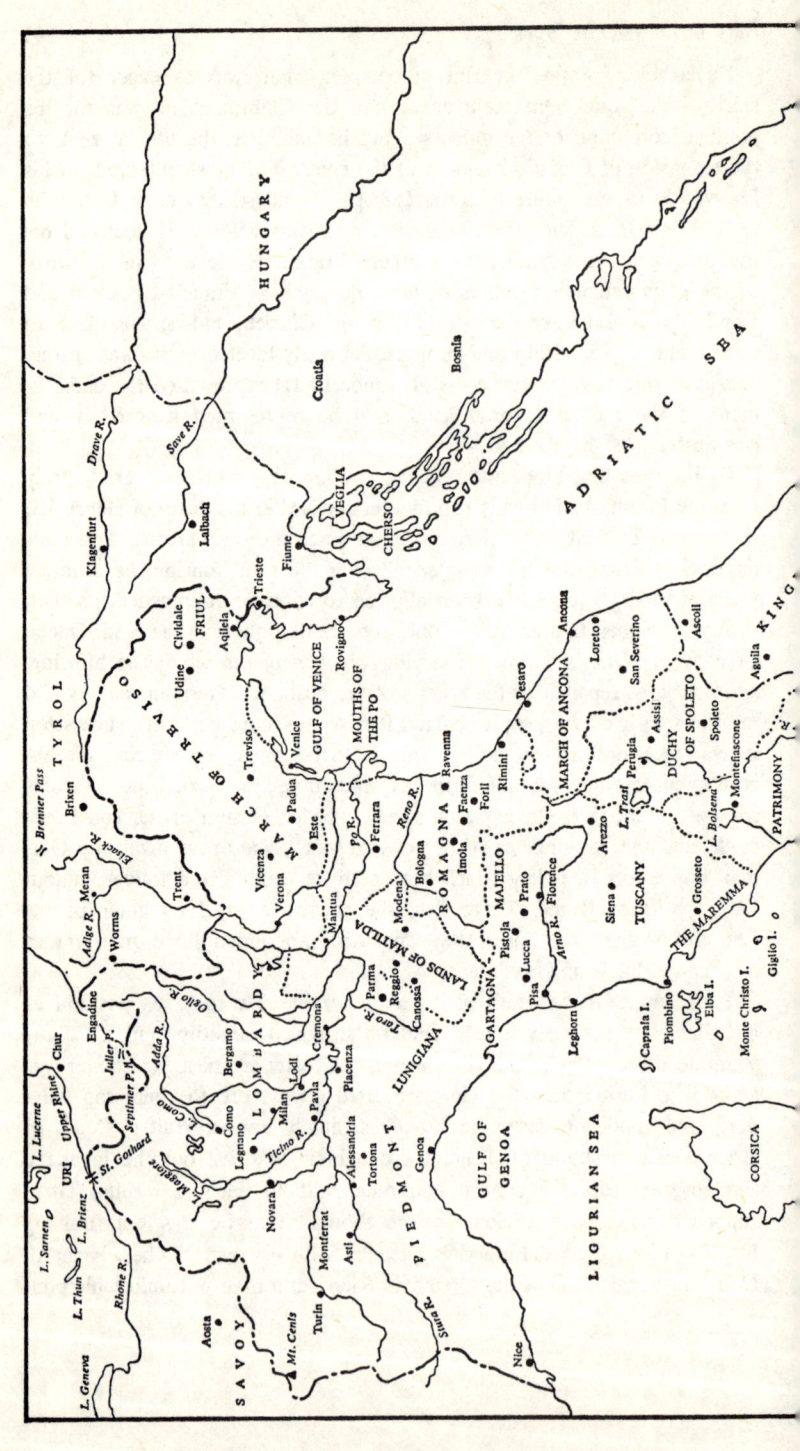

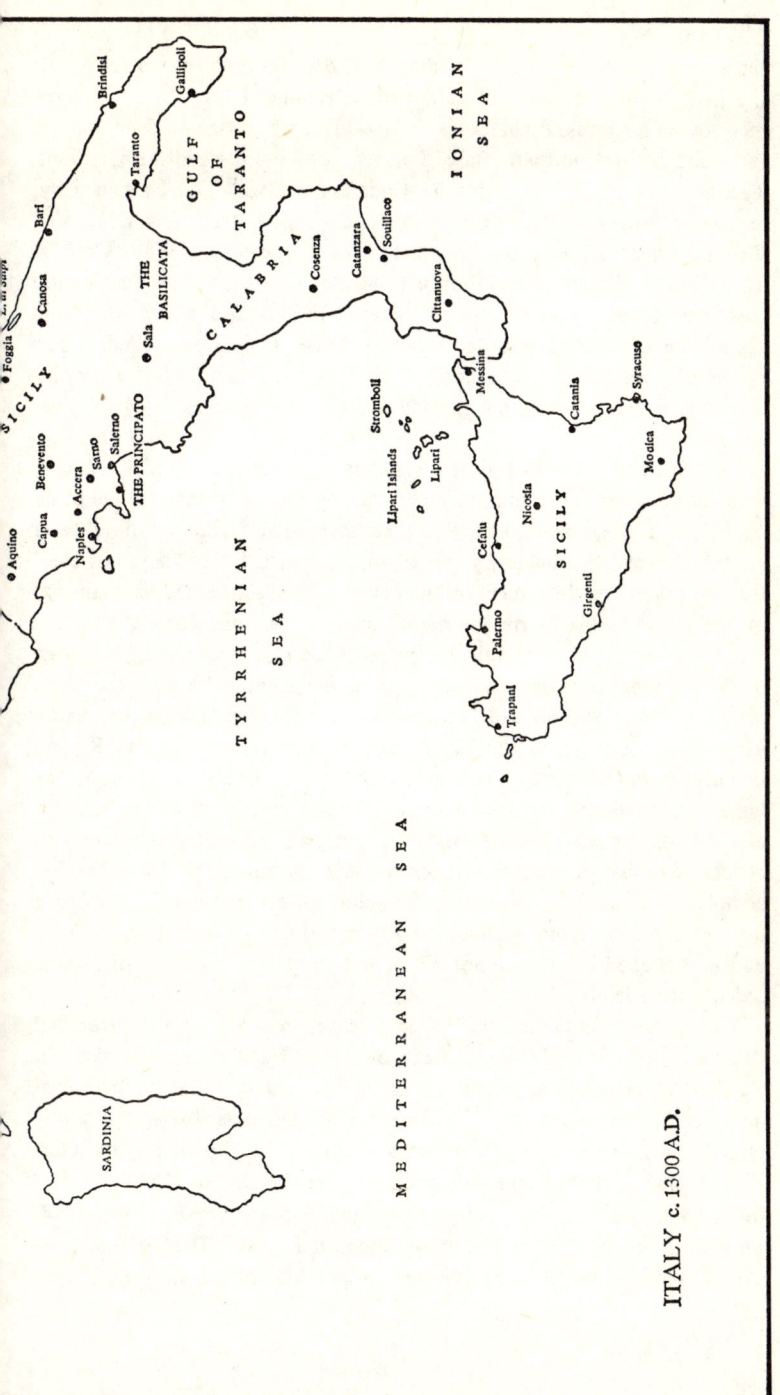

ITALY c. 1300 A.D.

tifical brother, was so successful that, by 1208, Innocent was able to visit the pacified kingdom of his ward and to arrange for its future government by native lords. Richard, as his reward, received rich lands in Apulia.

In central and northern Italy, Innocent was more rapidly triumphant. Tuscany and the domains of the Countess Mathilda, which that lady, legally or otherwise, had deeded to Pope Gregory VII, now renounced their allegiance to the Empire and asked for the protection of the Church. The cities of Tuscany then formed themselves into a new league, the leadership of which they implored Innocent to accept—a prayer which the pontiff could not find it in his heart to refuse. Only Pisa, proud of her power and her wealth, held aloof from this combination. After a century of delay, it seemed that the papacy finally was about to enjoy its Tuscan heritage.

To the north, it was Innocent's policy to maintain friendly relations with the cities of the Lombard plain, and by means of that expedient he managed to wield an influence among them that could not have been his through less peaceable means. It was in the center of Italy, however, that the pope scored his most brilliant success, by establishing his authority in Rome and in his Patrimony of St. Peter. When Innocent mounted the throne of the popes, he found the papal lands just throwing off the yoke of the German garrisons that had policed them under Henry VI. Within the City, power was divided between the Prefect of the City, who was an imperial appointee, and the Chief Senator, who represented the Roman nobility. Within a month, the Prefect was brought to his knees before the imperious Innocent and swore eternal loyalty; thenceforth, he held his office at the pope's pleasure. Within a year, the Chief Senator had also become a papal official, and Innocent now controlled the City. No less complete was his triumph over the nobility of the Patrimony. He drove the German lords from Spoleto, the Romagna, and the march of Ancona, and he obtained the recognition of his authority even in the most remote corners of his lands.

With respect to Germany, Innocent played the part of the giver and withholder of crowns. On the death of Henry VI, there was a disputed election. The Hohenstaufen party of the defunct Henry, fearing a prolonged minority on the part of the infant Frederick, had passed over the young prince and nominated Philip, Henry's brother. The rival party, the German Guelphs, rebelled and nominated, not Frederick, but Otto of Brunswick. Civil war followed, and both parties appealed to Pope Innocent, who, after much grave deliberation, supported Otto. "The settlement of this matter," he declared, "is the proper province of the Holy See, since it was the Holy See which translated the Empire from the East to the West, and ultimately because that same See confers the imperial crown. . . . We pronounce Philip unworthy of the Empire, and we absolve all who have taken oaths of fealty to him as monarch. Now, inasmuch as our dearest son in Christ, Otto, is industrious, provident, discreet, strong, and faithful, descended on both sides from a devout stock and himself devoted to the Church, we, by the authority of St. Peter, declare him to be king; and we will, in due course, bestow upon him the imperial crown." The price that Innocent demanded for this support of Otto was high. The new king and emperor-to-be was obliged to guarantee to the pope the strip of territory running from Rome to Ravenna, to concede those portions of Tuscany which were not fiefs of the Empire, to acknowledge papal suzerainty over the Kingdom of the Two Sicilies, and to promise to obey the pope in all matters having to do with the leagues of the Lombard and Tuscan cities.*

Despite the support of Pope Innocent, however, things were not going well for Otto. Philip's star was in the ascendancy, and the extravagance of Innocent's language in announcing his support of Otto led many bishops to join the nobility in protesting the pope's attempt to interfere in an imperial election. As time went on, Philip's Ghibellines got the better of Otto's Guelfs, and the latter's cause rapidly took on all the aspects of a hopeless one. Innocent, to whom the cause of the papacy was the cause of God, was not adverse to a bit of diplomatic double-dealing in such an emergency. And, in fact, he was on the point officially of shifting his support to Philip when that prince was murdered (1208) by a disgruntled vassal. Otto was now undisputed king, and providence had intervened at exactly the right moment to prevent a fatal blunder on Innocent's part. A grateful Otto, ignorant of his near sacrifice by the pope upon the altar of expediency, henceforth described himself as "King, by the grace of God and of the lord Pope." The next year he crossed the Alps and was crowned emperor at Rome—after being required to vow to respect the concessions he had already made to Innocent, to promise complete freedom in all ecclesiastical elections, and to support the papacy in its struggle against heresy. After ten years of waiting, Innocent, already master in Italy, had procured for his client prince both the Kingdom of Germany and the Empire of the Romans.

* These guarantees, once given by Otto, laid the first real legal foundation for the States of the Church. Hitherto, papal claims had been based on the various Donations which were, at best, vague and, at worst, spurious. Now, Otto's deed constituted an uncontestable grant, and conveyed unquestionable title to a well defined area.

Pope Innocent now declared to one and all that he hoped to spend the remainder of his pontificate in spiritual pursuits. It was not to be so. The coronation of Otto IV began, rather than ended, Innocent's problems with the Empire. Once back in Germany, Otto subjected his Christian conscience to a careful examination. Or perhaps he learned of Innocent's near perfidy. In any case, he decided that he could not, in good faith, be both true to the pope and loyal to his imperial duties. Guelf by birth though he was, he now turned into a thorough Ghibelline. He nullified his grants to the pope, attempted to restore the imperial feudal system in papal territories, and presumed to treat the Two Sicilies as a mere fief of the Empire. Even worse, he laid claim to the inheritance of Mathilda and, in 1210, he invaded and occupied the papal lands in Tuscany. Innocent, moved to terrible wrath, hurled the sentence of excommunication against Otto and released his subjects from their oath of allegiance to him. As in the time of Gregory VII and Henry IV, the German barons revolted against their monarch and deposed him; then they summoned the pope's ward, Frederick, from Sicily to assume the crown of Germany.

This was not altogether good news for Innocent, for it meant that once more the crowns of Sicily and Germany would rest on a single head. Yet, Frederick, an unknown quantity, was preferable to Otto, a known enemy; and so, Innocent sacrificed the long-range interests of the Holy See to an immediate advantage. He accepted Frederick as king, but exacted from him the same price that he had formerly demanded of Otto. Frederick, pressed by the need for Innocent's immediate support and confirmation, forgot the unhappy precedent of Otto and swore what was required of him:

> We, Frederick the Second, by divine favor and mercy King of the Romans, ever Augustus, and King of Sicily, do recognize the grace conferred upon us by God, and have before our eyes the immense and innumerable benefits conferred on us by you, most dear lord and reverent father, our protector and benefactor, lord Innocent, by God's grace the most venerable pope. Through your benevolence, labor, and guardianship, we have been brought up, cherished, and advanced, ever since the Empress Constance, of happy memory, confided us to your care, almost from birth. To you, most holy father, and to all your Catholic successors, and to the Holy Roman Church, our special mother, we shall discharge all duties of obedience, honor, and reverence, always with a humble heart and a devout spirit, as our Catholic predecessors, kings and emperors, are known to have done to your predecessors. Not one jot shall we subtract from these, but rather add to them, that our devotion may shine all the more.

Frederick then promised that he would not interfere in the election of bishops, and that canonically elected candidates would be installed. He confirmed the pope's title to the States of the Church: "I vow, promise, swear, and take my oath to protect and preserve all the possessions, honors, and rights of the Holy Roman Church, in good faith, to the best of my power."

From this time (1213) forward, Frederick advanced from success to success. Otto was driven into private life, and the papal legate placed the German crown on Frederick's head at Aachen, in 1215. Where great Innocent blessed, it was whispered throughout Europe, there success and prosperity followed; but where he cursed, there came death and destruction.

Pope Innocent was not reluctant to assert the papal prerogative elsewhere in Europe, and, despite his preoccupation with Italy and Germany, it was to his credit that no consideration of political gain ever prevented him from maintaining moral principles against sovereigns who could have been useful in attaining his political ambitions. The most conspicuous instance of this trait is found in his famous quarrel with Philip Augustus, King of France, a quarrel which he inherited from his predecessor, Celestine III. Philip had married Ingeborg of Denmark, sister of King Canute VI. When the advantages to France expected from this union failed to materialize, Philip put Ingeborg aside, commanded his obedient bishops to nullify his marriage, and then married Agnes of Meran. Celestine had voided the verdict of the French bishops, but, old and feeble as he was, he was able to do little more than urge Philip to return to Ingeborg. Innocent, however, could do a great deal more. He warned the King and the bishops of France that they were trifling with matters over which only the supreme pontiff had jurisdiction. "Recall your lawful wife," he commanded Philip, "and then we will consider what you may care to advance on your behalf. If you do not do this, however, no power on earth shall move us to the right or to the left until justice be done." When Philip still did not act, Innocent dispatched a legate to the French court who, in the most menacing tones, conveyed Innocent's message: unless Philip dismissed Agnes immediately, he would be excommunicated, his subjects released from the allegiance, and the kingdom placed under a papal interdict so that no religious services would be held anywhere in France. Under the threat of so awful a curse, the French barons and bishops withdrew their support of Philip. Yet, the king still held out, as much from royal pride as from love of the fair Agnes. The interdict was then pronounced, and all France shuddered. The dead lay unburied, the newborn went unchristened, sinners lived unshriven and, even more terribly, died unabsolved. Finally,

Philip, with his kingdom at the edge of revolt, promised to dismiss Agnes and to reinstate Ingeborg as queen—a promise which the death of Agnes, shortly thereafter, made easier of fulfillment. The repentant and bereaved king was welcomed with such paternal warmth back into the fold of the Church that he vowed to become—and indeed became—the stanchest ally of Pope Innocent.

Having dealt with Philip of France, Europe's most powerful prince, Innocent enjoyed easier victories over lesser potentates. It was his ambition to break through any separation of the spiritual and secular powers and to bind to the papal throne as many as possible of the kings of Europe by the ties of feudal vassalage. The now universally acknowledged feudal superiority of Rome over the Norman kingdom of Sicily had been the first precedent for this most unecclesiastical of all papal aggressions. Already, other small kingdoms, principally Portugal, had followed the example of the Normans. Peter of Aragon did the same in 1204. In 1213, a greater monarch was forced, after a long struggle, to make an ever more humiliating submission. John of England was opposed by the weapons of excommunication and interdict, and finally by the menace of deposition. He knew Innocent too well to believe that the pontiff would hesitate for a moment to release the English from their allegiance to the crown. He therefore surrendered the royal regalia to the papal representative, and, as a vassal of the papacy, received them back again. Nor were these the only kings who sought the support, or quailed at the threats, of the mighty Innocent. The heretic princes of the East vied with the orthodox kings of Europe in their quest for the pope's favor. Leo, King of Armenia, implored Innocent's protection. Prince John of Bulgaria begged the pope to elevate him to the royal dignity. In Hungary, Innocent acted as mediator of the claims of two brothers, Emeric and Andrew, who were contending for the crown of that country. Canute of Denmark, zealous for the honor of his sister, Ingeborg, was his humble petitioner. Poland was bound in abject obedience. The Duke of Bohemia meekly accepted a papal rebuke for maintaining "questionable political alliances."

Innocent's most prestigious accomplishment, however, was the *coup* by which he conferred upon a suppliant the imperial crown—not of the West, but of the East. An odd whirl of the wheel of fortune brought this to pass. Innocent had preached a crusade in the hope of recovering the Holy Land from the infidels. An army of Frenchmen and Flemings answered his summons. Deciding to avoid the deadly overland route, they applied to Venice for the means of transportation. The Venetians agreed, but when it came time to embark, it was discovered that the crusaders had no money.

The shocked Venetians refused stubbornly to extend credit either to the Frenchmen or even to Pope Innocent himself. For a time, it appeared that the expedition would come to naught. But the Venetians were as crafty as they were grasping. When the pious crusaders had been worked up to the proper point of desperation, the shipowners suggested that, after all, there might be a way. The crusaders could pay their fare by attacking the city of Zara, on the coast of Dalmatia, to which Venice had a hitherto unrecognized claim. Zara was taken (1202). But one detour now led to another. To Zara, now Venetian, came the son of the Greek emperor, declaring that his father's throne had been taken by a usurper, and pleading for assistance. Venice, wishing at least to wound two birds with one stone—Constantinople and Pisa (the new emperor favored Pisa over Venice)—persuaded the crusaders to turn aside, for the moment, from their holy quest and restore the deposed emperor to his throne. They did so, and the wronged emperor was back on his throne in short order. In Constantinople, however, matters did not go smoothly between Greeks and crusaders. Misunderstandings led to disagreements, disagreements to fights, and fights to open war. The devout crusaders took the Christian city of Constantinople by storm, plundering palaces, churches, shrines, and houses. Then, their appetites whetted by such minor spoils, they seized the Empire itself (1204) and divided it among themselves. Profit-conscious Venice, as might be expected, came out best; she took coast and island, town and country, all along from Zara round the shores of Dalmatia, Albania, Peloponnesus, and Thessaly, ending with half of Constantinople herself. One crusader, the Marquis of Monferrat, became King of Thessalonica. Another, Baldwin, Count of Flanders, was elected Emperor of a Latin Empire of Constantinople, and forthwith petitioned Rome for approval of his election to the purple. Innocent, as furious at the ruin of his crusade as at the sack of Constantinople, thundered against the warriors of Christendom and particularly against the Venetian entrepreneurs. But it was too late. Never would he be able, not even by excommunication or interdict, to force his good knights to disgorge their golden booty. So, he made the best of it and behaved with dignity and perception. After having roundly berated the crusaders for preferring the things of earth to those of heaven, and having commanded that they ask heaven's pardon for the desecration of holy places, he sent his legate to Constantinople to bestow the crown of Byzantium upon the suppliant Emperor-elect, Baldwin of Flanders.

Despite such vigor and authority, however, Innocent's constant meddling in the internal affairs of states did not pass altogether unchallenged. Even the kings who declared themselves his clients and vassals were constantly in conflict with him. Not only did the monarchy come to resent Innocent's imperious ways, but, for the first time, even the peoples of the European nations began to make common cause with them against the pretensions of the papacy. The nobles of Aragon protested King Peter's subjection to Innocent, declared that the surrender of their kingdom was invalid, and prevented the payment of the promised tribute to Rome. When John of England procured the pope's condemnation of the Magna Carta, the support of Rome was not sufficient to prevent the outraged nobles from combining to drive that unhappy prince from the throne. It was only by repudiating this condemnation that the papacy could secure the throne of England for John's son, Henry III, and thus continue, for a time, its precarious overlordship on that island.

Innocent's iron hand managed to crush opposition, but in adding the new hostility of the kings and the emerging nations to the eternal opposition of the Empire, he was entering upon a course of conduct which, within a century, was to prove fatal to his successors. The more political became the papal authority, the more difficult it was to maintain its prestige as the source of law, morality, and true religious belief. Innocent himself never lost sight of the higher ideals of Christianity, even while he strove for terrestrial might. But his successors were not always to be so able, nor so high-minded.

For the moment, however, the papacy reigned supreme. Innocent had created an ecclesiastical empire where even the most powerful of the earlier popes had merely asserted claims. He had confirmed the Two Sicilies in their dependency upon the Holy See; he had put the papacy at the head of the Guelf party in Italy, and he had made that party almost a national one; he had enforced the authority of the Roman Church throughout Europe; he had made and unmade kings, and he had seated emperors upon the thrones of the East and the West. No such spectacle had been seen in four centuries; and none such would be seen again for another six. The concept of Europe as an ecclesiastical organization had attained its fullest expression.

Toward the end of his life, Innocent held a General Council in the Basilica of St. John Lateran. Surrounded by hundreds of cardinals, archbishops, bishops, and secular princes, he lay down the law to the world. "Two things have we specially in our heart," he declared. "The deliverance of the Holy Land, and the reform of the Church Universal." In its seventy canons, the Council strove to carry out Innocent's wishes. It condemned the moribund Albigensian heresies of southern France. It attempted to rekindle enthusiasm for the spirit of the crusades. It drew up a radical scheme for reforming the internal life and discipline of the Church. It attempted to regulate the morals and the learning of the clergy, to limit their worldliness and their lust for money, and to restrain them from abusing the authority of the Church either through an excess of zeal or from baser motives. It invited bishops to set up free schools. It subjected existing monastic orders to strict supervision and forbade the establishment of new monastic orders. It outlawed superstitious practices. As a whole, the Council was aimed at the regulation and improvement of the influence of the Church on society. If many of the abuses dealt with were too deeply rooted to be corrected by mere legislation, the attempt at least speaks well for Innocent's character. All medieval legislation, secular as well as ecclesiastical, was but the promulgation of an ideal rather than the formulation of precepts meant to be executed literally. But no more serious attempt was made in the Middle Ages to root out evils than in this Council of Pope Innocent's.

The formal enunciation of this idealistic program of reform brought to an end the reign of Pope Innocent III. The pontiff devoted what little remained of his life to the preparations for a crusade which was to set out in 1217. But in the summer of 1216, Innocent expired at Perugia, after a reign of eighteen years, at the age of fifty-six. If not the greatest or the most saintly of the popes, he had been the most powerful of them all, and for nearly two decades all Christendom had resounded with tales of his doings.

4. The Fall of the Medieval Empire

By the time of Innocent's death, the chronic struggle between the Empire and the papacy seemed to have taken on a character of desperation. Although the Church had scored unprecedented triumphs and the Empire had been debased, the battle was far from over. Both institutions felt instinctively that they were near the end of their resources. They had exhausted their allies, emptied their treasuries, and decimated their populations by almost two centuries of continuous warfare. And, just as important, Christendom was growing weary of warlike vicars of the Prince of Peace and of ineffectual successors to Charlemagne. It was necessary, therefore, that matters be settled between the protagonists once and for all, and pope and emperor alike were aware that a final and decisive battle was imminent.

The fundamental antipathy of the two combatants had been aggravated by the union of the crowns of Germany and Sicily. Innocent III, pushed by circumstances into supporting the claims of the youthful Frederick II of Sicily to the German throne, had tried to protect himself from the consequences of his act by extorting elaborate and sacred oaths of loyalty from Frederick; but it must have been as obvious to Innocent as it was to Frederick that the ambitions of the latter must prove stronger than either his loyalty or his piety. For the moment, under Pope Honorius III (1216-1227), Innocent's immediate successor, the Papal States lay between Frederick's Kingdom of Italy to the north, and his Kingdom of the Two Sicilies to the south, like a ripe cherry between an upper and a lower jaw. This precarious situation is the explanation, though not necessarily an excuse, for the constant bitterness and the frequent duplicity of the popes in the ultimate stages of their contest with the Empire. The papacy was, quite simply, fighting for its life.

The struggle affected all of Italy, for Italy was—as it had been in the past—a convenient battleground on which Germany fought out its wars. The peninsula itself had divided its loyalties between the Chair of Peter and the Throne of Caesar. Among the Lombard cities, Milan and many of its sister cities were still papal and Guelf; but Pavia and a few others were imperial and Ghibelline because, while they loathed the Germans, they hated the Milanese even more. Florence and the other cities of Tuscany were Guelf—except for Pisa and Siena, who had learned from experience that the Empire could sometimes be trusted, while Florence never could be. Rome and the Patrimony of St. Peter were split into two constantly shifting parties, for permanent allegiances were as unfashionable as winners were unpredictable. A few of the great families, such as the Colonnas and the Frangipani, frequently were Ghibelline, while the Orsini and its satellite clans were often Guelf. The new religious orders—the Franciscans and the Dominicans, particularly—which swarmed from the Alps to the Straits of Messina, were, of course, steadfastly loyal to the papacy; so much so, their enemies claimed, as willingly to subordinate religious interests to political ends. The aristocracy of the peninsula, which was chiefly of Teutonic descent, generally held for the Empire.

The central figure in this last act of the drama of Empire and papacy is the Emperor Frederick II, who was just twenty years of age when Pope Innocent had allowed him to assume the German crown. He was a man of middle height, and well proportioned, although he became somewhat corpulent with the passage of time. His features were good, and he presented a pleasing demeanor. He had light hair which, like that of his father and grandfather, inclined toward redness, but in his later years he became totally bald. Despite his troubled childhood, passed in solitude and gloom at Palermo, amid wars and rebellions, he had been educated (at Pope Innocent's direction) with the utmost care. He was conversant in many tongues and versed in the literature of many nations. The half-Greek, half-Saracen culture of his native Sicily had fostered in him a curious combination of acute rationalism and dreamy mysticism. He had a true medieval love for the intricacies of dialectic, and he delighted in geometry and astronomy. His public and private life was regulated by the predictions of his astrologers (a not uncommon practice at the time, even among popes). He was a man of intellectual curiosity, and his great menagerie of strange animals was one of the sights of Europe. The camels and dromedaries employed in transporting his baggage excited the wonder and admiration of the Italians, and his prize, an elephant sent by the Sultan of Egypt, was the most famous animal of the age. He enjoyed hunting and hawking, as a naturalist as well as a sportsman, and he wrote a treatise on falconry that remained the standard work on the subject until well into modern times. In his concern for his health, he studied surgery and medicine and, with all his love of fresh air, he was something of a hypochondriac who consulted his physicians almost as much as he did his astrologers. He regulated his life and his diet carefully, and he had a thoroughly unmedieval penchant for cleanliness of person. His enemies counted among his crimes that he bathed "even on Sunday."

As Frederick passed from youth into maturity, his habits of life grew less European and more and more oriental. He secluded his wives from the public eye, eastern fashion, and he committed them to the care of eunuchs. At Lucera, he maintained a harem of concubines, the expense of which was borne by the realm and duly entered in the public accounts.

Though a competent strategist, Frederick did not regard himself as a warrior, and he took little pleasure in those feats of physical prowess and endurance which were the pride of his contemporaries. He was, however, a subtle statesman, indeed almost a great one, who sought to gain his ends by diplomacy rather than by force of arms. Courteous and polished in manner, he seemed to belong to a race other than that of his rude Swabian and Norman ancestors. His complex character had nothing of the simplicity and homogeneity of his Norman and German subjects, but reflected at one time the coloration of an astute and effeminate oriental and at another seemed to anticipate that of a Renaissance prince.

In most ways, Frederick outstripped contemporary thought, and in many he outstripped contemporary sympathy. His contempt for the ideals of his time comes out most strongly in his dealings with the Church, and he was said to have learned from his Arab and Jewish teachers an utter skepticism in all religious matters. Moses, Mohammed, and Christ, he is reported to have said, were three impostors who had deluded the world each in turn; and it is alleged that he believed the soul perished with the body. If Frederick maintained these views in private, he was careful to submit himself to all the outward observances of the Church, and to prove his orthodoxy not only by a formal denial of all such charges, but also by the most violent persecution of heretics. He was openly skeptical of political freedom and of most of the things in which his Italian compatriots believed most fervently. And while the Italians smiled at the theory of the "divine right" of Empire and of the blessings of a strong government, these were the things in which Frederick believed most devotedly.

In his lifetime, Frederick excited both love and hatred to extreme degrees—a quality which he continues to exercise among scholars to this day. As a poet, lawgiver, soldier, and statesman, he was the wonder of his world—*stupor mundi,* an English chronicler called him. Impetuous and terrible in anger, he was tender in friendship. Unpredictable save in the monomania of his ambitions, he was the prototype of the medieval *enfant terrible,* a crusader who was at once the terror of the papacy and the delight of Islam. He was undoubtedly the most arresting and influential Italian personality before the time of Dante.

Despite the protection of Innocent III, Frederick had had great difficulty in maintaining his position in Sicily against the descendants of the old Arab lords of Sicily on one hand, and against the turbulent Norman feudal aristocracy on the other. The years immediately after Innocent's death were occupied with renewed struggles against the Saracens in Sicily. It was not until 1225 that he was able to overcome them, and then he attempted to divide the Arab community by transporting large numbers of them to the rebuilt town of Lucera, on the mainland. The industrious Arabs, skilled workers in steel and silk, prospered thereafter; and with prosperity came gratitude and loyalty to their conqueror. Frederick cultivated these Arab subjects assiduously, for they were a military as well as an economic credit to his realm. They were impervious to the terrors of the spiritual weapons of the Church, and they were more than willing to fight for Frederick in his Italian wars. Moreover, they proved an adequate counterbalance to the Norman aristocracy, which was allied with the papacy, and an effective force in pacifying such cities as Messina and Syracuse, which rebelled against the substitution of a centralized royal authority for their ancient communal liberties.

With the Saracens, the Normans, and the cities all under his control,

Frederick issued a series of laws that were openly intended to replace the feudal system by a royal autocracy. He repossessed alienated royal domains, destroyed or occupied the fortified castles of the great lords, and forbade, under pain of death, private wars among his subjects. Criminal trials were removed from the feudal courts to those of royal judges, and towns were deprived of the right of electing their magistrates. The spiritual lords fared as badly as their temporal counterparts. They were required to pay taxes, and to give up any civil offices that they might hold. The jurisdiction of ecclesiastical courts was severely curtailed, and the increase of Church property by legacy was halted through legislation. On the ruins of the old aristocratic system of government there grew up a comprehensive administrative complex in which all laws emanated from Frederick, and matters at every level, from the court itself down to the meanest village, were controlled by royal functionaries.

The arts and sciences flourished under the aegis of this benevolent despotism. In 1224, Frederick established the University of Naples, "so that those who hunger for knowledge may find within our kingdom the food for which they yearn, and not be forced to go into exile to beg the bread of knowledge in foreign lands." It was the first European university founded by royal charter, and though it was to be an efficient instrument of education, its dependence on the state deprived it of that freedom which was necessary for it to play a real part in the intellectual history of Europe. Frederick revived the ancient school of medicine at Salerno, and no one who did not have a license from that institution was allowed to practice medicine in Frederick's kingdom. The royal palace itself was a center of intellectual vigor. There, Michael Scot translated many of the works of Aristotle into Latin, and Leonard of Pisa, who introduced Arabic numerals and algebra into the West, was Frederick's protégé. The king, it was said, dabbled in Latin poetry; and it is known for a fact that his compositions in Italian mark the beginnings of the vernacular literature of Italy. Dante himself regarded Frederick as the "father of Italian poetry," and, for a time, it seemed that the Sicilian dialect, rather than that of Tuscany, would become the literary idiom of Italy. So well did Frederick love art that he robbed Ravenna to adorn his palace at Palermo, and he collected—sometimes by purchase, sometimes by robbery—jewels, gold and silver plate, furniture, and, of course, manuscripts.

This high-minded, stubbornly autocratic prince, born centuries before his time, could hardly hope to live in peace alongside an inflexibly authoritarian papacy and obstinately autonomous communes. And, in fact, relations among them were soon strained to breaking. The rupture first occurred, as always, between emperor and pope. Honorius III was a gentle, sincere, mild-mannered Roman noble who, under his predecessor, Innocent III, had been charged with the administration of the papal finances. Honorius did not pretend to be a statesman, nor was he a zealot. He was, however, a devout man, and, like Innocent, intent above all things upon recapturing Jerusalem from the Arabs. It is not unlikely that Honorius' zeal for the Holy Places was sharpened by the consideration that Frederick in Palestine was considerably less dangerous to the papacy than Frederick in Sicily. Yet, Honorius had been young Frederick's tutor, and he wished him well. His conciliatory temper gave the young king time to work out his policies in the south and to consolidate his kingdom before Honorius pressed him in the matter of a crusade. Still, such things could not be postponed indefinitely. Frederick had bound himself by an oath to Innocent to embark personally upon a crusade. Moreover, he had promised Innocent to prevent the permanent union of Sicily with the Empire by investing his young son, Henry, with his Italian possessions, to be held as a fief of the papacy. But as success strengthened Frederick's love of power and his impatience with outside control, it became obvious to Honorius and to the world that the young king was unwilling to fulfill either of these promises. Honorius gently urged him to depart for the East in order to uphold the cause of the Cross, but Frederick exercised his ingenuity in devising excuses for delay which the meek pope was obliged to accept. At last, in April 1220, Frederick openly defied the pope by allowing his son, Henry, to be elected King of the Romans, and therefore his successor both in the Empire and in Sicily. He had the effrontery to explain to Honorius that the election had taken place without his knowledge or consent, and to profess his own complete deference to the Holy See in all things. The good pope, outmaneuvered, sighed and resigned himself to the inevitable. He crowned Frederick as Emperor of the Romans in November of that year, and, at the same time, exacted an oath from the new emperor that he would start on the crusade within one year.

The year passed, and then another, and yet another. Frederick, with his double crown safe upon his head, did not move a step toward Jerusalem. Honorius remonstrated, and he even hinted at the possibility of excommunication. Frederick swore great oaths, made excuses and fervent protestations of undying loyalty and devotion toward the Holy Roman Church. But still he did not go. The affairs of his kingdom, he claimed, necessitated his presence in Italy. It soon became clear what these affairs were. In 1226, the emperor convoked a great diet at Cremona, where he renewed the ancient imperial claims over Lombardy. In alarm, the Lombard cities revived their league and hurriedly blocked the roads by which the imperial armies could cross over the Alps from Germany. Frederick then declared the cities to be outside the law, and one of his submissive German prelates presumed to fortify the imperial lightning with spiritual thunder by placing the Lombards under an interdict. This was too much, even for the patient Honorius. He pronounced the interdict to be invalid, declared himself the ally of the Lombard cities, and prepared to renew the ancient co-operation between the papacy and the communes. Then, perhaps exhausted by this uncharacteristic display of energy, he died.

Honorius' successor, Cardinal Ugolino, who took the name of Gregory IX (1227–1241) was a man of a different stamp. He was a member of the great Conti family of Latium—a tribe so conscious of their rank that they took their name from their title—and a near relative of the late Innocent III. In addition to a common ancestry, he shared with Innocent an inflexible will and a most exalted concept of papal prerogatives. Blameless in his personal life, a warm friend and patron of St. Francis of Assisi and of St. Dominic, deeply versed in theology and in canon law, he was blessed with the face of a saint and the presence of a Roman emperor. But, despite Gregory's sanctity, his training, and his eighty years, he was a Tartar: fiery, impatient, and stubborn to the point of madness. It was he who, during the pontificate of Honorius, had put the crusader's cross into Frederick's hands and received his crusader's vow. And now, having controlled his holy wrath during the reign of the benign Honorius, he swore by everything sacred that the emperor, willing or not, healthy or ill, secure or in danger of rebellion, would fulfill that vow. Brushing aside the specious explanations which Frederick was so adept in formulating, Gregory had only one word to say to the emperor: "Go!"

Frederick knew Gregory's temper, and he began preparations for departure. At last, the gossips of Rome said, Frederick was in earnest for the crusade. Bands of Italian, French, and German soldiers gathered at Brindisi on Italy's heel, and, despite a pestilence which killed many of them, the fleet set sail on September 8, 1227, with Gregory's relieved blessing. But a few days later, the pope received word that the fleet had turned about and that Frederick and his soldiers had now disembarked at Otranto. The emperor's excuses arrived forthwith, saying that a sharp attack of fever had obliged him to return. There is little doubt that Frederick was telling the truth this time. Among the victims of the fever was the commander of his armies, the Landgrave of Thuringia, without whom the crusaders would have been in a poor state indeed. But Frederick had made excuses too often in the past, and by now Gregory was too exasperated to care what

Frederick's reasons were. He immediately circulated an encyclical letter to the bishops of Frederick's kingdom, setting forth the papal grievances and pronouncing the sentence of excommunication against the emperor—and adding an interdict for any city, town or village that might dare to receive him:

> Out of the spacious amplitude of the seas, the tiny bark of Peter, placed, or rather displaced, by whirlwinds and tempests, is so continuously tossed about by storms and waves that its pilot and rowers can hardly breathe in the inundating rains. Four special tempests shake our ship: the perfidy of the infidels, the madness of tyrants, the insanity of heretics, and the duplicity of false sons. . . . Now, in this time, when there is a need to destroy monsters of this sort, to rout hostile armies, to quiet disturbing tempests, this Apostolic See had cherished with great care a certain son, namely the Emperor Frederick, whom from his mother's womb she received upon her knees, nursed him at her breasts, carried him upon her back, rescued him often from the hands of those who sought his life, with much pain and at great cost educated him until she had brought him to manhood, and led him to a royal crown and even to the heights of the imperial dignity, believing that he would be a rod of defense and a staff for her old age.

The letter then recounts Frederick's false promises, his delays, his broken vows, and the false start from Brindisi, and prays that God will send men who are able "in purity of heart and cleanliness of hand" to lead the armies of the Christians. But, he adds,

> Lest, like dumb dogs who cannot bark, we seem to defer to men rather than to God, and take no vengeance upon him, the Emperor Frederick, who has worked such ruin on the people of God, we, though unwilling, do now publicly pronounce him excommunicated, and command that by all he be completely shunned; and that you, and other prelates who hear of this, publicly publish this sentence. And, if his contumacy shall require it, we will take even more serious steps.

The threat in Gregory's last sentence was clear. If Frederick did not make amends, the pope would deprive him of his crowns. It was the signal for the violent renewal of the battle between emperor and pope.

The ban of excommunication was published all over Europe. Bishops read it in their cathedrals, priests in the parishes, obedient friars told of it in pulpits from Sicily to Scotland, and laymen discussed it in their taverns everywhere. Frederick, however, did not flinch under the blow. Instead, he wrote letters to the monarchs of Europe, complaining that "no

Roman Emperor has ever been so badly treated by a pope. The Roman Church is so swollen with greed that the property of the Church itself is not enough to satisfy it; and it is not ashamed to disinherit and exact tribute from emperors, kings, and princes." To Henry III of England, he remarked that "the Church excommunicated your father, King John, and kept him under that sentence until he and his kingdom had become tributary to her. . . . We pass over her simony, her incredible demands, her open usury, and her deceits which infect the whole world. We pass over her words, sweeter than honey, smoother than oil—insatiable bloodsuckers. They say that the Roman Curia is the Church, our mother and our nurse, while in fact that Curia is the root and source of all evils. They send legates hither and thither, to excommunicate, to reprimand, to punish—not to sow the fruitful seed of God's word, but to extort money, to reap, and to bind where they have never sown."

Such heated exchanges demonstrated amply the temper of the protagonists; but they did not yet result in a clash on the field of battle. The fact was that the pope's emissaries had failed to undermine the allegiance of Frederick's subjects either in Germany or even in Italy, and that Frederick's Roman partisans had stirred up the City to the extent that Gregory found it necessary to spend Easter of that year (1228) at Viterbo.

Now Frederick did the unexpected. Hoping to confirm his posture as the wronged party in the dispute, and perhaps also to mollify Gregory, he once again embarked at Brindisi for the Holy Land. But Pope Gregory, scandalized at the prospect of a Holy War being waged by an excommunicate emperor, forbade Frederick to set foot in Palestine, and commanded the imperial armies to refuse to follow him. When Frederick persisted, the ban of excommunication against him was repeated and reinforced. The unfortunate emperor had now run the gamut of papal sanctions. He had been threatened with excommunication for not going on a crusade, excommunicated for returning from a crusade, and now excommunicated for going on a crusade. Little more could happen to him, and it was with a light heart that Frederick landed at Acre in September 1228. Although he found the Eastern Patriarch, the Knights Templar and Hospitaler, and the friars all turned against him, and although he was not unprepared for battle, Frederick almost immediately succeeded in reaching an agreement with El-Kamil, the Sultan of Egypt. The Sultan restored Bethlehem, Nazareth, and Jerusalem to the Christians, on condition that the Mosque of Omar remain in Saracen hands. This accomplished, Frederick, on a Lenten Sunday, took the crown of Jerusalem from the high altar of the Church of the Holy Sepulchre and placed it on his own head. By June 1229, he was back in Italy. In nine months, without a blow being struck in battle, and despite the lamentable state of his soul, Frederick had done more for the Christian cause than the hundreds of thousands of more orthodox crusaders who had preceded him.

During Frederick's absence in the Holy Land, Guelfs and Ghibellines had come to blows in Italy. Upon his return, however, a quick peace was made. Both pope and emperor had too many internal problems, and too little confidence in their respective chances of victory, to risk a final confrontation just yet. "The emperor," wrote Pope Gregory IX, "has come to seek me out with all the zeal of a devoted son, and he has assured me that he is ready to accomplish all my desires." And Frederick wrote that "the pope has opened his heart to me, and has calmed my spirit. I will remember the past no longer." The burden of the double excommunication was lifted from Frederick's shoulders, and he returned, in the words of Gregory, to his *consuetae deliciae,* his "customary amusements."

These amusements, as Gregory knew well enough, were not of the sort that any Christian, pope, prince, or peasant, could look upon with equanimity, and the gossips of Europe had long busied themselves with Frederick's morals and theological beliefs. He not only tolerated Saracens in his kingdom, it was said (and it was quite true), but he even lived on intimate terms with them, and he preferred the company of Saracen women to that of upstanding Christian ladies. Frederick's lifelong enemies, the mendicant friars, with that malice peculiar to the vowed celibate, embroidered upon these tales as well as upon rumors concerning the emperor's doctrinal orthodoxy. They delighted in reporting that Frederick had asserted that "If God had seen my beautiful Sicily, he would never have chosen that miserable Palestine for his kingdom," and that "There have been three impostors who invented religions; and one of them died on a cross."

Frederick's real offense, in the eyes of pious people everywhere, was not, of course, that he delighted in the company of Moslem women, or even that he was fond of making epigrams at the expense of dogma, but that he quite openly worked to subordinate the spiritual power to the temporal. It was an offense aggravated by the consideration that Sicily, as the result of Frederick's efforts, had replaced southern France as the cultural center —and, so far as the Church was concerned, as the heretical center—of Europe. Rome felt instinctively that a realm so fortunate in the good things of this world, so lax on so many points of morality, and so careless of the respect due to the successors of St. Peter, must be a menace to the well-being of Christendom in general and of the Holy See in particular.

Italy in the Middle Ages

In the nature of things, the tenuous peace that had been made upon Frederick's return from the crusade could not long endure. For the time being, however, since neither party was ready to strike the decisive blow for power, both sides watched each other with mutual suspicion and guarded hostility, and the rumor mills of both ground out tales and myths designed to discredit their respective enemies in the eyes of Europe.

The time of watching and waiting ended in 1237. In the years between Frederick's crusade and that date, the Lombard cities had watched with alarm the despotic and anti-municipal policies of the emperor, and they reckoned, not unreasonably, that the tyrant would soon turn his eyes to the north. As early as 1232, these cities had revitalized their league and extended it to the chief towns of the Romagna and the March. Other leagues sprung up in Tuscany and Umbria.

Frederick's suspicions were aroused by all this activity, and suspicion turned to rage when the cities formed an alliance with King Henry of Germany, Frederick's own son, who was in revolt against his father's authority in Germany. The emperor at once set about finding some Italian power antagonistic to the municipal leagues, and he saw his best support in the remnants of the feudal aristocracy that remained in Italy. Some of the more capable barons had been able to exercise some authority, by means of their wealth and influence, over the cities, and with such men Frederick now formed an alliance. Chief among these new partisans was the family of Romano—a house of German origin—two brothers of which had been able to establish themselves in Verona and Vicenza. It was an alliance which was to prove disastrous in the long run, but, for the moment, it seemed promising; after all, feudal barons were likely to be better fighters than Lombard merchants. Now, with the help of the Romano brothers, Eccelin and Alberic, and sustained by German troops and by his trusty Saracens from Lucera, Frederick soon outmaneuvered the cities, and on November 27, 1237, the entire army of the Lombard league was defeated at Cortenuova, between Milan and Brescia. The Milanese, as always the chief instigators of revolt, fled, leaving behind their standards and their commander in chief, a Venetian named Tiepolo. The victor celebrated his success by a sort of Roman triumph through the streets of Cremona, with his pet elephant leading, or rather dragging, the unhappy Tiepolo in the emperor's wake.

Most of the cities then made peace with Frederick, though a few irreconcilable Guelfic strongholds—notably Milan, Alessandria, Brescia, Piacenza and Bologna—persisted in their resistance. They saw a ray of hope in the possibility of securing a new ally, the pope. Nor was it a vain hope. Pope

Gregory had decided that the time was ripe for a final break with the Empire. After the triumph at Cremona, Frederick had sent the battle flags of Milan to the Roman enemies of the pope. The message was clear: Gregory's turn would come once the last of the Lombard cities had been reduced to obedience. Indeed, Frederick was now openly boasting of his intention to restore all of central Italy to imperial allegiance, and this threat tipped the papal scales in favor of war. Medieval popes had often had to swallow affronts to their spiritual authority, but none of them, so long as he could muster one soldier or count one ally, would countenance a threat to his territorial sovereignty. The willful Gregory IX, namesake of Hildebrand and heir of Innocent III, was not likely to be the first to do so. He immediately declared himself an ally of the Lombard league and, in March 1239, launched a new bull of excommunication against Frederick which, in addition to the usual penalties, formally deposed the emperor and released the subjects of the Empire from their oath of allegiance. Frederick was tolerably accustomed to the papal thunders, but he was also aware of the historic effect of formal deposition of an emperor, and he was understandably disturbed by this new development. His fears were shortly realized. Although the German princes remained faithful to him despite the papal ban, in the eyes of the Italians Frederick's condemnation by Gregory identified the imperial cause with that of the enemies of religion, and in such hitherto friendly cities as Parma the emperor began to lose ground rapidly. Even the Romans, those traditional foes of all authority, now flocked to the cause of Gregory—who was, they remembered, a Roman too.

This choosing up of sides marked the opening of the final phase of the struggle between Empire and papacy, the initial stages of which were fought with unprecedented bitterness and violence. Frederick denounced Gregory for supporting "heresy" in Lombardy, and he called on all kings and princes to aid him in putting down "the greedy and self-seeking priest" who intended to make the abasement of the Roman Emperor the first step in a campaign to subdue all the monarchs of Europe. Gregory, capitalizing on the gossip of the good friars, replied by accusing Frederick of the most shocking blasphemies and the most shameless immorality. In all this exchange of pleasantries, the only discernible facts are that both Frederick and Gregory were striving with all their might to win over public opinion, and that they both managed to attract a large body of the most ardent supporters.

The emperor opened his military campaign against Gregory by incorporating the March of Ancona and the Duchy of Spoleto, both papal pos-

Italy in the Middle Ages

sessions, into the Empire, and by absolving the inhabitants of those territories from their allegiance to the pope. Then he invaded the Papal States and took Ravenna, Faenza, Foligno, and Viterbo, which brought him to within striking distance of Rome itself. Shortly afterward, the City was surrounded by the imperial armies. Nothing but the miraculous and almost unprecedented loyalty of the Romans saved Gregory's city from capture. Thus circumscribed, Gregory now attempted to unite Christendom behind him by summoning a General Council to Rome, to join him in a new condemnation of Frederick. Only a handful of prelates answered the summons. The bishops of Germany were fearful of the consequences if they defied their emperor; those of Italy, France, and Spain were refused safe conducts through the imperial lines. The French, Spanish, and Italian bishops therefore gathered at Genoa, whence they were taken aboard ships engaged by the pope to bring them to Rome. Once at sea, however, the papal ships were attacked by an imperial fleet and, after a brief show of resistance, most of them were captured. Only those ships carrying the prelates of Spain managed to escape. The lord cardinals, archbishops, bishops, and abbots, along with their attendant prelates and secretaries, and the delegates of the Lombard cities, were, we are told by an observer of the scene, "packed together in oppression and chains, and tormented by such hunger and thirst" that, when they were eventually thrown into a Neapolitan dungeon, "heaped up like pigs, the very prison into which they were cast seemed to them a welcome place of rest." Frederick had, with small effort and little cost, captured a General Council of the Church. Flushed with success, he again advanced on Rome, and this time the Romans did not resist him. He was at the gates of the City when Gregory died, on August 21.

Frederick, to his credit, did not push his advantage, but immediately withdrew to Naples to await the outcome of the papal election. Perhaps he wished to demonstrate that it was not against the Holy See that he had been at war, but only against Gregory, "the greedy and self-seeking priest." Or perhaps his moderation was designed to impress Gregory's successor, whoever he might be. Whatever Frederick's motives, few of the cardinal-electors trusted him sufficiently to venture to Rome for the conclave. A mere handful of them assembled to elect Celestine IV (1241), an old man who died before he was able to be enthroned. Thereafter, the Apostolic See was vacant for eighteen months. Finally, in June 1243, a sufficient number of cardinals assembled to elect a Genoese cardinal, Sinobaldo Fiesco, a former professor of law at Bologna who was said to be a fervent Ghibelline, and who was known to be a trusted friend of the emperor. Frederick, however, was under no illusion about his chances with the new pope. He is said to have remarked—though the sentence is probably apocryphal—"I have lost a good friend; for no pope can be a Ghibelline." Authentic or not, the saying expressed the fact of the matter. Fiesco's first pontifical act was to assume the name of the predecessor whose virtues he proposed to emulate; and it was an ominous sign for Frederick that his former friend chose to be called Innocent IV (1243–1254).

Both parties, to show their good will, entered upon negotiations, but neither pope nor emperor were serious in these exchanges. Things had gone too far. Too many words had been spoken, too many outrages perpetrated, for either side to be content now with anything less than total victory. Within a year of Innocent's coronation, the imperial troops were again ravaging the papal possessions, and Innocent had fled first to Genoa and then across the Alps to Lyons. From there, he assembled a General Council to ratify the condemnation of the emperor.

The Council assembled at Lyons in June 1245, with a good number of prelates in attendance, although the bishops of Germany again demonstrated their loyalty to, or at least their fear of, their master by staying at home. In practice, the primary business of the assembly was the condemnation of the emperor, and the fathers proceeded to it without delay. On July 17, Innocent pronounced, in the name of the Council, the deposition of Frederick from the thrones of Germany, Italy, and the Two Sicilies. "And we command," Innocent concluded, "that those who hold the right of election within the Empire now proceed to a new election. As to Sicily, we ourselves, after consultation with our brothers, the cardinals, will do all that is necessary."

The German electors assembled and elected a new emperor—or rather, an anti-emperor, for Frederick refused to divest himself of his dignities—in the person of Henry Raspe, Landgrave of Thuringia. The majority of the German nobles, however, remained loyal to Frederick, and under the leadership of his younger son, Conrad, they were able to inflict a major defeat on Henry of Thuringia, who then fled back to his dukedom to die. For a time, the imperial crown went a-begging. It was offered to Hakon, King of Norway, who refused with the words, "Willingly would I fight against the enemies of the Church; but I will not fight against the enemies of the pope." Finally, the young Count of Holland, William, was prevailed upon to accept the imperial dignity, and for the rest of Frederick's life the control of Germany was in the hands now of one, and now of the other, of the claimants. Neither William nor Frederick, represented by Conrad, was able to win a decisive victory; but, under the hammer blows of their

Italy in the Middle Ages

constant efforts to do so, Germany gradually sank into that state of feudal anarchy which was to endure into the nineteenth century.

Everything now seemed to go against Frederick. His army in Italy was utterly routed at Parma in 1248, and the victorious citizens of that city captured, in addition to the emperor's soldiers, his entire harem. His favorite son, Enzio, was defeated and taken by the Bolognese at Fossalta, and spent the remainder of his days in captivity. Pier della Vigna, Frederick's closest friend and confidant—"he who kept both the keys of Frederick's heart," said Dante—was unjustly accused of treason, and he killed himself to avoid torture. Plots and conspiracies multiplied even in the south, and the barons of Apulia rose in revolt. Everywhere, the cities of Italy, Ghibelline and Guelf alike, were in flames.

Still Frederick fought on. He was sustained by that streak of mysticism, almost of madness, inherited from the oriental forebears of his mother, Queen Constance. Visions of grandeur, such as in earlier days he would have been the first to deride, now took form in his mind. He saw himself now not merely as emperor, but as God's anointed, destined to reform the Church and to restore it to its pristine purity. "God is our witness," he declared in a manifesto to the Christian princes, "that our intention has always been to force churchmen to follow in the footsteps of the primitive Church, to live an apostolic life, and to be humble, like Jesus Christ. In our days, the Church has become worldly, and we therefore propose to perform an act of charity in depriving these men of the treasure with which, to their eternal damnation, they are filled. . . . Help us to put down these swollen prelates, so that our mother, the Church, may have more worthy guides at her helm." The princes shook their heads sadly and did not bother to answer. It was as obvious to them as it would earlier have been to Frederick himself that the only reform he really proposed was to absorb the Church into the Empire.

Going from words to deed, Frederick now declared himself to be the head of the Church in his kingdom, and he proceeded to burn alive any "heretic" who supported papal authority or who, under any pretext whatever, spoke or acted against his own authority. He declared himself worthy of the adoration of his subjects, like the pagan emperors of old, and he claimed to be Christ's vicar on earth and, moreover, himself an emanation of the Godhead. His birthplace, the town of Jesi, was to be the Bethlehem of the West; and the unhappy Pier della Vigna was to have been the Apostle of this new Messiah.

The clouds parted once more for Frederick shortly before his death. News came to him that the Ghibellines of Lombardy at last seemed to be winning the upper hand in the north. And, from across the Alps, he heard that Conrad had won a major battle against William of Holland. Encouraged, Frederick started northward once more toward the end of 1250, but he was overtaken by a mortal illness a short distance from Lucca, at a hunting lodge named Fiorentino. "This is the spot long ago foretold to me," he said, "where I must die. The will of God be done." In great peace of mind he formally bequeathed the kingdom and the Empire to Conrad; he then appointed a bastard son, Manfred, to be regent in Conrad's absence. On December 19, he died. According to his friends, he died in the bosom of the Holy Roman Church, to which he was reconciled on his deathbed by the Archbishop of Palermo. According to the friars, however, he died a damnable heretic, forsaken by God and man, in misery and despair. Neither ending would have been out of character for Frederick. Innocent IV, upon hearing of the death of his archenemy, shouted for joy: "Be glad ye heavens, and let the earth rejoice!"

With Frederick died and was buried the Holy Roman Empire as a real factor in the destiny of the Christian world, although for another generation a furious battle was to rage over the disposal of its corpse. The name of the Empire was to continue for another six hundred years; and for centuries yet, an occasional German princeling was to come down across the Alps to receive the diadem at the hands of some new pope on the banks of the Tiber. But, with Frederick's passing, the old medieval Empire became no more than the shadow of a theory which had failed to be realized in practice.

The end of Frederick's Hohenstaufen dynasty itself reads like the final act of a Greek tragedy. In accordance with his last wishes, Conrad succeeded to the Empire and to the Kingdom of the Two Sicilies, while Manfred acted as regent for Conrad in the latter. These arrangements, taken to ensure the continued union of Sicily with the Empire, served notice to the world that the struggle was far from over. Pope Innocent was resolved not to undergo a repetition of his experiences with Frederick, and he laid his plans to root out the last of "the viper's brood," as he called Frederick's offspring.

In Germany, Conrad IV and William of Holland had fought each other to a standstill, and Conrad, abandoning the fight for the moment, appeared in Italy in 1252. After rallying the Ghibellines of the north, he sailed from Venice for Sicily, where Manfred and the southern nobility gave him a hearty welcome. But, perhaps inevitably, relations between the half brothers quickly deteriorated. Conrad regarded himself as absolute ruler of the southern kingdom; and Manfred, who had exercised royal au-

Italy in the Middle Ages 167

thority for two years, was reluctant to relinquish the reins of power into the inexperienced hands of Conrad. The rift between the royal brothers gave Pope Innocent the opening he had been seeking. In 1254, he excommunicated Conrad, and the friars proclaimed a holy war against the Hohenstaufens in Italy. A few months afterward, however, Conrad died, at the age of twenty-six, leaving Conradin, a child of two, as his heir. Excluding Manfred from power, he appointed one of his German lieutenants, Berthold of Hohenburg, as regent of the kingdom. Instantly, the age-old enmity between the Germans and the Italians erupted into bloody riots and battles, and Berthold, powerless to control either side, was happy to divest himself of the regency in favor of the willing Manfred. Meanwhile, the troops of Innocent IV had invaded the kingdom and seized several important strongholds. The local nobility, sensing an opportunity to best the detested Germans, vowed loyalty to the papacy and ranged themselves and their troops beneath the banner of St. Peter.

In the face of this coalition, Manfred had no choice but to negotiate. In 1254, a treaty was signed in which Manfred was reconciled to the Church and recognized as Prince of Taranto. Nothing whatever was said of the rights of Conradin. Manfred had hoped, however, that his submission would be rewarded by his recognition as King of Sicily; now he discovered that Innocent had clandestinely offered that crown to Edmund, younger son of King Henry III of England. Reversing himself, he thereupon called upon his father's Saracens of Lucera, and, with their support, he resolved to withstand the forces of Innocent IV. But before any action could be taken, Innocent died (December 7, 1254).

Innocent's successor was a nephew of Pope Gregory IX, who took the name of Alexander IV (1254–1261). The new pope was described by a contemporary as "kindly and pious, diligent in prayer and highly spiritual, but easily moved by flattery and inclined to avarice." Alexander was too unworldly to possess the inflexible will of his pontifical uncle or the ambition of Innocent IV, and he thought it wise to withdraw the papal forces from Naples and to content himself with excommunicating Manfred. He also renewed his predecessor's offer of the Sicilian throne to Edmund of England, and began an endless series of exchanges with Henry III to determine who would pay for what if the offer were accepted. It was a hopeless task, for Henry was every bit as parsimonious as Alexander, though not quite as rich.

Manfred, meanwhile, left on his own, showed that he was a son not unworthy of his father. Before the end of 1255 he had subdued the rebellious barons of Apulia and secured his position on the mainland. Then, crossing over to Sicily, he quickly established his authority on that island. Luck came to his aid. In 1257, a popular revolt in Rome drove Pope Alexander to take refuge at Viterbo, and a popular, though violent and bloody, democracy took over the Eternal City and entered into friendly relations with Manfred. By astute diplomacy, Manfred also came to an understanding with Genoa and Venice, with whom he entered into commercial treaties. At last he felt sufficiently strong to do for himself what the pope had been unwilling to do and, in August 1258, he crowned himself King of Sicily. For a short time, the Kingdom of the Two Sicilies enjoyed peace and prosperity under his rule, and the Hohenstaufen star seemed once more in the ascendancy. In the north, Manfred's strength was consolidated, ironically, by a defeat of the Ghibelline party. In 1259, Eccelin and Alberic da Romano, those redoubtable allies of Frederick II, had been killed in a pitched battle with the Guelfic armies of Cremona, Mantua, Ferrara, Padua, and Milan. The victory of the cities and the death of the Ghibelline leaders had the unwanted effect of making Manfred now the uncontested head of the Ghibelline party in Italy. An Italian writer of the next generation tells us that he "rose to great power and state, and all the imperial party in Tuscany and Lombardy increased greatly in power. The Church and its devout and faithful followers were much abased."

The cause of the papacy indeed seemed so hopeless that Alexander IV was reduced to offering to Manfred terms of peace that were humiliating to the successor of Gregory VII and Innocent III. As it turned out, even his humiliation was in vain, for Manfred refused absolutely even to discuss Alexander's offer. The hapless pope escaped his embarrassment by dying, in May 1261.

The next pope, Urban IV (1261–1264), the son of a French cobbler, was an active, energetic, headstrong and hot-tempered man, but one who, when he was at peace with himself, was capable of exercising excellent judgment. He was clear-sighted enough, and enough of a Frenchman, to realize that no Italian would willingly fight Manfred for the sake of some pale English prince named Edmund. Urban therefore withdrew the offer of the Sicilian crown from the son of Henry III, and offered it instead to Charles of Anjou, the brother of King Louis IX of France. Charles, ambitious, clever, and ruthless, accepted with alacrity; but before he could come to Urban's assistance, the pope died. His successor, however, Clement IV (1265–1268), also a Frenchman, took up where Urban had left off. He proclaimed a crusade against Manfred and, in 1265, Charles of Anjou appeared in Italy, where he was greeted with great cries of joy by the Guelfs. Florence named him *podestà*. Fickle Rome, where

Pope Clement could not show himself publicly for fear of insults, took Charles to its heart and acclaimed him Senator.

In June of the same year, a commission of cardinals formally conferred upon Charles the Kingdom of Sicily in the pope's name, and exacted his acceptance of the terms for his occupation of that papal fief. He was required to pay a tribute of eight thousand ounces of purest gold, to surrender the Duchy of Benevento to the Apostolic See, and to renounce the office of Roman Senator as soon as he had taken possession of Manfred's kingdom. Charles swore all that was required of him, and then he returned to France to raise an army. Before the end of the year, he was back in Italy with troops of Provencals, French adventurers, and Italian Guelfs. In January 1266, he and his wife, Beatrice, were crowned King and Queen of Sicily, and within a few weeks he had invaded Manfred's dominions. The Neapolitans were unprepared for a winter campaign, and many of the cities, towns, and castles fell without resistance to the French. The decisive battle was fought at Grandella, near Benevento, on February 26. Manfred's Saracens easily dispersed Charles's Provencal infantry, but they, in turn, were scattered by the mail-clad and mounted French knights. The latter then fell upon Manfred's German cavalry and quickly defeated them. The young Hohenstaufen king, seeing the utter hopelessness of his situation, resolved to die honorably rather than fall into the hands of his enemies. Spurring his mount into the thick of the fighting, he fought valiantly until he was struck down. It was, according to the standards of the time, a worthy end to a brilliant career.

On that one day of battle, the Kingdom of the Two Sicilies passed from the hands of the Hohenstaufen into those of the Anjou, or Angevin, dynasty. It was not, for the people of the south, a particularly fortunate change, for Charles's concept of kingship was to impose his will by systematic cruelty and oppression. Nonetheless, in Italy a cruel Frenchman was preferable to a German barbarian, and the kingdom soon settled into a state of comparative tranquillity. Charles then marched northward to help the Guelfs of Tuscany. In Florence, at the news of Charles's victory over Manfred, the Ghibellines were expelled from the city, and the Guelfs, now in sole charge, undertook to reorganize the municipal constitution along republican lines. They were uneasy, however, in their newfound power, and they soon asked Charles to occupy the city. A band of French cavalry came, and the Florentines, at the beginnings of democracy in their city and at the turning point in their history, elected Charles to be ruler of Florence for a period of ten years.

The final chapter in the history of the Hohenstaufen family is the story of Conradin, grandson of Frederick II and son and heir of Conrad IV. Conradin, in his fifteenth year when Manfred's death made him the sole survivor of his house, was a precocious and gallant lad. He longed to right the wrongs of Italy, as recited by the Ghibelline exiles at his court, and he was mature enough to understand that there was no future for him in a Germany which, because of the protracted wars of his father and William of Holland, was now divided into fiercely autonomous principalities. Conradin's romantic attraction to the sunny and populous southern land was sharpened by news of uprisings against Charles of Anjou in Naples and Tuscany. Anjou's triumph had been too rapid to be complete, and a strong reaction against him had set in as the result of the brutality and cruelty of his commanders. In Calabria, a full-scale revolt had broken out. In Rome, the Senate and the people, as well as the pope, had been alarmed at the victories of their French protégé; they had wanted him to be successful, but not too successful. Now they chose as Senator of the Romans an old enemy of Charles's, Henry of Castile, brother of King Alfonso X. In the north, the Guelfic tide continued its rise, and the Ghibelline cities, with Pisa at their head, struggled vainly to maintain the *status quo*. In the midst of all this unrest, Conradin thought that the time had come to try his fortunes in Italy. In 1267, the young prince entered the peninsula and entrenched himself in Verona. At the approach of the old imperial menace, however, the mutual jealousies and feuds of the cities vanished, and once more they united against the common enemy. Pope Clement IV feared Charles of Anjou; but he feared even more this sprig of the Hohenstaufen tree, and he roused all Italy against Conradin, whom he designated as "the basilisk sprung from the seed of the dragon."

At the beginning of 1268, Conradin had collected sufficient men and money to move. He marched southward, and after many false starts, his army met that of Charles of Anjou on August 23. The combined French and Italian forces totally annihilated the German army. Conradin was captured by an act of treachery and summarily beheaded. Thus perished the Ghibelline cause in Italy. Henceforth, the peninsula was to be left to work out her own destinies, without German interference.

5. *The Collapse of the Medieval Papacy*

The fall of the House of Hohenstaufen and the collapse of the Holy Roman Empire marked the beginning of the end of the Middle Ages. A new era was taking shape in Italy and throughout Europe, and its dawning was apparent to men of keen vision. Hohenstaufen and Empire both had crashed into ruin under the weight of papal hostility, leaving the popes supreme in Christendom. But the papacy itself—that Apostolic See to whom the domination of Europe now seemed assured, that Fisherman's Throne before which emperors knelt and lesser monarchs cringed, that "head of the world" at whose nod oaths and allegiances might be loosed or bound—it, too, insofar as it embodied the medieval ideal of a supranational and theocratic primacy, was tottering. It, too, was to fall at the irreverent touch of a new age. So long as the papacy stood untarnished by human corruption, it seemed mighty and sovereign, its power eternal, and its dominion unlimited; such had seemed its destiny under Hildebrand, under Alexander III, and under Innocent III. But the century which followed the death of Innocent was to work great changes in the omnipotent papacy of the Middle Ages. And, at a push, it was to tumble and fall with a crash that was to reverberate through the centuries.

There were signs, during the contest with Frederick II, that the weapons of the papal armory that had, up until then, seemed so terrible, were coming to be regarded in Europe as a mere arbitrary exercise in power. Excommunication and interdict had been used so prodigally, and so openly, for purely political ends that men, while they might believe that they were indeed the curse of the popes, could no longer bring themselves to accept them as the curse of heaven. Moreover, a new power was rising in Europe. The vigorous and united Kingdom of France had come into being, and it was determined to play that major role in European affairs which it regarded as its due. Henceforth, the Italian papacy and the German Empire had been the giants of the continent; now, they would have to contend with this new power, and it was one which would soon dwarf them both. In its belligerent self-confidence, France was to confront the arrogant papacy, strip it of its splendid robes, and lay bare the dessicated and fragile frame underneath.

Boniface VIII (1294–1303) was the pontiff under whom the medieval papacy, and the Middle Ages in Italy, came to an end. He was not, however, the sort of man who might be expected to preside over the disintegration of the mighty empire forged by his predecessors. To the contrary, he seemed cast in the mold of Innocent III: vigorous, energetic, arrogant, eloquent, vastly learned in the law, purposeful in politics, subtle in diplomacy, and terrible in anger. There is a bronze statue of him in the *duomo* at Florence which depicts him admirably, almost heroically. The only discrepancy is that it shows Boniface not only as a man of dignity and power, but also with his right hand raised in a gesture of blessing upon the world.

It is a posture at which Boniface himself might have smiled, for he was a man far more of this world than of the other, and his words, when he spoke, were more likely to be curses than murmured benedictions. Villani, a Florentine historian of the period (and an ardent Guelf), says of him that "he was high-minded and lordly, and coveted much honor. . . . He was greatly respected for his learning, and much feared for his power. He was very greedy for gold with which to enrich both the Church and his own family, but he did not try to dissimulate this greed and said that it was his privilege to do whatever he wished with the possessions of the Church. . . . He was very cautious and capable, and was gifted with much common sense . . . but he was excessively cruel toward his enemies and haughty toward his adversaries. He was more worldly than befitted his station, and he did many things that were displeasing to God." Dante, as passionately Ghibelline as Villani was Guelf, and a bitter enemy of Boniface's into the bargain, was less generous. He called Boniface "prince of the new Pharisees" and unhesitatingly placed him in Hell; but even he was sufficiently aware of the pope's human qualities to call him "the great priest." Another contemporary, perhaps more accurately, summed up Boniface as "a magnanimous sinner."

The first act of Boniface's reign was symptomatic of his sinfulness rather than of his magnanimity. His predecessor on the throne had been Celestine V (1294), a saintly monk who had been forced, much against his better judgment, to accept the tiara. After four unhappy months as the successor of St. Peter, Celestine had done the unprecedented: he abdicated the infallible papacy on the grounds of his utter fallibility, and immediately fled to a hermit's cave in the mountains. Boniface, upon his accession, was uneasy at the thought of a former, and possibly a rival, pope at liberty in Italy. He had Celestine arrested and imprisoned at Alatri, between Rome and Naples, where the former pope soon died.*

As soon as Boniface felt himself secure upon the throne, he turned to face the problems besetting him. In the City, a party of Romans refused to recognize his election, asserting that, since no pope could resign, Celestine's abdication had been invalid, and that therefore Boniface's election was null and void. To the south, the Angevin king of the Two Sicilies pretended to supremacy over the States of the Church. Across the Alps, the French king had embarked upon a line of conduct intended to cut off papal revenues from that kingdom. In Denmark, King Eric was indulging him-

* Boniface's enemies accused the pope of murder, and exhibited a large nail which, they claimed, had been driven into Celestine's skull by the pope's henchmen. There is no evidence, however, for suspecting Boniface of complicity in his rival's death.

Italy in the Middle Ages 173

self in the most open persecution of the clergy. Moreover, Christians everywhere were spilling each other's blood—the French fought against the English, the Genoese against the Venetians, the Pisans against the Florentines, Anjou against Aragon (for the crown of Sicily), and Adolph of Nassau against Albert of Austria (for that of the Empire). And everywhere, Guelfs and Ghibellines were battling in the streets and over the countryside of Italy. The magnitude of these problems would have made a lesser man than Boniface, or even a more humble one, blanch.

The chief threat for the moment seemed to lie, as always, in Rome itself. Boniface, by meddling in the private disputes of the great House of Colonna, had contrived to make enemies of two cardinals of that family. These two, who apparently did not have an exact knowledge of Boniface's character, hinted publicly that Boniface's election was invalid. The pope, in revenge, stripped them of their dignities, excommunicated them, and proclaimed a "holy crusade" against the Colonna family in the course of which the castles of that house were burned to the ground and its retainers slaughtered almost to a man. The most prominent Colonnas escaped a similar fate only by fleeing abroad, while Boniface had the satisfaction of seeing the renegade ex-cardinals on their knees before him, proclaiming him, for all the world to hear, to be the true and undoubted Vicar of Christ on earth. A few cardinals who grumbled at the indignities thus visited upon two of their number were silenced when Boniface, who knew his Sacred College, granted to the cardinals the right to wear the imperial purple—a privilege which the College retains to this day. The Colonnas could not be bought with such trifles, and in time Boniface would have to pay for this victory. But, for the time being, the new pope was triumphant in Rome, and he seemed, indeed, to sit as high as had the great Innocent a century before.

In Sicily, he was not as successful. The popes had never been pleased with the dynasty founded by Charles of Anjou. The Angevin were a haughty race, quarrelsome, imperious, and grasping. They not only oppressed the people of Naples and Sicily, but also treated the popes with an irreverent disdain which belied their protestations of loyalty and devotion. One of Boniface's predecessors, Nicholas III (1277–1280), had intrigued, along with the King of Aragon, with certain Sicilian exiles in an attempt to unseat Charles's descendant. Before these intrigues could come to fruition, however, the people of Sicily took matters into their own hands. An outrage, either real or imagined, perpetrated upon a Sicilian lady by a French officer, was the spark that ignited the fire of revolt among the inflammable islanders, and the French in Sicily were massacred in a conflagration known as the Sicilian Vespers (1283). By happy circumstance, the fleet of the King of Aragon was in the vicinity, and the Sicilians asked its protection from the certain revenge of the French, who still held Naples. In return, they offered to Aragon the crown of Sicily, which the king accepted and passed on to his younger son, Frederick. Pope Boniface attempted to dissuade Frederick from accepting, but the young Aragonese ignored the papal arguments and was crowned in Palermo amid great rejoicing. The pope thereupon excommunicated Frederick and pronounced an interdict against the entire island, both of which sanctions were ignored by prince and peasant alike. At length, Boniface was obliged to recognize Frederick's title (1300), on condition that, after Frederick's death, the Kingdom of Sicily should revert to the Angevin dynasty at Naples. No one actually expected that condition to be met, but everyone concerned, except the Neapolitan Angevins, declared themselves satisfied.

In the north of Italy, the papal curse was observed to hold even less terror for the faithful than it did in the south. Boniface, like all of his predecessors, yearned for a crusade to free the Holy Land from the Turks; and, like most of his predecessors, he was unable to elicit more than fine words from the princes of Europe and the municipalities of Italy. He threatened, and rustled sentences of excommunication and interdict, but no one budged. Early in his reign, he commanded that Genoa and Venice, locked in one of their chronic and commercially inspired feuds, sign a treaty of eternal peace. They ignored his command, peremptorily rejected his attempts at mediation, laughed at his talk of hell-fire, and fought on for three more years. In Florence he was even less successful in attempting to halt the war against Pisa, but he retaliated by placing the city under an interdict and then by inviting the French, under Charles of Valois, to enter and "pacify" Italy. He baited the hook by pointing out that it would be easy for Charles, in a land of rich cities, to indemnify himself for his trouble. Charles did indeed come to Florence, where he and his allies burned, pillaged, raped, stole, and murdered until, when he withdrew in 1302, he had earned the undying hatred of the Florentines both for himself and for Boniface.

Boniface's intrigues and little wars required funds, and the greed of which his contemporaries spoke was not slow in devising a way of collecting them. In 1300, he proclaimed a Jubilee, or "Holy Year," to celebrate the centennial. For centuries, Palestine had been the destination of Europe's pilgrims, and the shrines of Rome had been neglected. Now, however, Palestine was once more in the hands of the sons of Islam, and Rome reasserted herself as the pilgrim's city. Eager to endorse a practice which he

Italy in the Middle Ages

foresaw would increase the prestige as well as the income of the Holy See, Boniface issued his Bull of Jubilee, promising to all pilgrims who visited the basilicas of St. Peter and St. Paul during the year the same spiritual benefits as would previously have been gained by a voyage to the Holy Places of Palestine. An age that could laugh at excommunications still believed fervently in indulgences, and the pilgrims came swarming across the Alps and streaming into the Italian ports in numbers which astounded even Boniface. A contemporary writer states that no fewer than two million Christians visited the City in that year, and that, on an average day, there were no less than two hundred thousand pilgrims in Rome. Even allowing for normal exaggeration, the success of Boniface's idea was unprecedented. Dante, one of the pilgrims, tells us that the crowd was so great that "the Romans took measures for the people to be able to pass over the bridge [of Sant'Angelo], so that everyone on one side of it faced toward the Castello, and went toward St. Peter's, and on the other side of it they all faced toward the Mount [Mt. Giordano, a small hill on the left bank of the Tiber]. . . ." The contributions of the pilgrims matched their enthusiasm. Another eyewitness says that "two priests stood day and night with rakes in their hands, heaping up the gold and silver that were poured upon the altar of St. Paul's." Boniface, the delighted recipient of this largess, appeared frequently in public to bless the crowds, "dressed in imperial vestments, with two swords borne before him as symbols of his temporal and spiritual dominion over all the earth."

The Jubilee marked the zenith of Boniface's glory. Henceforth, his star and that of the medieval papacy was on a rapid decline. A long-standing quarrel with the Kingdom of France had broken out afresh, and it was not to be resolved until the popes became the captives of the Kings of France.

The French king, Philip IV, called *le Bel* ("the fair"), was the embodiment of the new spirit of disenchantment with papal claims to universal supremacy, and he was the personification of the theory of Gallic supremacy in Europe. In the pursuit of the latter, he had, in 1294, invaded and seized the English-occupied province of Gascony. Edward I of England had at once declared war. Both monarchs, however, were too impecunious to support an army, and both adopted the expedient of attempting to tax the clergy and the ecclesiastical property of their kingdoms. It was a scandalous exaction, particularly since the taxes were destined for the financing of what were regarded as "worldly ambitions." The French clergy, more independent than their English colleagues, refused to surrender to Philip the fifth of their revenues that he demanded, and they appealed to Rome for a ruling on the legality of Philip's levy. Boniface answered immediately: "We decree that if any clergy shall pay . . . any part of their income or possessions to a layman . . . without the permission of the Holy See, they shall incur excommunication. Moreover, we decree that all persons, of whatever station or rank, who shall ask or receive such monies, or who shall seize or cause to be seized, the property of the Church or of the clergy . . . shall incur excommunication."

But Philip was as adamant as Boniface was uncompromising. He refused to nullify the new tax laws, and proceeded then to retaliate by forbidding the exportation of gold, silver, precious stones, and food from France, and by ordering the ejection of foreign merchants (mostly Italian) and emissaries (mostly papal) from his kingdom. In one stroke, he cut off the chief source of regular papal revenue—that paid yearly by the French clergy—and banished the agents of Boniface who were in France preaching a new crusade and collecting funds for its support. In the face of such opposition, Boniface retreated and allowed the French clergy to make "voluntary" contributions to Philip's war. The king, for his part, rescinded the ordinances that were so fatal to the papal treasury. Moreover, he and Edward of England accepted Boniface as mediator in their quarrel, and even Edward acquiesced in the pope's verdict in favor of the French. For a time, peace prevailed between Boniface and Philip; but it was hardly likely that two such men, both arrogant, both ambitious, both convinced of their own righteousness, and both powerful, could continue for long without the appearance of some new dissension.

While Boniface was exulting in the triumph of his Jubilee Year, his old enemies, the Colonnas, still in French exile, were regaling the French court with tales of the pope's cruelty, greed, heresies, and injustices. In the atmosphere of hostility thus engendered, the French nobility were particularly sensitive to any encroachment on the prerogatives of their sovereign by one whom they regarded, and sometimes openly referred to, as a "degenerate Italian priest." Thus, when a disagreement arose between one of King Philip's great nobles and a papal emissary, the legate was summarily accused of attempting to stir up an insurrection, tried, condemned, and imprisoned (1301). Boniface demanded the immediate release of his representative, instructed the clergy to refuse payment of the hated taxes until Philip had complied, and announced that he would summon the French bishops to take the necessary steps for "the reformation of the kingdom, and the amendment of the king." The insulting bull was publicly burned at Paris, angry words flew on all sides, and the war was on between Boniface and Philip.

The pope, who had a marked fondness for vehemence of language, fired the next shot by issuing another bull, the famous *Unam sanctam* of 1302, which deserves to be quoted, not only for the effect which it was to have upon future generations, but also because it sums up the doctrine of papal supremacy in its most rabid form, and incidentally reveals how little Boniface understood the temper of the age:

> In this Church, there is but one Lord, one Faith, one Baptism. . . . And of this one Church there is only one body and one head, not two heads as though it were a monster: to wit, Christ and the Vicar of Christ, St. Peter and the successor of St. Peter. . . .
>
> We are told by the words of the Gospel that in His fold there are two swords; that is, a spiritual sword, and a temporal sword. Both swords are in the power of the Church; the first, indeed, to be wielded by the Church, and the second, for the Church; the one by the hand of the priest, the other by the hand of kings and knights—but at the will and sufferance of the priest. One sword, moreover, must be subservient to the other, and the temporal authority must be subjected to the spiritual. . . .
>
> A spiritual man judges all things, but he himself is judged by none. This authority, even though it is conferred on man and exercised through men, is not human, but rather divine, being assigned by divine lips to Peter. . . . Who, therefore, resists this power thus ordained by God, resists the command of God. Indeed, we declare, announce, and define that it is altogether necessary to salvation for every human creature to be subject to the Roman Pontiff.

These were words that Henry IV and even Frederick II might have heard in fear and trembling, for their thrones if not for their souls. But Philip the Fair, while he might be the equal of Henry and Frederick in ambition, was neither pious enough, nor sufficiently insecure in his own realm, to fear the rolling thunders of Rome's curse. Knowing that the nobility and people of France stood behind him, he convoked the States-General of the land, accused Boniface of every imaginable crime—among them: tyranny, witchcraft, sodomy, simony, murder, embezzlement, adultery, usury, idolatry, and heresy*—and called for a General Council of the Church to judge the matters in dispute and depose Boniface. Then Philip sent an ambassador to the pope, who was at the papal town of Anagni, to notify him of the appeal to a Council. Boniface, quite beside himself with fury, shouted that only a pope could convoke a General Council, and immediately ordered the

---

* From the standpoint of evidence, there is no indication that Boniface was guilty of any of the crimes charged to his account—except perhaps that of tyranny, which, however, was not a crime punishable under medieval law, either canon or civil.

preparation of a bull excommunicating King Philip and laying all France under the papal interdict.

Philip, however, was not content to sit at home and await Boniface's fulminations. Along with the message to the pope, he had prepared a plot to take him captive and bring him to France as a prisoner. William of Nogaret, his ambassador to Boniface, after delivering the king's message of defiance, met with a representative of the Colonna clan, and the pair arranged the details of the plot. They were joined by innumerable Colonnas and their dependents, and by dozens of Roman nobles who had been stripped of their properties to make way for Boniface's many nieces, nephews, cousins, sisters, brothers, uncles, and aunts. All told, according to one historian of the period, there were almost two thousand persons involved in the plot. Despite the multitude of conspirators, Boniface seems not to have been apprised of Philip's intentions. An old man of eighty-six, he was still at Anagni, a small town not far from Rome, which was the place of his birth. Here, from the pulpit of the cathedral where Roman emperors had been excommunicated and deposed, he proposed publicly to pass the same sentence on the French king. Two days before the time set for the excommunication, on a September morning of 1303, the noise of battle awoke the unsuspecting Boniface. While his nephews fought to keep the invaders at bay, the pope had time to rise and to attempt to negotiate with the French agents. But the intruders soon forced their way into the burning palace, from which everyone but the pope and two loyal cardinals had fled. They found Boniface awaiting them, and his death, seated upon his throne and holding a golden crucifix. "Since I have been betrayed like Christ," he cried, "I am ready to die like Christ." For a moment, all were paralyzed by Boniface's majesty. Then the spell was broken by Sciarra Colonna, who, being a Roman, had had some experience in dealing with popes. Seizing the aged pontiff by the arm, he dragged him from the throne, struck him full in the face, and would have dispatched him then and there had he not been forcibly restrained by the more coolheaded Nogaret. Boniface was chained, and his palace—that of it which had not burned—was turned over to the mob to be looted.

In a few days, public sentiment in Anagni, which had before been on the side of the French, shifted, and the townspeople, aghast at the thought of the Vicar of Christ, and an Italian, in chains and at the mercy of the hated French, stormed the palace and freed the pope. As soon as he was free, Boniface, who had been given nothing to eat during the three days of his captivity, made his way to the market place, where he begged, "If any good woman will give me alms of bread and wine, I will bestow upon her

God's blessing and mine." Then, escorted by a troop of horsemen sent by the Orsini family of Rome—the great rivals of the Colonnas—Boniface returned to the City, where, under pretext of protecting him from the French, the Orsini shut him up in the Vatican. He remained there, half mad with rage, until released by death in October 1303. Upon his death, a chronicler recorded a prophecy made by the unfortunate Pope Celestine V at the time of Boniface's election: "He shall enter like a fox, reign like a lion, and die like a dog." Thus during Boniface's pontificate was the hollowness of papal power revealed to the world. "Holy Mother Church," complained one ecclesiastic, "who in other days ruled her children, is now reduced to slavery; nay, even trampled underfoot."

Philip of France, however, was not content to see the papacy merely degraded. He wished to assure that it would never again rise to challenge his authority. In 1305, he engineered the election of a Frenchman to the papal throne. This pope, Clement V (1305–1314), never went to Rome, but took up his residence at Avignon, in the south of France, where Philip could keep his eye, and his thumb, on his pontifical creature. Thereafter, French popes succeeded one another, and here the papacy was to stay for nearly seventy years, almost completely in the power of successive French kings. They built on the banks of the River Rhone a gigantic fortress as the permanent papal palace, and they came to regard Rome, the source of whatever greatness they retained, as a dismal, dangerous, remote place. They believed wholeheartedly that the Seat of Peter had been uprooted from Italian soil and transplanted to France. In Italy, the period of the popes' absence became known as the "Babylonian captivity of the Church."

The political degradation of the papacy was not all that was accomplished during the subjection of the popes to the Kings of France. The Curia, hitherto a bureaucracy of devoted professionals, became a collection of great nobles in clerical dress, of men of pleasure. Of old, the popes and cardinals of Rome, even the most dissolute ones, had had a touch of greatness about them; when they sinned, they did so with magnificence, through pride, arrogance, hate, and ambition. At Avignon, even the vices of the popes and their court became the sins of the weak: the quest of wealth for its own sake, gluttony, sexual license, ambition for titles and honors rather than for power. The principal characteristic of the papacy until the death of Boniface had been that of strength; now, it was that of weakness and corruption. In the brief space of eleven years, from the election of Boniface in 1294 to the translation of the papacy to Avignon in 1305, the second great factor in the life of medieval Italy had expired.

With the Empire reduced to a shadow, and the popes under the whip of France, the old things had passed away.

6. *The Final Gasp of Empire*

After the popes had been dragged to France, the Empire, like a dying soldier who manages to rise long enough to emit one shout of triumph over his enemy's body, made a final effort to recover life and strength in Italy. It was very gallant, and very ineffectual. In the scale of history, it owes its celebrity to the great man who summed up and reiterated the imperial creed, rather than to the prince who attempted to revitalize the Empire, in much the same way as Pope Boniface VIII had summed up and reiterated the papal creed. Both were equally dead, to be sure; but each man believed in his system fervently, and as Boniface's bulls set forth the doctrines of Hildebrand and Innocent III, so do Dante's treatises and letters set forth those of Barbarossa and Frederick II.

The year of Boniface's Jubilee, 1300, is the year to which Dante assigns his own journey to the abodes of departed spirits; and as the Jubilee marked the close of the medieval papacy, so the *Divine Comedy* marks the close of medieval theology. Dante himself stands as the great monument at the boundary separating the old world, which was passing away, from the new, which was about to make its entrance. Giovanni Villani, who was about fifteen years younger than Dante, describes him in this way:

> He was deeply versed in almost all learning, although he was a layman. He was a great poet, a philosopher, and a master of rhetoric in prose and in verse as well as in oratory; he was a most noble writer, very great in rhyme, with the most beautiful style that has been seen in our language up to the present. In his youth, he wrote the book *La Vita Nuova,* and then, when he was in exile [from Florence], he wrote, among other things, twenty ethical poems and many admirable verses on love. And he wrote three noble letters; one he sent to the government of Florence, complaining of his exile; the next, he sent to the Emperor Henry, when he was at the siege of Brescia, blaming him, in the tone of a prophet, for having delayed; the third he sent to the Italian cardinals, during the vacancy after the death of Pope Clement [i.e., Clement V, the first Avignon pope], urging that they come to an agreement and elect an Italian pope. All these were in Latin, in a lofty style, with excellent reasoning and appeals to authority, which were much praised by men of judgment.
>
> This Dante was, however, by reason of his learning, somewhat arrogant,

haughty, and disdainful. Like an ungracious philosopher, he could not speak easily with unlearned men. Yet, because of his other merits, it is fitting to give him perpetual remembrance in this chronicle of mine, even though his noble works left to us bear witness in writing to what he was, and confer honorable fame upon our city.

Dante, by passages from the *Divine Comedy* and especially from his treatise *De Monarchia* (*On Monarchy*), explains how the Empire, sixty years after its last champion, Frederick II, had been buried, could again raise its head. In Germany, after an interregnum, the House of Hapsburg, in the person of Rudolph, Archduke of Austria, had claimed and obtained the imperial crown (1298). But Boniface VIII had refused to recognize him, and Rudolph had never ventured to cross the Alps nor attempted in any way to exercise imperial authority in Italy. Dante, however, and his fellow Ghibellines, could not bring themselves to believe that the familiar imperial institution had passed away. The concept of Europe as an aggregate of equal and autonomous nations had not yet arisen, and the Ghibellines were convinced that only the universal authority of a supranational Roman Emperor could cope with the confusion, anarchy, and political chaos of Italy. They believed in the emperor in the way that the Guelfs believed in the pope, or that the Saracens believed in Mohammed. If the emperor returned and established his authority, then peace would bloom, exiles (like Dante) would be restored to their homes and possessions, and Rome once more would shine as the center of a pacific and catholic Empire. In the *De Monarchia* Dante explains the reasoning by which he and his fellow Ghibellines arrived at that hope. First, he formulates an elaborate argument to establish that a universal empire is necessary to the well-being of the human race; then he demonstrates that that universal empire rightly belongs to the Roman people, proving his premise by appeals to the authority of Virgil and of the New Testament; finally, he shows that the supremacy of this universal and Roman empire is derived directly from God.

This extreme enunciation of the imperial creed was in flat contradiction, of course, to Boniface's theory of papal supremacy, just as the Ghibelline *credo* had always been opposed to papal pretensions. By Dante's time, the entire question seemed academic, for both theories had been relegated to a political limbo; but then, all of a sudden, the imperial theory started up afresh. A new King of the Romans, Henry VII, announced that he was coming from Germany to Italy to receive the crown of the Empire. The Ghibellines welcomed him with boundless enthusiasm (1310). The hope that Henry would restore peace and establish order permeated even the Guelfic cities, and almost all the communes—except Florence, the most rabidly Guelf of them all—sent envoys to greet him. Dante, in exile from Florence on account of his Ghibelline convictions, wrote a letter of encouragement to all the Italian princes:

> Behold, now is the acceptable time in which there are signs of hope and peace. A new day begins to shine, a new dawn begins to break that shall dissipate the dark night of our calamity. Now the eastern breezes have begun to rise, the lips of heaven begin to redden, and, with serenity, to comfort the aspirations of our peoples. And we who have passed a long night in the desert —we shall see the long-awaited joy.
> Rejoice, O Italy, an object of pity even to the infidels. Now will you be the envy of the whole world because your bridegroom, the comfort of the world and the glory of its people, the most merciful Henry, Divus, Augustus, Caesar, hastens to his wedding. Dry your eyes; remove your signs of mourning, you who are so fair. He is at hand to free you from captivity by the ungodly; he will strike the unjust man and destroy him with his sword and give over his vineyard to other husbandmen who will reap the fruits of justice in the time of harvest.

Clement V, the French pope, away in Avignon, did not know quite how to conduct himself in the face of this imperial claimant. On the one hand, he was not ill disposed to the appearance of an emperor who might subdue the Roman barons, restore some semblance of order in Italy, and act as a counterbalance to the French king. On the other hand, he could not afford to offend Philip of France by seeming to encourage a rival, or by allowing the Ghibelline party to gain strength in Italy. Finally, he decided to play a double game, encouraging Henry in the north while, in the south, he strengthened the Angevin King of Naples, who was the leader of the Guelfs. It was therefore with Clement's approbation that Henry entered Italy in his imperial quest.

Henry VII, called Henry of Luxemburg, was a brave man, honest, just, devout, and courageous. He was also hopelessly and dangerously idealistic, for it was his sole ambition to be the leader of all the people and to bridge the gulf between the Ghibellines and the Guelfs of Italy. He therefore presented himself in the peninsula as the supporter of the legal rights of the people, of public order, and, to a certain extent, of liberty. And he found Italy sorely in need of all three. The result of the constant feuding between Guelfs and Ghibellines, between towns and cities, had been to exhaust the citizens, to empty their treasuries, and to establish petty tyrants throughout the north of Italy. Every city and town had its lord, usually invested with dictatorial powers, who had attained his position simply because he had had sufficient strength to enforce the rule of law at a time when the alternative seemed to be anarchy. Sometimes the lord was a local noble, sometimes he was a foreign adventurer invited, with his soldiers, to maintain order in the city. The threat of anarchy was so great, and the desire of the people for respite so all-consuming, that the citizens demanded of their despots only one thing: the strength to punish, rapidly and severely, anyone who disturbed the peace.

These lords of Lombardy and Piedmont presented themselves to King Henry, offering their help and expressing their good wishes. Henry, however, was quite firm and sincere in his good intentions. Though he received the despots with every courtesy, he quickly pointed out that his sole interest in Italy was the establishment of order—and that by order he meant the order of things as settled by the Peace of Constance: an imperial governor in every city of the Empire. Then the lords began to bicker. Some of them decided to submit, some of them vowed to resist. Henry was already learning what a difficult place Italy could be; and it did not take him long to learn the rest of the lesson.

When he reached Milan, the city, that ancient citadel of revolutionary sentiment, lowered her flags in homage to the new Caesar, and the Guelf archbishop willingly placed the iron crown of the Lombards upon his head. Then Henry made his first mistake: he asked the Lombards for a great deal of money. He was poor, he said, and it seemed only right that the Italians should contribute to the support of their emperor-elect. Moreover, he asked Milan for fifty noblemen from each of the two parties—ostensibly to act as a guard of honor, but actually to serve as hostages for payment of the money. The Ghibellines assented readily enough, but the Guelfs, suspecting treachery, refused. Then the Guelf leaders, fearing for their lives, fled, and their houses were looted and burned by the Ghibellines. And that was the end of the peace. Henry had been forced into the usual role of German tyrant and chief of the Ghibelline party. The Guelfic cities rose in revolt. Cremona was sacked and her walls razed. Brescia was besieged and reduced. But Florence, the leader of the Guelfic cities and the center of resistance, was left untouched while Henry was engaged with these comparatively unimportant places. The Ghibelline party of that city was in a frenzy of impatience for Henry to "liberate" Florence. Dante wrote to Henry:

For a long time have we sat and wept by the rivers of confusion, and incessantly have we prayed for the protection of a just king. . . . When you, the successor of Caesar Augustus, crossed the Apennines carrying the insignia of Rome, then, like the sudden dawn, there rose new hope for the happiness of Italy. But now, men say that you delay, or even believe that you are turning back. Rise up, then, and delay no more. Take confidence from the countenance of the Lord God of Hosts, in the presence of whom you act, and vanquish this Goliath [Florence] . . . whose death shall strike fear into the camp of the Philistines, so that they will flee and Israel shall be set free. And as now we, exiles in Babylon, mourn when we remember holy Jerusalem, so then shall we, citizens in our own city, breathe in peace and turn the plague of confusion into joy.

Henry, moved as much by his imperial designs as by Dante's plea, did turn southward for the march to Rome. When he reached Florence, however, he found that enemy of the Empire secure behind barred gates and fortified walls. The Florentines, moreover, strengthened the anti-imperial sentiment by sending gold to other Guelf cities and by resurrecting, in some haste, the league of Tuscan and Umbrian cities. Henry, perhaps not yet convinced that the spirit of the age was against the universal empire, and that it was useless to try to revive the glories of the past, but doubtless discouraged by the increased hostility of the Italians, abandoned the attempt to subdue the Florentines and now marched toward Rome.

The plight of the City in the fourteenth century was such as to rouse pity, and even despair, in the hearts of men much less addicted than Henry to the memory of imperial splendors. While the popes dallied in Avignon, their former capital lay forlorn and almost deserted. While Florence was becoming the most prominent city in Italy, Rome was decaying into a small provincial town with interesting ruins and a famous name. The disorder which had prevailed in Rome and the surrounding countryside after the departure of the popes had led the citizens, in self-defense, to set up a popular government composed of a Council of Thirteen headed by a "Captain of the People" and a Senator. Pope Clement, however, soon managed to have himself declared Senator for life, and, from Avignon, he ruled Rome through a deputy. To the Romans, this seemed a more or less natural arrangement, for no one imagined that the popes were in Avignon for more than a brief sojourn. They were stupefied, consequently, by the announcement in 1308 that the papal Curia was being transferred, lock, stock, and barrel, to Avignon. Then, when the papal basilica of St. John Lateran was almost entirely destroyed by fire a few years later, and no effort was made to rebuild that historic edifice, the citizens of Rome finally began to suspect that the Roman popes were popes of Rome no longer. They were deeply moved by what they inevitably viewed as a judgment of heaven for their wickedness. Processions begging divine forgiveness crisscrossed the City; private wars were forgotten, and great sums of money were collected for the restoration of the Lateran. For a brief space, peace reigned in the City which had known little of peace for centuries. It was, however, an unnatural, and therefore a temporary, state of affairs. Good resolutions were soon forgotten in the heat of Roman passions; the great houses of Colonna and Orsini quickly resumed their private wars, and Rome, in the absence of the papacy and the College of Cardinals, was soon entirely given over to the malevolent despotism of its native aristocracy. The bishop who was the absent pope's deputy was moneyless, weaponless, and helpless. Pope Clement, despairing of the condition of the City, gave his support to the Council of Thirteen against the nobles—with the result that he was led, in effect, to recognize the Roman democracy, and to allow the people to choose their own representatives. Thus, the absence of the popes enabled the people to enjoy, to a certain, and limited, extent the blessings of a commodity that was even more rare in the City than peace: liberty. It was a quality that they were resolved not to abandon lightly, or to exchange for the yoke of an emperor—even one apparently so benign as Henry VII.

The news that Henry was on his way to Rome therefore excited extreme emotions among the citizens. Some loudly acclaimed the dawn of a new imperial day. But most, just as loudly, called for the assistance of Robert, King of Naples, to prevent the coronation. That monarch, who wanted no rival in Italy, was quick to oblige. When Henry entered Rome in May 1312, in full battle array and bringing with him a lion for the Capitol, he found half the City in the hands of the Ghibellines and the other half occupied by the Neapolitan army. He had little choice but to fight, and he managed to take the Capitol by a violent assault. But he failed to capture St. Peter's, or even to penetrate the barricades that had been set up on all approaches to the Basilica, and he reluctantly had to abandon the idea of being crowned where his predecessors had been raised to the imperial dignity. The commission of cardinals, who had been deputed by the pope to perform the coronation, then refused to carry out that function in any building other than St. Peter's. Their written instructions, they said, specified that Basilica and no other, and they had no authority to countermand the pope's wishes. Henry then appealed to the citizens of the section of the City which he controlled, and they voted in favor of a coronation in the Basilica of St. John Lateran. The cardinals, under threat of death, somehow discovered the necessary authorization, and Henry was crowned there, amid the ruins of the recent fire.

Henry soon discovered, however, that, while Holy Roman Emperor he might be, he was by no means master of the Romans. The Guelfs, supported by King Robert's Neapolitan troops, remained in possession of much of the City. The new emperor, too weak to turn them out, remained for a time in the Ghibelline section of the City, in the midst of material, political, and moral ruin. Finally, he could bear no more, and he quit Rome in disgust, muttering against the ingratitude of a people who could first welcome him and then treat him badly. He now marched against Florence, resolved to punish the city as the ringleader of civil disobedience in Italy; but the city's walls were too strong, and her money too abundant, for the imperial armies, and the impotent emperor could do little more than despoil the countryside. He fell back into Ghibelline Pisa, and set to work patiently to gather men and money for a larger army. The Pisans responded eagerly, and before long Henry was marching toward Naples, to punish King Robert for his part in the Roman fiasco. Death, however, cut short the emperor's vengeance, and he succumbed at Siena either to the fevers of the Tuscan summer or to the fanaticism of a Dominican monk.* He is perhaps best remembered as the quixotic figure who came, in Dante's phrase, "to set Italy straight before he was ready." But he was but a dim shadow in the drama of Italian history; yet, his brief and ineffectual adventure south of the Alps served to recall to the Germans the hopelessness of any attempt to revive the old connection between Italy and the Empire. The brave words of Dante's *De Monarchia* had proved to be, not the glorious prophecy of Empire that he had intended, but rather its epitaph.

7. Italy at the Close of the Middle Ages

With the disappearance of the two great actors, whose enduring quarrels had been the main thread of Italian history, the principal roles in the drama devolved upon elements which had, up to then, been lesser *dramatis personae*. These, the city-states and principalities of the peninsula, now stepped to the fore and carried on the plot of history.

In the south, as had already been noted, the former Kingdom of the Two Sicilies was torn in two. Charles of Anjou, conqueror of the Hohen-

---

* Henry's followers believed strongly, and their belief has been perpetuated in the form of a Roman legend, that the emperor was given poison in the sacramental wine while attending Mass. There is, however, no real historical evidence to this effect.

Italy in the Middle Ages

staufens and founder of the Angevin dynasty, shrewd and clever as he was, had outsmarted and overreached himself. In his palace at Naples, he was dreaming great dreams, and he had even turned covetous eyes on a glittering prize, the throne of the Byzantine Empire, when that rebellion known as the Sicilian Vespers had erupted in the southern island of his kingdom. The Sicilian nobles had then offered the crown of Sicily, as we have seen, to Dom Pedro, King of Aragon. Pedro accepted, and he and his son, Frederick, made good their claim to that kingdom against all attempts of the Angevins and of the feudal suzerain of Sicily, the pope, to oust them. Their tenacity kept Sicily separated from her sister kingdom, Naples, for over a century and a half (1282–1443).

In central Italy, as usual, all was in disorder. The popes, the legitimate sovereigns, had settled in luxurious exile in Avignon, and were whiling away their time in the pursuit of money, honors, and, frequently, sensuality. Although they attempted to govern their Italian possessions by deputies and legates, these representatives were the constant prey of the local nobility, just as the popes themselves had so often been in the time of the Roman residency, and the papal authority, though it continued to be recognized in principle from the Tyrrhean Sea to the Adriatic, was unenforceable. A few of the towns submitted to their papal vicars, but most of them took on the aspect of autonomous communes governed by a powerful baron or by a popular, but less powerful, democratic system. Rome herself, in the absence of her bishops, dwindled to a city of ruins, for the control of which petty nobles fought in the crumbling streets. Papal indifference had transformed the city into an unimportant town, where nothing any longer occurred of sufficient consequence to affect the course of Italian history.

It was to the north that the center of gravity had shifted, to Florence and the independent city-republics, where, at this moment, the future of Italy was being forged. Principal among these small states was Florence, the head of the Guelfic leagues; the Ghibelline strongholds of Pisa and Siena; the Lombard commune of Milan, Venice, and Genoa; the one a maritime oligarchy and the other a maritime aristocracy; and the feudal county of Savoy.

We have seen how these cities had shaken off both the tyranny of their own nobles and the authority of the emperors, and had begun their careers as independent republics. By the time of Hildebrand and Henry IV—that is, by the late eleventh century—these communities, most of them of ancient Roman foundation, had begun to emerge as individuals. They did, however, share certain common features. All of them were independent republics. All of them were built in conformity to a general pattern, according to which the city clustered around two main points: the *Duomo,* or cathedral, which was flanked by a belfry and a baptistery, and the *piazza,* or public square, on which fronted the *Palazzo Publico* (city hall) where the governing magistrates had their offices. On streets radiating from the piazza stood private houses and the palaces of the nobles and the merchant princes. And here and there the battlements of private fortresses towered above the neighboring buildings; for a characteristic of all these communes was that they were constantly prepared for violence. In the streets, homes, palaces, towers, merchant's stalls, and churches, the citizens all stood ready for warfare. It required only the ringing of the church bells to signal the beginning of battle.

The citizens of the city-republics were divided into three categories. The highest comprised the ancient nobility of the city, the upper clergy, and the wealthiest of the merchants and bankers. The middle class was of classic composition: the small merchants, the tradesmen, the master artisans, and the lower clergy. Below these two classes came the great majority of the population, the miscellaneous many: the laborers, the peasantry, the unemployed, and the unemployable. In some cities, the nobles, allying themselves to the proletariat by means of such expedients as the public dole, held political power. In the more fiercely democratic ones, however, such as Florence, the tradesmen and merchants controlled the government, thanks, in large measure, to the efficiency with which they were organized, for political as well as commercial action, into guilds. There were seven "greater guilds" of tradesmen, craftsmen, and "professionals": judges and notaries, wool·merchants, refiners and dyers of foreign wool, silk dealers, money-changers, physicians and apothecaries, and furriers. Tradesmen and artisans whose occupations did not qualify them for admission to these major guilds belonged to one of the fourteen "lesser guilds"—the butchers, shoemakers, carpenters, masons, and so on. Though the guilds might, on occasion, differ violently among themselves, they were able quickly to form a strong common front against any outside enemy. They were therefore the single most potent economic and political force in Florence, and their power was increased by a law which required every freeman who was not a noble to belong to one of the guilds. (Dante, for example, was enrolled in that of physicians and apothecaries.) Membership, moreover, like occupations, usually descended from father to son.

In the government of the cities, the executive, legislative, and judicial powers were generally distinguished in theory, though combined in practice. The executive power was vested sometimes in one man, as in Milan, or in several, as in Venice, who were assisted and advised by a council, or "cabinet." This council, in addition to its advisory function, occupied itself with such matters of public concern as weights and measures, the maintenance of public roadways, the imposition of fines, and so forth. Most often, there was a larger council as well, for election or appointment to which were eligible only those citizens who were legally enfranchised. The latter were never more than a small percentage of the population, for enfranchisement required that one's family have been resident in the city for several generations and, more important, that the candidate for enfranchisement be a man of substantial property. The operative principle behind this rather plutocratic form of democracy was that only men of long and undivided loyalty, and only those of considerable wealth, would be sufficiently concerned with the common weal to exercise mature and careful judgment in all instances. It had been noted, moreover, that wealthy men were less susceptible to bribery than poor men, or at least that their prices were so high that few could afford to offer them a sufficiently tempting bribe. For those citizens who did not enjoy the franchise, there was a formal assembly of all citizens which met regularly in the *piazza publica* and shouted approval or disapproval to such proposals and questions as were put to it by the government.

In the early days of the city-states, the executive power was often shared jointly by two or more men, who, in Roman fashion, were called consuls. Theirs was not an easy job. If they were impartial in the exercise of their office, they displeased their own party; if they were partial, they were subject to retaliation. Such difficulties led to the evolution of a new office, that of *podestà*—a title which, it will be recalled, was first introduced by Barbarossa. This official was elected by the free citizens of the cities in order to supplant the consuls in their more important functions. The *podestà* was almost always a nobleman, and he was almost always chosen from another city in the hope of lessening the danger of partisanship. The citizens, however, if of Guelphic persuasion, usually chose a Guelph; and, if Ghibellines, a Ghibelline. When the *podestà's* term of office (usually six months or a year) began, he came to the city, bringing with him his staff—two knights, several judges, councilors, notaries, and various attendants both official and personal—so that he would not be subjected to the pressures of local persuasion. Upon his entry, he took his oath of office in the *piazza:* to observe the laws of the city, to do justice to all men, and to wrong no man. His duties, and even his movements, were carefully defined. Sometimes he was not allowed even to enter any house other than that assigned to him, so as to lessen the danger of his official judgments being influenced by relations with private citizens. During the course of his term of office, the *podestà* could expect to be free from harassment, even by those citizens whom he might have wronged. After its expiration, however, he was required by law to remain in the city for a certain length of time, so that anyone who had a legitimate complaint could obtain redress; and it happened occasionally that a *podestà* who did not execute his oath of office faithfully never lived to leave the city at all. Such, more or less, was the ordinary form of communal government. Naturally, constitutions varied from city to city and from time to time, according to the dictates of class feeling, partisan enmity, and economic expediency.

Economics was a vital consideration in every aspect of life in the city-states, for prosperity and power were based on commerce and waxed and waned according to the degree to which trade flourished or languished. The tradesmen therefore received every civic encouragement to make their businesses prosper; and prosper they did, even in the face of difficulties which would have conquered less determined men. The wool guild of Florence was an excellent example of this spirit of enterprise. Tuscany yielded a poor quality of wool; so much so that it was impossible to weave any but the coarsest cloth from it. The Florentine wool merchants therefore imported a superior quality of wool from Tunis, Barbary, Spain, Flanders, and England, and wove it into cloth so expertly and so economically that foreigners—including the English, Spaniards, and Flemish—could not compete with them in respect either to price or to quality. The Florentines then exported this cloth to the principal markets of Europe—often to the very countries from which they had bought the raw wool in the first place.

Trade with trans-Alpine Europe, however, was of less importance to the cities of northern Italy than trade with the East. Merchandise could be carried over the seas more easily, and less expensively, than over the Alps; and, in many respects, the products of the East, received in exchange for the goods of Italy, were of better quality and more varied than those from northern Europe. The cities therefore loaded the galleys of the great maritime communes, such as Venice, Genoa, and Pisa, with silk and wool, oil, wine, pitch, tar, and common metals, and brought back from Alexandria, Constantinople, and the ports of Asia Minor and Syria such things as pearls, gold, spices, sugar, oriental silks, wool and cotton, goatskins, and dyes; and, sometimes, oriental slaves.

Such widespread and ever-growing mercantile enterprise eventually and inevitably outstripped the limited capacity of barter and the meager supply of cash, and gave rise to a new industry: a system of banking, with its attendant methods of credit and bills of exchange. The Florentines, nimble-witted as they were, excelled at this business, and the great banking houses of Florence, such as those of the Bardi and the Peruzzi families, by the end of the Middle Ages had branches or correspondents in all the chief cities of Europe and the Near East.

That commerce was able to flourish on such a scale, given the conditions of the time in Italy, is a tribute to the ingenuity and enterprise, and perhaps to the rapacity, of the citizens of the city-states. Florence, for example, was greatly hampered by the conditions in the surrounding countryside. Outside her walls, for a radius of fifteen or twenty miles, there were numerous castles, or rather lairs, of "robber barons," whose wealth was founded and multiplied almost entirely on the proceeds of highway robbery. Moreover, rival cities refused to allow Florentine wares to pass through their territories without payment of outrageous taxes and duties. Occasionally, Florence found it necessary to wage wars in order to force one city or another to moderate its demands. War was also sometimes necessary to enforce the rights of Florentine merchants in other cities. On all highways, at all bridges and fords, at every gate, there were tolls to be paid. From city to city a merchant had to exchange his own money for local currency, for each city had its own system of weights and measures (though eventually the *florin* of Florence came to be accepted everywhere). In addition, each city imposed customs on all foreign—that is, extra-urban—merchandise entering its walls; in the early days of commerce, it was so much per cartload; later, it was a more sophisticated percentage of the gross values of the wares. Sometimes a merchant, on entering a city other than his own, was obliged to wear a distinguishing badge; at Bologna, for example, non-Bolognese merchants had a bit of red wax affixed to the thumbnail of one hand, which they were forbidden to remove until they had left the city.

These were the ordinary obstacles to trade in time of peace. But peace itself was, at best, uncertain. Apart from the wars with the emperor, the cities fought their feudal nobility, or each other, with monotonous regularity. Venice habitually made war on Ravenna, Pisa on Lucca, Vicenza on Treviso, Fano on Pesaro, Verona on Padua, Modena on Bologna, and the greater cities, such as Milan and Florence, on all their neighbors, either discreetly or conjunctively. When a city had no important war abroad, the citizens kept in practice by fighting one another. Burghers and nobles periodically barricaded the streets, manned the towers, rang the bells, and hacked away at one another with uncontrolled fury. The burghers usually won. They then banished their adversaries by the hundreds and enacted laws to deprive those who remained of any real power. At Lucca, for instance, the nobles lost so consistently that they were at last formally excluded from any share in the government. At Pisa, if there were any major disturbance in the streets, the nobles were required by law to go immediately to their homes and remain there until order had been restored. In many cities, a register was kept to record the names of those nobles who were suspected of nurturing "anti-democratic" sentiments.

These two factions, the burghers and the nobles, generally identified themselves as Guelphs and Ghibellines, respectively. At first, the Guelphs were indeed the citizens of the communes and the partisans of the papacy, and the Ghibellines were the noble defenders of the Empire and of the feudal system. With the passage of time, however, these terms lost their meanings, and, by the end of the Middle Ages, they served merely to distinguish one political party from another, the principles of both of which shifted according to the mood of the age. Even when these two factions were at peace with one another, they were careful to distinguish themselves by different badges and customs. The merlons of the Guelph battlements, for example, were always square, while those of the Ghibellines were always swallow-tailed. Good men of both parties wore caps of special design, trimmed their hair in a certain way, and even sliced their bread and folded their napkins in a prescribed manner. It was enough that a leading Ghibelline should bow, or swear, or wear a certain color, for the Guelphic faction immediately to adopt the contrary fashion.

The rapid growth of population in the late Middle Ages, the accumulation of wealth on a large scale, and particularly the flourishing state of commerce, all demonstrate the error of emphasizing unduly the propensity of the Italian cities for fighting and war. In these petty conflicts and brawls, the numbers engaged were comparatively few, and, in the peculiar fashion of the times, little blood was shed. Moreover, most of the fighting of the time was the consequence of economic problems. It was the late medieval equivalent, and perhaps a comparatively healthy one, of the strikes, lockouts, boycotts, price wars, cut-throat competition, and other—often equally bloody—phenomena of the industry of a later age.

The maritime cities of Italy were in a position quite different from that of the inland cities, and they had a different history. So far as trade was concerned, they enjoyed a great advantage over their less fortunately situated neighbors. No feudal baron could bar the sea, and pirates, while always a danger, were no serious obstacle to maritime commerce. As trade prospered, however, commercial rivalry between the ship-owning cities grew more acrimonious. Pisan seamen grew to loathe all Genoese, and no Genoese could bear the sight of a Pisan standard without being roused to a pitch of fury. Since both cities did a thriving business in the Levant, and since they were geographically so near to one another, it was inevitable that they should become deadly rivals and enemies. And, in fact, they fought constantly and bitterly for years. The final confrontation came in 1284, a few miles from the mouth of the Arno. The Genoese, who greatly outnumbered the Pisans, won a great victory, destroying many Pisan galleys and taking, according to a perhaps exaggerated contemporary report, ten thousand prisoners. Pisa never recovered from this blow, and Florence and Lucca took immediate advantage of the Ghibelline city's predicament to unite with Genoa in forcing the latter to accept a Guelph government. From this time on, clever, greedy Florence, like some great hawk, kept her eyes fixed on Pisa, impatient for the time when she would be able to seize and gobble her prey.

The queen of the seas at this time, however, was not Genoa, despite her Pisan victory, but Venice. That city enjoyed a portion of fierce individuality even more generous than that of her sister city-republics. So much so, in fact, that she hardly seemed to belong to Italy at all. She had held herself aloof from the two dominant passions of medieval Italy, the Empire and the papacy, and no cries of "Pope!" or "Emperor!" had ever rippled the Grand Canal or roused to flight the pigeons of the Piazza San Marco. No misguided feudal loyalties circumscribed her mercantile passions. No excess of piety ever tempered the philosophy of reasonable profit to which she adhered. And there is no evidence that any Venetian ever lost a moment's sleep, or that any Venetian ship ever altered its course by a hair's breadth, because of papal excommunications and interdicts. For the interests of Venice, and her sphere in influence as well, lay not in Italy but in the Near East, in Constantinople. Even after the influence of the Greek emperors had long ceased in Italy, the loyalties of Venice were engaged on the Bosphorus, and the city was, in temper and aspect, more a Constantinople of the West than an Italian city. She was as untroubled by the political passions as she was by the religious enthusiasms of the West, and, even during the crusades, she concerned herself solely with the increment of her commerce, with the securing of foreign markets, and with the enrichment of herself. Such were the only objects which shaped her policies and directed her actions.

Originally, the Venetians, assembled in public meeting, had elected their Doge, or duke, and had exercised their right to vote on important matters of public interest. Little by little, however, the wealthiest families of the city had acquired control of the government and turned Venice into an oligarchy. The first major step in that direction had come in the time of Barbarossa, when the Lombard cities were fighting to free themselves from imperial domination. At that time, a Great Council was elected, comprising four hundred and eighty members, to which were given powers of legislation, of appointment to civil and military posts, of election of the Doge, and of appointment to vacancies in the Great Council itself. This concentration of powers in the hands of a self-perpetuating governmental organ resulted, foreseeably, in the suspension of the political privileges of the individual citizens and the concomitant supremacy of the oligarchy. This assembly of merchant princes, in whom patriotism, love of money, pride of place, and devout Christianity seemed to exist in remarkable harmony, was an egregiously competent body. The greatness of Venice was their overriding ambition, and they pursued it relentlessly. Beginning early in life, these patricians were trained for their future duties by service in the navy and the merchant marine, or by some employment in the government of the various cities, islands, and territories included in the Venetian empire. They were perfectly aware that the Republic existed and flourished solely by virtue of commerce, and they made every effort, by war, diplomacy, private enterprise, and deceit, to extend that commerce. After the conquest and division of the Byzantine Empire by the Crusaders in 1204, the Venetians became more eager than ever for a monopoly of trade with the Levant, and they entered into a deadly rivalry with the Genoese, who were every bit as aggressive, eager, and rapacious as their Venetian competitors. The subsequent wars between the two cities, destructive and expensive as they were in property and money, were of no little use to the Grand Council, for they brought home to the ordinary citizens of Venice the value of a compact and cohesive governing unit. And the merchant princes took advantage of that appreciation to abrogate whatever still remained of the civil rights of their subjects.

Throughout the thirteenth century, the Great Council, although in practice it was composed entirely of patricians and elected its own members, had theoretically been open to all classes and to all citizens. Any Venetian, so the theory went, was eligible for election. At the close of that century, however, the patricians enacted a series of measures which virtually divided Venetians into two classes: those whose ancestors had belonged to the Great Council, and those whose ancestors had not. They decreed that only the members of the first class would henceforth be eligible for election—a bit of legislation known, appropriately enough, as "The Closing of the Great Council." Naturally, all those who were eligible wanted to become councilors immediately, and the Council grew until it finally numbered some fifteen hundred members. Thus fortified, the

Council then gathered to itself some of the powers of the Doge by dividing the various functions of government among the main sections, or committees, of the Council—the Senate, the Senate of Forty, the Doge's cabinet, and the Council of Ten—until it arrived at that form of government which the republic was to retain for many centuries to follow.

At the other end of the spectrum, far removed from economically and otherwise opulent Florence and serenely magnificent Venice, was the wretched County of Savoy, perched on the Alps and maintaining a precarious control over both slopes, with no resources whatever except the muscles of its mountaineers and its possession of the Alpine passes. The Counts of Savoy were taken from the House of Savoy which, like many of Europe's dynasties, traced its origins into the mists of the Dark Ages. What is certain is that, about the year 1000, a certain Humbert of the White Hand, emerging from obscurity, obtained the city of Turin and a part of Piedmont as the marriage portion of his son, and thereby secured a foothold for his family in Italy. In the course of another century or so, the House of Savoy, in a succession of ubiquitous Humberts and Amedeos, all of whom were brave shrews and successful men, extended their domains by the means usual in that age: war, marriage, theft, and extortion. They made the most of their position, so to speak, as the doormen of Italy, and they exacted great privileges from needy emperors as the price of moving safely through the Alpine passes. They fought rival houses, waged countless petty wars, and, rightly or wrongly, acquired various territories which are now parts of Italy, Switzerland, and France. The succession of the backwoods Counts of Savoy reads like any other medieval genealogy, and their exploits, raids, and sieges, viewed from the perspective of centuries, suffer from a monotonous similarity. But survival proved the worth of the stock, and when, after long centuries, the people of Italy were to have need of kings, it was to be found that the only royal house that had retained power and general respect was that of Savoy. It would have greatly surprised glorious Florence and splendid Venice to learn that the rulers of poor, rustic Savoy would someday consolidate their holdings into a compact kingdom, Piedmont, and, from there, step to even higher honors.

8. The Transition from the Middle Ages to the Renaissance

Every historical era is, of course, an age of transition, since the human condition is ever changing, either for the better or for the worse. The late thirteenth and the fourteenth centuries, however, are, if one must speak of historical "ages," the age of transition *par excellence,* in that they were essentially a bridge between the Middle Ages and the modern world. As such, they shed light both on the preceding period and on the time following, since they incorporate elements of both.

In religion, this period was basically medieval. It was a time of passionate, and even excessive, faith, in which religious belief tended to manifest itself violently. In Perugia, for instance, there suddenly flared up, and thence spread throughout northern Italy, a mania for public penance. Thousands upon thousands of penitents, both adults and children, men and women, rich and poor, marched from one city to the next, half-naked in the snow, scourging themselves, lamenting their sins and those of the world, and praying frenetically. Thieves and nobles were both possessed by this frenzy, and both made restitution to their victims. Professional assassins threw themselves on their knees before the families of the slain and begged them to take vengeance. Ancient enemies embraced, exiles were recalled to their homes and their property restored, prisoners were freed with the blessings of their jailers, moneylenders forgave their debtors, husbands ceased to deceive their wives, and even some of the clergy put away their concubines and resolved to distribute their wealth to the poor. The movement spread beyond the Alps and, for a time, it seemed that this new faith, based upon self-mortification and self-inflicted pain, would replace Christianity as the religion of the people. Then, as suddenly as it had appeared, the movement vanished, without warning and without leaving evidence of its existence save in the chronicles of the time. Thieves began to steal again, and assassins to take on new assignments. Enemies flew at each other's throats, ex-prisoners were clapped back into their jails, and the clergy began to fornicate and pile up wealth anew. Perhaps the reaction of the various municipal governments of Italy had served to diminish the fervor of the Flagellants,* as the adherents of this movement were called, for the rulers took alarm at this appearance of a belief which not only had all the symptoms of a public mania, but also threatened the good order of the state. The rulers of Milan, for instance, threatened to hang any Flagellant who came near the city, and to make their point they caused six hundred gallows to be erected on the borders of their domain, and thereafter Milan was notably free of Flagellants. Such frenzied religious manifestations—and there were many such, not only in Italy but throughout Europe—were not without cause or effect. They served notice, upon those wise enough to understand, of a profound and widespread disaffection with the medieval Church.

* The name was derived from their practice of flagellating themselves publicly.

Other expressions of religious unrest were more rational, though equally ephemeral. In Italy, these often took the form of an all-consuming desire for peace after a thousand years of war and violence. Priests and laymen alike called upon warring cities to be friends. "O, when will dawn the day," one of them cried, "that will see Pavia say to Milan, 'Thy people are my people,' and Cremona to Crema, 'Thy city is my city.'" Even turbulent Genoa responded to the general sentiment. Early one morning, the citizens were alarmed to hear the ringing of the church bells—the traditional call to battle—and, dressing hurriedly, they seized their weapons and hurried to the public *piazza*. There, they witnessed their venerable archbishop, in full pontificals, exacting from the leaders of the city an oath, sworn on the bones of St. John the Baptist, to lay aside their quarrels. Pope Gregory X, no lover of the Empire or of its emperors, pleaded with Guelphic Florence to recall its Ghibelline citizens from exile and to live with them in peace. "A Ghibelline," he preached, "is a Christian, a citizen, and a neighbor. Are all these things of less importance than that one word, 'Ghibelline'? And will that single word—which is, in fact, an empty word, for no man knows what it signifies—have more power in exciting hatred than those three words in awakening love and charity? You say that you pursue this strife for the sake of the popes of Rome. If that be so, then I, the Pope of Rome, now embrace these prodigal citizens of yours, no matter what their offenses. I forget all the wrongs of the past, and I declare them to be my sons." Gregory's eloquence was not without effect. In obedience to his wishes, some one hundred and fifty Guelphs, and an equal number of Ghibellines, met on the banks of the Arno and embraced as brothers. But the most renowned of these peacemakers was not a pope or even an archbishop, but a simple friar of the Order of St. Dominic, a native of Vicenza. On one occasion, a great multitude—four hundred thousand people, a contemporary says, but the actual figure was probably less than one quarter of that—assembled to hear the friar preach on the text, "My peace I give unto you." From all the warring cities, people came, bishops and barons, merchants and artisans, serfs and freemen, women and children. During the sermon, the crowd wept and moaned for its sins, pleaded tearfully for forgiveness, and embraced one another as a sign of Christian love. When, in conclusion, the preacher raised his crucifix and cried, "Blessed be the man who shall keep this peace; but cursed forever shall be the one who breaks it," the auditors' great "Amen" thundered out, signaling, so it was believed, the end of war forever. But, within a few days, appetites sharpened by brief abstinence erupted again, and again Italy resounded to the clash of halberd and sword.

Of more lasting effect were the intellectual advances of the age. In the preceding century, universities had sprung up in many of the cities of northern Italy. The term "university" (*universitas*), however, did not signify a formal institution of learning, but rather a guild of students. This guild hired its own professors, and, to a large extent, determined its own curricula, and was virtually self-governing. It owned neither land nor buildings, but hired rooms in the town where classes could be held. Thus, it could easily shift from one city to another in case of trouble in one place, and it sometimes did so in the classic struggle between "town and gown." The students of these universities were often, as at the great University of Bologna, divided into two bodies, one Italian, and the other trans-Alpine, and these two bodies were subdivided according to city or state of origin. Each group elected representatives, and the representatives elected the rector, or "president," of the university. They were also charged with the negotiation of a formal treaty with the officials of the town or city in which the university was located; and they were frequently able to extract extremely favorable terms, such as immunity from municipal control, for the presence of a university was of great economic advantage to a town. Though the curricula of the great universities were generally similar, some schools excelled in and became famous for a specialty. The university of Bologna became Europe's foremost school of law, and that of Salerno was famous for its faculty of medicine. It was law, however, Roman law specifically, that attracted the great multitude of students, for the growing needs of commerce and the increasing complexity of social and political life demanded men learned in that discipline. Nonetheless, other branches of knowledge received due attention: theology, canon law, astrology, and the *quadrivium* of the ancients (music, arithmetic, geometry, and astronomy).

Some of the universities, though they represented the distinctly secular side of life, became famous as centers of theological thought. The University of Paris, for example, was the most eminent school of theology in the world, and it was there that Italy's most famous thinker, Thomas Aquinas, first as a student and then as a teacher, devised and began to enunciate that great philosophico-theological system known (inaccurately) as Scholasticism. His best known and most influential work, the *Summa Theologiae*, was a justification of Roman Catholicism by an appeal to human reason rather than to divine authority, and by appeals to medieval scientific principles. It was a revolutionary departure from the methodology of the time. The whole of Aquinas' work stands as a synthesis, a systematic and complete exposition of God, man, and nature as conceived by medieval man.*

* Until the middle of the twentieth century, the Scholasticism of St. Thomas, or Thomism as it came to be called, was the official theology and philosophy of the Catholic Church.

But Thomas, like any daring thinker, was ahead of his time, and his works were at first condemned and burned as heretical by the Archbishop of Paris. Within a short time after his death, however, less obtuse heads prevailed, and Aquinas was canonized by a grateful Church. As for the miracles required for elevation to the altar, his theological treatises were accepted as wonder enough.

Such emotional and intellectual traits were natural to an age of change and transition. It is significant that, at the same time, social life was undergoing a change from comparative simplicity to relative luxury in taste and in standards of living. The accumulation of wealth through trade had had its effect on every phase of Italian life. By the beginning of the fourteenth century, men of a certain turn of mind had already begun to long for a more simple life, and to look back on the uncomplicated requirements of their grandfathers as the sign of an enviable innocence. Dante, through the mouth of his ancestor, Cacciaguida, bewails the passing of that time of virtue when "I saw Bellincion Berti go girt with leather and bone, and his lady come from the mirror with unpainted face; and I saw dei Nerli and del Vecchio content to be in plain buff, and their ladies happy at their spindle and flax. . . . One kept watch, tending the cradle and, to sooth her child, would use the language that first delights fathers and mothers. Another, drawing the strands from the distaff, would relate to her family tales of the Trojans, of Fiesole, and of Rome." Another contemporary recalls the simple days of Frederick II with unconcealed approbation:

> In those times, the manners of the Italians were plain. A man and his wife did not need two plates, but one. There were no knives with wooden handles, and no house with more than two drinking cups. A servant held a torch during the evening meal, because candles of wax and tallow were unknown. The clothes of the men were of leather, and unlined, and they wore scarcely any gold or silver. The common people ate flesh only thrice a week . . . and many did not drink wine during the summer months. A small supply of corn seemed great wealth at that time. The dowries of women were small, and their dress, even after marriage, was plain. Men prided themselves only on being well armed and mounted, and the nobility aspired only to have lofty towers. . . . But in our days such frugality has given way to sumptuous luxury. In dress, that which is most exquisite is the most sought after: gold, silver, precious stones, silks, and fine furs. The wines of foreign lands and rich meats are required. Hence, in our days there flourish usury, theft, fraud, and tyranny.

Along with the newly acquired taste for luxury and intellectual activity, wealth conferred upon Italy a burst of energy in the arts, and an eager interest in life and the things of this world which manifested itself in a love of gaiety and amusement. Villani, the fourteenth-century historian of Florence, describes one instance of this new fondness of things terrestrial:

> In the year of Our Lord 1283, the city of Florence was prosperous, at peace, and in a state of much tranquillity, chiefly because of the Guelphs, who were in power. It was a condition very advantageous to the merchants and the artisans. In June, on the Feast of St. John, in the section across the Arno, where the Rossi family and their neighbors were the most important people, the nobles and the rich organized themselves into a company, adopted a white costume, and elected a chief called the Lord of Love. The purpose of this company was to hold feasts, games and dances for the ladies and gentlemen of the city and for other persons of birth. They paraded through the town with trumpets and other instruments, and had great dinners and suppers and all sorts of celebrations. These festivities lasted almost two months, and they were reputed to be the finest and most distinguished that Florence, and all of Tuscany, had ever seen. Gentlemen and troubadours came from all over, and all were welcomed and entertained lavishly. For it should be remembered that the city and the citizens were better off than they had ever been before. . . . There were then in Florence three hundred knights, and there were many companies of ladies and gentlemen who, morning and evening alike, maintained richly spread tables and had jesters in attendance, so that buffoons and players and jugglers came to Florence from Lombardy and from all of Italy, and they were welcomed there. Whenever a stranger of some distinction passed through the city, there was a competition among the companies to see which one would have him as their guest; and then the stranger was most politely escorted, either on foot or on horseback, all through the city and the surrounding countryside.

This was the lighter side of the renewed Italian interest in the joys of life. There was, however, a more serious aspect, one more concerned with the mind than with the senses. In literature, Dante Alighieri (1265–1321) was the first figure of lasting importance; but even he owed a debt to the poetic and literary revival which began under the aegis of Frederick II in Sicily. When the Hohenstaufen were destroyed by the Angevin dynasty, the intellectual and literary ascendancy of Sicily had been lost to Bologna, where, as befitted a university town, a few academics, such as Guido Guinicelli, composed correct, but not very inspired or inspiring, verses. Next, Tuscan, and particularly Florentine, poetry flourished, in the works principally of Dante himself and, earlier, of his friend Guido Cavalcanti. It has often been said that Dante's *Divine Comedy,* his undoubted masterpiece,

Italy in the Middle Ages

was the *Summa Theologica* of Thomas Aquinas in poetic form. Certainly, Dante was, chronologically, a man of the Middle Ages; yet, his appeals to the authority of the pagan authors, such as Virgil and Aristotle, his political views, his stress on the value of the individual, his preoccupation with life on earth, all characterize him as part of the new era rather than of the old.

Perhaps Dante's most important achievement, however, from the standpoint of literary history, was not so much that he wrote the *Divine Comedy,* but that he wrote it in the Florentine, or Tuscan, dialect, and thereby raised that idiom to the rank of the national Italian language. His Tuscan verses were recited in taverns, at public functions, in piazzas, and in homes in a way that would have been impossible had he written that work (as he almost did) in the usual Latin of the time. For Italy had almost as many dialects as it had villages and towns. One friend of Dante's tried to persuade the poet to write in Latin, for he claimed that there were "a thousand languages in Italy." Dante himself, in his treatise *On the Vernacular Tongue,* enumerates the most common of these: Sicilian, Calabrian, Apulian, Roman, Tuscan, Genoese, Sardinian, Romagnol, Lombard, and Venetian. These main dialects were further broken down into local dialects. In Tuscany, the people of Siena spoke one way, and those of Arezzo another. Such subdivisions reached a ridiculous extreme in Bologna, where the residents of the Via S. Felice spoke a subdialect different from that of their neighbors on the Via Maggiore. As though the dialectical multiplicity of Italian were not sufficient competition for the Florentine idiom, two other major languages fought for pre-eminence in Italy: Latin, which was the universal language of scholars, of the law, and of the Church, and French. Various Florentines, Venétians, Sienese, and Pisans all wrote in French, "because the French language is universal, and it is more delectable to hear and to read than any other." After Dante, however, Tuscan came to be generally accepted as the language of social and literary usage, the actual "Italian language." The use of the same idiom by two other Florentines, Petrarch and Boccaccio, in their sonnets and stories, respectively, established firmly the primacy to which Dante had raised the language of his city.

The sculptor's art, like that of the writer's, had also begun to flourish in the late thirteenth century. The great master of the time was Niccolo Pisano (1206–1278?), who, according to some, was an Italian from the south, and, according to others, was born in Tuscany. Whatever his origin, he went to Pisa early in his career—hence the surname *Pisano,* the Pisan. The first work that can be ascribed to him with certainty was the pulpit in the Baptistery at Pisa, which bears an inscription to the effect that Niccolo completed it in 1260. Pisa was then at the height of her mercantile glory. She had no inkling of the forthcoming, and fatal, conflict with Genoa, and she wished to build for the ages. She had completed the *Duomo,* the ("leaning") Tower, and the Baptistery, and now she wished to beautify their interiors. The pulpit was an unsurpassed beginning. An ingenious admixture of tradition in concept and realism in execution—which was in direct opposition to the two-dimensional Byzantine rigidity which was then prevalent—caused such a sensation that Niccolo was asked to carve another such for the cathedral of Siena. He worked also at Perugia, Pistoia, and Bologna, and possibly at Lucca. Niccolo's son, Giovanni (1250–1328) inherited his father's genius. His masterpiece, like his father's, was a pulpit, this time at Pistoia, which serves to demonstrate how far art had traveled in a single generation. In his eagerness to express action and life, Giovanni deserted entirely the classical—at least in concept—and went directly to nature. This eagerness for "the natural" was the same quality which gave to the *Divine Comedy,* and especially to the *Inferno,* that incredible vividness which makes it so memorable. These two, Niccolo and Giovanni, founded the great Tuscan school of sculpture, which was to attain its full glory at the end of the next century.

Italian architecture of this period, however, cannot boast figures of the eminence of Giovanni or Niccolo Pisano; nor does it show a definite step upward which can be called the beginning of a new period. Rather, the contrary is true. Throughout the Middle Ages in Italy, architecture, in comparison with the other arts, had thrived. In the old days of Theodoric the Ostrogoth, the Byzantine tradition had been transplanted to Ravenna, and for centuries afterward the Roman churches were built upon the pattern of the cruciform Greek basilica. By the middle of the twelfth century, the Lombard style was flourishing in Lombardy, the Tuscan Romanesque in Tuscany, and the Norman Sicilian in Sicily. The Gothic style had crossed the Alps before the triumph of the popes had destroyed the Germanic influence in Italy, and the struggle between the Gothic and Romanesque styles reflected, at the artistic level, the contest for supremacy between the Empire and the papacy. Despite the architectural continuity of the Italian Middle Ages, and the consequent need of a revolution in that field, there is one man who stands out above his contemporaries because of the monuments which he left and the master whom he had. Arnolfo di Cambio (1232–1300) was one of Niccolo Pisano's assistants at Pisa, and he proved so outstanding that, when Siena offered the master a contract for a pulpit, Arnolfo was requested by name. Despite his promise as a sculptor, however, he early interested himself in architecture, and it was he who built, in

Italy in the Middle Ages

Florence, the Church of Santa Croce for the Franciscan friars, who designed the Palazzo Vecchio, and who drew up the first plans for the cathedral.

If architecture had thrived in the Middle Ages, the same cannot be said for painting. For centuries, the most important factor in that art had been authority. The Greek painters of Constantinople had laid down a set of rules which were every bit as binding as the edicts of the emperors or the bulls of the popes. In every painting of the Madonna, for instance, every arm and every leg had to be depicted in precisely the same rigid position; the stiff, mosaic-like Infant had to be seated in the same way in the same unyielding lap; and the same inflexible figures of the same saints had to surround Mother and Child. Initially, it would have been considered near-blasphemy to infuse human life into these supernal beings. By the thirteenth century, however, side by side with this painting-by-edict, there gradually began to emerge another style, a freer, simpler way of depicting life. And it was in Tuscany that this revolution in painting, as in the other arts, began. The last of the masters in the Byzantine manner was also the first to popularize the new style. Cimabue (1240-1302), as devoted as he was to tradition and to the authority of the masters, was Tuscan enough to be infected by the surge of spiritual energy that was sweeping through the peninsula, and he was moved to attempt to portray the grace and beauty of living beings as they were in reality. By later standards, his style was indeed medieval; yet, his contemporaries were quick to perceive his innovational techniques. Charles of Anjou, fresh from his conquest of Naples, visited Cimabue's studio for a first view of a Madonna that the artist was painting for the Dominican monks of Florence, and great crowds pressed into the building to steal a glimpse of this novelty. When the picture finally was carried through the streets to its destination in the Church of Santa Maria Novella, its fame had preceded it, and an enormous procession of admirers followed in its wake.

As famous as Cimabue was in his time, and as widely regarded as a daring innovator, he had the misfortune to work at a time when a master artist and master revolutionary was abroad in the land, one whose fame was to obscure lesser artists for future generations. Giotto (1267-1336) was a contemporary of Dante's, born at a time when Niccolo Pisano and his son were sculpting the Sienan pulpit and Charles of Anjou was admiring the Madonna of Cimabue. He, like Arnolfo di Cambio, was a product of Pisano training, having studied under Giovanni; and he was Arnolfo's successor as the leading architect of Florence. The *campanile,* or bell tower, of the cathedral was his work. And being also a sculptor, he contributed some of the bas-reliefs that decorate the base panels. His favorite artistic exercise, however, was painting, and it is in that field that he has left his mark. He painted frescoes in the churches of Florence, Arezzo, Assisi, Padua, Ravenna, Rome, and Naples, and the people thronged from all parts of Italy to admire his lifelike figures. Other painters flocked to study under him, and in his lifetime and for a century afterward he dominated Italian painting by virtue of the revolution he wrought in freeing that art from the bonds of authority and subjecting it to human feeling.

Perhaps the most striking general characteristic of the economic, social, intellectual, and artistic activity in Italy at the close of the Middle Ages is the suddenness with which it appeared upon the scene, apparently almost fully developed. This rapidity of forward motion was not confined to those areas, however, for the political structures of the peninsula began to shift with equal rapidity. While artistic progress at first seemed to be correlated with the rise of the democracies of the north, no sooner had that progress bloomed into the works of Dante and Giotto than the democratic communes began to disappear. At first, the outward forms of democratic, or at least of republican, government remained intact. The *podestà* still exercised his authority. The major and lesser councils still busied themselves with the internal and external affairs of the state. The people still assembled in the *piazza* to vote on affairs of public interest. And everyone still paid lip service to the will of the people. But close observation would have revealed a dangerous flaw in the exercise of these republican forms: a lack of spontaneity. The councils and committees and public assemblies had ceased to be arenas for a free, and sometimes violent, exchange of opinions and of dissent from the consensus. They had become merely bodies which gathered in order to record an opinion previously arrived at. The members of these organs now began to go to one particular house or palace to be told how to vote; first, they did so secretly, and then openly, and finally with ostentation and braggadocio. The men who dictated these opinions, whether nobles or rich burghers, were undoubtedly men of intelligence and ability. They had been able, by adroitness or duplicity, or by an outright *coup d'état,* to gain control of a city, and then, after having ruled in their own lifetimes, to transmit their power intact to their heirs. It is not difficult to understand how such things were done, for they are common to every century and to every society. It is more difficult to understand how the members of the councils, the wealthy merchants, and prosperous guilds could have abdicated their hard-won places in favor of a despotism. The answer was probably that these worthy burghers preferred the stability of an autocracy to the political confusion of a democracy. It is impossible for

Italy in the Middle Ages

trade to flourish, for landlords to realize the maximum income from their properties, for luxury to display itself without restraint, for industrialists to achieve the greatest profits, so long as the law of the land represented, and depended upon, the whim and will of the common people. Liberty had to be paid for in an element of uncertainty in government, in legislation, and in commerce; and it was too high a price to pay. Gentlemen of property, of business, and of leisure preferred the stability of an assured income to the freedom of political choice.

Such preference, however, was not exercised in all the cities of Italy. In Florence, the democratic form of government was to prevail for many years yet. At Rome, the indisputable title of the popes and the very unruliness of the populace prevented the great clans of the Colonna and the Orsini from introducing a despotic form of government. The Kingdom of Sicily under its Aragonese kings and that of Naples under the House of Anjou had already become practically absolute monarchies, for Frederick II had, long before, crushed or circumvented the spirit of freedom in his domains. It was chiefly in the north that the main historical current of the century was to run.

Verona was perhaps the paradigm of the city-state under despotic rule. It was an ancient city, in which the amphitheater built by Augustus Caesar still stood while the churches of Theodóric the Ostrogoth had long since crumbled into dust. And it was a prosperous one, in which the Adige River in its rush through the city turned innumerable mill wheels. The cathedral had already been started, and the great Ghibelline tower already rose high above the market place. Altogether, it was a tempting prize for any enterprising tyrant. This fact had not been lost upon Eccelin da Romano, it will be recalled, one of Frederick II's nobles, who had established himself in authority there by means of a cruelty which still lives in the traditions and legends of the city. When Eccelin died shortly after Frederick's debacle, he was succeeded by representatives of the Scaligeri, or della Scala, family. These Scaligeri were a respectable and respected race, as benevolent as despots can be and still remain despots. Its most noble representative was Can Grande Scaligeri (1311–1329), the fifth of his line to reign in Verona, who was renowned in his own time, even in his own city, for his brilliance, courage, and munificence. Despite these qualities, however, he had, like his fellow despots of Italy, only two objects in life. The first was to render his authority secure in the city, and the second was to extend it beyond the city. As he was already secure in Verona, almost the first act of his reign was to fix a lustful gaze upon little Vicenza, some thirty miles to the north. But it turned out that Vicenza was no longer available; it had been snapped up by another neighbor, Padua, who had the advantage of being only twenty miles distant. Can Grande, however, was not to be put off by such trifles. With the help of the romantic Emperor Henry VII, Can Grande got himself appointed imperial vicar, or governor, of Vicenza. When Padua, which was Guelph, refused to surrender the prize to Ghibelline Scaligeri, a long and bloody war ensued. The fertile fields between Verona and Padua were laid waste; the peasants were dragged to one city or the other and held for ransom; the Guelphs of Verona, and the Ghibellines of Padua, were seized, imprisoned, and tortured. Finally, Padua found herself in a desperate state. Her control over the neighboring towns was loosened, her population was reduced by war and desertion, her citizens were fighting among themselves rather than against the Veronese, and her nobles were contending among themselves in the hope of becoming lords of the city. She therefore surrendered to Can Grande and gave up Vicenza. Other cities swiftly suffered the same fate, and Can Grande Scaligeri, by virtue of his conquests, became one of the great powers in Italy. He was steadfast, honorable, and generous to his enemies; but he never pretended to be anything more or less than a tyrant; and, on his deathbed, he bequeathed his signory to a nephew who, he felt, would be of the same inclinations.

Can Grande had chosen well. This nephew, Mastino, who ruled from 1329 to 1351, was a man after his uncle's heart. He began his career with a display of military virtuosity that left his enemies breathless, conquering in rapid succession Brescia and Parma. Inflated by his success, he became a *magnifico* of classic proportions. Soldiers, horse and foot, attended his every step. His palace was filled to overflowing with fawning nobles, clients, protégés and jesters, and there was always available the latest device for banishing care—music, dancing, jousting, and love. Everything about Mastino was on the grand scale. He himself, his men and his animals, all were covered with precious embroidery, cloth of gold, silks of the Orient, and laces from France. When he rode forth, all Verona rushed to the windows to look upon such magnificence. And when he was angry, all Verona trembled, for this lord was as terrible in wrath as he was splendid in appurtenance. He had little use for the observances of the Church, and he cared even less for the opinions of those who did. Episcopal remonstrances and papal interdicts alike he ignored with good humor.

His splendor and impiety, however, were less the cause of his downfall than was his ambition. It was rumored that he coveted a royal crown for himself, that of Lombardy, or perhaps even of Italy. And such ambitions, once they became known, were not calculated to render the other cities well disposed toward Verona. Finally, Mastino overreached himself in doing business with the citizens of Florence. The Florentines wished to control the city of Lucca and, according to a curious custom of the time, they expressed a desire to buy it. Mastino generously offered to act as intermediary between Florence and Lucca, and made a successful bid on the part of the former. But when he had possession of the city, he kept it for himself. The indignant Florentines immediately declared war, and induced some of Mastino's rival despots—the Visconti of Milan, the Gonzaga of Mantua, the Este of Ferrara—to join them, along with Venice (who had complaints of a commercial nature against the Scaligeri). This alliance was victorious and imposed hard terms upon Mastino. Venice took the towns near her, and thus acquired her first possessions on the mainland. Padua reverted to her primordial despots, the Carrara family. Milan's ruling Visconti family got Brescia. In one stroke, the great Scaligeri, and with them the power of Verona, was destroyed. From then on, the family dwindled in importance, degenerating from the idiosyncratic to the manic in an orgy of fratricidal feuds until, by the end of the fourteenth century, it lost Verona entirely.

The Scaligeri were archetypal. What they did in Verona, other families did in other places. The Gonzaga clan established itself in Mantua; the Este in Ferrara; the da Polenta in Ravenna; the Montefeltri in Urbino; the Malatesta in Rimini; the Baglioni in Perugia; and, the greatest of them all, the Visconti, in Milan. These latter had succeeded in surpassing its rivals and gaining control of Milan at the end of the thirteenth century, about the time that the oligarchy was tightening its grip upon Venice and popular government establishing itself firmly in Florence. And it was at this time that Florence, Venice, and Milan, all began that upward swing which was to end with their becoming three of the major political divisions of Italy (along with Piedmont, the Papal States, and the Two Sicilies). The Visconti were not, however, as firm in the seat of power as some of their contemporaries until Henry VII, Dante's Messiah figure, gave his support to this family and confirmed them in their position. By the time of Henry's death (1313), there was no one in Milan who dared stand up to them. Having thus attained security and additional stability by insuring that their signoral authority would descend, in despotic fashion, from one generation to the next, the Visconti began casting about for ways to extend that authority beyond the boundaries of Milan. By means of war, diplomacy, and treachery, they swallowed most of the smaller cities in the vicinity, and then, their appetite whetted, their eyes fell upon bigger game. There, they saw, were lovely Pisa, and thriving Bologna, and wealthy Genoa, all waiting to be taken. Pisa, however, presented an insurmountable obstacle, for Florence, whose love of liberty did not extend beyond her walls, had marked the city as her own prize. Similarly, the Visconti designs on Bologna roused the fury of the absentee popes of Avignon, and the familiar threats of excommunication, interdict, and an anti-Milanese crusade, rolled from the banks of the Rhone to hover over the palace of the Visconti, staying the hand of that pious tribe. Genoa, however, was a different matter. Crippled by her wars with Venice, she willingly surrendered herself to the mercies of Milan, hoping to receive peace and security in exchange for her liberty. Thus, Milan, despite setbacks here and there, prospered, and the power of the Visconti exceeded that of any of the other despotic dynasties of Italy.

The third great power of the north, Florence, had not substantially changed its form of democratic government since the preceding era, and despotism, in any but its commercial form, was regarded as intolerable by the citizens. Although there were symptoms of a new struggle between the nobles and the burghers, prosperity continued to make tyranny unnecessary. Indeed, the Florentine taste for luxury grew to such proportions that it became necessary to pass laws—which were, of course, universally ignored—governing such things as the fabric from which one's dress might be made, and how much gold or silver might be used for personal adornment. Such wealth was made to serve political as well as fashionable ends, and Florence gradually extended her authority, sometimes even by invitation, over her neighbors, until she had built for herself a sizable state in Tuscany.

At the other end of the spectrum among the major political divisions of Italy was the Kingdom of the Two Sicilies which, during this epoch, was split into the Kingdom of Sicily under the House of Aragon, and the Kingdom of Naples, under the House of Anjou. Sicily was in a condition of almost hopeless despondency. Its Aragonese kings were not men of sufficiently high intelligence, forceful character, or adequate means to impose their authority effectively, and the kingdom was retrogressing from the glorious days of Frederick II into political anarchy and into a position as an intellectual backwater. The Kingdom of Naples was, at first, better off, for King Robert, grandson of Charles of Anjou, was a man of unusual gifts. But he was succeeded, in 1343, by an empty-headed, frivolous granddaughter, Queen Joanna, who, in the thirty-eight years of her reign, managed to reduce Naples to almost the same state of degradation as its unhappy neighbor to the south. By the last part of the fourteenth century, therefore, Naples and Sicily were in such economic and political chaos that they were unable to participate in the great events that were about to manifest themselves in the north of Italy.

Hardly better off were the pontifical possessions to the north of Naples. From the fortresses of the Roman Orsini and Colonna families, to the towers of the Malatesta tyrants in Rimini, all was in confusion. With the popes still in Avignon, the City shrank to a vestige of her former greatness. The prospect of a return of the popes had faded, and as it faded the City fell into hopelessness, and from despair into material and moral decay. Armed bands prowled the shabby streets even by day. Sheep and cows grazed among the ruins of once splendid temples and churches. Robber barons squatted in the deserted and dilapidated palaces of the absent cardinals. The native clergy was submerged in ignorance, squalor, and immorality. Poverty was a state common to all Romans.

The element which gives life to Italy during this period, however, is not the political situation of the great divisions of the country, but rather the intellectual ferment which was beginning to make itself felt. Since the date of Niccolo Pisano's pulpit, the desire to learn, the wish to know, had increased in proportion to the growth of wealth and leisure. The two great medieval warehouses of human knowledge—nature and the classics of Rome and Greece—remained the same as before, and they contained approximately the same material as before. Nature, however, which heretofore had seemed to appeal so much to medieval man, began to lose its charm. The second factor, the classical heritage, seemed so much more precise and tangible, reflecting as it did an ancient world and a golden age in which intellectual giants had recorded their thoughts in magnificent prose and undying verse. These works seemed to comprise, as indeed they did, a secular Bible, a handbook of all rational truth. And the new generation now emerging into the dawning intellectual light of the fourteenth century turned to this source as men dying of thirst to a spring of cool water.

The leader of this new movement was a man named Francesco Petrarch (1304–1374), who, like Dante, was a Florentine-in-exile. He had studied law at the University of Bologna, and, as a result of his studies, became a confirmed Ghibelline. Along with a love for the Latin classics, this conviction seems to have been the only benefit that the young man derived from his studies, for while he loved the Roman law he came to despise the practice of law itself. "It went against the grain," he wrote later, "to acquire painfully an art that I was not willing to practice dishonestly, and that I could hardly hope to practice otherwise." After Bologna, he returned to his father's house at Avignon (for his father was also a Florentine exile), where all the most learned and brilliant men of the time were assembled around the papal throne. There, he happily abandoned all thought of a legal career and devoted himself to literature. During the next twenty-one years, he was to compose two hundred and seven sonnets and poems on his famous ladylove, Laura. These verses caught the fancy of all Italy, and they were read with admiration and envy by burghers, princes, and bishops alike. No one seemed to mind that Petrarch was, at the time, a cleric in minor orders, or that he, as a cleric, was the proud father of two little Avignonese bastards. He was the first of the humanists, and, in morals as well as in literature, the precursor of the Renaissance.

He traveled to Rome in 1336 to inspect the ruins of Roman civilization, and he was so moved that he pleaded with five successive popes to return to the City and establish Rome in its ancient glory. In 1341, Petrarch received the laurel crown as a scholar and poet from the Senate and people of Rome. The King of Naples was his sponsor, and his apotheosis was applauded by the princes of Europe and by the tyrants of Italy. After this triumph, he traveled about the peninsula, visiting Parma, Bologna, Verona, Florence, Arezzo, Naples, Milan, Padua, and Venice. He became the fashion of his age. The pope invited him to return to Avignon and become Papal Secretary. The King of France invited him to Paris, and the German Emperor to Prague. The Visconti of Milan, the Scaligeri of Verona, the Cararresi of Padua, all vied for his attention and favor. The Florentines offered him a chair at their university. And the Venetians, ever practical, offered him a house. But he was content to settle in a small house of his own at Vaucluse, east of Avignon, and to spend the remainder of his life in the pursuit and study of the wisdom of the ancients, and in encouraging his friends, and the world at large, to do the same.

The chief accomplishment of his life was not the sonnets, miraculous as they are in their exquisite subtlety, delicacy, and perfection of rhyme and meter, which occasionally make even Dante seem clumsy by comparison. It was rather the fact that he focused the attention of Europe on antiquity, and by so doing turned away their minds from the supernatural and toward the natural, toward man and the world, toward human pleasures, and established the validity of these things as replacements for the quest of spiritual immortality which had been the hallmark of the Middle Ages. In that sense, Francesco Petrarch was indeed, as he has been called, the "Father of the Renaissance."

The revival of interest in the classics flowered in Petrarch, so far as literature was concerned. In politics, it was to produce a bloom of a different sort, a young man named Cola di Rienzo (1314–1354) who, in his own way, had as passionate a love of ancient Rome and its civilization as did

Italy in the Middle Ages

Petrarch. Cola was a man of imagination, a poetic dreamer who, in his youth, had delighted in the works of Livy, Cicero, Seneca, and Virgil, and had gloried in thoughts of the ancient Roman republic. He was a man of the people, the son of a publican, handsome, eloquent, and charming. Thus equipped, he embarked on a meteoric public career which was to blaze brightly for a time, and then fade into nothingness. His first public charge was as a member of one of the embassies which Rome periodically dispatched to its absentee pope at Avignon to beg him to return to the Eternal City. The mission was, as usual, a failure, but young Cola seems to have made a good impression all around, and Pope Clement VI detained him for almost a year for the pleasure of his conversation. When Cola returned to Rome in 1344, with a minor papal commission in one pocket and a long letter of eulogy from Pope Clement in the other, he seems already to have decided to embark upon the course that he was to follow for the rest of his life: to restore the Senate and people of Rome to their former grandeur. His faith in his mission and his oratorical gifts soon inflamed the people with the same passion, and he led them in a successful revolt against the dominant nobles of the City. He forced the barons to submit and established the rule of Roman law, with himself as head of government under the resounding title of "by the authority of Our Most Gracious Lord, Jesus Christ, the Dreaded and Gracious, the Tribune of Freedom, Peace and Justice, the Liberator of the Holy Roman Republic."

But Rome without Italy was merely a head without a body, and Cola's intention was to restore the Roman Republic as it had been in its palmy days. He dreamed, therefore, of a confederation of all Italy under the leadership of Rome. His first step in that direction was to invite all the princes and powers of Italy to attend a general conference in the City; and, as all Italy responded to Petrarch's appeal to the literature of ancient Rome, so now it responded to Cola di Rienzo's appeal to its political aspirations. Milan, Genoa, Lucca, Florence, Siena, and many small cities answered sympathetically. Petrarch was delighted at Cola's success, and proclaimed the Tribune to be the Savior of Italy, Romulus, Camillus, Brutus. Indeed, such was the strength of the classical illusion that Cola's dream seemed to take on substance. In September 1347, he was able to write, and not to be thought mad with ambition, that "we have made Roman citizens of the citizens of the states of Holy Italy, and we admit them to the right of election. The affairs of the Empire have, by their nature, devolved upon the Holy Roman People. We now desire to renew and strengthen the old union with all of the principalities and states of Holy Italy, and to deliver Holy Italy herself from its state of abject subjection and to restore her to her former condition and glory. We mean to exalt to the position of Emperor an Italian who, by reason of his zeal for the union of his race, will be stirred to great efforts for Italy."

There is little doubt who the Italian was whom Cola had decided upon as emperor. But he was not to be allowed to realize his ambition for the imperial purple. The time was not ripe, and, just as important, he himself was no longer a suitable instrument. He had become proud, vainglorious, and cruel, one of the most oppressive tyrants of tyrant-ridden Italy. Moreover, he had grown fat and had lost the charm of youth, and he was no longer a novelty—a consideration that counted for much among the Romans. Also, the nobility and the upper classes of the City hated him for having deprived them of power. The end came when Cola, in need of money, attempted to increase public taxes. The Roman mob, thus provoked, stormed the Capitol, seized their Tribune as he attempted to steal away in disguise, and, in ancient style, murdered him on the very steps of the Capitol. His head was cut off, his body dragged by a jeering throng through the streets, and then burned and the ashes scattered. So perished Cola di Rienzo, one of the most poetic, and one of the least practical, men of Italian history. His career had lasted but ten years. His mad dream had been, of its nature, transitory. The classical heritage of the Middle Ages was too purely intellectual, too remote from the brutal realities of Italian politics and economics, to be applicable at the purely "practical" level of public affairs. Yet, the fact that, fourteen hundred years after the death of Julius Caesar, a new Roman Tribune should have been able to establish himself, however briefly, on the Capitoline Hill and to revive publicly the Roman Republic of the Gracchi, demonstrates the enormous impact of ancient Rome on the medieval mind, and leads to an understanding of how the classical heritage shaped and directed the intellectual revolution in Italy.

So far as the direction of that intellectual revolution—that is, of the classical revival—was concerned, Italy in the fourteenth century undoubtedly was specifically different from what she had been in the few preceding centuries. This difference, however, did not extend to all areas of human life. Social progress, as in every century, lagged behind intellectual development, and Italy did not escape, by virtue of her intellectual ferment, the woes that had beset mankind for a thousand years previously.

The most dramatic of these ills, and one which seems to have appeared with particular virulence in the fourteenth century, was the plague. Periodically, this dread disease—or diseases, for "plague" must be understood in its generic sense—swept across Europe, usually brought from the East by merchant ships. And since Italy was the prime Eastern trader of the day, it was natural that she should suffer the most. One such plague infested Tuscany in 1340; and another, Lombardy two decades later. The worst, however, and by far the most notorious, was the horrible Black Plague of 1348, which devastated large areas in Italy before moving northward across the Alps. Boccaccio describes the symptomatology in the *Decameron:* first, swellings about the size of eggs appeared, which turned black and hard. The victim then went into convulsions and died in terrible pain, usually only three days after the appearance of the first symptoms. Even animals were not immune, for Boccaccio records the death of two pigs who had chewed the clothing of a victim of the Death. Medicine was useless; and, in fact, it was usually not even thought of, for people ordinarily ascribed such plagues to wholly non-medical causes: the position of the stars, a drought or famine, witchcraft, Jewish plots (for the Jews were widely regarded as having a penchant for poisoning public wells), and, most often, the judgment of God on a sinful world. Some people thought that the best cure was to pray; others, that it was necessary to eat and drink well and to avoid all mention or thought of the disease; and others, not necessarily the most foolish, simply regarded death as inescapable and spent their time in merrymaking of all sorts.

At first, the bodies of the dead were buried, but as deaths mounted into the tens of thousands, they were abandoned in the streets to rot—and to spread the plague still faster. People fled into the country, and private houses and palaces lay deserted and open to looters. All loyalties vanished. Sons and daughters deserted their stricken parents, and lovers left one another to die in the streets. Many of the clergy, however, recalled from their dissipation by this visible evidence of divine wrath, were the sole attendants upon the dying; and many of them thus contracted the dread infection and atoned for their sins by a heroic death.

Between March and July of 1348, records Boccaccio, more than one hundred thousand people died in Florence. In Siena, some eighty thousand, about three quarters of the population. In Genoa, forty thousand; in Pisa, three out of every four, and the same in Rome, Venice, Naples, and Sicily. To an age accustomed to strict medical control of epidemics, such percentages and figures seem incredible. But Petrarch, a prophet as well as a poet, hastens to reassure us: "Posterity will never believe that there was ever a period in which the world was almost entirely depopulated, houses emptied of families, cities of inhabitants, and the countryside of peasants. How will the future believe, when we ourselves, who have seen it, can scarcely credit our senses? We go outdoors, walk through the streets, and see them full of the dead and the dying. We return to our homes, to find them empty of all life, for in our absence all have perished. O, happy that posterity to whom such catastrophes will seem but the dreams and figments of the imagination!"

Another evil, this one peculiar to Italy, and almost as deadly as the plague, was the mercenary soldiery which swarmed over the peninsula like locusts. In the old days, when Barbarossa had flourished, wars were fought between the militia of the cities on one side, and the imperial knights and men-at-arms on the other. By the fourteenth century, however, a great change had come about in the methods of raising armies and of waging war. Every feudal vassal had an obligation to serve his lord in the field for a maximum of forty days in the year. This arrangement worked well enough so long as wars were fought in one's own neighborhood or province. But when the emperors began crossing the Alps regularly to fight their wars in Italy, forty days were obviously too short a time in which to accomplish one's objective. The emperors, therefore, and the lords under them, were reduced to hiring soldiers whose only stipulation was that they would serve so long as they were paid. As years passed and the descent of the emperors into Italy took on the aspect of piratical adventures more than of military expeditions, the quality of these mercenaries degenerated. Men who would not have fought in a legitimate battle for any amount of gold now enlisted eagerly for campaigns that promised to be little more than exercise in rape, pillage, and murder. By Petrarch's time, the imperial armies were composed almost entirely of criminal elements who were periodically unleashed against any target that was too weak to protect itself, but too wealthy to be left in peace.

The Italian cities, however, must share the blame with the Empire for this state of affairs. The despots of the northern cities, for obvious reasons, did not wish their subjects to be trained in the use of arms. Moreover, the merchants and tradesmen of the mercantile cities did not wish to be away from their businesses during the period of a campaign, and they claimed that they could not afford to spare their employees for similar service. So they too hired professional soldiers to fight their battles for them.

Warfare itself, as practiced by these mercenaries, also changed considerably. It now required a state of discipline and training that the old communal militiamen, who were merely summoned from their homes and shops to their posts by the ringing of a bell whenever an emergency occurred, could hardly attain. Cavalry now required frequent exercise in maneuvers. Bowmen and pikemen required constant drill and training. There arose the need for a full-time military caste, and the need was filled by the appearance of professional soldiers-for-hire. Such men, in time of either peace or war, were formed into military organizations, usually called "companies," under the command of an aggressive adventurer or soldier of fortune who, in Italy, was known as a *condottiere,* or leader.

Generally, the use of mercenary soldiers was not wholly intolerable to the Italian people so long as there was a war to be fought or a city to be captured. These men, however, who had come down from the north to fight for the emperors, or who had sailed from Spain to fight for the House of Aragon in Sicily, were not always able to find employment, and it was in times of official peace that they were most dangerous; for they found their work agreeable, and, after a war, they frequently decided not to disband their companies but to continue to try their luck together. If they were then not able to sell their services to a city or to a despot who would pay them well, they wandered about the peninsula like nomads, capturing a helpless town if they could, or, if they could not, then living off the countryside, stealing everything that could be carried away and killing anyone who resisted. When they did find employment in the service of a prince or a city, they proved to be fickle and altogether undependable. When two armies of mercenaries faced each other across the field of battle, they fought only when absolutely compelled to do so, and then only as gently as possible. Their employers dared not remonstrate, for the *condottiere* was as likely as not to respond by turning his brigands loose upon the city that was so lately his master.

These companies of mercenaries, however, were often well organized and, when they chose to be, savage and effective fighters. Under a *condottiere*-general or a council of officers, they took such names as the Company of St. George, or the Great Company. Some of them, and some of their leaders, became famous in their own time and lived on as legends afterward. One such was a German named Werner, who called himself "Lord of the Great Company, Enemy of God, of Pity, and of Mercy." Another was an Englishman, the famed John Hawkwood, who began public life as a London tailor, but then abandoned his needle for the sword and alternately won Florence's battles for her and terrorized her citizens. There is a full-length fresco of him in the Florentine cathedral; but no one knows for certain whether it was painted in recognition of his great deeds or in gratitude for his early death.

For almost a century these latter-day Ostrogoths swaggered, fought, and looted up and down the peninsula, until at times it seemed that the age of the barbarian invasions was once more upon Italy. Even Petrarch was sufficiently moved by the devastation they wrought to turn from Cicero to Christ in a mournful jeremiad:

> O Jesus, Lord of the world, what has come to pass? Why do I sigh and weep in grief? A vile handful of bandits, vomited forth by their filthy dens, stalks and rides across the ancient queen of the world, Italy. Christ Jesus, in tears and supplication I turn to you. If we have abused your goodness more than was fit, if we have been too swollen with pride because of your aid and favor, if we have treated you ill, then you are right in depriving us of our freedom. But let not these murders, these sacrileges, these thefts, these rapes of wives and daughters, find favor in your sight. Make an end of this evil. To the fools who have said in their hearts, "There is no God," show that you do indeed exist; and to us give a sign that we are your children. Almighty Father, help us. We hope in you, and we call your name in prayer, weeping, and confessing that no one can save us other than you, O Lord.

As though the plague and the *condottieri* were not sufficient evil for the century, Italy suffered another affliction during the thirteen hundreds. It is one to which we have already adverted, and one which, for all its unpleasantness, was not as severe as the other two. This was the tyranny of the despots. The founders of the despotisms were certainly men of vigor and of political ability. In place of liberty, they provided for their subjects that security and order which the economic and social needs of the time required. Their descendants and heirs, however, as is often the case with descendants and heirs, were not of the same caliber as the founders of their dynasties. They often found hard work distasteful, and they avoided it religiously. They found it too demanding to exercise justice and benevolence, and so they gave themselves up to dissipation and cruelty. They could not imitate their forebearers' ability to lead the citizens, and they came to regard their subjects and their cities as private property, as chattels, provided solely for their amusement.

The Visconti of Milan exemplified this pattern of degeneracy among the despotic dynasties. In the middle of the fourteenth century, one Giovanni Visconti, Archbishop of Milan, became lord, as well as ordinary, of the city. He was an intelligent and cultivated man, an accomplished humanist and scholar, who exercised the offices of prince and priest for the intellectual, civic, and spiritual betterment of Milan during the few years (1349–1354) that he reigned. Upon his death, the archbishop was succeeded as lord of the city by three nephews who, in conformity with the uncle's express wish, reigned jointly. This princely trinity was made of unholy stuff, and the three brothers vied with one another in a contest of

Italy in the Middle Ages

incompetence and cruelty. The most infamous of them, however, was Bernabo Visconti (1354–1385), who was a tyrant to his fingertips, whose selfish whims made him hated and feared during his lifetime and a legend after his death. He loved to hunt, and he commanded that no Milanese citizen other than himself and his invited guests should participate in that sport. To make his point, he forbade that any resident of Milan should own a dog, although he himself had a kennel of some five thousand hounds. These dogs were billeted on the citizens of the city, as soldiers might have been in time of war, and the unwilling hosts had to feed and house Bernabo's dogs at their own expense. Periodically, Bernabo's kennel masters made tours of inspection, and if they found a dog that was too thin then the citizen responsible for his care was fined. If a dog died from other than obviously natural causes, then the citizen's entire property was confiscated. In the same vein, no one other than Bernabo was allowed to kill boars or rabbits for any purpose. Offenders were punished by being maimed or hanged. Sometimes, however, Bernabo, moved by Christian mercy, allowed the criminal to escape with his life and limbs if he would eat, raw, the entire boar or hare.

As might be expected, the Milanese were not overly fond of Bernabo, and he lived in constant fear of conspiracy and assassination. He imposed a curfew upon the city, and no one was allowed to leave his house after sundown for any purpose whatever; to do so was punishable by having one foot cut off by the public executioner. No one was allowed to refer to any subject that might cause political or civic unrest in the city; any man who even spoke the words "Guelph" or "Ghibelline" in any context, in public or in private, had his tongue cut out.

Such cruelty extended to the personal as well as to the public realm. On one occasion, Bernabo shut up his secretaries, for some minor error, in a cage with an enraged wild boar. On another, a young man who had prankishly pulled a magistrate's beard was sentenced to pay a fine; but Bernabo, when he reviewed the case, ordered the lad's hand cut off instead. The *podestà*, hoping that the boy's parents would be able to obtain mercy from Bernabo, delayed execution of the sentence. But Bernabo, hearing of the situation, then ordered both of the culprit's hands cut off, and, for good measure, also cut off the right hand of the *podestà*. Not even the clergy were exempt from his rages. A priest who had demanded too high a fee for a funeral service was buried alive in the grave prepared for the body of the deceased. Two other priests who came to protest this violation of clerical immunity were quickly hustled outside and burned alive for their insolence. Yet, Bernabo Visconti counted himself a devout Christian. He prayed often, and loudly. He built numerous churches, was scrupulous in the observance of fast days, and frequently abstained from meat even when it was not required by Church law that he do so. A man of excess in all things, he acknowledged himself the father of thirty-two bastards.

Bernabo's brother and joint ruler, Galeazzo II, was cast in the same mold, except that he was more intellectual than pious and professed an interest in the classics of Greece and Rome. He founded the University of Pavia, and is otherwise commemorated in the annals of literature for having exchanged figs, flowers, and flattery with Francesco Petrarch. Galeazzo's son, Gian Galeazzo, who succeeded his father as Bernabo's co-ruler, aspired to an official recognition of his despotic authority, and he was willing to pay for it. In exchange for three hundred thousand sequins, the King of France gave his daughter to Gian; but the king got the better of the bargain, for the frail girl did not long survive her transplantation to Milan's bloody soil. Gian then took for his second wife the daughter of Bernabo. Shortly afterward, he lured his new father-in-law to a meeting by some ruse, arrested him, had him tried and condemned for conspiracy—of all things—and then poisoned him. Gian Galeazzo II thus became Milan's sole ruler and, in 1395, he took the title of duke of that city.

The people of Italy, under the yoke of such tyrants, and afflicted, moreover, by recurrent plagues and predatory *condottieri,* sought desperately for some remedy. Only two possibilities presented themselves, and, by time-worn tradition, the Italians turned first to the Empire and then to the papacy. From time to time, German emperors came down into Italy; but these emperors were now Hapsburgs rather than Hohenstaufens, and their interests lay elsewhere. Their expeditions across the Alps were undisguised fund-raising campaigns, and their visits to Rome, ostensibly for coronation, were little more than a pretext for fleecing the City of what little wealth it still retained. They sold privileges and honors and titles to whomever could pay, gathered whatever taxes were available, and then locked their treasure chests and returned to Germany with their loot. They did nothing for Italy other than relieve her of her troublesome wealth.

When it became obvious to all that the Empire held no hope for them, the Italians began again to raise a great cry for the return of the popes from Avignon. There was no Italian, Guelph or Ghibelline, humanist or saint, soldier or monk, who was not inordinately proud that the papacy was an Italian institution. One might hate the popes, rob them, mistreat them, and, occasionally, kill them. But everyone believed that the popes should suffer these things nowhere but at Rome, and at the hands of no one but the Italians. If a pope was going to be a saint, then it was Italy who should benefit from his sanctity. And if he was to be a sinner, then it was Italy alone who had the right to witness, and perhaps to understand and forgive, his weakness. Sentiment in this respect grew strong and vociferous. Humanists wrote elegant letters to Avignon, recalling the Servant of the Servants of God to his duties in Rome. Friars summoned him from their pulpits. Saints, such as Catherine of Siena, being not bound by ordinary rules of human deportment, addressed insulting letters to His Holiness, commanding his presence in the Eternal City under pain of divine displeasure. And still the popes resisted. They were too comfortable and safe in their massive Avignonese fortress-palace, and too secure in the affection of their French subjects. Or perhaps it was, as Petrarch somewhat waspishly alleged, that they loved the wines of Burgundy so well that they could not bear to leave them.

It was the eminently practical Roman people who finally were able to devise a formula effective enough to bring their father home. The States of the Church, it was hinted officially, might well find it necessary to look elsewhere for a ruler, if the Most Holy Lord, Pope Gregory XI, did not see fit to return to his bishopric and to save his children from the woes that beset them. Gregory thereupon set out from Avignon, despite the most strenuous efforts of the French king to restrain him, and arrived in Rome on January 17, 1377, where he was received with an explosion of joy and enthusiasm. The Babylonian Captivity of the Church had finally ended, and Italy, after seventy years, once again—or at least so it was hoped—had a leader.

The Italians, however, had lived too long cheek-by-jowl with disorder and arbitrary government to be willing to submit quietly to an authority which they had rejected at every opportunity in the past. Once their exaltation at the pope's return to Rome had been dulled by the passage of time, the city-states came quickly to resent the smallest hint of the infringement of their own prerogatives and privileges by the pontifical government. The States of the Church themselves proved as unruly as ever, and the petty despots and nobles who were ensconced everywhere submitted only with the greatest reluctance to papal authority. Pope Gregory, however, was a realist. He had not been deceived by the elaborate welcome accorded him by his subjects; nor had he enjoyed any illusions about the political temper of the Italians. He sensed a strange mood in the land. Rumors of revolt were whispered in every corner, and uprisings seemed to threaten at every turn. The entire peninsula seemed in a state of suspense, as though awaiting a development the nature of which was only vaguely suspected. Resigning himself to the inevitable, he struggled patiently, and unsuccessfully, to bring some order out of chaos, until he died, a stranger in a strange land, in 1378.

It was then that came the storm. It took the form of a violent internal schism—known to history as the Great Schism—which split the Church and Europe into two, then into three, apparently irreconcilable parties. The trouble began with the election of Pope Gregory's successor. The College of Cardinals comprised two factions. One, the French party, had never reconciled itself to the papal return to Rome, and it lived only for the day when the Chair of the Apostle would be once again installed on the banks of the Rhone. The other, the Italian party, detested France, the French king, the French cardinals, and everything reminiscent of the humiliation of Avignon. The sentiments of this latter faction were fully shared, as might be expected, by the people and nobles of Rome.

Accordingly, when the cardinals assembled to elect Gregory's successor, they were greeted by a howling mob of Romans who demanded that they be given "a Roman, or at least an Italian" pope. The nobles, for their part, informed the cardinals that they required "a Roman pope, or, by heaven, we shall turn your heads as red as your hats." The frightened princes of the Church replied that a pope elected under threat of force would be no pope at all, but an intruder. But no one listened. And many of the electors took precautions. Their personal possessions were hidden away or sent out of the City, and guards were posted around their Roman residences. Several of the more cautious dictated their wills before the conclave began, and more than a few of them took to wearing armor under their scarlet robes. Finally, on April 7, 1378, the electoral consistory assembled in the Vatican, while all Rome swarmed in St. Peter's Square. "St. Peter's Square was black with people," a cardinal later recorded, "and as we approached the basilica the mob began to scream horribly, demanding, in its own idiom, a Roman or an Italian pope. There were some who threatened and cursed the princes of the Church." One of the leaders of the mob, a man gifted with an almost supernaturally Roman voice, climbed onto the shoulders of his friends and bellowed at the cardinalatial procession, "You will give us an Italian or a Roman pope, or, by the bowels of the everlasting God, you shall all die!" The young Cardinal Orsini, scion of one of Rome's great families and bred in the contempt of the mob, alone found the courage to reply. "O cursed men of Rome," he shouted, "do you imagine that you will thus get yourselves a pope? You are but starting this day a fire that will burn the whole world to ashes!" But the mob only howled the more, and the cardinals trembled, and the impetuous Orsini, muttering threats, withdrew into the conclave. Another cardinal led him to the chapel where the voting was about to begin. "Come, my lord," he said. "Let us give them their Italian or their Roman. It would be better to elect the Devil himself than to die."

As the hours passed and no news was forthcoming from the conclave, the threats of the crowd grew louder. A group of Romans attempted to spur their Eminences on to greater efforts by driving sharp spears up through the floor of the room in which the ballots were being cast. But there was still no news. Finally, just when the people were preparing to set fire to the building, a rumor spread through the Square that a Roman had been elected to the Throne of St. Peter. The mob, which had been mad with rage, was now insane with joy. Bursting into the conclave, they demanded to see their new Holy Father. The cardinals, however, did not have the courage to confess that they had indeed elected an Italian, but not a Roman, the Archbishop of Bari, who had taken the title of Urban VI (1378-1389). They hastily thrust Urban into a corner and, seizing one of their number, the aged Cardinal Tibaldeschi, a true Roman, carried him to the papal throne to receive the homage of his people. Then their Eminences fled precipitously. The pseudo-pope, meanwhile, was left with his Romans. They crammed themselves into the small chapel by the hundreds, crowding around the throne, pressing Tibaldeschi's gouty hands until the old man screamed with pain. When they asked his blessing, he cursed them instead, and feebly shouted the words, "This is a damnable comedy! How in God's name can I say I am pope?" A sudden hush descended upon the crowd. Someone shouted, "Who then is pope?" And old Tibaldeschi answered, "My lord of Bari." It is a tribute to Tibaldeschi's oratorical powers that he not only managed to escape with his life, but also to pacify the people by pointing out that they had demanded "at least an Italian" pope, and that God in his wisdom had granted their wish.

It is difficult to imagine, given even the peculiar circumstances of the consistory, what movement of the Holy Spirit had inspired the cardinals to elect Urban VI. There was hardly a man of the Sacred College less suited to the papacy at this time. What the Church needed was a man who could sooth the Romans, mediate between the French and the Italian cardinals, and repair the breach between the papacy and the French throne. What Italy needed was a conciliator and a healer. But Urban was none of these things. He was vain, cruel, petty, and tyrannical, as short-sighted as he was stubborn and as egotistical as he was domineering. His first official act was publicly to insult the French cardinals with such vehemence that the latter felt obliged, for the sake of their honor—and probably for that of their safety as well—to withdraw from the City. They did not go far. At Anagni, they stopped and convoked a rump conclave, in which they declared that Urban's election had been invalid, and that the Holy See was vacant. They had been forced, they claimed, "to elect an Italian pope that the Holy Spirit had not chosen. An insane mob compelled us to elect temporarily an apostate, a murderer, a heretic guilty of every conceivable crime. He acknowledged that his election would be only provisional, no more; and then, being without honor, he forced us, by threatening us with death, to raise him to the Apostolic Chair, and to set upon his guilty head the triple crown. . . . Now that we are safe from his anger, we declare solemnly that he is an intruder, a usurper, an anti-Christ. And we pronounce our anathema against him, and against anyone who accepts his rule." They then elected one of their party, Robert, Cardinal of Geneva, who took the name of Clement VII, to replace the deposed Urban VI. Urban naturally refused to submit, and remained in Rome surrounded by his Italian cardinals, while Clement installed himself at Avignon.

Europe was split in two, with some countries recognizing one pope and some the other, according to the dictates of policy or ambition. France, of course, adhered to Clement of Avignon; and Italy, just as naturally, obeyed the man who was "at least an Italian." At the level of individual Christians, there seemed to be no safe guide other than one's personal preference for one or the other pretender, for the authorities usually regarded as reliable were as confused, and as confusing, as everyone else. The enormously prestigious University of Paris first upheld Urban, and then reversed itself to support Clement. Even the saints were divided among themselves. St. Catherine of Siena, for example, heatedly defended Urban, while St. Vincent Ferrer just as rabidly gave his allegiance to Clement. Towns had two bishops, one Clementine and one Urbanist, and the faithful of the metropolitan centers were divided between two archbishops—all of whom exchanged anathemas, interdicts, excommunications, and a steady stream of pious curses. The revenues of both papal courts were greatly reduced by this divided loyalty, and the necessity of raising money reduced both to the most shameful expedients. Ecclesiastical offices were literally sold to the highest bidder, dispensations and indulgences were available only at a fixed price, divorces and annulments were forthcoming only for those who could afford to pay munificently for them. Under the impact of this example from above, the morals of the clergy deteriorated to the vanishing point, until the whole of the Church was one vast repository of scandal. Ludwig Pastor, the Catholic historian whose *History of the Popes* is a standard and unsurpassed work, concludes that "The amount of evil wrought by the schism of 1378, the longest known in the history of the papacy, can only be estimated when we reflect that it occurred at a moment when thorough reform in ecclesiastical affairs was a most urgent need. This was not utterly out of the question, and, indeed, all the evils which had crept into ecclesiastical life were infinitely increased. Respect for the Holy See was also greatly impaired, and the popes became more than ever dependent on the temporal power, for the schism allowed each prince to choose which pope he would acknowledge. In the eyes of the people, the simple fact of a double papacy must have shaken the authority of the Holy See to its very foundations. It may truly be said that these fifty years of schism prepared the war for the great Apostasy of the sixteenth century."

In this state of affairs, all Christendom came to feel that reformation was necessary, and that it must begin with the healing of the Great Schism. The two popes, under the pressure of public opinion, seemed willing enough. The Roman pretender made widely publicized overtures to Avignon, while he of Avignon bowed and smiled and vowed that all would be well. A meeting was discussed, and a reconciliation promised. But nothing was done. It must have been obvious even to the most optimistic observer that neither pope had the slightest intention of retreating one inch from his claim to absolute and sole authority in the Church. The princes of Europe, however, were as determined as the popes were stubborn, and, under pressure from the former, the College of Cardinals took matters into their own hands. They assembled in council at Pisa (1409), deposed both popes, and then elected another to take their place. The trouble was that neither Rome nor Avignon had agreed to this council, and therefore neither of the old popes would consent to abdicate in favor of the new. So, instead of solving the problems of the Church, the Council of Pisa had compounded them by creating a third pope.

This desperate situation required desperate measures. The man to take them was the Emperor Sigismund (1410–1437), who could see quite clearly, from his German throne, that Christendom was on the verge of total disintegration. The failure of the papacy to provide leadership had borne fruit, and other—and worse—troubles had begun to appear in the form of widespread heresy. In hitherto pious England, John Wyclif had denounced the popes and bishops for pride, greed and arrogance, condemned allegiance to the hydra-headed papacy, and formally denied the doctrine of transubstantiation.* In Bohemia, Jerome of Prague rejected the temporal authority of the Church, and John Huss stated publicly that

---

* The dogma which teaches that, at the consecration of the Mass, the substance of the bread and wine is changed into the substance of the body and blood of Christ.

the Emperor Constantine had wrought a great evil when he conferred temporal power upon the popes. As much as the orthodox temporal princes might rage against these newfangled ideas, they could do little to extirpate them. The preachers—or rather, the reformers, for such they were in fact—had the sympathy and the ear of the people. The papacy herself, having lost the respect of Christians everywhere for her vices and above all for her divisions, could do nothing against this new breed of theologians. The Emperor Sigismund, however, was clever enough to see where all this would lead. It was but a short step, he understood, from questioning papal authority to questioning that of the Christian monarchs of Europe, whose positions were, after all, founded upon the same theology as that of the popes. Sigismund, therefore, on his own authority and speaking as "the head of Christendom," convoked an Ecumenical Council at the city of Constance, for the purpose of adjudicating the various pretensions of the rival popes and of considering the lamentable state of the Church. And all Europe, by now sick to death of a helpless papacy and a degenerate Church, supported him and responded favorably to the invitation. Prelates, scholars, and princes assembled at Constance in 1414, determined to put an end to these scandals. This Council, which sat for almost four years, deposed the Pope of Pisa, John XXIII, for various crimes, including piracy, murder, rape, sodomy, and incest. Gregory XII, the Roman pope, the best intentioned of the lot, abdicated. Benedict XIII, a Spaniard, who was the pope of Avignon, was also deposed; but he refused to give up his throne and fled to Spain, where he died many years later, full of dignity and even of sanctity, universally ignored by Christians everywhere.* The

* From the standpoint of canonical justice, there seems little doubt today that Benedict XIII was the sole legitimate pope until the time of his death. The violence of the Romans had clearly, according to an undoubted principle of canon law, voided the election of Urban VI, and therefore the cardinals were free to elect another pope, which the majority of them did in the person of Clement VII, the Avignon pope who was Benedict's predecessor. The Council of Pisa was canonically invalid, since only a pope is allowed, by canon law, to convene a general council, and therefore the title of John XXIII was also invalid. As for the election of Martin V by the Council of Constance, the same principle applies; i.e., that it was an illegal gathering, since only a pope (an authentic one), and not an emperor, could call a general council. Moreover, according to canon law, only the College of Cardinals, and not a council (even a legitimate one) could elect a pope, and therefore the election of Pope Martin was also invalid. The complicating factor so far as election by the cardinals was concerned was that, if, as the Council of Constance claimed, the titles of the three popes were all invalid, then it followed that those of the cardinals they had appointed were also invalid. That left only one cardinal of the Holy Roman Church who had an unclouded title, for there was only one living cardinal who had received the red hat before the Schism, at the hands of Pope Gregory XI. And that cardinal was none other than Pedro de Luna—the man who was now Benedict XIII. It was a dilemma that

Council then proceeded to the election of a new pope. Their choice fell upon Martin V (1417–1431), a Roman of the Colonna family, who, upon mounting the throne, closed the rent which had disfigured Christianity almost to the point of ruin.

The other preoccupations of the Council of Constance (i.e., heresy and the reform of the Church) were another matter. It was easy enough to rid oneself of the reformers, and Jerome of Prague and John Huss paid with their lives for their temerity in questioning the authority of the papacy. But the extirpation of heresy itself, and the healing of the divisions of Europe, required strenuous reform of the Church, and the spirit of reform was resisted by the papal party of Martin V from the very beginning. The reformers wished to clean out the papal Curia and to give a republican cast to the Church, by virtue of which the pope would rule only in conjunction with the Sacred College of Cardinals. The papalists, on the other hand, were determined that the pope was to remain the absolute head of the Church, and that any reforms must be undertaken only at the pope's instigation. In pursuing this policy, the papal party ensured that the inevitable reforms, when they did come, would come not as the acts of a self-reforming Church of Rome, but as a Reformation imposed from beyond the Alps. In pursuing this willful course, the papacy demonstrated that it had learned nothing from the past. The popes, during their captivity in Avignon and during the Great Schism, had abdicated the leadership of Italy and of Europe. Now, in the wake of the Council of Constance, it refused to change with the times. Time, therefore, now began to leave her behind, and, from this moment, the Church was overtaken by events. It can no longer serve as the central theme in the course of Italian history. Its place

---

Benedict himself had pointed out to the Council. "You say my title is doubtful," he had told the Emperor Sigismund. "So be it. But before I was pope, I was a cardinal, made cardinal before there was a Schism. I am the only cardinal left alive from before the Schism of the West. If, as you say, all popes since that day are in doubt, then so are all their cardinals. And since it is the cardinals who must elect the pope, I who am the only true cardinal, I alone can elect a true pope . . . and there is nothing on earth to prevent me from electing myself." This announcement, a witness says, was greeted "with a great silence." Martin V himself seems to have adverted to the truth of Benedict's statement, for, after the latter's death, he assembled the Spaniard's three cardinals and, in return for confirmation of their titles, he insisted that they meet in consistory and formally elect him. From the standpoint of canon law, therefore, the pontificate of Pope Martin V can be dated only from that consistory, and the title which descended from Martin to the present incumbent of the Roman See owes its authenticity not to the Council of Constance but to that election. It is significant, in that regard, that the Catholic Church today recognizes the Council of Constance as ecumenical only with respect to its acts in 1417–1418—that is, after it had been formally convened by the newly elected Pope Martin.

henceforth is merely that of one among the several political entities of Italy, each of which contributes to the flow of events: the Kingdom of Naples, the Kingdom of Sicily, the Republic of Venice, the Duchy of Milan, and the Republic of Florence.

The Kingdom of Naples at this time had reached the nadir of misery. Its giddy queen, Joanna I, had chosen the wrong side—that is, the side of the Avignon popes, the losers—during the Great Schism, and the Roman popes had sworn vengeance. Retribution took the form of deposition, and Joanna, by papal edict, was replaced on the Neapolitan throne by her cousin Charles. The new king had Joanna strangled, and thus initiated a blood feud between his heirs and hers, which, to the disgust of the Neapolitans, was fought out for many years. Under their usurper kings, unhappy Naples was taxed, assessed, and otherwise almost robbed out of existence by the heirs of Charles and by their favorites and mistresses. Until the middle of the fifteenth century, the history of the kingdom is a sad tale of steady retrogression toward the Dark Ages. The only bright spot, and a temporary one at that, was the unification of Naples and Sicily in 1443, through the adoption of the King of Sicily, Alfonso of Aragon, by the Neapolitan monarch.

The Kingdom of Sicily was slightly better off than its mainland neighbor. The Norman royal line, as we have seen, had died out and been replaced by the House of Aragon (1409). When Alfonso of Aragon was adopted by the Neapolitan dynasty and attempted to claim his heritage, he was challenged by the House of Anjou, which still claimed Naples for itself. There followed a struggle of Spaniard against Frenchman in Italy which was to be so protracted as to prove disastrous to the entire peninsula. Alfonso eventually was able to assert himself in Naples, however, and he was recognized (1443) by the pope as King of the Two Sicilies. By the middle of the fifteenth century, therefore, the southern half of Italy was united and at peace.

In the north, several city-states had emerged as dominant powers in their respective areas. To the northeast, Venice had been growing in strength and wealth. The path to power, however, was one of violence, and the city made numerous and bitter enemies in the process. Her possessions on the Italian mainland, gained by aggression, had earned her the undying hatred of Padua. Her expansion along the Adriatic had stirred up the animosity of the Hungarians. Her mercantile enterprises in the Levant had made a deadly enemy of Genoa. And her policy of expansion in all directions and at almost any cost had embroiled her in war after war with almost every state with whom she came into contact. The most bitter of these was the struggle with Genoa, known as the War of Chioggia (1378–1381), in which Venice, after being drawn back from the brink of defeat by the genius of her two illustrious admirals, Vettor Pisani and Carlo Zeno, so completely crushed her rival that Genoa never recovered. Venice, however, regained her strength in short order, and soon she was busily extending her conquests. Padua fell to her in 1404, and the Paduan despots, the Carrara family, were strangled to a man. Verona fared little better, although her despots, the Scaligeri, managed to escape to the south. Under the Doge Francesco Foscari (1423–1457), the Republic of Venice reached her greatest extent on the Italian mainland by annexing the cities of Bergamo and Brescia and by carrying her boundary to the river Adda.

During this period of expansion, the Venetian oligarchy had been at work tightening its hold on the reins of government. There had been, however, numerous conspiracies and attempted *coups,* for the Venetians, bred in the tradition of freedom, did not all submit gracefully to despotism, however benevolent. The most famous, and the last, of these attempts to overthrow the oligarchy was organized by no less a person than the Doge himself, Marino Faliero, and its purpose seems to have been to establish a governing coalition comprising representatives of the people and the old nobility. Tradition tells us, however, that the motive of the insurgent Doge was the desire for revenge against a member of the oligarchy who had publicly insulted him. The plot became known, and ten of the conspirators were executed—nine of them being hanged from the windows of the Doge's palace, and the tenth, Faliero himself, being beheaded as the ringleader. The portrait of the fallen Doge in the great hall of the Palace was obliterated, and in its place was inscribed a warning to future rebels: "This is the place of Marino Faliero, who was beheaded for his crimes."

The determination of the oligarchy to maintain itself in power continued to be equaled, as earlier, only by its preoccupation with the prosperity of the city. Commerce was the very life of Venice, and the rulers tended it with loving care. They paid particular attention to the means of commerce, and the building and fitting-out of ships in the famous Arsenal of Venice was one of their primary concerns: carracks, with triple decks and enormous storage holds, for the perilous waters of the Atlantic; galleasses, with prodigiously high forecastles and poops, for the pirate-infested Mediterranean; and graceful galleys, with long rows of oars and lateen sails, for the familiar Adriatic.

The riches brought to the city by these ships, the stability of the government, and the security of an island homeland, all combined to make of Venice a city unique in the peninsula. Instead of being a place of fortresses, surrounded by massive walls and grim towers, she bloomed with light and elegant palaces, whose balconies and marbles reflected gaily in the canals. All seemed wealth and tranquillity, and—in contrast to the kingdoms of Naples and Sicily, which were at this moment moving backwards, both together and separately, and to the tumultuous Papal States—Venice appears as a stronghold of prosperity and peace as she passes through the fifteenth century.

Venice's chief rival for the primacy of power in the north was Milan, which had been raised, as has been noted, to the dignity of a dukedom under Gian Galeazzo Visconti. Gian Galeazzo, though he had left much to be desired as a Christian, had been, in many respects, an able ruler, and under his iron rule Milan had flourished as never before. The most unpopular and exorbitant taxes were reduced, and many others were abolished altogether. The administrative and judicial systems of the city were reformed, and ducal legislation was, for its time, a model of wisdom and fairness. Gian Galeazzo shared the pride of the people of Milan in their city, and he planned Milan's great Gothic cathedral on a scale calculated to satisfy that emotion. He completed the palace at Pavia, where he deposited the two great joys of his life, his famous collection of books, and his equally famous collection of the bones of saints. His was a truly royal ambition, and under him Milan acquired, sometimes through force but more often through rapacious diplomacy, the cities of Verona, Padua, Siena, Assisi, Perugia, Pisa, and Bologna. Rumor had it that Gian Galeazzo cast covetous eyes even on the states of the pope; and history records that he aspired at least to a unified Kingdom of Lombardy. Venice, however, and Florence were too powerful for the success of Milan's plans. Venice, with her eyes turned perpetually to the East, might have thought it not worth-while to oppose Milan single-handed. But Florence was irredeemably democratic, and she would not tolerate any suggestion of foreign domination. The people of that city had not hesitated to oppose emperors and popes when their liberties were threatened; they would hardly treat more gently a mere Visconti upstart in Milan. They therefore organized a league against Gian Galeazzo, and a balance of power was established which left northern Italy suspended, for the moment, between the determination of the Florentines and the ambitions of the Visconti.

There the situation remained until the loosening of tensions resulting from Gian Galeazzo's death in 1402. His premature demise left the Milanese duchy in a state of undisguised chaos. The possessions of Milan, accumulated with so much care, were left to the government of an inexperienced widow-regent, a short-sighted ducal council, and three young boys. The subject cities and towns fell away, one by one, into the hands of the local despots so recently deposed by Gian Galeazzo. Some fell prey to powerful neighbors—Padua and Verona to Venice, Pisa to Florence, Bologna to the papacy. Thus was the splendid patrimony carved up until Duke Filippo Maria (1412–1447), Gian Galeazzo's second son and the last of the Visconti, achieved maturity and succeeded in restoring the duchy very nearly to its earlier boundaries.

Florence, the last of the major political powers of Italy, seemed always to be engaged in a state of internal struggle. She was forever occupied in exiling, deposing, or attempting to suppress her aristocrats. The Florentines had been compelled by circumstances, in the days of danger from the emperors, to accept foreign lords as military leaders. They expelled the last of them, Walter of Brienne, who called himself Duke of Athens, in 1343, and then they speedily legislated against the possibility of an equally unpleasant domination by passing laws against the aristocrats of their city. The burghers, then secure and confident, managed the affairs of Florence for the next generation. At that time, there appeared, for the first time in Florentine public life, the name of Medici, in the person of a certain Salvestro de' Medici. Salvestro was *Gonfaloniere,* or chief executive officer, of the city, and he attained fame, and laid the groundwork for the rise of his family, by proposing laws in favor of the common people. The latter, their appetites whetted, wanted and demanded more. The mechanics and artisans of the lower guilds, however, were outraged at this sharing of privilege, and they rioted, and then revolted, with the *Ciompi,* or wool carders, at their head, and overthrew the government. In 1378, they put one of themselves, Michele di Lando, at the head of the city. Now the Florentines prided themselves on being a democratic people; but no human being, they pointed out, would submit to the rule of a wool carder. And if the rich burghers were too proud to submit to a king, they could not be expected to accept a tradesman as their chief. After a moderate upheaval, therefore, the government passed into the competent hands of a small group of distinguished and wealthy citizens who, under the leadership of Maso degli Albizzi and Niccolo da Uzzano, ruled prudently and wisely, resisting the aggressions of the Milanese and making it their policy to maintain a balance of power in Italy.

It was the peace and prosperity which flourished under the rule of this oligarchy that allowed to be felt in Florence, and then in all Italy, the first stirrings of that movement known to posterity as the Renaissance.

IV
AN AGE OF RENEWAL:
The Renaissance
(1400–1580)

By the fourteenth century, much of what had been characteristic of the Middle Ages in Italy had begun to decay. With the collapse of the Holy Roman Empire and the loss of prestige and of universally recognized authority by the papacy, the dominant religious or spiritual interpretation of every phase of human life was effectively undermined. Scholastic philosophy, hitherto the inflexible guide of every respectable intellect in Europe, had, as the result of its own logical excesses, fallen into disrepute and was now the object of ridicule and the target of popular jokes. In commerce, the ancient and tightly knit system of guilds in trade and industry had served its purpose and was now giving way to the spirit of individual free enterprise. As these buttresses of medieval civilization gave way, there gradually appeared new institutions and new ways of thinking and living. These new things were founded, of course, on man's accomplishments during the Middle Ages; sometimes they were a logically evolved continuation of them, and sometimes they reflected a revolt against medieval ideals. But they were sufficiently different from the old ways, in either case, to stamp their time with a new character and a new civilization. The age during which this new civilization flourished in Italy—roughly from the beginning of the fifteenth century to the end of the sixteenth—is traditionally known as the Italian Renaissance.

The term is not a particularly fortunate one. "Renaissance" means rebirth; and, in that sense, the word Renaissance implies that that great cultural, spiritual, and social revolution of the fifteenth and sixteenth centuries was merely a "rebirth" or "revival" of interest in the classics; that is, in

An Age of Renewal

the learning of ancient Greece and Rome. Indeed, until a few years ago, such was the common textbook definition of the Renaissance. The truth of the matter, however, is something quite different. Interest in the classics was merely the starting point, rather than the culmination and the specific difference, of the Renaissance. As far back as the time of Charlemagne, as we have seen, there was an intense interest in the ancient Greek and Latin authors—and, in that sense, it is correct to speak of a Renaissance of the ninth century. From that time on, such of the classical authors as were available were assiduously cultivated and revered, and, in some instances, regarded with an awe usually reserved for the saints of the Church. Virgil, Cicero, and Seneca, for example, were regarded as great authorities on almost every subject under the sun, and no man could make a plausible claim to erudition during the Middle Ages unless his conversation was liberally seasoned by quotations from these masters. No one excited more admiration than Aristotle, whose work was studied, analyzed, memorized, and finally synthesized by Thomas Aquinas into that Scholastic system which, from the early thirteenth century, became the dominant factor of medieval intellectual life. It is difficult to believe, therefore, that the cultivation of the thinkers of ancient Greece and Rome was the element that separated the men of the Renaissance from their medieval forebears. For the Renaissance was much more than the revival of pagan learning. It covered a multitude of new achievements in art, literature, philosophy, politics, education, science, and religion, some of which had little or nothing to do with the Greeks and Romans. Moreover, the Renaissance is distinguished from the previous age by the introduction of a new complex of concepts, ideas, and ideals, a complex which, it is generally agreed, have set the standard for the modern world. Of these ideals, the most important, because the most far-reaching, was that of humanism; that is, of the exaltation of what is human and natural in life, rather than of what is divine and supernatural. If any one element may be said to have been *the* characteristic of the Renaissance, then that element must be humanism, for it included in itself practically all of the ideals which the man of the Renaissance found worthy of pursuit: optimism, individualism, hedonism, skepticism, and materialism. As such, it is accurate to say that humanism, the emphasis on this world and on human values, was the heart and soul of the Renaissance.

Humanism, however, did not spring full-blown from the brow of Italy. In many ways, it was closely related to the spirit of the High Middle Ages, a spirit which manifested itself in the human pride reflected in the great Gothic cathedrals of the thirteenth century, in the pursuit of learning evident in the universities, in the earthy stories of Boccaccio, in the sonnets of

Petrarch, in the religious questioning of such "heretics" as John Huss and John Wyclif, and, ironically, in the rampant secularism of the Church. When, to this incipient humanistic spirit, certain other factors were added, then the whole produced a new culture—part medieval, part Greco-Roman, and part new or "modern." And it was that result of the interaction of the ancient, the recent, and the new which we call the Renaissance.

These new factors have already been touched on, for, in general, they were the same ones which had stimulated the intellectual and artistic revival in the twelfth and thirteenth centuries: contact with those two great cultural reservoirs of the Middle Ages, the Byzantine and Saracenic civilizations; the emergence of the spirit of commerce and capitalistic enterprise; the growth in wealth and influence of the Italian city-states; the revival of interest in classical studies, begun centuries before by Charlemagne's Alcuin, but emphasized more recently by Petrarch; the birth of critical and skeptical attitudes as exemplified in the philosophies of such men as Roger Bacon and Abelard; the gradual escape, by the Church as well as by secular governments, from the supernatural preoccupations of the period up to the twelfth century. This latter factor was of particular importance, especially as regards the Church; for the advent in the late Middle Ages of popes who were more concerned with this world than with the other—popes such as the great Innocent III and Boniface VIII—not only disabused Europe, and Italy especially, of its illusions concerning the papacy, but also set the precedent for a series of magnificent Renaissance popes—Nicholas V, Pius II, Julius II, Leo X—whose concerns were not with theology, but with art, literature, and politics, and whose patronage was of incalculable value, and perhaps indispensable, to the progress of the revolution in art, science, and literature.

When all those elements are considered as a whole, it seems entirely natural that it was in Italy that the Renaissance was born, and where it flourished and grew to maturity. It was in Italy that the classical tradition had been preserved more intact than elsewhere; and it was the Italians who logically regarded themselves as the heirs of the ancient Romans and who prided themselves exorbitantly on this heritage. Something of the ancient Empire's liberal paganism also survived in Italy, where, it has been noted, there was little of the dread which the Church and its sanctions inspired north of the Alps. The Italians simply lived too much cheek-by-jowl with the Church to have any illusions about it; and therefore, while the Church often controlled the bodies of the Italians, it never quite attained that domination of the mind and soul of Italy which characterized its reign elsewhere. This attitude was reflected everywhere in Italian life.

An Age of Renewal

The great universities, for example, were founded for the study of such subjects as law and medicine rather than (as elsewhere) of theology and Scholastic philosophy, and none of them had any ecclesiastical connection whatever. Moreover, it was Italy who lived in closest contact with the Byzantine and Saracenic civilizations and who absorbed the impact of their cultural influence. And, perhaps most important of all, it was in Italy that the cities flourished from commerce with the East, and that the accumulation of wealth gave leisure and the means for intellectual and artistic interests. And so, it seems inevitable that Italy, who in ancient times had ruled the world, and who under the medieval papacy had remained its center and head, should now, as a new era dawned, lead the world from its medieval twilight into the bright light of day.

1. The Early Renaissance (1400–1464)

It was from Florence, as has already been seen, that the glimmerings of the glory that was to be the Renaissance first appeared, in the persons of Petrarch and Boccaccio. And, just as Florence gave birth to those beginnings, so too, the Renaissance itself, like a burst of energy summoned by a divine touch, came into vigor in that city, in the first half of the fifteenth century. The Renaissance, however, as it manifested itself in Florence, must not be thought of merely as an artistic movement—unless, of course, one regards life, as did the Italians, as an art. In reality, only a small portion of the deepest feelings and interests of the Renaissance found expression in artistic or literary form. The great majority of them were expressed instead in life itself. The celebrated Florentine artists of this period—known as the Early Renaissance—were merely representative of their fellows. They were surrounded by their fellow citizens, all of whom were crammed full of the ardor of life, of expression, of discussion, of accumulating wealth, and of glorifying their city. The epitome and paradigm of such citizens, and the most important figure of the Early Renaissance, was Cosimo de' Medici (1389–1464), who, though himself without pretensions to artistic accomplishment, was the patron and friend of every artist of distinction. It is due to Cosimo, perhaps more than to any artist of the time, that the intellectual and artistic movement of the early fifteenth century flourished and gained momentum until it burst out into Italy, and thence into the rest of Europe.

Cosimo's father, Giovanni de' Medici, the richest banker of Italy and one of the principal citizens of Florence, had been active in politics, and, at the time of his death in 1429, was chief of the party which was opposed to the ruling oligarchy. Cosimo, according to the custom of the Florentines, succeeded to his father's position, and, when the oligarchy fell, he became the actual head of the city, although he was always careful to maintain the pretense of being merely a private citizen. His lively intelligence and his broad education put him in keen sympathy with the intellectual ferment of his time, and his enormous wealth and power enabled him to express that sympathy in those ways which artists and intellectuals appreciate most. Wealth was his great instrument, and of it he lent and gave lavishly. In later life, he was heard to say that his chief error had been that he had not begun to spend money sooner than he did. He was basically a serious man, concerned with things of the mind, and adverse to buffoonery of any kind, though not to laughter and to gaiety. By virtue of wide experience in affairs of state, of extensive reading, and of a remarkably retentive memory, he was both an interesting talker and good company. With men of letters, he discussed literature; with theologians, divinity; and with philosophers and astrologers, the subtleties of their specialties. And, in every case, the wealth of information which he had accumulated on these subjects won the respect and admiration of his listeners even if, as occasionally happened, his money and position did not. As a ruler, he exemplified and embodied the new ideas on politics and government, which maintained that every individual state, regardless of its size, should be absolutely free from external control—a belief, however, which he did not always put into practice with respect to Florence's weaker neighbors. He rejected the medieval belief in limited government and in an inflexible ethical basis of politics. In practice, he held that the authority of the state—that is, of the ruler—was subject to no limitations whatever. That which was necessary to maintain the power of the state provided its own justification; what was necessary, he held, was *ipso facto* good. Through the careful application of these principles, he gradually attained absolute power. The outward forms of democracy were meticulously preserved, while every thread of government responded to the slightest twitch of Cosimo's hands. He was indeed, as he was called by the Florentines, *Pater Patriae,* the Father of his Country; and, in the fashion of a father, he was at once benevolent, loving, and despotic toward the people of the city.

Cosimo de' Medici is chiefly remembered today, however, not for his despotism, but for his benevolence, his love of beauty, his determination to make Florence the glory of Italy, and his liberality toward anyone with talent. He employed the architect Michelozzo Michelozzi to build his palace (now known as the Palazzo Riccardi), his villa, and also the Domini-

An Age of Renewal

can convent of San Marco. He employed the famous Filippo Brunelleschi to rebuild the abbey of Fiesole. He was fond of sculpture, and he had statues by the best masters of the day in his palace; among his favorites was Donato Donatello. He employed Fra Angelico to paint in the convent of San Marco, and Benozzo Gozzoli to decorate his private chapel. Cosimo's greatest interest, however, was in the humanities. He built several buildings for libraries in Florence, and one in Venice, and he interested himself enthusiastically in the preservation and increase of book collections. For the library in the abbey of Fiesole, he employed a man of letters, Vespasiano da Bisticci, his biographer, who hired forty-five copyists and, in twenty-two months, finished the two hundred volumes then thought necessary for a good library. Among this collection of indispensable works was, naturally, the Bible, along with concordances and commentaries; the works of St. Ignatius, St. Basil, St. Gregory Nazianzen, St. John Chrysostom, and as many of the works of the other Greek fathers as had been translated into Latin; St. Cyprian, Tertullian, and the four doctors of the Latin Church; the medieval masters St. Bernard, Isidore of Seville, Hugo of St. Victor, and St. Anselm; the works of Albert the Great, Alexander of Hales, Thomas Aquinas, and Bonaventure. There were books of law, both canon and civil, and all of the available works of Aristotle, with commentaries. Of the Latin writers, there were Livy, Caesar, Suetonius, Plutarch, Sallust, Quintus Curtius, Valerius Maximus, Cicero, Seneca, Virgil, Terence, Ovid, Lucan, Statius, Plautus, and, as Cosimo ordered, "all the other books necessary for a library." While engaged in this activity, however, he never forgot that he was the prince before he was the patron of art and literature, and he viewed his accomplishments in that light. "I know the moods of Florence," he used to say. "Not fifty years will pass before the Medici are drived out of the city. But then, at least these buildings will remain."

Cosimo's words were prophetic. Later generations remember him not so much as *Pater Patriae,* or as the founder of the House of Medici, which was to rule for centuries in Tuscany and mingle its blood with the royalties of Europe, but as the patron of the arts, the friend of artists, and the central figure around which to group the men of genius of the Early Renaissance.

In architecture, the most memorable name of Cosimo's time is that of Filippo Brunelleschi (1377–1446). His biography by Vasari opens with these words: "Many men are created by nature little in person and features, but with their souls so full of greatness and their hearts so full of the unbridled fury of genius that, unless they work on things difficult almost to the point of impossibility, and unless they finish them to the astonishment of the spectator, they never give themselves any rest all their lives. Such a man was Brunelleschi, no less insignificant of person than Giotto, but of so lofty a genius that it may be said he was commissioned by heaven to give new form to architecture, which for hundreds of years had gone astray [such was the Renaissance view of the Gothic and Romanesque styles, which Vasari, himself an artist of the Renaissance, shared fully]. Moreover, Brunelleschi was adorned with the greatest virtues. Among these was the gift of friendship, to such a degree that there never was a man more kind or loving than he. His judgment, however, was wholly free of passion. Wherever he saw the worth of another man's merits, he totally disregarded any advantage to himself or to his friends. He knew himself, and he inspired others with his own noble qualities. . . . He declared himself a deadly enemy of the vices, and a lover of those who practiced virtue. He never wasted time, for he was always busy with his own affairs or with the affairs of others when they had need of him. . . ." Brunelleschi was no scholar; but, being a Florentine, he was excessively fond of conversation and debate, and he did not hesitate to engage learned men in discussion. He was particularly fond of debating the Holy Scripture, and then, a friend said, "he talked like a second St. Paul."

Brunelleschi began life, as did most architects of that time, as a member of the guild of goldsmiths, from which point he developed naturally as an architect. A great event of his life was a trip to Rome with Donatello. There, the two artists examined all the classical remains of the city and in the surrounding countryside, measuring everything they laid eyes on, and learning all that they could of the art of the ancients.

In Florence, besides the abbey of Fiesole, built for Cosimo de' Medici, Brunelleschi designed the Church of San Lorenzo for Cosimo's father, and he designed and began construction of the lordly Pitti Palace across the Arno. His greatest achievement, however, was the dome of the cathedral of Florence. The church, first begun by Arnolfo di Cambio, had been in the hands of a succession of famous architects, and was nearing completion. The gap at the intersection of the nave and the transepts, nonetheless, presented a problem which demanded the talents of a man such as Brunelleschi. The diameter of this gap was about one hundred and thirty-five feet, and its height above the ground was one hundred and forty-five feet. No such span had been vaulted by man since the rebuilding of the Pantheon in the second century after Christ. A public competition for a dome was held, in which Brunelleschi took part. After apparently interminable discussions—for Florence was "a city where every one speaks

An Age of Renewal

his mind"—Brunelleschi was chosen for the work. His great dome, though no slavish copy of Roman forms, was thoroughly classic in its simplicity and its spirit, and it is the great architectural achievement of the Early Renaissance. Brunelleschi no doubt wished to revive the old Roman art, as did his fellow architects. And, indeed, these men did so as far as they were able; but their problems were peculiar to their own time, and there were few models intact from the days of Roman splendor. They were therefore forced, for the most part, to rely upon their own ingenuity in principles of construction, and to limit their use of Roman forms to ornament and detail. They thus evolved a style all their own, one which was adopted by other Florentine, or at least Tuscan, architects and spread throughout Italy. To Brunelleschi and his contemporaries is really due the foundation of the various schools of Renaissance architecture which sprang up in Milan, Venice, Pavia, Bologna, Rimini, Brescia, Siena, Lucca, Perugia, and in almost every city of northern Italy.

In sculpture, the dominant figure of the Early Renaissance was Brunelleschi's friend, Donatello (1386-1466), or, as he is sometimes known, Donato. Donatello was a realist. He shows classical influence at times, particularly in technique and in sundry bits of detail; but his primary instinct was to reproduce what he could see and touch. His vigor, his energy, and his impatience with artificiality produced a profound change in sculpture and also in painting. His early works were statues for the exterior of the *Campanile* of the cathedral, and for the Church of Orsanmichele, of which the most famous are the *Zuccone* (*Baldhead*), and the St. George. Later, he modeled a youthful David, the first nude bronze since the time of the ancient Empire, and the statue of Gattamelata at Padua, the first equestrian statue since that of Marcus Aurelius in Rome.

In addition to Florence and Padua, Donatello worked in Venice, Mantua, Modena, Ferrara, Prato, and Siena, whence he introduced the Renaissance into the sculpture of northern Italy. He was a man of strong character and poetic spirit, striving in his art to be true to nature and to the beautiful, to mingle pagan art and Christian sentiments, tradition and freedom. He liberated his art from the mannerisms of the Gothic, and he introduced a note of individualism into sculpture—an accomplishment by virtue of which he and his pupils affected the whole plastic art of Italy.

Donatello's peer and contemporary was Lorenzo Ghiberti (1378?-1455), a native of Florence, whose glory it was to cast the bronze doors of the city's Baptistery—a work whose twenty right panels required twenty-one years for completion. As the work progressed, Ghiberti was aided by Donatello, Michelozzo, and an enormous group of assistants. When the doors had been finished and installed on the north side of the Baptistery, the Signory immediately commissioned another pair, this time for the east side, and Ghiberti, without stopping to catch his breath, set to work again. This time, assisted by such men as Brunelleschi, Antonio Filarete, Paolo Uccello, and others, the project took twenty-seven years. Michelangelo, upon viewing this masterpiece for the first time, was so astonished at its perfection of detail and perspective that he declared the double door to be "worthy of gracing the entrance of Paradise." Vasari pronounced it "the finest masterpiece in the world." Even the difficult Florentines were so pleased that they elected Ghiberti to the Signory and gave him a substantial income, in perpetuity, to support him in his old age.

Luca della Robbia (1400–1482), a pupil of Donatello's, and like his master and Ghiberti, a friend and protégé of Cosimo de' Medici, used his long life to perfect a new material of art: terra cotta. His purpose was to find a way by which clay, a highly tractable substance, might be made as beautiful in texture as marble. He achieved this end, after much experimentation, by molding the clay into the desired form, covering it with a glaze of various chemicals, and then baking it in a specially designed kiln. His new process was an instant sensation in Florence, and he was commissioned to make terra-cotta representations of the Resurrection and the Ascension for the cathedral sacristy, and to furnish an abundance of figures for Cosimo's palace. His fame grew and spread throughout Italy, and orders for his new material poured in. He was not able to resist the temptation to accumulate a fortune by the Renaissance version of mass production, and some of his work during this period is hardly up to the standard of his masterpieces, the *Coronation of the Virgin* in the church of the Ognissanti, and the *Visitation* in Pistoia's church of San Giovanni. Nonetheless, he opened a new door in the realm of art, and he founded a dynasty of artists that would bring fame to Florence for years to come.

In painting, Tommaso Guidi, known as Masaccio (1401–1428), stands conspicuous, even among many painters of rare talent. "Masaccio" is an unflattering diminutive of Tommaso, and it recalls the only personal trait we know of him. Vasari says: "He was a most absent-minded person, and very casual, like a man who has fixed his will and his whole mind on art only, and who cares little about himself and still less about others. He never wanted to interest himself in any way in the things or cares of this world, even in his own clothes, and he never attempted to collect money that was due to him except when he was in the most extreme need. Instead of Thomas, everyone called him Masaccio; not because he was bad, since he was good nature itself, but because of his absent-mindedness.

Nevertheless, he was as affectionate and amiable as could possibly be wished." This "marvelous boy," as Vasari called him, died at the age of twenty-seven, but he left an ineffaceable mark on Italian painting. Across the Arno River, in the rather ugly church of S. Maria del Carmine, there is a chapel in which, mingled with the work of contemporaries and imitators, are Masaccio's frescoes, figures of St. Peter and St. John, of a shivering boy, and a few others. Of these, Leonardo da Vinci was moved to say, "After Giotto, the art of painting declined again, because everyone imitated the pictures that had already been done. And so it went, until Tommaso of Florence, who is called Masaccio, showed by the perfection of his works how those labor in vain who take for their standard anyone but Nature herself, the Mistress of all masters." To that same obscure chapel, Michelangelo, Raphael, Leonardo himself, Fra Angelico, Fra Lippo Lippi, Verrocchio, Ghirlandaio, Botticelli, Perugino, Piero della Francesca, Fra Bartolommeo, Andrea del Sarto, and dozens of Italy's other great artists, came to study, admire, and copy. Masaccio had been the first to apply the new principles of perspective to his art; and he thus began a new era in pictorial art.

The most famous painter of the period, however, was not to be Masaccio, but a humble Dominican friar, a Tuscan named Guido di Pietro (1387–1455), who took the religious name of Fra Giovanni, but whom an admiring Italy rechristened Fra Angelico—"the angelic brother," or Brother Angel. And he was, in fact, an angel, according to all reports. His patience and humility surpassed the wholly natural, and, in his sixty-eight years of life, it is recorded that he never once showed the least sign of anger, and that no one ever succeeded in offending him, although many tried. For him, painting was but a manifestation of his intense spiritual life, a rather unusual form of prayer. His work is indeed a canticle of divine love, and its aim was to inspire piety by overwhelming the viewer by the beauty and majesty of the Christian faith. In the assembly hall of the friars in his own convent of San Domenico at Fiesole, he painted a powerful *Crucifixion,* to recall to his confreres the reason for their existence. In each of the fifty cells of the convent, he painted frescoes of some Gospel scene, each one according to the particular need of the occupant. In that to which Cosimo de' Medici retired from time to time to contemplate the vanity of worldly glory, he painted his famous *Adoration of the Kings.* In his own cell, he depicted his favorite subject, the Coronation of the Virgin, and he painted the same scene in the dormitory of the Convent of San Marco. This work, along with other works in his own house—such as the *Descent from the Cross,* the *Last Judgment,* and *The Annunciation*—

spread his fame throughout Italy, so that Nicholas V, the reigning pope, summoned him to Rome. There, he obliged Nicholas by decorating the papal chapel with scenes from the lives of St. Stephen and St. Lawrence. Nicholas was so struck by the beauty of Angelico's paintings and by the splendor of his soul that he offered to make him Archbishop of Florence; but the humble friar recoiled in horror from such worldly glory, protesting that he was too weak to accept the archiepiscopal dignity without grave danger to his soul.

Fra Angelico lived with one eye on heaven and one on earth; and he painted in much the same way, with the brush of the Middle Ages dipped in the colors of the Renaissance. His simplicity of form is reminiscent of Giotto, and his choice of ethereal colors—blues, greens, scarlets, golds—reflects his happy view of creation and of man's place in the universe. The overall effect of his work, however, is supernal rather than earthly; idealistic rather than realistic. The world is but a pale reflection of heaven, and his men and women but corporeal prefigurements of supernatural souls enjoying the beatific vision. His work is of the Renaissance in its perfection; but, in its spirit, it is almost wholly medieval. Fra Angelico himself was not unaware of that position, and his epitaph exemplifies the same dichotomous commitment: "Let it not be said of me that I have been, as it were, another Apelles; but rather that I gave all that I gained to your faithful, O Christ; for there are some works that are of this earth, and others that are of heaven. I, Giovanni, was a child of the Tuscan city of Florence."

The antithesis of the angelic Giovanni was another child of Florence, Fra Filippo Lippi (1406–1459), a Carmelite friar. He left his convent at the age of twenty-six, but continued to call himself "Fra," or Brother, a title which proved no impediment to the pursuit of that which, even more than his art, he loved best in life. Vasari summed it up nicely: "Filippo is said to have been so amorous that, when he saw a woman who pleased him, he would have given all his possessions to have her. And if he could not succeed in this, he quieted the flame of his love by painting her portrait." One of his amours was a nun, with whom he eloped and who thereafter served as the model for many of his exquisite and tender Virgins. On another occasion, Cosimo de' Medici shut up the hot-blooded monk in a house so that he might not waste time while working on a commissioned painting; but, Vasari reports, "Filippo remained so for two days; then, overcome by his amorous and bestial desires, he cut up his sheet with a pair of scissors and let himself out of the window, and then devoted much time to his pleasures. . . . From that time, Cosimo gave him the freedom to come and go as he chose. . . . And afterward he sought to hold Filippo by the bonds of friendship, and was thus served by him with greater readiness."

A man as susceptible to feminine beauty as Fillippo could not help painting superb Madonnas; and, indeed, his finest works are his various depictions of the Virgin—where, naturally, she appears, not as the idealized woman of Fra Angelico's conception, but as a figure of earthly beauty and warmth. Similarly, Filippo's Holy Family is simply a portrait of a contemporary Italian family, homey, intimate, and wholly of the Renaissance. His greatest work, according to the critics of his own time (for they are now in a state of advanced deterioration), are the murals he painted in the cathedral of Prato, depicting scenes from the lives of St. John the Baptist and St. Stephen the Protomartyr. He died in 1469, while engaged in decorating the cathedral of Spoleto. The fire of passion seems to have burned to the last, for, according to Vasari, the cause of his death was poison administered by the indignant family of a young girl whom Fra Filippo had casually seduced. He left behind him, in addition to a great body of splendid work and a mountain of debts, a son, Filippino Lippi, who was to attain fame in the succeeding generation.

The element which gave volume and impetus to this stream of creativity in the plastic arts was humanism—a word that, for the man of Cosimo de' Medici's time, had a rather restricted meaning and signified enthusiasm for the classical writings because of their inherent human interest. For if man and earthly experience were now to be the object of human celebration, it was in the literature and art of ancient Rome and Greece that the perfect exemplar of that celebration was to be found.

At the beginning of the fifteenth century, virtually all of the Latin classics familiar today, and many of the Greek, were known, at least in imperfect form, to the most learned of the scholars of the Middle Ages; and the universities, through the efforts of such men as Albert of Cologne and Thomas Aquinas, were thoroughly familiar with the works of the Greek philosophers in their Latin translation. Greek poetry, however, was woefully neglected. It was not until the time of Petrarch and his disciples that these treasures began to be unearthed—some in dusty monastery cells, some in garbage heaps, and some covered by pious tales of medieval miracles. In the first half of the century, humanists rummaged through the libraries and bookstalls of decaying Byzantium in search of precious manuscripts. In this way were brought to Italy hundreds of "lost" works, and hundreds more whose more accurate texts could be used to purge the old Latin versions of their corruptions. Among such discoveries were the plays of Aeschylus and Sophocles, the texts of Herodotus, Thucydides,

Polybius, Demosthenes, Aristotle, and seven dramas of Euripides. The final collapse of Constantinople (1453) resulted in an exodus of Byzantine scholars to Italy, and with them they brought not only their knowledge of the Greek tongue, but their precious manuscripts. The way had already been prepared by the intensive study of Greek by Italian humanists under Byzantine scholars who had been lured to the universities of Italy by the promise of fabulous rewards, and under Greek ecclesiastics who had come to Italy for the Council of Florence (1439) and stayed to reap the reward of their scholarship.

In a short time, Italy was in a frenzy of editorial revision. The new texts were being compared with the old, and the latter were being corrected and commented upon with a passion and accuracy that would have seemed excessive to the scholar of the Middle Ages. Plato, particularly, astounded and charmed the Italian humanists. In 1445, Cosimo de' Medici, under the influence of Gemistus Pletho, founded a Platonic Academy at Florence, and set up a fund to enable one of his humanist protégés, Marsilio Ficino, to undertake the translation and explication of Plato's works. Under the impact of the enthusiasm for Plato, the philosophy of the schools, Scholasticism, finally gave up its intellectual throne, and was replaced by Platonism.

Italy, however, remained wholly Latin, despite her admiration for the Greeks, and the first place in her heart was reserved for the art and literature of Rome. Latin was revived as a medium of literature, and the model of prose was Cicero, while that of poetry was, of course, the incomparable Virgil and, occasionally, Horace. The classical authors of Rome were imitated, slavishly and without restraint; and, inevitably, form became more important than substance, and rhetoric replaced reality. The literature of the period, therefore, was almost uniformly grandiose and grandly sterile. It served a purpose, nonetheless, for, in its preoccupation with form, it enunciated the canons of good taste and style, which were to be the standard for the vernacular of later generations.

As in the plastic arts, Florence, under the gentle aegis of Cosimo, was the center of literary humanism, and Florentines were the leaders and teachers of the movement. The most famous of these was Niccolò de' Niccoli (1363–1437) to whom writers submitted their manuscripts for correction. He filled his house with manuscripts, and opened his collection to all who were interested in studying them. His library provided the foundation for the great Laurentian Collection of Florence. Leonardo Bruni, himself no mean humanist, deferred to Niccolò as "the censor of the Latin tongue." It was high praise, for Bruni (1370–1444) was the man whose translations of Plato into Latin revealed to Italy the full splendor of the

An Age of Renewal

Greek's style. He also wrote a Latin *History of Florence* in which he forsook the model of dry medieval chroniclers and attempted, not without success, to give an orderly account of his native city in the manner of such ancient historians as Livy.

One of the most remarkable, as well as the most famous, of the early humanists was Poggio Bracciolini (1380–1459), a friend both of Niccolò de' Niccoli and of Leonardo Bruni, who unearthed a huge number of ancient manuscripts of the classics. In the Swiss monastery of St. Gall, he found the *Institutiones* of Quintilian buried in a cellar, and a number of Cicero's orations at Cluny, as well as texts of Lucretius, Columella, Vitruvius, Frontinus, Valerius Flaccus, Tertullian, Plautus, Petronius, and Ammianus Marcellinus. His passion for manuscripts was equaled by his devotion to the archaeological treasures of Rome, and he devoted as much time and money to the collection of coins, inscriptions, and statuary, and to the description of Rome's monuments, as he did to the accumulation of literary treasures. As quick tempered as he was learned, Poggio quarreled with all and sundry, and he did not hesitate to attack his enemies, and sometimes his friends, in elegant Latin. So talented did he prove in this respect that, as a contemporary assures us, "the whole world was afraid of him." Latin also was turned into an instrument of extortion, and, on one occasion, Poggio had only to hint to King Alfonso of Naples that a sharp pen could pierce a king's hide more effectively than any sword for that monarch hastily to dispatch a gift of gold with the request that the trigger-tempered humanist sheathe his pen. Much to everyone's relief, Poggio died in 1459. But he could not resist having the last laugh on his generation. After he was buried in the Santa Croce, his statue by Donatello was erected on the exterior of the cathedral of Florence; but, in 1560, in the course of some alterations in the church, it was set up inside the building—where it has remained for centuries as a representation of one of the Twelve Apostles.

Such confusion is particularly ironic in view of the fact that for such men as Poggio, Leonardo Bruni, Niccolò de' Niccoli, and the humanists in general, Christianity, in the medieval understanding of that term, had more or less ceased to have any meaning. Their heroes were no longer an Augustine, a Jerome, a Bonaventure, or an Aquinas, but rather Plato, Virgil, and the lesser denizens of the literary and intellectual pantheon of ancient Greece and Rome. The virtues to be cultivated were no longer those of Francis of Assisi; humility was to be replaced by pride, obedience by freedom, chastity by the enjoyment of love in any form, and poverty by the pursuit of luxury—sometimes as a means, but more often as an end in itself. Lip service, to be sure, was still paid to Christian belief, for Christianity was, in the view of the humanists, necessary to the well-being of the masses; but it was not to be taken seriously for a moment by minds liberated by immersion in the greater glories of antiquity.

For a century, the beliefs and the teachings of the humanists were to be the principal factor in Europe's intellectual and artistic life. They made writers and public figures conscious of the subtleties of language, and of the artifices of rhetoric, but at the same time their preoccupation with antique Latin delayed for a hundred years the evolution of a vernacular— i.e., Italian—literature. They freed the reason from the yoke of theology; and then they impeded the free use of reason by subjecting independent thought to the exaltation of erudition. In a word, they progressed, but they also stood still. And what they produced, almost inadvertently, was a necessary moment of consolidation, a pause in march of progress, during which the necessary work of translation, explication, and dissemination of the thought of the ancients was accomplished. The tools of scientific thought, rather than the progress of science itself, were their concern, and they gloried in the work of grammar, lexicography, rhetoric, and the critical revision of classical texts rather than in the creative opportunities afforded by the new-found learning. Through their efforts, and despite all their failings, a bridge was built by which the heritage of Greco-Roman antiquity was enabled to cross over into the modern world. It was no mean accomplishment; and that it occurred in the time, and under the patronage, of Cosimo de' Medici, is perhaps the chief boast of that munificent prince.

2. The Golden Age of the Florentine Renaissance (1464–1492)

Cosimo died in 1464, to be succeeded by his son, Piero de' Medici who, while well intentioned and of good character, lacked his father's intelligence, and, to an even more conspicuous degree, his father's tact. Within a matter of months, the city was in revolt. Although the Medicean party finally prevailed, it was clear that Piero's reign was to be an uneasy one; and it is probable that all Florence, Medici partisan and anti-Medicean alike, was quietly pleased when death cut short the unhappy Piero's tenure.

Piero's son, Lorenzo—he who was to become known as "the Magnificent"—took his father's place, became lord of Florence in all but name, and, like his grandfather, stood as the center of a brilliant group of scholars, artists, sculptors, and poets. Under him, the Renaissance spread and kindled enthusiasm from Lombardy to Calabria, but Florence still maintained her primacy. All the other cities of Italy lagged far behind her, while toiling and panting to make themselves as beautiful and as famous as the city of the Medici.

Lorenzo de' Medici was, in many ways, the embodiment of the ideal Renaissance prince. Though not handsome, he was tall, healthy, and broad-shouldered, and looked more like an athlete than a statesman. In public, he bore himself with modesty and dignity; yet, in private, he had the gift of making those in his company forget his station and his power. After the cares of statecraft, his chief interest was the pursuit of knowledge in all its forms, and so keen was his mind and so avid his curiosity that he was able to hold his own with such protégés as Politian, Ficino, Pico della Mirandola, and Pulci. His morals reflected those of the humanists of his time. He wrote profoundly devout hymns and licentious verses with equal facility and enthusiasm. He was scrupulous in maintaining the outward appearances of religious devotion, while amusing himself by a steady succession of mistresses who, as often as not, turned out to be the wives of prominent Florentines. He contributed with open-handed liberality to religious causes, and supported with equal generosity an uncounted number of virtually pagan artists, writers, poets, sculptors, scholars, and hangers-on. Though a subtle and expert diplomat, whose intrigues entangled Italy in a web of Florentine design, he was also a poet of much talent. Indeed, his verses are among the best of the age and are surpassed only by those of his friend Politian. It is to Lorenzo's credit that, while an accomplished Latinist, he preferred to write in Italian, and thus restored to its primacy the vernacular of Dante, which the humanists had overthrown a century before. He was, in short, the central character of the High Renaissance, as his grandfather, Cosimo, had been that of the Early Renaissance, and, at the same time, its most magnificent patron. He ruled a powerful state, managed and increased one of Europe's great fortunes, wrote remarkable verses, supported and patronized the great artists and writers of his time, toyed with mistresses, outwitted the mightiest princes of his time, fathered a pope, and ended as he began—the greatest Italian of his time, magnificent in fact as well as in title.

Under Lorenzo's guidance, the literary men of Florence now began to write more and more in Italian rather than in Latin, and slowly was formed the language which was to become the literary standard of the entire peninsula: Tuscan. At the same time, he continued to give evidence of the reverence in which he held the great works of the Latins and the Greeks as models of style and erudition. Representatives were dispatched throughout Europe in search of manuscripts, and he encouraged the fledgling art of printing as the means of reproducing the classics with the greatest possible accuracy. The old university at Pisa was restored and enlarged and magnificently endowed, and the Platonic Academy, founded by Cosimo de' Medici, flourished under Lorenzo's care and encouragement.

Drawn to Florence by the munificence of Lorenzo and by the city's reputation for the love of art and learning, scholars and artists flocked to the Medici court, among them such men as Politian, Michelangelo, Ficino, and Pico della Mirandola. The vast majority of Lorenzo's circle, however, were native Florentines. And not all of them were grave scholars, or even temperamental artists. Luigi Pulci (1432–1487), for example, won fame as a wit and humorist, and for providing the popular note of Lorenzo's day. He early in life won the friendship of Lorenzo, who thereafter employed him on diplomatic and business missions. Under Medici patronage, he composed his famous, and infamously ribald, *Il Morgante Maggiore,* in which he drew from the wealth of medieval tales to fashion a parody of the romances of chivalry by applying to those tales the language, prejudices, and views of the bourgeoisie. He succeeded in convulsing with laughter the Medici court, Florence, and then all Italy. But such irreverence could not go unpunished, and when Pulci died he was refused Christian burial on the grounds that some of the ancient figures whom he had held up to ridicule were, after all, saints.

A writer of a different sort was Angelo Poliziano, or Politian (1454–1494), who, at the age of twenty-six, was appointed Professor of Classical Languages at the University of Florence. A great scholar, Politian, who early won fame by his translations of Homer, was led by Lorenzo's example to write in Italian, and, as court poet of the Medici, he produced *La Giostra* (*The Tournament*), a poem celebrating the alliance in 1475 between Florence and Milan. A more important creation, however, was his *Orfeo,* a tragedy dealing with the love of Orpheus and Eurydice, which marks the secularization of the old liturgical drama of the Middle Ages. *Orfeo,* although modeled on classical works, was written in Italian, and it illustrates the giant strides made by the vernacular as the medium of the new culture. After the time of Politian, Latin was to become the language merely of the learned few, of pedants and churchmen.

Perhaps the most remarkable man of Lorenzo's circle was Pico della Mirandola (1463–1494). This Pico was an extraordinary man, the paradigm of the universal genius of the Renaissance. A scion of the counts of Mirandola (a town near Modena), he was persuaded by Lorenzo to make his home in Florence after completing his studies in Paris and Bologna. He was interested in everything—philosophy, poetry, architecture, music

—and in everything he studied he achieved some excellence. According to Politian, who knew him well, Pico combined in himself all the gifts of nature: beauty, "with something of divinity shining from his face," energy, miraculous intelligence, remarkable memory, universal erudition, the gift of languages, and an agreeable personality. Thus armed, Pico took as his life's work the reconciliation of the religions of the West (Christianity, Islam, and Judaism) among themselves; and then of those religions with Platonic philosophy, and Platonic philosophy with Aristotelian thought. Pico labored long and hard at this task, and he wrote a number of treatises on the subject. Naturally, Pico's orthodoxy was suspected at Rome, particularly when he had the courage to publish in the City some nine hundred theses which he offered to defend against all comers. No one accepted the challenge, but pope and curia condemned a good dozen of the theses, whereupon Pico fled back to Florence to spend his remaining years in the company of Lorenzo and the Platonic Academy. There, he became a devout follower of a strange reformer who had appeared on the scene, one Savonarola, and turning to religion, he burned his five volumes of poetry, distributed his wealth among the poor, and lived a life of seclusion. His death, at the age of thirty-one, came at a time when he was preparing to become a friar of the Order of St. Dominic.

Pico's determination to reconcile pagan Platonism with Christianity was shared, with considerably more success, by Marsilio Ficino (1433–1499), he who had been commissioned by Cosimo de' Medici to spend his life in translating Plato into Latin and who formed part of Lorenzo's heritage, as it were, from his grandfather. As a young man, Ficino was so incredibly handsome, we are told, that he was pursued relentlessly by the ladies of Florence; but he had only one love, Plato, and only one occupation, his books, and feminine charms held no attraction for him. In the pursuit of his studies, he came to lose his faith in Christianity, for Platonism seemed to him infinitely superior to the teachings of Paul and the Fathers. He was won back, however, by the writings (and the excellent Latin) of St. Augustine and, at the age of forty, he became a priest. He remained, however, an enthusiastic Platonist, for he saw no contradiction between the monotheism of Plato and Socrates and that of Christianity, and he affirmed that the pagan philosophers had been the recipients of a divine revelation quite as valid, and perhaps more explicit, than that with which the Prophets of the Old Testament had been favored. It was a belief that found favor with Lorenzo and the other humanists, whose conviction it was that medieval Christianity could be salvaged only by reinterpreting it in terms acceptable to philosophers and men of learning.

Lorenzo's patronage and his interests were not confined, of course, to literature, but, like those of Cosimo, extended themselves to artistic endeavor in every form. As a prince, he was particularly addicted to that avocation of princes, building; and so, architecture, and that decorative handmaiden of architecture, sculpture, consumed much of his time and his fortune. "Those who wished to please him," wrote a contemporary, "used to collect, from every part of the world, medals, coins, statues, busts . . . and whatever bore the stamp of antiquity." He placed his architectural and sculptural treasures, along with those of Cosimo and Piero, in a garden adjacent to his palace, and he admitted everyone who wished to study the collection. To any student who showed promise in architecture or in sculpture, he gave a pension so that he might have leisure for study, and among these promising young men was a fiery-tempered lad from Caprese, named Michelangelo Buonarrotti.

Lorenzo's enduring love in architecture was somewhat the style of ancient Rome, and he used his money and his influence to propagate that taste. During his reign, Florence came to be adorned with the most elegant residences and public buildings of Europe, an undertaking in which some of Florence's wealthiest families vied with Lorenzo in their patronage of architects and sculptors. The Strozzi family of bankers, for example, outdid him in commissioning Benedetto da Maiano to build a splendid residence in the Tuscan style, a building known as the Strozzi Palace. Lorenzo himself, in addition to completing the "family church" of San Lorenzo, and the abbey at Fiesole, commissioned Giuliano da San Gallo to design a monastery, and to build for him a magnificent villa at Poggio a Caiano. Moreover, he encouraged the Signory to modify and beautify its home, the famous Palazzo Vecchio.

In addition to these men, Lorenzo encouraged and employed such versatile architects and sculptors as Giuliano da Maiano (Benedetto's brother), Antonio Pollaiuolo, and his nephew Simone, Mino da Fiesole, Antonio Rossellino, and a dozen others, all of whom produced works, chiefly of sculpture, whose beauty survived the centuries. The master sculptor of the age, however, was Andrea di Michele Cione, known to posterity as Verrocchio (1435–1488)—True Eye. A disciple of the great Ghiberti, Verrocchio was a master of anatomy, and he possessed an unrivaled talent for imparting action, grace, and delicacy to his creations; and he thus brought to perfection the concepts of that other student of Ghiberti, Donatello. Perhaps his greatest work was his *David,* with its perfectly molded body bursting with youthful energy. On the face, there is the thoughtful expression which was the hallmark of all Verrocchio's works. The Florentine Signory was so delighted with the work that it placed it at the head of the main stairway of the Palazzo Vecchio. On a par with the *David* was Verrocchio's massive *Colleone,* an equestrian statue of the terrible *condottiere,* Bartolommeo Colleoni, which was commissioned by the Venetian Senate and which stands to this day in the Campo di San Zanipolo. Both epitomize Verrocchio's determination to combine anatomical accuracy with beauty and action, a determination which, in execution, made of him one of the great artists of Lorenzo's time.

Sculpture, however, at this time was gradually being replaced by painting as the favorite form of artistic expression in Florence. Unlike the sculptors, the painters had few—and those obscure—models from antiquity to copy. They were therefore quite literally forced by circumstances into originality, and, lacking exemplars from which to work, they took men and nature as their models. There is therefore, in their work, an immediately perceptible change of attitude toward life, a new conception of human existence. It was a conception which was engendered, of course —as so much else in Florence at that time—by the heightened interest in Greek thought; and that is the readiest explanation, and perhaps the best (so long as it is not accepted as completely adequate) for this new direction in painting. It is perhaps more accurate to say that it was Greek thought as the Florentines understood it—that is, Platonism, with its admixture of mystical Plotinism—and the impulse which it gave to a subtler and more complicated conception of life.

This influence is most conspicuous in the work of Sandro Botticelli (1447?–1510), whose spirit wandered about half in the world of pure reality, which he ill understood and depicted badly, and half in that of fantasy, which he knew better than anyone else. After serving his apprenticeship in the studio of Fra Filippo Lippi, Botticelli began to receive commissions from the Medici. For Lucrezia Tournabuoni, Lorenzo's mother, he painted *Judith;* and for Piero, Lorenzo's father, he painted the *Madonna of the Magnificat* and the *Adoration of the Magi.* Under Lorenzo's patronage, he moved into pagan mythology, and it was for Lorenzo that he painted his masterpiece, *The Birth of Venus,* in 1480, an incomparable achievement in design and composition. This was shortly followed by *Mars and Venus* and then by *Primavera* (Spring). Botticelli, Vasari reports, "painted plenty of naked women . . . in many houses," and then went on to conclude, in all self-righteousness, that there were "serious disorders in his life." The rise of the great reformer Savonarola, in Florence, again turned Botticelli's mind to Christian subjects, and he produced several memorable pictures in the aftermath of his reconversion: the *Madonna of the*

Pomegranate, the *Coronation of the Virgin,* the *Annunciation,* and, finally, the *Nativity,* which latter ranks almost on a par with the *Venus.* Then, there is silence. From the age of fifty-six until his death ten years later, Botticelli painted no more. Overcome by a species of religious depression, he was content to sit in poverty and inactivity while contemplating the ruin of the Christian world. On the *Nativity,* he describes the mentality which led him to that state: "This picture, I, Alessandro, painted at the end of the year 1500 . . . in the time of the fulfillment of the Eleventh Chapter of St. John, in the second plague of the Apocalypse, when the devil is loosed for three and one-half years. Later, he shall be chained, according to the Twelfth Chapter of John, and we shall see him trodden down, as in this painting."

Considerably less ethereal than Botticelli, and notably less pessimistic, was Benozzo Gozzoli (1420–1497), who lavished his skills upon nature, people, and events, rather than upon the depiction of allegories. He was a remarkable storyteller, as attested by his series of pictures on the life of St. Augustine in that saint's church in San Gimignano, and by his *Visit of the Magi* on the walls of the Medici Palace, in which events and people are depicted as though they had taken place and lived in fifteenth-century Italy. His Old Testament scenes, in the Campo Santo at Pisa, possess similar qualities, and some of them are regarded as among the greatest frescoes of the Renaissance.

Gozzoli was a student of Fra Angelico, and the influence of the master is perceptible in his work. But Angelico's major heir was not Gozzoli, but Domenico Ghirlandaio (1449–1494), whose style, like that of Gozzoli, was narrative, popular, and descriptive. At the age of thirty-one, he painted what is perhaps his greatest work, the series of frescoes in the refectory of Florence's Ognissanti: *St. Jerome,* the *Descent from the Cross, Madonna of Mercy,* and the *Last Supper.* For Pope Sixtus IV, he painted two frescoes for the Sistine Chapel, the success of which earned him numerous commissions in his native Florence, including his magnificent, and altogether Angelesque, *Adoration of the Shepherds.* To Angelico's ideal approach, Ghirlandaio added harmony of composition, faithful perspective, and realistic depiction, and, in so doing, he brought the technology of his art to its epitome in his century.

Of less fame, but no less skill, was Filippino Lippi, the illegitimate son of Fra Filippo Lippi, who was as gentle, affable, and courteous as his father was boisterous and hot-tempered. A pupil first of his father and then of Botticelli, he produced, while still a young man, his *Vision of St. Bernard* and the frescoes in the Carmelites' Brancacci Chapel. After a brief sojourn

An Age of Renewal

in Rome, he returned to Florence to paint his frescoes of St. Philip and St. John in the Strozzi Chapel. In the last years of his life, he was called to Prato to paint a Madonna, which was reputed to be his best work (until it was destroyed during the Second World War). The gentleness of Filippino's character and the excellence of his work, Vasari assures us, was sufficient "to eradicate the stain of his birth."

Such were the chief figures who comprised the circle of Lorenzo the Magnificent during the Golden Age of the Florentine Renaissance. Lorenzo himself was survived by many of them, for he died in the midst of all this activity that he loved so well. On his deathbed, his one concern was that the glory of Florence should continue, and he expressed to Pico della Mirandola and to Politian his regret that he must die before completing the collection of manuscripts that he had undertaken for their benefit and for the use of students. Then, on April 9, 1492, he expired, after having received the sacraments of the Church, at the age of forty-three. "He lived long enough for his glory," said King Ferdinand of Naples, "but he lived too short a time for Italy."

Lorenzo was by far the most remarkable prince of the *quattrocento,* or fifteenth century, but there were many others who patronized scholars and artists as generously as he, according to their means. Alfonso of Aragon, who had temporarily united the Two Sicilies, was wholly devoted to the humanities, and it was his custom to listen to the works of Virgil as he sat at dinner, and to take volumes of Livy with him on his military campaigns. But his dual kingdom had little or no part in the Renaissance, for, poverty-stricken and lawless, it responded only feebly to the efforts of individuals who, here and there, attempted to emulate the great Florentines. In the north of the peninsula, however, it seemed that all the world was mad for art, and its princes led the fashion. Federigo da Montefeltro, Duke of Urbino (1422–1482), was the foremost scholar among the warrior-princes of his time, and the foremost soldier among the scholars. He collected a great library (now housed in the Vatican), and he built a palace which was the wonder and the envy of all Italy. Taking the Medici as his model, he employed and supported artists and scholars with great liberality. Federigo's neighbor, Alessandro Sforza, the tyrant of Pesaro, was likewise a soldier by profession, but he passed the time between wars in collecting books. Duke Ercole d'Este of Ferrara was likewise a patron of art and of artists, and, combining taste with the means to indulge that taste, he decorated his capital and his palaces with the masterpieces of his own time as well as of antiquity. Milan herself was eclipsed by Ferrara and Urbino, her less powerful neighbors, for Francesco Sforza was busy making good his defective title to the duchy and he had little time for art or scholarship. But even he kept humanists at his court, and continued to work on the Certosa (the Carthusian monastery) of Pavia.

Not only princes, but private citizens as well, were lovers and patrons of art. In almost every city of the north—excepting only in Piedmont—there was some artist of whom the city was inordinately proud. Nonetheless, so long as Lorenzo the Magnificent lived, Florence continued to be the most outstanding of the cities of Italy, and the most envied, as she had been for generations before him. Upon his death, however, intellectual and artistic primacy was to pass from Florence to Rome. By chance, that superiority seemed to follow the fortunes of the Medici. Under Cosimo, Piero, and Lorenzo de' Medici, the Renaissance seemed to have made Florence its home. In the next generation, it was to find its fullest expression in Rome; but even there it took its name, the Age of Leo, from another Medici, Lorenzo's son. It was not primarily to Pope Leo X, however, but to his immediate predecessors, that the City was indebted for that pre-eminence. At the summons of the papacy, men of genius went to Rome from all Italy, but chiefly from Florence. A distinguished Tuscan —almost, but not quite, a Florentine—who went from Florence to Rome in this way serves as the personification of this migration. Tommaso Parentucelli was born in a small town near Lucca, and was educated at Florence and Bologna. He entered the Church at an early age, and, returning to Florence, he soon became a member of the circle of humanists who surrounded Cosimo de' Medici. He was an outstanding student, and he enjoyed so high a reputation for learning that it was to him that Cosimo came for advice concerning the proper volumes for the library at Fiesole. Tommaso's character, talents, and accomplishments were recognized at Rome as well as in Florence, and he quickly became a bishop, a cardinal, and finally pope, under the name of Nicholas V, in 1447.

To Rome, Pope Nicholas brought the characteristics of the Renaissance. He fostered learning, encouraged art, and generally worked to raise the intellectual caliber of ecclesiastics and of the turbulent Romans—not only because of his own interest in intellectual subjects, but also because he thought that by this means he might overcome that rumbling spirit of reform which was already beginning to make trouble in Germany and Bohemia. It was his dream to make of the papacy a center of learning and culture that should be the universally acknowledged and admired head of Christendom. To that end, he gathered together scholars from every field, collected together books and founded the Vatican Library. He rebuilt or restored numerous churches and public buildings, began construction of the Vatican Palace, and planned a new church in place of the old Basilica of St. Peter's, which he intended to be the finest temple of Christendom. He summoned to Rome architects, painters, goldsmiths, artists, and artisans of all sorts. With him began that brilliant period of the papacy as a secular power devoted to art and culture, a period which was shortly to culminate in the Age of Leo X.

3. The Barbarian Invasions (1494–1537)

At the time when the Renaissance was making its way from its home in Florence to its culmination in Rome, a complete change was being prepared in the political condition of Italy. It is a change that can only be compared to that effected by the barbarian invasions of a thousand years before. It was, in fact, a period of fresh invasions by *barbari,* or barbarians, as the Italians of the period—not without some justification—called foreigners. The fatal year of 1494 marked the first invasion of the French. From that time onward, there was a series of invasions by the French, the Austrians, and the Spaniards, until finally Italy was parceled out according to the whims of the invaders. Before that time, Italy was in an unusually peaceful and prosperous condition. The Florentine historian Francesco Guicciardini (1483–1540) thus recalls the time of his youth: "Since the fall of the Roman Empire, Italy had never known such great prosperity, nor had she experienced so desirable a condition as in the year 1490 and the years just before and after. The country had been brought to profound peace and tranquillity, agriculture had spread over the roughest and most sterile hills as well as over the most fertile plains, and Italy, then subject to no master but herself, abounded in men, merchandise, and wealth. She was embellished to the utmost by the munificence of many princes, by the splendor of many noble and beautiful cities, by the center and majesty of religion. She was rich in men most adept at public affairs, and in intellect she was most noble for all kinds of knowledge. She was industrious and excellent in every art. And, according to the standard of those days, she was not without military glory as well."

In the happy years described by Guicciardini, and in the decades that preceded them, Italian politics was a domestic game played between the five major powers—the papacy, Naples, Florence, Venice, and Milan—who treated one another's border cities as stakes. They formed leagues and counterleagues, fought innumerable petty wars, engaged in countless bloodless skirmishes, rattled their swords and blew their trumpets, and

ITALY IN THE 15TH AND 16TH CENTURIES

An Age of Renewal

generally made a good deal of commotion. But they were all Italians, and they all knew the rules of the game—however irregular and confused those rules might appear to an outsider. In 1494, there came a change. History seemed turned back a thousand years. The French poured over the Alps from the northwest. The forces of the imperial House of Hapsburg came from the northeast. And from the south, from their province of Sicily, came the Spaniards.

All Italy was to suffer from one or another of these oppressors. And some, like Milan, were to be subjected to more than one. In that city, on the death of Francesco Sforza in 1466, Galeazzo Maria Sforza, his son, had succeeded to the ducal throne. Galeazzo Maria was a fairly typical Italian ruler of the time, brilliant in display, liberal in giving, harsh in taxing, interested in art and scholarship, subtle and cruel in government, and dissolute in his private life. Fearful stories are told of his brutality, and he was, almost inevitably, assassinated in 1476. The story goes that a schoolmaster of Milan burst out one day in the classroom with the words, "Will none of my pupils rise up, like Brutus and Cassius, to free his country from this vile yoke, and thereby merit eternal renown?" Three of his students, filled to overflowing with Plutarch and stimulated by private wrongs, were moved to follow the classical example, and they succeeded in murdering Galeazzo Maria in a church. All three, of course, were caught and put to death. The last one to die—from being skewered on iron hooks and then cut to pieces alive—stated before his death: "I know that for my wrongdoings I have deserved these tortures, and more besides if my flesh could endure them. But as for the noble act for which I die, that is the comfort of my soul. Instead of repenting it, were I to live my life ten times over again, and ten times to perish in these tortures, still would I consecrate all my life's blood, and all my strength, to that noble purpose."

The murder, however, for all its drama, had little effect. In politics, as in the arts, the classical impulse affected only details. Lodovico Sforza, nicknamed *Il Moro* ("the Moor"), Galeazzo Maria's brother, seized power and supplanted the lawful heir, his nephew, in every respect except in the title of duke. Il Moro was a man as brilliant as he was devoid of moral sense, and for a time he basked in the full sunshine of the opening High Renaissance, patronizing Bramante and cultivating Leonardo da Vinci. But Lodovico's political talents were not equal to his intellectual gifts, and he did not understand the larger forces of European politics.

At the time, Milan was at odds with Naples, and Lodovico Sforza thought to introduce a new piece, in the form of a foreign power, into the game of Italian politics, in order to overawe the Neapolitans. He therefore invited the King of France, Charles VIII, who represented the claim of the House of Anjou to the crown of Naples, to come into Italy and take what was rightfully his. Other Italian princes, with no more knowledge than Lodovico of European politics, joined their names to his in the invitation. Charles VIII, an unattractive man of limited intelligence, but strong in a compact and vigorous kingdom, had visions of playing the part of a new Charlemagne; and he therefore accepted the invitation with alacrity, got together an impressive army, and crossed the Alps in 1494. He received the obeisance of Lodovico, and then swept triumphantly down through the peninsula. No resistance was attempted. Florence made a treaty with him, as did the pope, and Naples watched her king run away and the French march in with mingled indifference and delight. King Charles's brilliant success, however, was a mere blaze of straw. The powers of Europe took alarm at an exclusively French appropriation of the wealth of Italy. While Charles was reveling in Naples, a league was formed in which Venice, the papacy, and Lodovico Sforza joined. Charles, his army decimated by disease, was no match for this combine, and he fled northward as fast as he could, barely escaping across the Alps. This episode, short-lived as it was, was full of portent for Italy. The barbarians had once more broken through the barrier that nature had set up to protect Italy, and they had sampled the delights that the peninsula had to offer. The second period of the barbarian invasions had begun.

Milan herself was to pay a heavy price for the treachery of Il Moro. The succeeding King of France, Louis XII, was a grandson of Gian Galeazzo Visconti's eldest daughter, and, as such, had at least as good a title to the duchy as did Lodovico. The desire for revenge lent strength to Louis' claim, and, in a few years (1499), the French again crossed the Alps into the plains of Lombardy, captured Milan, took Lodovico prisoner, and locked him up in a French dungeon for the remainder of his life. Thereafter, the sovereignty of Milan was tossed back and forth among the powers of Europe, during the struggle for domination between Francis I of France and the Hapsburg emperor, Charles V. The Empire upheld the cause of the Sforza heirs and re-established them on the Milanese throne. Then, France won the Battle of Marignano (1515) and once again claimed Milan; but the Emperor conquered the French decisively at the Battle of Pavia (1525), and once again the Sforza dynasty ruled Milan. The male line of the family, however, became extinct in 1535, and the Duchy of Milan, though it continued to be a nominal fief of the Empire, was annexed by Charles V to the crown of Spain (Charles was King of Spain as well as Holy Roman Emperor). It thus passed, as a part of the Spanish inheritance, to a line of Spanish kings, and for the next three hundred years it was to be ruled by a succession of Spanish viceroys.

Florence fared somewhat better than Milan, for, although she too was fated to lose her liberty, she did so not without glory. And if she was to be ruled by a despot, at least that despot was to be one of her own. Florence entered upon her destined road with the death of Lorenzo the Magnificent in 1492. The politic statesman, whose sagacity had contributed so much to the pleasant state of Italy prior to the French invasion, was more responsible for Florence's primacy in Italy than even the Florentines suspected; for, with his death, the great period of Florentine superiority ended. The city continued to pour forth genius, it is true; but that genius was no longer gathered together at home in the Medici circle, and so it chose to emigrate to honor in other places. Nonetheless, Florence still challenges the admiration of posterity. The ancient citadel of republicanism once more asserted its pre-eminence in a burst of moral enthusiasm. Nowhere else in Italy throughout the Renaissance was such a spectacle seen, and though the leader of it, Girolamo Savonarola, (1452–1498) was a native of Ferrara, yet it was in Florence and among the Florentines, that he kindled enthusiasm and acted out his meteoric career.

Savonarola was the reincarnation of a Hebrew prophet, a veritable Habakkuk of Florence, passionately sure of the government of God, passionately convinced that the wickedness of Italy must bring its own punishment and purification, and passionately certain that God had chosen him to preach repentance to the profligate Italians. Shortly before Lorenzo's death, Savonarola rose to eminence as a preacher. He spoke of righteousness, and of judgment to come unless Italy mended her ways. He foretold spiritual evils and, more frightening still, political punishments, and he proclaimed that God would stretch forth his hand and send an avenger to punish Italy. The prophecies were so definite, and they fitted the invasion of Charles VIII so accurately, that Savonarola was hailed as a prophet. In the excitement of the French invasion, Lorenzo's heirs were driven out of the city, the former republican constitution was reestablished, and Savonarola was raised, by a burst of popular enthusiasm and devotion, practically to the position of ruling and guiding the city. The extent of Savonarola's influence becomes clear through the diary of a contemporary Florentine, an ordinary citizen named Luca Landucci, who was an apothecary:

> December 14, 1494. On this day, Fra Girolamo greatly urged in the pulpit that Florence should adopt a good form of government. He has been preach-

ing in Santa Maria del Fiore [the cathedral] every day; and this day, Sunday, he preached, and he did not want women as his audience, but men; and he especially wanted the officers of the city, and no one stayed in the Palace [the Palazzo Vecchio, the City Hall] except the Gonfaloniere and one other. All the officials of Florence were there, and he preached about matters of state, that we ought to love and fear God and love the common good, and that no man henceforth should wish to hold his head high or wish himself great. He always inclined to the side of the people, and insisted that no blood should be shed, but that punishment should be carried out in some other way. And he preached like this every day. . . .

April 1495. Today Fra Girolamo preached and said that the Virgin Mary had revealed to him how the city of Florence would become more wealthy, more glorious, and more powerful than she had ever been, but not until she had suffered many troubles. And he spoke all of this as though he were a prophet, and most of the people believed him; particularly the better sort of people, who had no political or partisan passions. . . .

June 17, 1495. Fra Girolamo is today held in such high esteem and devotion in Florence that there are many men and women who would obey him promptly if he should say, "Walk into the fire." Many believe that he is a prophet; and he himself has said that he is one. . . .

February 16, 1496. The Carnival. Fra Girolamo preached a few days ago that the children, instead of foolish pranks, throwing stones, etc., should collect alms and distribute them to the worthy poor; and, thanks to divine grace, such a change came about that, instead of foolishness, the children collected alms for days beforehand, and today six thousand or more of them, carrying olive branches and singing hymns, marched to the Duomo where they offered up what they had collected, so that good and sensible men wept from tenderness and said, "Truly this new change is the work of God." . . . I have written this because it is a fact, and I saw it, and I felt the greatest happiness to have my own children among those blessed innocent hands. . . .

August 15, 1496. Fra Girolamo preached in Santa Maria del Fiore, and there was so much holiness in the church, and it was so sweet to hear the children sing . . . that, in truth, it seemed that the church was full of angels.

The friar's political enemies, however, were strong and influential, and it was not difficult to convince the reigning pope, that notable Borgia, Alexander VI, that a monk who preached poverty, humility, and peace was a menace to orthodoxy. Alexander therefore excommunicated Savonarola, and ordered the Signory of Florence to forbid him to preach. There was much excitement over this action, and feeling ran to a passionate height among the Florentines. In the midst of this, one of Savonarola's disciples, a Dominican friar, challenged one of his master's enemies, a Franciscan friar, to an ordeal by fire. Let them both walk through the flames, the

Dominican said, and God would spare him who had justice and right on his side. The Franciscan accepted, and, on the day appointed for the test, all Florence flocked to the piazza. The Dominican and his adversary were there, and the fires were lighted. But nothing was done. One delay followed another. There was disagreement as to conditions, as to whether the two participants should carry crucifixes, or the Eucharist, or both, or neither. When it became clear that there would be no ordeal, and therefore no proof of God's favor for one side or the other, the populace, now enraged, turned on Savonarola. They had believed him a prophet, and they had expected to see a judgment of God. He lost his power and his influence as quickly as he had gained them, and he retired to his convent friendless except for his faithful fellow monks. Pope Alexander, however, was not to be satisfied by Savonarola's downfall. Who knew, he reasoned, when the fickle Florentines might raise him up again, mightier than before? And so the pope demanded that the friar be tried by the Signory. Savonarola was indeed tried, and subjected to the torture, during the course of which a confession was extorted from him. Our apothecary recorded the fact, and his own reaction, which was the reaction of Florence as a whole:

> April 19, 1498. The confession of Fra Girolamo was read before the Council in the Great Hall, which he had written down in his own hand—he whom we held to be a prophet—and he confessed that he was not a prophet, and had not received from God the things he preached; and he confessed to many things in the course of his preaching which were the opposite of what he had given us to understand. I was there to hear the confession read; and I stood astonished and stupefied. My soul was in pain to see such an edifice tumble to the ground because it rested on a lie. I had expected Florence to become the new Jerusalem, from which should proceed laws, glory, and the example of a good life, and I had expected to behold the restoration of the Church, the conversion of the infidels, and the comfort of good men. And now, I behold the opposite; and I can do no other than accept it. In thy will, O God, stand all things!

As a result of his confession, Savonarola was condemned to death for heresy. He was hanged, his body burned, and his ashes thrown into the Arno. Florence quickly reverted to her old ways, and so ended the single moral effort to which the Renaissance gave birth.

After the reformer's death, the republican government which he had condoned, and for a time controlled, survived for a few days; but the Medicean party forced its way back into power in 1512, and Lorenzo's sons grasped the reins of power. Shortly afterward, the second of these sons,

Giovanni (1475–1521), following the path set by the art and humanism of Florence, went to Rome, where he assumed the papal tiara under the name of Leo X. As pope, he was in a position to strengthen his family in Florence and to consolidate their power. Republicanism flared up once more, briefly, in 1527, but it was powerless before the hostile spirit of the times. By then, another Medici, Clement VII, was on the throne of the Apostle, and the Emperor Charles V was induced, for reasons of policy, to suppress what he called "the rebellion of the Florentines." Florence resisted gallantly; Michelangelo strengthened her walls, and the courage of the defenders threw the last light of glory over the city. But it was all in vain. A great-grandson of Lorenzo, Alessandro de' Medici, was placed into power by Charles V, and given one of the emperor's daughters as his wife. He was succeeded by a distant cousin, Cosimo (1537), who was honored by the pope with the title of Grand Duke of Tuscany. Thus, Florentine liberty and freedom were extinguished, and the Medici were finally established as princes of the city in name as well as in fact.

In the midst of these misfortunes, Venice, to the northeast, still led a brilliant career, like a famous soldier who has received a mortal wound and does not know it but instinctively fights more fiercely than before. Her fatal wound was the conquest of Constantinople by the Turks in 1453. At first, the only obvious evil effect was war. Venice, almost inadvertently, stepped into the place of fallen Byzantium and became "the bulwark of the West" against the forces of Islam. She waged war after war with the Turks, and thus maintained her reputation for valor and determination. But the Turks were too strong for her, and, little by little, the city was stripped of her empire of coastland and islands. But an even worse blow was the cutting off of the great trade route with the East upon which Venice depended for her wealth and her strength. The merchants of Europe then discovered a new road to Asia, by rounding the Cape of Good Hope; and commerce was thus able to continue, and to avoid the Turks. But it also abandoned the Mediterranean, the great center and source of civilization, and left Italy's maritime cities, and Venice particularly, stranded, as it were, on the shores of a forsaken lake.

Venice's doom, however, was still hidden in the obscurity of the future, and the city appeared to be at the height of her prosperity. A French ambassador, Philippe de Commines, at this critical epoch, called her "the most triumphant city I have ever seen." And, indeed, the Venetians were a people apart. They had never suffered from foreign invasion or from domestic revolt. They lived in isolation from the rest of Italy, maintained their own customs and usages, and enjoyed, in proud security, a joyous

An Age of Renewal

and opulent life. Venice was undoubtedly the richest, the most comfortable, and the most efficiently governed city in the world. In military strength, she was commonly recognized as the first power of Italy, with the papacy, Naples, and Milan about equal in second place. Thus encouraged, Venice had no thought of decay or decadence, and she continued her greedy career of annexation on the mainland with an arrogance worthy of ancient Rome. She seized part of the Romagna, and angered the popes who thought that they had a better title to this land. She irritated the Emperor Maximilian—father of Charles V—by her pretensions to Verona; and, to the west, she came into dangerous competition with the French invaders of Lombardy. These enemies, taking their cue from the piratical seizure of Naples by the French and Spanish (1500–1501), conspired to partition the territory of Venice, and invited all the powers of Europe to join them in taking a share of the booty. This coalition, called the League of Cambrai, first stripped Venice of all her territory on the Italian mainland, and then threatened the city herself (1508). The allies, however, soon fell out among themselves; and Venice, by carefully biding her time, soon managed to recover most of what she had lost. So, although the barbarians had brought the city to her knees for a short time, Venice weathered the storms better than had Milan or Florence, and she continued to maintain her independence, albeit precariously, for another three centuries to come.

The least fortunate of the Italian powers was, as usual, the Kingdom of the Two Sicilies. It will be recalled that Sicily and the Kingdom of Naples had been united under King Alfonso. On Alfonso's death in 1458, however, the two parts split apart again. Sicily, as part of the Kingdom of Aragon, devolved on a legitimate brother of Alfonso's, whereas Naples, claimed as a conquest, was bequeathed to a bastard son, Ferdinand, aptly called "the Cruel." The two kingdoms followed their separate paths for nearly half a century, until Sicily came, by inheritance, into the hands of Ferdinand of Aragon, the widowed husband of that Isabelle of Castile who had been the patroness of Christopher Columbus. The crafty, and eminently successful, Ferdinand was not satisfied with Castile, Granada, Sicily, and vast domains in the New World, but coveted also the Kingdom of Naples. He therefore allied himself with Louis XII of France, who now represented the traditional Anjou claim, and the two invaded the kingdom and divided it between them (1500–1501). The two despoilers soon quarreled over the booty, and their armies fought the matter out in southern Italy. The Spaniards were victorious, and Ferdinand got what he was after. The Kingdom of Naples was annexed outright to the crown of Spain. In this way, the Kingdom of the Two Sicilies was reunited under the Spanish king, and on Ferdinand's death, in 1516 it passed to his grandson, the Emperor Charles V. For the next two centuries, the unhappy Neapolitans and Sicilians were to remain subjects of the King of Spain.

While the powers of Italy were falling to the north and south of Rome, the papacy, not unexpectedly, found itself in an exceedingly difficult situation. Its problems, however, were quite different from those of the other Italian states, for it was not merely one of the five principal political divisions of the peninsula, but a supranational force which enjoyed, or at least claimed, the allegiance of all of Europe. Its principal problem was to adapt an ecclesiastical system, matured in the Middle Ages, to new political situations, to the new knowledge and the new thought of the Renaissance; in short, its task was to adapt itself to a new world. In the medieval period and in its struggle with the Empire, the papacy's course, however arduous, had been plain enough: to abase the emperors. During its captivity at Avignon, its duty to return to Rome—though individual popes might have been blind, or indifferent, to that duty—had been to return to Rome. During the Great Schism, the one end to be aimed at was union. But now, everything had changed, everything was new; and a new policy had to be devised.

There were three matters which required particular consideration: the demand for reform which came from across the Alps; the great intellectual awakening of the Renaissance; and the ambitions of the other powers. In the face of these problems, the papacy adopted a twofold solution: to establish a strong pontifical principality, and to use the new intellectual forces as a motive power to keep itself at the head of Christendom. By a strong political principality, the papacy hoped to secure itself against the ambitions of the other states, Italian and otherwise. By harnessing the new intellectual forces, it hoped to range them on its side, and so to choke off, or at least to outshout, the trans-Alpine cry for reform. This plan was not, of course, worked out in detail from the beginning; rather, it was a course which the papacy gradually adopted, partly on the basis of theory and partly under the stress of circumstances.

It will be recalled that the Council of Constance had, in 1417, healed the Great Schism, and that Pope Martin V (1417–1435) had been enthroned as sole and undoubted pope. Martin's pontificate marks the end of the old Republican commune which had made so much trouble for popes and emperors in days past; and it therefore marks also the first definite stage in the transformation of the papacy into a local secular power. Rome, although she did not deny herself an occasional uprising or rebellion in memory, as it were, of the good old days, now settled down as a papal City.

It was in these circumstances, as has been noted, that Pope Nicholas V, hoped to maintain the papacy at the head of Christendom by means of the new intellectual forces unleashed by the Renaissance. Such a conception was purely Italian, and it showed plainly enough that the papacy had ceased to represent Christianity as a whole, had ceased to be the head of a truly universal Church, and had become a purely Italian institution. But while Nicholas and his successors were dreaming of culture and of becoming Italian princes, the pious Christians across the Alps, comparatively indifferent to the intellectual excitement of the Renaissance, were thinking instead of sin and of the remedies for sin. The papal curia, for all its experience and cleverness, did not foresee that, to subordinate the old conception of the papacy as the head of the religious and ecclesiastical organization of Europe to the new conception of it as an Italian principality, would surely alienate the Teutonic peoples of Europe; and it did not foresee that the Renaissance, with its spirit of free examination, free criticism, and its encouragement of the free play of human reason, must inevitably prepare the way for a theological crisis within the Church. The curia did, however, perceive the opposite difficulties—difficulties to which later generations, from the misty distance of centuries, are generally blind: that, unless the papacy did establish itself as a temporal power, it might well be reduced to another Babylonian Captivity by a Neapolitan or French king, by a Duke of Milan or a Holy Roman Emperor, or even by some ambitious *condottiere*. And it perceived clearly that other difficulty as well, that if the papacy turned against the intellectual movement, or even was indifferent to it, then the intellectual movement would, in self-defense, turn against the papacy.

The popes did indeed seek to revive the old role of the papacy in one respect. They tried to arouse the sentiment of Christendom against the Turks, and to lead a crusade against them; but the time for such a course had long passed. The kings and princes of Europe were busy with their own affairs, and they would not budge from their kingdoms and principalities; and so the papacy had to abandon the plan. Discouraged by this failure once more to rally Europe round its standard, it naturally turned to the new theory of a papal kingdom, and it vigorously strove to put the theory into practice. The three popes who accomplished this task were Francesco della Rovere (Sixtus IV, 1471–1484), Rodrigo Borgia (Alexander VI, 1493–1503), and Giuliano della Rovere (Julius II, 1503–1513).

Francesco della Rovere was the son of a peasant. Educated by the Franciscan friars, he won distinction as a theologian, philosopher, and diplomat, and he was chosen as general of the Franciscan order. As pope, it was he who embarked on the last, futile attempt to rouse a crusade, and it was he who thereafter openly abdicated the role of universal pontiff and became an Italian prince. Energetic and masterful in all that he did, he set to work to consolidate the loose and unruly papal territories into a compact and obedient state. It was not an easy task, and one of the chief obstacles in Sixtus' way was the lack of trustworthy men. Obviously, there was little advantage in gathering together an army or capturing a city if the papal general or governor found his own interests in opposition to those of the papacy. Loyalty was held in little esteem by Italians of the Renaissance. Sixtus met the difficulty by employing his nephews as his chief assistants. This expedient was merely the revival of the ancient and almost time-honored custom of papal nepotism, and marked no departure in policy. But it happened that these nephews happened to be young men of extraordinary greed, ferocity, and dissipation, and they brought the system into particular notoriety. To one of these nephews, Sixtus gave a cardinal's hat, four bishoprics, an abbey, a patriarchate, and, most important of all, free access to the papal treasury. When this young man died of dissipation, the rank of favorite papal nephew descended to his brother. For him, the pope procured a wife from the ducal house of Sforza, and he began to carve out a dukedom for him in the Romagna, with the intention of adding slices cut from neighboring states. The nephew, however, was arrogant, ignorant, and brutal, and, in the natural course of Italian politics, he was murdered. This more or less put an end to Sixtus' nepotic tendencies, for there were no more nephews; but the policy had served its purpose. The pope had made himself feared in Italy, and he had advanced the project of a papal kingdom to a point where his successors would be able to take it up and complete it. Sixtus also pursued Nicholas' plan to make Rome the first city of the world in art and in magnificence. He brought together artists, architects, and scholars, and he patronized art and literature. But this aspect of the plan to maintain the papacy at the head of Christian Europe belongs rather to the story of the High Renaissance, and will be examined there.

The next pope, Innocent VIII (1484–1493), was undistinguished except by his willingness to recognize publicly his illegitimate children, and by what then appeared to be a whimsical desire to preserve the peace of Italy. His successor, however, was the notorious Rodrigo Borgia, Pope Alexander VI. It was during Pope Alexander's pontificate that the French invasion of 1494 took place. The introduction into Italian politics of this new and terrible element frightened the pope as well as the other rulers of Italy, for he knew that the papal principality would never be sufficiently strong to resist single-handed such an army as that of the French king. He tried, therefore, to form a union of the Italian powers for common defense, but his policy met with little success—especially since he himself, seeing advantages to be gained from a French alliance, completely reversed himself and signed a separate treaty with Charles VIII (1499). He did no more than any other Italian prince of the time would have done—indeed, Florence did precisely the same thing—but he must bear a share of the responsibility for the fate of Italy. It was a deliberate sacrifice of Italian interests to his own immediate ambitions. The pope wished to establish a pontifical domain, and he acted in the manner which he thought would be most likely to bring about success.

Alexander VI also followed the example of Pope Sixtus IV in raising his family to power, partly from affection and partly in order to strengthen the papacy. His task was to reduce the papal vassals in the Pontifical States to obedience, and to create a strong central government. The instruments he employed were his children—his daughter, Lucrezia, who became a marriage pawn in the market place of Italy, and who finally ended up as the Duchess of Ferrara; and particularly his son, the famous Caesare Borgia. Caesare Borgia has won a great reputation in history, largely owing to Machiavelli's admiration for him. He was an athletic man, handsome, taciturn, quick, cunning, and cruel. He began his career in the Church, but, at the time of his father's reconciliation with France, he found it expedient to give up his cardinal's hat, and he was created Duke of Valentinois by the French king. Caesare made an excellent instrument for rooting out the disobedient vassals of the Pontifical State. They were crafty, greedy, and untrustworthy; but he was craftier, greedier, and more untrustworthy than they. He therefore dispossessed them with ruthless vigor, and established himself in their places. His energy and success were extraordinary, and he was generally regarded throughout Italy as a very devil and as an object of awe and dread. None knew how far his ambitions might reach, or how far the papacy might be able to push him. The direct military power of the Pontifical State was not very great, and it could readily be measured; but the indirect power of the papacy was indefinite, and therefore alarming. Nonetheless, Caesare's principality, which rested wholly upon the papacy—that is, upon the position of his father, the pope—fell to pieces when Alexander VI died; and thereafter Caesare was reduced to the sale of his military genius as a paid commander in the armies of Europe.

The attitude of Pope Alexander VI toward the arts, like that of Pope

Sixtus, belongs to the history of the Renaissance. But, in respect to them as well as to the Pontifical State, he followed the dual policy established by Sixtus. That policy undoubtedly had its advantages; but it also had its disadvantages, and these appear more conspicuously in the reign of Alexander VI than in any other. The establishment of papal dominion encouraged, if it did not necessitate, nepotism; and nepotism involved prodigality and dissipation. The popes used their families to strengthen their position; and the upstart families, giddy with sudden wealth and power, misbehaved scandalously. The nephews of Sixtus rendered some service to the papacy, but they caused great scandal, particularly across the Alps. Caesare Borgia rendered greater service, and he caused even greater scandal. The other branch of the twofold policy, by a different path, led to the same result. Patronage of arts and letters involved great expense and encouraged luxurious tastes; luxury led to idleness, and idleness, at least in the case of the Romans, to vice. The atmosphere of the City had never been favorable to spiritual life, and now, surcharged with the classical spirit of the Renaissance as well as with the secular ambitions of the papacy, religious attitudes were practically extinguished.

For centuries, the Roman curia had been the butt of satire. The minnesingers of Germany and the troubadours of Provence had all paused in their amorous ditties to compose bitter gibes against the greed and luxury of the great Roman prelates. Dante had not hesitated to place priest, prelate, and pope in hell. Petrarch had written scathing verses. It had become axiomatic throughout Europe that *Curia Romana non quaerit ovem sine lana*—"the Roman curia is not interested in sheep who have no wool." One of the best tales of the *Decameron* turns on the conversion of a Jew who goes to Rome, sees the conduct of the pope and of the cardinals, and becomes a Catholic because he is convinced that only a truly divine Church can survive under such a burden of sin. In the time of Pope Alexander VI, the Curia outdid itself, and Alexander led the way. He openly acknowledged his children and just as openly alienated the possessions of the Church in their favor. He bestowed a cardinal's hat on Alexander Farnese in return for the love, or at least for the acquiescence in his lust, of the beauteous Giulia Farnese, the new cardinal's sister. He allowed, and attended, ballets, banquets, and entertainments of a scandalous nature in the palace of the Vatican. And he encouraged his sons and his cardinals, not only by his example but by his words, in a dissolute way of life. His weaknesses, however, were not limited to mere vices. The odor of crimes, so shocking that they scandalized even the blasé Romans, filled the air. The pope's eldest son, the Duke of Gandia, was murdered, and so was his son-in-law, one of the husbands of his daughter, Lucrezia. Cardinals were observed to die with increasing frequency and always under mysterious circumstances; and their property, by some equally mystifying canonical process, reverted to the Holy Father. The common voice, whispering low in Rome and loudly elsewhere, ascribed most of these murders to Caesare Borgia, and in some cases the name of Alexander himself did not escape implication. The pope himself seemed, on occasion, to share the common opinion of Caesare. "Caesare," he once said in paternal indulgence, "is a good-natured man; he cannot, however, forgive offenses." Lucrezia, too, became the object of the grossest slanders. No doubt common gossip then, as always, raised a great tree of falsehood from a mustard seed of truth; but, from the standpoint of historical causality, the most important consideration is not whether such charges were true, but that they were accepted everywhere as true. North of the Alps, the simple-souled Germans shuddered at the doings of the diabolical Romans. But even the Romans were surprisingly fastidious when it came to the Borgia pope. When Alexander died—inevitably, it was rumored that he had been poisoned, and, just as inevitably, some even ascribed the deed to Caesare—no man could be found who would touch the body of the deceased pope. The cadaver was dragged by a rope fastened to its foot from the bed to the grave, and there tumbled in. No one in Christendom doubted for a moment that Pope Alexander VI had gone to join his master in hell.

Pope Alexander managed, during his reign, to violate every rule of domestic morality. His successor, Pope Julius II (1503–1513), was a man whose character and behavior as pope were as foreign to the priesthood as Alexander's had been; but his behavior seems, at least to later generations, less repulsive than that of his predecessor. Julius, a nephew of Sixtus IV, was above all not a pontiff, but a fiery soldier, a high-aspiring prince of the Renaissance, a man of great military and administrative qualities, a *magnifico* in every sense of that term. Had he been Duke of Milan or King of Naples, he would have presented a noble figure; but a Vicar of Christ, armed and armored from head to foot, entering a conquered city astride a magnificent charger through a breach in the walls created by the papal cannon, was a sight for which even Renaissance Italy was not ready. More important, it was as clear a defiance of the evangelical spirit of the German reformers as had been the private profligacy of the Borgia pope.

Pope Julius II pursued the policies of the papacy with greater zeal, and with more marked success, than any of his immediate predecessors. His irrepressible energy completed the work, begun by his uncle Sixtus IV, of transforming the incohesive States of the Church into a compact and obedient principality. He is the real founder of what was to be the absolute Papal State, the first real pope-king. He achieved as much success in the other branch of papal policy, and he reveled in the kindred spirit of the High Renaissance. He raised up Rome to the place of the capital city of the world; and, if the world had asked the papacy for art rather than for religion, it would have had nothing of which to complain. But while Pope Julius was thinking of crowns and principalities and art, Germany was thinking of sin, and of simony and taxation, and the Germans were becoming conscious of an extreme national antipathy to Italian rule. When a young German monk named Martin Luther went on a visit to Rome, instead of taking pleasure in the architecture and the painting and the sculpture that adorned the city, he was horrified at the pagan spirit of the Church and of the clergy.

Despite these failings, Pope Julius, at his death, was no doubt entitled to a sense of accomplishment. He left to the Church a small kingdom in the middle of Italy, and he had made Rome the center of Europe's artistic and intellectual life. It was not to be until the days of Julius' successors that the failure of that policy was to appear. By a kind of poetic justice, the utter inability of art to satisfy the demand for reform, for spiritual purity, for religion, was proved during the pontificates of the two Medici popes, Leo X and Clement VII. The Medici patronized and canonized the arts, first at Florence and then at Rome; and the arts repaid the Medici with enjoyment and renown. But the Medici had done nothing, either at Florence or at Rome, for the spirit of reform; on the contrary, they had helped to crush Savonarola. And therefore the spirit of reform turned on them. Germany hoisted the standard of schism during the pontificate of Pope Leo, and an army of Germans sacked Rome during that of Pope Clement.

Leo X was a good-natured, fat, clever, and cultivated man, who had no great virtues and no great vices. "Since God has seen fit to give us the papacy, let us enjoy it." Such is the sentiment, which legend, if not his own convictions, has put into Leo's mouth. It characterizes his reign admirably. Bred as he was in the intellectual circle of his father, Lorenzo the Magnificent, and a member in good standing of the luxurious society of Rome, Pope Leo shared the tastes of both groups. He was a connoisseur of art, and he derived great pleasure from artistic works. He derived equal enjoyment from good company, good cooking, and good hunting. His political conduct was not of much consequence—or of much interest, even to himself—for matters had gone too far for the policies of a single Italian prince to be of real importance to Europe as a whole. In the perennial struggle for supremacy between the Emperor Charles V and King Francis I of France, the pope generally tried to hold a balance of power, and he bargained with both sides; but, as the Emperor, in possession of both Milan and Naples, was the stronger and the closer neighbor, the papacy usually found its advantage on that side. As to the ecclesiastical unity of Christendom, there was practically nothing that Leo could do effectively. The causes which split the Teutonic world from the Latin were already matured. It was too late to stop the Reformation. Luther himself might indeed have been dealt with more shrewdly, but the forces (political as well as spiritual) which supported him could not, by Leo's time, have been kept in check by any means. Leo excommunicated Luther (1520), and the Imperial Diet at Worms, under the Emperor Charles, condemned him and his doctrine. But the unity of the Church was already doomed.

Leo was succeeded by his cousin, Clement VII (1523-1534), after a brief pontificate by the last non-Italian pontiff, Hadrian IV (1522-1523). Clement had few of the minor vices, and none of the minor virtues, of his pontifical relative. He was, in a word, incompetent; and he failed to realize the gravity of the situation in which the papacy found itself. The prevailing state of public opinion may be inferred from this extract from the diary of a young Roman citizen:

"I saw the pope the first day of May 1525, come, in the morning of the Feast of SS. Philip and James, to the Church of the Holy Apostles, and, after celebrating high mass, remain all day and all night in the palace of the Colonna. . . . It was an old custom in the Colonna palace, which connects with the church and had windows looking into it, to throw various kinds of fowl and animals into the church to the people who were there, all of the lowest sort. They also put a pig in the middle of the church, out of reach, and whoever was able to climb up and take it, won it; and on top of the roofs were kegs and pots of water, which they poured on the people who climbed up. It amused those gentlemen, and the on-lookers, to see the crowd in a mess, battling, shrieking, pushing, shoving, like beasts —a form of merrymaking not fit for any church or sacred edifice." The diarist adds: "Now let people learn to know the souls of the great, and especially of priests, how wicked, deceitful, and false they are, how full of fraud and knavery."

Pope Clement seems to have had little idea, beyond the pursuit of such amusements, of what policies to follow. He was totally at a loss in attempting to decide whether to incline toward the Empire or toward France. At precisely the wrong moment, he made exactly the wrong choice and joined a league against the Empire. Charles V, when he heard of it, was enraged. "I shall go into Italy," he swore, "and there will I revenge myself on those who have wronged me—and especially on that rascal, the pope!" Charles was a man who swore but rarely; and, when he did swear, those who knew him trembled. And so, Pope Clement drew upon himself and upon the City the punishment due to a long course of papal politicking. The imperial army of the emperor—a ruffian mob of German mercenaries (mostly Lutherans), with a sprinkling of Italians and Spaniards, under the command of a renegade French duke, Charles de Bourbon—was encamped in the north. Unpaid for many months, they now began to clamor for plunder. Bourbon, who had no means with which to pay them—the emperor was notoriously tight-fisted—pacified them by promising them rich Italian booty. Thereupon, he led them toward Rome. At last, the Romans realized what was in store for them. On Holy Thursday, April 8, 1527, the pope was publicly accosted by a wild-eyed hermit from the mountains. "Thou bastard of Sodom," the zealot screamed at the frightened pontiff. "For thy sins, Rome shall be destroyed. Repent! If not, then in fourteen days thou shalt see it come to pass."

On May 6—only a little over the hermit's deadline—the imperial army was under the walls of the City. Their initial assault was repelled, but they found an opening in the neglected walls, and poured through the breach. Bourbon himself was killed, but this served only to remove the only authority who might have exercised some control over the imperial troops. The Roman militia fought bravely, as did the Swiss Guard, but it was useless. All resistance was put down brutally, and the City was given over to plunder. Now Rome was not a large city. Its population of 90,000 had been reduced, in recent years, by an outbreak of the plague. But it was rich in the oblations and tribute money of Christendom. The churches were decked with gold and silver, the palaces stuffed with precious paintings, tapestries, and ornaments of every kind. Popes, cardinals, and princes had, for centuries, vied with one another in the accumulation of works of art and articles of luxury. All this was thrown open to the mercy of the invaders. But they had no mercy, and for eight days the City was subjected to a fate which she had been spared even by the barbarians of a thousand years before. The soldiers killed every man, woman, and child who crossed their path. They pillaged every church, every monastery and convent, every palace and house which could not find gold with which to ransom itself. Nuns were raped in their convents, or carried off to the soldiers' dens to become the common property of the entire barracks. Hundreds of priests, bishops, and archbishops were slaughtered after they had paid the ransom required of them. Women were violated by entire companies of soldiers before the eyes of their husbands, fathers, and lovers. One citizen, Domenico Massimi, was forced to watch his sons killed, his daughter gang-raped, and his house burned, before he himself was accorded the kindness of death. Altogether, it is estimated that between twelve and fifteen thousand Romans perished—perhaps twenty per cent of the population. The destruction of works of art and of scholarship was carried out apace. Everything that was movable and obviously valuable was carted off to the German camp. The rest—manuscripts, paintings, entire libraries—was burned. The Vatican Library itself was saved only because the Prince of Orange, who had succeeded Bourbon as nominal leader of the barbaric horde, made his headquarters in it.

As the sack went on, Pope Clement and his cardinals looked on from the towers of the Castel Sant' Angelo, where they had taken refuge. There they remained until December 1527, when it pleased the Emperor Charles to release them. Charles, still in Spain, was delighted to learn that Rome had been taken, though he professed to be shocked at the savagery of his soldiers. Nonetheless, he was quick to take advantage of Clement's situation by exacting a humiliating treaty of peace. The pope was required to pay a personal ransom of some four hundred thousand ducats, and to surrender to Charles the cities of Piacenza, Parma, and Modena, as well as several fortresses and castles, including Sant' Angelo. Clement himself was to be removed to Gaeta or to Naples, until such time as the emperor had decided what to do with him. In the meantime, the various cities of Italy grasped as much as they dared of the papal territories on which Charles made no claim. Ferrara seized Reggio, and Venice took Ravenna. Florence, which Clement, like Leo X, had ruled through his Medici kinsmen there, expelled them forthwith and proclaimed itself a republic with Jesus Christ as its king. The papacy, as a spiritual power and as a political force, seemed sunk irredeemably in ruin. Even those who had opposed the sins of the papacy, the greed and corruption of the Curia, the luxury of the clergy, and the scandal of an irreligious Church, were moved to pity. Erasmus of Rotterdam—himself no pillar of domestic morality, but a moderate reformer, nonetheless—wrote: "Rome was not only the center of the Christian faith, the nurse of noble souls, and the home of the Muses, but she was also the mother of nations. To how many was she not more dear and more precious than their own native land? In truth, this is the ruin, not of one city, but of the whole world."

4. The High Renaissance (1499-1521)

The flood of devastation and suppression which was to overtake Italy was, at the opening of the sixteenth century, but dimly perceptible, and then only to the most acute observer. Most intelligent Italians had not the time to worry about the future. The intellectual and artistic revolution that had had its beginnings in Florence and had flourished under the aegis of the House of Medici was now approaching its period of culmination, a period in which the greatest masters were to do their work and which separates the earlier and more experimental stage from the later stage of exaggeration and decadence which followed it. The movement toward the apex of the Renaissance swept all the arts along with it. It produced the greatest men in literature since Petrarch; the greatest architects since the Gothic masters of the Ile-de-France; the greatest sculptors since Praxiteles; and the greatest painters that the world had ever seen.

Italian literature, which had not had a man of unquestionable authority and stature since Dante, now roused itself brilliantly. Niccolò Machiavelli (1469-1527) was by far the most famous—and perhaps also the most infamous—writer on the policy of government since the opening of the Renaissance, a policy to which he gave full expression in his most celebrated work, *The Prince*. Moreover, he was the author of one of Italy's most popular *novelle,* a satire on marriage entitled *Belfagor arcidiavolo,* as well as of the outstanding comedy of the Renaissance, *Mandragola*. This latter, bordering on the obscene though it did, so pleased the reigning pope, Leo X, that His Holiness commissioned Machiavelli to compose a history of Florence. The resulting work, *Storie Fiorentine,* embodied as revolutionary an attitude for historiography as *The Prince* did for political philosophy. Machiavelli was not satisfied merely to record events; he sought out causes and traced their effects. He discarded the fables with which previous generations of Florentine writers had flattered the vanity of their compatriots. And most important of all, he imposed an intelligible unity upon the flow of history by tracing a dual theme of Italian political interaction: first, that the cause of Italy's fragmentation was due to the papacy's eternal policy of raising up discord so as to preserve its own independence; second, that Italy's great advances through the centuries had come under the rule of such princes as Theodoric—and, of course, Cosimo and Lorenzo de' Medici.

After Machiavelli, the most famous name is that of Count Baldassarre

Castiglione (1478-1529), whose *Book of the Courtier* is, in its way, an enduring masterpiece. On this book, which portrays fashionable society at the elegant court of Urbino, Tasso wrote: "So long as there shall be princes and courts, so long as ladies and gentlemen shall meet in society, so long as virtue and courtesy shall abide in our hearts, the name of Castiglione will be held in honor." The count's work purports to be a series of conversations between the Duchess of Urbino and her guests concerning the proper qualities of a perfect gentleman. The society whose portrait emerges from Castiglione's pages is, no doubt, more than a little affected, stilted, and snobbish; but it is dignified, well behaved, and high-minded. The characters discuss deportment, athletics, propriety of speech, whether one should confine oneself to the Tuscan vocabulary of Petrarch and Boccaccio or make use of the vernacular spoken elsewhere, whether painting is a nobler art than sculpture, what a gentleman's dress should be, and so forth. The discussion proceeds to the proper behavior of a lady, and, by natural and wholly predictable steps, to the subject of love. At this point, Bembo, a famous littérateur, takes the floor to argue that higher love, governed by reason, is better than lower love, and will lead to the contemplation of universal beauty. As pseudo-Platonic as such sentiments may seem to later generations, they were the genuine emotional currency of the time, and, as such, they were familiar to Lorenzo de' Medici and his friends; and they are as characteristic of the period as its cruelty, treachery, and sensuality.

Poetry, with the delightful spontaneity and capriciousness of Italian genius, chose Ferrara, the dominion of the House of Este, for its abode. There Matteo Boiardo (1430-1494) wrote the *Orlando Innamorato,* an epic of chivalry concerning the court of Charlemagne and the love of Roland for the beautiful Angelica. The work was left unfinished, and Lodovico Ariosto (1474-1533) picked up the thread and carried it on, far more brilliantly and far more ironically, under the title of *Orlando Furioso* ("Roland Crazed"). Ariosto's work, which was immensely popular, was intended to entertain; and, in that, it succeeded. Its variety, wit, irony, sarcasm, and levity make it entertaining even in the twentieth century. Its interest is strengthened by the light which it sheds on the attitudes of educated Italians of the Renaissance, especially in regard to religion. Biblical allusions, regarded as sacred north of the Alps, here are lugged in to give a touch of humor. In one instance, a knight, Astolfo, rides out in search of poor Roland's lost wits; he meets St. John the Evangelist who, among other improbable things, drives him to the moon in Elijah's chariot. In another passage, Michael the Archangel finds that the goddess of Discord has not obeyed his orders, and he "seized her by the hair, kicked and pounded her without pity, broke a cross over her head, until Discord howled for mercy and embraced the knees of the divine envoy." Like most of the irreverent humanists of his time, however, Ariosto conformed to the rites of the Church. He accepted them as conventional forms, tinged possibly with supernatural power, and, like his contemporaries, he was never quite able to rid himself of the suspicion that, after all, it might all be true; and, if so, what then? But, until he resolved that doubt, he could not resist poking fun at the Church, and thus at himself and his own hesitant agnosticism.

Ariosto was a gentleman of birth and position. He spent most of his life in the service of his sovereigns, the princes of the House of Este. He wrote the *Orlando Furioso* between 1505 and 1515, and thereafter he devoted most of his time to improving and polishing it. Basking in the sunlight of fashionable admiration, he had no idea that another man, who had spent his life in mighty works of architecture, painting, and sculpture, would, in his old age, turn one day to literature, and write sonnets that would be read and reread, like a breviary, by men and women who ignored his own luxuriant rhetoric. These sonnets, by Michelangelo, are the noblest embodiment of those high ideas of love which descended from Plato to the philosophers of the Medici palace in Florence and the courtiers at the ducal palace in Urbino, and, despite the imperfection of their style, they are crammed to bursting with a passionate intensity and a rugged elevation of sentiment which make them *sui generis* in Italian literature.

In the fine arts, the High Renaissance produced a score of famous men. Among them, three or four stand head and shoulders above their fellows. Each is marked by an extraordinary individuality of talents, character, and disposition: Michelangelo, by passionate fury—his famed *terribilità;* Raphael, by sweet serenity; Leonardo, by his noble curiosity; and Bramante, by his unusual combining of poise and ardor.

Of Leonardo da Vinci (1452–1519), an admiring Vasari wrote: "Sometimes according to the course of nature, sometimes beyond and above it, the greatest gifts rain down from heaven upon the bodies of men, and crowd into one individual such a supernatural abundance of beauty, grace, and excellence, that, to whatever that man may turn, his very act is so divine that, in surpassing the work of all other men, it makes manifest that it is by the special gift of God, and not by human art. This was true of Leonardo da Vinci, who, besides a physical beauty beyond all praise, put an infinite grace into whatever he did; and such was his excellence that, to whatever difficult things his mind turned, he easily solved them."

Leonardo was a Florentine, the son of the extramarital union of a prominent lawyer with a woman of humble station. He was trained by the subtle Verrocchio, from whom he learned the smile—if it be a smile—on the faces of his portraits of women. By the time he was twenty-five, he was already sufficiently distinguished as a painter to win the attention and the favor of Lorenzo the Magnificent. After several years of Lorenzo's patronage, however, he seems to have grown disenchanted with the intellectual and artistic views of the Medici circle, and he accepted an offer of employment at the court of the Sforza despots in Milan. There, he spent sixteen years, and he did a hundred different things: he modeled a great equestrian statue of Francesco Sforza (since destroyed), painted portraits, drew architectural designs—for everything from a triumphal arch to a bathroom—executed hydraulic works, studied the cultivation of the grape, and played his lyre, which, we are assured, was of the purest silver. In the refectory of the Dominican monastery of S. Maria della Grazie, he painted one of his surviving masterpieces, a fresco of the Last Supper. One of the Dominican novices used to watch the painter at work, and has recorded that Leonardo would sometimes paint from sunrise to sunset without stopping even to eat; sometimes he would stand for hours contemplating his figures; and sometimes he would dash up the scaffold, make a few strokes with the brush, and then hurry down.

The *Last Supper* is a study of psychological reactions. Christ, serene on the threshhold of his fate, had just announced to the Apostles that one of them will betray him to his enemies. Leonardo's purpose was to depict the emotions of astonishment, horror, terror, and guilt that are reflected upon their faces as they grasp the meaning of what their master has said. Leonardo's best known work is perhaps the *Mona Lisa,* which portrays a similar interest in the moods of the human heart. The painting is a portrait of the wife of one Francesco del Giocondo, a Neapolitan, but it is much more than a portrait of one woman. One critic has called it a universal likeness of woman, "a perpetual life, sweeping together ten thousand experiences." The *Mona Lisa* is noteworthy, too, as the supreme example of Leonardo's skill in depicting the interplay of light and shade. He did not, as had his predecessors, show a gradual transition from light to dark, but instead punctuated dark areas with spots of light, and vice versa. The effect, in this painting as in others, is to surround the face with a light haze, which accentuates the look of pensiveness. The third of Leonardo's greatest surviving masterpieces is his *Virgin of the Rocks,* a work less well known than the other two but their equal in technical skill. It is also distinctive for illustrating the artist's passion for science and his belief in the universe as a place of order and symmetry. The figures are disposed in geometric composition, with every rock and plant depicted in the most meticulous and painstaking detail. For Leonardo was greatly impatient with the practice of imitating classical models, and it was his unshakable belief throughout his life that art should have, as its foundation, a scientific study of nature—that is, that the artist should examine the structure of a plant or rock, and delve into the mysteries of human emotion, as carefully and as methodically as the anatomist would dissect a cadaver. For the same reason, he would often roam the streets for hours in search of a face that would reveal the beauty, horror, truth, falsehood, sincerity, or hypocrisy of the person behind it.

Leonardo returned to Florence for several years, a stay broken by a brief employment as military engineer and architect to the redoubtable Caesare Borgia, and then, from 1506 to 1516, he alternated between Milan and Rome. Three years before his death, he bade farewell to Italy, and accompanied Francis I, King of France and a royal lover of art, to that kingdom. Little remains of all that Leonardo planned during those years— a few pictures, some incomparable drawings, some treatises on the arts, some apothegms. These, however, would have been more than enough to justify the fame of a lesser man. One of his apothegms, *Tu, o Iddio, tutto ci vendi a prezza di fatica,* ("Thou, O God, sellest us everything at the price of hard work"), is poorly borne out by his own vast portion of genius —a situation which inclines one to support Vasari's view that Nature makes special gifts.

The greatest architect of the High Renaissance was Donato d'Agnolo, called Bramante of Urbino (1444–1514). He, like Leonardo, worked in Milan during the resplendent reign of Lodovico Sforza, and there he did much powerful work and imposed his personality upon Lombard architecture. But it was in Rome that his great reputation was made, a city to which he was drawn by the great Rome-ward flow of art when the French invasion drove the fine arts from Milan. In Rome, Bramante became the papal architect of Innocent VIII and Julius II. He shares with Raphael and Michelangelo the honor of making of the Basilica of St. Peter and the Vatican palace what they are. In 1505, Pope Julius decided to tear down the old church which, according to tradition, had been built in 326, and build an entirely new one over what was said to be the tomb of St. Peter. Several architects were invited to submit proposals, and it was Bramante's design that won Julius' approval. Bramante's plan was as grandiose as Julius' ambition. The new Basilica was to be in the form of a Greek cross, crowned with a vast dome—"the dome of the Pantheon upon the Basilica of Constantine," as Bramante described it. The edifice was to cover almost twenty-nine thousand square yards (St. Peter's today covers only slightly over seventeen thousand). On April 11, 1506, Pope Julius laid the foundation stone, amid high hopes. But, as time progressed and Julius grew more and more interested in war, his enthusiasm for the new Basilica diminished, as did the funds available for the project. In 1514, Bramante died, happily unaware that his magnificent project was never to be carried out. A Roman legend has it that Bramante, on reaching the Gate of Heaven, was confronted by an outraged St. Peter, who demanded to know why the architect had torn down his ancient Basilica. Bramante attempted to justify himself, and pointed out that the new Medici pope, Leo X, would surely build another one. "Well, then," said the Apostle, "you will wait here at the Gate until it is finished." The new Basilica of St. Peter was completed some one hundred and twelve years later.

Upon Bramante's death, the reigning pope, Leo X, appointed as his successor one Raffaello Sanzio, better known as Raphael (1483–1520), a painter who was to find fame not as the architectural director of the new St. Peter's but as history's most successful, most beloved, and happiest artist. Raphael, whose creations were to rank with those of Leonardo as the expression of Italy in the High Renaissance, was born in Urbino, where his father, Giovanni de' Santi, was court painter and poet to the duke, Guidobaldo. The boy had the advantage of growing up in an atmosphere of cultivation, to which he responded with the ready ease which marked his intelligence. He was orphaned at the age of eleven, and began studying painting under a local master. In 1500, he went to Perugia, where he worked under the celebrated Perugino. There, that ability to absorb ideas and methods which characterized his life came to the fore, and, Vasari tells us, "his copies cannot be distinguished from the original works of the master."

Raphael soon exhausted Perugino's possibilities, and he resolved to go to Florence where, he had heard, Leonardo da Vinci and Michelangelo Buonarotti were doing magical things. He immediately became a pupil of both of his heroes, and under their tutelage his technique began rapidly to evolve. At this time, he painted a series of Madonnas—the *Madonna of the Grand Duke,* the *Madonna of the Goldfinch,* the *Madonna of the Meadow,* the *Madonna of the Chair,* the *Fair Gardener*—all of which, in their carefully triangular arrangement, reveal the influence of Leonardo. By 1508, his fame had already penetrated to Rome, and Pope Julius invited him to come to the City. There, Raphael achieved some of the noblest monuments of the High Renaissance, his frescoes in the Vatican palace:

The School of Athens, Parnassus, the *Deliverance of St. Peter,* and the *Meeting of Leo I and Attila,* to name only a few.

It was under Pope Leo X, however, that Raphael flourished, perhaps because he and that amiable pontiff were so similar in temperament. Leo overwhelmed the artist with commissions, wealth, and honor, and Raphael became the lion of papal society. He dressed like a nobleman, and lived like a prince. On one occasion, the austere Michelangelo remonstrated with him, saying, "You travel around with a retinue, like a general." To which Raphael, no mean wit himself, replied, "And you go about all alone, like a hangman." Raphael, however, did not take pleasure in such exchanges, for he was the personification of modesty and affability to all around him. He delighted in presenting valuable works of art to his friends, and he was generous, in a wholly Medicean way, when it came to supporting and encouraging struggling young artists of promise who were less fortunate than himself. That his affections extended themselves to a series of mistresses alarmed no one, least of all his pontifical patron, Leo X, who regarded such indulgence as only fitting for a man of such genius.

These amusements did not deter Raphael from his work, as they did Leonardo, whom Leo X had dismissed as a dawdler. In 1514, he began work on the *Incendio del Borgo,* which, whether he himself completed it or not (critical opinion has it that Raphael drew only the cartoon for this work, and left its completion to a pupil), is an episodic narrative in the best Raphaelesque style. At the same time, he completed cartoons for other frescoes, which were to be finished after his death by other pupils: Gianfrancesco Penni, and Perino del Vaga. Similarly, the frescoes which decorate the *Loggie,* or open galleries, built by Bramante around the Vatican's Court of St. Damascus, were designed by Raphael and executed by Penni, del Vaga, Giulio Romano, Polidoro da Caravaggio, and others. Leo X also commissioned Raphael's last work of importance, the famous tapestries depicting scenes from the Acts of the Apostles, which were intended to complement, and perhaps to outshine, the ceiling of Michelangelo and Julius II in the Sistine Chapel. Raphael completed the drawings of these tapestries, lavishing upon them all his accumulated knowledge of and experience in composition, dramatic effect, and anatomy, and they were then transferred (in Brussels) to silk and wool, and sent back to hang in the Sistine Chapel. At the end of December 1519, the tapestries were put on display for the edification of the Roman aristocracy. One of those who attended the exhibition recorded the opinion which has endured to our own time: "The whole world was struck dumb by the sight of these tapestries. By universal consent, there is nothing more beautiful in the entire world."

Raphael, like Leonardo, was a man of all-encompassing interests. He designed mosaics, woodwork, jewelry, and pottery. He designed, with equal ease, stables and a chapel for the Chigi family of Rome, and Florence's unsurpassed Palazzo Pandolfini. The enduring quality of his style in all his endeavors, however, is due primarily to its simple humanistic charm rather than to the intellectual power which Leonardo brought to his works, or to the emotional intensity which characterized all that Michelangelo did. Although he was influenced by both of these great contemporaries, Raphael remained loyal to the tradition of gentle piety inherited from Perugino. He was not bothered by philosophical questions, or tormented by the mysteries of human feeling. Instead, he devoted himself to the cultivation of ideal beauty as an end in itself. And it is this quality—which is, at the same time, a human failing—that has endeared Raphael as much to succeeding generations as it did to his own.

The giant among these giants, the towering figure of the High Renaissance, was not the universally accomplished Leonardo, nor the loved and loving Raphael, nor the fiery Bramante, who is said to have told St. Peter, "I will pull down this Paradise of yours, and I will build another, a much finer and more splendid place, for the saints to live in." It was Michelangelo Buonarroti (1475–1564), a native of the little town of Caprese near Florence. When he was six, his family moved to Florence, where he attended school. But he preferred drawing to writing and reading, and, at the age of thirteen, he was apprenticed to the city's most popular and successful painter, Ghirlandaio, where he was to learn what he could of painting. He had been in Ghirlandaio's studio only a short time, however, when a visit to the Medici sculpture collection turned his attention away from painting to sculpting. His work in that line quickly attracted the friendship and patronage of the great Lorenzo, who took Michelangelo into the Medici palace, where he became, along with Lorenzo himself, Ficino, Pico della Mirandola, Politan, and Pulci, a member of that prince's most intimate circle. Here he stayed until Lorenzo's death in 1492, and then returned briefly to his father's house, and then to Bologna where he carved a graceful *Kneeling Angel*.

Returning to Florence in 1495, he found the city under the rule of the firebrand monk, Savonarola; and he also found that a reformed Florence offered little chance of livelihood to an artist. In the following year, he went to Rome, where he secured the patronage of Cardinal Raffaello Riario. During this first stay in the Eternal City, his most memorable work was the *Pietà* which is now one of the glories of St. Peter's Basilica, and which is, in the opinion of many, the finest work of Michelangelo, and perhaps the finest in the history of sculpture.

The success of the *Pietà* not only brought fame and money to the artist, but also a commission from Florence. The cathedral of that city had had in its possession for a century an enormous, but irregularly shaped, block of marble. Now, Michelangelo was asked to chisel a statue out of it. The result was a statue which the Florentines called *Il gigante*—The Giant—and which has since become known as *David,* perhaps the most popular, and the most copied, work of sculpture in the world. It has flaws—one hand too large, one leg too long, a buttock too flat, the neck too elongated—but the overall impact of this massive creation silences criticism today as it did in Michelangelo's time. In the opinion of Vasari, "It surpasses every other statue, ancient or modern, Latin or Greek."

In 1505, a year after the completion of the *David,* Michelangelo was summoned to Rome by the imperious Julius II. The pope wanted a tomb for himself, one that would be worthy of his greatness, and it was this project that he entrusted to the Florentine sculptor. Marble was brought in enormous quantities for the colossal monument that Michelangelo designed, and brought to Rome. But, at this point, the pontiff's preoccupation with death receded before his enthusiasm for war, and the project was allowed to fall. Michelangelo, disgusted, returned to Florence. But Julius II's repeated and peremptory summons back to the Holy City could not be ignored. He returned in 1508, and was dismayed to find that the pope wished him not to carve the great tomb, but to paint the ceiling of the Chapel of Sixtus IV. Protesting that he was a sculptor, not a painter, he gave in to the pontiff's urging, and from May 1508 to October 1512, he worked on the Sistine ceiling. To the problems of perspective and foreshortening in painting a ceiling sixty-eight feet above the floor were added those of the pontiff's temper and of Michelangelo's own irascible nature. The work was punctuated by a series of confrontations, which can most accurately be described as fights, between the pope and the painter. To Julius' almost daily demand for more speed, and to his continual question, "When will it be finished?," Michelangelo replied with equal brusqueness: "It will be finished when I believe that I have done all that has to be done." On one famous occasion, tempers flared to such an extent that His Holiness threatened to hurl the artist bodily from the scaffolding.

Julius' original plan for the ceiling had been simply a series depicting the twelve Apostles, but Michelangelo insisted upon a more complex scheme. He divided the vault of the chapel into over a hundred panels by the use of painted columns and moldings. In the larger panels, he painted scenes from Genesis—creation, the Garden of Eden, the Flood. In the spandrels of alternating arches were magnificent figures of the prophets Daniel, Isaiah, Zecharia, Joel, Ezekiel, Jeremiah, Jonah. In the other spandrels were figures of the Sibyls, who were believed to have foretold the coming of Christ. In the triangles at each end of the ceiling were more scenes from the Old Testament: Moses in the desert, David and Goliath, the hanging of Haman, the beheading of Holofernes by Judith. The only concession to the New Testament are scenes from the genealogy of Mary and Jesus, depicted in the lunettes and recesses above the windows. And Julius, though at least nominally a Christian, and certainly the head of the Christian Church, made no objection, either to Christianity's meager representation on the ceiling of the chapel of the popes, or to the ever recurrent nudity of Michelangelo's figures—both of which aspects shocked some of Julius' more delicate courtiers. Perhaps the bellicose pope recognized, as death approached, that it would not be his interminable wars which would immortalize him, but this incredible work of art which he had sponsored, supported, and upon its completion, blessed.

Pope Julius II died early in 1513. He was succeeded by that pontifical patron *par excellence* of the arts, Pope Leo X, Giovanni de' Medici, son of Lorenzo the Magnificent. Leo at once retained Michelangelo to take up the work on Julius' abandoned tomb, although, to be sure, it was to be a monument of lesser proportions than envisaged by Julius himself. Once again, however, Michelangelo was obliged to interrupt his work on Julius' memorial long before it was finished. (Indeed, it was never to be finished, and the statues that the artists had already completed were to be scattered about Rome and Italy—the most famous being Michelangelo's *Moses,* now in the Church of S. Pietro in Vincoli in Rome, which is an ill-proportioned and confused work reflecting many interruptions.) Leo destined Michelangelo's talents for something more noble, as he thought, than a monument to a dead Julius: a monument to the living House of Medici. There was at Florence a church called San Lorenzo, the family church of the Medici in which were buried Cosimo, Lorenzo, and many other members of the family. The church had been designed and built by Brunelleschi, but its facade had never been finished. Leo now commanded Michelangelo to finish this work. The artist grumbled, but he went to Florence. There, he fought with his assistants as well as with everyone with whom he came into contact, and did no work. Finally, in 1520, Leo relieved him of the commission, and excused himself from giving any more work to the difficult artist. "He is a difficult man," he complained, "and there is no way to get along with him."

In the following year, however, Leo died, and, after a brief interval, another Medici, Clement VII (1523–1534), ascended the Throne of the Apostle. This pope was an admirer of Michelangelo, and, unlike Pope Leo, he was perfectly willing to put up with the artist's temperament. "When Buonarotti comes to see me," he told a friend, "I always ask him to be seated, otherwise I know that he would do so without permission." Under Clement, Michelangelo undertook what was to be the culmination of his career as a sculptor: the *Nuova Sagrestia,* or New Sacristy, of Florence's Church of San Lorenzo. He was to design the sacristy as a mausoleum for the Medici, to execute the tombs according to his own plans, and to adorn them with appropriate statuary. The sacristy itself, completed in 1524, was a simple building, a quadrangle crowned with a modest dome. But it was the perfect setting for the magnificence which Michelangelo had planned for the tombs themselves. There were to be six of these, but only two—those of Giuliano the Younger and of Lorenzo, Duke of Urbino—were ever completed. Nevertheless, they are the culmination of Renaissance sculpture, as the same artist's work in the Sistine Chapel are the apex of Renaissance painting. The tombs show the two Medici in the prime of life, Giuliano in the armor of a Roman commander and Lorenzo in the pose of *il Penseroso,* the Thinker. On the sarcophagus of the former are two figures, both nude; to the right, a male, supposedly representing Day, and, to the left, a female, Night. On that of Lorenzo are two more nudes, Dawn and Sunset. Whether these allegorical figures were intended to symbolize the disasters which had overtaken the republic of Florence, as some maintained, or to reflect the artist's own sense of disappointment in the world, as others have asserted, or merely to exemplify Michelangelo's obsession with the human body, is unknown.

Work on the tomb was interrupted by the Sack of Rome and Clement's imprisonment in Sant' Angelo. But when that pontiff was again safe, he ordered his Medici relatives in Florence to find Michelangelo and to induce him to complete the work. Michelangelo agreed, and managed to complete the *Madonna de' Medici* before Clement's death in 1534. At that point, however, the sculptor feared that, with his protector gone, the Florentine Medici would imprison him for having opposed their return in 1529, and so he fled to Rome.

In the City, he was welcomed with open arms by the new pope, Paul III (1534–1550), who immediately put him to work on what was to be perhaps his most famous painting, *The Last Judgment,* behind the altar of the Sistine Chapel. After six years of labor, the work was unveiled (1541), and it was universally admired. Vasari, that ubiquitous critic, called it the most wonderful of all paintings, and artists came from all over Europe to study the anatomy, the musculature of the figures, the foreshortenings, and the amazing sense of perspective.

In 1546, Michelangelo undertook, at Pope Paul's insistence, his last great work, the completion of St. Peter's, upon which he set to work with an energy not to be expected in a man of seventy-two years. The commission was continued during the reigns of succeeding popes, Julius III, Paul IV, and Pius IV, and in 1557, after years of making and rejecting designs, the sculptor-artist turned architect had ready a model of the cupola. It was to be the only part of the Basilica for which Michelangelo himself was directly responsible, for, at his death in 1564, it was found that he had left no definite plans for any portion except the dome. It may be that, in addition to his duties at St. Peter's, he attempted to do too much, for, as late as his eighty-ninth year, he was transforming the ancient Baths of Diocletian into the modern Church and Convent of S. Maria degli Angeli, and designing one of the City's gates, the Porta Pia.

He died at the age of eighty-nine, at peace with heaven and the world, leaving "his soul to God, his body to the earth, and his possessions to his nearest relatives." He was buried in Florence, where, appropriately, Giorgio Vasari, Michelangelo's greatest admirer, designed a sumptuous tomb for him. The judgment of time has not been unlike that of Vasari himself, that Michelangelo Buonarroti was the greatest artist who ever lived.

It was not chance that brought Michelangelo, Raphael, Bramante, and a score of other great artists to Rome. They assembled there because the papal court, pursuing its policy of maintaining the papacy at the head of Christendom by means of culture, had summoned them to come. Rome herself never produced great artists. She was never herself artistic, just as she had never been spiritual. But, as in earlier times she had drawn spiritual forces to herself, so, during the High Renaissance, she attracted and made use of the artistic forces of Italy. For years, the policies of the papacy had prepared the way. Step by step, as the ambitions of the popes had become more and more secular, they had become also more and more artistic, more intellectual. For seven decades, every pope contributed to this end. Eugenius IV had opened the door by employing distinguished humanists as his secretaries, and by inviting the most notable painters and sculptors of his time to Rome. Nicholas V had conceived the splendid scheme of making Rome the mistress of the intellectual and cultural world, and he had transformed the Vatican into a huge Academy. Lorenzo Valla came, as did Miccolo Perotti and Filelfo. Leon Battista Alberti was assigned to plan palaces and piazzas, and Bernardo Rossellino was commissioned to restore the churches of the Lateran, S. Maria Maggiore, St. Paul, and S. Lorenzo. Andrea del Castagna and the beatific Angelico were invited to decorate the walls of the Vatican. His successor, Pius II, had, as Enea Sylvius Piccolomini of Siena, achieved fame as one of the most eminent men of letters of his age. Paul II was a virtuoso in objects of art, and he prided himself upon increasing the grandeur of the papal court. Sixtus IV embellished Rome with new public buildings and churches. He restored the Hospital of Santo Spirito and reorganized the University of Rome. Under him, the Sistine Chapel was begun according to the plan of the architect Giovannino de' Dolci; and under him were its walls decorated by Perugino, Signorelli, Rosselli, and Cosimo, with scenes from the life of Christ and that of Moses. He added greatly to the Vatican Library, and the mathematician Regiomontano was employed to reform the old Julian calendar. John Argiropulo was summoned to the City to give a series of lectures on Greek literature, and Sixtus encouraged every initiative aimed at the sparking of interest in the art and culture of antiquity. Pope Innocent VIII brought Mantegna from Padua, and Pinturicchio from Perugia, further to embellish the Vatican. Pope Alexander VI made Pinturicchio his court painter, and that charming master decorated the papal apartments with the great bull of the Borgia coat of arms, and with portraits of the pope's children. One painting, Vasari whispers, depicted the pope's mistress, the lovely Giulia Farnese, as the Virgin, with the pope worshiping her.

Popes and cardinals alike felt the great movement of the Renaissance, and many of them strove to lead it. But the fiery master of the High Renaissance was Julius II, whose plans in the arts were even more grandiose than in politics. He was the center of the period, as Cosimo and Lorenzo de' Medici had been in their generations. Less astute than Cosimo, and far less subtle and accomplished than Lorenzo, he was, nonetheless, a much more heroic leader than either of the Florentine princes. His hardy, weather-beaten face in Raphael's portrait, with its strong, well-shaped features, reveals him to be noble as well as imperious, arrogant, and irascible. It was Julius who brought to Rome the greatest genius of the Renaissance, Michelangelo, and commanded him to build a tomb more splendid than any ever built before. It was he who, with his architects Bramante and Giuliano da Sangallo, resolved to pull down the old Basilica of St. Peter, founded by Constantine and Pope Silvester II, despite a thousand years of sacred associations, and to build "the wonder of Christendom" in its place. The greatest architects of Italy were to succeed one another as masters of the works: Bramante and Sangallo from Florence, Fra Giocondo from Verona, Raphael, Antonia da Sangallo the younger, Baldassare Peruzzi of Siena, and Michelangelo Buonarroti.

At this time, too, classic art, owing to the discovery of antique statues, had its fullest effect. The *Nile,* now in the Vatican, had been found in a Roman garden, the *Apollo Belvedere* in a vineyard near the City, and the *Laocoön,* and many others here and there. Of the discovery of the *Laocoön,* a record remains. "I was at that time a boy in Rome," wrote Francesco, the son of Giuliano da Sangallo, "when one day it was announced to the pope that some excellent statues had been dug out of the ground in a grape patch near the church of S. Maria Maggiore. The pope immediately sent a servant to Giuliano da Sangallo to tell him to go directly and see what it was. Michelangelo Buonarroti was often at our house, and, at the moment, he happened to be there. Accordingly, my father invited him to accompany us. I rode behind my father on his horse, and thus we came to the place designated. We had scarcely dismounted and glanced at the figures when my father cried out, 'It is the *Laocoön* of which Pliny speaks!' The laborers immediately began digging to get the statue out. And after having looked at them very carefully, we went home to supper, talking all the way of antiquity."

Thus these various forces—the discovery of antique works of art, the passion for art, the eager Italian intellect, the conception of Rome as mistress of culture, the character of Julius II, and the genius of Bramante, Michelangelo, and Raphael—worked together to cover the papacy with a pagan glory at the very moment when its needs were of a religious nature. Moreover, as these monumental strivings of the popes required money, the sale of indulgences and the exaction of tribute, to which Germany objected so strenuously, continued with more rapacity than ever.

The age in which all this occurred is often known as the Age of Leo X. But Pope Leo, for all his affability and culture, is not deserving of the honor. He had an inborn Medicean interest in and enjoyment of artistic and intellectual matters, but it was his fate to build upon the work of others —upon that of his Medicean ancestors of Florence, and upon that of his pontifical predecessors in Rome. It is instead his distinction to stand in history as the last pope to wield the Italian scepter over all Europe; the last to send his tax collectors from Sicily to England, and from Spain to Norway; the last to enjoy the full heritage of Imperial Rome. To his magnificent predecessors, Rome owed her rebirth. Under them, the Church had been transformed into a great artistic, intellectual, and cultural enterprise, and had shifted its interest to the plane of temporal values at the expense of spiritual values. And under them the gods of the Renaissance had entered the churches of Europe, and the God of the Christians had left.

5. The Cinquecento: *Italy in the Sixteenth Century*

Erasmus of Rotterdam had called the Sack of Rome in 1527 "the ruin, not of one city, but of the whole world." It was a prophetic insight, although, by virtue of poetic license, it exceeded the bounds of absolute fact. The truth of the matter was that, as the Renaissance now moved beyond the Alps into those "barbarian lands" which the Italians had always held in such contempt, Italy herself stood at the threshold of a centuries-long period of national degradation—a period to which the Sack of Rome served as an ample foretaste and introduction.

The struggle between France and Spain for the mastery of Europe in general, and of Italy in particular, was decided once and for all by the Battle of Pavia (1525), in which the King of France lost all but his life and his honor. France was too proud to acquiesce humbly in this defeat, and, from time to time, she was to march her troops across the Alps into unfortunate Piedmont, sometimes on her own initiative and sometimes at the invitation of an Italian prince. But the grip of Spain was too firm to be shaken, either by virtue of French intervention or by that of Italian resistance, and, from this time on, Italian politics were to be determined by foreign kings. Two treaties between France and Spain, that of Cambrai (1529) and that of Cateau-Cambrésis (1559), embodied the results of their elaborate bargains and their interminable wars. The sum and substance of them was a practical abandonment by France of her Italian claims. Henceforth, the map of Italy would be drawn to Spanish taste.

To the north, Milan was ruled by Spanish governors, while, in the south, Naples and Sicily were subjected to Spanish viceroys. The business of a Spanish viceroy was simple enough: to raise money. Taxes were therefore unbelievably oppressive. It was said that, in Sicily, the royal officials nibbled; in Naples, they ate; and in Milan, they devoured. In addition to regular taxes, special imposts were laid on every conceivable pretext— when a new king succeeded to the throne, when a royal heir was born, when war was waged by Spain in defense of its vast empire, or when it entered the head of a Spanish king to persecute the Protestants. In the south, particularly, this taxation, coupled with unwise government and extended over several centuries, caused a gradual increase in ignorance and poverty, conditions which have continued to the present day as part of the legacy of Spanish greed.

In Florence, the sagacious Grand Duke Cosimo I (1537–1574) ruled with severity tempered by prudence. He understood that his position depended entirely on his fidelity to Spain and to the papacy, and he acted accordingly. He married a Spanish lady, Eleanora of Toledo, daughter of the Viceroy of Naples. He reduced Siena, once Florence's dangerous rival, to the role of a Florentine satellite, and he crushed the last remnants of republican sentiment in both cities. He employed Vasari to design the Uffizi, completed the building which houses the Laurentian Library, and emulated the luxurious style of his ancestors to the extent that his purse would allow. He was, in effect, what one would expect an ungifted member of the House of Medici to be: an imitator.

North of Florence, the petty duchies of Ferrara, Urbino, Modena, Parma, and Mantua formed a ducal coterie of the sort that was to become characteristic of the next two centuries. The papacy was to swallow up Ferrara (1598) and Urbino (1631), but Ferrara's famous dynasty, the House of Este, moved on to Modena, where it remained ensconced until the Napoleonic era. In Parma, Pope Paul III (1534–1550)—the Alexander Farnese who owed his cardinal's hat to Pope Alexander VI's amorous designs on Giulia Farnese—erected a ducal throne for his son. This young man was weak and dissolute, and the nobles of the city quickly murdered him; but his Farnese descendants eventually made good their title, and the little Duchy of Parma, with its palace, its barracks, and its pictures, emerged as one of Italy's petty states and remained so for three centuries. Of the other cities of the north, only two of any importance—Genoa and Lucca—were permitted to retain their republican form of government.

To the northwest, there begins to take shape, for the first time, a well-defined picture of Savoy. This duchy, built up piecemeal by war, marriage, and diplomacy, was a composite state comprising much of Piedmont and portions of what are now France and Switzerland. Unfortunately, the lands of the Dukes of Savoy lay directly in the path of the French armies on their marches into Italy. During the wars of Francis I and Charles V, the reigning duke had hoped to preserve his independence of action by maintaining neutrality. Instead, he succeeded in losing all. France thought it more convenient to own, rather than to rent, her line of march into Italy, and she annexed Savoy; and for two decades thereafter, the duchy served as a camping ground, and occasionally as a battleground, for France and Spain. For a time, it seemed that Savoy might be blotted from the map of Europe. Then, one of its dukes, Emanuele Filiberto (1553–1580), known to his contemporaries as "Iron Head," an accomplished soldier, had the good judgment to pick the winning side. He served in the Spanish Army and, in the Peace of Cateau-Cambrésis, secured, as his reward, the restoration of his duchy. That portion of Emanuele Filiberto's policy which is of special interest is that which gave Piedmont precedence over the France and Swiss provinces of Savoy, established the seat of government at Turin, put the university in that city, substituted Italian for Latin in public documents, and so proclaimed himself an Italian prince and Savoy an Italian state. This duke gave to Savoy the general character which it was to retain. He checked the power of the clergy, built up the army, reformed the legal system, converted the duchy's old feudal system into an absolute autocracy, and altogether put Savoy on the road which ultimately was to enable it to play its great role in the liberation and unification of Italy three hundred years later. Emanuele Filiberto, for that reason, is reputed one of Italy's national heroes.

Venice, in contrast to Savoy, was losing ground rather than gaining it. She had recovered most of the territories on the Italian mainland which had been wrenched from her by the League of Cambrai; but, in the east, the Turks were steadily depriving her of city, island, and province. After a long period of war, one gallant and successful encounter gilded the fortunes of the losing side. A coalition against the Turks was effected between Spain, the papacy, and Venice, and the united fleets of these three states, under the command of Don Juan of Austria, won the famous sea battle of Lepanto (1571); but, except for the chopping off of a fair number of infidel heads and arms, little was accomplished. Soon afterward, peace was made on terms hard for the proud Venetians, but beneficent in that it was destined to last until the middle of the seventeenth century.

In central Italy, of course, was Rome; and in Rome there was still the papacy. In view of the events of the immediately preceding years, one might expect to find, as elsewhere, degeneration and decay. One would, however, be mistaken. As before and afterward in history, the Roman Church and the papacy had once more, phoenix-like, risen from their ashes and taken on new vigor and renewed energy. Ever since the fall of the medieval Empire, when the political union of Italy and Germany had been broken, disruptive forces had been at work to break the ecclesiastical union of the two countries. Finally, in the pontificate of Leo X, Martin Luther had affixed his theses concerning indulgences to the door of the Castle Church at Wittenberg, burned the papal bull, and thrown off his allegiance to Rome. All of the north of Europe had followed him. The record of the papacy at that time had been one of utter failure, and worse.

An Age of Renewal

It had smeared itself from head to toe with the tar of simony, nepotism, and vice. It had cast religion to the winds. An observer might reasonably have predicted that all Europe would dismember and suppress the papacy, and adopt a system of national churches. Nevertheless, by the end of the sixteenth century, the papacy once more stood erect and vigorous, with the Society of Jesus on its right hand and the Holy Inquisition on its left, draped in righteousness by the reforming Council of Trent (1545–1563), and dealing with kings and emperors, as of old, on terms of equality. The process which effected this change—a process which was a felicitous combination of virtue, wisdom, policy, and bigotry—is variously known as the Catholic Reformation, the Catholic Revival, the Catholic Reaction, and the Counter-Reformation. Borne upward and onward by this reaction to the Protestant schism, and by the forces of reform and conservatism within the Church, the modern papacy rose, militant and triumphant, upon the ruins of the papacy of the Renaissance.

The same spirit which had caused the Reformation in the north started the Counter-Reformation in the south. A wave, comparable to the old movement for Church reform in Hildebrand's time, swept over the Catholic Church and lifted the reformers within the Church into power. Then, the south emulated the north. Catholic zeal for reform matched Protestant ardor, and Catholic prejudice equaled Protestant bigotry. Moreover, a reformed papacy was able quickly to find allies. The logical consequence of Protestantism had been the introduction of personal independence into religion; the next step, it was foreseen, would be personal independence in politics. Indeed, Protestant subjects, especially when their rulers were Catholic, tended to become unruly and disobedient; and their princes, who stood for absolutism and conservatism, found themselves strongly drawn to an absolutist and conservative pope. The kings of Spain and the Roman popes, so recently at sword's point, thus became fast friends and allies. Within three years after the Sack of Rome, Pope Clement VII crowned Charles V with the imperial diadem in Bologna, where, for the last time in Italy, an "Emperor of the Romans, always August, Lord of the World," was proclaimed; and the papacy, now invigorated by its league with the omnipotent Charles, lifted its head.

Strength, however, came from other sources. A brilliant young Spaniard named Ignatius of Loyola, who had been a soldier but had abandoned the battlefield for the Church, founded the Society of Jesus (called the Jesuits), which vowed itself to poverty, chastity, and to unquestioning and absolute obedience to the papacy (1534). Another fountain of strength, the Inquisition, was also imported from Spain. From the time of the great Pope

Innocent III, the friars of the Order of St. Dominic had been charged with the preservation of the purity of the faith and with the punishment of heretics. Over the centuries, they had performed this function with what, at the time, seemed adequate zeal. But, in Spain, then in the throes of that great anti-Islamic struggle which culminated in the capture of Granada and in the virtual unification of Spain under "the Catholic Kings," Ferdinand and Isabella, still greater zeal was deemed necessary, and the Spanish Inquisition was established. Its fame spread far and wide, and the Spanish viceroys of Naples introduced it, in a modified and less malevolent form, into their domains. At the urging of the most fanatic reformers, the Inquisition then was adopted at Rome, where it was known as "the Holy Office" (1542). Heretics were frightened into conformity, or were punished. Some were driven into exile, and a few were burned to death. Freedom of thought and of expression—a quality dear to the heart of Italians of the Renaissance and even of the Middle Ages—came under heavy attack, and the *Index Librorum Prohibitorum*—the infamous "Index" —was promulgated, condemning any written work which might serve to raise doubts concerning the Catholic faith in the mind of a reader, and passing a sentence of *ipso facto* excommunication on anyone who might dare to read a book listed therein. The great and growing power of the Catholic reformers may be measured by the fact that the pope who sanctioned these great bulwarks of orthodoxy and of the papal system was none other than the once gay and worldly Paul III, Alexander Farnese, who very likely had gained the papacy through simony, as he had once gained a red hat through his sister's easy virtue.

The culmination and consolidation of the movement of Catholic reform was the Council of Trent. Europe had been too long accustomed to the idea of ecclesiastical unity not to attempt some reconciliation between Catholics and Protestants. It was hoped that a general and ecumenical Council might heal all wounds, smooth all difficulties, and revive the cohesiveness of an earlier age. The popes, however, resisted the idea. They had come to regard Councils as unfriendly bodies, with dangerous tendencies toward hostile investigations and new canons; and they were inclined to take the risk of losing the Protestant regions of Europe altogether rather than to make use of so dangerous a tool to recover them. But the Holy Roman Emperor, the perennial Charles V, was insistent. His Empire, as well as the Church, was split between Catholics and Protestants, and it was in imminent danger of breaking in two. The Council of Trent was therefore convoked (1545). Its primary object was reconciliation; but everyone knew that no reconciliation was possible without radical disciplinary and dogmatic reforms within the Church, and so the papal party played its cards with exceeding care. The Lutherans, though invited, did not deign to attend; and the papal party, in order to forestall such reforms as might have compromised what they regarded as the doctrinal purity of the Roman Church, plunged into the definition of dogma; and they defined it in such a way as to shut out, once and for all, all of the Lutheran schismatics. The Catholic reform party, for its part, managed to sandwich in, between the definitions of dogma, various decrees for the reform of Church discipline.

In theory, an Ecumenical Council of the Roman Catholic Church acts under the direct inspiration of the Holy Ghost. From the secular point of view, however, the guiding spirit of the Council of Trent seemed rather to be the conflicting interests of pope, bishops, Holy Roman Emperor, Spain, France, and the Italian states. In fact, the Council was twice broken up. The first time, the pope, having taken alarm, declared the Council adjourned. The second, the Lutherans, then at war with the Emperor Charles, came perilously close to Trent, and the conciliar fathers fled in panic from the city. The Council met again, for the third time; but by then all hope of reconciliation with the Protestants was dead. The prelates therefore set to work as a purely Roman Catholic body. It soon became clear that, in the interval since the summoning of the Council, the Church's reform party had won complete control. Pope Paul IV (1555-1559), a man of high character and a former head of the Holy Office, had promulgated many edicts concerning reform. His successor, Pius IV (1559-1566), who was pope during the final sessions of the Councils, followed his lead. Pius, an astute diplomat, instead of wasting energy in attempting to persuade his disputatious bishops, had gone directly to the Catholic sovereigns of Spain, France, and Austria, and had secured their approval for the embodiment of his ideas for reform into the decrees of the Council. Nothing, however, could have been accomplished without the reforming spirit within the Church itself; and it was to Pius' credit that he did his best to remove such obstacles as advocates of the old order placed in the way of that spirit. Stern rules were made against corrupt practices. Canons regulated the conduct of the clergy, the duties of bishops, the affairs of monasteries and convents, and all matters connected with the world-wide organization of the Roman Church. These reforms came too late to affect Protestant opinion, but they served to rally the doubtful, to confirm the faithful, and to give to the papacy the moral support of the Catholic powers of Europe.

In this way, the papacy prospered during the very generations in which the greatness of Italy was dwindling away. The fortunes of the two had wholly parted company. The papacy, indeed, had made itself an Italian institution, and never again would a non-Italian occupy the Chair of St. Peter. But, in other ways, it had ceased to have any national affections. Italy, her genius faded, her fervor faint, not only deprived of what might have been a powerful support, but even oppressed by her own greatest creation, the Roman Church, ceased to be a country. She became, in the famous phrase of another age, "a mere geographical expression," an aggregate of little states, with no tie among them except that of juxtaposition and common subservience to foreign powers. Over them all—Spanish provinces, independent republics, little duchies and principalities, and the Papal States—falls the shadow of the royal standard of Spain. Next to the consciousness of that dreaded banner, the most vivid impression of the period is the contrast between the strength of the papacy and the weakness of Italy—a contrast which leads perhaps to the conclusion that the fortunes of the two have not only parted company, but that they have become virtually irreconcilable.

The *Cinquecento* exhibits in the arts the same disintegration and decay that is found in the political life of Italy. Honesty, independence, and genuineness have now faded away, and in their place there are cleverness and effort. The high tide of the Renaissance was during the pontificate of Julius II; but the flood lingered on at the full until 1540, and then the ebb began. This change from maturity to decay was all-pervasive; but it was gradual, and a period of excellence intervened between the High Renaissance and the beginning of the Baroque period. This process is most clearly marked in architecture. During the High Renaissance, the basic law of architecture was dignity; the grand manner dominated, and charm determined the disposition of subordinate parts. Domes were noble; loggias, elegant; pilasters, decorative; cornices, well proportioned; ceilings, splendid. After 1540, indications of decline appeared; but this fading brilliance was a kind of *götterdämmerung,* and, though it heralded the excesses of the Baroque, it displayed at times a purity of detail and a noble restraint worthy of the earlier period.

Of the architects of this intermediate stage, the greatest was Giacomo Barozzi (1507–1573), called Vignola, after the town where he was born. Vignola was a man of theories. He had a superb knowledge of classical architecture, and he wrote a manual on the architectural orders which enjoyed great authority for almost two centuries. He built various edifices at Bologna, and designed a vast palace for the Farnese family at Piacenza. The art of making gardens, of using cypress trees, greensward, pools, terraces, and clumps of ilex as joint partners with stone, brick, and stucco, had come into being in the sixteenth century, and Vignola was one of the masters of this new art. He designed the Farnese gardens on Rome's Palatine Hill—a wonder known to the twentieth century only by representation and fame, since the gardens have been destroyed by time, neglect, subsequent owners, and eager archaeologists. He was an artist of great ideas; and occasionally he captured the grand manner of his predecessors. On the other hand, he also helped to bring on the worst of the Baroque. His famous church at Rome, the *Gesù*, despite its vast, high-arching nave, lent itself with fatal facility to a gorgeous hideousness of decoration and set the fashion for many imitative Jesuit churches. These latter, while missing the grandeur of their exemplar, caught only its vulgar decorative excesses.

The next in rank, Bartolommeo Ammanati (1511–1592), a Florentine, was virtually the court architect of Tuscany's grand duke, Cosimo I. He built two bridges across the Arno (the Ponte alla Carraia and the Ponte Santa Trinità), finished the main body of the Pitti Palace, which had been designed by Brunelleschi, and completed the pleasure grounds behind the palace known as the Boboli Gardens. Among his contemporaries was Giorgio Vasari (1511–1574), an architect, painter, and biographer, who designed the Uffizi at Florence, painted many pictures of indifferent worth, and wrote *Lives of the Painters,* a garrulous, discursive, often inaccurate but always delightful book. Another was Galeazzo Alessi (1512–1572), a Perugian, who built the stately, tourist-haunted palaces of Genoa, once occupied by opulent merchant-princes, and the gigantic church of S. Maria degli Angeli. Jacopo Tatti Sansovino (1486–1570), of lesser renown, though a Florentine, is known chiefly for his many noble buildings in Venice. Andrea Palladio (1518–1580), a citizen of Vicenza, embodied a passionate love of classical architecture in palaces and churches in his native city and in Venice. During the revival of classic enthusiasm in the eighteenth century, he was to be regarded as a demi-god. Palladio captivated Goethe, among others, and as soon as the great German arrived at Vicenza, he hurried to see the Palladian palaces: "When we stand face to face with these buildings, then we realize their excellence; their bulk and massiveness fill the eye, while the lovely harmony of their proportions, admirable in the advance and retreat of perspective, brings peace to the spirit."

Such men kept alive the traditions of the great period of Renaissance architecture, but only for a time. As the years passed, artificiality and exaggeration usurped the place of elegance and power. A servile imitation of Roman models, an absolute acceptance of classical correctness, prevailed.

The classic orders—the Corinthian, especially—spread themselves everywhere. In one place, barren and formal simplicity obtruded itself; in another, all was pretentious magnificence. After 1580, the transition is complete, and the Baroque is triumphant. Sham rules all. Wood and plaster mimic stone. Columns, supporting nothing but the architect's pride, twist themselves awry. Monstrous scrolls, heavy moldings, gilt deformities, senseless statues, and all the contortions to which stucco and other cohesive materials will submit, hang and cling everywhere, inside and out.

In sculpture, the same degeneration came to prevail. Michelangelo, in his statues for the Medici chapel at Florence, *Night* and *Day, Evening* and *Dawn,* had achieved the utmost which thought and expression could express in marble. They stand, pillars set up by Hercules, at the end of the noble sculpture of the Renaissance. Michelangelo's successors attempted in vain to imitate him. They produced only bulk, or writhing, or distortion. And yet, some men of this period did remarkable work. Benvenuto Cellini (1500–1571), a talented goldsmith, sculpted the Florentine *Perseus.* John of Bologna modeled the *Flying Mercury.* Taddeo Landini of Florence designed a charming fountain in Rome. After these men and a few others, sculpture followed architecture in its facile descent into the Baroque, and thereafter expressed itself in prophets, saints, and popes who stand, in swaying and vacillating postures, in nave and aisle, on roof and balustrade.

In painting, similarly, the same story is repeated. At Florence, after the close of the High Renaissance, twilight darkened rapidly into night. There are few artists of note except two fashionable portrait painters, Agnolo di Cosimo, known as Bronzino (1502–1572), and Iacopo Carrucci, called Pontorma (1494–1556). After them come, in dreary succession, the decadent painters, who painted figures bigger and bigger in would-be Michelangelesque attitudes. Elsewhere, also, the generation bred under the great masters began to fade away—the gentle Luini of Milan, Leonardo's disciple; the facile Giulio Romano, Raphael's pupil; the beauty-loving Sodoma of Siena; the romantic Dosso Dossi of Ferrara. Such names show how reluctant was the genius of painting to leave Italy. But she obeyed fate and, at the end of the century, we have the Caracci beginning to paint in Bologna, and Caravaggio in Naples. It had been only a hundred years since Botticelli painted Venus, fresh from the salt sea foam.

In literature, likewise, at the opening of the *Cinquecento* there was the historian Guicciardini; the political writer Machiavelli; the poet Ariosto; the cultivated Castiglione. At the end, there is only Torquato Tasso (1544–1595), who stands drooping, like a figure of Italy. Tasso was the last great genius of the Italian Renaissance; and he stands there facing the oncoming decadence in gifted helplessness. He had many talents, a noble nature, a melancholy temperament, and a weak character. His story is a tale of court favor and success, of rivalry and suspicion. His home was Ferrara, but he wandered about a great deal, attempting to ease his melancholy. Eventually, his mind gave way, and he was put in a madhouse by his patron, the Duke of Ferrara, where he remained for seven years. He spent his last years in the monastery of Sant' Onofrio, on the Janiculum at Rome, where, for a long time, tourists used to stop and gaze at the remains of an ancient oak under whose shade he was accustomed to sit in the Roman afternoon. One poet and critic said of Tasso: "Italy's great literature, her living, national and, at the same time, human literature, with which she reconciled Antiquity and the Middle Ages, and with which she, in an altogether Roman way, represented a renewed Europe, ended with Tasso." His sad life is a fitting epilogue to the Italian Renaissance.

This general course of ascent, culmination, and decline holds true of Venice, also, although the chronology differs. For Venice, in her art, preserved her independence from the normal Italian experience as resolutely as she did that independence of action in politics. She produced no literature—piqued, perhaps, because Italy had adopted the Tuscan dialect rather than her own for the national language. But in the arts, after decay had elsewhere set in, she bloomed in the fullness of perfection, as late roses blossom when other bushes show nothing.

In architecture and sculpture, the Lombardi, a Venetian family probably from Lombardy, flourished for nearly a century (1452–1537), and left their mark on Venice in the form of tombs and statues, churches and palaces. Contemporary with the last generation of Lombardi came the gifted Alessandro Leopardi (d. 1522), who completed the great statue of Colleoni designed by Verrocchio, and gave a new impulse to Venetian sculpture. While the sculptors of Tuscany had been studying Roman remains, the Isles of Greece had been giving Greek models to their Venetian conquerors; and Leopardi in particular profited greatly by them. In the sister art of architecture, the first memorable name after the Lombardi is that of the Florentine Jacopo Sansovino, who spent most of a long life in Venice, where he built the Zecca, the Loggetta, the Libreria Vecchia, and the Scala d'Oro, or Golden Stairway, of the Palace of the Doges. Palladio, of whom we have already taken note, came to Venice from Vicenza, and bequeathed his name to the neo-classic style known as Palladian.

In painting, first came the famous Bellini family, Japoco (1400–1464?), and his two sons, Gentile and Giovanni. After them came Vittore Carpaccio (1455–1526), painter of St. Jerome and his lion and of St. George and his dragon. Then followed in rapid succession the most gifted group of painters that ever lived at the same time, all born within twenty years of one another, as if to prove how prodigally Nature could endow a petty province that had had the good fortune to please her. There was Giorgione, from Castelfranco on the Venetian mainland; Titian, of Cadore, noblest of the portrait painters; Palma Vecchio, from Bergamo, creator of the superb women of Venice; Sebastiano del Piombo, pupil of Giorgione and friend of Michelangelo, who painted the Fornarina in the Uffizi Gallery; Lorenzo Lotto, of Bergamo, another painter of exquisite women, aristocratic men, noble saints, and poetical angels; Giovanni Antonio da Pordenone, a painter of portraits second only to those of Titian; Bonifazio, of Verona, depicter of patrician luxury; Paris Bordone, of Treviso, so uncertain in merit, yet, when at his best, so rich in hue, so admirable in his pictures of Venetian ceremonial; and, at the close of the century, the giant Iacopo Robusti, called Tintoretto (1518–1594), and Paolo Veronese (1528–1588). This cluster of names serves to demonstrate that, while elsewhere in Italy art was dwindling into mannerism and exaggeration, Venice was putting forth an extraordinary burst of pictorial magnificence. And yet, even in Venice, by the end of the sixteenth century, none of these great names were left.

The causes of the end of the Renaissance in Italy are far from clear. Probably, the most important one was Italy's loss of economic supremacy. The brilliant achievements of Florence and of the other centers of the Renaissance had rested, to a large extent, on a foundation of commercial prosperity. That prosperity, in its turn, depended upon the Italian monopoly of Near-Eastern trade after the fall of the Byzantine Empire. The discovery of the New World, however, caused a shift of the centers of international trade from the Mediterranean to the Atlantic coasts, and, as a result, Italy's life-blood—commerce—was gradually drained away. The Catholic Reformation, too, like the Protestant Reformation to the north of the Alps, had a stultifying effect upon the intellectual life of the country, in that it promoted, as an ineluctable by-product of its fervor, attitudes of bigotry and intolerance—attitudes obviously hostile to the spirit of free investigation and free expression which is so necessary to the survival of any intellectual and artistic movement. Other causes might be speculated upon: the persistence of ignorance and superstition among the great masses of the people of Italy; the political instability of the peninsula; the oppressive effects of foreign domination. Indeed, as many causes may be adduced as there are points of view regarding the Renaissance. The truth of the matter is, very likely, that the expiration of the Italian Renaissance was the effect of all of the causes cited, and of many more besides, none of which in itself would have been sufficient to extinguish the brilliant light which had been lighted in Florence and then carried to Rome, but all of which, taken as a whole, formed a hostile and repressive force which not even the natural exuberance of the Italians could resist. And so, the twilight of a new "middle age" was about to descend upon Italy, a time of stasis, if not of decay, while the revolution which the Renaissance had unleashed moved beyond the Alps and into the "barbarian" kingdoms of Europe.

V
ITALY IN THE MODERN WORLD
(1580–1814)

1. *The End of the* Cinquecento

By the end of the sixteenth century, Italy had fallen, as we have seen, like a ripe apple into the hands of foreigners. She lay helpless under ambitious Jesuits, zealous inquisitors, petty princelings, and ambitious Spanish viceroys. The glories of the preceding age had faded into memory; and the will to think, as well as the freedom to act, had almost vanished entirely from art and intellectual life as well as from political life. Italy was on her way to a new phase of her history, one which was to last for almost two and one-half centuries. It was a phase characterized by stasis and stagnation at every level and in every place—except in Venice, always individual; and in Rome, where a freshly revivified papacy now flourished, phoenix-like, after the debacle of the Reformation. Her political life had become, as it were, grand-ducal, like something out of a Lehar operetta. Her religion had become formal, superstitious, and a matter of dread obligation rather than of spontaneity and willing belief. Her literature was now affected, stilted, and, like that of ancient Rome in decline, it glorified rhetoric for the sake of rhetoric. Her architecture magnified the excesses of the Baroque, and her sculpture was steeped in mannerism and exaggeration. The entire peninsula had become, it seemed, a theater, where plots were spun and lines recited for the delectation of Europe.

The history of these two and a half centuries is not to be found so much in the solemn volumes of historians as in the journals of German, French, and English travelers; for during this time Italy was not a country, either geographically or sentimentally; it became instead a place of recreation for gentlemen on the Grand Tour, for pious folk bound for the Eternal City, for virtuosi seeking classical reliques, and for elderly statesmen hoping to find a cure for their gout. It was the Italian *opera bouffe,* played out on the most beautiful and charming stage in the world. The best description of Italy during the century following the end of the *Cinquecento* lies in the journals of a keen-witted Frenchman, Michel de Montaigne, who, in the company of friends, spent several months in Italy (1580–1581). Confusingly enough, Montaigne's diary is sometimes written in the second person, and sometimes in the third. Nonetheless, this is a small enough burden to bear in return for the Frenchman's vivid descriptions of life in the peninsula.

At Verona, which was within the territory of the Republic of Venice, he was introduced to the Italian love of bureaucratic formality. "Without the health certificates which they had obtained at Trent, they would not have been able to enter the city. There is no plague, nor any rumor of one; it is simply the custom—so that they may cheat us of the few pennies that they cost. We went to see the cathedral, where Montaigne thought the behavior of the men at High Mass to be very peculiar indeed. They chatted even in the choir of the church, standing up, with their hats on and their backs to the altar, and seemed not to pay the slightest attention to the service except at the elevation of the Host. The Mass was accompanied by the music of organs and violins. . . . We went to see the castle and were shown about by the officer in charge. The government [of Venice] keeps a garrison of about sixty soldiers there; but, according to what Montaigne was told, they are there to be used against the people of the city rather than against foreign enemies. We also saw a congregation of monks called the Gesuati of St. Jerome. These men are not priests, and they neither say Mass nor preach. Most of them are ignorant men, but they carry on a business, both in Verona and elsewhere, of distilling lemon-water. They are dressed in white, with little white caps and a dark brown gown over it. Handsome young men." The travelers also visited Verona's ghetto, or Jewish quarter, and then the Roman amphitheater, which Montaigne thought "the noblest building he has ever seen."

From Verona, Montaigne went to Vicenza, which he described as "a large city, though a little smaller than Verona, all full of the palaces of the nobility." Here, he ran into the Gesuati of St. Jerome again, selling their lemon-water. "These monks tell us that they whip themselves every day; each one has his own switch at his place in the chapel." From Vicenza, Montaigne traveled along a broad straight road, running through a fertile countryside to Padua. The inns here, he complained, could not compare with those of Germany; they were redeemed, however, by the fact that they were cheaper by a third than those of that country. "The streets are narrow and ugly, with few people about and few handsome houses. We went about all the next day and saw the famous schools of fencing, dancing and riding, where there were more than a hundred French gentlemen together." In fact, young men went there in great numbers—Frenchmen in particular —less to acquire a knowledge of books than to acquire those accomplishments which were then necessary to a man of fashion.

In Venice, Montaigne dined with the French ambassador. The latter confided to him "that he had no social relations with anybody in the city, because the people were so suspicious of foreigners that anyone who spoke to him more than once would immediately become an object of distrust." Montaigne thought that the four most remarkable things about the city were its canals, the police, the Piazza of St. Mark's, and the crowds of foreigners. He was delighted, and a bit alarmed, to receive as a gift a little book of *Letters* from a Venetian lady, one of that celebrated class of courtesans who, while outside the matrimonial pale, managed to live in ostentatious luxury and to be cultivated by masculine society. Returning by way of Padua, Montaigne passed the renowned sulphur springs, frequented in spring and summer by the wealthy and fashionable sick, who took mud or vapor baths and drank the waters. He noted the canals, the system of irrigation in the plains where rows of vine-laden trees intersected fields of wheat, the enormously strong oxen, the broad mud flats, which were once swamps and which the government was attempting to reclaim.

At Rovigo, a small town in Venetian territory, he found "as great an abundance of meat as in France . . . and though they use no lard for the roast, they do not take away the flavor. The bedrooms, because there is no glass and the windows are never shut, are not as clean as in France. The beds are well made, smooth, and well supplied with mattresses; but they have nothing but rough coverings, and they are very close-fisted with white sheets; if a man travels alone, or with little style, he will not be given any."

Crossing the Po, as he had the Adige, upon some kind of pontoon bridge, Montaigne went on to the Duchy of Ferrara, where he was delayed on account of his health certificate. The ducal regulations on this point were very specific. On the door of every room in the inn was written, "Remember your health certificate." Lest anyone forget, the names of all travelers were reported to the police as soon as they arrived at an inn. The traveler found most of the streets broad and straight, and paved with brick. There were many palaces, but few people. He did what any visitor to Ferrara did at the time: paid his respects to the duke, went to see Tasso in the madhouse, and observed the odd Gesuati of St. Jerome again.

At Bologna, in the Papal States, Montaigne found a thriving city, larger than Ferrara and with many more people. There, also, he found young Frenchmen come to learn riding and fencing. He admired the fine porticos that covered almost every sidewalk, the handsome palaces, the buildings of the School of Sciences, the famous bronze statue of Neptune by John of Bologna. "The cost of living is about the same as at Padua—that is, very reasonable. But the city is less peaceful in the older sections, which are a sort of no-man's-land between the partisans of the different nations. On the one side are always the French; and, on the other, the Spaniards, who are there in great numbers."

This national factionalism was not confined to Bologna, but was found everywhere in the Papal States. Even fifty years later, a perplexed visitor to Ravenna wrote: "The city is divided, as you know, into Guelfs and Ghibellines; so much so that one man will not go into another's church, and each side has its own place in the public square. A tailor who sews for one side need not look for business from the other, and it is the same in all the trades. They distinguish one faction from the other by the style of wearing one's hair, one's cap, and so forth." But the pale ghosts of once-great parties were slight inconveniences compared to the *banditti* who overran the pope's domains. These marauders, who also decked themselves out with ancient names, under pretense of fighting one another, succeeded in robbing, burning, pillaging, raping, and murdering with perfect impartiality. The soldiers and the common people sometimes united against these rascals, but the latter were too strong and too numerous, and often too well connected, to be completely extirpated. In the Papal States, one highwayman named Piccolomini, the scion of a famous Sienese family, who had given popes and princes to Italy, raided wherever he chose with impunity. Once he led a band of two hundred men up to the very walls of the City. On that occasion, the pope could do little more than buy him off, for he was under the protection of the Grand Duke of Tuscany. As part of the bargain, Piccolomini, after confessing publicly to three hundred and seventy murders, was absolved and pardoned.

Leaving Bologna, Montaigne hesitated in the choice of roads because of brigands. Apparently he chose wisely, for he was not robbed. He crossed the Apennines by a road which, he says, is the first one he found in Italy that could be called bad, and entered the Grand Duchy of Tuscany. One village on the way, still in papal territory, was famous throughout Europe for the knavery of its innkeepers, who made extravagant promises until the traveler was safely housed, and then rendered only the scantest services, and that reluctantly. At another village, this one in Tuscany, rival innkeepers rode out to meet Montaigne and struggled to secure him for themselves. One offered to serve a rabbit for dinner, gratis, if Montaigne would lodge with him. The Frenchman, however, prudently rode around to all the inns, inspecting food and wine and beds and making bargains. He finally decided upon one particular inn; but the host managed to sneak "extras" into the bill for candles, linen, firewood, and food.

Florence, capital of the Grand Duchy, seemed to him smaller than Ferrara. He went to see the ducal stables, the ducal menagerie, Michelangelo's statues, Giotto's campanile, and finished by remarking that he had never seen a country with so few beautiful women as Italy. Lodgings he found inferior in comfort to those in France, and the food was less well served, and served in smaller portions, than in Germany. The windows were large, and always open, for there was no glass, and if the shutters were shut they excluded light and air as well as wind. The beds were uncomfortable, the wines too sweet, the sauces and seasonings inferior; moreover, Florence was held to be the most expensive city in Italy. Montaigne dined with the Grand Duke, Francesco I (son of Cosimo I), and his second wife, Bianca Cappello, who sat at the head of the table. She had a handsome face, was reputed handsome, and seemed to have been able to keep her wandering husband devoted to her for a surprisingly long time.

From Florence, Montaigne went to Siena. Along the way, he noted that the soil seemed tolerably fertile, and that there was hardly a plot of ground that was not under cultivation. In the city, he noted the Duomo, the palaces, the splendid *piazza,* the fountains, and—a very important point—that the wines are "good and fresh." He observed that, in Tuscany, the city walls are allowed to fall into ruin, while the citadels are carefully fortified and no one is permitted to go near them; which showed, he concluded, that the Grand Duke feared domestic insurrection more than foreign attack. He took occasion to comment that "the French are kept in such affectionate remembrance here by the people of the country that any mention of them brings tears to their eyes, for war itself, with freedom in some form, seems to them far sweeter than the peace which they enjoy under this 'tyranny.'" The French had aided Siena in its brave struggle for liberty, and a valiant remnant of French and Sienese had held out until the Peace of Cateau-Cambresis (1559) when France abandoned the city to Cosimo de' Medici.

From Siena he rode southward past Bolsena, Viterbo, and a pleasant valley covered with wood, "a rare commodity in this country." He commended, incidentally, the customs of the area. In good houses, dinner was served at two o'clock and supper at nine. If there was a play, it began at six and was over by suppertime. "It is a good country for a lazy fellow, for everyone gets up late."

Montaigne's first interest in Italy was Rome; and, in Rome, the chief attraction was the papacy. Soon after his arrival, he was received by the sovereign pontiff, Pope Gregory XIII.

"On December 29, M. d'Abain, who was then our ambassador, a learned gentleman and a long-standing friend of M. de Montaigne, advised him to go and kiss the feet of the pope. M. de Montaigne and M. d'Estissac went in the coach of the ambassador, who, after he had been granted an audience, caused them to be called by the pope's chamberlain. According to custom, only the ambassador was with the pope, who had by his side a bell which he would ring when he wished to summon someone. The ambassador was seated, uncovered, at the pope's left hand. The pope himself never uncovers his head before anyone, but no ambassador may remain covered in his presence. M. d'Estissac entered first, then M. de Montaigne. . . . After taking a step or two into the chamber, in a corner of which sits the pope, the visitor, whoever he may be, kneels and waits for the pope's blessing. This given, he rises and advances to the middle of the room. A stranger, however, must never approach the pope by going directly across the room; he must turn to the left upon entering, and then, after making a detour along the wall, approach his chair from the side. When a visitor has gone half the distance to the chair, he must kneel again for another blessing; then he advances as far as the carpet spread out in front of the pope. Here, he must kneel on both knees, while the ambassador who presents him kneels on one. The ambassador moves back the pope's robe from his right foot, exposing a red shoe with a white cross embroidered upon it. The kneeling visitor must keep himself in the posture until he is close to the pope's foot, and then bend down to kiss it. M. de Montaigne swore that the pope raised the tip of his foot a little. They all kissed it one after another, each making room for the other as the ceremony proceeded. Then the ambassador covered the pope's foot, and, having resumed his seat, said what seemed fitting on behalf of M. d'Estissac and M. de Montaigne. The pope, with a courteous expression, then encouraged M. d'Estissac to cultivate learning and virtue, and M. de Montaigne to maintain the devotion he had always exhibited toward the Church and the interests of the Most Christian King. He added that, whatever service he might render them, they could depend on receiving, this being an Italian figure of speech. They said nothing, but, having been blessed again as a sign of dismissal, they left the room in the same order. Each one leaves in the manner that seems best; but the usual custom is to walk backwards, or at least sideways, so as to avoid turning one's back to the pope. As in entering, one kneels for another blessing at the halfway mark, and again at the door for a final benediction."

Some time afterward, M. de Montaigne visited the Vatican Library. "On March 6 I went to see the library of the Vatican, which is housed in five or six connecting rooms. There are many rows of desks, each one having a great number of books chained to it. Also, in the chests, which were all opened for my inspection, I saw many manuscripts, of which I remember particularly a Seneca and the *Opuscula* of Plutarch. Among the noteworthy sights I saw was a statue of the good Aristides, with a fine head, bald and heavily bearded, a grand forehead, and an expression of great gentleness and majesty. The base of the statue is very ancient and has Aristides' name written on it. I saw likewise a Chinese book written in strange characters, on leaves made of a certain material more tender and transparent than our paper. . . . It is said that these sheets are made of the bark of a certain tree, as is a fragment of ancient papyrus which I saw. I saw also the Breviary of St. Gregory in manuscript, which has no date; but the account given of it states that it has come down from one hand to another since the time of St. Gregory himself. It is a missal similar to our own, and it was taken to the recent Council of Trent as an authority for the ceremonies of the Church. Next, there was a book by St. Thomas Aquinas, containing corrections made by the author himself, who wrote badly, using small characters even worse than my own. Next, a Bible printed on parchment, one of those which Plantin has recently printed in four languages. . . . Next, the original manuscript of the book which King Henry of England wrote against Luther and sent, fifty years ago, to Pope Leo X. . . . I inspected the library without any difficulty; indeed, anyone may visit it and make what extracts he likes; it is open almost every morning."

Montaigne shared with his contemporaries the firm belief that sermons were an entertainment as well as a method of spiritual instruction, and he took great pleasure in listening, particularly to Lenten preachers. "There were many excellent preachers. In particular, there was one, a renegade rabbi, who preached to the Jews on Saturday evenings in the Church of the Trinità. Here, there was always a group of sixty Jews who were bound by the laws of Rome to be present. This preacher had been a famous doctor among the Jews, and he attacked their beliefs by their own arguments, even out of the mouths of their rabbis and from the words of the Bible.

He had much skill and knowledge of the subject, and of the languages necessary for the elaboration of the same. There was another, a priest called Padre Toledo, who preached before the pope and the cardinals, who was a man of extraordinary ability in learning, in appositeness of expression, and in the mustering of his arguments. Still another, who preached at the church of the Jesuits, was distinguished for his beauty of expression. The last two were members of the Jesuit society. It is remarkable how great is the part played by this society in the Christian community; it is my belief that never before has there existed any confraternity which has risen to such eminence, or which may affect so strongly the destinies of the world, if it is able to prosecute its designs in the future."

Naturally, Montaigne missed none of Rome's magnificent Holy Week ceremonies. "On the morning of Holy Thursday, the pope, in full pontificals, accompanied by the cardinals, climbed to the second platform of the great portico of St. Peter's. In his hand he held a lighted torch. Then, a canon of St. Peter's, who stood to one side of the balcony, read in a loud voice a Latin bull, by which an infinite variety of men were excommunicated. Among others, the Huguenots were specially named, and all those princes who have seized and hold any of the lands of the Church—an article which elicited great shouts of laughter from the cardinals Medici and Caraffa, who stood close to the pope. The reading of the bull lasted a good hour, for when the canon had read a paragraph in Latin, then Cardinal Gonzaga, who stood on the opposite side of the balcony, would translate it into Italian for the people. When the reading was over, the pope threw his lighted torch down among the people, and Cardinal Gonzaga, perhaps in jest, threw another. This caused a great disturbance below among the people, for everyone scrambled to pick up a fragment of the torches, in the course of which many a great blow was given with fist or cudgel. . . . On these days it is the custom to exhibit the veil of St. Veronica. This is a face, wrought in needlework, of a dark and somber tint, and framed in the fashion of a mirror. It is shown with great ceremony from a high pulpit, and no spectacle provokes such a great show of reverence as this. The people all prostrate themselves on the ground, the greater part of them weeping and uttering cries of woe. . . . On these same occasions, they show to the people also, with equal ceremony, a lancehead enclosed in a crystal vessel. This display is made several times during the day, and the crowd which comes to witness it is so huge that, as far as the eye can see, there is nothing but an endless throng of men and women. Here is the true papal court."

Montaigne also had occasion to observe the bizarre religious confraternities which were fashionable at the time. "There are more than a hundred confraternities, and there is no distinguished man who does not belong to one. Our kings belong to that of the Gonfalcon. Each particular society exercises, especially during Lent, certain functions of religious significance, and, on a special day, they walk about in companies clad in linen gowns, each company wearing its own color—white, red, blue, green, or black—almost all with their faces covered. . . . The whole city, as night approached, seemed to be on fire as these companies marched in procession toward St. Peter's; every man bore a lighted candle of white wax in his hand. I am sure that at least twelve thousand torches must have gone by the place where I stood; for, from eight o'clock until midnight, the street was filled with the procession, marshaled and regulated in such excellent fashion that, though there were many different companies coming from various directions, the ranks were never broken nor the progress delayed. Each confraternity had a fine choir of musicians, who sang as they marched. In the midst of the ranks was a file of penitents, about five hundred in number, who scourged themselves with whips, which left their backs all raw and bloody. This is a riddle which baffles me, but there is no denying that they were bruised and cut in cruel fashion, and that this self-torture went on without ceasing. Judging by the aspect of their faces and the assurance of their walk, and the steadfastness audible in their speech and visible in their demeanor (for I heard several of them speak), it would never have occurred to me that they were engaged in a painful task. Among them were youths of twelve or thirteen years; and right in front of me was one, very young and handsome, over whose wounds a woman lamented loudly. But the boy turned toward us with a laugh, and said, 'Enough of that. What I do, I do for your sins and not for my own.' Not only was there no appearance of distress or pain, but they even went about their flagellation with an appearance of pleasure. . . . Along with them went certain men carrying wine, which was offered to them now and then, and some of them took a mouthful of it; and sometimes sweetmeats were given. The winecarriers often took wine in their mouths and then spat it out and so moistened the lashes of the whips, which were of cord and were becoming coagulated with blood, in order to separate the thongs. They also spewed the wine over the wounds of some of the flagellants. The appearance of their shoes and breeches suggested that they were people of low condition, and that the majority of them had sold themselves to this service. . . . And on this day great liberty is granted to all women, and throughout the night the streets are filled with ladies nearly all going about

Italy in the Modern World

on foot. Nevertheless, the city seems to have greatly mended its manners, for all amorous glances and manifestations are suppressed."

M. de Montaigne, it is obvious, was an impassioned gawker. There was nothing he loved better than watching life in the streets. For such a man, Italy is a God-send; and Rome is paradise itself. "The most common exercise of the Romans is to walk in the streets; and there are streets especially set aside for this purpose." Pretty women, noble men, splendid courtesans—everything and everyone enchanted him. On one of his walks, he witnessed the public hanging of one Catena, a notorious bandit of the time. "On January 11, in the morning, as M. de Montaigne was leaving the house on horseback, he met Catena, a famous robber and chief of *banditti,* whom they were leading from the prison. This man had caused panic in all Italy, and monstrous tales were told about him. One such concerned an occasion on which he captured two Capuchin monks. He promised the two priests that he would spare their lives if they denied God; and when the unhappy men did so, he slew them immediately, without any motive either of gain or vengeance. M. de Montaigne halted to witness this spectacle. Over and above the escort, which is customary in such countries as France, here they allow a huge crucifix, draped in black, to precede the criminal. At the foot of this cross is a crowd of men wearing cloaks and masks; these are said to be gentlefolk of Rome, members of a confraternity sworn to accompany criminals to execution and corpses to the grave. Two of these helped the condemned man into the cart, preaching to him the whole time. One of them let him kiss continually a picture of Our Lord, so that those in the street might not see the man's face. At the gibbet, which was a beam upon two posts, they held this picture before his face until he was pushed off the ladder. He died as criminals commonly do; that is, without movement or cry. He was a dark man, of about thirty years. After he was dead, they cut the body into four quarters. It is the custom here to kill criminals without torture, and then, after death, to subject the corpse to barbarous treatment. . . . The crowd, who had not felt any pity at the hanging, cried out in sorrow at every stroke of the ax. As soon as the man was dismembered, Jesuits, and other clerics, went up to a high place and shouted to the people on all sides that they should observe and learn from this example."

Even the gossip of Rome tended to be encrusted with moral lessons; and Montaigne, sophisticated traveler though he was, was not above repeating some of the common talk in the City. "A certain man was with a courtesan, lying in bed and enjoying the situation to the utmost, when, at the twenty-fourth hour, the *Ave Maria* was rung, whereupon the girl sprang out of bed and knelt down on the floor to say her prayer. Shortly after, he was with another, when suddenly the good mother (for these girls are always in the hands of some old bawd whom they call their 'mother' or their 'aunt') knocked at the door and, having entered in a great rage, tore off of the girl's neck a ribbon from which was hanging a medal of Our Lady, so that it might not be contaminated by the sinful act of the wearer. The young girl, it seems, was greatly depressed by the fact that she had neglected to remove this medal first."

Leaving Rome regretfully, Montaigne went first on pilgrimage to Loreto, and thence to the baths at Della Villa. There he decided to give a ball. "Five or six days before the date, I had caused notice of my entertainment to be given in all the neighboring villages; and on the day previous I sent invitations to all the gentlefolk then at either of the baths. I bade them come to the ball, and to the supper afterward; and I sent to Lucca for presents—which must be numerous—so as to avoid the appearance of favoring one lady above all the rest, and to steer clear of jealousy and suspicion. . . ." At the appointed hour, the guests arrived and the ball began. M. de Montaigne had recourse to the advice of the most distinguished lady in choosing the most beautiful young women in the gathering, who were to be given prizes. "For the distribution of these prizes, the girls were called one by one from their places to come before the lady and myself, sitting side by side; whereupon I gave to the lady the gift which seemed appropriate, having first kissed it. Then the lady, taking it in her hand, gave it to the young girl, and said: 'This is the gentleman who is giving you this charming present. Thank him for it.' I added, 'No, rather your thanks are due to the gracious lady who had designated you, out of so many others, as worthy of reward. I much regret that the offering made to you is not more worthy of such merit as yours.' . . . I also invited all to supper, as the meals in Italy are like the lightest of our repasts in France; and on this occasion I only provided a few joints of veal and a pair or two of fowls. . . . I also found a place at table for Divizia, a poor peasant woman who lives about two miles from the baths. She is unmarried, and supports herself by her handiwork. She is ugly, about thirty-seven years old, and unable to read or write. But it happened that in her childhood there came to live in her father's house an uncle, who was always reading aloud from Aristo and the other poets. Divizia seemed to take a natural delight in poetry, and she soon was able not only to make verses with amazing readiness, but also to weave into them the ancient legends, the names of gods of various countries, of sciences, and of illustrious men, all as though she had received a liberal education. She recited some of her verses in my honor, which, to be truthful about it, were little more than verse and rhyme; but the diction was elegant and spontaneous. I entertained at my ball more than a hundred strangers, even though the time was inconvenient for them, seeing that they were then in the midst of their silk harvest, the principal crop of the year. During this season they work, morning and evening, regardless of feast days, at plucking the leaves of the mulberry for their silkworms; and all my peasant guests were engaged in this work."

After this pastoral interlude Montaigne felt once more the call of Rome. On this occasion, however, he seemed in a less indulgent mood. Making a comparison between freedom in Venice and that in Rome, he argued for Venice, and gave these reasons: "Item, that in Rome houses were so insecure that those who had large sums of money were advised to leave their purses at their banks, so as not to find their chests broken open. Item, that it is not safe to go out at night. Item, that the Superior General of the Cordeliers was dismissed from his position and thrown into prison because, in a sermon preached before Pope Gregory XIII and the cardinals, he accused prelates of laziness and luxury. Item, that his luggage had been examined by customs officials on entering the City, and had been ransacked down to the smallest article of clothing . . . besides that, they had taken all the books they found in order to examine them, and they took so long about it that one who had something to do might as well mark them off as lost. Add to that that their rules were so extraordinary that the 'Book of Hours of Our Lady' fell under suspicion because it came from Paris rather than from Rome. And they also confiscated books which were written by some German theologians against heretics, because in combating the errors of the heretics these theologians had described the errors." Another book belonging to Montaigne, a history of Switzerland, was confiscated because the translator was a heretic.

Montaigne's own work, the *Essays,* had been submitted to the Master of the Sacred Palace—i.e., the pope's theologian—who examined them. They were returned after a long delay, and the Master stated that he left it to Montaigne's own conscience to correct what seemed to be in bad taste, if not outright dangerous. Item, that Montaigne had used the word "luck." Item, that he had named poets who were heretics. Item, that he had suggested that a man at prayer ought to be free from any unworthy inclination. Item, that he thought death sufficient punishment for any crime, and suggested that any torture before execution was cruel.

In Montaigne's rambling but perceptive and critical account of his Italian sojourn is captured the spirit which prevailed in the peninsula from the end of the sixteenth century until almost the middle of the nineteenth. It is an Italy of olives, mulberries, and chestnuts; of fertile fields and vine-laden trees, of irrigated plains and treeless valleys; of innkeepers, good, bad, and indifferent; of garrisons and citadels, of ducal palaces and daredevil *banditti;* of beggars, professional flagellants, perfuming friars and perfumed cardinals; of prelates in coaches, and antique ruins and Renaissance glory. It is an Italy where all stands still for the inspection and the delight of the visitor. In short, it is Italy in an age of stagnation.

2. The Age of Stagnation: Politics (1580–1789)

One advantage of stagnation, of course, is stability. And, in fact, this era in Italy was one of comparative political stability. The dukes, viceroys, and sundry autocrats and oligarchs were settled in their domains with a security that seems a little tame, and perhaps dull, after the whirlwind of foreign invasion. The wars of Europe, naturally, continued to be fought out in the north of Italy, and conflicts between France, Spain, and Austria—waged at first to contain the ambitions of Austria's Hapsburg dynasty, and then to abate the over-greatness of France's Bourbons—were bitter, bloody, and usually inconclusive in result; and the Italians were the principal victims. Nonetheless, the period of confusion, of shifting boundaries and ephemeral regimes belonged to the past, and each of the Italian principalities now enjoyed a consecutive political history over a span of two hundred years.

Of these political entities, Venice was the wealthiest and the most influential. Still ranked as one of Europe's great powers, she was courted, flattered, bribed, sought as an ally, and feared as an enemy. She formed part of the councils of Europe, and she bore herself with dignity and pride. Nonetheless, a change was being worked, slowly but irreversibly, in the fortunes of the city. So slow was its progress, however, and so subtle and well trained in the arts of diplomatic simulation were the statesmen of Venice, that the city's reputation and prestige remained untarnished long after the power upon which they rested had shrunk almost to the vanishing point. Despite the glories of the Battle of Lepanto, for example, Venice lost the island of Cyprus to the Turks; but her accomplished diplomats secured a peace which lasted for two generations—a surprisingly long time, considering that Venetians and Turks were destined to fight each other until both lay utterly exhausted.

Venice was less successful in her relations with her Christian neighbors. Her most spectacular quarrel was with the Holy See. A celebrated and irritating papal bull, entitled *In Coena Domini* ("At the Lord's Supper") had been issued and reissued under the stimulus of the Catholic Counter-Reformation. Read every Maundy Thursday, it was probably the very bull that Montaigne heard translated from the balcony of St. Peter's. This document, besides excommunicating Europe's multitudinous heretics, asserted papal claims of an extreme character wholly reminiscent of those of Boniface VIII in the High Middle Ages and generally gave convincing evidence of the papacy's renewed vigor and ambition. The other states of Italy bowed and accepted, at least to outward appearances, this declaration of papal supremacy; but Venice not only rejected the claims of the Holy See but also forbade that the bull be read in her territories. The city, while constantly professing her profound respect for Rome, had, in fact, always been self-willed and opposed to papal pretensions. By nature, she was worldly rather than other-worldly; and, by preference, she was free-thinking rather than Catholic. The quarrel over *In Coena Domini* was aggravated by festering disagreements over territory and politics. For one thing, Venice insisted upon her right to tax Church property and to bring to trial clerics accused of secular offenses. Acting upon the latter right, in 1606 she arrested and tried, and then condemned, two priests guilty of a felony. Since, by this act, Venice openly defied the doctrines laid down in the papal bull, Pope Paul V laid the city under a general interdict. The Signory retaliated by issuing a decree of banishment against all priests who should honor the interdict. The pope, however, stood firm. All the world knows, he said, that "there can be no true piety without complete submission to the Spiritual Power." But "all the world" was not of the same opinion. The Protestant powers rushed to the aid of Venice; and the Catholic powers, including the states of Italy, declared their support of the pope. Each camp outdid the other in hurling defiance, insults, and threats in the faces of their opponents. War hung like thunder in the air, and it seemed that all Europe was about to be plunged into a religious conflict of major dimensions. But Henry IV, who had just finished pacifying his own Kingdom of France and saw that the country could not support another major upheaval, now intervened as a peacemaker. A compromise was patched up between Pope Paul and the Signory by means of which both parties were able to save face. Swords were sheathed, apologies were offered all around and accepted, and Christendom breathed more easily for a time.

Out of this quarrel emerged at least one noble reputation. Fra Paolo Sarpi, a priest, has properly been called the last of the great Venetians. In his youth, he was so precocious a scholar that at the age of eighteen he was already Professor of Theology; by the time that he was twenty, he had won also the chairs of philosophy and mathematics. As a man, he was, after Francis Bacon, the foremost scientist of his time. He discovered the valves of the veins and—independently of Harvey—the circulation of the blood. He experimented with heat, light, sound, color, pneumatics, and the magnetic needle. In the field of astronomy his accomplishments were such that Galileo called him *il mio padre e maestro*—"my father and my master." Sir Henry Wotton, the English ambassador at Venice, wrote that "Fra Paolo is as expert in the history of plants as if he had never perused any book but that of Nature." To his scientific talents the priest added those of the historian, and he wrote a celebrated history of the epoch-making Council of Trent. During the conflict between Venice and Pope Paul V, Fra Paolo sided with his native city, and he was appointed Theologian to the Republic. Although he was in Holy Orders, it was not Rome, but Venice, who had first claim on his loyalty, for he was above all else a patriot; and he argued Venice's case, brilliantly and successfully, before the nations of Europe. At his death in 1623, his last thought was of Venice, and his final words were, *Esto perpetua*—"may she live forever."

The good friar's dying wish, however, was not to be granted. Venice was at the dusk of her splendid day. True, some moments of glory still remained to her. In the middle of the seventeenth century, the war with the Turks was renewed, and the Venetians valiantly and single-handedly resisted the mighty Islamic empire for twenty-five years, although in the end she was forced to cede Crete to them (1669). A second war between the Venetians and the Turks later in the century met with at least ephemeral success. In 1682, with the Emperor Leopold and the Polish king, John Sobieski, as her allies, she conquered the Morea, Egina, Santa Maura, and several fortresses in Dalmatia, all of which were assigned to her by formal treaty in 1699. But the Turks could not allow so weak an enemy to retain one of the fairest provinces of Islam. Before their very eyes—or at least before those of their innumerable spies—the ancient Republic was disintegrating. Supreme power was in the hands of an oligarchy which was becoming daily more irresolute and incompetent. Half of the nobles belonging to the Grand Council had been reduced, over the years, to a condition of extreme poverty, and they lived by selling their votes to whomever could afford to buy them. The Council of Ten came to regard the state as a private preserve provided for their own benefit and profit. Justice was for sale at every court, the state treasury was emptied, the fortifications were falling into ruin, and the armed forces had become a refuge for those who were otherwise unemployed or unemployable. The government exacted taxes without restraint, and for the exclusive profit of the nobility, until the distant provinces of the Republic were forced to plead for mercy.

The newly acquired provinces in Dalmatia came to long for their lost prosperity under the comparatively benign yoke of the Turkish sultan. This sultan, Achmed III, was of course informed in detail of everything. Banking on Venetian disorganization and on the unrest of the citizens, in 1714 he sent his forces into the Morea, and in one month he reconquered that fortified peninsula. Not a hand had been raised to resist him.

The fact was that, by now, Venice had lost not only the means, but also the will, to resist. Centuries of continuous struggle and intrigue had taken their ineluctable toll, and the hearts, minds—and the pocketbooks—of the citizens of the Republic were exhausted. Henceforth, throughout the eighteenth century, the city, once the envy of Europe and the bulwark against the spread of Islam into the West, must perforce maintain a policy of neutrality. During the war of the Spanish Succession (1701–1714), she had been forced by weakness to stand aside as Europe combined to resist the overbearing power of Louis XIV of France. During that of the Austrian Succession (1740–1748), in which the Empress Maria Theresa secured her throne, Venice was similarly compelled to stand idly by while northern Italy once again became Europe's battleground. Like an old dog who has fought many good fights in its prime and now, lame and battle-scarred, maintains a dignified aloofness from the fray, Venice lay back. She no longer intervened in the affairs of Europe; indeed, she no longer had a voice in them. Of her vast empire, now only bits of Illyria and a few of the Ionian Islands remained to her outside of Italy. She therefore shut her eyes reluctantly to the past, and concentrated her attention on making herself "the revel of the earth, the masque of Italy." Frivolity, rather than greatness, now occupied the citizens; and the entertainment of travelers replaced the conquest of commercial markets as the preoccupation of the Most Serene Republic. It is true that her old glory flashed up once more, briefly, under the last great admiral, Angelo Emo, who, on the eve of the French Revolution, courageously cleared the seas of Algerian pirates. But it was too late. By then, Venice had run her course, and her end was at hand.

To the west of Venice, the unhappy duchy of Milan was fulfilling its melancholy destiny of being the prize of Spain while being coveted and fought for by France. The Spanish viceroys of the period fade into uniform anonymity. One after another they appear, levy exorbitant taxes, scheme how to circumvent the French ambitions of Cardinal Richelieu, Cardinal Mazarin, and Louis XIV, intrigue to extend Spanish domination, and then, after a few years, return to Spain a little richer but without leaving a clear imprint upon the pages of history. The dominant impression is one of ignorance, bigotry, cruelty, and inefficiency, overlaid with the elaborate ceremoniousness of rigid Spanish etiquette, and nothing more.

During this period, Milan, like the other Spanish possessions of Italy, slowly passed from Spanish hands into those of other foreign powers. Like mere parcels of valuable land, the provinces of Italy were traded back and forth, awarded as the spoils of wars between foreign powers, granted in consideration of familial love and affection, or assigned for the sake of the political equilibrium of Europe. Following the War of the Spanish Succession and then that of the Polish Succession (1733-1735)—matters in which Italy had no concern—the European powers, by an intricate system of treaties, attempted to re-establish European equilibrium by an elaborate system of weights and counterweights. Where the balances tipped too much to one side or the other, a province of Italy invariably was thrown in to restore them to a level. Milan was subject to only one such transfer, from Spain to Austria, by the treaties of Utrecht and Rastadt (1713-1714) which closed the War of the Spanish Succession. The same treaties took Naples and the island of Sardinia from Spain and gave them to Austria, and transferred Sicily from Spain to Savoy. Spain, however, perhaps understandably, was dissatisfied with this arrangement, and attempted to recover what she had lost; but a new European coalition against her forced her to renounce her claim. In the general pacification following this war, it was felt that a more satisfactory arrangement was needed, and provinces were again shuffled around. Savoy gave up Sicily to Austria and, in return, received Sardinia (1720). Finally, after the War of the Polish Succession, Austria, by the Peace of Vienna (1738), ceded Naples and Sicily to younger sons of the royal family of Spain, the Spanish Bourbons; it was stipulated, however, that these provinces should never be united with the crown of Spain. In exchange, Austria received the little duchy of Parma, which had fallen to a Spanish Bourbon upon the extinction of that city's native dynasty, the Farnese family. But ten years later, Parma was back in the hands of the Spanish Bourbons as a result of the War of the Austrian Succession.

Tuscany, once the gem of Italy, shared the fate of her sister states. After the first Grand Duke, Cosimo, six successors had followed, each one less capable than his predecessor. By the time that the last Grand Duke of the Medici line died in 1737, that once magnificent family had, through incapacity, an exaggerated taste for luxury, bigotry, and a penchant for homosexuality, dwindled into insignificance. Then, by virtue of that general reapportionment prescribed by the Peace of Vienna, the Grand Duchy was handed over to the Duke of Lorraine, the husband of the Empress

Maria Theresa of Austria. It thus became an appanage of the Hapsburg empire, and eventually came under the rule of the younger sons of the imperial house.

The record of these transactions—for they cannot be called otherwise—while it seems complex, actually is reduced, so far as final results are concerned, to this situation: Milan belonged to Austria; Naples, Sicily, and Parma belonged to the Spanish Bourbons; and Sardinia belonged to Savoy. In all of Italy, there remained only two powers who were not available for international barter: Savoy and the papacy.

The Dukes of Savoy, after their acquisition of Sardinia in 1720, and after seven centuries of being mere dukes, decided that the time had come to assume a more magnificent style. They therefore took for themselves the title of Kings of Sardinia. It was not an unmerited, nor a wholly illogical, elevation. The ancient duchy of the new Kings of Sardinia had had the misfortune to lie in the way of three powerful and warlike nations, France, Spain, and Austria. Savoy's plain of Piedmont made an admirable battleground, and the combatants chose it on all possible occasions for their wars. So, of course, the duchy was subjected to unremitting pillage, rape, and massacre. The entire blame, however, must not rest upon the shoulders of Spain, France, and Austria. The fact of the matter was that the Dukes of Savoy were every bit as ambitious and rapacious as their great neighbors. Whenever one of them thought he perceived an opportunity to seize a bit of neighboring territory, he caught at it recklessly and without regard to the consequences. Invariably, however, the French, Spanish, and Austrians conspired to deprive Savoy of its booty; and often, in exasperation, they not only took away the new territory but also deprived the ambitious dukes of some of their legitimately acquired domains. In this way, bit by bit, Savoy lost its old Swiss provinces and its old French provinces; and, gradually, Piedmont emerged as the most important—indeed, the only important—province of the Dukes of Savoy, until, in the general division of spoils in the first half of the eighteenth century, they ended up with Sardinia. The new Kingdom of Sardinia, therefore, had as its head the province of Piedmont; and the territory of the Kings of Sardinia became known, almost interchangeably, as both Sardinia and (more commonly) Piedmont.

For Italy as a whole, however, the most important fact of political life at this time was not Piedmont's union with Sardinia. Instead, it was that, while the people of the other states whiled away the time in entertainments and frivolities of all kinds, those of Piedmont, through constant warfare and a spirit of fierce independence, were gradually becoming a nation of soldiers. In devastation, war, and ruin, Piedmontese valor and Piedmontese courage were trained and developed. Eventually, it was to become obvious that Piedmont, and she alone, was the sole refuge and hope of whatever patriotic sentiments still remained in Italy.

To the south, strength of a different kind was obvious in the other of Italy's two living powers, the Papal States. The papacy at the end of the sixteenth century was in the full flood of revival, and the individual popes were carried along on the tide. The bold and successful front opposed to the Protestant enemy by the Counter-Reformation was supplemented with a renovation of discipline within. Heresy was suspected everywhere, and it was traced and tracked relentlessly. Papal inquisitors roamed about, spying what they might, and frightening the learned from publishing, printers from printing, and almost all thought of freedom from the minds of the people. Thus, it was thought, traitors—that is, heretics—would be extirpated. At the same time, faithful soldiers of the Church were being trained. Seminaries for priests of various nations were founded in Rome, and the schools of the Jesuits were everywhere. Pope Sixtus V (1585-1590) was a pope worthy of an earlier age. He formulated a plan—vainly, as it turned out—to reconquer Egypt for Rome, and to make the Mediterranean and Red seas a highway for Christian armies and navies to attack and destroy the Turkish empire. He attacked the *banditti* of the Papal States with the same energy that his predecessors had exhibited in attacking its barons, and, for a time at least, he succeeded in suppressing them. He prided himself upon being a builder, and he completed the dome of St. Peter's, set up the Egyptian obelisk in the *piazza* before that Basilica, and substituted statues of St. Peter and St. Paul in place of those of Trajan and Marcus Aurelius in the Foro Trajano and the Piazza Colonna. He constructed a system of aqueducts to bring water into the City from over twenty miles away, and he gave to Rome once more its ancient appearance of the capital of the Latin world. He fixed the number of cardinals at seventy; he revised the Vulgate; and he formulated many grand designs for which, as he himself noted, his strength would have been inadequate, even had he lived for a hundred years.

Such popes as Sixtus, however, who put into effect the papal principles of the Council of Trent, vigorous and admirable as they often were, scarcely belong to the history of Italy. The papacy at this time had a far wider scope, and a far wider reach, for it was intimately bound up with a great Roman Catholic effort to restore or extend Catholic and Latin supremacy throughout the world. In the isles of Britain, in Scandinavia, in Poland, in Russia, in Germany, Austria, France, and Switzerland, the

Italy in the Modern World

Church now fought, as of old, with the Roman spirit of conquest. Everywhere there were Jesuit priests, busy, devoted, and often heroic. The ardor of a St. Francis Xavier, the self-discipline of a St. Francis de Sales, the passionate mysticism of a St. Theresa of Avila and of a St. John of the Cross infected, inspired, and controlled tens of thousands of disciples. Everywhere there was great activity. In South America there were militant bishops and archbishops, supported by hundreds of monasteries and countless priests. In Mexico, schools of theology were flourishing for the training of native clergy. In India, thousands upon thousands of converts clustered around the city of Goa. Even in China and Japan, the Jesuits built churches and made Catholics out of adherents of Confucius and Buddha. The popes of the Counter-Reformation founded, in fact, an empire upon which the sun never set.

But the history of that empire is not the history of Italy, and the popes who founded it belonged to the world rather than to the peninsula. This line of pontiffs cast in heroic mold, however, soon ended. The new line, starting early in the seventeenth century, is remembered as builders of palaces and villas, and as collectors of pictures and statues, rather than as successors of Caesar and Augustus. First there came Paul V (1605–1621), an ineffectual man whose prime distinction was his famous quarrel with the Republic of Venice. Gregory XV (1621–1623) showed more promise, but his short reign allowed him to accomplish nothing more than the establishment of the Congregation for the Propagation of the Faith. The next pope, Urban VIII (1623–1644), devoted his long reign chiefly to the enrichment of his family, the Barberini, and to the suppression of "heresy." In the first instance, he allowed his relatives to build palaces from materials torn from the ancient Roman ruins; and for this the Barberini became the target of a famous Roman squib: *Quod non fecerunt barbari, fecerunt Barberini*—"What the barbarians did not do, the Barberini did." In the second instance, Urban is remembered as the man during whose pontificate Galileo was brought before the Holy Office (the Inquisition), where his opinion that the earth moved and that it was not the center of the universe was condemned as "absurd, false in philosophy, and essentially heretical."

Under Urban's successor, Innocent X (1644–1655), Catholic Europe stopped fighting Protestant Europe, and the Thirty Years' War was terminated by the Peace of Westphalia (1648). As a result of this agreement, the Catholic powers gave up their attempt to overturn the Protestant states and acknowledged their independence. Innocent launched a fiery bull against this treaty, but Europe, Catholic and Protestant alike, was weary of war, and everyone disregarded the old man's curses.

Long before the end of the century, the forces of renewal which had inspired and sustained the Catholic revival had begun to fade. The great Catholic potentates of Europe—the kings of Spain and France, and the Austrian emperor—now lost interest in a cause that had cost them so much blood and so much treasure with so little result, and they began to turn their minds and their energies to the fulfillment of their own ambitions. The popes, perhaps as weary as the monarchs, also seemed to give up. As had happened a thousand years before, the pontifical throne now became the prize of the great "papal families," and a succession of Barberini, Chigi, Rospigliosi, Odescalchi, and other popes devoted themselves, and the papal revenues, to the glorification of their families and to the maintenance of the archaic glories of a Renaissance court. The period of reform was now over, and the papacy settled down to enjoy its little Italian monarchy. It was content simply to maintain, more or less intact, the ecclesiastical empire which it had inherited from the preceding age.

3. The Age of Stagnation: The Arts (1580–1789)

The dreary picture of Italy's political situation is relieved somewhat, though not dramatically, by a certain activity in the sciences and the arts. After the moral vigor of republican Florence, however, and after the freshness of the Renaissance and its later grandeur, after the elegance of the courts of Rome, Urbino, Ferrara, and Milan, it requires a certain amount of time to adjust oneself to a different standard, and to acquire a taste for this period of petty dukes and dissipated princelings. It is not that Italy was without an element of seriousness at this time. There has always been, in Italy, a factor of virility and masculine strength which manifests itself throughout the history of the peninsula. In this period, that strength found its chief expression in science and the arts.

The first lights to emerge after the Renaissance, however, were neither scientists nor artists, but philosophers. Giordano Bruno (1548–1600) and Tommaso Campanella (1568–1639) were thinkers whose philosophies ran counter to the scholastic system sanctioned by the Church. Inevitably, they collided with the stern spirit of Catholic reaction to Protestant "heresy." On account of his numerous works, and principally because of his celebrated political Utopia, *Civitas Solis* (*The City of the Sun*), Campanella spent a considerable portion of his life in prison. Bruno, the most famous of the so-called "philosophers of Nature," did not escape so easily. He was arrested by the Venetian Inquisition in 1592, and in the following year he was handed over to the Roman Inquisition and spent some years in prison. Finally, as he refused to make a public retraction of his opinions, he was burned alive at Rome and his ashes scattered to the winds.

Greater than either of these, however, was Galileo Galilei (1564–1642), one of the most accomplished men of his time and one of the most famous names in astronomy. He was born at Pisa and educated in the university of that city, where he became a professor of mathematics. In 1609, he heard that a Dutchman had fabricated an instrument which, in some strange way, by means of a lens, magnified distant objects. Acting on this hint, Galileo constructed a telescope; and, if not actually the inventor of the instrument, he was at least the first to use it in astronomy. In the next year, he made various eventful discoveries: that there are mountains on the moon and spots on the sun; that Venus has phases; that Saturn has an appendage (which later was discovered to be rings); that Jupiter has four satellites—a discovery which increased the number of celestial bodies from the sacred and perfect number seven (sun, moon, Mercury, Venus, Mars, Jupiter, Saturn) to the uninspiring one of eleven. These discoveries, and his additional researches, persuaded Galileo to adopt the Copernican theory; that is, he came to believe that the earth, far from being the center of the universe, was merely one of several planets which revolved around the sun. He set forth his discoveries and his conclusion in a book, the *Dialogo,* or *Dialogue,* which appeared in 1632 and met with prodigious success. The reigning pope, Urban VIII, was furious, and attempted to forbid distribution of the book; but it was too late, for the first edition was now spread throughout Europe. He then adopted the expedient of insisting, both publicly and privately, to anyone who would listen and to some who would not, on the absolute and specific declarations of the Bible, which prove that the sun and the heavenly bodies revolve around the earth. To contradict these assertions, he said, is nothing less than to dispute divine revelation. "To dispute divine revelation," of course, was tantamount to heresy of the worse kind; and Urban, having laid the groundwork, proceeded to the next step: both Galileo and his book were placed in the hands of the Inquisition. In vain did a member of the papal court, a Benedictine monk named Castelli, plead that Galileo was entirely respectful to the Church and to the Bible, and that "nothing can now be done to prevent the earth from revolving." Castelli was dismissed in disgrace, and Galileo was forced to appear before the dread Inquisitors without defender or adviser. There, by order of Pope Urban, he was again and again threatened with the most excruciating tortures—although he was never actually subjected to anything more than the acute mental and physical discomfort usual in an inquisitorial dungeon. Finally, Galileo, now an old man, sick in body and mind, without friends, broke. On his knees, and publicly, he pronounced his recantation: "I, Galileo, being in my seventieth year, being a prisoner and on my knees before your Eminences, and having before my eyes the Holy Gospel, which I touch with my hands, do now abjure, curse, and detest the error and the heresy of the movement of the earth." (1634) To complete the Church's triumph, Pope Urban annexed to the *Index of Forbidden Books* a papal bull forbidding "all writings which affirm the motion of the earth." Then Galileo was released, to spend his remaining years in exile from his family, his friends, and his work. He lived long enough to see the truths he had established carefully weeded out from all the Catholic colleges and universities of Europe.

One of the most famous Italian thinkers of this period was Giambattista Vico (1668–1744), a Neapolitan philosopher and jurist. In his writings are found the beginnings of modern sociological and anthropological methodology. Vico attempted, with some success, to apply to the study of human history the methods of scientific analysis proposed earlier in the century by Francis Bacon. The result was a revolution in the writing of history, which had previously taken the form of biographies of illustrious men, or of the manifest development in time of God's will. Vico (along with Grotius, a Dutch jurist) regarded social institutions as human, rather than divine creations, and he explained them in terms of human, living forces. By the scientific analysis of the rise and decline of societies he evolved a cyclical interpretation of civilization, by virtue of which he is commonly regarded as the originator of the philosophy of history. His chief work, the *Scienza nuova* (1725), in which his major theories were developed, influenced thinkers for generations after his death—from Auguste Comte in the nineteenth century to James Joyce in the twentieth.

Science, however, and serious thought are not the abiding characteristics of this period. In the seventeenth and eighteenth centuries, science was too new, art too old, and life too brief, for Italy's grand-ducal society to give much thought to anything but the art of life, and, occasionally, to the arts in their usual forms. Life, as an art form, was cultivated religiously, as we gathered from the journals of M. de Montaigne, by the end of the *Cinquecento*. This trend was continued into the seventeenth and eighteenth centuries, and its chief panegyrist was Johann Wolfgang von Goethe—a name that one does not normally associate with frivolity—who sojourned in Italy from 1786 to 1788. The picture that Goethe paints is enchanting.

Rome, as before, was the artistic and spiritual center of Europe, and there was preserved the gorgeous pageantry of the Renaissance. The pomp and vanities of the papal court, the sumptuous entertainments of the cardinals and of the Roman nobility, the treasures of the libraries and museums —all these things attracted to the City not only the most brilliant names in Europe but also poets, writers, sculptors, and painters from everywhere. Anyone who was anyone at all came to Italy; and Italy, of course, meant Rome. Fun-loving Venice, with its boisterous carnival, also welcomed great crowds of visitors, as did Florence with its incredible wealth of Renaissance architecture and painting. Even Naples, with its bad inns and vicious *banditti,* attracted its share of indefatigable English, French, and German travelers. Everyone came, was entertained, and admired, and then, like Goethe and Montaigne before him, went back to their own countries full of praise for, and fond memories of, that miraculous land where people, indeed, knew how to live life at its fullest.

There was an aspect of Italian life, however, which these aesthetic and noble visitors did not see, one which fell considerably below the level of the artistic. Along with overwhelming poverty, crime was everywhere rampant in Italy, to a degree that make Montaigne's mild observations on that subject seem quaint. During a ten-year period in the Papal States in the latter part of the eighteenth century, there were actually recorded some thirteen thousand murders. In Milan, there were even more. In the Republic of Venice, every year, between seven and eight thousand criminals were condemned either to death or to life imprisonment. Conditions in the south, where violence was a way of life rather than a sporadic condition, were assuredly worse, but no records were kept. So frequent were major crimes that the various municipalities set up traveling courts of justice comprising judge, prosecutor, defense attorney, confessor, and executioner, who patrolled the cities on horseback. They had the power summarily to try and to punish (usually by execution) any criminal brought before them.

The social condition of Italy at this time, brilliant as it was on the surface, and horrifying as it was underneath, was able to produce a respectable artistic movement. It was the age of the Baroque in Italy, in art as well as in life; and, as much as that style may suffer by comparison to the achievements of the Renaissance, it is certain that there is hardly an Italian city of any size that would not be the poorer for the absence of it. Modern Rome, for example, owes much of its charm to these decadent generations and to that excessive style—to the Villa Medici, the Villa Borghese, the Spanish Steps, the Trevi Fountains, the Piazza Navona.

The master spirit of the Italian Baroque was a Neapolitan, Giovanni

Lorenzo Bernini (1598–1680), who excelled in architecture as well as in sculpture. His most famous and certainly his greatest achievement is the splendid colonnade which he designed for the *piazza* in front of St. Peter's. To him also we owe the extraordinary bronze canopy under the dome of the same Basilica, the two extravagant fountains in the Piazza Navona, and the royal staircase in the Vatican. His best-known sculpture is the group of Apollo and Daphne which stands in the Villa Borghese. Bernini's statues, his fountains, and decorations reflect the story of his time. They undoubtedly reveal decadence; yet they are respectfully imitative of the best achievements of the Renaissance. It was left to his disciples to produce works of grotesque contortion, obvious effort, and a straining for effect merely for the sake of effect. There is a maximum of visible exertion, with a minimum of real accomplishment. Details are multiplied beyond reason, and ornaments bear little, if any, relation to the organic structure of the buildings which they adorn. Yet, that practice is an Italian trait of the period, and even its excess has the merit of being at least picturesque. It endured until the eighteenth century, when, after the storm of ornamentation, an architectural calm prevailed in reaction, and facades became rectilinear, at least for a time.

In painting, the school of Bologna, led by Lodovico Caracci (1555–1619) and his nephews, Agostino and Annibale, set the style, and their work remained the cynosure of tourists' eyes until the late nineteenth century. They had the merit, or at least the courage, to attempt to combine a faithfulness to nature with all the virtues of preceding ages. Their efforts were greatly admired by their own generation as well as by those of a later time. Sir Joshua Reynolds was one of the travelers who admired them, and some of their disciples were briefly regarded as the equals of Raphael. Domenichino's *Last Communion of St. Jerome,* for example, was accorded a place of honor in the Vatican galleries on a par with that of Raphael's *Transfiguration.* Though the Bolognese school has now lost its vogue under the scorn of the critics, its work is still sufficiently powerful to elicit a gasp of astonishment from the unwary tourist. Many a visitor to Rome still manages to escape from critical friends long enough to admire, in secret, Guido Reni's *Aurora* painted on one of the ceilings of the Palazzo Rospigliosi.

Another school, almost as famous as that of Bologna, was that devoted to Naturalism—that is, to the depiction of the wholly secular and unpleasant side of life, of starving beggars, and of poverty, squalor, and misery. Of these painters, the principal were Michelangelo da Caravaggio (1569–1609), a Neapolitan, and his pupil Ribera, known as "Lo Spagnoletto" (the little Spaniard) because he was born in Spain. A later group, the eighteenth-century Venetian school, comprised the minor talents of Canaletto, Bellotto, Guardi, and others who painted, over and over again, the limpid canals and pleasure palaces of Venice. The greatest and best known of this group was Giovanni Battista Tiepolo (1693-1770), who attained, to a surprising extent, the grand manner of the masters of the sixteenth century.

The spirit of the Baroque in Italy expressed itself also in literature, and nowhere more fully than by means of an institution called the Academy of Arcadia. The Academy was founded in Rome in 1692 by a group of dilettanti for "the ennoblement of literature," for the "purification of taste," and for other laudable purposes, and so successful was it in epitomizing the unreality of the Italian world that it soon had branches, imitations, and colonies all over the peninsula. The members called themselves Arcadian shepherds and shepherdesses, assumed pastoral names, composed precious sonnets by the bushel, wrote one another's biographies, and altogether were remarkably, and sometimes delightfully, light-headed. Carlo Goldoni (1707-1793), the playwright, gives a glimpse of these eighteenth-century *litterati* as he observed them in Pisa.

One day, he chanced to pass a garden gate and saw within a group of ladies and gentlemen grouped around an arbor. "This assembly that you see," he was told, "is a colony of the Arcadia of Rome, called the colony of Alpheus, named after a very celebrated river in Greece which flowed through the ancient Pisa in Elis." Intrigued, Goldoni went up to the group and listened to an endless number of gentlemen reciting poems, ballads, sonnets, *canzoni,* and so forth. At one point, he noticed that some members of the company were looking at him curiously, as though to ask who he was and what he was doing there. Eager to satisfy their curiosity, he asked the president if a stranger might be allowed to express—in verse, of course —the satisfaction which he experienced in witnessing so interesting an assembly. Goldoni tells us that he had a sonnet in his head, composed by him several years previously, for some similar festival. Now, he simply changed a few words to adapt it to the present occasion and then recited the fourteen lines with the tone and inflection which set off the sentiment and the rhyme to the best advantage. The sonnet, being accepted as wholly extemporaneous, was loudly applauded, and Goldoni was invited to become a member of the colony. At the next meeting, the president, whose proper title was Guardian of the Shepherds, presented the playwright with two documents. One was a certificate of membership in the Arcadia of Rome, under the name of Polisseno (Polixenes). The other was a legal deed which bestowed upon him the Fegean Fields in Greece. Whereupon, the entire assembly hailed him under the name of Polixenes Fegeus and embraced him as a fellow shepherd.

This general fondness for playacting eventually found expression on the stage, in an art form highly characteristic of the seventeenth and eighteenth centuries. The drama had never been successful in Italy. Machiavelli and Ariosto had tried their hands at the writing of comedies, but the product of their efforts had left much to be desired from the dramatic standpoint, and had been generally ignored by the public. After this acknowledged failure of serious comedy, another species was launched and established itself at about the beginning of the Baroque. It was called the *commedia dell'arte,* in which the *dramatis personae* were masked and always impersonated certain definite characters. These characters were Pantalone, a Venetian merchant who always wore a black robe and red stockings and spoke the Venetian dialect; il Dottore, the doctor, a pompous ass from Bologna; Arlecchino (Harlequin), a scatter-brained servant, and Brighella, a clever and dishonest servant, both of whom spoke the patois of Bergamo; Colombina, (Colombine), the soubrette of the piece, a pretty maidservant from Tuscany; Capitano Spavento (Captain Terrible), a fire-eater from Naples, and so forth. The dialogue of the piece was wholly extemporized, except that the playwright provided a skeleton plot, or *scenario,* for the actors to follow. The *commedia dell'arte* had great vogue, and troops of Italian comedians traveled all over Europe to great applause.

By the middle of the eighteenth century, however, the *commedia* had run its course and become mere vulgar horseplay. It was given the deathblow by the work of Carlo Goldoni, the only brilliant comic playwright that Italy has produced. Goldoni was a Venetian, and an embodiment of the happy, careless, amiable, entertaining society of the time. He led an unfettered life, going to Tuscany to learn proper Italian and ending his career with a twenty-year visit to Paris. Some of his plays were written in the Venetian dialect, and two were composed in French. Altogether, he left more than a hundred pieces, counting tragedies, interludes, etc. The chief virtue of this corpus is its utter lightness. Everything is made of foam, like a delicious comedic *soufflé*. Sustaining the fluff are mobs of counts, barons, marquesses, and charming ladies, with their maids, innkeepers, footmen and valets, cobblers, and adventurers—all united in elaborate mockery of the idle habits of the time. These pieces retained their popular appeal as late as the beginning of the twentieth century, when, in the hands of such spirited Italian performers as Eleonora Duse and Ermete Novelli, their charms seemed as much suited to the era of the Romantic as to that of the Baroque.

In addition to the *commedia dell'arte* and Goldoni's comic drama, Baroque Italy gave to the world another and far more important gift, the opera. Once more, Italian genius flared up and led the world in music. As far back as the days of the Council of Trent, the reforming spirit of the Church found its noblest expression in the work of Palestrina (1524?–1594); but, after his death, after the Catholic revival had lost its deeply serious feeling, music took another step. Florence, the old home of genius, was once more the garden where the new flowering took place. A group of music lovers, full of classic theories about art, wished to revive the antique Greek drama with its combination of poetry, music, and dance. It was their opinion that, of these elements, words were the most important factor, and that the music must be subordinated to the full emotional expression of the poetry and must serve to intensify the dramatic significance of the story. To translate that opinion into practice, they devised a method of setting music to declamation, in an early form of *recitativo*. In their attempt to revive the Greek drama, however, they succeeded in producing the opera. After a few years of work over the new ideas, in 1600, at the Pitti Palace, an opera was publicly performed in honor of the betrothal of Marie de' Medici and King Henry IV of France. This was the first public performance of a secular opera. Not long afterward, Claudio Monteverdi (1567–1643), a revolutionary genius in the history of music, began to produce his operas at Mantua. In 1637, the first public opera house was opened in Venice; others quickly followed, and the opera became Italy's favorite diversion. Italian musicians and singers carried it to France, Germany, Austria, and England. Naples soon eclipsed all the other cities of Italy in the composition of music. Alessandro Scarlatti (1659–1725) wrote a vast number of operas, oratorios, and ecclesiastical music. He was followed by his son, Domenico Scarlatti, by Durante, Leo, and Jommelli, by Pergolesi, Piccinni, Cimarosa, and Paisiello—all of whom followed one another, like a flight of brilliant tropical birds, through the eighteenth century. Even at that comparatively early date, Italian opera had a tendency to subordinate dramatic propriety and realism to the exigencies of the all-important arias; but it was not to be until the beginning of the nineteenth century, with the advent of Rossini, Bellini, and Donizetti, that the operas of Italy became, as it were, liquid Baroque.

The Italians led the world not only in the composition of operatic music, but also in its production. Among Italy's musical geniuses, one must surely number the great violin makers—the Amati of Cremona, the greater

Stradivarius (1644–1737), and the other famous makers of Cremona, Brescia, and Venice—as well as the great organ builders, the Antinati of Brescia, and the greatest of the librettists, Metastasio.

This Metastasio (1698–1782) had a career that can be compared only to that of a successful prima donna. As a boy, he was adopted by one of the founders of the Arcadia of Rome, from whom he learned the delights of verse and music. After the death of his protector, and having spent his inheritance, Metastasio fell into the company of singers and musicians at Naples. There, at the age of twenty-five, he composed the words of an opera, *Dido,* which had a phenomenal success. From that time on, Metastasio poured out play after play in words that went halfway, and more, to meet the accompanying music. His fame was on the lips of Europe, and he became the idolized darling of lords and ladies, kings and popes. He flitted from court to court, worshiped and flattered by all, drinking the sweet nectar of facile success. He serves as the embodiment of the Italian opera; or, more accurately, as a poetic spirit, a kind of Baroque nightingale, as it were, chanting the spell which conjures up the sweetness and the unreality of these two make-believe centuries, the seventeenth and the eighteenth, in Italy.

4. The Napoleonic Era (1789–1815)

The story of Italy in the late eighteenth century is largely that of the beginnings of a *Risorgimento,* a "resurrection" on a national scale, during which the Italian people at last began to awaken from the torpor that had engulfed them since the end of the *Cinquecento.* The spirit which engendered this resurrection or reawakening was, to a great extent, imported from France where, under the impact of the so-called *Philosophes* or *Encyclopaedistes* (terms applied generally to the radical thinkers of France during the pre-Revolutionary period), such heretical ideas as that of "Liberty, Equality, and Fraternity" were being propagated. These concepts, in the guise of philosophical philanthropy, wafted across the Alps quickly, where, perhaps surprisingly, they infected some, but not all, of Italy's autocrats.

In Piedmont, no such outlandish notions warmed King Victor Amadeus III. He wrapped his cloak tighter around him and announced that the old ways, which had been good enough for his forebears, were good enough for him. He continued to maintain his court in imitation of Versailles, and continued to drill his soldiers in imitation of Frederick the Great of Prussia.

In all things, the *ancien regime* remained. Only nobles were employed in the higher ranks of government service, and only nobles were commissioned as officers in the army. But it was not easy even for the nobles; they were treated like schoolboys, and the slightest deviation from the prescribed path in policy or behavior was rewarded by severe punishment. The clergy preserved all the privileges of the old days. Their tribunals alone had jurisdiction over clerics, and their tribunals alone had competence in any crime that smacked of sin. Everyone, king, nobility, and clergy, clung to the autocracy and were determined to maintain it in full vigor. Even the poverty-ridden and hard-working peasants rallied to their king with unswerving loyalty and to their clergy with unshakable faith. They were a devout people, whose religion was an inseparable part of their lives; and loyalty to throne and to altar was one of the basic principles of their behavior. Moreover, a system of double censorship, enforced by Church and state, crushed all freedom of thought or expression, while the activity of the ancient Inquisition guaranteed strict orthodoxy in political as well as in spiritual matters.

Surprisingly enough, it was in the Austrian provinces of Italy that the spirit of reform showed itself most vigorous, for the Hapsburgs regarded themselves as benevolent despots and, under the Empress Maria Theresa (1740–1780) and her son, Joseph II (1765–1790), the Austrian government took a comparatively enlightened interest in the well-being of its subjects. In Lombardy, except for the Viceroy and a few high officials, local government was left in the hands of the Italians themselves. Military government disappeared, and natives of the province were exempt from military service. The tax system was reformed, clerical privileges were curtailed, superfluous monasteries and convents were suppressed, the Inquisition was abolished, agriculture and trade were favored, and manufacture was encouraged and subsidized. More important for the future, a certain liberty of speech and freedom of the press were allowed, and new ideas came into circulation. The ideas of the *Philosophes* were freely discussed. Cesare Beccaria (1738–1794) published his celebrated *Essay on Crimes and Punishments,* which began the attack on capital punishment and on penal cruelty, and, in other works, preached the reform of wage and labor laws. Austrian garrisons were still on duty, and, in the final analysis, Milan was still ruled from Vienna; but now Lombardy thought and talked and prospered as it had not done for three hundred years.

In Tuscany, reform likewise bounded along under the Hapsburg Grand Duke, Leopold I, who proposed to destroy there every remnant of the Middle Ages. He attacked the power of the clergy, granted free trade

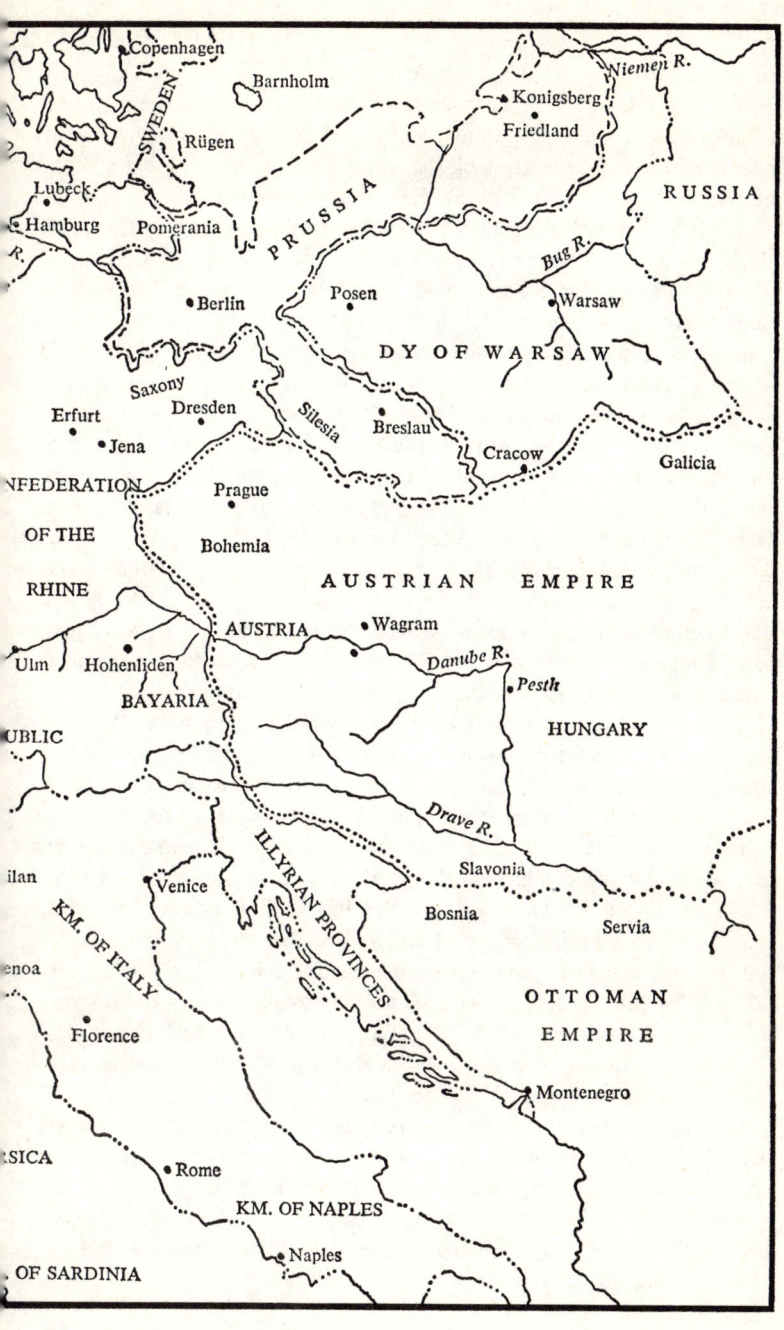

in grain, and reformed the tax system—even to the detriment of his own estates. He improved the universities of Pisa and Siena, drained and reclaimed the marshes of the Maremma, and led the way in abolishing torture and capital punishment. He took the unheard-of step of rendering a public accounting of the state's finances. He had no use for the military, and he disbanded the army and sold the navy (which comprised only two small ships) to Russia. In short, Leopold put into practice the most advanced philanthropic ideas of his time, and the result was to make Tuscany one of the best-governed states of Europe.

In Venice, the new ideas affected the government not at all. The old system of government by stasis continued. The Great Council of Patricians sat in indolent conservatism. The Doge, by now merely an expensive ornament, shuffled about his great Palace, while the Senate talked endlessly and the Council of Ten maintained its petty despotism. Venice was moribund. Her voice was shrunken to a mere whisper in the affairs of Europe. Only gaiety, luxury, vice, and entertainment were cultivated triumphantly. To the west, similarly, Modena lay still and concentrated its attention on avoiding all possible offense to its more active neighbors. The adjacent duchy of Parma at first had inclined, under the ministership of a Frenchman, toward reform; but the ascension of a new duke, at once devout and dissipated, announced the slipping back of Parma into the old ways.

In the Papal States, similarly, medievalism lay heavy upon the land. There was no commerce to speak of, no manufacture, and little agriculture. Priests were everywhere, and the greedy relations of the pope almost everywhere; and the country was run for their exclusive benefit, for no layman could hold office. The finances were in such hopeless confusion that, as one cardinal commented, "only the Holy Spirit can make some sense out of our accounts." The offerings of the faithful from all over the world, the sale of ecclesiastical and civil offices, and the multiplication of taxes did little more than pay interest on the bonded debts; there was nothing left over for education, roads, agricultural improvements, or social reforms. Rome herself had become a little, relatively unimportant ecclesiastical city. Only at Ancona, a seaport, and at Bologna, with its university, were there exceptions to the general wretchedness.

In Naples, however, even the Bourbons felt the fresh breath of reformation. A progressive minister tried to reduce the number of superfluous priests, monks, and nuns, and to root out the old feudal privileges. The pope retaliated by refusing to fill vacant bishoprics, to which the minister, Tannucci, responded by expelling the Jesuits and by refusing to pay the ancient tribute to Rome of seven thousand ducats. King Charles III and

Tannucci had even greater difficulty in their attempt to suppress feudalism, mainly because the judges responsible for enforcing the laws which they enacted were themselves appointed by the feudal barons. In practice, therefore, these reforms had little effect. In Naples, however, a considerable company of men gathered together, cultivated the new ideas, and followed the general lead of the French *Philosophes*. But in Sicily, the people were so unsusceptible to the new spirit that even the reforming prime minister and the king could do nothing to budge the dead weight of custom. In the end, despite the best intentions of the government, the Two Sicilies were hardly better off than the Papal States.

Such, briefly, was the condition of Italy toward the close of the eighteenth century. There was, to be sure, a spirit of reform in the land; but in no sense can it be regarded as a national movement. There was no popular demand for reform. Reform was imposed, as despotism had been, from above. And, ironically, it was the foreign rulers of Italy who promulgated reform; the native rulers did nothing. Moreover, each reforming state aimed simply at eradicating the social and economic evils that were peculiar to itself. Neither rulers nor ruled yet dreamed of a united Italy, any more than did the writers and thinkers of the time. Even such a man as Vittorio Alfieri (1749-1803), a species of the true antique Roman, who boldly expressed his hatred of foreign oppression and his love of liberty in somewhat tedious classic tragedies, stands in history not as an advocate of Italian unity but as an example of that rebirth of virility which was to come to fruition only in the nineteenth century. They were above all men of their time, liberal and skeptical, philanthropic and sophisticated. They were vitally interested in the theory of reform, and in its practice insofar as applicable to their own states. But no thought of Italy as a single political entity entered their minds.

As French revolutionary sentiment developed abroad, it was inevitable that it should penetrate the Alps not only by means of books but also through organizations. And it was in the Masonic Lodges that the doctrines of Liberty, Equality, and Fraternity came to be preached most effectively. As early as 1733, an English tourist, the Duke of Middlesex, had founded a lodge at Florence, from where, under grand-ducal patronage, it spread rapidly to Venice, Vicenza, Verona, and Milan. In the south, Freemasonry spread more slowly—despite the numerous liberals at Naples—because of Pope Clement XII's condemnation of the society in 1733; but in 1749, the influential Duke di Sangro succeeded in founding a lodge among his aristocratic colleagues, which survived until a second condemnation by Benedict XIV. When it emerged again, it had become middle class rather than aristocratic in membership, and political rather than social in purpose. It went underground, became a club on the French model, and became saturated with the revolutionary thought of French agitators. Italian Freemasonry, however, served primarily as an organ of propaganda for the coming Revolution in France. It was never "patriotic" in the usual sense of that term; it was anti-Church, Francophile, and a-nationalistic.

In the four years that followed the beginning of the long-anticipated and much-dreaded French Revolution in 1789, Italy—Piedmont and Naples, particularly—was subjected to an ever-growing flood of French agents whose work it was to awaken sympathy for the Revolution and, not coincidentally, antipathy for France's enemies in Italy: the Austrian Hapsburgs in the north, and the detested Bourbons in the south. Although the intellectuals and the upper classes of Italy, following, as always, the example of the French aristocracy, expressed an academic enthusiasm for Liberty, Equality, and Fraternity, the real support for the ideas propagated by these agents came from militant and restless extremists. There were arrests in Milan and Genoa. At Turin, the capital of Piedmont and, at that time, the stronghold of irreformable despotism in Italy, a plot was discovered to murder the royal family and to seize the government. It is indicative of the state of Italy at this moment that the entire peninsula—the aristocrats, the middle class, the intellectuals, the Masons—except for a tiny number of fanatic egalitarians, reacted in horror to this discovery. The ground in Italy had been prepared for a revolution; but for a French, not an Italian, Revolution.

Down into this world came the fury of that French Revolution. In 1793, the French, having executed Louis XVI and Marie Antoinette and declared themselves a republic, now felt free to deal with the enemies abroad. War was declared on Austria, and, almost inadvertently, on Piedmont, which had allied herself with Austria in 1792. As far as Italy was concerned, the war was without consequence for three years. Then, in 1796, a young Corsican named Napoleon Bonaparte, who, at age twenty-seven, was a general of artillery, was given command of the French troops who were camped, more or less inactive, on the Alpine border. He had been sent by the revolutionary government of France in order to rid themselves of this brilliant, successful, popular, and therefore dangerous phenomenon. Paris undoubtedly regarded Bonaparte's new command as a form of polite exile. But Bonaparte regarded it as a golden opportunity. The enemy, he knew, was asleep in winter quarters—the Austrians in the east of Lombardy, the Piedmontese in the west of the Lombard plain; and fragmented Italy, with its petty states and duchies, expected no attack at all. Arriving at the

French camp, he found his troops freezing, starved, diseased, and unpaid. He had brought no food, no medicines, and no money. But he had brought inspiration. "Soldiers of France!" he addressed the troops, "you are half naked and half starved. The government, which owes you so much, can do nothing for you. Your patience and your courage do you honor; but they bring you no glory, and no advantage. But I will lead you into the richest plains of the world! There you will find flourishing cities, teeming provinces. There will you find honor, glory and—yes—wealth! Soldiers, will you now be found wanting in courage and firmness?"

Then he led his famished army like a whirlwind into the north of Italy. Before them, the French saw the rich plains of Piedmont, blossoming in the spring. "All this is yours!" Bonaparte told them. True to his word, he met the Piedmontese army, crushed them, and forced them to sign the disastrous Treaty of Cherasco by which Piedmont, quite literally, was put at the disposal of the French. In less than three weeks, General Bonaparte had kept his word to his army. Henceforth, their enthusiasm could hardly be restrained. Advancing into Lombardy, he defeated three Austrian armies in quick succession, and made himself master of northern Italy. In October 1797, by the Treaty of Campo Formio, he extinguished the ancient Republic of Venice and handed it over to Austria, while the rest of the north he retained for France.

To the Italians, Bonaparte presented himself as a liberator rather than as a conqueror. And, for them, he was, after all a man of Italian blood, with an Italian name, speaking Italian as his mother tongue. He set himself up as the herald of liberty and equality, and he spoke of Athens, Sparta, and classical Rome. "People of Italy! The armies of France come to break your chains. It is a friend to all peoples. Have confidence in us. Your property, your customs, your religion, all shall be respected."

Under the watchful eye of France, Italy's little despotisms transformed themselves into republics after the French model. Genoa became the Ligurian Republic. Ferrara, Reggio, Bologna, and Modena combined into the Cispadane Republic. Another group of cities, with Milan and Brescia at their head, became the Transpadane Republic. The two latter, however, for some reason seemed to Bonaparte to be unwieldy, and, at his urging, they amalgamated into a single Cisalpine Republic. Then the French liberator graciously granted to them a constitution. For the first time, the future conqueror of Europe and Emperor of the French had himself raised a political structure. And now, by this juggling back and forth of cities and provinces in the old manner, in the wake of taxes and requisitions which exhausted both public and private funds, in the heavy-handed and cruel suppression of any disorders, the Italians realized that the French, with their *liberté* and their *egalité,* were no different from what the Austrians, the Spaniards, the Bourbons, and their own little princes had been. The initial enthusiasm for the French gave way to disenchantment, and disenchantment to sullen resentment. On the eve of the Treaty of Campo Formio, one of Napoleon's soldier-politicians, M. Carrion-Nisas, witnessed the estrangement of the Italians from their "liberator":

> On drawing near his capital [Milan], I saw a numerous train of horses and vehicles. The fiery victor, on whom were focused the eyes of the world and the hope of the nations, was going away, escorted by his officers and surrounded by his troops. A woman at his side [Josephine] was ablaze with diamonds and happily delighting in her splendor. He himself seemed gloomy and distracted, but on his cold and immobile countenance there was no remorse, no grief, no emotion. In letters of ice, insensitivity was written across his brow.
>
> Now there were no shouts and cheers, no accompaniment of blessings and acclamations such as that with which the people used to greet him in the time of conflict. Everywhere, silence reigned. The farmer and the workman turned away at the sight of him and left without uttering a sound. Their attitude and their looks proclaimed the contempt and scorn that their lips dared not utter.

The Italians, however, for all their discontent, were in no position to do anything about the situation. Italy was almost entirely without means of opposition. Neither Tuscany nor the Papal States, which were still unoccupied, had troops, while in Naples there was an ill-equipped and badly organized army of only twenty thousand men. Moreover, in 1792, a French fleet had sailed into the Bay of Naples and compelled the Bourbon king there to agree to complete neutrality. By the end of 1797, Bonaparte left Italy for Paris, and then for his ill-fated expedition to Egypt. Italy was left under the command of General Berthier—the same Berthier of whom Bonaparte had only recently said, "Berthier, bah! He is not fit to command even a battalion!" The new commander seized the opportunity presented by the murder of a French agent in Rome to occupy the City. The pope fled to Tuscany, and the Papal States became the Roman Republic. The presence of the pope in Tuscany, the French decided, was an invitation to trouble; they therefore moved into Florence, dispossessed the Grand Duke, and Tuscany henceforth was known as the Etruscan Republic.

Only Naples now remained outside the circle of French power. But not for long. The witless Spanish Bourbon, Ferdinand I, under the urging of his wife and of the English government, assembled an army under an Austrian, General Mack, and, in December 1798, when the French troops were away in winter quarters, he marched unopposed to Rome. Now this Ferdinand was a weak and effeminate man, devoid of talent either military or administrative. He, and the Two Sicilies, were completely under the thumb of his wife, Queen Maria Carolina, an Austrian, a strong and masculine woman, who, when she could spare the time from childbearing (she bore Ferdinand twelve children in almost as many years), governed king and kingdom ruthlessly. Ferdinand, once in Rome, and probably giddy with his unaccustomed freedom from Maria Carolina's domination, recalled the pope, rattled his sword, and, in the words of one contemporary historian, "in the voice of a rabbit, he proclaimed to all Europe that 'the Kings are awake.'"

Neither Ferdinand's nor Rome's freedom was to endure. The French attacked almost immediately, and the Neapolitan army fled back to Naples with King Ferdinand leading the way. There the king paused in his flight long enough to collect his queen, his prime minister, and all of the national treasury that he could carry; then, under the protection of the English fleet, he sailed to Sicily. Naples offered a brave resistance to the French, but it was no match for the veterans of Bonaparte's campaigns in the north. The kingdom was occupied as far as the Straits of Messina, and a French-style government was proclaimed under the resounding name of the Parthenopean Republic. Italy was now a group of French-imposed republics, dominated by the French, and kept in existence by French troops. Only eighteen months had passed since Bonaparte first appeared south of the Alps.

No sooner had Italy been converted, albeit forcibly, to republicanism, than French power in the peninsula evaporated as quickly as it had materialized. The Allies—that is, England and Austria—won over Russia to their side and, in the early part of 1799, Austrian and Russian armies crossed the Adige and thrust the French out of the north of Italy. French troops in Rome and Naples were hastily summoned northward, but in vain, for soon only Genoa was left of all France's Italian possessions. The Italians themselves quickly completed the work that the Russians and the Austrians had begun. The peasantry attacked and exterminated, with their farm implements as tools, whatever isolated French outposts and garrisons they could find. Bishops and pastors put aside their breviaries, took up the sword and led their flocks effectively, and often heroically, against what remained of the atheistic and godless spawn of the Revolution. In Lombardy, the Austrians went even further. They arrested and shot all available supporters of the Cisalpine Republic. In Naples, an army dispatched by King Ferdinand from Sicily and under the command of Cardinal Ruffo was victorious. The republican government surrendered, on terms which included a safe-conduct for themselves and transportation to France. The terms were agreed to by Ferdinand's representative and by Cardinal Ruffo. At that moment, the English fleet of the Mediterranean, under the command of the redoubtable Lord Horatio Nelson, sailed into the harbor. Nelson unilaterally repudiated the armistice, seized the republican leaders, and, on his own authority, hanged Admiral Caracciolo, a Neapolitan who had deserted the royal cause and taken command of the republican forces. All Europe, and even England, was shocked by Nelson's actions; but nothing was done about it in London, and nothing could be done about it elsewhere. Nelson's dishonorable fury, however, was more than matched by the savagery of the now reinstated King Ferdinand and Queen Maria Carolina. More than a hundred of the republic leaders were shot, hundreds were sent to the galleys for life, and hundreds more exiled or given lengthy prison terms.

Ferdinand and Maria Carolina were soon to pay for their acts. But, unfortunately, so was the rest of Italy. In October 1799, Bonaparte, of whom little had been heard for a while, was back in France after the fiasco of his Egyptian campaign. Furious at the loss of his Italian conquests, he quickly descended into the peninsula through the St. Bernard Pass and crushed the Austrians utterly at the Battle of Marengo (June 1800). Italy was once more at his feet. By the treaty of Lunéville, in February 1801, Bonaparte gave western Venetia to Austria, while France received all of northern Italy to the Adige. In the few years following Marengo, the peninsula was organized into three units. Piedmont, Tuscany, and the Papal States, including Rome, were annexed to France. The former Cisalpine Republic was rechristened the Italian Republic, and then, when Bonaparte declared himself Emperor of the French (December 2, 1804), it became the Kingdom of Italy (*Regno d'Italia*), and Napoleon put upon his head the iron crown of the Lombard kings with the words, "God has given it to me. Woe to him that touches it!" To the south, Naples remained, for the moment, under Ferdinand. But in 1806 Napoleon decided that the time had come to settle accounts with the Bourbon tyrant. As the French troops approached, Ferdinand fled once more to Sicily, and his place on the throne of Naples was taken by Napoleon's brother, Joseph, who reigned for two years. King Joseph was then transferred to the Spanish throne, while that of Naples was bestowed on one of Napoleon's marshals, Joachim Murat, a former army sergeant, who became King Joachim I. Italy again, from top to bottom, was under French rule.

Politically speaking, Italy had never been nearer a condition of unity than when, divided into two French kingdoms, she began to feel the benefits of compactness and uniformity in government. Into the Kingdom of Italy, the Kingdom of Naples, and the annexed Papal States, Napoleon introduced an orderly administration, a uniform and enlightened legal code, and an effective system of internal reform. Also, he once more promised them liberty and equality. And once more the people of Italy trusted Napoleon and, relying upon his promises, gave him support and material aid. But they soon discovered, again, that his imperial word was as ephemeral as the smokes of Vesuvius. He ruled Italy more despotically even than he ruled France. He gave to the Italian people, as he had given to the people of France, social equality; but he denied them political liberty. He gave them a well-organized government, and a competently administered country; and he gave them more comfortable cities to live in—cities which, nonetheless, he had stripped of most of their artistic treasures. But he demanded in return the absolute obedience and submission to his will that he exacted from all those that he ruled. He made them sharers in his military glory; but he imposed upon them that heaviest and most repellent of burdens, military conscription. He gave them protection; but at the same time he made them feel the weight of his police system and the reality of his despotism by suppressing freedom of speech and freedom of the press, and by placing in their path a thousand obstacles to freedom of movement and freedom of trade. In order to gain a more efficient force to aid him in his wars, he heaped promise upon glittering promise; and, above all, by the promise of an unhoped-for unity and independence did he play upon the chords of Italian sentiment. Before the eyes of Italy he held out the picture of a state freed from foreign princes, applying its energies to its own upbuilding, a *patria*, a fatherland, a national home. Under the spell of these promises, Italy waited, trusting to see with each new treaty, each alteration in her governments, each reshaping of the political boundaries of her states, some indication that her conqueror would redeem his word. But the years passed, and nothing happened. Finally, it again dawned upon the Italians that they could hope for nothing from the Emperor of the French.

By 1812, at the time of Napoleon's retreat from Moscow, when the once invincible Empire had begun to disintegrate, Italy had discovered that force, subterfuge, and shameless political intrigue were to be the only reward for the support she had given to her conqueror. From that time, a spirit of opposition to Napoleon became increasingly prominent. The clergy and the nobility, longing for the fleshpots of the old regime, came to desire the return to Austria of the domination of Italy. But the reformers, the romantics, the intellectuals, all began to see that the salvation of Italy, if it was indeed ever to come, must be found in Italy's own power and resources. This latter opinion was earnestly propagandized by ubiquitous secret societies—offshoots of the pre-Napoleonic Masonic Lodges—who spread everywhere their gospel: that tyrants (by which was meant Napoleon, primarily, but also the Austrians) must be destroyed; and that Italy must be granted a constitution. The idea of independence under a constitution was preached so unceasingly that it sank into the national consciousness and became the foundation upon which the future of Italy was to be built.

At that moment, Napoleon was being forced back by the Allies, step by step, toward the original boundaries of France. Hoping to win Italy to their side, the Allies offered the crown of Italy first to Eugene de Beauharnais (Napoleon's Viceroy of the Kingdom of Italy and stepson); but Eugene refused to abandon the man to whom he owed everything. "I shall never be king at that price," he wrote to Marshal Bellegarde, commander of the Austrian forces. But King Joachim Murat of Naples had been formed in a less heroic mold. Ambitious to retain his throne, and unable to discover a middle road between devotion and defection, he abandoned Napoleon in the hope that the inevitable success of the Allies would make him king of the entire peninsula, and signed a treaty with Austria in January 1814. Hardly was the ink of Murat's signature dry, however, when the Allies, through Lord William Bentinck, the English representative in Sicily, declared for the return of King Ferdinand to the Neapolitan throne. Murat had sacrificed his honor only to be caught in the intrigues of the Powers whose cause he had decided to support.

That each of the European powers who wished to win the support of the Italian people appealed to their desire for liberty is striking proof of the longing that Italy, by 1813, had developed for peace, independence, and national consolidation. Napoleon had discovered that the word "liberty" was an open sesame to the hearts of the Italians. Lord Bentinck had appealed to them as lovers of liberty, and not tyranny, when he sought to further the cause of King Ferdinand. "Holland, Portugal, and Spain," he said, "can testify to the disinterestedness of our efforts. Shall Italy alone remain in chains? Shall Italians war against other Italians to aid a tyrant to destroy their liberty? Italians, do not hesitate; be Italians!" The Austrian representatives, General Nugent and General Bellegarde, touched the same chord when, in 1813 and 1814, they promised liberty and independence as the reward for Italian support of the Allied cause. "We come to you as liberators," said Nugent. "Long enough have you groaned beneath the weight of oppression. You shall become an independent nation, happy, if only you prove loyal to those who love you and will protect you. . . . Do not fear that, under new masters, you will be forced back into the old state of weakness and dependence. No, Italians! This is not the purpose of the Allies. Your independence, the maintenance of your civil and political existence are among the causes of the present war, so that you may be, among the nations around you, a single body, a single nation worthy of the respect of others, and free from the dominance of foreigners."

To a people who had long felt the evil effects of Napoleon's rule, who were impoverished by his exorbitant taxations, whose industry and agriculture were almost at a standstill because of his military exactions, whose foreign trade and commerce were restricted by a continental blockade, such words seemed to hold the promise of redemption. Piedmontese, Lombards, Romagnols, Tuscans, Romans, and Neapolitans, all were now beginning to feel the need of a union of forces and interests, of a state worthy of the respect of the world, in which local differences might be reconciled by the desire to work for the welfare of a common fatherland.

With Napoleon's fall and his exile to the island of Elba in April 1814, Italy was once more freed from foreign domination. Then the victorious Allies announced that a great congress would be convened at Vienna in September of the same year, to discuss the future of the lands which Napoleon had seized by force. In a prominent place on the agenda of the Congress of Vienna was to be "the Italian problem." In view of the promises and reassurances of the English and the Austrians such a short time before, it seemed that Italy's dream of independence and unity was on the verge of realization. But that was not to be. The people of Italy had made, once more, the fatal error of relying upon the pledges of the trans-Alpine powers.

VI
FROM ABSOLUTISM TO INDEPENDENCE
(1814–1870)

1. A Time for Conspiracy (1814–1848)

To the emperors and kings assembled at the Congress of Vienna in 1814, the "Italian problem" at first did not seem much of a problem at all. The guiding principle of the convocation was that of legitimacy—that is, that states belonged to their legitimate princely dynasties—and the work of the delegates seemed cut out for them: to restore to the Italian princes the domains from which Bonaparte had ousted them. But it was not that easy. The two dominant figures of the Congress, Prince Talleyrand of France and Prince Metternich of Austria, soon made of the Italian states the subject of a duel as bitter as it was intricate. Talleyrand was a devoted believer in legitimacy, particularly when legitimacy was to the advantage of France; he therefore insisted that all of Italy's pre-Napoleonic dynasties, without exception, be restored. Metternich, for his part, while professing an equal reverence for legitimate sovereignty, was determined that the former royal dynasty of Naples, that of the French Bourbons, should not be restored. Neither man would budge an inch from his stated position, and, for a time, it seemed that the Congress of Vienna was fated to sit in perpetuity while the two diplomatic giants, one immovable and the other irresistible, glared at each other across the conference table.

The cause of this impasse was Joachim Murat, King of Naples, Marshal of France, brother-in-law and friend of the deposed Napoleon. In return for Murat's desertion of the French emperor in 1814, Austria had guaranteed the former's throne by formal treaty. This treaty, however, was the

From Absolutism to Independence

pretext rather than the motive for Metternich's intransigence. Austria had already secured for herself, by the Treaty of Paris in the preceding year, the territories of Lombardy and Venetia. Now Metternich saw his chance perhaps to extend Austrian influence throughout the peninsula by placing a grateful Murat in her debt.

Talleyrand's motives were equally complex. In principle, he considered it an intolerable insult to France's restored Bourbon dynasty that a branch of that family should be deprived of its legitimate place as kings of Naples, and particularly that they should be replaced by a creature of Napoleon's. Moreover, he found it essential that Austrian influence in the north of Italy be counterbalanced by a French regime in the south. In this, he was supported by almost all of the other powers at the Congress. England saw a threat to her control of the Mediterranean in a neo-Napoleonic Naples. Russia's Tsar Alexander I, an emotional man, was opposed to Murat on the grounds of personal antipathy. Prussia, violently against any reminder of her humiliation by France, had declared from the very first that no vestige of the Napoleonic regime must be allowed to survive in Europe. Spain supported Talleyrand for the sake of consistency, since she wished to see her own branch of the Bourbons restored to their duchies of Lucca and Parma.

In the face of these considerations, Talleyrand and Metternich were persuaded finally to postpone the settlement of the Neapolitan succession until the end of the Congress, so that the delegates might move on to other matters. In the meantime, the Congress confirmed the Italian arrangements that had been agreed upon in Paris the preceding year. Genoa was incorporated into Piedmont, and King Victor Emmanuel returned to Turin. The former French empress, Marie Louise of Austria, was imposed, along with her lover, upon the duchy of Parma, while another Marie Louise, this one a Bourbon, was given the duchy of Lucca; and both were wholly under the control of Austria. Francis IV, the Austrian archduke, returned to Modena, Pius VII to Rome, and Ferdinand III to Tuscany, where he alone, of all the princes, made some attempt to preserve the reforms of the earlier period and to temper the tradition of absolutism.

The thorny question of the Neapolitan succession eventually was settled by events rather than by diplomacy. Murat was not unaware of the precariousness of his position. All that stood between himself and deposition —and possibly a firing squad—was Metternich's support; and he knew, from experience, how ephemeral a thing that could be. When Napoleon returned from Elba for the famous "Hundred Days," Murat therefore decided to gamble everything on one last throw of the dice. He offered his services once more to the French emperor and, without waiting either for permission from Napoleon or for the consent of the pope, he marched his troops northward, across the Papal States, to forestall an attack by Austria. At the same time, he issued a proclamation calling on the people of Italy to rally around him to defend their liberties. But, except for the co-operation of a few unimportant towns, this appeal went unheard, and, having been badly defeated by the Austrian armies at Tolentino on May 4, 1815, Murat fled first to France and then to Austria. Metternich now seized the opportunity to sponsor Ferdinand's restoration to the throne so hastily vacated by Murat, and, while Talleyrand watched helplessly, the new king, with Vienna's blessing, was escorted to his kingdom by Austrian troops. Talleyrand's candidate had won the Neapolitan throne—but he had won as Austria's puppet. To complete Talleyrand's humiliation, the Congress, at Metternich's dictation, declared Ferdinand to be not merely King of Naples, but King of the Two Sicilies, and it united Naples and Sicily under a common administration. To seal the bargain, King Ferdinand quickly negotiated a treaty of perpetual alliance and friendship with Austria. The influence of Austria—that is, of Metternich—was now as complete in the south as in the north of Italy.*

The disappearance of Murat removed the last obstacle to the complete supremacy in the peninsula of the principles of the restoration. The diplomats of the Congress of Vienna had done the very worst thing possible, and they did it so effectively that the cure was not only worse than the disease, but it actually brought Italy into a condition more serious than before. The absolutism of 1815 and of the years following was more complete than it had been in the era preceding the Napoleonic conquest. Even the good results of the progressive revolution of the last quarter of the eighteenth century were swept away by the determination of the Congress to destroy as effectually as possible all traces of Napoleon's influence. So far as possible, the old dynasties were in their old places, and the old methods of government were in full operation. Not a thought had been given to the Italian desire for independence. Italy had become, in the words of one Italian diplomat at Vienna, "just money, with which to pay for other things."

Despite these circumstances, the returning rulers were received with displays of joy. The Roman people welcomed Pope Pius with the enthusiasm which they usually reserved for street riots. In Turin, King Victor

---

* In October 1815, Murat made a final attempt to win back his kingdom, but he was quickly captured by Ferdinand and put to death by a firing squad of Neapolitan soldiers.

Emmanuel was so moved by the warmth of his reception that he vowed never to forget it. Francis of Modena—who, within a year, was to reimpose the double yoke of autocracy and clerical hegemony on his people—was greeted with cheers and adulatory verses. Even the controversial and never-popular Ferdinand of the Two Sicilies was met by happy crowds. Thus gratified, the princes set to work at once to turn back the clock. At Rome, the pope, a good man but a weak one, gave way to his cardinals and once more placed all governmental offices into clerical hands, restored feudal privileges, and reintroduced into the City, and into the nineteen provinces into which the Papal States were divided, that air of theocratic and paternalistic despotism which had been the hallmark of the eighteenth century. In Venetia and Lombardy, where Austria ruled directly, Metternich established a typical Austrian administration. Its methods, though not always bad in themselves, were aimed at the suppression of all local privilege and at the creation of loyal Austrians out of disaffected Italians. The Austrian emperor, Francis I, put it candidly enough. "It is necessary," he declared, "for the Lombards to forget that they are Italians. Obedience to my will is the bond that will unite my Italian provinces to the rest of my states." To this end, a system of military government was established, punishments were frequent and severe, and judicial tribunals were managed in the interests of Austrian absolutism. Austrian coinage and the Austrian legal code were introduced. Italians were driven from the professorial chairs of the universities and replaced by Austrians—who, often enough, could barely speak Italian. Needless to say, such methods served only to defeat the purpose for which they had been adopted. Instead of making Austrians out of the Lombards and the Venetians, they made them more intensely Italian. "Our Italian possessions," wrote one observant Austrian to Metternich, "are guaranteed to us only by physical force. Moral force is altogether lacking here. . . . They [the Italians] have only contempt and detestation for our uniform system of administration, by which they are put on a level with Germans, Bohemians, and Galicians." As the result of this "uniform system of administration," the industry of Lombardy and Venetia, hampered by the petty restrictions of the Austrian bureaucracy, began to deteriorate. And since trade was directed by Austrian policy rather than by rational economic laws, the historic lifeblood of Venice, commerce, came to be neglected almost entirely. Matters were hardly better in Piedmont, where Victor Emmanuel, giving full vent to his hatred of everything Napoleonic, plunged the country into unprecedented confusion in one stroke: he issued an edict declaring null and void any law passed since the Constitutions of 1770. In the new Kingdom of the Two Sicilies, Ferdinand bound himself, by his treaty of friendship with Austria, to grant no constitution to his people, and to refuse any offer of union with other Italian states. The Neapolitans and the Sicilians muttered, of course; but Ferdinand had little fear of trouble. After all, he was supported by a large body of Austrian troops—who were paid, fed, and lodged by the taxes of Naples and Sicily. In Tuscany alone, under Ferdinand III and his minister, Fossombroni, was the situation more encouraging. A comparative competence and honesty in government began to make itself felt; the clergy was kept in its place, and the people were molested as little as possible in their businesses and their daily lives. Tuscany became the envy, and then the refuge, of those who suffered oppression in other parts of Italy.

In this general atmosphere of absolutism in Italy, Metternich was busy attempting to implement his overall policy for the peninsula. What he seems to have had in mind was a loose and informal federation of states, comprising those of Germany to the north and those of Italy to the south, bound to Austria by treaty and prepared to support her by arms in case of war. King Ferdinand of the Two Sicilies, for example, had, in addition to his other commitments, promised twenty-five thousand men to Austria in case of war. Now Metternich attempted to extend this policy to the other Italian states. Tuscany was approached first with the offer of a treaty of friendship and mutual aid, and, because she was still too weak to resist, she accepted and committed herself to supply six thousand soldiers. Encouraged, Metternich now approached Rome, but both his persuasive art and his threats failed to move Pope Pius, who declared firmly that the Church, by virtue of her mission, must live at peace with the whole world, and that she could bind herself to no one nation. Piedmont, encouraged by this example, also resisted successfully, being convinced that her only chance of independence was to hold herself aloof both from France on the one side, and from Austria on the other.

With the failure of this plan to link the Italian states to Austria individually, Metternich now turned to an alternate policy: to form an official Confederation of Italian States, in which Austria, as the ruler of Venetia and Lombardy, would have a loud—and, it goes without saying, dominant —voice. Again, however, Pope Pius refused to join, declaring that it was as impossible for him to bind the Church to Italy as it had been for him to link her with Austria. And again King Victor Emmanuel of Piedmont gave the plan the *coup de grâce* by refusing to abdicate his authority in favor of Austrian hegemony. Not only that, the hardy Sardinian attempted to resist Austrian aggression by setting up, on his own, a confederation of small states not only of Italy but of southern Germany as well. In this case, however, Naples was too far along the road of subservience to Austria to be willing to join; and also, once more, Rome put the universality of the Church before her political interests in Italy. Victor Emmanuel's inspired scheme therefore came to naught.

Metternich was too occupied by his plans for the future of Italy to notice that, in the years following the settlement of the "Italian problem," the Italians were growing restless under Austrian-inspired absolutism. This discontent was fostered, and indeed, in some cases, initiated by the secret societies, of which Italy was the motherland of dozens. These societies, all of which aimed at revolution, flourished under grotesque names at every level of society, in the universities, the army, among the aristocracy, and among the peasants. Of these, the most numerous, the most famous, and the most feared was the *Carbonari,* or "Society of Charcoal Burners," which appeared to have taken on an organized form in Naples during the reign of Joachim Murat, about 1811. This association, the most typical of all the secret societies, represented both the undercurrents of popular unrest and in its more noble aspect, the influence of the revolutionary ideas that had evolved out of the events of the preceding two decades. Therefore Carbonarism is, for the student of Italian history, not a great political movement, nor even a great organized revolt, but rather a widespread political symptom indicative of the spirit that was coming to mind of the people of Europe everywhere. In France, it protested against the Restoration of the Bourbons, and in Spain it resisted the wretched government of Ferdinand VII. In Italy, its function was to oppose Austria and everything for which that state stood. Its cardinal principles were liberty of the individual, constitutional government, and national independence; and its chief means of action were popular agitation and armed revolution.

The first notable outbreak of the Carbonari was in Naples and in Piedmont in 1820—scarcely a year after Metternich had declared to his emperor that Italy was "perfectly tranquil." It was an important year in Italian history, for it represented the first major attempt of the people to gain constitutional liberties. In that year, the Neapolitans, inspired by the example of the people of Spain, who had just forced a constitution out of their King Ferdinand, began to clamor for the introduction of a similar guarantee of liberty into the Kingdom of the Two Sicilies. At first, the situation seemed full of hope. At the first sign of organized popular revolt, King Ferdinand yielded and conceded all that the Carbonari demanded.

On July 13, he publicly took a solemn oath to grant a constitution, an oath which concluded, temptingly, with these words: "Almighty God, who with infinite knowledge knows the soul and the future, if I lie now or intend to break this oath, may you at this instant strike my head with the lightning of your vengeance." Nothing happened, and the trusting Neapolitans went to their homes full of joy and enthusiasm. The Carbonari were hailed as the saviors of the people, and they now stepped to the front as the leaders of the liberal cause. Their praises were sung throughout Italy, and their lodges and membership increased phenomenally.

But the victory so easily gained had to be maintained in the face of a double opposition: that of the king, who had disgracefully perjured himself, and that of Metternich, who saw in the Neapolitan movement an unfavorable augur for absolutism everywhere. It was not until March 1821, however, that Metternich was prepared to move. ("If our fire-engines had been full in July," he said, "we should have set to work immediately.") An army of eighty thousand Austrian soldiers was ordered to march on Naples and put down the revolt. On March 23, Naples fell, and Ferdinand, greatly relieved, took up once more the old despotic regime. The constitutional government which he had vowed to defend was instantly swept away; the leaders of the Carbonari were imprisoned; the army was reduced; all co-operators in the revolution were executed, imprisoned, or exiled. The Two Sicilies were turned over to incompetent government, corrupt officials, financial bankruptcy, intrigue, and brigandage of all kinds—all supported by the military power of Austria.

While the movement in Naples was being extinguished, an uprising in Piedmont brought new distress to Metternich. However reactionary King Victor Emmanuel may have been after 1815, he was consistently stubborn in his determination to resist becoming an Austrian protégé. The king genuinely loved his good Piedmontese and Sardinians, and he had more than once proved himself loyal to them. Notwithstanding the fact that he had taken an Austrian wife, he had rejected every Austrian proposal for a treaty. When, therefore, the liberals of his kingdom demanded a constitution, and the Carbonari of Turin added the argument of an agitation which threatened to become a revolution, the king found himself on the horns of a dilemma. He was eager to conciliate his people and to prevent bloodshed; but he was convinced that Austria would be as quick to prevent a constitutional government in Piedmont as she was proving to be in Naples, and that any concessions to the agitators would furnish Metternich with the pretext for direct intervention in Piedmont. Unable to resolve the problem, he avoided the responsibility of a decision by abdicating in

From Absolutism to Independence 347

favor of his brother, Charles Felix, who was absent in Modena, and by appointing Charles Albert, Prince of Carignan, as Regent during the absence of the new king. Charles Albert immediately promulgated a constitution almost identical with that which had just been granted in Spain; and then, being unsure of himself, requested that King Charles Felix send further instructions. The new king lost no time in doing so: the constitution was declared null and void, and it was stated the Austrian troops would be called in, if necessary, to restore order. To these commands the Regent submitted. He, too, abdicated, while the revolutionaries mustered their forces to meet the Austrian army which they knew would shortly be upon them. They were not mistaken. They were met by an overwhelming force of Austrians and royalists at Novara and were crushed. In September, King Charles Felix, as absolute as any of his ancestors, took up his residence at Turin. Metternich, in order to prevent future uprisings, ordered twelve thousand troops to be stationed in Piedmont, at Alessandria. In addition, he compelled the pope to allow, and to pay for, an Austrian garrison in the papal city of Ancona, and the Grand Duke of Tuscany for one at Florence. These troops, in addition to the forty thousand already quartered in Naples, would, he felt, be sufficient to take care of any further trouble. Thus, the storms of revolution swept by, and the dukes and princes of Italy, under Metternich's hawklike eye, deemed themselves secure once more.

Indeed, the two almost simultaneous revolutions were followed by a decade of outward peace. Times were hard for lovers of independence, but hope and purpose had been let loose in the land; and in dark corners, hiding themselves as best they could, the friends of freedom looked to the future. Openly, little could be done; but indirect aid came from, and popular sentiment was stirred up by, literature which loudly proclaimed the revolutionary ideal. There was Ugo Foscolo, the poet, half Venetian and half Greek, who refused to take the oath of allegiance to Austria and fled instead to England, thereby giving to Italy, it was said, "a new institution: exile." There were Giovanni Berchet of Milan, a poet and man of letters, and Gabriele Rossetti, the father of Dante Rossetti and himself a poet, and many others. The most distinguished by far of these literary revolutionaries was Alessandro Manzoni, a deceptively sedate and gentlemanly Milanese, who occupied himself by the writing of patriotic plays and the famous romance, *I Promessi Sposi*. Perhaps greater than Manzoni, though less widely known, was a melancholy poet, Giacomo Leopardi, who raised Italian self-respect, as did Manzoni, by proof that the genius of the race lived still. His verses, however, were calculated to inspire Italians to action as well as to restore their pride in their country:

> O my country, I see the walls, the arches,
> The columns, the statues, the defenseless towers
> Of our forefathers.
> But the glory, I do not see.

Leopardi's sadness was matched by that of Italy. Austrian soldiers, the ubiquitous government spies, and often the clergy, did their best to destroy all vigor, life, and freedom. The press was closely censored, and no allusion to liberty or independence was allowed to appear before the eyes of the public. Even the arts were not exempt from government control. In a chorus of Bellini's opera, *I Puritani,* the word *liberty* was crossed out by a bureaucrat and replaced by *loyalty.* A tenor who forgot the change, perhaps unintentionally, was sent to prison for his offense. Things were at their worst in the Two Sicilies, where Ferdinand I, a rake, a bigot, a coward, and a complete autocrat, practiced the utmost and most arbitrary cruelty. After an insurrection in a small village, twenty-six heads—those of all the participants—were cut off and publicly exhibited for the edification of the people. Once, when a mother begged Ferdinand's mercy on behalf of her two sons who were condemned to death, he commanded her to choose one. She chose one. The other was shot, and the woman went mad, to Ferdinand's great delight.

The ten long years of inaction, repression, and suffering at last passed away, and another wave of exasperated independence and patriotism swept over the peninsula. In 1830, owing to the stimulus of the success of revolutions in France and Greece, a new effort was made in Piedmont, Modena, Bologna, and the Papal States to throw off the burden of absolutism. Once more recurred the phenomena of a decade before; once more the movement took a revolutionary form; and once more failure led to bitter reprisals, imprisonment, exile, and death. Tyranny and despotism gained, rather than lost by these uprisings, and absolutism settled down upon the agitated people more heavily than ever.

Among those suspected of complicity in these revolutions was one Giuseppi Mazzini, who was arrested by the government of Genoa because, as he himself said, he "was a young man of talent, fond of solitary walks at night, and habitually silent as to the subject of his meditations." And, he added, "the government was not fond of young men of talent, the subject of whose meditations was unknown to it." He was imprisoned at Savona, and there it was that he began to lay his plans for the establishment of a new association, Young Italy, which was to accomplish, through the education of the younger generation, what the Carbonari had failed to accomplish through the agitation of the old: the regeneration of Italy. Acquitted of the charges against him, Mazzini went to Marseilles, and there, surrounded by exiles from Parma, Modena, and the Papal States, he prepared to carry out his design and to avoid the faults of the Carbonari, whom he believed to be actuated by principles as dangerous as they were erroneous—"their complex symbolism, their hierarchical mysteries, their political faith . . . their tyranny of invisible chiefs, their ignoble blind obedience, their spirit of revenge." His own organization, by contrast, was to be simple in organization, entirely free of symbolism and graduated degrees; it was to consist of central and provincial bodies, and to have in each city an organizer, aided by propagandists. Its purpose was simply stated: the establishment of a free and united Italy, an independent nationality composed of twenty million men. This state was to be independent; that is, from its soil was to be driven every hostile foreigner; and it was to be republican; that is, privileges were to be abolished, clerical aristocracy suppressed, the class that bought and sold labor gradually reduced, individual faculties developed. A legislative system was to be inaugurated that should be "adapted to the wants of the people and calculated to promote the unceasing progress of national education." Young Italy was to obtain these results through the methods of education and insurrection, and one was to supplement the other. Education was to teach the need of insurrection; and insurrection was to become the means of national education.

Mazzini was a master conspirator, a veritable St. Paul of the religion of Italian independence. His whole life was a passionate renunciation of all the pleasures and comforts for which most men live, and a passionate dedication of himself to his ideals. Unlike his Pauline paradigm, however, Mazzini was never a successful man of action or a ready and energetic organizer. He was too obstinate in adhering to the doctrines that he enunciated, too uncompromising in dealing with the more practical side of life, too inexperienced in the ways of the world to succeed in any attempt to make a practical application of his ideas, and too ready to demand of others the same dedication and sacrifices which he exacted from himself. Consequently, when it came to the actual working out of his plans by the organization that he had founded, the defects of the whole scheme became clear, and Young Italy never succeeded as a revolutionary body, nor was the insurrectionary part of the program ever successfully carried out.

In 1834, because of the persecution in Piedmont of members of Young

Italy, an invasion of Savoy by the movement was attempted from Switzerland, but proved a lamentable failure. From 1841 to 1844, a series of attempts was made to rouse the Neapolitans and the citizens of the Papal States; but the watchfulness of the governments, aided by wholesale arrests and imprisonment, prevented the movements from reaching fruition. In 1844, the Bandiera brothers, sons of a noble family of the south, roused to a frenzy of patriotism by Mazzini's appeals—and despite the protests of those with better judgment—attempted to excite a revolt in Calabria. They were quickly captured and executed by the government of the Two Sicilies. This unfortunate episode served to check the revolutionary propaganda of Mazzini's party, and seriously injured the cause that he still continued to promote. The party of action, as Mazzini called his followers, practically ceased, after 1844, to be a political factor in Italy, and its work became more underhand and indirect. With Mazzini now in exile in London, weaving his impractical plots, the organization in Italy pursued its work quietly, and often effectually. By its moral efforts, Mazzini's Young Italy undoubtedly hastened the time of unity and independence, but by its political narrowness and encouragement of revolutionary fiascoes, it retarded the work of others who possessed better judgment and greater insight. So greatly did its reputation decline that, by the next decade, leaders among Italy's moderates would call the once promising Young Italy "one of the scourges of Italy."

While Young Italy, along with the Carbonari, were reduced to working in secret, literature continued to carry on the task of arousing enthusiasm for national achievements and national ideals. Silvio Pellico's *Le Mie Prigioni* was a scathing denunciation of Austrian aggression. The plays of Giovan Battista Niccolini, a Florentine, were rousing appeals for action against civil and ecclesiastical despotism. The romantic novels of Massimo d'Azeglio, of Piedmont, a painter and statesman as well as a writer, reminded youth of the bygone glories of Italy. Other novels, passionately patriotic, by Tomasso Grossi of Belluno and by Francesco Domenico Guerrazzi of Leghorn, followed the example of Massimo d'Azeglio's work. These romances, which seem so incredibly dull today, did much to sharpen a universal sense of dissatisfaction and unrest in Italy. But a book of a different sort had, in its way, a more brilliant career. Its author was Vincenzo Gioberti, a native of Milan who, early in life, had taken Holy Orders. He was converted to patriotism, suspected of complicity in revolutionary movements, imprisoned, exiled; in exile, he studied, taught, and thought. In 1843, he published, in Brussels, his book. It was entitled *Il primato morale e civile degli Italiani* (*The Moral and Civil Primacy of the Italians*), and it was a review of the ancient glory of Italy and a guide to new ways in which that splendor might be revived. Gioberti's basic proposal was for a confederation of the Italian states—excluding the Austrian provinces—with the pope at its head; and for that reason his followers became known as Neo-Guelphs. The book had tremendous success. Its ideas were accepted and became a political credo. And, strangely enough, for a time it seemed that his plan was on the threshold of execution.

In 1846, Pope Gregory XVI, a conservative man, died, and a ferment of interest arose as to his successor. In the College of Cardinals, a bitter struggle took place between two factions, one comprising the conservatives and the other the moderate-progressives. Finally, a compromise was effected whereby Cardinal Giovanni Mastai-Ferretti, Bishop of Imola, became Pope Pius IX—the famous "Pio Nono," as he was universally called. The new pope, an amiable, smiling, charming, handsome, and liberal prelate, lost no time in showing where his heart lay. Within a month or two, as an apparently immortal Metternich watched in horror from Vienna, Pius granted amnesty to political prisoners, appointed a commission to study necessary reforms in the Papal States, permitted (tacitly, at least) freedom of the press, organized a Council of State consisting of laymen, and authorized the organization of a civic guard. Pope Pius was hailed enthusiastically throughout the peninsula. Here was Gioberti's ideal pope. Here was the man, it seemed, to lead the Italian Guelphs and once more to drive the barbarians from Italy. Shouts of "Long live Italy, the Pope, and the Constitution!" echoed throughout the land.

While the pope was winning the good will of the people by his liberal policies, two other states were also feeling the influence of the new spirit and were undertaking promising reforms. Tuscany, under the mildly paternalistic rule of its Grand Duke, had for years enjoyed peace and prosperity. The news from Rome, however, fanned into flames the spark ignited there by the revolutionary writers. In order to avoid a conflagration, Grand Duke Leopold was obliged to yield to popular demands. In the latter part of 1847, he modified the press law, appointed a commission to revise the legal codes, summoned an advisory council of distinguished citizens, and agreed to the formation of a municipal guard. He discarded his Austrian uniform and adopted Tuscan dress; and then expressed his good will in less symbolic fashion by appointing reform-minded Tuscans to his cabinet. Public enthusiasm in Tuscany knew no bounds, and the Grand Duke, a modest man, was astonished to find himself vying with Pio Nono as a national hero.

Piedmont was slower, but it, too, came into the ranks of the reforming states. King Charles Albert—who had succeeded Charles Felix in 1831—was already involved in a dispute with Austria over salt and wine customs payments, and this episode in 1846 had begun a confrontation with Austria that was to end in actual war. Charles Albert so far supported Pope Pius' reforms that he sent him letters of congratulation, offering aid and saying, "Whatever may occur, I will not separate my cause from yours." To his people, he declared, "If ever God shall give us the grace to undertake a war of independence, no one but I shall command the army. Oh, what a glorious day will that be, when we shout the battle cry of a war for the independence of Italy!" To words Charles Albert added deeds. He reorganized his cabinet by dismissing reactionary councilors, authorized the revision of the legal code, modified the police system, and increased the local powers of the communes. Finally, he promised other reforms that were greatly needed. He promised other, less tangible, things also. Summoning Massimo d'Azeglio to the palace, he bade his astonished subject to tell the people that when the occasion should present itself, his own life, his sons' lives, his treasure, and his army, all would be spent unstintingly for the cause of Italy.

Thus encouraged by king and pope, patriots from Piedmont to Sicily waited in tremulous expectation for the coming of great events. The period of waiting was short. While Metternich was announcing in a circular letter to the European powers that Italy was but a geographical expression, and that the complete sovereignty and independence of each state of the peninsula must be maintained, Italy from end to end was on tiptoe with excitement. And then the year 1848 came rushing in with swashbuckler fury.

The new year began with the Tobacco Riots at Milan, which were a symptom of rapidly rising tensions in Lombardy and which involved clashes with the police and several fatalities among the rioters. There were vociferous cries of sympathy from Piedmont and Rome, and the funerals of the victims took on the character of national mourning. It was a first indication of the national quality of the revolt. Then, on January 12, a mob attacked the Bourbon soldiers of King Ferdinand II and drove them out of the city. This example was followed throughout Sicily. Across the channel, Naples also arose and demanded a constitution. The frightened king granted it (January 29). In Piedmont, at an assembly of journalists, the editor of a newspaper called *Il Risorgimento* declared loudly that the time for petitions for the banishment of the Jesuits and for the institution of a national guard had passed, and that a constitution should be demanded. The speaker was a rather stout man of thirty-eight with a square face and high forehead. He wore spectacles, and under his chin a fringe of beard ran round from ear to ear. He looked like an amiable and distinguished professor—except that there was a pinch to his nostrils and a compression to his lips that suggested arrogance and a devotion to power. His name was Camillo Cavour, and it was on this occasion that he first became a man to watch.

The city of Turin took up Cavour's cry, and the king acceded. Then, in quick succession, the Grand Duke of Tuscany and Pope Pius IX both granted formal constitutions perpetuating and expanding their liberal reforms. In the Austrian provinces of Lombardy and Venetia, there were riots, arrests, assaults upon the police, cavalry charges, and martial law. Then came word that Vienna herself had revolted, that the hated Metternich had been driven into exile, and that the terrified emperor had promised a constitution. Venice accepted the promise; but Milan, where a citizen had been killed by the police, broke into rebellion. Carts, carriages, tables, chairs, pianos, bedsteads were all heaped into barricades to defend the streets. Everyone took part. Men, boys, children, and priests snatched up knives, hammers, axes, stones, and sticks. These were the renowned "Five Days" of Milan. Every street, every house was a battleground, and the Austrian commander, Field Marshal Radetzky, with his garrison of fourteen thousand men, was driven from the city. From Milan, revolt spread throughout Lombardy. When the news reached Venice, the citizens rose, forced the Austrian governor to capitulate, and proclaimed anew the ancient Republic of Venice, of which Daniele Manin was named president.

This glorious news—Venice republican, Milan victorious over Radetzky—flew to Turin. Every liberal went mad with excitement. Now, they cried, had come the hour for which Piedmont had disciplined and trained itself, for which it had longed for so many years; now should Piedmont lead Italy and fight the nation's battle. Cavour cried that there was but one possible course: immediate war with Austria. On March 23, King Charles Albert stepped out onto his balcony and waved the tricolor standard of revolutionary Italy. The next day, a royal proclamation stated that the Piedmontese army would march to the aid of Lombardy and Venice. A shout of joy went up throughout Italy. Modena and Parma cast out their Austrian dukes and sent recruits to help. The Grand Duke of Tuscany, the King of Naples, and even Pio Nono, each sent an army. The war had become a national crusade.

At first, the campaign went well. The Italian allies numbered more than ninety thousand men, and Charles Albert, leading the main body, forced the Austrians under Radetzky back into the quadrilateral formed by Verona, Peschiera, Mantua, and Legnano. But the king was no general; he was a novice, unlearned in strategy and ignorant of tactics. While he dawdled, not knowing quite what to do, Radetzky received reinforcements. This situation noticeably cooled the first glorious burst of feeling for union and freedom. Pope Pius, for one, began to feel doubts. What right had the Vicar of Christ to take part in war? Were not Austrians and Italians one in the sight of God? What had the Universal Church to do with national divisions? He declared that he would not fight, but such great tumult greeted his announcement in Rome that he was forced to reverse himself. Nonetheless, his hesitation had dealt a fatal blow to the cause of Italian independence. In Naples, the watchful Ferdinand II, eager for any pretext, took advantage of some rioting in the streets to dissolve parliament and order his army home. One general, with a few hundred men, disobeyed, but the rest turned back.

In the north, the ancient jealousies and rivalries between the Italian states intervened and broke the new-made union. Venice, instead of uniting with Piedmont in a political confederation, insisted upon retaining her autonomy, and Milan hesitated out of jealousy of Turin. Of these discords Marshal Radetzky was quick to take advantage. Within thirty days, the Tuscan army had been destroyed, the papal army taken prisoner, and the Piedmontese army isolated. The issue finally was decided at the battle of Custoza, July 23-25, after which the Piedmontese were made to surrender Milan and to retreat across the river Ticino into their own territory. Austria returned, triumphant, into full possession of her provinces, except for the city of Venice; and the dukes of Parma and Modena returned to their domains under her protection.

Elsewhere in Italy the current of events ran with equal swiftness. In Sicily, King Ferdinand bombarded his rebellious city of Messina (hence his universal nickname, Bomba) and forced it to surrender; thereafter, he was at pains to ignore the constitution throughout the Kingdom of the Two Sicilies. At Rome, utter confusion reigned. Pius appointed an energetic and popular statesman, Pellegrino Rossi, as prime minister, hoping that this action might restore peace and order within his realm. Rossi, however, was shortly assassinated. Shots were even fired at the papal palace on the Quirinal, while rioters and looters wandered at will through the streets of the City. Pio Nono, thoroughly frightened, fled to Gaeta, at the Neapolitan border. The City begged him to return and even went so far as to promise obedience; but the pope, in what can only be described as a sulk, peremptorily refused. The revolutionary leaders of Rome therefore convened an assembly of citizens to decide what form of government to adopt and, though Pope Pius hurled excommunications at all partici-

From Absolutism to Independence

pants, the delegates met (February 5, 1849), declared the temporal power of the papacy to be at an end, and established the Roman Republic. At the head of the new Republic, presiding over a triumvirate, the citizens placed that fiery but ineffectual revolutionary, Giuseppe Mazzini. In Tuscany, the republican fire likewise blazed, and the Grand Duke joined Pio Nono in furious exile at Gaeta. As at Rome, a provisional government was set up, with a triumvirate at its head.

As the Romans and the Tuscans were establishing a precarious peace within their boundaries, the Piedmontese and the Austrians renewed the war in the north. On March 23, at Novara, a small town on the Piedmontese side of the Ticino, the final battle was fought. Once more, the Austrians were victorious. When King Charles Albert asked for a truce, Radetzky's terms were so savage that the king, unable to accept them, and feeling himself to be the chief cause of this severity, felt it necessary to remove himself from the scene. He abdicated in favor of his son, Victor Emmanuel II, and went into exile, where he soon died. The new king was left to accept Radetzky's terms.

Although all rational hope for the cause of Italy was now at an end, still the dismembered parts of the coalition struggled on. The men of Brescia defended themselves gloriously for days, barricading every street, and making fortresses of their homes, but they were overpowered. The Austrian commander, General Haynau, inflicted atrocities that made his name an object of horror throughout Europe. He himself confesses, "I commanded that no prisoner should be taken, and that everyone found with weapons in his hands should be put to death on the spot; and also that the houses from which shots came should be burned to the ground." In Sicily, the revolutionaries resisted bravely but in vain, and King Ferdinand's authority was re-established throughout the island. In Naples, all liberals were in grave danger of imprisonment, exile, or death. In Tuscany, the mild citizens, aghast at what they had wrought and at their own radical government, invited the Grand Duke to return. He came, bringing an Austrian garrison with him.

At Rome, even more notable things were happening. Mazzini, at the head of the government, was in a difficult position. Pope Pius had asked the Catholic Powers of Europe to re-establish the temporal power of the papacy, and France, Spain, Austria, and reactionary King Ferdinand at Naples, all were eager to obey. France's new president, Prince Louis-Napoleon Bonaparte, a nephew of the Emperor Napoleon I and himself soon to become emperor under the title of Napoleon III, was required to tread a careful course. He needed desperately the support of France's clerical party, and so he felt obliged to protect the pope from his enemies. Yet, at the same time, he dared not lose the support of France's liberal party. He therefore pursued a wavering course of action. In a statement curiously prefiguring the governmental morality of a later age, he declared that he would indeed send an army to Rome, but that its purpose would be to defend "real liberty," to give the Romans sufficient freedom of action to decide for themselves what they wanted. The French soldiers then advanced to the walls of Rome (April 29, 1849). The Romans, however, feeling that they had already spoken their minds with sufficient clarity, would have none of President Bonaparte's "real liberty." Skirmishes were fought, and the French were forced to retire to a distance from the City. Meanwhile, an Austrian army came from the north, a Neapolitan contingent from the south, and the Spaniards landed at the mouth of the Tiber. The French explained to the Austrians that this was not an Austrian affair; and the Austrians, not without some feeling of relief, withdrew northward. The men of Rome, reinforced by the troops of a fiery adventurer named Giuseppe Garibaldi, drove back the Neapolitans. The Spaniards, for the part, chose to retire quietly, leaving the French to deal with the situation as they thought best. French reinforcements arrived, and the fighting began anew.

The Romans defended themselves for three weeks, although their troops were untrained and ineffective against regular French regiments. The hero of the period was Garibaldi. The last of the knights-errant, he was the very incarnation of Romance and Revolution. Bred to the sea, this Savoyard from Nice (which was part of Savoy at the time), always retained the jaunty, gallant bearing of the professional mariner. His countenance, with its broad, tranquil brow, kindly eyes and strong mouth, in youth always joyfully sparkling, later changed under the weight of care and disillusionment; but still he kept the seaman's mien, and the seaman's lightsome eye. He was the *beau idéal* of a romantic hero. After serving under Mazzini in the latter's abortive invasion of Piedmont in 1835, he had fled to South America, where he lived a life of guerrilla warfare, fighting like a Paladin on behalf of republican revolutionaries struggling for their freedom. And, all the while, he was training a band of Italian adventurers, his famous "Legion," so that they should be ready when their country had need of them. These men had first, under Garibaldi's command, joined the forces of King Charles Albert, and then, after the latter's defeat and abdication, had rushed to the defense of Rome. Their entry into the City had been extraordinary enough to excite to enthusiasm even the sophisticated Romans. The gaunt soldiers, wearing red shirts and pointed hats topped with plumes, their legs bare, the beards full-grown, their faces tanned to copper, their long hair flowing and unkempt, looked like so many Fra Diavolos. At their head, Garibaldi himself, in his red shirt, with loose kerchief knotted round his throat, the regular beauty of his noble, leonine face set off by his waving hair, mounted on a milk-white horse, rode like a demigod.

Besides Garibaldi's Legion, troops of volunteers came from all over Italy to fight against the detested foreigners. But it was all in vain. On June 3, 1849, the French general, Oudinot, with an army of thirty thousand men, opened the attack on the City. The Roman defense was desperate and valiant, full of heroic exploits which live on in the annals of history as in the legends of the Romans. Nonetheless, early on July 1, while Mazzini in the Assembly still urged resistance at any cost, Garibaldi, haggard with exhaustion, entered the hall and announced to the deputies that defense was no longer possible. The next morning, Garibaldi left Rome with several thousand troops and began his retreat across Italy to Ravenna. Pursued by four armies, his little force defied capture and eventually disappeared among the Apennines. He himself, after many close brushes with arrest, found refuge in Tuscany. General Oudinot marched into silent Rome, dissolved the Republican government, and sent the keys of the City to be laid at the feet of Pio Nono, with the compliments of the French Republic. A committee of cardinals arrived to rule Rome, with the aid of French bayonets, until the pontiff should return.

Venice alone amid her lagoons held out and, under Daniele Manin, her valiant president, maintained a stout defense until August. But cholera and famine came to the enemy's aid and, on the 24th, the city capitulated. Marshal Radetzky heard an Austrian *Te Deum* sung in St. Mark's, while all Italy lay prostrate under the forces of triumphant reaction. Piedmont alone was left to become the center of whatever hope of independence and unity still existed.

2. *A Time for Diplomacy* (1848–1859)

After the uprisings of 1848–1849, it seemed that the old tyrannies were more firmly entrenched than ever in every state of Italy except Piedmont. Liberalism in any form and of any tincture was immediately suspect, and known liberals were in an unhappy position: the lucky ones were in disgrace, and the others were in prison. Those who had been most unequivocally compromised had fled abroad; Garibaldi was now in America, Mazzini in England, and Manin in France. But the cause of Italian liberalism, whether in exile abroad or under suspicion at home, was as fragmented and confused as ever. Some swore that Italy's sole hope lay in the establishment of a unified republic. Others were for a free confederation of autonomous states. Still others maintained that total unity under a constitutional monarch was the only possible solution. Some looked to Piedmont for inspiration and aid; others, to France; and others, to England. The means proposed for these diverse ends were as various as the ends themselves, and ranged from lawful agitation to outright insurrection and foreign invasion.

The old regimes were as uncompromisingly decisive as the liberals were confused. In Naples, for example, King Ferdinand, now universally known as "Bomba," formulated an inflexible policy: to imprison anyone suspected of any form of liberalism, and to keep the suspect in prison "pending further developments"—that is, indefinitely. It is generally believed that between fifteen and thirty thousand men thus fell victim to the royal paranoia. Among them was one Baron Carlo Poerio, a former minister to the king and a gentleman known and esteemed throughout Europe. Poerio's trial took place in 1850, at a time when William Gladstone, the future prime minister of England, was in Naples. Gladstone attended the trial, and in his famous *Letters to the Earl of Aberdeen* he described in detail the "horrors amidst which the government of that country [the Two Sicilies] is now carried on." The policies of Ferdinand's government, he said, "are an outrage upon religion, upon civilization, upon humanity, and upon decency." He deplored "the incessant, systematic, deliberate violation of law by the Power appointed to watch over it and maintain it." Ferdinand's policy was "the wholesale persecution of virtue, the awful profanation of public religion, the perfect prostitution of the judicial office. This is 'The negation of God erected into a system of government.'" And then Gladstone, with that rhetorically pious sense of self-righteousness that seemed to come so naturally to British statesmen of the Victorian era, ended by declaring that "It is time that either the veil should be lifted from scenes fitted more for hell than earth, or some considerable mitigation should be voluntarily adopted. I have undertaken this wearisome and painful task, in the hope of doing something to diminish a mass of human suffering as huge, I believe, as acute, to say the least, as any that the eye of Heaven beholds." These letters of Gladstone's fell into the hands of Lord Palmerston, the then prime minister, and were sent by him to every government in Europe. They accomplished a great deal in awakening general sympathy for the oppressed peoples of Italy. And so, not for the first time in history and not for the last, the genius of the Bourbon family for doing the wrong thing at precisely the wrong time, and for being caught at it, was to be a major factor in their downfall.

In the Papal States, it seemed that Pius IX had fallen almost completely under the influence of the reactionaries and the Jesuits (at that time, the two were almost indistinguishable), and the old order was restored by papal decrees and enforced by foreign arms. The Romans, however, were more delighted by the return of Pio Nono than saddened by the loss of the Republic; for the papacy was a proved asset, while no one knew quite what a Republic would have brought. The City therefore settled down under the accustomed system without undue complaint. Modena, Parma, and Tuscany, all ruled by sprigs of the Hapsburg tree, as usual did whatever they thought would be pleasing to the government of Austria, which, in this instance, meant the imprisonment of liberal agitators. Lombardy, of course, was occupied by Austrian troops under the redoubtable Marshal Radetzky; but this was hardly enough to keep the Lombards from exercising their natural talent for conspiracy. Mazzini, in London, had formed a "National Italian Committee" for the purpose of raising a loan through private subscription in England and Italy. One of the committee's favorite and most effective projects was the establishment and maintenance of an anti-Austrian printing press at Capolago, on the Swiss border, which published and distributed imflammatory leaflets and pamphlets in Austrian territory.

That Italy was relatively calm at this time did not mean that the liberals had accepted a reversion to the *status quo*. It is true that the masses had never, except in Piedmont, taken a really active part in the liberal movement, and so it could hardly be expected that the people as a whole would rise up in defense of a movement in defeat to which they had never rallied when it was flourishing. In the cities, however, there were numerous liberal groups, and it was there that lay the strength of the movement and its guiding spirit. In those circles, a new determination was beginning to show itself. Up to 1848, the purpose of the liberal movement had been largely one of reform—to reform the Austrians, the Bourbons, the popes, by means of exacting constitutions from them. Now, however, reform was what the liberals did not want; for a reform movement could too easily lapse into apathy or be misled, as in the past, by false promises. What was now to be under attack was the entire political system and its *raison d'être*. The only way to establish Italian independence was to overthrow the old system entirely; Austria, the princelings, the temporal power of the popes—all must be swept away. But just how this was to be accomplished, no one could yet tell.

The logical, and perhaps the only realistic, hope of Italy seemed to lie in Piedmont. And, indeed, the history of Italy during the ten years that followed the collapse of the national effort of 1848–1849 will center in the political life of that small kingdom, and in the work of one man, Camillo Benso, Count di Cavour. The only liberal survivor of the wreck of 1848 was the constitution granted by King Charles Albert. Although by modern standards that constitution hardly qualified as "liberal," yet, in nineteenth-century Italy, it seemed a model of enlightened government. It provided for a Premier or "President of the Council," who was nominated by the King. There was a Senate, also appointed by the King, and a Chamber of Deputies elected by the comparatively few citizens of Piedmont who were allowed to vote.

After the Battle of Novara, the new king, Victor Emmanuel II, persuaded his friend Massimo d'Azeglio to accept the premiership. The new Premier was not a statesman, nor did he claim to be one. By profession, he was a painter; by avocation, a writer and a soldier. Of political gifts, he had few; and of political experience, none. In almost his first exercise of office, the negotiation of the peace treaty with Austria, he was forced to dissolve the lower Chamber and to call for a new election. Following an appeal by the king for support and loyalty, a new Chamber was elected, and it dutifully approved the treaty as it stood.

Among the newly elected deputies was Count Cavour, editor of *Il Risorgimento,* who represented his native Turin. Cavour had been a vehement liberal all his life and, at one point, his unconcealed hostility to the old regimes had forced him to resign from the army. He then took up farming, and made a fortune at it by introducing modern machinery and methods onto his family estates. He had traveled widely in England, France, and Switzerland, and he was acquainted with the leading political figures of those countries. Politically, Cavour stood between the reactionary tendencies of the right and the excesses of the left; in consequence, he was often condemned by both sides. Among his gifts were two that were to prove of particular value to the future of Italy. He was a born parliamentarian, with a profound knowledge and practical grasp of constitutional questions; and he was what might be called a "modernist." That is, he took little interest in Italy's past glories, and her art and literature were beyond his range of interests. His entire outlook focused on the future, and his interests were centered on the modern notion of "progress"—on scientific advance in industry and finance. Cavour was, then, far removed from the classic Italian ideal of the "complete man"; but he was peculiarly suited to the needs of his time. He was, in fact, the one great statesman that Italy was to produce in the nineteenth century; and he was to be the architect of Italian unity and independence.

The policy of Massimo d'Azeglio as premier—strangely enough for that old revolutionary—was aimed primarily at the avoidance of any disturbance both within and without Piedmont, and he was determined to postpone indefinitely any reforms that might "upset" Italy or Europe. Cavour, on the other hand, realized that if the new constitution did not deal effectively and quickly with the abuses that it had been established to correct, then the people of Piedmont would be hardly better off than before. Cavour's policy as Deputy, therefore, was intended to force as many reforms as possible as rapidly as possible. The foundation of his greatness was laid in March 1850, when he spoke in favor of the Siccardi Laws, which abolished the *Foro Ecclesiastico,* or Church Court—a system which had duplicated the civil court and doubled the costs of litigation in such common matters as matrimonial cases, probate, and so forth. After the passage of this reform and the enthusiastic public response to this legislation, Cavour's rise was rapid. A few months later, he was made Minister of Agriculture, Commerce, and Marine, and he quickly committed Piedmont to a policy of free trade which, while cutting import tariffs to a minimum, also opened up enormous new markets to Piedmontese products. The success of this scheme led to Cavour's appointment as Minister of Finance, in which capacity he negotiated a sizable loan from Great Britain and paid off what remained of the war indemnity to Austria.

It was now obvious that Cavour's star was in the ascendant, and Cavour himself, always a realist, began to deal with some of the problems that he would face when, as seemed inevitable, he would be called upon to replace Massimo d'Azeglio. The most important of these was that of uniting his own moderate party in the chamber with the group of moderates led by Rattazzi, in order to secure a majority that would enable him to carry out his plans. The *coup d'état* in France (1851) which gave dictatorial powers to President Louis-Napoleon Bonaparte, and the pressure exerted on Piedmont by France to stifle public criticism of the new regime, brought Cavour and Rattazzi together, and ensured that majority. This union forced D'Azeglio's resignation, but King Victor Emmanuel refused it, and ordered that D'Azeglio form a new ministry—one in which the troublesome Cavour would not be included. This, however, obviously was a condition that could not endure, and D'Azeglio was perceptive enough to know it. In November 1852, he resigned again, and insisted that the king ask Cavour to head the new government. The king acquiesced, and the government known in history as "The Great Ministry" came into being under Cavour.

Cavour, unlike Massimo d'Azeglio, knew exactly what was to be done, and he knew precisely how to go about doing it. His single purpose was to eject Austria from Italian affairs, and to establish a unified Kingdom of Italy. Italy's best hope, he reasoned, lay in the co-operation of Austria's traditional enemy, France; but France's new Bonapartist absolutism might prove dangerous, and therefore it would be necessary to enlist the sympathy of England to serve as a counterbalance. Nothing would be more effective, Cavour knew, in winning foreign support for Piedmont than for his country to gain a reputation for law, order, and prosperity. Moreover, a sound and progressive government in Piedmont would focus the eyes of Italy on that country and enhance her position as the most capable leader of the Italy of the future. For the next two years, therefore, the new government concentrated on civil reform, on roads, docks and railways, and on all the accouterments of progress in a modern state. Parliamentary government, too, flourished, and business was now conducted in the Chamber of Deputies in a way well calculated to impress the parliamentary-minded government of Great Britain.

In foreign affairs, Cavour held firmly to a course of moderation—which by no means meant that he was willing to allow Piedmontese rights to be infringed by foreign powers or Piedmontese prestige to suffer. In a diplomatic clash with Austria over the sequestration of the property of Lombard *émigrés* in Piedmont, he drew up and circulated throughout Europe a full, clear, and objective statement of Piedmont's case, and then recalled the Piedmontese minister in Vienna. This "civilized" behavior, particularly when compared to the insults and threats which emanated from Vienna, elicited the sympathy and admiration of Great Britain—as it was intended to do—and Piedmontese (and Cavour's) prestige abroad grew to considerable proportions.

What Cavour's policy now required was a "European complication" which Piedmont could use to draw England and France to her side and away from Austria. The opportunity presented itself in the form of the Crimean War (1854), with France, England, and Turkey aligned against Russia. The issue, as so often is the case in modern wars, was one about which the combatants cared little: the guardianship of the Holy Places in Palestine. Cavour immediately offered Piedmontese troops to the Allies. There was much cautious and time-consuming negotiation, for England and France would have preferred the aid of powerful Austria to that of Victor Emmanuel's little Alpine kingdom. But Austria hesitated, and finally refused to commit herself; and so, the Piedmontese offer was accepted. The troops went, fought bravely, and brought credit upon Italy and upon

From Absolutism to Independence

Cavour. The bad impression left by the disastrous campaigns of 1848-1849 was effaced, and public esteem for Piedmont and Italy increased throughout Europe—except, of course, in Austria. More important, a wave of national pride swept over Cavour's country, and over all of Italy. The shame of Novara had been wiped out.

The Crimean War ended in early 1856, when the Austrian emperor offered his services as mediator, and the fruits of victory were reaped at the Congress of Paris later that year. The preliminaries of this Congress caused some trepidation in Piedmont. Would that small country be admitted to the negotiations on an equal footing with the great powers? Or would it, and Cavour, suffer the shame of being relegated to a position of secondary importance? The theory of the question was never resolved, although there was some discussion of it among Austria, France, and England. In practice, as soon as Cavour arrived in Paris he was accepted as an equal by the delegates of those countries, and even by Count Buol, the Austrian representative. It was a significant preliminary victory, and one which contributed substantially to Cavour's self-confidence in pursuing other objectives. He had come to Paris with two such objectives firmly in mind. One was to obtain for Piedmont the Duchy of Parma, a Hapsburg possession. The other, and the chief one, was to call the attention of Europe to the sad condition of Italy, and, if possible, to obtain a condemnation of Austria's presence and policy there. So far as the question of Parma was concerned, all hope soon was abandoned. The ruler of France, the erstwhile President Louis-Napoleon Bonaparte, who, by a referendum of 1852 had been transformed into Napoleon III, Emperor of the French, stated emphatically to Cavour that it was impossible. "Austria," he said, "would prefer to go to war rather than let you have Parma." There remained therefore only the Italian question, and, on April 8, at the instigation of Napoleon III, the subject was introduced.

At that session, Lord Clarendon, the British representative, discussed, in detail, the situation of Italy. He declared forcefully that the presence of foreign troops upon Italian soil was a menace to European equilibrium, and that the government of Pius IX was the worst in Europe; he denounced the King of the Two Sicilies for his cruelty, and the petty princes of Italy for their uselessness and incompetence. "No Italian statesman," said Cavour in his dispatch to Turin, "could have formulated a more forceful, or a more exact, accusation." Count Buol of Austria, greatly offended, replied that the subject was irrelevant to the business of the meeting, and that he had no instructions to cover it. Then Cavour spoke in a spirit of moderation—for, as he wrote to D'Azeglio, he meant to be as calm in speaking as he ought to be bold in acting. He repeated the grievances of Italy, and, after reciting the sins of Austria in Italy, showed that the Austrian presence was contrary to treaties, destructive of the political peace of the peninsula, and dangerous particularly to the kingdom of Victor Emmanuel.

No action was taken by the Congress, but Cavour had gained his point. Austria, who had entered the negotiations as mediator, now left them as the accused. Moreover, Buol's obstinate attitude had annoyed Napoleon and made him more receptive to Cavour's arguments; and France and England, by permitting discussion of the subject, had openly admitted that Italy's wretched condition was a matter of European interest. The Congress of Paris was to become the turning point in the history of the Risorgimento.

It also marked the end of the first phase of Cavour's policy. Hitherto, Cavour's acts had been based on the hope that Italy's problems could be solved by negotiation. Now, it became clear to him that nothing short of force would make Austria surrender her Italian provinces. He therefore began to concentrate his energies in preparing for the coming struggle, and in winning over the indispensable support of the two sympathetic powers, England and France, and particularly of the latter. He had every reason to believe, as he informed King Victor Emmanuel, that the kingdom was safe from attack by Austria unless the latter was prepared to face also England and France, for he did not doubt that his Crimean allies would come to his aid in the event of an unprovoked attack. The sense of safety which this belief engendered became the cornerstone of his new policy: to adopt a course of exasperation which would prod Austria into an attack.

Austria recognized the gravity of the situation. Although enraged by her treatment at Paris, she resolved to change, at least superficially, her Italian policies. Acting upon English advice, she tempered the rigor of her police system in Lombardy and Venetia, pardoned political criminals, and promised an amnesty. The Emperor Franz Joseph himself visited Milan, made strenuous efforts to conciliate public opinion, and appointed his brother, the Archduke Maximilian, the most lovable and esteemed of all the Hapsburgs, as viceroy there. In Cavour's eyes, however, Austria's self-reform was an even greater menace to Italian freedom than Austria's aggressions. In his determination that war should come, he used every means to frustrate Austria's projects, and to encourage whatever might provoke her anger. He not only built a naval base at Spezzia and urged the completion of the Mt. Cenis tunnel, but openly collected funds in Austrian territory for a fortress at Alessandria and accepted, if he did not initiate, a Milanese proposal to erect a monument to the Piedmontese army of the Crimea "as a symbol of a common faith and a common hope in a better future." Piedmontese journalists were encouraged to increase their attacks on Austrian despotism. Finally, in Parliament, Cavour threw down the gauntlet of war, crying: "Italy has been considered as a beautiful woman, oppressed by a barbarous and tyrannical husband, made for eternal subjection because incapable of governing herself. But this is no longer so. Italy is now marching toward independence and liberty." Austria's patience now gave way, as was expected, and Count Buol issued a note strongly denouncing Piedmont and demanding apologies. Cavour, in language equally strong, rejected the demand, and the Austrian ambassador was recalled to Vienna.

The situation was immensely to Cavour's liking, and he began to prepare in earnest for the struggle. First, he rallied the old revolutionary elements to his cause. He had already spoken, at Paris, to Daniele Manin, the former republican President of the Venetian republic, and won him over. He got in touch with Garibaldi and urged him to prepare for what was to come. Of all the republican elements of Italy, only Mazzini and his followers did not grasp the idea that the country, if she was to be saved, could not depend any longer on futile insurrections and upon the outdated ideal of conspiracies. He enlisted the aid of La Farina, through whose efforts a National Italian Society was formed in 1857, which worked openly in Piedmont, but secretly in the rest of Italy. Its purpose was to propagandize the idea of unity among the people, and to prepare the way for the consolidation of Italy when the time should come.

In the meantime, Cavour maintained an attitude of cold propriety toward Austria, even though diplomatic relations between the two countries had now ceased entirely. This practice, however, was rendered difficult by a new republican uprising, in 1857, under Mazzini. There was an attempted invasion of Naples, and a simultaneous revolt at Genoa. Both attempts were, as usual, complete failures, and the republican forces in both instances were captured or killed. Cavour had now to patch up as best he could the damage done by Mazzini's latest display of ineptness, for from London and Paris there issued a flood of protests, and from Vienna a torrent of recriminations. Cavour was equal to the task. He instructed his ambassador in London to magnify the effort of the Mazzinians, pointing out that the "great European revolutionary party" had its headquarters in England, and that Europe's most dangerous radicals were constantly hatching their plots under cover of English liberty. With the Emperor Napoleon III, he took the contrary line, minimizing the seriousness and size of the uprising and emphasizing that, if this was all that the revolutionaries were capable of then there was really nothing to fear. Under the balm of Cavour's double talk, the storm soon blew over and both Napoleon and the British government became once more quite friendly.

The hopes thus roused, particularly the French emperor's increasing sympathy, were for the moment dashed by an event which seemed to destroy all prospect of military aid from France. Early in 1858, an Italian refugee, Orsini, made an attempt upon Napoleon's life. The news was followed by violent accusations from Paris, coupled with threats and demands, while, in London, a parliamentary crisis was created in the course of which Lord Palmerston's friendly government was forced to resign. A scapegoat was needed, and Cavour decided upon the hapless Mazzini who, for once, was probably quite innocent. Mazzini's republican partisans throughout Victor Emmanuel's domains were arrested and many of them exiled. Mazzini's newspaper, *L'Italia del Popolo,* was hounded to death by prosecution and, finally, by confiscation. A law was passed which strictly limited criticism of foreign governments and rulers. But none of this was enough for the frightened Napoleon III, who had his Foreign Minister send a blistering letter to the French ambassador at Turin. It was, however, the pride and candor of King Victor Emmanuel that saved the day. The king had sent General della Rocca to congratulate Napoleon upon his escape from death, but the general's report upon the emperor's words was so insulting to Piedmontese dignity that Victor Emmanuel's anger was aroused. "If what you write to me are the Emperor's very words," he told the general, "then you must tell him, in your own words, that one does not speak to a faithful ally in such a manner. Tell him that I have never tolerated compulsion from anyone; that the path which I must follow is that of unsullied honor, and that, for this, I must answer to none but to my people and to my God. For eight hundred and fifty years my family has held its head high; and no one shall make me lower it now." Cavour added a postscript, hinting that it would do no harm if Della Rocca committed the indiscretion of reading the letter aloud to Napoleon. The general did as he was told; and the enigmatic *parvenu* on the French throne reacted in a way that was altogether unexpected. "Now, that is what I call courage," he told Della Rocca. "Your king is a courageous man. I love his words. Write to him at once. Put his mind at ease, and tell him that I regret having caused him pain." Thus, Orsini's bomb, far from causing a breach between Turin and Paris, had strengthened Napoleon's determination to go to the aid of Italy and face war with Austria. The exact character of Orsini's influence has never been satisfactorily explained; but the appeal which, as an Italian patriot, he made from prison in France, begging the emperor to make Italy free and the Italians one people, seems to have had a desirable effect. Shortly after Orsini had expiated his crime upon the scaffold, a French envoy appeared in Turin and informed Cavour of Napoleon's intention of visiting Plombières, near the Swiss border. It was intimated that the emperor would be pleased to receive Cavour informally there. "The drama approaches its resolution," Cavour wrote to his friend, General La Marmora. "Pray heaven that I do not blunder at that supreme moment!"

At Plombières, Napoleon broached the crucial subject without preliminary or preface. He promised to aid Piedmont in a war against Austria, on condition that an acceptable provocation could be discovered. Cavour said little, waiting for the emperor to show what remained of his hand. The garrulous French monarch was quick to oblige. There was to be a Kingdom of Upper Italy under Victor Emmanuel, a Kingdom of Central Italy under the Duchess of Parma, the Papal States under the pope, and the Kingdom of the Two Sicilies. These four entities were to be confederated under the presidency of Pius IX. To achieve this confederation, approximately three hundred thousand troops would be required, of which France would supply two hundred thousand, and Italy the balance. In exchange for her help, France must be given Savoy and the city of Nice. The bargain was to be sealed by the marriage of Prince Napoleon (commonly called "Plon-Plon"), the emperor's cousin, to Victor Emmanuel's daughter, Princess Clothilde.

There was little likelihood that the Italian states would consent to be shuffled about by the French emperor, and Cavour knew it. But, wisely, he held his tongue. The principal thing was to get a French army into Italy and to expel the Austrians. The settlement of accounts with Napoleon could come later. Leaving the emperor with every expression of gratitude for his generous proposal, he hurried back to Turin, where, with some difficulty, he was able to persuade Victor Emmanuel to consent to the betrothal of Princess Clothilde, aged fifteen, to the thirty-seven-year-old Plon-Plon. That disagreeable task accomplished, Cavour then conferred with the leaders of the army and the National Society—La Marmora and Garibaldi, and then La Farina—as to the steps to be taken in order to prepare the country for war. The conflict, everyone agreed, would start late in the spring of 1859. It was left to Cavour's wisdom to discover a *casus belli,* which must be clearly non-revolutionary and in which Austria would appear to be the aggressor. After some thought on the subject, Cavour decided that the best way would be to exasperate Austria to the point where she would be goaded into a declaration of war herself.

By the beginning of 1859, every diplomat in Europe knew that the decision for war had been made. These were the days when the most casual words of monarchs were examined for hidden meanings, and, on the first day of the New Year, the French emperor's words to the Austrian Ambassador at Paris reverberated throughout the chancelleries of Europe. "I deeply regret," he said, "that my relations with your country are not so good as I might wish. But I beg you to write to your Emperor that my personal sentiments toward him remain unchanged." In the nuanced cadences of diplomatic jargon, these sentences were heavy with meaning, and they were understood as such: war was inevitable between France and Austria. Wrote Cavour: "The Emperor has opened the year with an outburst that is reminiscent of the style of his late uncle [Napoleon I] on the eve of a war."

A few days later, Prince Napoleon arrived in Turin with a signed treaty of alliance in his baggage. And, on January 30, the treaty was confirmed by the prince's marriage to Princess Clothilde.

A diplomatic struggle now began to forestall the coming war. England, Russia, and Prussia all mistrusted Napoleon III. They had not forgotten the first emperor of that name, and, if the French succeeded in routing the Austrians, then the ancient specter of French domination once more would be conjured up. Prussia urged caution; Russia expressed neutral sentiments; and England, with Lord Malmesbury as Foreign Secretary, stated that, according to the stipulations of the Congress of Vienna, no territorial changes would be acceptable in Italy. But since it was the stated purpose of Napoleon and of Cavour to change the Italian map—the one to rearrange it, and the other to unite it—there was little chance of finding a common denominator with British policy. The two conspirators were well aware that Britain would not fight against them; for public sentiment in England was not with Austria, but strongly with Italy.

Cavour therefore set about most urgently his task of forcing Austria to make the first move toward war. After Napoleon's fateful conversation with the Austrian ambassador on New Year's Day, Austria had thought it wise to send an army corps into Lombardy; for she put more trust in her generals than in her diplomats. This act strengthened Cavour's position. He demanded from the Parliament, and got, fifty million lire, "for defense." In fact, both sides, throughout their preparations for war, insisted, as always in the history of aggression, on the purely defensive nature of their military moves. "We shall not declare war," Count Buol announced for Austria; and Cavour was equally emphatic. The appropriation of fifty million lire was followed by a bill for the reorganization and strengthening of the militia. Hundreds of volunteers flocked to Piedmont to join the army, from the Papal States, from Naples, from Lombardy, and the small duchies. They were trained as a special force to be commanded by Garibaldi, and they were a particular source of irritation to Austria—for most of these twelve thousand men were Austrian subjects.

As Cavour was making these final preparations for war and, in the process, applying ever greater pressure on Austria, Napoleon was under pressure of a different sort. England was escalating her peace offensive, and every day notes were arriving from the Foreign Office and even personal appeals from Queen Victoria. There were disconcerting rumors of Prussian mobilization. Napoleon was forced to make public the nature of his treaty with Piedmont, but he emphasized that the document would come into force only in the event of an Austrian attack. England then sent an ambassador to preach peace in Vienna, where the Austrians were quick to assure everyone that they had no intention of attacking. In the meantime, Austria was increasing her forces in Lombardy, France was hastening her preparations for war, and Cavour, with Napoleon's consent, was calling up the reserves in order to bring all of his regiments up to maximum combat strength. It was, in effect, full mobilization on all sides.

Then Russia intervened by proposing a conference. Cavour, who now was determined on war at any cost, fought the proposal with every means at his disposal. England asked Victor Emmanuel to disarm as a gesture of "good faith"; Cavour agreed—but on condition that Austria disarm first. Austria, naturally, refused. Then England proposed that France, Austria, and Sardinia disarm simultaneously. Napoleon acquiesced, on condition that his Italian ally be admitted to the peace conference—a condition that Austria heretofore had refused to admit. A joint note from England and France informing King Victor Emmanuel of this agreement drove Cavour to attempt suicide, but he was saved at the last moment by a friend. Cavour was then obliged to yield.

The decision for peace or for war now rested in Austria's hands. If she also agreed to disarm, then it would be peace; if not, war. To Europe's astonishment—and to the vast relief of Cavour and Napoleon—Austria categorically refused, sabotaged the proposed conference, and issued an ultimatum giving Victor Emmanuel three days in which to order unilateral disarmament. Cavour's policy of defensive provocation had triumphed. Austria was exposed as the apparent aggressor before the world, and the terms of the alliance with France were now in force. It was war.

3. A Time for Violence (1859–1870)

In the war thus begun the advantages seemed to be all on the side of Austria, for, with almost two hundred thousand men in Lombardy, she had only to cross the Ticino, disperse the Piedmontese, and capture Turin. Had she done so, she would have been able to prevent the junction of the French and Italian forces. But Austria compounded the diplomatic error of the ultimatum by putting the command of her forces into the hands of the inefficient General Giulay, who was hampered both by a natural timidity and by an almost preternatural fear of the name Napoleon. He permitted the allies to make their junction on schedule, and then, convinced that they intended to invade Lombardy by way of Piacenza, he remained quietly inactive between the Lesia and the Ticino. It was not until June 1 that he discerned the plans of the enemy, which were indeed to invade Lombardy, but by way of Novara. By then, it was too late for the Austrians. Hurrying northward, Giulay suffered a resounding defeat at Magenta on June 4. The road now lay open to Milan, and four days later, amid wild rejoicing, Napoleon and Victor Emmanuel entered the Lombard capital. The Austrians could do nothing but evacuate Lombardy altogether.

At this point, however, Napoleon found his troubles in Paris increasing, for the role of liberator involved several inconvenient consequences. For one thing, Cavour's far-flung Italian intrigues were beginning to bear fruit. The people of the Romagna now refused any longer to submit to papal rule. In Tuscany, there was a popular revolt, the Grand Duke was deposed, and Victor Emmanuel was offered, and accepted, the dictatorship of the country. The Duke of Modena prudently fled to Vienna. The Duchess of Parma remained at home, but her authority in the duchy vanished entirely. As promising as such events were for the future of Italian unity, they did little to please the emperor. What would France's Catholics say about all this? And had Cavour forgotten the magnificent designs discussed at Plombières? Moreover, there was disturbing news of civil unrest in France, of hostility in Germany, of Prussian indecision, and English displeasure. All these rumors and reports reached Napoleon; and all of them awakened in him a doubt, in the midst of victory, as to the wisdom of his adopted course. Nonetheless, the future seemed bright enough. On June 11, the allies marched out of Milan to complete the conquest of northern Italy and to drive the Austrians from Venetia. The Austrians, now under the personal command of the young Emperor Franz Joseph—the vacillating

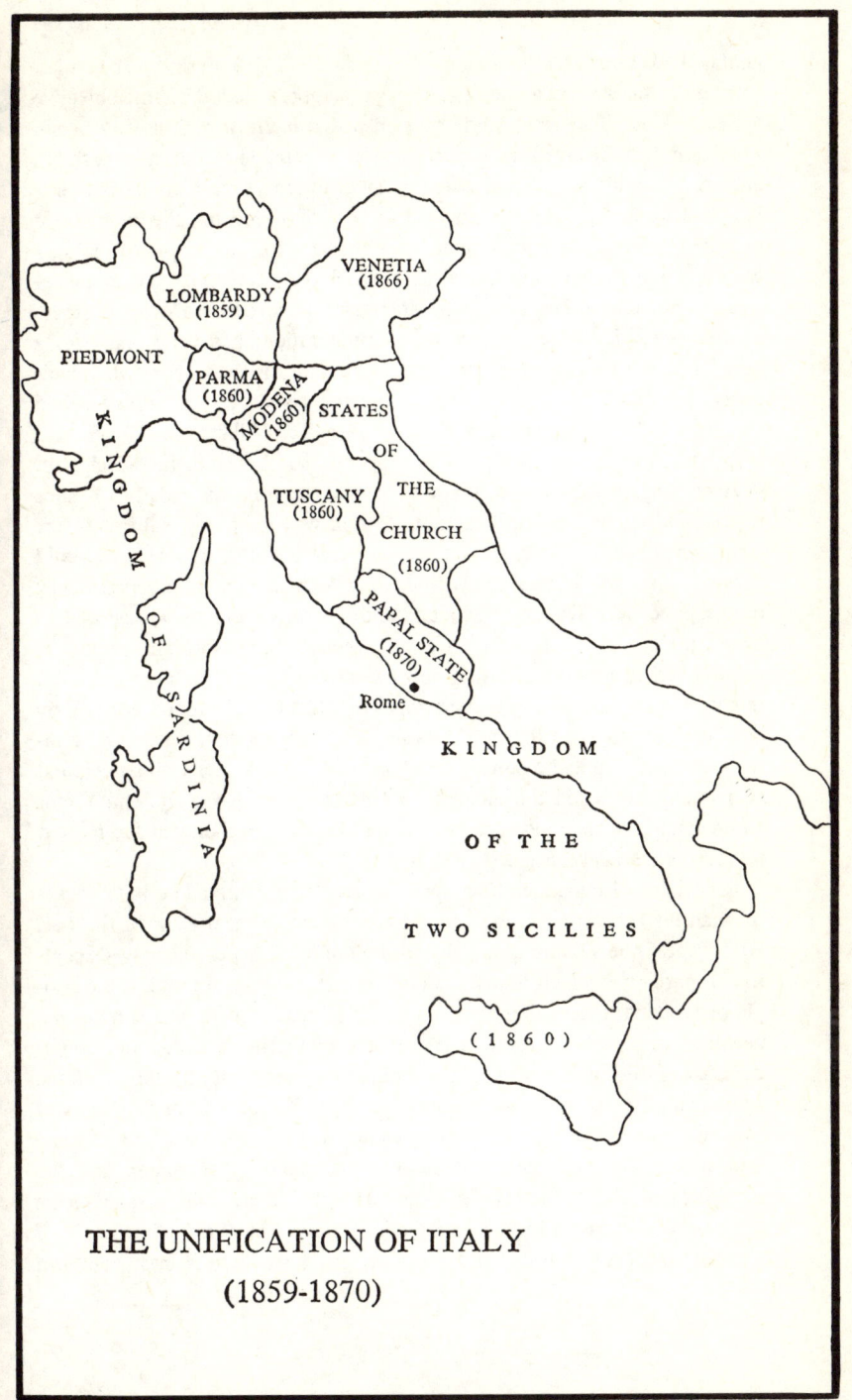

Giulay had been recalled—were advancing toward Solferino. The allies, ignorant of the Austrian line of march, were approaching the same objective from the west. They met, and there ensued a battle which, having begun as a skirmish between two reconnaissance companies, soon engaged a quarter of a million men and lasted, without intermission, from early morning until dusk. The French attacked at Solferino, and the Piedmontese at nearby San Martino; both fought bravely and well; but it was to the successes of the French that the victory was largely due. The Austrians retreated, but the allies were unable to pursue them because of a shortness of provisions. By June 6, however, all preparations had been made for a decisive battle at Verona. Everything was ready for the attack, when suddenly, on July 7, a piece of astonishing news arrived. An armistice had been concluded by Napoleon and Franz Joseph at Villafranca. The French emperor's doubts, first awakened at Magenta, had borne their logical fruit.

According to the terms of the armistice, Lombardy was ceded to France to be handed over to Sardinia; but Venetia was to remain subject to the Emperor of Austria. Italy was to be made into a confederation that should consist of all the Italian states, including Venetia, under the presidency of the pope. The Dukes of Modena and Tuscany were to be restored to their thrones, and they were to grant a general amnesty. The pope was to be asked to introduce certain indispensable reforms into his states. And this was to be the end of the high hopes of Italian freedom and unity. Italy had received a slap in the face. Cavour, naturally enough, was beside himself with rage. He had a stormy interview with King Victor Emmanuel, and he passionately urged the monarch not to assent to the treaty. But Victor Emmanuel had the good sense to see that he had no choice in the matter. Cavour immediately resigned.

King Victor Emmanuel, however, with greater insight and political sagacity than his famous minister, was able to discern the real gains of the war. He accepted the situation, and signed the preliminary peace treaty—excepting all parts of it which touched on his own rights and on those of the people of Modena, Parma, Tuscany, and the Romagna. Then, having formed a new ministry with Rattazzi in place of Cavour, he accepted the consequences of his half victory and prepared to carry out the terms of the agreement. He recalled the Piedmontese commissioners from the states of Modena, Parma, and the Romagna, confident that in the end the national aspirations of Italy would win out over the fears of Napoleon and the ambitions of Franz Joseph. And he was right. Even while arrangements were being concluded for a meeting of the powers at Zürich, the people of Tuscany, Modena, Parma, and the Romagna took matters into their own

From Absolutism to Independence 373

hands. In Tuscany, a parliament was summoned which deposed its grand-ducal dynasty and voted for annexation to Piedmont. In September, a month later, Modena did the same. Parma followed the same path a short time afterward, and the Romagna, though still a part of the Papal States, declared through a special assembly that it also wished to be ruled by Victor Emmanuel. Victor Emmanuel, however, hesitated, in fear of the uproar throughout Europe that the situation would create. Nobody but Cavour, it was decided, could manage the complex problem; and Cavour was called to office again. He quickly decided to appeal to the doctrine of the popular will by declaring that a plebiscite would be a help in order that the people of the various Italian states could thus publicly and freely determine their own status. The Emperor Napoleon, himself no stranger to plebiscites, hesitated to give his consent; but Cavour dangled the province of Savoy and the city of Nice temptingly before the imperial gaze, and he acceded. The province and the city were reluctantly handed over by Victor Emmanuel, the plebiscite was held, and Parma, Modena, Tuscany, and the Romagna were united with the Kingdom of Sardinia under the name of the Kingdom of Italy (April 15, 1860).

While these momentous events were taking place to the north, King Ferdinand II of the Two Sicilies died, hated and despised by all Europe, but nowhere more than in his dual kingdom. He was succeeded by his son, Francis II, who was a weak, ignorant, and bigoted prince, in every respect the worthy offspring of such a father. He contemptuously refused an invitation from Victor Emmanuel to join in the struggle against Austria, embraced the reactionary party, and formed an alliance with Pope Pius IX. The liberals of the south quickly swung into action. A revolt broke out at Palermo in April 1860, and was put down, but not before its spirit had infected the entire Kingdom of the Two Sicilies. Two young patriots, Francesco Crispi and Rosalino Pilo went about stirring the people to revolt. Garibaldi was begged to place himself at the head of the proposed revolution. On the night of May 6, two ships, the *Lombardy* and the *Piedmont*, secretly left Genoa. On board was Garibaldi and a thousand volunteers, known as *i Mille*. On May 11, the ships docked at Marsala. Two Neapolitan cruisers were also in the harbor, but two English men-of-war happened to be there too. The English captains, under the pretext of a courteous exchange of greetings with the Neapolitan ships, distracted the latter long enough to allow Garibaldi and his men to land undetected. Once ashore, the invaders ran to secure the telegraph office. They arrived just as the operator had finished sending a message to the effect that two Piedmontese ships, filled with troops, had come into the port. A Garibaldian quickly added this phrase to the message: "I have made a mistake. They are two merchant ships." An angry answer came back immediately: "Idiot!"

I Mille then marched inland virtually unopposed. A provisional government was organized, with Garibaldi as president and Crispi as first minister. The universal cry was "Italy and Victor Emmanuel!" Garibaldi was shortly joined by insurgents from Sicily and, thus reinforced, he engaged and roundly defeated the Bourbon army. Victory followed victory. Palermo fell, and then Milazzo and Messina. Garibaldi crossed the straits and invaded the mainland in August. King Francis, now thoroughly frightened, acted in panic. He proclaimed a constitutional monarchy, appealed to Napoleon, to Victor Emmanuel, and indeed to anyone who would listen and to many who would not. But he was too late. His armies fled, and Garibaldi swept on victorious. The king fled on September 6, and, on the next day, Garibaldi marched into Naples. The Kingdom of the Two Sicilies was his.

Of these developments, England alone approved. The rest of Europe expressed shock at such irregular proceedings, and Cavour and Victor Emmanuel began to feel uneasy lest the Great Powers—France and Austria, in particular—should intervene in Italy. It was a difficult situation, for Garibaldi, in the flush of his Neapolitan victory, was now moving northward, proclaiming his intention of seizing Rome, regardless of the French army stationed there, and then of marching on Venice, regardless of the treaties which gave that city to Austria. These were perfect opportunities for foreign intervention, and Cavour saw that he must act quickly if Piedmont was to retain control of the situation. He requested Pio Nono to dissolve his army, and, when the pope refused, the Piedmontese army marched into the Papal States. They took possession of the entire country except for the City itself and its immediate environs, and then marched on across the Neapolitan frontier. Here, the last remnants of the Bourbon army was attempting to hold back Garibaldi. The arrival of the Piedmontese quickly settled the matter. A man less noble than Garibaldi might have shown resentment at having another come, at the eleventh hour, and seize, or at least share, the fruits of victory. But Garibaldi hailed Victor Emmanuel as King of Italy, refused all offers of honors and rewards, and then, feeling that his work was done, he retired to the little island of Caprera. He went into retirement as poor, and as untouched by corruption or personal ambition, as he had been when he first emerged from obscurity. The Two Sicilies and the liberated parts of the Papal States now voted to join themselves to the united Kingdom of Italy. In February 1861, the first Italian parliament was held, and Victor Emmanuel formally was invested with the title of King of Italy. Except for Rome and Venice, Italy was free and independent for the first time in almost fifteen centuries.

The new kingdom's most pressing problem was, predictably, Rome. A history of twenty-five centuries, a profound national sentiment, a patriotic, poetic, and romantic love for the City dictated that Rome alone, the ancient mother of empire, must now become the capital of a united Italy. Opposed to this determination was historic Catholic sentiment which, while widespread in Europe, was strongest in France. The pope, logically enough, deemed his Italian nationality to be of less importance than his obligation to the Church. Catholics everywhere agreed with him. How could one believe in the universality of the Church, or in the impartiality of the papacy, if Rome were under the thumb of an Italian national government? Such differences in point of view, strongly felt and bitterly expressed, brought papal partisans and ardent nationalists to mutual injustice. The Italians began to look upon Pius IX as their most dangerous and obstinate enemy, while the Roman Curia branded the new government as a collection of brigands and excommunicates. French sympathy, of course, lay with the papacy; and the presence of a French army in Rome made the question exceedingly delicate.

As though this were not enough, a special circumstance aggravated the difficulty, and the delicacy, of the problem. The dispossessed King of the Two Sicilies, Francis II, had taken refuge in Rome. From there, he gave his blessing and his financial support to gangs of adventurers who raided the Neapolitan provinces and committed unspeakable atrocities there. When pursued by the Piedmontese army, these rascals crossed over into the Papal States and were saved. It was an intolerable situation, but little could be done about it diplomatically. Pio Nono, though he deplored the excesses of these criminals, refused to recognize the authority of Victor Emmanuel in the Two Sicilies, and therefore he could not release the guilty ones to him. King Francis—in the eyes of Rome, the "legitimate" sovereign of Naples—for his part refused to take any action whatsoever against the brigands.

In the midst of these difficulties, Cavour was planning and working with his accustomed diligence. He had many times previously stated his basic principle with respect to the Church: "A free Church in a free State." He, along with every other Italian, was convinced that Rome must become a part of the Kingdom of Italy. But, unlike many of his compatriots, he believed that this could be accomplished only by moral, not physical, force. In parliament, he defended and clarified his position by putting forward two propositions. First, the pope's temporal power did not give him independence. Second, the pope would find independence when Rome became the capital of Italy. What he envisaged was a complete separation of Church and State—a "free Church" and a "free State." Today, he stated, there was complete liberty of speech and of assembly; next, there must also be complete religious freedom—not only for the individual, but also for the Church. It would therefore be necessary, first of all, to convince Rome of Italy's sincerity in its guarantees of liberty; then, he believed, Rome would complete the unification of Italy, and bring peace to the nation, by voluntarily accepting Victor Emmanuel as her sovereign.

Shortly after this statement, Cavour died (June 6, 1861). Upon his deathbed, he declared himself a true believer in the Holy Roman Church, confessed his sins, and was absolved and anointed by a local priest. But the Roman Curia was as little impressed by Cavour's repentance as it had been by his diplomacy. The priest was summoned to Rome, severely reprimanded, deprived of his parish, and sent to finish his days in a remote monastery. Cavour, for all his greatness, had greatly underestimated the strength of Roman emotion.

Cavour's death was a national calamity. In his hands had been all the threads of national policy. In his mind was the sketch for the future. The course that he had pursued had been one of personal conviction as much as of national expediency, and it had succeeded as much because of Cavour's personal prestige and strength of character as because of its basic good sense. Now, with Cavour gone, uncertainty and ambiguity prevailed. His successors, first Baron Ricasoli and then Urbano Rattazzi, followed Cavour's policies as best they could, but with little success. Ricasoli, a haughty aristocrat, alienated King Victor Emmanuel, the French emperor, and the Italian parliament—all in the nine months of his tenure. Rattazzi, while a more genial man, lacked support in parliament, and he was obliged to resort to political "deals" and underground machinations in order to achieve any sort of workable government. In a word, he was an intriguer. Garibaldi said of him, "One can always do something with Rattazzi."

During Rattazzi's government, Italy's exhilaration at the achievement of unity and independence began to give way to a realization of the problems that confronted the new nation. The most serious of these difficulties, as always, was that of money. It had been taken for granted, for instance, that unity would alleviate the burden of taxation; whereas in fact the opposite was the truth. The debts of the seven states all had to be taken over by the new government, and provisions had to be made for administration, defense, education, and means of transport on a national scale. Some of these—education, for example, and military and naval expenses—had been things on which such states as Tuscany and the papal provinces spent nothing; now, they had to bear their share of such burdens, and taxation grew steadily heavier.

The conviction of Italy that she was now a Great Power, on a par with England, France, and Russia, added to her difficulties. A disproportionately large army was planned, along with a navy in keeping with Italy's ambitions as a Mediterranean power. Then there must be, of course, an extensive railroad system, and a national system of schools—but only after a sufficiently impressive military establishment had been built up. Such ambitions were greatly frustrated, but not destroyed, by economic reality. The fact was that, from the industrial standpoint, the new kingdom was hardly equipped to assume such a burden. The Italian economy was chiefly agricultural, and the nation's chief exports were wines and silk, lemons and oranges. Some sulphur was mined, but there was no iron, and no coal. The machinery and weapons that such magnificent dreams required were to be purchased from England or France, or perhaps from far-off America; and for this money was required. The taxpayer, therefore, who perhaps shared the vision of Italy as a Great Power, was compelled to assume this burden also.

To these problems were added those which were to be expected in achieving the true unification of a nation as fragmented as Italy. The proclamation of the Kingdom of Italy, while it had signified a basic political cohesion, had not miraculously welded the Italians into a single social and economic unit, and the individual states in their own territories continued much as before. They all had their own laws, their own customs and traditions, their own hatreds and jealousies, and their own dialects. Northern Italy was relatively prosperous, while the provinces of the central and southern portions of the peninsula were, to a large extent, sunk in poverty. Similarly, the north enjoyed a long tradition of education and literacy, while, in the former Kingdom of the Two Sicilies, ninety per cent of the population could neither read nor write. And, as always, southerners hated, envied, and mistrusted the men of the north; while the latter looked down with contempt on their compatriots of Naples and Sicily.

The Italian parliament—the Chamber of Deputies—fairly reflected these divisions. The party of the Right comprised a hard core of Piedmontese deputies and a more loosely knit circle of supporters of the other Italian states. This party had as its aim the continuance of Cavour's policies both at home and abroad. The party of the Left was composed of the supporters of Mazzini and Garibaldi; to it belonged most of the southern deputies, and a few from Tuscany and central Italy. The Left was held together by its opposition to Piedmontese domination, and by its determination that the cities of Rome and Venice must be added to the kingdom by any means, including force. The inspiration of the latter sentiment was the group known as the Party of Action, of which Garibaldi was the leader.

Such was the legislative body to which Italy entrusted the solution of its problems. Its first step was to extend, by decree, the political system of Piedmont to the whole of Italy. The system was comparatively enlightened and liberal, and guaranteed, among other things, freedom of speech and of assembly. Yet, because only Piedmontese officials knew how the system worked, it became necessary for the various states to place themselves under the leadership of Piedmontese officials; and there quickly followed loud and frequent charges of "Piedmontism"—a policy of making over all of the peninsula in the image of Piedmont. The Chamber's next move was to adopt a system of administration. Cavour himself had proposed a decentralization of government which would have placed considerable power in the hands of the regional officials of the states. In this instance, however, his policy was overridden by the Chamber. It would have encouraged separatism, the deputies decided, and encouraged the continuance of the ancient regional jealousies. Instead, a system was adopted which was modeled after that of France. Each of the former states was divided into provinces or "departments"—of which there were to be fifty-three—and over each province was installed a Prefect. This official was responsible directly to the government in Turin. Under this regime, customs and tariffs, coinage, weights, and measures were standardized, and commissions were set up to deal with the adoption of a common legal code and with the establishment of a network of communications throughout the nation. Such measures, of course, required time before they could bear visible fruit. For the moment, however, all that the good citizens of Italy could see was confusion and inconvenience everywhere and in every phase of their lives. And so, they grumbled and complained, and some were even heard to wonder aloud whether the whole thing had not been a mistake; whether they had not been better off "in the good old days," under their own princes and their own antiquated regional systems.

But no satisfactory settlement of Italy's difficulties seemed possible so long as the greater problem of complete unity remained unsolved. So long as Austria remained in Venice, so long as France's troops remained in Rome, Italy's obligation to arm herself would continue; and so long as that obligation remained, then her financial problems would grow worse rather than better, and they would make concord at home impossible. As early as March 27, 1861, Cavour had asserted that Rome ought to be, and would be, the capital of Italy; and, recognizing that, for the time being, it was impossible to eject the Austrians from Venice, he had concentrated upon the Roman question. Having failed to make his point, either by direct negotiations with the papacy or by intrigue in Rome through secret agents, he had turned to France with a proposal that, if French troops were withdrawn from the City, the Italian government would abstain from any attack upon the states of the Church. The negotiations initiated by Cavour might have succeeded had he lived. After his death, they were carried forward first by Ricasoli, and then by Rattazzi. Although Pio Nono rejected every advance with his famous *non possumus*—"we are not able," the Emperor Napoleon III seemed not disinclined to withdraw his troops from Rome.

At this point, however, negotiations were brought to naught by the impatience of the Party of Action. Garibaldi, chafing under the apparently dilatory policies of the government—and believing that Rattazzi, a liberal, would secretly favor any aggressive action—began to collect volunteers on the Tyrolese boundary and in Brescia for an attack upon Austrian territory. When the government promptly checkmated this move by arresting some of the Party's leaders, Garibaldi started for Sicily with the cry of *Roma o morte!*—"Rome or death." As he went, he gathered followers for an attack upon the City. For the government of Italy to sanction such an action would inevitably have involved Italy in a war with France. Victor Emmanuel therefore had no choice. When Garibaldi, with a small army of hot-tempered radicals, crossed into Calabria, he was met by government troops at Aspromonte, near Reggio. There, General Cialdini, in command of Victor Emmanuel's troops, pleaded with Garibaldi to withdraw. He refused. Shots were fired—which side fired first is uncertain—and Garibaldi was struck in the ankle and taken prisoner (August 29, 1862).

The effect of this embarrassing incident was disastrous for Italy. The government of Premier Rattazzi resigned at once. France broke off negotiations and, instead of withdrawing her forces from Rome, greatly increased their number. Moreover, in September, when the government at Turin, in order to soothe the indignation of the Italians over the wounding of Garibaldi, declared that Italy would persist in her efforts to obtain Rome, Napoleon recalled his ambassadors in Turin and appointed a militant papalist as his foreign minister. Yet, despite this act, the sympathies of the Emperor Napoleon were still with Italy. In 1863, when he realized that his concessions to French clericals had not won him their support, that Pio Nono was as unyielding as ever, and that the presence of the French in Rome was a continual source of irritation to all concerned—the French generals and the Roman Curia were constantly at each others' throats—he became more ready than ever to come to an agreement with Italy.

At the same time, Italy was ready now to negotiate with the French emperor on the basis of a compromise. Napoleon agreed to withdraw gradually his troops from Rome. Victor Emmanuel, in exchange, guaranteed that Italy would respect the sovereign authority of the pope over the territory that remained to him. This agreement, known as the Convention of September 1864, was duly ratified; and Victor Emmanuel, in order the better to carry out its terms, consented to move his capital from Turin to Florence. The Convention perhaps postponed, but eventually made inevitable, the solution of the Roman question. France now not only officially recognized the previous annexations of papal territory, but tacitly agreed that the occupation of Rome by the Italians was a political as well as a moral necessity.

The Convention of September, though an excellent diplomatic maneuver on Italy's part, moved to rebellion the people of Turin who feared, in losing the capital, to lose the leadership of the country. It equally outraged the pope, who looked upon an agreement between his erstwhile protector and his enemies as an intolerable offense against the Church. Despairing of temporal support, Pius IX issued in December 1864, the encyclical *Quanta cura* and the famous *Syllabus,* or catalogue of errors of the age, in which he defined the claims of the papacy and the authority of the Church over the state and over society. Not only did he condemn religious freedom and liberty of conscience and the laicizing of education, but he also inveighed, in the strongest terms possible, against liberal Catholics as well as against Protestants and "rationalists." Notwithstanding the fact that parts of the *Syllabus* were openly directed against the Italian government, and that all of it was hostile to the Italian constitution, Victor Emmanuel allowed both it and the encyclical to be circulated freely throughout Italy. In thus giving, as it were, enough rope to Pio Nono for him to hang himself, the king made considerably easier the final settlement of the Roman question.

Once established at Florence in February 1865, the government turned its attention to finance, internal reform, and, above all else, to the acquiring of Venice. General La Marmora, Victor Emmanuel's minister, first proposed to buy the city from the Austrians. When that failed, he proposed, through Napoleon, that Rumania be divided and that part of it be given to Austria in exchange for Venice—a proposal that both Russia, of whose empire Rumania was a part, and Austria, understandably refused even to consider. Next, and after much hesitation, he consented to an alliance be-

From Absolutism to Independence

tween Italy and Prussia against Austria, hoping to win Venice as Cavour had won Lombardy, through the intervention of an outside Power. It was a natural combination. Prussia, under the leadership of Bismarck, "the Iron Chancellor," occupied a position in Germany somewhat similar to that of Piedmont in Italy. Both had somewhat similar problems. Both felt antagonism toward Austria, and both distrusted France. Austria, for her part, was greatly distressed by this alliance. As all Europe knew, Austria and Prussia would shortly be at war, and Vienna had little desire to fight her battles on two fronts. At the suggestion of the French emperor, therefore, Austria offered to cede Venice to Italy if the latter would abandon her alliance with Prussia. Victor Emmanuel refused indignantly, and the war began, on schedule, in June 1866. The Italians were beaten both on land and sea, to their great mortification and chagrin. A crushing Prussian victory at Sadowa, however, forced Austria to her knees. She had little choice but to accept the victor's terms—which included the cession of Venice to Italy. On November 7, Victor Emmanuel made his entrance into the city, after a plebiscite in which the people of the province voted 650,000 to 49 for annexation to the Kingdom of Italy.

Now, only Rome remained. In 1867, Garibaldi, encouraged by the final withdrawal of French troops from Rome, once more announced his determination to invade the pontifical territory. Though immediately arrested by the government and returned to his home on Caprera, he escaped; and, having raised volunteers in Tuscany, he noisily crossed the papal frontier. In this crisis, Victor Emmanuel issued a proclamation against the Garibaldians and prepared to send the Italian army against them. At the same time, he pleaded with the French government not to intervene. Napoleon, however, fearing that Italy would not hold to the Convention of September, dispatched a body of French troops which, joining the papal forces, met the insurgents at Mentana, and killed and captured many of Garibaldi's men under the very eyes of the Italian army.

At this juncture, when the French were once more in the City guarding the interest of the pope, Pius IX made a historic effort to compensate himself for the temporal and political losses of the preceding years. On December 8, 1869, he convened at Rome an ecumenical council, known as the First Vatican Council, which was the first to meet since the Council of Trent in the sixteenth century. The council's most notable achievement was the promulgation of the doctrine of papal infallibility, which declared that "when the Roman Pontiff, in the fulfillment of his mission as the first teacher of all Christians, defined that which ought to be observed in matters of faith and morals, he cannot err." The supremacy of the pope in the

Church was thus established dogmatically, and Pius IX was raised to a height of spiritual authority more exalted than any attained by even his most ambitious predecessors. In placing Pius IX above the episcopate and all councils, the doctrine of papal infallibility, by constituting him as sole interpreter of the faith, made inevitable a stricter definition of the doctrines of the Church along the lines of the *Syllabus* of 1864. And the situation was even more striking in that, even before the dispersion of the conciliar fathers in October 1870, the troops of the Kingdom of Italy had invaded the pontifical territory and stripped Pio Nono of the last remnants of his temporal power. He, whom the bishops and cardinals had greeted, on July 20, as "the Infallible Pope," by September 20 had become "the Prisoner of the Vatican."

For the opportunity of thus settling the Roman question, the Italians were indebted to the Franco-Prussian War. During 1869 and 1870, Italy and France had discussed the matter of their future relations. Among the issues treated was that of the advisability of an alliance between France and Austria against Prussia; but Italy had made it a condition of her assent that French troops must once more be withdrawn from Rome and that the Convention of September be once more observed. But, as Napoleon had refused to accept any such condition, all negotiations between the two countries had been suspended. Therefore, when war broke out, in July 1870, between France and Prussia, there existed between Italy and France neither treaty nor understanding. With the defeat of Napoleon and the downfall of the Second Empire at the battle of Sedan, French troops were withdrawn from Rome. On September 8, the Italian army crossed the frontier, and before the end of the month, was in possession of the City. A plebiscite was held, and, by a vote of 133,681 to 1507, the Romans voted to become a part of Italy. In June 1871, the seat of government was formally removed from Florence, and Rome, after fifteen hundred years, became once again the capital of Italy.

One more step remained to be taken, however, before the Roman question could be regarded as fully resolved, and before Italy, who was now approaching the close of her period of formation could enter upon her career as a Great Power, free from the disturbances to which she had been subjected by the political and religious controversies of the past. By the Law of Guarantees, adopted in May 1871, one of the most remarkable of modern documents dealing with the relations between Church and state, the complete spiritual independence of the papacy was secured, and the place of the Church in civil society was determined. The person of the pope was declared sacred and inviolable, and any attack upon him was to be regarded as an attack upon the person of the king himself. He was granted royal honors, as befitting a great sovereign, and the right of free correspondence with Catholic bishops throughout the world. He was allowed to convoke ecumenical councils, whose meetings were to be protected by civil authorities; to maintain his own courts, to have his own diplomatic service, and his own postal and telegraph services. In the way of material concessions, he was allowed to enjoy in full the palaces of the Vatican and the Lateran, as well as the papal villa at Castel Gandolfo. The Holy See, moreover, was to receive the sum of 3,225,000 lire per year. In all that concerned the relations of the state with the Church, the government of Italy showed itself more liberal than any other Roman Catholic country in the world. Papal decrees were not subject to the approval of the Italian government. Bishops were not required to take the oath of loyalty to the king. In all matters of spiritual discipline of the clergy and faithful, the judgment of Rome was to be final. In fact, insofar as the control or interference of the state was concerned, the Church was to be absolutely and totally independent. It was, it seemed, Cavour's dream come true: a free Church in a free state. Yet, Pius IX—by nature a kind and lovable man, but one who had passed, out of fear, from an early liberalism to the other extreme—refused even to consider the advantages that such a settlement might offer. Instead, he excommunicated the invaders of his territory, refused to accept the annual indemnity provided by the Law of Guarantees, and declared himself a prisoner in the Vatican. He refused to recognize the Kingdom of Italy, or even to enter into relations with it, and he instructed Catholics in Italy to take no part in the elections either as electors or elected. The fact remains, however, that at no time in the modern history of the papacy was the pontiff to become so powerful, influential, and secure as after 1871. Pius' successors, however reactionary they might be in doctrine, became liberal and conciliatory in tactics. Though in all official acts and statements they expressed themselves as hostile to Italy and unresigned to the loss of their temporal power, nevertheless, in practice they accepted the protection that Italy offered them, and in time they came to recognize as inevitable the permanent loss of their territory. It was not to be until the passage of almost six decades, however, that this recognition was to be translated into a state of reconciliation.

Italy's final attainment of national independence and total political unity is the most significant event of European history between the fall of the first Napoleon in 1815 and the Franco-Prussian War (1870). For the very first time in the history of the nations of Europe, the old principles of the inviolability of treaties and of hereditary sovereign rights were compelled to give way to the doctrine of the rights of a nation. For the first time, the supporters of the narrow and conservative theories of the old system were forced to acknowledge themselves vanquished by the enlightened methods of government and administration that characterized the modern, or new, regime. The Italians had won nothing less than a victory over Europe, whose traditions, principles, and prejudices were all against them; over Austria, and the petty princes, who had sought by every means in their power to oppose their national aspirations; over the Roman Catholic Church, whose fundamental principles regarding the temporal power of the pope were essentially hostile to Italian unity, and whose teachings on government and politics were basically opposed to political freedom; and, finally, over France, who, under Napoleon III—and despite the fine words of that prince—had no intention of allowing Italy to become more than a loose federation of autonomous states. These were the victories of Italy. But they were also the victories of King Victor Emmanuel, who had conquered himself, his traditions and his prejudices, who had been willing to sacrifice both his daughter and his own kingdom, for Italy. Perhaps most of all, they were the victories of Cavour who, though he did not live to see the final victory of his policies, had forced the world to recognize a new international principle based on the affinities of peoples, and had inaugurated, not only a new regime for Italy, but also a new public law for Europe.

VII
THE NEW ITALY
(1871–1920)

1. The Opening Years (1871–1896)

When, on February 18, 1861, Victor Emmanuel opened the first Italian Parliament at Turin and received, "by the grace of God and the will of the nation," the title of King of Italy, a new state had taken its place among the nations of the world. As a new state, Italy had been eager to justify its existence by the adoption of policies, both internal and external, that were at once honorable and effective. But the obstacles to be surmounted were legion. The most pressing problem, of course, had been that of achieving complete unification—that is, of bringing Venice and Rome into the kingdom. So long as that had not been attained, other problems had had to be relegated to a position of secondary importance. By 1871, however, with the Austrians gone from the north and King Victor Emmanuel installed in Rome's Quirinal Palace, these now came to the fore and demanded the immediate attention of the government.

Such difficulties generally fell into two classes: internal problems, and external problems. Under the first heading, of prime importance was the necessity for imposing at least a modicum of political, social, economic, and cultural cohesiveness on the Kingdom of Italy. D'Azeglio had expressed the problem admirably as early as 1861: "We have united Italy. Now, let us unite the Italians." The great impediment to such unity obviously was to be found in the history and traditions of the Italians. In this respect, Italy differed from Germany, who, though long fragmented, had always been conscious of the oneness in blood of all her peoples; and, similarly, from Austria, who, though her empire comprised a kaleidoscope of disparate nationalities, found her strength in the devotion of all her peoples to the Hapsburg dynasty. In Italy, however, from the fall of Romulus Augustulus in the fifth century to the Napoleonic era, there had never been a single important unitive factor. Divided into small and fiercely independent states, ruled by rival, and often warring, dynasties who had no interest either in the common name or the common country, the country had been virtually a mosaic of races and governments. Feudal suzerains, municipal consuls, Renaissance despots, popes, and princes, had all controlled, at one time or another, the different parts of Italy. At the same time, German, French, Spanish, Byzantine, Norman, and Saracenic influences had left their indelible imprint upon the history and traditions of the various states. Moreover, though geographically suited to be a single state, Italy had few natural bonds binding her people together. Lombards, Piedmontese, Tuscans, and Romagnols possessed, it is true, certain traits in common, and they resembled one another in the character of their industry and social organization. But each of them differed from the people of the south in all of these particulars. The sub-Alpine region was unlike the Neapolitan in climate, fertility of soil, and nature of its produce, and the Lombards differed from the Neapolitans in temperament, traditions, and culture. The Ligurians and the Venetians, who had been schooled for centuries in commerce and municipal independence, were wholly unlike the volatile and comparatively slothful Sicilians, who had suffered for centuries from incompetent government and political oppression. In the north, where government tended to be less despotic, and existence was less precarious than elsewhere in Italy, the population was more dense, wealth more abundant, and industry more highly developed. In the south, however—notably in Apulia, Basilicata, and Calabria—there existed a scattered population which was content to subsist by means of primitive agriculture and husbandry, and which was afflicted physically by disease and morally by superstition and ignorance. Northern and southern Italy were, in a word, two different countries, and the welding together of them, as pressing as it might be, was to be the work, not of a day or a year, but of decades.

In this welter of different traditions and cultures, however, there was one constant element which ran through the whole: poverty. Italy, united or otherwise, was a poverty-ridden country. The day was long past when trade with the East and with Africa had poured a steady stream of gold and of luxuries into the cities of the peninsula. By the sixteenth century, a decline had set in; by the eighteenth, the nadir had been reached; and,

The New Italy

in the nineteenth, the new nation was harvesting the fruits of that retrogressive trend. Since the middle of the seventeenth century, moreover, a new factor had come to widen the breach that separated Italy, economically, from such nations as England, France, and Germany. That factor was the Industrial Revolution, the sign and badge of which had been the application of steam to power by James Watt in 1769, and which had begun in the key industry of cotton textiles. The process of mechanization had spread to other industries by virtue of such innovations as the Bessemer process for the manufacture of steel from pig iron, by giant strides in chemistry and other fields, and, perhaps most important of all, by the manufacture of machines which manufactured machines. In England and France, and then later in Germany, factories sprang up everywhere and towns grew up around them. Railroads crisscrossed the countryside, canals were dug and roads built; and capitalism appeared as the industrialists marshaled their sources of labor and material. Italy, however, continued, for the most part, to live as she always had. To a certain extent, the reason for this stasis had been political. The absolutist regimes of the peninsula, with Austria's Prince Metternich at their head, had recognized the connection between the new economic forces of the age and the new political ideas of liberty and equality, and they had consistently and forcefully opposed the introduction of economic progress. To this obstructionist policy was added a further liability, Italy's almost complete lack of known natural resources. By 1870, therefore, although Italy had a few railroads and a certain amount of industrial development in the north, the country was, as it had always been, overwhelmingly, almost exclusively, agricultural. To make matters worse, agriculture itself was carried out at a primitive level, particularly in the former states of the Church and in Naples and Sicily, and the methods generally employed were those that had been handed down from generation to generation for a thousand years. Along with this poverty went, partly as cause and partly as effect, backwardness at the political, social, and intellectual levels. In the former Kingdom of the Two Sicilies, for example, it had been the firm policy of the Spanish Bourbons to keep the great (and dangerous) masses of the people in abysmal ignorance, and, in 1870, it is estimated that ninety per cent of the Italians of the south were totally illiterate. Such conditions, permeating as they did the entire social structure of Italy, would be immensely difficult to correct. But it would have to be done, before the new nation could take her place among the powers of Europe.

Internally, therefore, Italy's government faced a dual task: to abolish the regionalism, both natural and artificial, that fragmented the country into provinces of disparate ambitions, ideals, and aspirations; and to break through the closed circle of the antique social and economic system which acted as a restraint upon any tendency toward improvement.

So far as Italy's external situation was concerned, the problem was less complex in its statement, but as difficult in its resolution as her internal problems, for the solution to the former depended almost entirely upon that of the latter. Italy still had to find its place in the European community. As a nation of some twenty-five million citizens, she was in a position, quantitatively, to demand a role in international affairs comparable to that of England, France, or Germany. Qualitatively, however, she was weak, disorganized, disunited, and poor. She would have to decide whether to participate in international power politics to the extent that her resources permitted, or to demand a place among the Great Powers, and then to expend her limited resources and energies in attempting to live up to that position. And that decision hinged upon what reforms the new government would be able to effect in the internal situation of the country.

The period of the 1860s was, as has been already noted, one which saw the extension to the whole of Italy of Piedmont's system of government, and which witnessed the emergence of Piedmont as the dominant factor in Italian politics. It was a predictable development, given Piedmont's role in the liberation and unification of Italy under Cavour's inspired direction. Cavour, however, had died in 1861, and King Victor Emmanuel, shaken by the irretrievable loss of his minister and friend, had taken up the task that Cavour had begun. Supported by a loyal majority consisting of the representative from Piedmont and central Italy, he had appointed Baron Bettino Ricasoli as prime minister; and it was under Ricasoli that the organization of the new Italy had begun, and under his successors who, like himself, belonged to the party of the Right Center. This succession of ministers of the Right, schooled in the methods, policies, and aims of Cavour, saw the country successfully through the critical period of national unification; and if its practices were sometimes more cautious than Cavour himself might have thought desirable, they were, nonetheless, sound in concept and effective in application. Even while every mind was preoccupied with the question of Rome and Venice during the years before 1870, Ricasoli, Marco Minghetti, General Menabrea, and Giovanni Lanza—all of whom served successively or alternately as premier during this period—were far from ignoring Italy's economic and social problems. As has been mentioned, the railway system of Piedmont was extended to Bologna, Ancona, Foggia, and afterward to Brindisi, so that the government was placed in communication with the former Papal States and Naples. At the same time,

The New Italy

projects had been initiated for improving agricultural yield; fens and marshes were drained, wild land transformed into arable fields, and waste regions colonized. In order to bring the country into closer economic relations with the outside world, commercial treaties had been negotiated with France, England, Sweden, Holland, Belgium, and Prussia. Of more importance than all else were the government's efforts to meet its heavy financial obligations—due to the assumption of the debts of the old states, to the cost of reorganizing the administrative system and of creating a new army and navy. By 1867, the debts of the Kingdom of Italy came to almost six hundred million lire, and a large part of the government's revenues were being used simply to pay the interest due on that amount. Consequently, in that year, the government was obliged to reimpose taxes that had been suppressed a few years before, and to consider the possibility of secularizing ecclesiastical property. Shortly afterward, the territory of the monasteries of Italy was confiscated, and then all Church lands that were not actually in use were seized for the benefit of the state. Still, the condition of the finances did not improve because of the obligation that remained of maintaining a large army to ward off any attempt to restore, by force, the Papal States to Pius IX. After 1871, further measures were adopted. The "convent law" of 1866, affecting monastic lands, was extended to Rome and the former ecclesiastical provinces in 1873, and a large amount of money was thus obtained for use in education and hospital building. As this bonanza was still inadequate to the needs of the government, *specie* payments were suspended in 1874, and an inconvertible paper currency was introduced; then, new and exorbitant taxes were legislated. The country groaned under these burdens, and disaffection was rampant. But this radical surgery was successful. In 1876, the national budget showed a surplus. The cautious conservatism of the Right had paid off.

In foreign affairs, the government's policy was equally prudent. Despite the exigencies of national defense, a succession of tight-fisted premiers kept close watch over the expenditures of the military branch, and the government's consistent policy in that regard was one of rational parsimony. At the same time, Italy was making strenuous efforts to strengthen its position with respect to the nations of Europe. It was difficult to achieve a stable relationship with foreign states, however, because of the refusal of Pio Nono to acknowledge the loss of his territory, and because of the efforts of the papalists beyond the Alps to bring their governments to support the pope. For nearly a decade, Italy lived in fear that the monarchists and clericalists of France would overturn the Republic and enter upon a crusade to restore the temporal power of the pope. But in other particulars

Italy's position, through the efforts of Victor Emmanuel, seemed better secured. In 1870, Amadeus, the king's son, was elected King of Spain. In 1873, Victor Emmanuel visited Vienna and Berlin and, to the joy of the Italians, he received a visit in the following year from the Austrian emperor, Franz Joseph, and in 1875, from William I of Germany.

Such were the chief characteristics of the few years of Italy's history as a kingdom. The party of the Right had piloted the ship of state past many of the dangers of the period up to 1876, and, with occasional mistakes of judgment and a basic political insagacity, it had performed a good work for Italy. In 1876, however, as the result of a generally unobserved, but far-reaching political revolution, the Right lost control of the government to the Left Center, or Left—a party that had twice already, in the person of Urbano Rattazzi, attempted to direct the policy of Italy. This change was due to many things, chief among which were discontent with taxes and with the policy of the Right regarding railroads; the transference of the capital from Turin to Rome, which carried the center of political life southward; the refusal of loyal Catholics (at the command of the pope) to vote or otherwise participate in national politics; and, finally, the promises of the Left to extend the franchise to a larger number of citizens and to reduce the burden of taxation.

The replacement of a government of the Right by one of the Left was considerably more than a mere shift of party supremacy. The Right, which had stood for northern Italy, for business activity, parliamentary experience, and loyalty to France, had been replaced by the Left, which represented central and southern Italy and the peoples of Naples and Sicily, where radical views were more prevalent and personal rivalries more common, where parliamentary methods were little regarded, and where an appreciation of the monarchy, of the Church, of France, was less kind. Instead of Piedmont, Lombardy, and Tuscany, now Naples and Sicily took the direction of national affairs, and Minghetti and Menabrea were replaced by a succession of new premiers: Agostino Depretis, Benedette Cairoli, and Francesco Crispi. The effect of this change was to place the government in the hands of party leaders who, while loyal to the constitutional monarchy, were committed to a program more radical than that which the Right had been willing to adopt; who were equipped to become, not the leaders of a single united party, but the heads of personal claques often hostile to each other as well as to the conservatives and to the Church.

As might have been expected, during the first few years after 1876 the disorder in the country increased steadily. Republicans and socialists were surprisingly successful in spreading liberal ideas, while a new party, that of the Irredentists, came into existence with the program of an "unredeemed Italy" (*Italia irredenta*). The aim of the Irredentists was simple enough: the annexation of all Italian-language territories in the possession of foreigners—that is, of the Tyrol and Istria, Nice and Corsica, Malta and the Swiss canton of Ticino. These demands naturally endangered Italy's good relations with Switzerland, France, and England; and they led to open threats of hostility on the part of Austria and Germany. Depretis was followed in the premiership by Cairoli, and Cairoli, in his turn, by Depretis; and while Italy was in this condition of unrest and instability, King Victor Emmanuel, the one man whose good sense and universal popularity might have set things aright, died (1878). He left behind him, as the most impressive monument to his memory, a grateful nation and an imperishable name. A few months later, Pio Nono also died, whose persistent *non possumus* of his later years tended to blot out the memory of his earlier career as a liberal pope, and whose official intolerance had too often hidden from view his kindly nature. Thus, before the close of 1878, the leaders of Italy had entirely changed. The Left had taken over the place of the Right; Humbert I that of Victor Emmanuel II; and Leo XIII that of Pius IX.

The effect of such important changes was to throw Italy for a time into a state of even greater political confusion and disorder. From 1876 to 1882, Parliament was given over to personal rivalries and personal ambitions. The ministries of Cairoli and of Depretis lacked consistency of principle and practice, and the ministers themselves seemed to be without judgment and breadth of view. In the country, agitation increased, while republicans, Irredentists, socialists, and anarchists vied in arousing disturbances and tumults in the great cities of the nation. In 1878, an attempt was made at Naples against the life of King Humbert. Throughout the south, underground groups—called Barsanti clubs, after an Italian corporal who had been executed by the government for disobedience to orders —sprang up and became clearinghouses for socialist plots and conspiracies. The intrigues of the Irredentists, meanwhile, who were carrying on their work in Trieste and the Tyrol in the interests of annexation, finally culminated in a scheme for the assassination of the Emperor Franz Joseph at Trieste. The assailant, a man named Oberdank, was executed by the Austrian government, and, like Barsanti, he was immediately elevated to the altar of political martyrdom and became the hero of the socialists and republicans.

All these events made extremely difficult the establishment of a fixed and logical foreign policy. It was the wish of Depretis to sever all connection with France and to form a close alliance with Germany. Cairoli, for his part, preached loyalty to France, inclined toward toleration of the Irredentists, and was unwilling to assume the burdens that would be entailed by a formal tie to Germany and Austria. With the passage of time, however, the atmosphere cleared somewhat. In 1880 and 1881, France, over vigorous Italian protests, launched an aggressive campaign in Tunis for the purpose of establishing a colonial empire. The resulting outcry served to rouse the Italian people and press, and there were demonstrations in all the large cities in favor of an alliance with Germany. Cairoli was forced to resign from office, and Depretis was swept into the premiership on the wave of anti-French sentiment. The new government at once inaugurated that policy which Italy was to follow for fifteen years, that of resistance to all enemies of the monarchy at home, and of close alliance with Germany and Austria abroad. In 1882, having suppressed the Irredentist movement and all republican agitation—which had heretofore been rather encouraged by the Left than otherwise, since its accession to power—he formally brought Italy into the Triple Alliance, a secret agreement which bound the country to Austria and Germany.

Since 1876, the financial condition of Italy had steadily improved. The efforts made to reduce expenses had so far succeeded that a balance between receipts and expenditures was regularly achieved, notwithstanding considerable spending for improvements in communications, industry, and agriculture. So satisfactory did the situation appear to be that, in 1883, the paper currency was withdrawn and *specie* payments resumed; and in 1884, amid general rejoicing, taxes were reduced. A program of compulsory education was introduced in 1877, and one of reform for higher education was enacted in 1884. Measures were taken for increasing the fertility of farmland, for the expansion of public works, and for bettering the sanitary conditions in the south. In 1882, a proposal for extending the suffrage —which had been under heated discussion for several years—was put into operation; by reducing the voting age to twenty-one years, and by lowering the tax qualification to under twenty lire, the number of enfranchised voters was increased from 627,000 to slightly over two million.

The noticeable economic amelioration of the Italian people, the adoption of a consistent foreign policy backed by public sentiment, and the passage of years, was now beginning to have its effect. Piedmontese and Sicilians alike began to speak of "Italy," and "Italian policy," and "the future of Italy." The southerner began to see money from the north spent to build schools for his children and hospitals for himself. His own countrymen, rather than the Piedmontese of twenty years before, were now at the helm of affairs, and he began to identify with the Kingdom of Italy in his thoughts and in his conversation rather than, as before, solely with Naples or Calabria or Sicily. Italy as a whole was beginning, for the first time since the Napoleonic conquest had ended briefly the fragmentation of fourteen centuries, to appreciate the advantages of political unity.

With the advent of relative order and prosperity at home, Italy now began to turn her attention more and more to affairs abroad. Thus far, she had had but little desire to emulate the colonial ambitions of her more powerful neighbors by attempting to extend her influence beyond her own boundaries. At this point, however, the same motives that had led Depretis to form an alliance with Germany and Austria, and to keep on terms of amity with England—that is, the increasing of Italy's importance and prestige among the Powers—induced him to undertake a colonial adventure in Africa. Some time before, a Genoese combine of merchants had established itself on the coast of the Red Sea just north of Babel-Mandeb and had acquired a strip of territory around the Bay of Assab. In 1882, the Italian government had purchased this land. In 1885, Depretis, his appetite for empire whetted by this taste of colonial grandeur, dispatched troops to Africa and seized the seaport of Massowa. Before two more years had passed, Italy found herself at war with Ethiopia. The prime minister, greatly embarrassed by the unusually heavy expenditures arising from this colonial adventure and from the increased armaments made necessary by a European war scare in 1886 and 1887, refurbished his cabinet by the addition of Francesco Crispi as Minister of the Interior. In 1887, Depretis, overwhelmed by the burdens of office, died, and was replaced by Crispi.

The new premier had little choice but to follow the policies established by his predecessor in office. He continued the war preparations, built new fortresses, and adhered rigidly to the Triple Alliance. In the latter instance he was supported vigorously by King Humbert, who viewed the Alliance as "a pledge of that peace which not only Italy, but all states, desire as necessary to the welfare of nations, and to their progress and civilization." At the same time, Crispi took up the banner of colonial imperialism and carried on the war against King John of Ethiopia, for which Parliament, encouraged by news of Italian victories at Zula, Keren, and Asmala, somehow found the funds. At the death of the Ethiopian king in 1890, he prudently supported the claims of the most powerful among the rival pretenders to the vacant throne of that nation. When that claimant, known as Menelik II, had established control over most of the country, Crispi negotiated friendship and commerce with him, and, for the moment at least, the African conflict was resolved in Ethiopia.

Italy's aggressive expansionism under Depretis and Crispi brought certain rewards in national prestige, self-esteem, and territory. But it also destroyed the financial equilibrium of Italy. Once more, deficits appeared in the accounts of the kingdom. In 1891, Italy spent 191,000,000 lire in excess of her revenues—a trend which increased so rapidly that, in the years that followed, it seemed impossible to restore the balance. The levying of new taxes therefore became necessary, and the additional burden thus entailed provoked, as always, great discontent and complaints among the people. This atmosphere of unrest was one in which the socialists and republicans flourished, and riots took place in Rome, Milan, Turin, and Apulia. Crispi, however, prided himself on being a man of strength and resolution. Having declared in Parliament his firm intention of defending the monarchy and of suppressing all revolutionary parties, he put down the rioters, attacked the Irredentists, abolished organizations clamoring for the annexation of Trieste and Trent, dissolved the Barsanti and Oberdank clubs, and in general denounced all "radicals"—that is, everyone who was actively engaged in abolishing the *status quo*. The victory of these rascals, he stated, would mean "war in Europe, the overthrow of the monarchy, and the complete ruin of the fatherland."

Undisguised strength is seldom popular in statesmen; and Crispi, unfortunately, combined strength with a certain arrogance of demeanor and intemperance of language. He created a great disturbance in Parliament when, in 1890, he violently attacked the leaders of the Right and charged them with "servility toward foreign powers" during the period when the government had been in their hands. It was an offense which those sensitive gentlemen were not able to forgive, and, by the following year, they had managed to infect their colleagues with their own sense of resentment at Crispi's unbridled energy and boundless egoism. At that point, the premier, convinced that the entire nation shared his view of his own indispensability to the well-being of Italy, imprudently demanded a parliamentary vote of confidence over a comparatively trivial matter of financial policy. The Right had its revenge; Parliament returned a vote of no confidence, and the stupefied Crispi had no choice but to resign.

His successor, the Marquis di Rudini, lasted but a year. During that time, he followed Crispi's policies to the letter, adhering to the Triple Alliance and to Italy's commercial commitments to Germany and Austria. In the following year, he resigned in desperation at his inability to ameliorate, by any means, the financial condition of the country. He was followed by Giovanni Giolitti, a man of ability and judgment who was, in the next two decades, to exercise enormous political influence. At the present time, how-

The New Italy

ever, Giolitti's term was brief. He had the misfortune to become premier at a time when the great Banca Romana scandal was about to break. The "Bank Scandal," as it was generally known, had its roots in the practice of allowing the more important banks of the capital city to issue paper money on their own initiative, regardless of their ability to cover such issues by gold reserves. Such unwise policies resulted, quite naturally, in abuses; and abuse resulted in loss of confidence in the banks on the part of business and industry. Loss of public confidence, inevitably, led to the failure of several large banking houses and a resulting financial crisis. Finally, rumors were circulated that the Bank of Rome itself was in difficulty. A government inquiry was instituted, the results of which the government deliberately concealed. Parliament then insisted upon a new inquiry, and upon the publication of a report. The revelation of fraudulent practices and of Giolitti's role in the deliberate concealment of them shattered public confidence in the new government, and the premier was forced to resign. Once more, Francesco Crispi was asked by King Humbert to form a government (November 1893).

Crispi brought to the premiership the vigor which had characterized his previous term, and he adopted generally the same policies as before. But he defined them more exactly: "We belong," he said, "to no one faction of Parliament more than to any other; we belong instead to a great party, whose sole purpose is the welfare of Italy. . . . We need only firmness and perseverance. Let us rally around the king, the symbol of our unity; for only the monarchy marks the union, and guarantees the future of the fatherland." Thus, during the three years of his current ministry, Crispi was to stand out as the advocate of the monarchy, the protector of the middle classes, the upholder of the Triple Alliance, the promoter of an aggressive colonial policy, and the open enemy of all popular movements —whether Irredentist, republican, socialist, anarchist, or even comprised merely of discontented workmen. In 1894, therefore, he carried on a campaign against the peasantry of Sicily, who had rebelled against the heavy taxes imposed by Giolitti; and, while he honestly tried to lighten the misery of workmen and peasants all over Italy, he was severe, and even brutal, in punishing socialists or republicans who actively furthered organized rebellion against the state.

The socialism against which Crispi reacted—or perhaps, as his enemies insisted, overreacted—was not of the relatively benign variety which was to become endemic in the West during the following century. It was rather a virulent form of anarchism, as preached by a Russian, Bakounin, who had spent some time in Naples a few years previously. When Italy's industrial movement began in the north in the 1870s, socialism was adopted by organized labor in reaction to capitalist abuses, even though Bakunin's anarchist tenets were, by then, generally rejected, and the first socialist newspaper, *Critica Sociale,* was established in 1891. At about the same time, socialist ideas became popular in Sicily, where they were applied as the basis for an agrarian policy. The network of unions (*fasci*) thus organized grew powerful quickly, and the landowners and upper classes grew frightened apace. There were clashes between the workers and the police; violence followed violence, and the movement spread from Sicily to Rome, Rufo, Spezzia, Pisa, Leghorn, Carrara (where the marble workers were, for the most part, anarchists), and Milan. Such were the early manifestations of that socialist movement which was to have such far-reaching consequences on the life and liberty of modern Italy.

In this instance, Crispi's response to violence was greater violence. Forty thousand troops were sent to subdue Sicily—which, Crispi insisted, the peasants and socialists were in the process of selling to England, or even to Russia. Martial law was declared and military courts were set up. Crispi carried through Parliament laws designed to make these courts more dreaded even than those of the hated Bourbons of the old days. For all those accused of "making and using bombs"—a cover-all phrase usually interpreted to mean anyone sympathetic to socialist ideals—sentences were imposed of from three to twenty-four years' imprisonment at hard labor. Moreover, through the prefects of the provinces—men who were, for the most part, Crispi's political creatures—the premier proceeded relentlessly to pursue the parties of revolution by forbidding the formation of unions, by prohibiting public assembly, by greatly circumscribing freedom of speech, by muzzling the press through political pressure, and by the hundred ways in which personal political dictatorship may be exercised even in a purportedly free society.

The revolt in Sicily was stamped out; and the landowners and the ruling classes applauded Crispi as a man capable of confronting a crisis. Among the people of Italy as a whole, however, alarm was expressed at this retrogression to the ways of the Bourbons and the Hapsburgs. Was this the "liberty and equality" which had been promised to them by Cavour and by Victor Emmanuel? The question soon began to be asked, not only in homes and saloons, but in Parliament; and many of Crispi's measures, which were at best of questionable legality, were vehemently criticized. His personal popularity was now a thing of the past; but his position was still too strong for concerted action by his enemies. He still had the support of the great conservative forces of the country—of the Church, of the landowners, of "big business," and against this combine of powers the common people could do nothing. It was to be left to Crispi to destroy himself. And when he did so, he made use of an unexpected weapon.

Since 1893, Italy had steadily continued her advance in eastern Africa. The army had won a victory over the Mahdi at Agordat, and, in 1894, had captured Kassala, the gate of the Sudan. In 1895, however, the government, encouraged by these successes, declared to the world that the Treaty of Uccialli, by which Italy and Ethiopia had formed bonds of friendship and commerce, was in reality an agreement which granted Italy a protectorate over the African nation. The Ethiopians, under King Menelik II, were outraged, declared war on the Italians, and inflicted a resounding defeat on them at Adua, or Adowa, where the Italian army, under the impulsive General Baratieri, left upon the field four thousand five hundred dead (including two generals, of which Baratieri was not one), and over two thousand wounded. The victorious Ethopians moreover carried off some fifteen hundred prisoners of war.

It was the end of Crispi's political life. Riots throughout Italy expressed the public's disapproval of the entire African campaign, and the general spirit of national grief and disappointment found voice in Parliament. Without waiting for a vote, Crispi resigned from office (1896). He lived for five years more in retirement, and was recalled to public notice only once, in 1898, when Parliament passed a vote of censure against him. He died in poverty and disillusionment, deprecating Italy for her ingratitude and convinced to the end that, under his leadership, the Italians could have learned, but for their obstinacy, to run before they had learned to walk. He was not an evil man, nor even a personally ambitious one. His aspirations, like his energies, centered around the well-being of Italy. His failing, however, had been to impose what one of his contemporaries called his "megalomania" upon national policy, and to pursue goals beyond the strength and beyond the will of the nation.

2. *The New Italy and the New Nationalism* (1896–1915)

The Marquis di Rudini, Crispi's successor, took office at a time when Italy's position was full of difficulties, and many of the obstacles to her progress seemed almost insuperable. She was burdened with a heavy national debt, which, notwithstanding the fact that taxation was excessive, tended to increase rather than to diminish. The people, agricultural rather than industrial, frugal but not thrifty, patient but not persistent, and taxed out of all proportion to the productive capacity of the country which they inhabited, were fast becoming socialists and republicans—less from conviction than from discontent and even despair. The enormous government expenditures, which were the cause of this condition, had been due not to the ordinary cost of administration, but to such governmental "luxuries" as the subsidizing of railway systems, to extravagance in the civil service, to the reduction of governmental contract awards to the state of a massive exercise in graft and peculation, and, above all, to the enormous armaments and expensive colonial expeditions which the Italian government felt bound to support. Both the government and the people had seen, after the debacle in Ethiopia and Crispi's resignation, the wisdom of abandoning an aggressive colonial policy; but the nation, still proud of its past and still unwilling to resign its place as a Great Power and enter upon a period of recuperation, still upheld its government in its policy of supporting an expensive army and navy. It mattered little, apparently, that the country was poorly endowed by nature with the sources of wealth, and that she could ill afford the expense of maintaining a prominent international position; and it seemed to matter even less that the attempt to do so was leading to mass emigration on the one hand, and to well-organized socialistic insurrection on the other.

The power of socialism in Italy had been rapidly increasing. Crispi's attempts at savage repression, of course, had been ineffective; even more, they had forced together Italy's leftist groups—the Socialists, the Republicans, the Radicals—until they formed a recognizable, though loosely bound, coalition of forces, in which the Socialists were the dominant element. It was natural, perhaps, that the Socialists should dominate; for, unlike the Radicals and the Republicans, they drew much of their membership from the middle classes and from the intellectuals of Italy. Rather than harangue crowds at street corners, the leaders of socialism propagated their beliefs by way of respectable and respected journals—the *Critica Sociale*, the *Lotta di Classe* (*Class Struggle*), and *Avanti!* (*Forward!*), all of which rivaled the best metropolitan newspapers in quality of reportage, and often far surpassed them in literary quality and topical interest. All of this, however, would have come to nothing had the Socialists had nothing worthwhile to sell to the public. What it had, in fact, was something that the public had been demanding for years: a comprehensive, progressive, and clearly stated social program. And such a program was what was lacking in the plans of the Italian government. Parliament, with its lack of organized political parties, with its personal rivalries and shifting intermural coalitions, with its basic policy of "pork-barrel" legislation, was incapable of visualizing and enacting a system of social reform based upon the needs of the country, needs which were being multiplied at an alarming rate because of increasing industrialization. The Socialist program, the so-called "Minimum Program" of 1895, which was received with public acclaim, proposed the vote for adults of both sexes, non-intervention of the government in disputes between capital and labor, religious freedom, a reformed penal code, and the abolition of the standing army in favor of a national militia. It also proposed the nationalization of the nation's mines and railroads, an eight-hour and six-day work schedule, medical care and pensions for the aged, workmen's compensation insurance, the establishment of government-supported school cafeterias, and several other elements of an enlightened and progressive program.

Even the traditionally conservative Catholic Church was infected, perhaps in self-defense, with the socialist spirit of reform. Pope Leo XIII, Pio Nono's successor, could not ignore the socialistic sentiments of Catholics throughout Europe. Hoping to guide such sentiments rather than allow them to be turned to the profit of purely secular societies, he issued an encyclical entitled *Rerum Novarum* ("Of New Things"), calling for broad social reforms and focusing the attention of Catholics the world over on such matters as fair labor practices.

Such was the situation that the new prime minister, the Marquis di Rudini, was called upon to face. He himself was a man not uninclined to liberal views. Upon taking office, he immediately announced a basic change of policy: the controversial African possessions would be transformed into a civil and commercial colony, known as Eritrea, and no further attempts would be made to extend their boundaries; economy would be introduced into government expenditures; reforms would be effected in Sicily; an amnesty would be proclaimed for political prisoners; a *modus vivendi* with the Socialists would be found. This program was partly carried out. A treaty was in fact arranged with Ethiopia, and a project was introduced for revising the tax system. Rudini, however, though a well-intentioned man, had neither the personal nor the parliamentary strength to accomplish most of his ambitious designs. Moreover, his unabashed liberalism served to exacerbate the dislike of the Church for the government; and, at the same time, it failed to win for him, as he had expected it to do, the support of the Socialists.

Rudini's precarious situation was rendered absolutely untenable in the following year (1897), when revolt broke out in the country. It started, as do most Italian revolts, in the south. Hunger, and indignation at the high price of bread led to riots, to the looting of shops, to violence and bloody confrontations with the police. The disturbances spread northward to Bologna, Piacenza, Parma, and Ravenna, and then to Tuscany. From Florence the movement reached Milan; and there it erupted into a massacre. Street demonstrations were organized everywhere, and the government, in a panic, called out the army. Shots were exchanged, patrols ambushed, civilians shot down in the streets. Cavalry charged the demonstrators, and the latter retaliated by erecting barricades in the streets. A hundred citizens were killed in three days, and three hundred wounded. Military courts sentenced thousands of civilians for such offenses as "stirring up class hatred." Finally, the city quieted under the bludgeon blows of the commander of the government forces, General Bava-Beccaris, who, for his part in this incident, is known to history as "the Butcher of Milan." The government, as is the wont of governments, was convinced that the disturbances of the preceding few months were the result of a vast Socialist conspiracy to overthrow the government; and King Humbert bestowed the Grand Cross of Savoy on General Bava-Beccaris "for his great services to the State in the suppression of the revolution."

Rudini had little choice but to resign in the face of this wholly artificial crisis, and the government's panic was revealed in its choice of an army veteran, General Pelloux, as his successor. With Pelloux came a flock of other generals, whom the new premier distributed among the various ministries. The people of Italy did not expect a great deal from General Pelloux; and they were not disappointed. Although he promised moderation, he shortly introduced a series of so-called "Exceptional Provisions," by virtue of which the government would have the right, among other things, to exercise censorship of the press, to prohibit public assembly of the citizens, to send political offenders to penal settlements, and to put public services under military control. The bill was strongly opposed in Parliament by the Left and by the Center (or Moderates) headed by Giovanni Giolitti, who, with a mixed bag of parliamentary tactics, including the filibuster, prevented a vote being taken before Parliament adjourned for the summer. In the fall, the battle resumed, and an attempt by the government to have obstructive parliamentarians silenced by the presiding officer, or to have them ejected, reduced the solemn assembly to chaos. Nevertheless, the rule was adopted, and the Left walked out in protest while their colleagues voted to approve the offensive "Exceptional Provisions." Pelloux then dissolved Parliament and called for general elections, in the hope that the Left would be defeated and that a new group of Deputies would enable him to carry out the program stipulated in the Provisions. The electorate, however, decided otherwise. The Right not only did not increase their majority, but lost so many seats that their majority was now extremely thin. Daily, Pelloux' government's position became more and more precarious until, with all hope gone of compromise between the Left and the Right, he resigned, and took his claque of satellite generals with him. An entire parliamentary year had been wasted in a vain attempt to promulgate the dictatorial conditions of the "Exceptional Provisions," and King Humbert was now resolved to avoid a repetition of this fiasco. He chose as premier an aged and inoffensive Deputy of the Right, P. Saracco, who formed a bipartisan cabinet, and under whom life returned to normal, or rather, under whom parliamentary procedure returned to normal. For there had been a radical change in the four years since Crispi's resignation, and political life was never to be the same again.

The old designations of Right and Left in Italian politics had been born during the early days of the *Risorgimento,* when Right designated the party of liberty and independence, and Left that of Garibaldi and his followers with their doctrine of insurgency. In 1870, however, the final occupation of Rome had robbed both parties of their *raison d'être,* and indeed of their very existence. By the end of the nineteenth century, the terms had come to have completely different meanings from those they had conveyed for Cavour or Garibaldi. The Right now designated the party of conservatism and of the *status quo,* of Piedmontism and of the monarchy. The Left was the party of progress, or at least of change; it was consistently anti-military, and frequently pacifist, middle-class, interested in industry rather than in colonial expansion or war, and preoccupied with the future rather than with the past. The Right was, in a word, the party of the monarchy, of the aristocracy, and of the military caste; while the Left was that of the intellectuals, the industrialists, and shopkeepers, and of the people at large. These were the forces that emerged with clear definition during the critical premiership of General Pelloux; and these were the forces that were to shape the destiny of Italy during the twentieth century.

At the threshold of the new century, Italy suffered a loss which, while not of the far-reaching import of the death of Cavour or of the passing of King Victor Emmanuel II, was sufficiently tragic to send a tremor of shock through the nation and to dramatize the differences which rent the people. In July 1900, King Humbert was assassinated by an anarchist at Monza. The murderer was captured, and he confessed that it had been the king's letter of congratulation to General Bava-Beccaris, on the occasion of the latter's brutal suppression of the disorders at Milan, which had motivated him to kill Humbert. The deceased monarch had not been a great king, or a remarkable man. He was kind, passionately patriotic, and genuinely and wholeheartedly concerned for the good of his people. In times of public need, he was unstintingly generous with his own resources, and he was a man of such sensitivity as to merit the appellation of "the poet of the House of Savoy." Yet, for all these qualities, he was a man out of Italy's past. He was enchanted with the idea of an Italian empire, and he supported Crispi's policy of colonialism—a course which, after the Ethiopian fiasco, was the cause of considerable personal unpopularity for him. A man of the Right to his fingertips, he was a firm supporter of the military on all occasions; and, most important of all, he was blind and deaf to the new spirit of liberalism that had emerged in Italy. Since, under the influence of the court aristocracy and of his generals, King Humbert had refused to move forward with the age, the age left him behind, and during his reign the hold of the House of Savoy on the mind and heart of Italy was loosened. He died ignorant of the deluge, or rather of the torrent of fire, that was to overwhelm his only son and successor, King Victor Emmanuel III, largely because of that failing.

The young king had hardly ascended the throne when the government of Premier Saracco fell. He appointed to replace Saracco a man of firm liberal bent, Zanardelli, who labored under the handicap of being obliged to work with a Parliament of equally unyielding conservatism. In his two years in office, Zanardelli's reform projects—a revamping and equalizing of the tax structure, for example, and a divorce bill—were consistently blocked by the deputies of the Right. In 1903, in frustration, he resigned, and died shortly thereafter.

The new premier appointed by King Victor Emmanuel was, once again, Giovanni Giolitti who, since his last term during the Bank Scandal a decade before, had been serving as Minister of the Interior. Giolitti differed from Zanardelli as night from day. For a principle of conduct, he had only ambition. As a policy of state, expediency was enthroned during his regime. He was cool, calm, superficially reasonable, and deeply cynical of men, motives, and the political process. His method of government was to bind men to him by the bestowal of political gifts, and then to demand payment in the form of support. Since, as premier, innumerable political plums were in his gift, he had innumerable supporters in Parliament. One contemporary observer remarked that Giolitti, in the course of his career, "nominated nearly all the Senators, nearly all the Councilors of State, and absolutely all of the Prefects and other major officials of the administrative, judicial, political, and military branches." That is, of course, an exaggeration; but not much of one. He was, above all, as a modern historian has said, "highly endowed with the happy gift of leaving the sinking ship."

The New Italy

Throughout his long dominance of Italian politics, Giolitti survived crisis after crisis by the simple stratagem of resigning at the first sign of heavy weather and leaving one of his disciples in the premier's office to handle things as best he could. When calm had been restored, he returned, and life went on as before. He was a past master of that practice known in Italian politics as *trasformismo,* or transformism, by virtue of which a premier assured support for himself in Parliament by forming a cabinet based on political expediency rather than upon principle, or confidence in the appointee, or the good of the nation. Once when the King remonstrated with Giolitti for having appointed a conspicuously unsuitable politician to a cabinet post, the premier was quite honestly puzzled. "But, after all," he replied, "I have only given him the Foreign Office!" And the two men could only stare at one another, each unintelligible to the other; for the King was a moral man, to whom Good and Evil were clear, unequivocal terms; while to his minister the only important logical categories were those of Necessary and Unnecessary.

Giolitti's ministry coincided with a notable increase in prosperity in Italy. Foreign trade increased greatly, the important automobile industry was founded and prospered, the use of electricity was constantly on the rise, and factories were erected throughout the north for the manufacture of textiles and machinery. Even the mass emigration of poorer Italians from the south to America, which initially was viewed as a blow to the labor force of Italy, proved to be an economic advantage. In Italy, many of the emigrants had been a burden upon the taxpayers; whereas, from the New World, a steady flow of money emanated to poverty-stricken relatives left behind. Under the impact of this new prosperity, the treasury, for the first time in many years, began to show a surplus. The measures taken by Giolitti's government, however, did not cause this upsurge so much as reflect them. There were trading agreements with Germany and Switzerland, a plan for the establishment of industry in the south, and legislation for reform in the penal system, public health and welfare. Such measures seemed too little, too moderate, and too long in the execution to those who had no share in the country's rising standard of living. In 1904, there were disturbances in Sicily and Sardinia, a general strike instigated by the Socialists, and then violent attacks on the government by the latter. Shortly thereafter, a crisis presented itself in the guise of a railway strike—and Giolitti resigned, naming one of his protégés as his successor. This nominee lasted for an uneventful year, and then was succeeded by Sidney Sonnino, an able man but a tactless one who quarreled with the Socialists and was obliged to resign. And then Giolitti came back, as he knew he would.

The second ministry of Giolitti, which lasted from 1906 to 1909, is remarkable not for the importance of its accomplishments (only two important measures were enacted, the Railway Bill and the Bill for the Conversion of the National Debt—and both of those were holdovers from Sonnino's administration), but for the fact that, during that period, the government accomplished so little while Italy was accomplishing so much. Under Giolitti's iron fist, his political debtors in Parliament did little that was either good or evil; they had steadily abdicated their power in favor of the all-powerful premier, lost interest in and contact with the national life, and were content to debate, collect their salaries, and grow fat at the taxpayers' table. The Italian people, however, had long ago learned that government was one thing, and life another. As the deputies idled and Giolitti intrigued for more and more power, the people ignored both and worked. Everywhere business was increasing. Co-operative ventures, particularly in the form of People's Banks, were introduced and became enormously popular. Italy's resources were supplemented by the introduction of foreign—particularly German—capital. Foreign interest in Italy was further stimulated, and the self-respect of the Italians encouraged, by a series of art and industrial exhibitions held throughout the country.

Despite such progress, conditions in Italy among the poor were, even by the standards of the time, unspeakable. In the south, millions lived in a state of absolute want, deprived of dietary necessities and housed in hovels, lean-tos, and even in caves. Nor was there much hope that one could improve one's position through education, for education was sadly neglected. The tradition of education had not died; but it was now confined to the upper strata of society. The law of compulsory education was hardly enforced; and when it was enforced the quality of the instruction imparted at the primary level of schooling hardly justified the effort involved on the part of the student attending. Teachers were always miserably underpaid, and very often they were not paid at all. The good ones therefore left for greener pastures; and the poor ones stayed and taught, but usually without managing to share a fragment of even their meager store of learning with their resentful pupils. Of all these things, Giolitti spoke resoundingly and movingly. But he did nothing.

On the whole, however, it must be said that Giolitti's supremacy was beneficial rather than otherwise to Italy. Notwithstanding his personal dictatorial tendencies, his intrigues, and the stasis of his government so far as active reforms went, his very presence as a stable force kept Italy quiet while she went on with her material advance of her own accord. His basic liberalism, which was founded on a realistic appraisal of the inevitability

The New Italy

of social and economic progress, kept him from interfering unduly; and, indeed, some of the measures which he thrust before the gaze of his compliant Parliament for their automatic approval were of positive aid. It is ironic, however, that the same liberal spirit, just as it was permitting such strides forward in Italy, was crumbling beyond the Alps under the impact of a double blow. The first was that of Marxism, with which Italy had already been infected by means of socialist thought which preached reform —but reform through legislation rather than through revolution. The second, which was to prove more dangerous in its Italian manifestation, was the nationalistic movement known as Bismarckianism—after Otto von Bismarck, the Prussian chancellor, under whose aegis Prussia had come to dominate first Germany, and then the Continent. Bismarckianism, with its doctrines of the supremacy of the state, of economic and political expansionism by the right of might, of racial supremacy and the *Herrnvolk,* or "Master Race," was to have important consequences in Italy. There, recast in the Italian mold, it engendered a credo of nationalism which was to dominate the state and to put it upon the perilous path of imperialism. It was a creed, however, which, while it overlay the Italian mind for a time, never permeated the Italian soul. For fifteen hundred years, the Italians had manifested little enthusiasm for militarism, and even less—except briefly during the rise of the city-states during the High Middle Ages—for imperialism. The Italians had seen too many governments come and go, caught too many princes, so to speak, with their hands in the till, and seen too many "master races" come out of nowhere and vanish into nothingness, to regard the state, in whatever dress, as anything more than a necessary evil, to be borne patiently and ignored generally. Moreover, Italy, as a political entity, was still too new, and her national consciousness still too embryonic, for her to be amenable to a truly nationalistic movement. Yet, the advocates of an Italian Bismarckianism were determined to change all this. And it seemed that the time was perhaps not unpropitious to change. With comparative prosperity had come a decline of enthusiasm for socialism as such; and with the gradual decline of illiteracy, the masses as well as the intellectuals were exposed to the give-and-take of propaganda and counter-propaganda, and to the crosscurrent of ideas from the world over. With such exposure was introduced an element of choice, and socialism, under attack by such able figures as Benedetto Croce and the idealistic school of thought, had come to be regarded, particularly by the young, as outdated. In its place, something new, attractive, and at least momentarily promising was needed. It seemed that nationalism might fill that bill.

What the nationalists offered was, briefly, glory—*grandezza;* the revival in the modern world of Italy's ancient grandeur. To these men, Crispi, with his colonial adventures and imperial visions, became a saint, and his ambitions became their faith. One of the exponents of nationalism, Alfredo Oriani, stated that faith briefly and exactly: "Greatness as the end; heroism as the means." The field of greatness and of heroism was to be that of Africa, where ancient Rome, in the person of Scipio, Caesar, and others had worked such wonders, "conquering Hannibal," as Oriani said, "imprisoning Jugurtha, suppressing the Ptolemies, and routing the Saracens." To convert the Italian people to this doctrine, the modern media of communication were employed strenuously. Newspapers were founded and widely circulated, particularly *Idea Nazionale,* whose editor, Enrico Corradini, made a career of fulminating against parties, classes, individuals, and humanity at large, and of pleading for passionate devotion to the fate and renewed glory of the nation. Nationalism found other powerful and eloquent advocates in such men as the realist poet, Gabriele D'Annunzio, who preached the love of power and of adventure and sang the glories of war and violence, and Giovanni Papini (now remembered, strangely enough, for his later *Life of Christ*), editor of the nationalist *Voce,* of Florence, who urged that "Italy, without a unity to its vision, needs someone to beat it, so that it may awaken, and someone to incite it, in order that it may act." Croce, in *La Critica,* among many others, was quick to point out the dangers inherent in the doctrines of superstate and superrace, but such efforts were too little to stop, or even to impede effectively, a movement which rested on such deep human emotions as pride, self-esteem, and the conviction of one's natural superiority. The traditional Italian "patriotism" was to be transformed into "nationalism," to assert itself in deeds and words, and deliberately to attempt to spread Italian commerce, culture, and government beyond the natural borders of the country. Even Francesco Nitti, a future prime minister and, at this stage, the leader of Italy's liberals, was tainted with the new doctrines, and publicly expressed regret at his earlier pacifist leanings. The Socialists, likewise, caught the spirit of the times and began preaching the need for a wider interest in international affairs. The Church itself, though only at levels below the papal throne, was noted to incline toward national self-assertion and energetic fulfillment of the will of the nation in the exercise of a certain "sacred egoism." There was a corresponding spread of nationalism in the groups that one might expect naturally to profit from national expansion—the military, the wealthy industrialists, the upper middle class, and the Italian nobility.

As these ideas were born, grew, and propagated themselves in Italy, Giolitti and Parliament sat, not knowing, or at least not caring, where it would all lead. In 1909, Giolitti resigned again over a minor crisis, and was succeeded again by Sidney Sonnino. After a brief term, Sonnino's place was taken by one of Giolitti's creatures, Luzzatti, who remained in office until April 1911, when it suited Giolitti to oust him and reinstate himself in office. And as this unending game of musical chairs, political-style, went on in Turin, militant nationalist societies, such as the *Dante Alighieri,* were springing up all over Italy and sending delegates to other countries to spread the gospel of Italian culture and to maintain the ties of Italian immigrants with the homeland. Irredentism grew stronger and more vociferous, and the Italians of Dalmatia, Istria, and Trent were encouraged, organized, and more or less secretly aided, in their efforts to unite their provinces to the Kingdom of Italy. The winds of doctrine were now blowing ever more violently. Through Milan and Florence, there came the impetus of William James, of Georges Sorel and Henri Bergson. From France, there blew the hysterical breeze of the Futurists—if not toward a certainty of its own, then at least against the certainty of anyone else. And, in that country, the authoritarian, absolutist, monarchical nationalism of Charles Maurras combined with the Catholic authoritarianism and nationalism of Maurice Barrès to incite Europe's new generation. All this, taken in conjunction with European political tensions—the simmering unrest of the Balkan countries, the Adriatic ambitions of Austria, the precarious renovation of the Ottoman Empire—all brought Italy's idealist, nationalist, action-at-any-cost militants to a pitch of hysterical enthusiasm. Thus fortified, they proselytized unceasingly among the young and gathered about them a zealous and ambitious force which proclaimed openly the approaching overthrow of the liberal state. The new Italy was embarking upon that course of "high moral tension" which, two decades later, a man named Benito Mussolini, by then the leader and director of the storm, was to proclaim to be "one of the fundamental necessities" for the triumph of the Fascist regime.

The first major expression of the new nationalism came in 1911–1912, with the Italian occupation of Libya. Italy had long had designs on that country, designs the fulfillment of which Europe, as a whole, regarded as inevitable. As far back as 1902, on the occasion of the renewal of the Triple Alliance, the Italian government had attempted to have her two allies, Austria and Germany, acknowledge her claim. Both refused, although Austria privately agreed not to interfere if Italy should move into North Africa. Germany, for her part, had her own plans for the territories of the Turkish Empire, to which Libya belonged, and she was strongly opposed to the extension of Italy's influence to any part of the Ottoman sultan's domains. England, France, and Russia, however, with their own expansionist programs, could hardly oppose Italian colonialism—particularly so far as regarded as valueless a strip of desert as Libya—with any degree of conviction; and they therefore gave their blessing to Italy's modest African ambitions. Even with such sanctions safely in its pocket, it is unlikely that Premier Giolitti would have moved with respect to Libya had it not been for the vociferous urging and intense pressures of the Nationalists. Giolitti was essentially a liberal and moderate bureaucrat, not an imperialist or a conqueror. His victories were won in the "smoke-filled rooms" of political legend, and not on the battlefield. He believed in the steady maintenance of the *status quo,* with occasional little steps forward at home; and not in giant steps onto another continent. Still, he could hardly afford to ignore Libya. Thousands of Italian immigrants lived in that country, where they prospered as merchants. Moreover, Libya was not without a certain political importance for the Kingdom of Italy, for it was the last strip of the North African coastline not yet occupied by one or another of the Great Powers; and Italy lived in dread lest she lose her only possible foothold on the southern shore of the Mediterranean.

The nationalist case for an African adventure was given its final impetus in 1911, by the "incident of Agadir." As French forces were busily putting down one of Morocco's perennial revolts in that year, there suddenly appeared at Agadir, a small port on the Atlantic coast of Morocco, the German cruiser *Panther;* its mission, it was announced, was "to protect German property." Europe was immediately thrown into consternation. German intervention obviously was a threat to French domination of North Africa; moreover, it confirmed in the minds of the French, and of the English, the deep-rooted suspicion that imperial Germany was determined, in one way or another, to claim some share of the African booty to which France and England had been helping themselves so generously. There followed three months of high tension, with England and France on one side and Germany on the other, during which it seemed that war was inevitable. But a settlement was finally reached, according to which Germany—in exchange for a sizable portion of the French Congo, agreed to recognize French domination in Morocco. Europe, except for Italy, breathed a sigh of relief and went back to its customary occupations.

In Italy, however, the situation was different. The incident of Agadir had aggravated the Libyan question to the point where it now became a national crisis. Africa was being carved up, the nationalists stormed, and

The New Italy

Italy was being left out in the cold. Germany had now openly embarked on a colonial program on that continent, and Libya undoubtedly fell within the ambit of those ambitions. Was not the country already full of German "archaeologists" and "geologists," whose activities, as all the world knew, were notoriously unarchaeological and ungeological? Italy, the nationalists wrote, preached, and urged on every possible occasion, must act now or she would be deprived of her last chance for a vital port across the Mediterranean. The crisis came in the summer of 1911, when the Bank of Rome, the principal source of funds for Italian merchants in Libya, announced that it could no longer afford to maintain its commitments there, and that it was considering selling its interests to a German combine. Under the stimulus of the public outcry which greeted this announcement, the Giolitti government finally acted. An expeditionary force was dispatched and, after a year's campaign, Libya was ceded to Italy by the Turkish sultan by the Peace of Lausanne (October 1912). Modern Italy had taken her first step as a Great Power; and she had had her first taste of imperialistic glory. Everywhere, the spirit of nationalism was triumphant.

Italy's joy at her triumph, however, was not unalloyed. The Libyan campaign had, as usual, been more protracted, and had consumed more in men and armaments than King Victor Emmanuel's military experts had predicted. The treasury was exhausted, and at the end of 1912, there was a deficit of twenty-five million lire, and the "emergency taxes" enacted because of the war had to be extended. In addition, the railway workers were on the verge of a general strike—an eventuality which, if it came to pass, would virtually paralyze Italian commerce at a time when that situation would be most troublesome. Finally, Giolitti's majority in Parliament was, for the first time, being seriously threatened. At the end of 1912, the premier had enacted a measure for universal suffrage, whose purpose was to quell the unrest aroused by the financial situation of the state. What Giolitti did not foresee, apparently, was that the new franchise would raise the number of voters from slightly over three million to eight million; and that the five million new voters would be drawn largely from the intellectuals and the middle class—that is, from the element of the Italian population least likely to be content with Giolitti's plodding and unimaginative government. The general elections of 1913, in fact, returned a Parliament in which Giolitti, although he still held a majority of the votes, did not feel safe. The revolt of the Radicals within the ranks of his own followers, the imminent railway strike, and the desperate condition of the finances, all combined shortly to persuade him that the safest course would be once more to resign. He did so, in March 1914, hoping, no doubt, to return to office, as was his custom, when the sky was less threatening.

The new premier, Antonio Salandra, a "liberal of the Right," as he called himself, managed to settle the railway strike by calling up the army reserves. But no sooner had he caught his breath after that crisis than a new and more menacing problem appeared. The Socialist party had, by the early twentieth century, faded into relative insignificance in Italy. It was, in fact, no longer even a party so much as an association of independent and mutually jealous local groups. At that moment, however, an obscure former stonemason and schoolteacher, Benito Mussolini, began to breathe new life and fire into the socialist body. As editor of the party organ of Milan, *Avanti,* his literary and oratorical talents, and his emphasis on the inevitability of class struggle attracted widespread attention and comment. Under his aegis, socialism—or rather, Mussolini's brand of socialism—again became an influence in the country. Now, with Salandra in office, and perhaps chiefly as the result of Mussolini's agitation, socialist-inspired disturbances erupted in the south. Roving bands of poverty-ridden and desperate peasants roamed the countryside, looting and committing outrages against the "upper classes"—that is, against anyone who had more than they themselves did. Less violent peasants organized boycotts and committed acts of sabotage against those whom they suspected of profiting beyond measure from peasant labor. Short-lived republics were proclaimed in Emilia and the Romagna, and everywhere disorder and anarchy seemed to be on the verge of triumph. The movement, however, was disorganized and unclear in its aims; and, inevitably, it fell of its own weight. Government troops moved in, and sheepish peasants returned to their barren farms. Order was restored—but not until the editor of *Avanti!* had had a taste of satisfaction in his ability to move men to action and bend them to his will.

Italy's internal troubles, however, and Giolitti's legacy of unrest and dissatisfaction quickly faded into comparative unimportance alongside the momentous events being enacted on the larger stage of international affairs. On June 28, 1914, the Archduke Franz Ferdinand of Hapsburg, heir to the throne of the Austro-Hungarian Empire, was assassinated at Sarajevo, in Bosnia, by a Serbian nationalist. The assassin's pistol shots provoked a European sensation; but it was the sort of sensation to which Europe was accustomed. There had been too many rumors of wars in recent years, and almost everyone was confident that, as in the case of the Agadir incident, matters would be settled by the annexation—this time, by Austria—of this or that part of Serbia. Then, a month later, on July 23, like a thunderclap of doom, came the Austrian ultimatum to Serbia, a demand for virtually total Serbian submission to an infringement of that nation's national rights, pride, and honor by the Austro-Hungarian monarchy. To later generations, accustomed to the disposal of small countries by Great Powers, the ultimatum does not seem unduly harsh in view of the provocation. To Europe of the early twentieth century, however, the ultimatum had a single meaning: "It can be interpreted only as a deliberate attempt to provoke war," editorialized the German newspaper *Vorwärts*. Predictably, Serbia, urged on by Russia, rejected the ultimatum, and sealed her own fate. This act was immediately followed by general mobilization —Russia to support Serbia, France to support Russia, England to support France, and Germany to support Austria-Hungary. By the first week of August, the intricate system of alliances and counteralliances by means of which the "balance of power" had been maintained since the Congress of Vienna a century before came into effective play, and formal declarations of war were exchanged between France, England, and Russia on one side, and Germany and Austria-Hungary on the other. World War I had begun and, before it was to draw to a bloody end four years later, the Western world was to be changed almost beyond recognition.

Italy had no clear obligation to enter the war on either side. She was, it is true, a member of the Triple Alliance with Germany and Austria; but her obligations under that agreement were quite clear: she was bound to aid her allies in a defensive war, only, and not in a conflict provoked by them. Nor had she any direct or important interests involved in the struggle between the Allies, as the Anglo-Franco-Russian combine called itself, and the Central Powers, as Austria-Hungary and Germany came to be known. She had had in the past ample cause to quarrel with Austria, and yet the two countries were still bound together by treaty. Neither England nor France had, in the past decades, given Italy any overwhelmingly strong reasons to join them in a major war. If her interests and her duty were therefore unclear and rather divided, so was public opinion in Italy and in Parliament. The issues raised by the Libyan war still agitated opinion. The elections of 1913 had been fought out in a spirit of irreconcilable bitterness, with general accusations of corruption and violence. The Nationalists had obtained parliamentary representation, and the Catholics, the Radicals, and the Socialists had been much strengthened. The year 1914 had, moreover, as has already been noted, been one of special unrest in Italy. The war therefore burst upon a restive and divided nation, governed, for the time being, by a coalition of conservative groups under the rather ineffectual leadership of Antonio Salandra. Salandra did as circumstances dictated. On August 2, just as hostilities were about to erupt, Italy officially declared her neutrality—an act which earned her the gratitude of France and England, and the contempt of Austria and Germany.

As the war progressed through 1914 and into 1915, the whole of Italy debated the eventual role that the nation was to play in the conflict. Giolitti, whose influence was still great, was a strong advocate of neutrality, and argued that much could be extorted from Austria through diplomacy without involving Italy in any danger or loss. Some prominent conservatives, such as former premier Sidney Sonnino, were prepared to enter the war on the side of the Central Powers, partly out of a rather quixotic regard for their engagements in the Triple Alliance and partly in order, as they thought, to safeguard Italy's commercial and financial position. Some Nationalists also were for war on the side of Germany and Austria, for Germany's Bismarckian concept of a "strong state" pleased them. Other Nationalists, along with the Irredentists, thought the war a good opportunity to win back such Italian-language territories as Trentino and Trieste from Austria, and were for a declaration of war against Germany and Austria. Still other Nationalists and Irredentists proposed neutrality, with the threat of war, as a safer way to the same end. The Catholics were strong neutralists, not only because the Church enjoined peace, but also because Austria was a Catholic power, and because they despised anti-clerical France. The Radicals, who, despite their name, were representatives of large industry linked to French capital, were in favor of war on the side of the Allies. Most of Italy's Socialists, under the orthodox leaders of the party, took the stand they had taken during the Libyan war—that is, they were uncompromisingly against all "capitalist national wars." A splinter group, however, under Benito Mussolini, broke away from the main body of the Socialist party and loudly advocated intervention. In order to propagate their ideas, a new Socialist daily was founded under Mussolini's editorship, called *Popolo d'Italia (People of Italy)*. And Mussolini now turned his flaming rhetoric against the neutralists of all classes: "We are not, and we do not wish to be, mummies, everlastingly immobile, with our faces turned toward the same horizons and enclosed within the narrow walls of subversive hypocrisy, where formulae are mechanically mumbled like the prayers of ritualistic religions. We are men! Live men! We wish to give our contribution, however modest, to historical creation! . . . If Prussian reaction should triumph in Europe and, after the destruction of Belgium and the planned annihilation of France, if it should lower the level of human civilization, then the deserters and the apostates will be those who did nothing to avert the catastrophe!" Mussolini's break with the Socialist party was, in effect, the beginning of the Fascist movement in Italy; for it was the beginning of an agitation which set the people against Parliament, which showed that small groups, filled with revolutionary zeal, could stir and command a nation and dominate a government.

Now, all over Italy small "Groups for Revolutionary Action" as they were called (*Fasci di azione revoluzionaria*), sprang up to agitate for entry into the War. Mussolini, along with D'Annunzio and various Nationalists, Irredentists, and university groups, traveled from town to town encouraging new groups, speaking at meetings, and spreading pro-war sentiment throughout the land. By the spring of 1915, a good part of the nation—though certainly not a majority—was inflamed to the point of urging intervention. With public opinion in this state of flux, the government of Salandra was busy negotiating with both sides. It was inevitable, in Salandra's opinion, that Italy must enter the war; but when she entered, she must do so on the side from which she could gain the most advantage. To that end, both sides were approached. From Austria, however, little satisfaction was to be obtained. Italy, as the reward for her intervention on behalf of the Central Powers, demanded, among other things, the province of Trentino (Trent), which Austria was altogether unwilling to cede. Negotiations were then opened with the Allies, whom Italy found eager to make generous promises. After the war, Trentino, and a good deal more, was to be Italy's, in exchange for a declaration of war against Germany and Austria. This offer was confirmed by the secret Treaty of London, on April 25, 1915. On May 3, the Triple Alliance was repudiated by Italy, and from the 13th to the 16th there were pro-war demonstrations all over the country, for the trend of public sentiment was now clearly toward intervention on the side of England and France. And on May 24, Italy declared war on her erstwhile allies, Germany and Austria.

3. The War and the Peace (1915–1920)

The beginning of the war in 1914 had found Italy woefully unprepared for engagement in the struggle. At the time, neutrality was the fashion in Parliament, and when the Minister of War requested twenty-four million lire to rectify the situation, the Deputies indignantly cut the sum to eight million. In the ten months of neutrality, some progress in military preparations had been made, thanks chiefly to the ability and tact of the Commander in Chief, General Cadorna. Still, when Italy entered the war, she was scandalously deficient in the modern implements of combat—in munitions and heavy artillery, particularly. She was equally poorly prepared from the standpoint of personnel, for the army was top-heavy with colonels and generals, while of lieutenants and captains there were hardly any at all. Moreover, of the officers available, too few were more than place holders who owed their rank to family connections or to political influence. Cadorna's first task, therefore, was to remove this superfluous weight and replace it with men of ability. The situation was hardly better among the enlisted men, among whom morale was as low as their training for combat was poor. Italy's situation, then, in May 1915, was that of a nation entering upon a struggle for which she was ill prepared.

As hostilities began, Cadorna's strategy was perforce dictated by that consideration. Surmising that Austria knew of Italy's inadequate preparations, and that she therefore did not expect an attack for several months, he decided to gamble upon surprise and launch an offensive along the entire Austro-Italian frontier. The order was given and, as Cadorna had suspected, the Austrians were taken completely unaware and forced to retreat. By the beginning of August, Italian troops had crossed into Austrian territory along almost the entire frontier. The offensive was renewed in October. The army was now fully mobilized, and greater force was employed; but Italy's lack of material now began to make itself felt. Artillery support was lacking for the infantry, and the latter suffered terrible losses. In addition, the element of surprise which had given the Italians the initial advantage no longer existed, and the Austrians had now been substantially reinforced by troops withdrawn from the Russian front. Although the Italians managed to hold on to their previous gains, new advances were negligible. Finally, in November, the cold forced the combatants to retire to winter quarters in order to prepare for renewal of the battle in the spring. The first round of the war was over for Italy; and, in General Cadorna's two offensives, she had lost a quarter of a million men.

All through the winter, artillery pieces and munitions were collected in desperate haste. Fortresses throughout Italy were stripped almost completely, and even the navy, over the protests of its officers, was compelled to surrender whatever it possessed in the way of mobile guns. General Cadorna's plan, for which this material would be required, was, as in the previous year, an offensive along the Isonzo River, extending from Tolmino to the Adriatic. On May 15, however, before the plan had a chance to go into execution, the Austrians turned the tables on Cadorna and launched a surprise offensive under the imperial commander, Marshal Conrad, and broke through the Italian center. Cadorna called for reinforcements which, although they were promised, never arrived. The Italian troops, however—by now veterans of some experience—dug in, and, on

June 3, Cadorna was able to report that the Austrian offensive had been contained along the whole front. Austrian pressure was further relieved when Marshal Conrad's promised reinforcements, in their turn, failed to arrive.

The line was now stabilized, and Cadorna decided to take advantage of the situation by following through with his plan for an offensive along the Isonzo, "in the hope that by great speed in execution, we shall take the enemy by surprise; for he does not expect an attack upon the Isonzo front when we have just contained the offensive from the Trentino." The offensive was launched on June 16 and continued until August, at which point the Italians had advanced to and created a new line beyond the Carso plateau and well on the way to Trieste. Fighting continued sporadically during September and October, but without significant result for either side, until the advent of winter made further combat impossible. Again, important advances had been made; but, again, the cost had been high. The Isonzo offensive alone—without counting those killed during Austria's Trentino offensive—had taken the lives of some one hundred thousand Italian soldiers. Thus far, after hardly more than a year of war, Italy had spent the lives of over a third of a million of her youth. And thus far all she had to show for it was several hundred square miles of Austrian territory.

This startling contrast was not lost on the opponents of the war in Italy, on the Giolittians, the Socialists, and other neutralists. They spoke out, freely and loudly, criticizing Premier Salandra's government, the conduct of the war, the army, and the monarchy. Trouble brewed in Parliament, and the neutralist leaders watched for an opportunity to tumble Salandra's government while, at the same time, mobilizing sentiment in the cause of peace. The occasion presented itself over a minor matter—the interpretation of an unhappy phrase in one of the premier's speeches—which consolidated opinion on the side of the neutralists. Salandra was compelled to resign under fire, and he was replaced by Paolo Boselli, a popular, but not very effective, Deputy. Boselli had the intelligence, however, to surround himself with men who possessed the talents that he himself lacked. Sidney Sonnino was retained in the Foreign Ministry, and the Ministry of the Interior was given to a man who had been in and out of government for a dozen years, Vittore Orlando.

Upon this government fell the burden of general discontent with the heavy losses of the recent campaigns. To Italy's own problems was now added the events of early 1917: the inception of unrestricted submarine warfare by the Germans, which threatened to reduce England to starvation;

then, the loss of a major ally by the collapse of Russia and the abdication of the Czar. The former event meant that supplies of food and ammunition from England—at their best never very plentiful—would now be even more sorely restricted; the latter, that Austria, now free of the necessity to supply troops for the Eastern front, would be able to throw the full weight of her forces against Italy. The entry of the United States into the war during the same year did little to dispel the general gloom, for it was estimated that it might be almost a year before the Americans could effectively participate in European military operations. 1917 was, therefore, a bad year for Italy. Her offensives made little or no headway, casualties were enormous, and, for the first time, there was a discernible note of pessimism regarding the eventual outcome of the war. The public was weary of the apparently endless and fruitless series of battles; and it was tired of shortages of food, skeptical of propaganda, and resentful of war taxes. Soldiers and officers home on leave found a dispirited Italian people openly expressing the desire to end the war by compromise rather than by victory; and they returned to the front with their morale shaken. So serious did the situation become that Cadorna complained to the government that "If the defeatist spirit in the country is not countered, the results on the army will be disastrous." The neutralists responded with the cry, "Not a man in the trenches next winter!"

It was in these inauspicious circumstances that Italy's French and English allies now urged Italy to launch another offensive against the Austrians. Cadorna, thinking that a victory would restore confidence in Italy and the army's confidence in itself, resolved on a bold attack. As his target, he chose the Bainsizza plateau, on the Isonzo and immediately south of the Austrian bridgehead of Tolmino. The plateau was the collecting point for the entire Austrian front, and its capture, in addition to its psychological effect, would throw into disorder the Austrian defense system and open the way to Trieste.

For three months, Cadorna patiently collected men, artillery and munitions, until the Italian forces along the rest of the front were reduced to skeleton units. Along a proposed offensive front of some twenty miles, he deployed his fifty divisions, over five thousand artillery pieces, and almost two thousand mortars. On August 18, the opening bombardment began, and the same night bridges were hastily thrown over the Isonzo to the north of the plateau and an attack was launched on the slopes leading to the plateau. The assault was successful. Cadorna's troops advanced halfway across the plateau before lack of artillery support (the big guns were still across the Isonzo) forced them to halt their advance. There they re-

The New Italy

mained, awaiting the construction of roads and bridges in order for their artillery to be brought up. By the end of August, the fighting on the plateau died down. In September, the assault was suspended, and orders were issued to consolidate the conquered sectors and return to the defensive.

At that moment, however, rumors were heard to the effect that a great concentration of not only Austrian but also German troops were massing behind the Austrian line in the Bainsizza plateau, under the command of a German, General von Bülow. These reports, soon verified by Italian reconnaissance teams, caused little consternation in General Cadorna's headquarters. The Italians were entrenched in positions of immense natural strength, positions which, moreover, had been heavily fortified. In addition, Cadorna had at his disposal some five hundred and sixty battalions, whereas, according to his best information, the enemy had only slightly over four hundred. The Italian commanders, however, took every precaution in case of an assault. But they did so in all confidence that their position, if not impregnable, was at least highly defensible against a numerically inferior force.

Early in the morning of October 24, at a time when rain and fog reduced visibility to almost zero, General von Bülow opened the attack by a heavy bombardment which included the use of gas shells. Shortly afterward, the combined German and Austrian troops advanced, and the Italians, under heavy fire, retreated. By the middle of the afternoon, von Bülow's troops had occupied the town of Caporetto, north of Tolmino on the Isonzo. The next day, the advance continued across the Isonzo valley and westward through the mountains. Creda and Staroselo were taken, now placing the Austro-German troops behind the Italian frontal position. Here and there, Cadorna's troops fought bravely and well; but in most places the entire front was disintegrating. Whole battalions lay down their arms in surrender; others turned and ran in complete disorder. By the night of the 26th, there was nothing to do but withdraw what remained of the Italian forces behind the Tagliamento River, some twenty miles to the west of Caporetto. No sooner had that position been stabilized than it was threatened anew, this time not by Austrian and German troops but by a mass of unarmed, fleeing civilians numbering almost four hundred thousand, who succeeded in disrupting almost completely the Tagliamento line at its most critical point. It was therefore decided to withdraw once more, this time to the Piave River only a few miles north of Venice. Now the Italians must hold; otherwise, the detested Germans and Austrians would once more be on the soil of Italy itself. And they held. Twenty-nine Italian divisions withstood fifty Austro-German divisions for almost three weeks of the most ferocious and savage fighting of the entire war. By November 25, the battle was over, and the exhausted Italians were relieved by French and English troops. The first Battle of the Piave was essentially the turning point of the war, and it had been fought and won by Italy, alone and unaided, against overwhelming odds. It was a glorious victory, thoroughly in the Italian style. And as thoroughly unpredictable as had been the collapse along the Isonzo only a few weeks previously, a debacle which became known as the Battle of Caporetto.

For several months now, the Italian front was quiet. In March 1918, the German divisions were withdrawn for the great German attack on the Western Front, as were those of France and England. In April, Italy, now feeling secure, dispatched an army corps of fifty thousand men to fight in France. The events of late 1917, however, despite their eventually happy outcome, had important political repercussions. The disaster of Caporetto outweighed, in the public mind, the victory of the Piave, and it brought home with overwhelming impact the meaning of defeat. Tens of thousands of refugees from the areas occupied by the German and Austrian troops of General von Bülow streamed across Italy, homeless, penniless, and friendless, and with blood-curdling tales to tell of the horrors of war. All Italy shuddered; and Boselli's government trembled and then fell. As his new premier, King Victor Emmanuel named Vittorio Orlando, Boselli's former Minister of the Interior, a man whose political acumen was matched only by his oratorical gifts. In his very first address to Parliament he struck the keynote of his government: "The situation will not be debated. It will be faced." Here, at last, was a man who was determined to lead, rather than to be led, by events. A wave of reaction swept over the country. Caporetto, which until now had sounded like a great *Dies irae* over the land, now became a memory around which rallied the national will to resist. "Caporetto has saved Italy from moral collapse," said one Minister. It would perhaps have been more accurate, and undoubtedly more diplomatic, to say that Vittorio Orlando had done so.

During 1918, the final year of the war, Italy, under the stimulus of inspiration provided by Orlando's leadership, was to know only victory. In June, a vehement Austrian attack on the Piave front was just as vehemently repulsed by the troops of General Armando Diaz (General Cadorna had been relieved of his command after the Battle of Caporetto), as were assaults on the Monte Grappa sector and the Tonale Pass. The June offensive continued for several weeks, and took a fearful toll of Austrian lives—some 150,000 of Conrad's troops were killed before he finally gave the order to withdraw. It had been Austria's last gasp, and her last bid for victory. Gen-

The New Italy

eral Diaz, however, was not prepared to rest on his laurels. On October 24 —significantly, the anniversary of the Battle of Caporetto—the Italian army, supported by a French and an English army also under Diaz' command —launched the final offensive of the war. The Austrian line broke along the entire front, and Diaz and his men advanced almost unhindered to the north, east and west. On November 3, all Italy rejoiced at the news that Trent had been taken, while, from Venice, a motley fleet of warships and private boats crossed the Adriatic and occupied Trieste without firing a shot. In all, more than half a million Austrian prisoners had been taken, and almost all of the weapons and materiel of Austria's Italian army. Caporetto had been doubly avenged by the Battle of Vittorio Veneto, as it was known. Moreover, Austria was now wholly open to invasion from the south, an invasion which would give to the Allies access to southern Germany as well. The position of the Central Powers was now hopeless. On November 4, Austria capitulated, to be followed, on November 11, by Germany. The war was over, and now Italy might anticipate gaining the rewards of her sacrifices at the peace conference.

The Battle of Vittorio Veneto, immediately preceding as it did the collapse of the Central Powers, threw Italy into a fever of nationalistic enthusiasm. The completeness of her triumph overwhelmed the nation and convinced her that Vittorio Veneto had been not only the final, but also the decisive, battle of the war; and that the battle, and therefore the war itself, had virtually been won by Italy. In one fell swoop, she saw herself elevated in fact, as well as in theory, to the charmed circle of the mighty, on a par with Britain and France, and entitled to the lion's share of the spoils of victory. No longer would Italy be content merely with Trent or Trieste. Visions of empire were conjured up by the press and enlarged upon in public oratory: Italian domination in the Balkans; Italian spheres of influence in Asia Minor; Italian colonies in North Africa and East Africa. Forgotten, in this frenzy of national pride and ambition, was a single sentence spoken across the Atlantic almost a year previously. The American President, Woodrow Wilson, had enunciated before Congress his famous Fourteen Points, which were to play such a vital role in the making of the peace. Point IX, which dealt with Italy, stated clearly and simply that "a readjustment of the frontiers of Italy should be effected along clearly recognizable lines of nationality." There was no thought of spheres of influence in the Balkans or Asia Minor, or of colonies in Africa, in that sentence. One might hope, at most, for Trent, and perhaps for Trieste. And, unfortunately for Italy, the Central Powers, in negotiating the armistices, based themselves on the acceptance of the Fourteen Points. The secret

Treaty of London of 1915, which effectively drew Italy into the war, seemed conveniently forgotten by its French and English signatories. Nothing was heard from London or Paris regarding its stipulations, or the rewards that Italy was to receive for her participation in the war: Trieste and Trent, and, going past purely ethnic lines, a good strategic frontier in the northeast; on the Adriatic, the northern half of Dalmatia, and, in the south, Valona—so that the Adriatic was to become an Italian lake; of Turkish possessions, "a just share of the Mediterranean region adjacent to the province of Adalia"; in Africa, "some adequate compensation" in the form of boundary adjustments between her existing East African and Libyan colonies and the adjacent French and English possessions.

Although the Italian people as a whole were not aware of Wilson's Fourteen Points, and still less of the (still secret) Treaty of London, Premier Orlando was painfully cognizant of both. At the end of October and the beginning of November 1918, when the chief Allied spokesmen met with Wilson's representative, Colonel Edward M. House, to discuss the Fourteen Points, Orlando attempted to introduce a qualifying interpretation of the all-important Point IX. His motion, however, was brushed aside with the comment that it did not bear on the conditions of the German armistice—which, in the eyes of France, England, and America, was the overriding business of the coming Peace Conference. Orlando, for some reason, did not insist, and the matter was dropped, while the Wilsonian program was formally accepted as the basis of the peace.

The chief reason for this cavalier dismissal of Italian claims at this early stage was primarily that Italy was still regarded by her Allies as a mere junior partner in the coalition of powers. Of the Allies, she had suffered the smallest losses—six hundred thousand dead, as against almost a million for the British and almost a million and a half for the French. Similarly, while northern France had been devastated by the war, in Italy the battles had been fought out in a comparatively small area, with proportionately less destruction of property; and, again, her expenditures for war had been far less than those of France or England. No one thought to mention, nor did Orlando think it expedient to point out, that, of all the Allies, Italy was the nation which, because of her poverty, could least afford *any* expenditure at all of men or money, and that, proportionately, her sacrifice had been at least as great as that of her wealthier co-combatants. In the same vein, Orlando neglected to inform President Wilson of the provisions of the Treaty of London, both before the Fourteen Points were made public and on the occasion of the American president's visit to Rome in January 1919, before the opening of the Peace Conference.

The Conference therefore opened, at Paris in the spring of 1919, with Italy at a decided disadvantage. Lloyd George for Great Britain, and Georges Clemenceau for France, who would have been in a position to honor the Treaty of London, had already committed themselves—as had Orlando, for that matter—to the Fourteen Points. And no one, thus far, had bothered to inform President Wilson that there existed a Treaty of London. To add to the difficulty, the reception of the Italian delegation, headed by Orlando and by his Foreign Minister, Sidney Sonnino, was notably unenthusiastic. The French, British, and American delegations—already irritated by a rising tide of criticism in the Italian press for the Wilsonian program—insisted on regarding Italy's share in the war as negligible, the Italian front as secondary, and the Battle of Caporetto (rather than Piave or Vittorio Veneto) as representative of Italy's contribution to victory.

In the midst of this indifference to Italian claims—not to say hostility to them—Orlando came to the Conference with two principal diplomatic aims in view. Both points had to do with Italian prestige. First, he was determined that the Italian peace treaty with Austria was to be signed at the same time as that with Germany, so as not to relegate the former to a position of inferiority in the eyes of the world. The second was to assure that the new nation of Yugoslavia (or the Kingdom of the Serbs, Croats, and Slovenes, as it was officially known until 1929), composed of the two previously sovereign states of Serbia and Montenegro and of several former Austro-Hungarian provinces, should not be treated on an equal footing with Italy. From the standpoint of territorial expansion, Orlando was of two minds. On the one hand, he was not opposed to Wilson's concept of nationalism based on self-determination; but, on the other hand, he was absolutely and irrevocably determined that Italy should have the Adriatic seaport of Fiume in Croatia. His Foreign Minister, Sonnino, for his part, put his trust in treaties rather than in men, and, from first to last, he held firm to the provisions of the Treaty of London—a divergence of opinion between him and his chief which did not help matters at all.

During Orlando's first meeting with Wilson, the Italian premier put forward his country's claims with great frankness; and Wilson, with equal candor, stated his position. Italy might have the Brenner line in the north as its boundary. But, so far as her claims to the east were concerned, it was not possible to agree. Fiume, with its fine port, was an absolute necessity for Yugoslavia; and Dalmatia, since the majority of its inhabitants were Slavs, must logically go also to Yugoslavia. As for Italy's security to the east, Wilson said, that would be sufficiently guaranteed by the neutralization of the eastern coast of the Adriatic, and by Italy's possession of the islands of that sea. Orlando replied that Italy would accept the Brenner line to the north, and possibly the cession of Dalmatia to Yugoslavia on the basis of ethnic grouping. But if Yugoslavia got Dalmatia because most Dalmatians were Slavs, he asked, not illogically, then why should Italy be deprived of Fiume, which was overwhelmingly Italian in population and which, furthermore, had already expressed a strong desire to be united with the Kingdom of Italy? Having stated their respective positions, neither man would budge an inch either to the left or to the right. Wilson was immovable, out of conviction; Orlando, because a great cry had arisen in Italy for "Fiume and Dalmatia," and he dared not give in to Wilson. France and England, while still paying lip service to the Treaty of London (which, of course, had promised Fiume and Dalmatia to Italy), were content to sit back and allow the American president and the Italian premier to settle the matter. But settle it they did not; and there the question remained, to the consternation of everyone concerned.

As might be expected, Italy was the most disturbed of all. America, England, Yugoslavia, and particularly France were daily excoriated both publicly and privately. France became the special target of public indignation perhaps because so much had been expected of her. But now, instead of supporting Italy in her just claims, she had become the foremost advocate of the new nationalities, of security by alliances with Britain and America, and of anti-Italian sentiment at the Conference. So virulent did anti-French agitation become that even so prestigious a journal as Milan's *Corriere della Sera* could editorialize that "It is now necessary to tell Italy, in plain terms, that there is a Power who seeks to dominate Europe. This Power is not, and cannot be, Italy. On the day when the weight of her conquests becomes too heavy to be borne, it will be necessary once more to rise; and Italy will rise anew. Let us not trust in illusions. Already, we have suffered too much. Let us rather prepare for the approaching war!"

In the midst of these harangues, the Italian question was taken up by the Conference (April 19). A paper stating Wilson's position was handed to the Italians. The Italians replied. Days of discussion followed, but nothing was accomplished. So far as an Italian settlement was concerned, the Conference was as far from agreement as it had been at the time of Orlando's first meeting with Wilson. Wilson then took an unprecedented step. On April 23, he released to the French press a Manifesto to the Italian People which was, in effect, an appeal to Italy over the head of her premier. The document contained nothing new. It merely restated the Fourteen Points and outlined the principles of the League of Nations, congratulated Italy on her bravery and courage, and pleaded for understanding and acceptance. But the Manifesto, rather than weakening Orlando's position, had the effect of strengthening it, for it rallied the outraged people of Italy around their premier. Parliament hailed Orlando and Sonnino as heroes and almost unanimously endorsed their demands. The Conference was now more deadlocked than ever. A variety of solutions were offered, all of which were strenuously modified by all of the powers, and then invariably rejected by Orlando.

On June 4, the Austrian treaty, by which Italy received the Brenner line, was made public. It seemed small enough recompense for Italy's part in the war, particularly with public indignation over Fiume and Dalmatia still keen. Orlando's position was undermined by these disappointments, and, upon his return to Rome for the opening of Parliament in the middle of June, he was defeated on a motion for a secret session to discuss foreign policy. Tired, disappointed, and frustrated at his lack of positive achievement in Paris, he resigned and was replaced by his former Finance Minister, Francesco Nitti.

Under Nitti's government, which was represented in Paris by the Foreign Secretary Tittoni, the problem of Italy's eastern boundary remained unsettled. In other areas, however, some progress was made. Italy was given a vast tract of desert in the Libyan hinterlands, and a tiny extension of Italian Somaliland in East Africa. And with that, the Italian people, who had dreamed of a vast colonial empire, had to be content. The question of Fiume was not resolved for another year. It was further complicated by the fact that, in September 1919, while negotiations were still going on, Gabriele D'Annunziò, at the head of a free Italian corps (called the *Ariditi*), occupied the city. This *coup* had the effect of narrowing the problem of Fiume down to a direct issue between Italy and Yugoslavia. A few months afterward, Nitti's government fell, and he was succeeded by the perennial and inevitable Giolitti, who appointed a new delegate to Paris, Count Sforza. Sforza was able to accomplish what Orlando and Nitti were not. Moreover, the defeat of Wilson in the American elections of 1918 had robbed the Yugoslavs of their chief advocate, and there was now a more conciliatory tone in their communications to Italy. On November 12, 1920, by the Treaty of Rapallo, a settlement was finally reached. Italy was to have the Istrian peninsula, while Yugoslavia was to get Dalmatia. The problematic city of Fiume was declared to be a free state, along with a strip of coastline which connected it to Italy's Istrian peninsula. D'Annunzio was handily ejected from the city, and Italy and Yugoslavia bound themselves in perpetuity to respect the sovereignty of the new state. And thus were brought to a close Italy's claims upon the Paris Peace Conference.

On the whole, the work of the Italian delegations at Paris was not very impressive. Rather than assert themselves as the representatives of the Great Power which they claimed Italy to be, they seemed to accept the English, French, and American estimate of Italy as a junior partner, to be given a small share of the booty, thanked for her efforts, and then dismissed. They took little part in the more important work of the Conference, such as the drawing up of the treaties of peace with Germany and even with Austria, and they expended their energies—and their credit—on a single question, that of their own frontiers. Even this narrow view of affairs was further circumscribed, as negotiations went on, by their concentration on the relatively unimportant question of Fiume. It is small wonder that the opinion of the Italians carried little weight with the American, British, and French delegations. And it is small wonder that the results of the Conference were so disappointing from the Italian standpoint, or that their effect in Italy was to exacerbate the already vivid sentiments of anger, bitterness, and disillusion. These were dangerous sentiments to awaken in a nation which had already tasted, however briefly, the pride of nationalism and the joys of victory. And they were sentiments which, in a few years, were to bear a deadly fruit.

VIII
THE AGE OF FASCISM:
Benito Mussolini
(1920–1945)

1. The Rise and Triumph of Fascism (1920–1922)

The history of Italy, from the final settlement after the First World War until the collapse of the country during the Second World War, is chiefly the story of one man, Benito Mussolini. This man, who represented, and, in many ways, personified Italy for so long, was born in 1883, of a peasant family, in the tiny village of Predappio in the Romagna. The family was poor, but, we are told, they were all of remarkably robust physique—an important heritage for a man destined to rise to power by insurrection. Mussolini himself, who shared the superstitions of rural Italians, often remarked that, on the day of his birth, "the sun had, eight days before, entered in the constellation of Leo"—a point which revealed that he "was destined for greatness, glory, and power."

Mussolini's father was the local blacksmith, and the Mussolini smithy was the club for his political cronies, the Anarchist-Socialists of the school of Bakunin, a branch of which had been established at nearby Forlì in 1874. Socialism, for the peasants of the Romagna, was not a middle-class intellectual exercise as it was to become in the cities, but a revolt against the bitter oppression of the great landowners, the municipalities, and the government. For the national government at that time, as has already been noted, regarded persecution, and not reform, as the proper remedy for Italy's economic and social ills. There were long prison sentences for "sedition" and "conspiracy"—words which were often interpreted to mean any public expression of political sentiment with which the government did not agree.

Yet, despite this oppressive policy, Socialism prospered and spread. Mussolini's father became the leader of the local Socialist group, and, in the year in which his son was born, he was arrested for carrying in procession a banner with the words, "If we can work, we will live free; otherwise, we will die fighting."

Mussolini as a child was doubtlessly sufficiently curious about politics to share the indignation felt and stirred up by his father. Every day, there were new stories of oppression, of neighbors' troubles with the officials of the municipality, of outrages by the landowners, and of the great world beyond the village which the peasants had only lately discovered in the pages of the new Socialist newspapers. No exaggeration was needed to make the tactics of the government appear in a dim light. There was the brutal and bloody repression of the Sicilian *fasci* in 1893 under Premier Crispi; and there were the anti-anarchy laws of 1894 and the enforced dissolution of all Socialist clubs and societies, and the systematic persecution of Socialist leaders. Only four years later, in 1898, came the "Terrible Year" of the Bread Riots, when four hundred people were killed in Milan alone, and almost a thousand arrested. There was unceasing social war, punctuated by short truces, and then social war again, and martial law. Such was the stuff on which the young Mussolini was nourished.

At elementary school, where, in his earliest years, his mother was the teacher, Mussolini was regarded as precocious but restless, pugnacious, and domineering. There are stories of fights, and of stone throwing, and they may be true. (Similar stories are told of Napoleon's boyhood. And many other boys also throw stones, and fight.) He was not a good mixer with other boys; he preferred his own company to that of his peers, and he was fond of walking alone in the fields and lonely places.

Mussolini's mother early discerned unusual talents in her son, and the boy was sent on to a secondary school maintained by a religious order (although Mussolini *père* was a violent anti-clerical). There, he won a reputation for being quick, intelligent, clever, and studious; and still he was a lover of solitude. There was, even at that stage of his life, a certain reserve about him which no one, not even those few whom he honored with his friendship, could breach. From this school Mussolini went on to a Training College, or Normal School, with the idea of becoming a teacher. It was a career which he regarded as the quickest exit from the lower classes for an intelligent and ambitious young man. Upon graduation, he attempted to secure a position as a clerk in the local municipality, but he was refused the job because of his father's political affiliations, and, since there was nothing else to do, he became an elementary-school teacher.

Mussolini's forty pupils occupied only his mornings. His afternoons and evenings were his own, and it was then that he, now nineteen years of age, began that process of self-tuition which was to become his substitute for the university education of the young men with whom he would later have to contest the leadership, first of Socialism and then of the nation. As an autodidact, he had all the weaknesses of the breed, including envy, and it is not surprising to hear him state publicly, years after he had come to power, his view of "university culture": "I advise," he said, "that it be assimilated rapidly; and that it be forgotten no less rapidly."

At the end of the school year, Mussolini went to Switzerland, where he remained from the middle of 1902 until the spring of 1904. He lived a life of shocking poverty, economic and social anxiety, and intellectual elation. Mussolini himself relates that he earned an incredibly meager living as a bricklayer and mason, and that he thus learned to hate the race of proprietors who, because they owned some capital, were placed in a position to vent their spite on the disinherited. He learned the bitter lesson which, added to those of his childhood, made of him an almost hysterical hater of the well-groomed young Socialists from the middle classes, and of their polite nineteenth-century liberalism and reformism.

Still, his own strivings seemed to be toward middle-class goals. As soon as he could, he left the ranks of the manual laborers and became a clerk in an Italian wine-dealer's shop. At the same time, he was assiduous in pursuing his self-tuition, and he was able, by the most diligent application, to master both French and German. In his free time, he attended lectures at the University of Lausanne, where he was most impressed by Vilfredo Pareto and his "theory of imponderables." Margherita Sarfatti, one of Mussolini's most admiring biographers, explains that "Pareto taught him his characteristic method of investigating problems by means of experimental, alert and wide-awake research, rather than by starting from some theory." Indeed, it was to be Mussolini's boast in later years that Fascism "does not possess an armory of theoretical doctrines, because every system is an error, and every theory a prison."

During this period, Mussolini also frequented Socialist and Anarchist clubs organized by Russian refugees, and, as a result of these associations, and because of some obscure journalistic efforts of his, he got into trouble with the police. He had already had some difficulty with them during his first days in Lausanne for being "without visible means of support." So now, in order to demonstrate his respectability, he took a job as a teacher in the little French village of Annemesse. Villages, however, did not provide a sufficiently large stage for either his interests or his ambitions. Soon, he was in Zurich, in the mainstream of Socialist and Anarchist discussion. Those were critical days for Marxism, which was fighting for its life against the criticisms of the Reformist school. From the conflict, there was to emerge Reformism for Germany, Revolutionary Syndicalism for France and Italy, and Bolshevism for Russia. All of these Marxist schools agreed, however, on at least one thing: that the "bourgeois world" was incorrigibly corrupt and must be destroyed. Mussolini, still embittered by the memories of his childhood and by his early experiences in Switzerland, publicly agreed with them; and the authorities, as soon as this became known, expelled him from the country for his "dangerous political views." He hated the "bourgeois masters" none the less for that.

In February 1909, there came a turning point in his career. He became Secretary of the Chamber of Labor in Trent, which was then Austrian. Two Socialist newspapers appeared in the city, of which one, *Il Popolo,* was the organ of the Italian Socialists who looked to the integration of the Trentino into the Kingdom of Italy. Mussolini became editor of *Il Popolo* and, inspired by the patriotic Socialism of Cesare Battisti, the founder and director of the paper, he was an outstanding success in the job. In this position, he first came into direct everyday contact with the issues which were to make a nationalist out of him. His Italian Socialist friends were treated with contempt, and then abandoned, by the Austrian Socialists. The Italian conservative bourgeoisie (the liberals were all Irredentists) lived quite satisfied under Austrian rule, acquiescent in the oppression of their working-class compatriots so long as their own economic and social situation was secure. And it was indeed secure, under the yoke of a trans-Alpine emperor (generally referred to by the Italians not as *il Imperatore,* the emperor, but as *il Impiccatore,* the hangman) whose officials ruled by means of political persecution. Within a few months, Mussolini personally felt the heavy hand of the Austrian government. For having written in *Il Popolo* that "The Italian frontier does not stop at Alà," he was expelled from Trent.

Mussolini was now well launched on a career as a publicist and organizer, which meant, in the Italy of that time, that he was an agitator in the Socialist cause. As his reputation grew, he was called to the secretaryship of the Socialist Association at Forlì, in his native province, where, in 1910, he founded a newspaper called *La Lotta di Classe (The Class Struggle).* He had already contributed to the organ of Socialism's revolutionary wing, the *Avanguardia Socialista (Socialist Avant-Garde)* of Milan, which had been founded in 1899 to oppose the orthodox leaders of the party. The title of his paper was a sign of his alignment with the militant Socialists of

Milan led by Arturo Labriola, for when first founded, it had been called *Lotta di Classe*—the name which Mussolini appropriated.

Mussolini held the Forlì secretaryship until he passed onto the stage of national politics at the Socialist Congress of 1912. His two years in that position were eventful ones. The character of the man, now nearing thirty, began to show traits which, in the not-too-distant future, were to become familiar to the world. He was, and he was to remain, possessed above all by the need for action, often action unprepared for by a foregoing consideration of its possible effects and consequences. He led the crowd to the Town Hall to get the price of milk reduced by threatening the lives of the Mayor and the Town Council. He led the peasants in a demonstration against the reaping machine. He led the mob in the destruction of a certain pillar in the Piazza of Forlì, which had long been a bone of contention among local politicians. By 1910, he had already been before the courts twice for disturbing the peace. In that same year, he was found guilty of publishing defamatory articles. In 1911, a series of articles on anti-militarism earned him a short prison term. Against the do-nothing Socialist deputies in Parliament he conducted a campaign of gross insults, describing them as "parliamentary paralytics."

Mussolini's impassioned utterances were being quoted in *Avanti!* (*Forward!*), the national Socialist newspaper. Then, at the Congress of Milan in 1910, he made a special mark by his attack on the policy of collaboration between the Socialist party and the democratic parties of the left. He urged the party to "live dangerously." His reception was mixed, and the attack had little practical effect. But it served to bring him more into the public view, a most important consequence in a time when personalities, perhaps more than policies, were apt to be the decisive factor in politics.

A critical time had now arrived for Mussolini and for the middle-class leaders of the Socialist party. In September 1911, Giolitti undertook his colonial adventure, the Libyan war. This was, it will be recalled, the culmination of a long series of efforts on the part of the Italian government to secure concessions from the Turkish government, then the ruler of Cyrenaica and Tripolitania, areas in which Italian immigrants and interests were numerous. It was particularly feared that these areas might be claimed by France, who had obtained Tunisia under the very nose of a frustrated Italy, or by Germany. This raised a serious crisis of conscience for the Socialists. Italy was an overpopulated country, and even her annual emigration, though very large, gave only little relief, especially to the South which most needed it. How would the issues involved in the war square with Socialist objections to the exploitation of backward peoples, militarism, and war? In fact, a large number of Socialists had come to accept the view that poor countries had a right to fight the rich nations for a distribution of the world's wealth, even as the proletariat had the right and duty to fight the capitalists. When the war for Tripolitania broke out, many Socialists supported it, although the party officially opposed it and had committees of protest set up all over the country. Mussolini himself was not an opponent of all wars, as his later career was amply to demonstrate; but he was an opponent of this particular war. His sentiments were shared by a sufficient number of articulate Socialist leaders—including Treves, the editor of *Avanti!*—to make themselves felt. Committees of protest were set up all over the country; a strike was engineered; barricades were erected in the streets. For two days, there were disturbances, cavalry charges into the ranks of the demonstrators, and dozens of casualties. Mussolini, as one of the most violent anti-war speakers and as a proponent of open resistance to the government, was arrested. The charges brought against him are an indication of the extent of his activities at this time: "Resistance to public authority; personal injuries to public officers; infringement of the freedom of the men called to arms; violent stoppage of industrial work and establishment, with consequent cessation of production; violent stoppage of the trains of the Romagna Lines, and the overturning of railway cars; damage to State telegraph lines by the destruction of poles and the cutting of wires; violent stoppage of a railway engine; the placing of a telegraph pole across a railway line . . ."

From such an array of charges, Mussolini could hardly expect to escape with impunity. In fact, he was convicted and sentenced to serve five years in prison; but he appealed, and as a result was required only to serve five months of the sentence. Five months, however, was sufficient to accomplish what five years of vitriolic journalism and violent sabotage could not. When he emerged from prison, he was hailed by the Socialists of Italy as a hero and martyr, and, at the Congress of Reggio Emilia in 1912, he was made editor of the Party newspaper, *Avanti!*, and advanced into the highest council of the Party.

The next years, 1913 and 1914, saw great civil strife in Italy, and Mussolini quite naturally used *Avanti!* to support the cause of revolution. In the south, government troops fired upon demonstrators; thereupon the unrest spread to the north, where it seemed at the point of becoming general. It was even expected in some quarters that at any moment a Republic might be proclaimed at Rome. Such was the state of the country at the end of 1913, just before the general elections of November—the first such to be held under the recently enacted universal suffrage. Mussolini officially entered the election as the candidate for Forlì, though he had little hope of winning as the city was known for its adherence to Republican principles. He campaigned vigorously, both orally and in the pages of his newspaper, on behalf of his own candidacy as well as for the principles of Socialism. He was defeated at Forlì, as he had expected to be; but the Socialist Party won a total of fifty-three seats in Parliament—an impressive victory, for which it was generally acknowledged that the editor of *Avanti!* was largely responsible. Mussolini himself was delighted with the results. "Now we can see that there will be only two parties," he said, "the one, conservative; and the other, revolutionary." This accomplishment, coupled with his success at the Congress of Anacona, raised him to the virtual leadership of the Party. He was "now the heart and the brain of the Socialist party," wrote Ivanoe Bonomi, a Socialist parliamentary leader who had seen his own influence wane as that of Mussolini waxed. "To the crowd, and particularly to the new recruits, who are the largest and the most enthusiastic element, he is the speaker and writer who is most esteemed, most loved—and most followed . . . his will has become law, and his authority has become that of a dictator."

It was one thing, however, to be the acknowledged leader of Italy's Socialist Party, and another to be the leader of Italy. Socialism undoubtedly was a growing power in the land. *Avanti!* itself, under Mussolini's editorship, had increased its circulation from thirty thousand to over one hundred thousand readers—no mean audience for a provincial weekly. But the Socialist was still a minority party, albeit a vociferous one, and, moreover, one whose leader could exercise only indirect influence on national policy since he himself was not even a member of Parliament. The tenor of Mussolini's life had thus far revealed certain characteristics which, while perhaps unusual, were not so rare as to be a passport to automatic power: an uncompromising hatred for bourgeois values; the will to subvert such values, even through violence; a broad, vague, but nonetheless genuine sympathy for the workers and peasants of the nation; and the conviction —or rather, the knowledge—that the shape of history is determined by energetic minorities rather than by lethargic majorities. In addition, he had been endowed by nature with that quality known as *presence*. The impression was not of a cold, intellectual nature, but of an emotional, moving and moved one. There was something altogether elemental about him. One sensed power; and one sensed sympathy; and one sensed ambition. He was what a later generation would come to designate as "a charismatic personality"; not merely as a leader, but as a leader to whom men were attracted almost in spite of themselves. However, if this had been all, Mussolini might well have remained, as have so many other equally gifted men, merely a figure in the front rank of his political party. What was needed was a crisis by virtue of which this "charisma" might be unveiled before the nation. Such an opportunity was at this moment in the making. Mussolini was to ride to his destiny on the wings of a rising Fury, the World War of 1914–1918. By making that conflict and its aftermath his own, he was to possess himself of the Italian people.

Mussolini, as was seen in the last chapter, was one of the advocates of Italian intervention in the conflict. That, however, was not the position that he maintained in August 1914, as the Allies and the Central Powers exchanged declarations of war. At that time, he was as divided as the national mind was. He began by adopting the official Socialist attitude, and he signed the official anti-war position paper of the Party. But Mussolini was a revolutionary in temper. Moreover, he was by no means, as will be recalled, a natural friend of "the German hordes" whose racial theories were so unflattering to the Latin peoples. Therefore he was strongly opposed to Italian intervention on the side of the Central Powers. And his basic sympathy with the Allies now began to emerge more and more clearly. The Socialist Congress of September 1914, declared strongly for neutrality at any cost, but Mussolini was already wavering. "I am not ashamed to confess that, in the course of these two tragic months [August and September of 1914], my mind has suffered oscillations, uncertainty, trepidation. And who, let me ask, among men of intelligence, in Italy and abroad, has not suffered, more or less profoundly, this inner crisis?" By the end of October, he asked the Executive Committee of the Socialist Party to reverse itself and declare against neutrality. The Committee refused, indignantly and unanimously. Mussolini was a minority of one. In a rage, he resigned from the party; and the Committee, in equally high dudgeon, dismissed him as editor of *Avanti!*. The Socialists were even more inflamed against their former leader when, barely two weeks later—on November 15—there appeared a new newspaper, *Popolo d'Italia,* a Socialist daily, under the editorship of Mussolini. There were immediately charges that Mussolini had deliberately engineered his break with the Party, and that the astounding feat of organizing a daily within so short a time had been accomplished by means of a subsidy from the government of France. There seems little doubt that such was indeed the case; and that, in addition, funds had also been forthcoming from the Italian government which was, at that time, as will be recalled, attempting to bargain with both sides in order to discover which of the combatants would offer Italy the better terms for her aid on the battlefield. In any case, *Popolo d'Italia* made a mystery of its position. As its motto, it bore a Napoleonic inscription: "Revolution is an idea which has found bayonets."

Mussolini's break with the Socialist Party, and the establishment of *Popolo d'Italia* marked, as has been noted, the beginnings of Fascism in Italy. Now, the *Fasci di Azione Revoluzionaria,* spoken of in the last chapter, were formed; and now Mussolini, along with compatriots who shared his convictions, began actively campaigning for intervention. Among these co-operators were men who were to be among the first of the post-war Fascists, such as Michele Bianchi, first Secretary General of the Party. These groups of speakers and writers clamored for general revolutionary action, and the monarchy came under particularly violent attack. By the spring of 1915, a large part of the nation had been converted to Mussolini's position. The government of Premier Salandra, having been offered a giant bribe in the secret Treaty of London, repudiated the Triple Alliance on May 3. From May 13 to May 16, there were pro-war demonstrations all over the country. On May 24, war was declared. Mussolini noted that "the terrible week of Italy's passion closed . . . with the victory of the people. . . . A will to war was declared by the people above the parliamentary herd. On the body of the nation, many parasites had feasted: Giolittians, Clericals, Socialists. But the nation, with one great shrug, has liberated itself from its troublesome and insidious burden."

It is surprising that Mussolini, in this mood, did not leave for the trenches at once, as his friends and associates were all doing. It was not until the end of August 1915, that he entered the army—the 11th Bersaglieri Regiment—and then only when he was conscripted. As a soldier, his conduct was commendable, if unexceptionable, and he rose to the rank of sergeant. (He explained later that his political reputation made it impossible for him to be proposed for training as an officer. It is likely that this was indeed the case.) He served in the front lines, in the trench war of the Isonzo area, for about nine months—a tour which was interrupted at the end of 1915 by an attack of paratyphoid fever. He made use of the subsequent sick leave to put some order in his personal affairs, and it was at this time that he married Rachele Guidi, his mistress of long standing, who had just borne the second of his children. In February 1916, he returned to the front lines. Though a competent soldier and a popular non-commissioned officer, he was given no opportunity to win distinction, nor was his unit involved in any important battle. He was careful, however, that the people of Italy should be kept informed of his doings and whereabouts through the pages of *Popolo d'Italia*. At the beginning of 1917, he was wounded—not dangerously, but painfully—when an (Italian) mortar shell exploded accidentally in his trench, and from that time until August 1917, he was in the hospital. His newspaper, of course, created something of a sensation out of his wound, a fiction in which it was joined by other, less partisan journals, who seized on every pretext to boost national morale. King Victor Emmanuel, who had already visited Mussolini during his bout with paratyphoid, again visited him in the hospital. And Mussolini, revolutionary though he was, expressed pleasure at this mark of royal favor. He never returned to his unit. Upon his discharge from the hospital, he applied for release from duty on the grounds of his indispensability to *Popolo d'Italia,* a request which was quickly granted. He returned to his newspaper office in Milan as soon as he was able, now no longer a simple political leader, but a war hero as well.

From his editorial chair, Mussolini continued the war which he had so lately fought in the trenches. Italy, indeed, had need of all the help she could get, for her situation, it will be recalled, was nearly desperate. The Russian Revolution had permitted the massing of Austrians and Germans on the Italian front. The army, poorly equipped and poorly led, suffered enormous losses and the severest physical hardships. And it received little comfort from the home front, where defeatism was endemic. There were hundreds of thousands of deserters. The manufacturers, the financiers, the contractors, and the landowners were, as always, profiteering. Parliament, which, as a body, had never been in favor of the war, was wavering in a cause which it had not chosen to support. Socialist anti-war propaganda was increasing daily. The peace efforts of Pope Benedict XV further weakened morale. And then, at the end of October 1917, there came the terrible debacle at Caporetto.

The reaction which followed Caporetto, which has already been noted, was the turning point. The spiritual renewal and the material reorganization which marked the rise of Italy's defensive instinct marked also the second important step toward the Fascist state, the first having been intervention itself. As in the first step, Mussolini led the way in the second. No voice was louder than his in calling for unity, for discipline, and for a massive national effort. Every sacrifice should be made, he declared, and he called for strong government action against defeatists, against the newspapers of the Socialists, and against slackers of every kind. The nation rallied, and it played a prominent, if not decisive, part in the autumn victory of the Allies in 1918. Mussolini joined in the peace celebrations with enthusiasm, almost hysterically; his sister, Edvige, recalled that he seemed "almost transfigured with joy." His hopes for the future ran high, as did those of all Italy. On November 11, he wrote: "It is necessary that victory should also realize the domestic aims of the war: the redemption of labor. From now on, the Italian people must be the arbiters of their destinies, and labor must be saved from speculation and misery." But Mussolini's hopes, along with his elation, were soon dashed, for Italy was soon deep in trouble, both at home and abroad.

At home, the smell of revolution was in the air. The men who had returned home from the trenches found neither recognition of their efforts nor prospects of employment. In part, perhaps, they had cheated themselves, in hoping unreasonably that the world could be made dramatically better by the mere fact of war. Undeniably they had been cheated by the fantastic promises of social reform made to induce them into the trenches. Instead of dramatic amelioration, however, and instead of social reform, they found that the old Philistine world had asserted itself with its ancient vigor, and that the old routine awaited them. Thousands of men who had been officers were now expected peaceably to resume their occupations of clerks, craftsmen, and students, to go back to work after so long a moral holiday. Yesterday, to murder had been a glorious act, the proof of a superior civilization, acclaimed as heroism. Today, they were expected to sell ribbons, to repair shoes, to study the causes of the Punic Wars.

There were causes of dissatisfaction that were peculiar to Italy. Most important of all, the country was made to feel not that it had contributed to the victory of the Allies, but that it had, in fact, been defeated. The Allies had spilled Italian blood for their own ends, and now they were in the act of cheating Italy of her just share of the booty of war—as witness the treatment of Orlando and Nitti in Paris. Italy, in the person of Orlando, and later in the ill-timed Manifesto, was rebuked by Woodrow Wilson for her claims on Dalmatian territory—territory which had been promised her in the Treaty of London. The redemption of Italian territories, so long preached by the Nationalists and the Irredentists, and now demanded also by the nascent Fascist movement, had been frustrated. And now, the Socialists added to the bitterness of Italy by a constant campaign of derision against those who had fought, designating them as dupes and fools.

The situation was exacerbated by the incompetence of the government, which had made no provisions for speedy demobilization. It had not provided demobilization pay to tide over the veterans until the economy could find its natural peacetime balance—thereby giving substance to the Socialist claims that Italy, and particularly the Italian soldier, had been used as a tool to further capitalist oppression. Moreover, there had been no effective planning for the conversion of the national economy from a wartime basis to one of peace. The swollen industries of war suddenly slumped—and it would be months before they could be re-equipped to produce the goods required by a nation at peace. Unemployment rose, until over ten per cent of the nation's work force—some four hundred thousand out of slightly under four million workers—were without income. Prices also rose until, in 1919, they were five times what they had been in 1913. Inevitably, the national debt and municipal debts had doubled and tripled; and now, in the midst of widespread unemployment, spiraling prices, and universal discontent, a rise in taxes was proposed in Parliament. A series of strikes erupted throughout the land, and there was talk of violence, and of revolution. The government tottered while the people demonstrated, and, for a moment, it seemed that there was no one who could set things aright again.

On March 23, 1919, five days after a momentous Communist demonstration in Milan, Mussolini assembled a group of friends and associates in a room at the Piazza San Sepolcro, and here, with the several dozen people in attendance, he revived his *Fasci,* which he now called *Fasci di Combattimento,* as a political party. It was the formal inauguration of the Fascist Party. For a party born in the midst of such economic and social unrest, however, its program was surprisingly mild. It congratulated veterans of the war, declared itself against imperialist ambitions (both foreign and Italian), endorsed the Wilsonian principle of national unity in the sense that it demanded the annexation of Fiume and the Dalmatian coast, applauded striking workers, and declared that it would oppose the election of "neutralist" candidates of any party. Mussolini himself recalled, years later, that, at the time of the meeting, he "had no particular doctrinal position in mind."

Hard upon this rather tame beginning, the new party leader traveled around the country, making revolutionary speeches and attacking the Socialists—an effort which he backed up by a flood of vituperative articles in *Popolo d'Italia.* From this torrent of words, a Fascist program began finally to emerge. The new party, Mussolini claimed, aimed at, among other things: universal suffrage; abolition of the Senate; reformation of the Constitution; enforcement of the eight-hour day; a minimum wage; reorganization of railways and public transportation; nationalization of all armament industries; a graduated tax on wealth; confiscation of all property belonging to religious congregations; the abolition of stipends paid by the state to bishops; and a foreign policy designed to enable Italy to take her "proper place" among the civilized nations of the world. As part of the latter aim, he urged, on every occasion, the annexation of Fiume and Dalmatia.

There was a little of something for everyone in the program—for Nationalists and Irredentists and Republicans and Liberals, and even for the Socialists, whom Mussolini was attempting to wean away from the Socialist Party, which he described as "perfectly autocratic, absolutist, imperialist, bourgeois . . . definitely reactionary, completely conservative." The program outlined by Mussolini had sufficient appeal, and, in its attacks upon the Socialist Party, contained sufficient truth to exercise considerable attraction upon the Italian people, and the fledgling party soon began to grow. It did not, however, grow rapidly enough either to suit Mussolini's plans, or to capture a single seat in Parliament during the elections of 1919. Discouraged, Mussolini spoke of quitting politics, since, as he said, "Fascism has come to a dead end." In the elections, his bitterest enemies, the Socialists, had a brilliant success, capturing 156 seats, while another new party, the Catholic *Partito Popolare,* won the third largest representation with 101 seats (the Liberals were second, with 129 seats). It was enough to discourage a man of much less volatile nature than Mussolini, who himself had been humiliatingly defeated (he received 1.5 percent of the vote) in his bid for a parliamentary seat from Milan.

It was as though Italy herself shared Mussolini's disappointment. Immediately following the elections, a new wave of unrest swept over the country. The Socialists called a general strike. There was, in addition, a postal strike, a railway strike, a strike in the textile mills, and then another railway strike. These were accompanied by clashes with the police and the army, and a general show of contempt for the authority of the government—a popular sentiment which had been aggravated greatly by the occupation, by D'Annunzio and his *Ariditi,* of Fiume, and by their eventual expulsion by government forces. These developments awakened new hope in the editor of *Popolo d'Italia.* The people, and particularly the workers, he concluded, were ready, as never before, for Fascism. And he was right. D'Annunzio's frustrated followers flocked around Mussolini, who had openly supported their former leader, as the last hope of Italian nationalism. Young people, disillusioned by disorder at home and reverses abroad, turned from the old parties to the new, and began to look to Fascism for salvation. The small landowners, fierce in the defense of their holdings, regarded Fascism as their final resort in the struggle against the claims of their tenants and workers; and Mussolini, who publicly claimed to be the champion of the peasant and the worker, gladly accepted the paradoxical role thus thrust upon him, and bands of black-shirted Fascist thugs, known as *Squadre,* and often simply as "Black Shirts," were organized to terrorize Socialist agitators and organizers. The police usually pretended not to notice this activity; indeed, they were grateful to Mussolini for relieving them of the task of keeping the Socialists in order, and many of them, in turn, joined the Fascist Party. The new popularity of the Party began also to attract men of ability, to whom the movement seemed to offer a road to power: the anti-clericalist Italo Balbo, from Ferrara; and Dino Grandi of Bologna, highly regarded both for his intelligence and for his love of violent means.

In the midst of this agitation, violence and counterviolence, the government of Premier Nitti vacillated between the policy of violent oppression and that of doing nothing at all in the hope that Italy's troubles would solve themselves. When neither course proved effective, Nitti resigned (June 1920), and was replaced by Giovanni Giolitti. For the first few months of his term, Giolitti's attitude toward the Fascists was one of mere toleration, for he hoped to win the support of Fascism's bitterest enemies, the Socialists. By 1921, however, that hope was gone, and, under his influence, the government now began to give active support to Mussolini who, with his vigilante Black Shirts, had now come to be regarded as Italy's champion of law and order because of Fascism's bloody opposition to Socialist-inspired unrest. Now the government not only protected the *Squadre* from arrest for arson, assault, and even murder, but also provided them with arms and money. The support of Giolitti—who naively thought to use the Fascists to destroy the Socialists, and then to control Mussolini for his own ends—combined with that of the small landowners and of the industrialists, who were grateful to the Fascist Party for their disruption of Socialist strikes, assured the political future of the Party. In the elections of 1921, Fascism won thirty-five seats in Parliament. Among the successful candidates was Benito Mussolini, who was elected as a Deputy of Milan, as well as of the district comprising Bologna, Ferrara, Ravenna, and Forlì. Dino Grandi was also elected from Bologna. Compared to the debacle of the 1919 elections, it was a striking success for the Fascists.

To Giolitti's delight, the Socialists had lost thirty-four seats. Parliament was now composed of four major blocs: the Socialists with 122 seats (the Communists, who had recently splintered from the main body of Socialism, held an additional 16); the Liberal Democrats, with 159; the *Partito Popolare,* with 104; and, of course, the Fascist Party with its 35 seats, to which were quickly added, for voting purposes, the 10 seats of the Nationalist Party. The rest of the seats were divided among the Agrarians, the Republicans, the Slavs and Germans, and so forth. But Giolitti's delight was short-lived. What he had accomplished, in fact, was a parliamentary division of power which made it impossible for a premier of any party to govern effectively. He shortly recognized the fact and resigned—for the last time, finally—and was replaced by Ivanoe Bonomi, a moderate Socialist and one of Mussolini's enemies of longest standing.

The establishment of the Fascist movement in Parliament did not, as might have been expected, abate to any degree the activities of the blackshirted *Squadre*. To the contrary, Socialist heads were being broken with increasing frequency, labor union headquarters were being burned by the dozens, Socialist centers being destroyed by the hundreds, and Socialists killed, in the process, by the decades. The losers in the battle between the Black Shirts and the Red Shirts were indeed the Socialists—who appealed, in vain, to the police, the army, and the government for protection—but, most of all, the Italian people, who could never be sure, in the midst of these civic disruptions, whether they might not inadvertently be caught up in some Fascist street brawl, whether the trains would run or not, and whether food would be delivered to the market on any particular day. Quickly, almost abruptly, public opinion began to shift, and the Fascists, although they still retained the support of landowners and employers, of the police, the army and the government, now began to be viewed with exasperation by the masses. Mussolini, sensitive as always to the popular wind, was quick to agree when, in July 1921, Premier Bonomi proposed a truce between the Fascists and the Socialists. The agreement was greeted with widespread mistrust among the leaders of Fascism and among the rank-and-file members, and, at a tempestuous meeting at Bologna in August, Mussolini angrily resigned from the Executive Committee of the movement, though he retained his status, as he said, of "an ordinary private soldier in the Milan *Fascio*." It was generally recognized, however, that Fascism would ill afford to do without the influential editor of *Popolo d'Italia,* and a process of reconciliation was begun almost immediately. At the Congress of Rome, in November, Mussolini, protesting that the truce must be honored, at least in the public forum, promised that he would not attempt to enforce its terms, and he was accordingly reestablished on the Committee. He had won, rather than lost, in the contest, for his resignation had extorted the public admission from his followers that Fascism could not hope to survive without the presence of its founder and most articulate exponent. Henceforth, his position in the Party was to be that of the ultimate and final authority on all questions of policy. As such, while advising restraint, he did not forbid further depredations by the *Squadre*, and there was widespread violence in Piedmont, Lombardy, Tuscany, and the Marches, and particularly in Ravenna and Parma. As the result of these activities, by the middle of 1922 the power of the Socialist Party had been effectively broken and Fascism was everywhere in the ascendancy. Moreover, as a result of Mussolini's policy which forbade the *Squadre* to offer any resistance to government troops, the army was now almost universally well disposed toward him and toward Fascism.

As the result of the economic and social crises inspired, at least in part, by the Fascist-Socialist confrontation, the government of Premier Bonomi fell in February 1922. As an expression of the exasperation of the public with ineffectual governments and do-nothing parliaments, crowds demonstrated in the streets shouting, "Down with Parliament! Long live military dictatorship!" And Mussolini, as always a weather vane in the wind of public opinion, declared that the Fascists would not participate in any government. King Victor Emmanuel, in a quandary, appointed as premier a man of little guile and smaller talent, Luigi Facta. Facta's government fell in July, when he failed to deal to anyone's satisfaction—including that of the Fascists—with a Fascist demonstration in Cremona. No one, however, could be found to put together a new government, and the king was forced to recall Facta.

The reappointment of this nonentity as premier was to prove the deathblow to Italy's already moribund parliamentary system. Under him, control of the country was to pass from the hands of the constitutionally elected representatives of the people into those of the Fascists. Only twenty-four hours after his reinstatement in office, the Socialists, on August 1, called for a general strike to protest Fascist attacks (under Italo Balbo) in the Romagna. Mussolini, in a public statement, gave the government forty-eight hours in which to deal with the situation. Facta did nothing, whereupon the Fascists took over the essential services—transportation, etc.—which had been immobilized by the Socialists, and the strike accordingly collapsed of its own weight. Everywhere, the Fascists were hailed as the single force for order in the country, and everywhere there was talk of a Fascist coup, of a Fascist march on Rome. But Mussolini, despite the urgings of his friends to give substance to these rumors by taking strong action against the government, did nothing. With the actor's fine sense of timing, he had decided that the moment was not yet ripe. And, as he watched, the nation continued on the path toward virtual anarchy, until public disaffection became so great that even those who were not Fascists began to look to Fascism as the sole hope of the country. In the space of a few weeks following the Fascist ultimatum to the government and Mussolini's show of strength during the Socialist strike, even the army, sensing where power now lay in Italy, virtually abandoned the morally bankrupt government of Premier Facta to its fate, and the Prefect of Milan was able to report to his superiors in Rome that, in the event of an emergency, the armed forces of Italy could "not be counted on to act on behalf of the government."

Nothing could have pleased Mussolini better than this complete disenchantment with the parliamentary system. Judging correctly that his moment had now come, he began a series of public addresses on order, on government, and on the monarchy. Declaring that public peace could be restored by a strong government acting within the framework of the monarchy—for he knew that a large section of the Italian people were emotionally attached to the House of Savoy—he proposed the abolition of the democratic framework of the past, represented by advocates of "parliamentary mystification" who have "consistently surrendered to that swollen-headed puppet, Italian Socialism." The "strong government" which he proposed was, of course, a Fascist regime: "Our program is simple: we wish to govern Italy. But it is not programs that are necessary for the salvation of Italy, but men of strength and will power." As to the means of attaining power, Mussolini was equally candid: "If the whole of Rome were not suffering from softening of the brain, they would summon Parliament at the beginning of November and, having passed the Bill for Electoral Reform, leave the matter to the electors in December. . . . If the government does not, however, follow this path, then we shall be obliged to take another path. . . . When it is a question of assaulting the State, it is no longer possible to have recourse to little intrigues. . . . We must give orders to hundreds of thousands of men, and it would be ridiculous to keep it a secret. We are now playing an open game."

Under the stimulus of such words, it was now impossible for Fascism not to act. Everywhere that Mussolini spoke, cries were heard of "To Rome! To Rome!" Finally, on October 16, 1922, at a meeting in Milan, plans for a coup were laid, and a quadrumvirate—comprising Michele Bianchi, Italo Balbo, Emilio De Bono, and Cesare Maria de Vecchi—was nominated to assume full powers under Mussolini. On October 21, a great convention of Fascists was held at Naples, where Mussolini announced to Italy that the moment had come: "It is time for the arrow to leave the bow, or the cord, stretched too tautly, will break. . . . I assure you, in all solemnity, that the hour has struck. Either they give us the government, or we shall take it by falling on Rome. Now it is only a matter of days or of hours. Each of you, return to your homes, so that we may be in a position to act simultaneously and that in every part of Italy we may together seize by the throat the miserable political dominating class."

Premier Facta, of course, did nothing. Worse, because the congress at

Naples passed without public disorder, he thought that the worst was over. He told the king, "I believe that the prospect of a march on Rome has faded away." In the meantime, Mussolini and the quadrumvirate was making the final arrangements for the March on Rome. The date was set for October 28, and the object of the march was to be nothing less than the overt seizure of power and the formation of a cabinet, under Mussolini, which would comprise no less than six Fascist members in the most important ministries. As Mussolini and his chief disciples worked out their plans, bands of Black Shirts roamed the streets of the cities, singing the songs of Fascism and shouting, *"A Roma! A Roma!"*

October 28 came and went, however, without the march. At the last moment, Premier Facta had been galvanized into what was, for him, frantic action. At his behest, the King offered to accept Facta's resignation, and to appoint Antonio Salandra, a protégé of Giolitto and a former premier, to replace Facta, and to include Mussolini in the new cabinet. Mussolini replied: "For a Salandra-Mussolini solution, it was not worth mobilizing a Fascist army, causing a revolution, killing people. I will not accept."

King Victor Emmanuel was shrewd enough to grasp the situation. De Vecchi, who was Mussolini's spokesman in Rome, was summoned to the Quirinale, where the monarch spoke with him at some length and ended by instructing him to request Mussolini to come to Rome—to receive the royal appointment as Premier. A few hours later, Mussolini, still in Milan, telephoned his wife. "I have made contact with the Palace," he said. "Please pack my bag with some things, and a suit. I have to go to Rome." On that night of October 29, 1922, Mussolini crossed the Rubicon in a sleeping car of the Milan-Rome express.

2. Il Duce (1922–1939)

The world of government, of high officials, and of rigid protocol, was one that was wholly foreign to the former editor of *Popolo d'Italia*. Mussolini had had a short term as a Deputy in Parliament, but his dealings with governmental departments had been nil. Indeed, one of the stratagems which he was to employ to disarm visitors and foreign diplomats in the first year of his rule was to admit his complete ignorance of the workings of foreign relations and of the mechanics of government. Such self-avowed lack of knowledge, however, did not prevent the newly constituted premier from reserving to himself the two most important cabinet posts in his government: Foreign Affairs and the Interior. For the rest, he surrounded himself with men of some ability in a truly non-partisan government. Of the thirteen major cabinet posts in his gift other than the two which he kept for himself, only three ministries were given to Fascists: Aldo Oviglio in Justice, Alberto de Stefani in Finance, and Giovanni Giuriati in Liberated Provinces. The Fascists did a little better in the distribution of the eighteen subministries, of which they received eight. It was a move shrewdly calculated to convince the nation, and the world at large, that Mussolini intended to govern by parliamentary means, and that he was far from being the wild-eyed anarchist and sinister revolutionary that his critics made him out to be. Even the King, who, though of somewhat limited ability, was not without a native shrewdness himself, was pleased by this display of moderation. "He is a man of purpose, and I have the impression that he will last a long time. He has, if I judge correctly, the will to act, and to act well. I told him to put together a government of capable men founded on a broad basis, and I sensed that he was of the same opinion and views. I confess that my previous opinion of him was quite different." The "previous opinion" to which Victor Emmanuel referred was probably much like that expressed by an Italian diplomat who, upon Mussolini's appointment as Premier, was asked what sort of man the Fascist leader seemed to be. "I have no idea," he answered, "but everyone says that he is a wild man from the north."

In his first few months in office, Mussolini continued to polish his image as a cool-headed and even moderate statesman. To the British and French ambassadors, he protested that his government would honor all of Italy's foreign commitments whether or not they seemed to be to the country's advantage, and that his greatest desire was for a close friendship with Italy's former Allies. At home, he conciliated public opinion by assuring the Deputies that he wished to govern through Parliament. At the same time, he reminded the Deputies of his power, and of their own precarious position: "I could have punished those who defamed and opposed Fascism. I might have made, of this bleak hall, a camp for my platoons. I might have dismissed Parliament and created a government of Fascists alone. But such, at least for the time being, is not my intention." Finally, he came to the crux of the matter. "This Chamber must understand the peculiar position in which it finds itself, according to which it is liable to dissolution in two days or two years. We therefore ask for full powers, because we wish to take full responsibility." And the Parliament, assured of at least its temporary liberty to exist, exhibited that degree of docility which Mussolini would come to expect of the organs of government. It voted Mussolini the "full powers" which he demanded. It was a striking success for the fledgling premier, and it greatly added to his prestige both at home and abroad. On the heels of this victory, Mussolini took steps to assure that the powers that he had just been granted would not evaporate in the time-honored fashion of parliamentary politics, by some minor crisis or other in which a vote of "no confidence" in the government might be elicited from the temporarily cowed, but still unpredictable, Deputies. In July 1923, he introduced and secured passage of an Electoral Reform Bill, according to which the old system of electing Deputies by constituency was abolished. In its place was established a new system, by virtue of which the party that obtained the largest number of votes in a national election

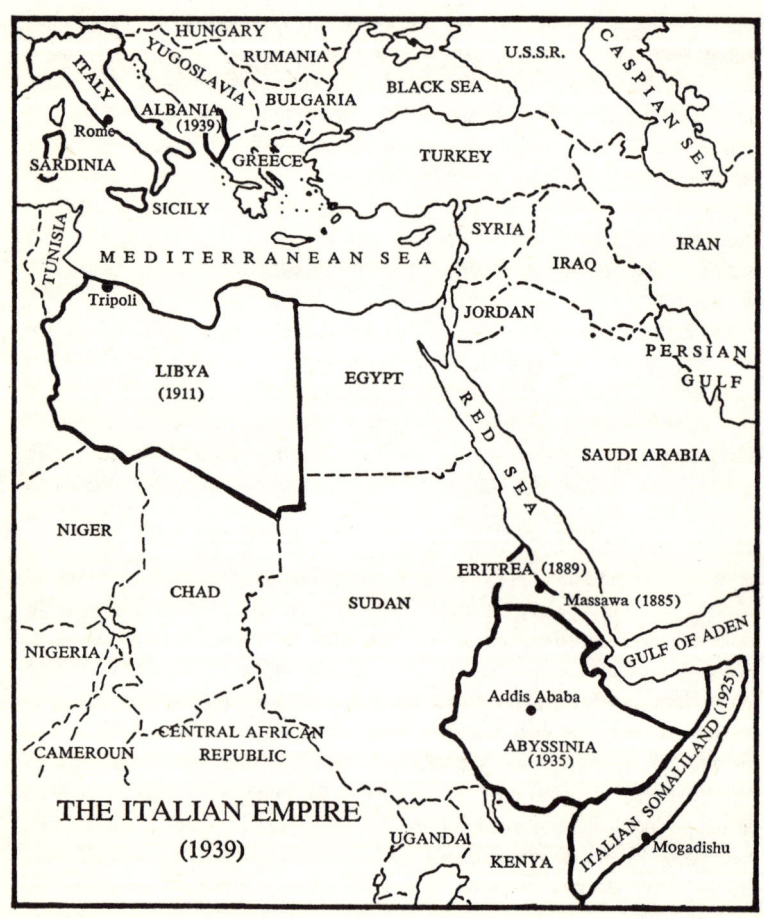

The Age of Fascism

would automatically receive two-thirds of the seats in Parliament (i.e., 357 out of 535 seats). Since Mussolini had the backing of the nation as a whole, there was little mystery as to who would be the beneficiary of the new system. And, in fact, in April 1924, general elections were held, and Mussolini's list of candidates received three-fifths of the over seven million votes cast, and the premier thereby secured a two-thirds' majority in Parliament. Henceforth, he had a captive Parliament at his beck and call, and the forms of constitutional government would receive only casual attention.

In the meantime, Mussolini's reputation as Italy's Man of the Hour was enhanced by a series of successes in both domestic and foreign affairs. At home, there was an automatic improvement in the situation by the fact of Mussolini's ascension to power. Fascist Black Shirts no longer felt the need to roam the streets in search of their Socialist enemies, since the latter had been effectively deprived even of the possibility of political power by virtue of Mussolini's electoral reforms. Socialist-inspired strikes were, as a result of the same causes, a thing of the past. Moreover, Mussolini struck at the very heart of domestic discontent by simplifying the tax system in such a way that the wealthy were made to bear a larger, and more just, share of the burden.

It was abroad, however, that Mussolini scored the successes which convinced the Italian public that, under him, Italy would achieve that share of glory which was its proper destiny. In August 1923, an Italian general and his staff were assassinated on Greek territory while on an official mission for the Conference of Ambassadors in Paris. Mussolini immediately issued an ultimatum to the Greek government, demanding humiliating apologies, capital punishment for the assassins, and reparations of fifty million lire. The Greeks indignantly rejected the ultimatum, and, for a few days, Mussolini seemed determined to resort to force to exact acquiescence in his demands. At the last moment, however, the Conference of Ambassadors intervened, and presented Italy's demands in a more acceptable form, to Athens. The Greeks, with the British, French, and Italians all arrayed against them, could do nothing but submit, and the incident was hailed in Italy as a great diplomatic victory for Mussolini and as a vindication of Italy's status as a Great Power. It was, however, with respect to the perennial question of Fiume that Mussolini did the most for Italian self-respect. In January 1924, he negotiated an agreement with the government of Yugoslavia whereby the status of Fiume as a Free State, as defined by the Treaty of Rapallo, was abolished, and Italy, in return for minor concessions to the Yugoslavs, received the controversial port, as well as the Delta and Port Barros. For the brilliant *coup* of the

Pact of Rome, as the agreement was called, Mussolini received the acclamation of all Italy, and Italy's highest honor, the Collar of the Annunziata. The former anti-monarchist, anti-aristocrat and "workman among workmen," received the title, by virtue of the decoration, of Cousin to the King —in which he seemed to take inordinate delight. D'Annunzio, on this occasion, in recompense for having been so badly treated with regard to Fiume by an earlier government, was consoled with a singularly appropriate title: Prince of Monte Nervoso.

Now, while Mussolini was riding the crest of the wave of popularity, there occurred an incident which, while it was to demonstrate to *Il Duce*— "The Leader"—as Mussolini liked to be called, the ephemeral nature of success and the fickleness of the mob, was also to be the turning point in the character of the Fascist regime. This incident is known as "the Matteotti murder." Giacomo Matteotti was a Socialist, a Deputy, and a forceful opponent of Fascism. On June 11, 1924, he disappeared, after having made a particularly virulent attack on Mussolini in Parliament, and after having made the ill-timed boast that he would shortly expose certain financial scandals involving prominent men in the government. At the time of his disappearance, it was recalled that Mussolini, in the heat of parliamentary passion, had turned upon the unfortunate Deputy and shouted, "What you need is a charge of lead in the back!" Immediately, wild rumors began to circulate throughout Italy, to the effect that Mussolini had, in effect, ordered the murder of Matteotti. Charges and countercharges flew. Three men—all good Fascists—were arrested and tried, and duly convicted; but not until it had come out that Mussolini had let it be known privately that Matteotti must be taught a lesson for his impudence. There was no suggestion, however, that the Duce had meant that his adversary should be killed. Indeed, one of the several ways in which the Fascists were in the habit of teaching "a lesson" to their more articulate critics was by forcibly administering to them epic doses of castor oil, thereby inducing a condition which not only immobilized them for a time, but also wholly humiliated them. Nonetheless, there was a violent public reaction to this evidence. There were whispers of a secret Fascist organization for the liquidation of enemies; of the scandalous protection afforded by the police to Fascist thugs; of the arbitrary nature of governmental practices; and even of the mental stability of the Duce, who could be so inordinately upset by the criticism of an obscure Deputy. In a quick *volte-face,* the public swung from undiluted admiration for Mussolini to an orgy of agonizing over the future, of disillusionment, and of hostility to Fascist policy.

For a time, Mussolini was completely demoralized. Even in Parliament, hitherto docile, there had been unprecedented criticism of Fascist tendencies toward violence. And the foreign press, of course, made a *cause célèbre* of the affair. As a gesture, Mussolini dismissed all members of his government who were, in any way, suspected of being implicated in the Matteotti affair, including Aldo Finzi, Undersecretary of the Interior; and he himself resigned the Ministry of the Interior.

For a time, public disenchantment continued, and the Duce even thought briefly of resigning and asking the king to form a new government. But, in the end, he prevailed. His enemies and critics in Parliament were too irresolute, too much out of the habit of direct action to be able to organize themselves effectively, and they missed their chance to sweep the now-tottering Fascist regime from power. Also, in the provinces, Mussolini's disciples were hard at work in the propaganda mills, charging that the Matteotti affair was merely a plot on the part of the Socialists to discredit Mussolini. Their efforts soon bore fruit, in the form of demonstrations and declarations of loyalty and support from the provincial population. By the end of July, the Duce had so far recovered his equanimity, and his influence, that Parliament was induced to pass a law giving the government the power to suppress newspapers for publishing false news or news "calculated to disturb the public order," for inciting to crime, for evoking class hatred, for attacking the king, the pope, religion, or the state. It was Mussolini's first overt move against the constitutional freedoms of Italy, and one to which he was pushed by—or at least for which he took the pretext from—the storm of criticism provoked by the Matteotti murder.

The suppression of the liberty of the press was merely the beginning. The years from 1925 to 1929 marked the transformation of Mussolini from the leader of a political party and the constitutionally appointed premier of Italy into a dictator. There was no pretense of writing a new constitution for Italy. The monarchy was retained, which allowed, and gave the color of truth, to Mussolini's declaration that it was his intention not to subvert the constitution, but to restore to it its original meaning. Within that framework of interpretation, Mussolini, aided by a Parliament now as subservient as ever, and allowed by a hopelessly disorganized opposition, was able to accomplish specific changes. He himself was transformed from Premier into Head of the State—*Capo di Stato*. As such, he was no longer to be responsible to Parliament, but to the Crown alone. Moreover, by the same act of legislation, he was granted the power of ruling by decree. And his power therefore, by the beginning of 1926, had become essentially dictatorial.

This virtual abandonment of a parliamentary regime in favor of dictatorial rule, which was hastened, if not actually caused, by the sense of political insecurity which the Matteotti affair had aroused in Mussolini, was fortified by other "reforms." Henceforth, Italy was to be represented in Parliament by a one-party system. At each general election—the first under the new dispensation was held in 1929—the candidates were to be hand-picked by the Fascist Party and submitted to the voters. The latter were left the freedom either to affirm or reject the four hundred individuals on the list. In the elections of 1929, therefore, it was not difficult to understand how the Fascist regime could boast of having won an immense vote of confidence from the people of Italy. Only 1.5 per cent of the eight and one-half million voters registered opposition to Mussolini's list of candidates. It is even less difficult to understand that, after 1929, there was not even a disorganized opposition in Parliament; there was no opposition at all.

The absolute control of the State, the Party, and Parliament which Mussolini now exercised was supported, of necessity, by the bureaucracy of government. The Duce achieved this by the process of giving over into the hands of the Fascists the entire structure of the administrative and civil services, while maintaining the outward forms—the offices, titles, and responsibilities—of traditional value. To control the vast web of interrelated responsibilities thus set up by Mussolini, the Fascist Party was reorganized to render assistance to the Duce. It became the function of the Central Directorate of the Fascist Party—later to be known as the Grand Council of Fascism—to advise Mussolini on matters of policy and practice.

Under the weight of this absolutist Fascist control of the state, it was inevitable that the internal freedom of Italy should break down, for absolutism by its nature requires the abolition of all opposition. Accordingly, beginning in 1925 with the legislation against freedom of the press, Fascist control of the media of communication grew until, by 1930, the government was issuing detailed instructions to the press not only regarding the news that it was allowed to print, but also concerning such things as the relative importance to be attached to each newsworthy item, and the place on the page that such-and-such an item was to occupy. Any editors or journalists who could not bring themselves to agree with the state on these matters were visited by Mussolini's *Opera volontaria repressione antifascista,* or O.V.R.A.—the inevitable secret police. Continued resistance to the dictates of Fascism was rewarded by an indefinite stay on one of Italy's tiny islands, many of which served as concentration camps, although relatively comfortable ones.

Particular stress was laid upon the formation of Italian youth in a mold

The Age of Fascism

acceptable to Fascism. As early as 1922, Giovanni Gentile, the philosopher, was commissioned to undertake a plan for the reform of the Italian educational system. This "reform" was aimed at producing a generation schooled in the values of Fascism rather than in the customary humanistic studies, and in producing a political elite rather than an intellectual one. To that end, teachers were carefully screened, a good part of the curriculum was devoted to obvious exercises in indoctrination, and textbooks were rewritten shamelessly to reflect the doctrines of the Fascist state. Parallel to these policies was the organization of clubs of Young Fascists, whose purpose it was to complement the work of the schools by instilling into the minds of Italy's new generation the ideology of Fascism, and to provide military training.

The grip which Mussolini thus obtained on the organs of government and of communication, and on the minds of the youth of Italy, would have been unavailing, however, without considerable attention to the economic problems of Italy. It was, after all, the existence, in an aggravated state, of those problems which had brought Fascism to power. Shortly after his accession to power, Mussolini had been able, as has been noted, to eliminate the strikes that had crippled the Italian economy for so long, and, with commendable diligence, he had succeeded in putting order into the finances of the government. But he was not long content with these achievements. After 1925, he worked steadily to extend Fascist control to every area of the economy. Declaring that class struggle was archaic, and that capital and labor had, in the Fascist state, common rather than opposing interests, the Duce and his advisers began to evolve what came to be known as the Corporate State. According to that concept, "the Italian nation is an organism endowed with a purpose, a life, and means of action which transcend those of individuals or groups of individuals." The state, therefore, was a "corporation"—or, perhaps more accurately, a "co-operative" of which the government was the manager—and this Corporate State "considers that, in the sphere of production . . . the private organization of production is a function of national concern, and that the organizer of the enterprise is responsible to the State for the management of its production." And, finally, the conclusion was clearly drawn: "State intervention in economic production will arise where private initiative is lacking or is proved to be inadequate, or when political interests of the state are involved. This intervention may take the form of control, or of assistance, or of direct management." In its final form, the concept of the Corporate State was to be implemented by three units: an association of employers; a syndicate of workers; and a governmental agency to represent the interests of the state. The system was rather slow in evolving. It was not until 1934 that the economic activity of Italy was broken down into corporations —twenty-two of them. By 1938, however, it had progressed so far that the Chamber of Deputies, the lower house of Parliament, was abolished and replaced by a Chamber of Fasces and Corporations, on the principle that it was more sensible to have a political body in which representation was granted on the basis of economic roles rather than on that of geographic location. That principle was to be discarded, along with the entire apparatus of Fascist government, in 1943; yet, the fact remains that it was one of the few truly progressive concepts of Fascist ideology, one based on recognition of the fact that geographic representation answers to the needs of an agricultural society, it is inadequate and unsatisfactory within the context of the modern industrial state.

As Mussolini worked at the revolution of the political and economic life of Italy during the late 1920s, he was also busy, less openly but nonetheless diligently, in an enterprise which was to prove the most enduring achievement, and the most brilliant success, of his career: the reconciliation between Italy and the Vatican. Since 1870, the pope had been the self-proclaimed "prisoner of the Vatican." Pius IX at that time had refused to recognize the nascent Kingdom of Italy, refused to accept an offered annual subsidy from the Italian government, refused to allow Catholics to participate in the political life of Italy, and refused generally to accept the fact that, for better or worse, the little kingdom which had been established during the Renaissance and bequeathed to him by his predecessors was irrevocably gone. His attitude was that he had been deprived of what was rightfully his, and he laid formal claim to the property of which he had been forcibly dispossessed. Leo XIII, Pius' successor, had been of the same mind, and under him what might have been, in Pio Nono, merely the understandable desire to salvage what remained of one's pride, became a policy of the Church. And there matters remained, until the time of Mussolini.

Mussolini, for his part, had, early in his career, proclaimed the need for a reconciliation between state and Church. In 1922, upon the elevation of Pius XI, he had publicly demonstrated his openness toward the Vatican by going to the Piazza San Pietro to witness the white smoke which marked the election of a new pope. At the end of 1925, he and his (civil-law) wife of many years, Rachele, had had their union blessed in a Catholic church in Milan—an obvious gesture toward the Vatican, as well as toward public opinion. On the other side, the reigning pope, Pius XI—a man no less resolute than Mussolini, and hardly less dictatorial—had demonstrated the same conciliatory spirit by showing himself outside St. Peter's to bless the faithful—the first time in half a century that a pope had done so.

The work of reconciliation itself was long and difficult. Negotiations were begun as early as 1926, with an exchange of memoranda on a non-committally low level. There were stops and starts, misunderstandings and misinterpretations, deliberate and accidental, with both sides playing an elaborate game of semantic chess. By the end of 1928, however, most of the difficulties had been removed, and the King appointed Mussolini to act as his delegate in concluding the negotiations. Pius XI appointed, for a similar function, his Secretary of State, the formidable Cardinal Gasparri, and Francesco Pacelli, brother of the future Pius XII. The final treaties were signed at the Lateran on February 11, 1929, by Mussolini for Italy and by Gasparri for the Holy See. Under the terms of these agreements—there were two separate treaties: the Lateran Treaty and the Concordat, the former regulating the terms of the reconciliation of Church and state regarding the status of the Vatican, and the latter governing future relations between the papacy and Italy—Italy recognized the Holy See as a sovereign power, while the Holy See recognized the existence of the Kingdom of Italy and declared itself satisfied as to the "Roman question." The pope received as his "state" the palace and grounds of the Vatican, and the Basilica of St. Peter and its adjacent piazza, along with an indemnity of one billion, seven hundred and fifty million lire. According to the terms of the Concordat, the state was to guarantee religious education in schools up to and including those of the secondary level, and religious marriages were declared to be legally binding. Divorce was not to be allowed under any circumstances, and all annulments were reserved to the ecclesiastical rather than to the civil courts—the latter being a point on which Mussolini was sorely disappointed, but concerning which he had found Pius XI intractable. "The trouble is that we both have the same mentality—that of the peasant," he admitted ruefully.

The Lateran Treaty and the Concordat were hardly to assure enduring harmony between the papacy and Italy, and, between 1929 and Mussolini's fall in 1943, there were to be many severe and public clashes regarding education, persecution of Italian Jews, and so forth. For the moment, however, it appeared that the agreement between Church and state had put the final seal on Italian unity, and there was great rejoicing in the streets, in government buildings, and at the Quirinale.

Mussolini was fortunate enough to be able to follow up this brilliant diplomatic success with others of a more immediately practical nature. At the same time—in the period between 1929 and 1935—he began to lay the foundations of the policies which were eventually to become his nemesis. In the former category, he brought Italy through the difficult years of the Depression with comparatively little trouble. By means of stringent wage and price controls, the lira was forcibly stabilized while the value of other European currencies was falling precipitously. Similarly, in order to prevent the outflow of capital, it became necessary to reduce imports greatly, and, so as to offset the losses thus incurred, Mussolini instituted a system of competitive production among the various provinces. The system—dramatically called "the Battle of the Grain"—was so successful that, by 1933, Italy had reduced the importation of grain by ninety per cent. But Mussolini's most striking success was to be in the area of public works, in a project of land reclamation known as the *Bonifica Integrale*. Included in this program was the draining of the Pontine Marshes—a vast malarial bog between Rome and Terracina—by which about 150,000 acres of fertile land were added to Italy's resources. Similar reclamation work was undertaken in Sardinia, Tuscany, Venetia, the valley of the Po, and Puglia; by the end of 1933, over nine million acres had been reclaimed. At the same time, roads and canals were constructed, public services were instituted, new towns were built, and malaria was virtually eradicated. The *Bonifica Integrale,* in all of its aspects, was Mussolini's most enduring, and therefore his most valuable, gift to Italy. And it was the one of which he was most proud.

Italian affairs at the international level during this period did not hold nearly the same promise for the future as those at home. For one thing, Italian bitterness toward France, which had begun as a result of Italy's disappointment in the peace treaty following World War I, was now exacerbated by an acrimonious debate over naval power; that is, over control of the Mediterranean, which Mussolini, with wholly Italianate pride, insisted in regarding as *Mare Nostrum* (as the Romans had called it), "Our Sea." Things reached such a pass in this respect that the British Foreign Office was already fearful that Italy might well leave the Anglo-French bloc in order to form a closer relationship with its erstwhile enemy, Germany.

As it turned out, such fears were not without some foundation in fact. As an unabashed dictator and self-proclaimed champion of Italian glory and nationalism, Mussolini was in basic sympathy with Adolf Hitler, the fiery National Socialist and advocate of "German destiny" who came to power in 1933. He was not ready, however, either to reject his understanding with Great Britain and France, or to ally himself with the growing Nazi power to the north. Hitler's destiny was still far too uncertain, and the power of the British and the French still far too certain, for prudence to counsel such a move. Mussolini therefore decided to play a waiting game before finally choosing sides, and, in the meanwhile, to extract as many advantages as possible for Italy from the situation.

It was in the spirit of this rather dangerous game that Mussolini invited Hitler to visit him at Venice in June 1934, and thus began that long association which was to endure to the end of his life. Nonetheless, at this first meeting, Mussolini was not impressed by his German counterpart, and he described him later—in private, of course—as *un buffone*, "a clown." Hitler, for his part—although Mussolini had seized the opportunity to lecture him severely on the folly of persecuting the Jews of Germany—came away from the visit under the spell of Mussolini's considerable personal charm. "He strikes the Caesarean pose that is necessary for Italians," he said, "but . . . in personal conversation he becomes human and quite agreeable." Mussolini's "Caesarean pose" was, however, something more than a pose, as Hitler soon discovered. In the month following Hitler's visit to Venice, Engelbert Dollfuss, Chancellor of Austria, to whom Mussolini had committed himself for the defense of Austrian boundaries, was brutally assassinated by a group of Nazi thugs. There was little doubt that the German government was behind the crime, or that, despite Hitler's repeated denials, the assassination was the first step in a planned German takeover of Austria. Mussolini acted promptly. He ordered a concentration of troops on the Austrian frontier and publicly assured the government of Austria of his determination to defend, by force if necessary, the independence of Austria. At this show of force, Hitler quickly changed his mood from one of jubilation to one of public penitence. He expressed his condolences to the Austrians, and then turned over the assassins to them, while the German minister in Vienna was recalled in disgrace.

Mussolini's action had very likely saved Austria, at least for a time, from German conquest. And it had greatly increased the Duce's prestige both in Italy herself and throughout the world, for by now people everywhere were becoming uneasy at the transparent ambitions of the German dictator. But it also had an unforeseen and ironic effect: that of beginning the process of driving Mussolini into the arms of Germany. Mussolini was able to conclude on the basis of this incident that France and England, for all their brave words, were not likely to offer much resistance to Hitler's plans in Europe. The two nations who had had the most to fear from a resurgence of German militarism had sat idly by during the Austrian crisis, while Italy, the weakest of the former Allies, had been left alone to face the threat of a possible war with the Nazi state—a state to which Italy, because (as Hitler was fond of pointing out, quite rightly) of a "common ideology," should be bound by ties of friendship and shared ambitions.

The process of alienation from England and France, and the alternate process of forging the Italo-German "Axis" (the word was coined by Mussolini himself), was virtually completed by the circumstances attendant upon the realization of Italy's ambitions in Abyssinia in 1935. Mussolini had long kept an eye on that East-African state. During the decade of his rule, he had attempted to secure for Italy a special place there, and he had concluded an agreement with the Emperor of Abyssinia to that effect in 1928—an agreement the terms of which were thereafter studiously ignored by the Abyssinians. In 1932, however, he had determined that treaties of friendship were no road to Italian domination in Abyssinia, and he accordingly dispatched his Minister for Colonial Affairs, Emilio De Bono, to East Africa to report on the prospects of an outright conquest. De Bono's report was favorable, and thereafter Mussolini's plans for Abyssinia became increasingly obvious. Early in 1935, active preparations for an invasion were under way on the pretext that Abyssinian forces had attacked an Italian garrison at Wal-Wal, near the junction of Italian Somaliland, British Somaliland, and Abyssinia. Europe buzzed with reports that a million Italians were under arms. The British and French governments made numerous clumsy attempts to dissuade Mussolini from the proposed African adventure, but the Duce was intransigent; he could see no reason why Italy should refrain from a course of action that England and France had both pursued so successfully, and with such impunity, for such a long period of time. Finally, the French Foreign Minister, Pierre Laval, and the British Foreign Secretary, Sir Samuel Hoare, realizing that Mussolini could not be moved by mere words, let it be known that, if Italy moved into Abyssinia, the League of Nations would intervene. They were as good as their word and, on October 11, 1935, the League imposed, or attempted to impose, a series of economic sanctions on Italy as "an aggressor," by virtue of which all shipments of oil, coal, steel, and iron to Italy were to be forbidden. By the beginning of November, however, it had become clear that the members of the League of Nations were unwilling to sacrifice a possible profit for the sake of Abyssinia, who was also a member in good standing. In Italy, of course, the proposed sanctions were denounced as "a plot to suffocate the Italian people economically," and public indignation over the perfidy of Britain and the duplicity of France reached fever pitch. There were daily reminders in the press that it was France and England who, having deprived Italy of her just share of the spoils of the World War, were now determined to exclude her from a colonial empire. In the

The Age of Fascism

midst of this storm, Hitler was reported to have remarked that, although he feared that Mussolini was hostile to Germany, nonetheless he wished the Italians well in their Abyssinian ambitions for the sake of their "common ideology." This comment of course made its way to Rome, as it was intended to do, and was widely commented upon and contrasted with the attitude of Italy's French and English "allies."

By the end of the year, Mussolini had become convinced that no European power would dare to marshal more than words against the complete subjugation of Abyssinia. On January 12, 1936, therefore, the Italian commander in East Africa, Marshal Badoglio, launched a major offensive against the forces of Haile Selassie, the Emperor of Abyssinia. On May 5, after a campaign of four months in which disorganized companies of native soldiers, equipped with spears and bows and arrows fought against twelve Italian divisions with air and artillery support, Addis Ababa, the Emperor's capital city, fell. A few days later, Mussolini announced the annexation of Abyssinia, and the assumption by the King of Italy of the title of Emperor of Abyssinia. The King returned the favor by offering to Mussolini the title of Prince, which the Duce refused, and Italy's highest military decoration, the Grand Cross of the Order of Savoy, which he accepted. Crowds of joyful and proud Italians danced in the streets, and mobs milled about in Rome's Piazza Venezia under the balcony of Mussolini's office, shouting in hypnotic unison, *"Du-ce, Du-ce!"* It was the proudest moment of Mussolini's long career, and one which was fully shared by the people of Italy, from King Victor Emmanuel to the meanest peasant. It disturbed no one in the land that Mussolini, encouraged by Germany, had undertaken an adventure which, while adding little to Italy's practical well-being, had alienated her from France and England and, at the same time, seriously depleted her financial, economic, and material resources. No one seemed even to have an inkling of the fact that Italy was being driven into an association with Germany against which her instincts, her history, her traditions, and her judgment all rebelled. No one, that is, except perhaps the Duce himself, for in the next year, he was to recall that "the Axis was born in 1936."

Events now moved forward at a pace which, in little more than three years, would complete the work begun by the Italian annexation of Abyssinia. In July 1936, only two months after the Italian victory in Africa, General Francisco Franco, commander of the garrison in Spanish Morocco, staged a military revolt against the military government of Spain. The conflict spread and flared up into civil war, with the Insurgents under Franco on one side, and the Loyalists or Republicans, on the other. Mussolini had little use for democracies or for democratic forms of government —a taste in which he had been lately strengthened by his experiences with France and Great Britain—and his natural inclination was to support the ambitious, if somewhat idealistic, Franco. The latter, aware of the Duce's sympathy for right-wing convictions, requested Mussolini's help, in the form of several airplanes. The aircraft were sent secretly, and more followed. But by the middle of 1936, Italian aid had increased to the point where secrecy was not possible, and Mussolini, throwing caution to winds, allowed a volunteer force of Italians to join Franco's forces in Spain. Thereafter, the Duce's devotion to Franco's cause increased until there were an estimated seventy thousand Italian troops fighting against the Republicans in Spain. At the same time, the other European powers were also becoming involved in the struggle. France and Russia sent aid to the Loyalists. England recognized the Republican government as the only legal one, but a distaste for fighting alongside the Russian Communists kept her from sending material aid to that government. Germany, meanwhile, made a careful choice, and joined Italy on the side of Franco. It was a choice dictated, not as Mussolini's had been, by ideological considerations, but by reasons of practical policy. "We do not desire a complete victory for Franco," Hitler said later. "Rather, we are interested in a continuance of the war and in keeping up tensions in the Mediterranean area." At the same time, the German ambassador in Rome was explaining exactly what Hitler meant:

> The role played by the war in Spain . . . could be similar to that of the Abyssinian conflict. It would bring out clearly the actually opposite interests of the powers and thus prevent Italy from being drawn into the net of the Western powers. . . . The struggle for political dominance in Spain lays bare the natural opposition between Italy and France, and, at the same time, it emphasizes the competition, in the western Mediterranean, between Italy's position and that of Great Britain. Thus, all the more clearly will Italy recognize the advisability of confronting the Western powers shoulder to shoulder with Germany.

Time proved the German ambassador to be a prophet. As the Spanish Civil War dragged on, and as the scale of Italian intervention increased, the rift between Italy and France and England became more pronounced. By 1937, Italian submarines were attacking British supply ships bound for Spain—an act of virtual piracy that the proud British would not easily forgive. At the same time, Hitler was working unceasingly to draw Mussolini and Italy into a net of his own weaving. In 1936, Count Galeazzo

Ciano, Mussolini's Foreign Minister and son-in-law, was invited to visit Hitler in Germany. He went, and he returned to Italy with stories of Hitler's respect for Mussolini and for Italy. "Mussolini," Hitler had said, "is the greatest statesman in the world, and no one can begin to compare to him." Together, Germany and Italy were more than a match for the rest of Europe, and, Hitler reminded Ciano, "German and Italian rearmament is proceeding much more rapidly than is possible in England. . . . In three years, Germany will be ready; in four, she will be more than ready." Mussolini, flattered, listened carefully, and remembered.

By 1937, relations between Germany and Italy were so cordial, and those between the latter and France and England had deteriorated to such an extent, that Mussolini himself was invited to visit Hitler at Munich. He went, and he was as much impressed by the evidence of military strength that he saw as he was pleased by the personal deference that the German dictator showed to him. Later in this visit, at Berlin, Mussolini proclaimed to the world that the two "revolutions," the Fascist and the National Socialist, shared a common purpose; that Italy and Germany were irrevocably bound together; and that Fascism would march to the end with National Socialism. A crowd of a million Berliners applauded the Duce's words, and Mussolini returned to Italy absolutely convinced now that Italy's future lay with Germany. He acted accordingly. Only a few weeks after the visit to Germany, Italy signed the Anti-Comintern Pact, originally conceived by Germany and Japan, and committed herself with the other two powers to the containment of world Communism.

With Italy now firmly in his camp, and the rest of Europe still distracted —as he had intended that they should be—by the Spanish Civil War, Hitler now felt free to proceed with the plans that Mussolini had interrupted a few years previously. At midnight, on March 11, 1938, German troops marched into Austria. Earlier in the day, Hitler had sent Mussolini a message explaining the forthcoming move, and pleading that the *Anschluss,* as the rape of Austria was known, was necessary on the grounds of self-defense. Mussolini, the man who, only a few years before, had been willing to go to the brink of war for the sake of Austrian independence, now refused to question the prudence, let alone the justice, of his German colleague's action. Prince Philip of Hess, Hitler's representative in Rome, reported the Duce's reaction to his master: "The Duce accepted the whole thing in a very friendly manner. He sends you his regards. . . . Schuschnigg [the Austrian Chancellor] had given him the news, and Mussolini replied that Austria was immaterial to him."

Barely two months later, Hitler was in Rome on a state visit to his new ally, and no expense or trouble was spared to convince the German that Italy was a worthy ally of the Third Reich. There were military parades, and an impressive naval display at Naples. As Hitler prepared to return to Germany, the Duce, in his farewell, took the hand of his guest and said solemnly, "From now on, there is no power that will be able to pull us apart." Hitler's eyes, a witness reports, filled with tears.

Hitler doubtless had reason to be grateful for the Duce's declaration of solidarity. One of the things which he had discussed with Mussolini during the visit was the question of Czechoslovakia, a nation which figured in Hitler's mind as the next victim of the Third Reich. Mussolini several times disclaimed any interest in the fate of that nation. He knew that it was useless to attempt to dissuade Hitler; and he believed, moreover, that Germany was perfectly capable of taking over Czechoslovakia without precipitating a European war.

By September, German Storm-Trooper formations were openly operating within Czechoslovakia, and all Europe was now aware of Hitler's intentions. Any doubts that may still have existed were banished by an ultimatum, amounting to a demand for total capitulation, from Germany to Eduard Beneš, the Czech president. Mussolini was still convinced that war would be avoided, although there were reports that both England and France, who were bound by treaty to protect Czechoslovakia from aggression, were on the point of complete mobilization. "The Duce . . . agrees that the situation is very serious," Ciano recorded, "but he believes that Beneš will end up by accepting the ultimatum." In order to bring pressure on Beneš to do so, Mussolini, on September 18, in a speech at Trieste, announced to the world that, in the event of war, Italy would "know who her friends are." A week later, he assured the German ambassador in Rome that, if war broke out, Italy would enter the conflict on Germany's side as soon as there had been a declaration of war from England. On September 26, he ordered mobilization for the following day.

Mussolini, however, for all his saber rattling, was still convinced that open conflict would be avoided. And, as though to confirm his irrational position, fate intervened, in the form of Neville Chamberlain, the British prime minister, who, on September 28, requested that Mussolini should mediate with Hitler in order to preserve world peace. The Duce agreed, and immediately contacted Hitler, offering, as the basis for an agreement with England and France, that Czechoslovakia would cede to Germany the Sudetenland. Hitler agreed, and Mussolini proposed that the representatives of Germany, France, England, and Italy meet immediately to effect the transfer. Again, Hitler agreed, stipulating only that Mussolini himself attend the meeting as Italy's representative.

Of the four leaders who assembled in Munich for the conference on the following day (September 29), only Mussolini had reason to look forward to the negotiations, and only he acquitted himself reasonably well. Mr. Chamberlain for Great Britain, and Edouard Daladier for France, traveled to the meeting place with the consciousness that they were about to betray an ally and, for the sake—or rather for the flimsiest hope—of "peace in our time," to sacrifice a nation to German ambition. Hitler, for his part, was furious at Mussolini's interference. The Sudetenland, with its large German population, had been the pretext of his threats, but not its purpose. He had envisaged nothing less than the conquest of the whole of Czechoslovakia. Mussolini, on the other hand, had fulfilled his obligation to Germany by publicly pledging support in the event of hostilities. And now, he was being acclaimed all over the world as the man who had preserved the peace of Europe. The Duce, in fact, was the guiding spirit of the conference, and, under his highly informal but nonetheless effective chairmanship, the surrender of the Sudetenland was accomplished while Hitler sat in sullen silence. Mussolini's sense of triumph accompanied him back to Italy, where he was greeted everywhere by enthusiastic crowds, and in Rome by a grateful King Victor Emmanuel. The sole voice that was heard to protest in Italy was that of Pope Pius XI, who, in a peace message, chose to speak of St. Wencelaus, a Czech martyr, in words clearly intended to refer to the martyrdom of the Czechoslovak nation. The words were more prophetic than the pope knew, for the final act of the tragedy of Czechoslovakia was about to be played out. In March 1939, barely four months after the Munich conference, German troops moved into the Czech provinces of Bohemia and Moravia. That night (March 15), Hitler proudly announced to the world that "Czechoslovakia has ceased to exist." France and England sat quietly in a mortified silence, and did nothing. Mussolini, who had not been privy to this new facet of Hitler's plans, complained that "every time Hitler occupies a country, he sends me a message." But he, too, could do nothing to halt the now virtually irreversible march toward catastrophe.

3. *The End of a Dream* (1939–1945)

In the eyes of Italy and Germany, and indeed of the whole world, Mussolini had, by his acts and attitudes, almost inextricably linked the destiny of the Italians to that of the Germans. All that was lacking was a formal military alliance between the countries, and that was not long in coming. Joachim von Ribbentrop, Hitler's Foreign Minister, had approached his Italian counterpart, Count Ciano, on the matter in the fall of 1937; but Mussolini had been frightened off by Ciano's conclusion that "He [Hitler] does not name the enemy, nor does he mention his objectives; but he wants war during the next three or four years." Moreover, Italy was, as Mussolini knew, unprepared, either militarily or from the standpoint of public opinion, for such an engagement. Nonetheless, the Duce was quick to assure the Germans, he agreed in principle to the necessity for such an alliance, and he would revert to the matter as soon as public opinion could be won over.

A double opportunity for Mussolini to act came within the next few months. In Spain, General Franco's forces had captured Madrid on March 28, 1938, and Valencia on March 30. With the occupation of these two cities, the Spanish Civil War ended. Italy celebrated the event with great joy and much acclamation of the Duce; and, in the public mind, Franco's victory appeared as the first sampling of the glories that awaited a joining of arms between Italy and Germany, as had occurred in Spain. At the same time, Mussolini was preparing a *coup* that was at once to even the score between Italy and Germany and to demonstrate conclusively—if such proof were needed—that Italy had entered upon the path already marked out by Germany. For some years, the Duce, encouraged by Ciano, had been itching to emulate Hitler's territorial acquisitiveness; and now the time seemed right to do so. England and France had already shown, by their acquiescence in the rape of Austria and Czechoslovakia, their unwillingness to intervene in favor of "a faraway country, between people of whom we know nothing," as Neville Chamberlain's unhappy phrase had it. And Germany itself, now comfortably in possession of the territory, people, and resources of two countries to which it had not the shred of a legal claim, could hardly object if its unofficial ally across the Alps helped itself to a bit of loot. This was particularly true since the object of Mussolini's ambitions was Albania, a poor and insignificant country across the Adriatic which was already virtually an Italian protectorate. On the day of the fall of Madrid, therefore, Mussolini issued an ultimatum to King Zog of Albania, which that monarch—as the Duce fully expected him to do— rejected. On April 7—Good Friday—Italian troops landed in Albania, and on April 8, the capital city, Tirana, fell to the invading forces while King Zog and his family fled toward Greece. On April 16, King Victor Emmanuel united to his Italian crown that of Albania, and the latter country became an Italian province.

Reaction in Europe was about what Mussolini had expected. The French government seemed hardly to have noted the Italian aggression. The British made a vigorous protest—and then were content to let the matter drop. And Hitler was delighted. The Italian action—which Mussolini had intended to a certain extent as the assertion of Italian independence—was recognized by the astute German dictator for what it was in fact: the forging of a bond between Italy and Germany which emphasized the common position between the two countries *vis à vis* those defenders of the *status quo,* Britain and France. It was now time, Hitler concluded, to press Mussolini for the promised military alliance. Accordingly, von Ribbentrop was once again dispatched to Italy, where he met with Ciano in Milan on May 6. In his briefcase, Ciano carried a memorandum from the Duce emphasizing that Italy required, absolutely, a period of peace of at least three years. To this stipulation, the Nazi Foreign Minister was perfectly willing to agree. He frankly informed Ciano that Hitler intended to recover for Germany the Free City of Danzig, and to close the "Polish corridor" which separated East Prussia from the rest of the Reich. But, he declared, "Germany also is in need of a period of peace of certainly not less than four or five years." Thus reassured, Ciano, the following day, announced that the terms of an Italo-German alliance had been agreed on. And, on May 22, the famous Pact of Steel was signed between the two powers, the significant sections of which are the second, third, and fifth articles:

> Article II. Should the common interests of the contracting parties be endangered by international events of any kind, then they will enter immediately into discussions over the steps to be taken for the protection of those interests. If the security or vital interests of one of the contracting parties should be threatened from without, then the other will give to the threatened party its full political and diplomatic support in order to neutralize this threat.
> Article III. If, contrary to the wishes and hopes of the contracting parties, it happens that either one of them becomes involved in hostilities with another Power or Powers, then the other contracting party will come immediately to its side as an ally, and will support it, with all its military forces, on land, on the sea, and in the air. . . .
> Article V. The contracting parties undertake now that, in the event of a war conducted in common, they will conclude an armistice and peace only in full agreement with one another.

Mussolini was immensely pleased with this agreement; and even Ciano, who distrusted the Germans, seemed at ease. The Italian people, however, expressed little enthusiasm for the alliance; and the King, who usually was one with his people in their sentiments, spoke to Mussolini of the Teutonic insolence and duplicity of the Germans and called the new allies of Italy "rascals" and "beggars" who would, at the first opportunity, reveal their true colors. But Mussolini was not concerned. Germany had guaranteed at least three years of peace. And, in three years, Italy would be ready for anything.

It is interesting to speculate on what would have been the outcome for Europe, and for the world, if Mussolini indeed had been granted the three years' respite on which he banked so confidently. But, while the Duce was beginning, at a leisurely pace, to prepare Italy for a distant and hypothetical war, Adolf Hitler was already laying detailed plans for an immediate conflict. On the very day following the signing of the Pact of Steel, he announced to his military war council in Berlin that "Danzig is not the object of our activities. It is a question of expanding our living-space in the east and of securing our source of food and of settling the Baltic problem. . . . There is no question of sparing Poland; we are left with this conclusion: to attack Poland at the first suitable opportunity. We cannot expect a repetition of the Czech affair. There will be war . . . The basic principle is: conflict with Poland, beginning with an attack on Poland. . . ." Within a short time, there were unmistakable signs that something was in the air in Berlin. Dr. Goebbels, Hitler's Minister of Propaganda, made a violent and public attack on Poland for suppressing the rights of the German population of Danzig—a statement ominously reminiscent of the deluge of abuse that had preceded the Nazi takeover of Austria and Czechoslovakia.

Everyone, it seems, interpreted these signals correctly except Mussolini and Ciano. Bernardo Attolico, the Italian ambassador in Berlin, sent repeated and urgent warnings that matters were taking a fatal course. Sir Percy Loraine, the British envoy in Rome, brought a personal message from Chamberlain stressing the perilous nature of the situation. With respect to Attolico, the Duce and his Foreign Minister concluded that their ambassador "has allowed himself to be taken in by the war scare." And to Chamberlain's warning, Mussolini, feeling that, with war several years away, he could afford to be insolent to the British, answered that "if England is going to fight in defense of Poland, then Italy will take up arms with her German ally." It was not until the end of July 1939, after reports by Italy's military attaché in Berlin of strong troop concentrations along the Polish frontier, and after another torrent of warnings from Attolico, that the Duce and Ciano began to suspect that, after all, Hitler may have been less than candid with them about his intentions. Ciano immediately proposed that he meet with Ribbentrop to discuss the situation. Mussolini agreed, and once more prepared a memorandum stating that, while war might be inevitable, the chances of German and Italian victory would be far better if the conflict were postponed for three or four years.

Ciano and Ribbentrop met at Salzburg on August 11, and spent ten hours together. The Italian pleaded, with all the considerable eloquence at his command, for a postponement of the "solution to the Polish question," but Ribbentrop was totally deaf both to rhetoric and to reason. "He gives the impression," Ciano noted, "of an unreasonable and obstinate determination to bring about this conflict." Ciano then tried to elicit some explicit information concerning Germany's immediate plans; but once more the German refused to co-operate, pleading, in Ciano's phrase, that "all decisions were still locked in the impenetrable bosom of the Fuehrer." The Italian diplomat now tried a different line of approach, suggesting that the matter of Poland in general, and of Danzig in particular, might be settled to everyone's satisfaction at a conference attended by Germany, Italy, France, Britain, Poland, and Spain. But Ribbentrop dismissed the notion with a brusqueness that bordered on the insulting. The next day, Ciano met with Hitler himself at the Nazi leader's mountain retreat. Hitler was more courteous than Ribbentrop, but equally adamant. He was determined, Ciano reported, "to take advantage of the next political provocation to attack Poland within forty-eight hours and to solve the problem in that way." To Ciano's protestations that Italy was unprepared for war, and that she had never been informed by Germany of the seriousness of the situation, Hitler loftily replied that, in view of Italy's unpreparedness, he was prepared to dispense with Italian aid during the campaign against Poland. It was an outraged and disappointed Ciano who wrote in his journal that night: "I am returning to Rome completely disgusted with the Germans, with their leader, and with their way of doing things. They have betrayed us, and they have lied to us. Now, they are dragging us into an adventure which we do not want and which may well compromise the regime and the country." From that conference until the end of his life, Ciano remained implacably anti-German.

Mussolini, meanwhile, vacillated between the extremes of fear and ambition. Basically an indecisive man, he was torn between the dread of Hitler's reproaches if Italy seemed afraid to honor her commitments under the Pact of Steel, and the conviction that, if Germany waged a successful war without Italy, then Italy would be deprived of a share in the spoils. One day, the Duce would assure Ciano that neutrality seemed Italy's only hope; on the next, the Foreign Minister would find Mussolini drafting a telegram to Hitler stating that "As soon as you cross the [Polish] frontier, I shall be at your side." It was Hitler who finally decided, albeit tentatively, the issue. On August 21, Ribbentrop telephoned to inform Ciano that Germany was about to sign a non-aggression pact with the Soviet Union. The news fell like a bombshell in Rome, for the Italians, while they were aware of Hitler's wish to reach an agreement with the Russians, had had no idea that a pact was imminent. Mussolini's first reaction was a conviction that a German victory in Poland was now assured, and that France and England would not dare intervene. Yet, after a few hours' thought, he realized that Italy's lack of preparation for a major war, and the chaotic state of the Italian army, made it necessary—now that he obviously must make up his mind one way or the other—to decline to participate in Hitler's war. At Ciano's insistence, therefore, on August 25 he composed a letter to the German dictator in which, after expressing his understanding and appreciation of Hitler's position in seeking a pact with Moscow, he stated:

> As for the *practical* position of Italy in the event of a military confrontation, my attitude is as follows: If Germany attacks Poland and the conflict remains localized, Italy will afford Germany every form of political and economic assistance that is requested of her. If Germany attacks, and Poland's allies open a counterattack against Germany, I must warn you now that it would be better if I did not take the *initiative* in military operations in view of the *present* state of Italy's war preparations, of which we have repeatedly and in good time informed you, Fuehrer, and Herr von Ribbentrop. Our intervention can, however, take place at once if Germany delivers to us immediately the military supplies and the raw materials to resist the attack which the French and the English would direct against us.

Hitler was both shaken and angered by Mussolini's decision. "The Italians are behaving just as they did in 1914," he exclaimed to his staff. Still, he could not afford to alienate the Duce, on whose eventual military assistance he still counted.

His response to Mussolini's letter, and to the Duce's further protestations of his good intentions, was carefully sympathetic:

> Duce, I respect the motives and influences which have determined your decision. Perhaps it will nevertheless be for the best. It is my opinion, however, that, until the outbreak of the struggle, the world should have no hint of the

attitude which Italy intends to adopt. I therefore ask that you support me psychologically, with your press and by other means. I also ask, Duce, if at all possible, that you compel Britain and France, by obvious military measures, to tie down some of their forces. . . .

Thus reassured, and publicly absolved of any obligation to act in the event of war between Germany and Poland, Mussolini might have been expected to be considerably relieved. But such was not the case. By August 29, he was again restless. He felt that a German attack on Poland was imminent, and that Italy would be regarded as cowardly for not joining in alongside her German allies. "The idea of neutrality weighs heavily upon him," Ciano noted. "Not being able to wage war, he makes all the necessary preparations, so that, in case of a peaceful solution, he can say that he would have waged it. . . ." On August 31, the Duce made a final attempt both to regain his lost prestige and to pose as the peacemaker of Europe, by proposing that an international conference be called for September 5 in order to settle matters peaceably. Before any answer could be received from the Powers concerned, however, the news came that, on September 1, 1939, German armies had crossed the frontier into Poland. On September 3, France and Great Britain declared war on Germany. Hermann Goering, whom Hitler had just named as his successor, expressed the reaction of the German people as a whole: "If we lose this one," he muttered, "then God help us."

Italy, as in 1914, remained neutral at the beginning of the conflict. The Duce's attempt to play the part of the mediator came to nothing, since when England and France finally gave an answer to his proposal for an international conference, they stipulated that all German troops must be withdrawn from Poland before the Powers could meet. Nonetheless, as late as the end of September, Mussolini still believed that he could engineer "some possibility of a rapid conclusion to the conflict." It was not until October 6, after Prime Minister Chamberlain's speech in Commons to the effect that "the present German government" was wholly untrustworthy and that "acts alone, not words, must be forthcoming," that Mussolini glumly concluded that "every possibility for an agreement has now disappeared."

During the nine months between the Russo-German invasion of Poland and Italy's entry into the war in June 1940, Mussolini never ceased to bewail Italy's inaction. He was irritated beyond measure, particularly, at the enthusiasm with which the Italians viewed their own neutrality. It was a policy and an attitude vigorously upheld by Ciano and the rest of Mussolini's cabinet, and imposed by Italy's lack of preparedness for war. Yet, it galled the Duce inordinately. Filippo Anfuso, Ciano's secretary, reports that, at this period, "I always found Mussolini in the state of mind of a man who, having decided not to play the game, is nonetheless determined to get into it as soon as he has gathered his strength. . . . I still see Mussolini at that time as a virile recluse, held down by chains." A source of particular irritation was that Hitler and the German armies were covering themselves with the glory of military victory, while Italy, and the Duce himself, who so longed to play the role of conqueror, did nothing. His preoccupation with his own and with Italy's public image was reinforced by an almost irrational jealousy of his German friends. He complained to his intimates that Italy, "having heard my warlike propaganda for eighteen years, cannot now understand how I can play the part of the apostle of peace now that Europe is in flames." And Ciano records that "For Mussolini, the idea of Hitler's waging a war, and worse still, winning it, is altogether unbearable."

It is unlikely, however—despite Ciano's unflattering portrait of Mussolini at this time—that the Duce's restlessness was inspired wholly by wounded pride and a childish desire for action at any cost. Mussolini was, after all, an intelligent man and, at times, an acutely perceptive one. Italy was playing a dangerous game, he knew, in accepting neutrality. If the war developed into a stalemate—as had World War I for a long period—then Italy might hope for a few crumbs from the German table, as Russia had during Germany's invasion of Poland. But if England and France were decisively defeated, then the spoils would be great indeed, and Italy, if she continued to sit on the fence, would have, by her neutrality, deprived herself of an opportunity for such spoils as she had not known for two thousand years. In Africa, there would be the vast possessions of France, an empire which Mussolini had long contemplated with frustrated envy, and in which it was realistic to assume that the Italians might replace the French. In Europe, there were Nice, Corsica, the eastern coast of the Adriatic, perhaps even Greece. An Axis victory, Mussolini estimated reasonably, could well make the Mediterranean once again an Italian lake, *mare nostrum*. But such antique splendor, the Duce also knew, could be purchased only at a heavy price: Italy's active entry into the war on Germany's side.

As Mussolini brooded, events in Europe were proceeding more rapidly than anyone had anticipated. The unbelievably rapid destruction of Poland, and that nation's partition between Germany and Russia, proved to the world the effectiveness of German arms. And then, after a short period of quiet in the West—a time which the Germans called the *Sitzkrieg,* or "sit-down war," or "phony war"—Germany began to move again. In the spring of 1940, Denmark, Norway, and, ominously, Belgium were overrun, events which demonstrated amply, in the eyes of Mussolini and those of the world, German might and Allied weakness, and which raised Winston Churchill to power in Great Britain and Paul Reynaud in France. On May 10, Germany attacked in overwhelming force in a drive aimed at the total reduction of France. "The democracies have lost the race," Mussolini announced. And convinced now that a German victory was inevitable and that Italy must move immediately if she were to claim a share in Hitler's booty, he made it clear that he intended to take the nation to the battlefield at the first opportunity. Pleas from Reynaud and from President Roosevelt for continued Italian neutrality produced only sharp answers from Mussolini, to the effect that "Italy is, and means to stay, the political and military ally of Germany in adherence to the Treaty of May 1939, an agreement which Italy, as a nation which cherishes its honor, intends fully to respect." With Winston Churchill, Mussolini was even more candid and took advantage of the opportunity to recite the litany of Italian grievances against England: "I remind you of the steps taken in 1935 by your government to organize sanctions at Geneva against Italy, who was then engaged in securing for herself a small place in the African sun without causing the slightest injury to your own interests and territory or to those of anyone else. I remind you, moreover, of the real and actual condition of servitude in which Italy finds herself at present in her own sea. If it was to honor a treaty that your government has declared war on Germany, then you will understand that an identical sense of honor and of respect for commitments . . . guides Italian policy today and tomorrow, in the face of any event whatever."

From this moment, it was clear that Italy would enter the war against the Allies. It was a matter only of weeks, and perhaps of days. On May 30, Mussolini formally signified this intention to Hitler: "I want to announce to you my decision to enter the war as of June 5." Upon Hitler's advice, however, the date was quickly changed to June 11; and, on June 10, Ciano officially notified the British and French ambassadors of his government's position. The British representative maintained a dignified silence, but his French colleague could not resist a parting shot. "The Germans," he icily informed Ciano, "are hard masters. You will have ample occasion to learn this." Such sentiments were too close to Ciano's own to leave him unmoved. "I am sad, very sad," he wrote in his diary that night. "The adventure begins. May God help Italy!"

Italy's entry into the war was to set the tone for the events of the next few years. It happened that, only a few days before Mussolini's official declaration of war, the armies of France collapsed utterly and the entire country lay open to the Germans. It was a development as dramatic as it was unexpected, and as humiliating for the Duce as it was gratifying to Hitler. The fall of France was exclusively a German victory, and one in which Italy, to Mussolini's chagrin, had made no contribution. And now, in the eyes of the world, as Mussolini well knew, Italy was cast in the role of "a jackal among nations," who rushed in at the last moment to rip what she could from the carcass of a noble but fallen foe. In fact, in the few days in which Italian troops were able to participate in the actual fighting, they managed to penetrate only a few miles into French territory and to stage only a few ineffectual air raids on French cities. Under the circumstances, when the French government—now under the tragic Marshal Henri-Philippe Pétain—requested an armistice from Germany and Italy, it was Germany who dictated the terms both to France and to Italy. It was a situation only slightly less humiliating to victorious Italy than it was to defeated France. Germany reserved to herself more than half of the French mainland, including the Atlantic coast; and Italy was given, grudgingly, a minute strip of land along the Franco-Italian frontier which did not include even the much-coveted city of Nice. In Africa, where Mussolini had had such brilliant hopes, Italy fared even worse. Tunisia, after which successive Italian governments had lusted for half a century, was placed in the hands of Marshal Pétain's government. As a sop to Italian feeling, however, Hitler offhandedly promised Mussolini the use of the port of Jibuti. "Mussolini," Ciano noted, "is very much embarrassed. He feels that his role is that of a junior partner." And the Duce's sensitivity to his position was such, in fact, as to compel him to order that the terms of the armistice were to be given no publicity in Italian newspapers.

Coupled with Mussolini's humiliation as a "victorious" partner in the Axis was fear—fear that the war would end and Italy, once again, would have been deprived of any tangible gain from her participation. Ciano said, "The Duce fears that the time of peace is coming close, and he sees that unattained dream of his life, glory on the battlefield, fading once more. . . . He fears that the English may find a pretext . . . to begin negotiations. That would be sad for Mussolini, for, now more than ever, he wants war." As the summer of 1940 wore on, however, the "peace scare" faded. And, as Great Britain and Germany both prepared for that great operation which was never to materialize, the invasion of the British Isles, the Duce began to cast about desperately for a suitable battlefield for Italian arms. On August 4, the Duke of Aosta, led an invasion into lightly defended British Somaliland. Encouraged by the duke's middling successes, Mussolini began to speak of an invasion of Yugoslavia, and of an offensive against Greece. Hitler, however, quickly pointed out that all resources of the Axis were needed for the battle against England, and he virtually forbade any action against either of the Balkan countries. Nonetheless, by the middle of September the German dictator had come to appreciate the difficulties involved in his projected invasion of Britain ("Operation Sea Lion," the Germans called it), and to turn ambitious eyes toward a more immediate, and apparently more attainable, prize: Russia. And Mussolini, sensing the change in the wind from the north, now considered himself free to act on his own accord. On September 13 (and against the strong recommendation of the Italian commander in Libya, Marshal Graziani), Italian troops began to cross the Libyan frontier into British-held Egypt. Within a few days, they had advanced over sixty miles to Sidi Barrani, where they remained for the remainder of the year. Mussolini, according to Ciano, was "radiant with joy."

Thus buoyed up, the Duce's confidence grew, and soon he was bursting for more action. His enthusiasm reached a crisis in September when Hitler, without consulting his Italian ally, ordered German troops into Rumania. Mussolini was indignant. He himself had been forbidden by Berlin to move into the Balkans, which he regarded as a properly Italian sphere of influence; and now Hitler, without even informing Rome of his intentions, had done so on the flimsy pretext of protecting the Rumanian oil fields from Russian ambition. Mussolini therefore determined to act quickly and freely. "Hitler always presents me with a *fait accompli*," he roared at Ciano. "This time I am going to pay him back in his own coin. I am going to occupy Greece, and he is going to find out about it from the newspapers. In this way, we will be even again." In this instance, at least, the Duce was as good as his word. On October 26, Italian troops crossed the Albanian frontier into Greece. And, on the same day, Hitler—returning from an unsuccessful attempt to enlist Spain's Franco in the Axis cause—was greeted at Florence by a smiling Duce. "This morning at dawn," Mussolini announced to his ally, "victorious Italian troops crossed the Greco-Albanian frontier." Hitler received the news, as one of his staff records, "with bitterness in his heart," and he returned to Germany complaining about "ungrateful and unreliable friends." He was of the opinion that Mussolini had committed a major error the results of which were difficult to foresee. And he proved to be right. Mussolini, upon his return to Rome, was met with the news that the initial momentum of the Italian offensive had been lost, that the attack had been strongly met and repulsed, and, indeed, that it was now the Greek army, and not that of Italy, which was on the offensive. This intelligence was shortly followed by an equally devastating blow to Italian pride. On November 11, the British naval forces in the Mediterranean attacked the Italian fleet based at Taranto. The battleship *Cavour* was sunk, and two others were seriously damaged along with the Tarantan dockyard. This British victory, coupled with the occupation of Crete, Lemnos, and other Greek islands, confirmed the supremacy of England in the Mediterranean—a position which it had been a major policy of the Duce to contest. Hitler, of course, was not pleased. To his generals, he described the Italian invasion of Greece as a "regrettable blunder" which had endangered the Axis position in the Balkans and in the entire Mediterranean, and he ordered them to prepare plans for a German invasion of Greece so as to salvage whatever could be salvaged from Italian ineptitude. To Mussolini, he addressed himself so strongly on the subject that the Duce commented ruefully, "He really smacked my fingers." Thereafter, the situation in the Balkans worsened to the extent that the Italian commander, General Ubaldo Soddu, reported that a military solution was no longer attainable and that an armistice must be sought. Mussolini sent a message to Hitler requesting "immediate aid," which the German dictator, after again complaining bitterly of Mussolini's decision to attack Greece and of the conduct of Italian troops, dispatched in the form of transport planes.

Italy's humiliation in Greece was soon duplicated in Africa. On December 9, the British attacked Marshal Graziani's garrison at Sidi Barrani, and the Marshal telegraphed to Mussolini that "we have had a licking." Sidi Barrani fell the next day, to be followed, within a few weeks, by Tobruk and Bardia. Over a hundred thousand Italian troops were taken prisoner, and some seven hundred big guns fell into the hands of the advancing British. By the end of the year, Mussolini was gloomily speaking of the possibility of a "real defeat in Libya." All in all, the year 1940, which had opened with such high hopes for the Axis, had ended in a series of embarrassing defeats for Italy. In the Mediterranean, the fleet had been badly damaged. In the Balkans, the Duce had been forced to beg Hitler for aid in order to avoid a complete catastrophe. And now, in Africa, it seemed that the victorious British were on the point of seizing not only Libya, but also Italy's possessions of Abyssinia, Eritrea, and the Somaliland. Faced with the prospect of the loss of their hard-won African empire, the Italian public reacted passively but noticeably. Morale reached a nadir, and it was to remain there for the rest of the war. The prestige of the government, and Mussolini's personal popularity, suffered a similar fate. For the first time in many years, strong dissent began to be expressed in

The Age of Fascism

official circles; and Ciano noted that "the ushers at the Palazzo Venezia were instructed to lead prominent Italians into separate waiting-rooms so as to prevent a general brawl."

Despite the note of pessimism on which the new and fateful year of 1941 opened, the prospect of a total Axis victory over the Allies had not yet become a hopeless dream. Notwithstanding reverses and embarrassments in the Mediterranean area, there were still impressive victories in store for the Axis. But they were to be German, not Italian, victories, as Mussolini knew. Italy's dependence on Germany was now such that the Duce's hope now was not so much to achieve glory as to avoid humiliation. To Ciano he observed bitterly that, in Hitler's New Order for Europe, Italy was merely a major confederated province of the Third Reich. And, he concluded, "we must accept these conditions; any attempt on our part to rebel would result only in our being reduced from the status of a confederated province to that of a colony. Even if they asked tomorrow for Trieste . . . we would have to bow our heads."

There seemed to be one chance, however, to free Italy from total German domination; and that chance lay to the east, in Russia. Mussolini, desperate, now determined to take that chance, and to request from the Soviet Union both economic aid and co-operation in the Balkans. Moscow, in the person of Vyacheslav Molotov, seemed interested, and negotiations proceeded to the point where an agreement in principle was reached. At this stage, however, it was necessary, or at least it was judged prudent, for Ciano to inform Berlin of his country's approaches to the Soviet Union —which was, at the time, a power still officially friendly to the Third Reich. Ciano's announcement was greeted by a verbal explosion in the German capital. Ribbentrop, acting on Hitler's instructions, ordered the Italian Foreign Minister immediately to cut off all parleys with Russia, and told him, moreover, that Italy had no business meddling in Balkan affairs. This ukase was obeyed forthwith. All hope of aid from a non-German source disappeared; and with it vanished Italy's last chance to salvage its national pride and to maintain a limited independence of action. At the same time, the Italian position abroad was further deteriorating. In Africa, Libya seemed on the point of falling entirely into British hands. By the end of February, the Somaliland had been lost; and by May 5, Eritrea was cleared of Italian troops and Abyssinia was once more in the hands of its indomitable Emperor, Haile Selassie. Again, the Duce reflected on the irony of his position. "We have lost our empire," he sighed, "while the French retain theirs."

The cup of bitterness, however, was not yet full to overflowing. Mussolini now was required to witness, and even to applaud, the retrieval of the situation which his own fumbling had created. On April 6, Hitler's armies swarmed across the frontiers of Yugoslavia and Greece. On April 13, Belgrade fell, and Yugoslavia—on whose Dalmatian coast Mussolini had long had designs—passed under the iron fist of the German dictator. By April 23, Greece shared the same fate; and, a week later, Crete fell to a German airborne invasion. In Africa, at the end of March, General (later Field Marshal) Rommel had attacked the British forces and, in less than two weeks, he recaptured all that the Italians had lost. In the space of a single month, the Germans, singlehandedly, had gained virtual control of the Mediterranean area while the Italians were compelled to sit idly by and endure publicly their humiliation. "It doesn't matter that the Germans acknowledge our rights on paper," Mussolini stormed privately, "when in practice they grab everything and leave us only a small pile of bones. They are dirty dogs; and I tell you that this cannot go on much longer. . . . Personally, I've had more than enough of Hitler and the way he acts. These meetings, called by the ringing of a bell, are not to my taste. A bell is rung to call servants. . . . But, for the moment, there is nothing that can be done. We must howl with the wolves. Today, in the Chamber, I will cajole the Germans, but with a heart full of bitterness."

By the end of May 1941, Europe hummed with rumors of an imminent German attack on the Soviet Union. At one of "these meetings" which Mussolini deplored, however, on June 2, Ribbentrop categorically informed the Italians that such reports were "devoid of any foundation in fact." By now Mussolini and Ciano were accustomed to German lies, and they were not surprised, therefore, when, on June 22, at three o'clock in the morning, a German diplomat appeared to inform the Duce of Hitler's invasion of Russia and to explain the reasons for this action. Mussolini, grumbling, could do nothing but accept the announcement with whatever grace he could muster. In an attempt to salvage what remained of his pride, he offered to send to Russia four Italian divisions—an offer which Hitler accepted with obvious reluctance.

The invasion of Russia ended whatever hope Mussolini had for a quick end to the war, either by military or by diplomatic means. He did not doubt for a moment that Russia would be crushed, but he was skeptical about Ribbentrop's boast that "within eight weeks, the Russia of Stalin will be erased from the map." Italy, already economically and militarily exhausted, with her morale catastrophically low, could not possibly endure a prolonged war effort. Nonetheless, in the situation in which he had placed himself and his country, Mussolini knew, he could do nothing but "howl

The Age of Fascism

with the wolves" and hope that eventually the results of his loyalty would bear some tangible fruit. Henceforth, he seemed determined to follow Hitler into whatever path, however predictably fatal, he might choose. Thus, when on December 3, the Japanese ambassador informed him that war was likely to break out at any moment between Japan and the United States, and that the Japanese government expected Italy to honor her commitment under the Tripartite Pact and, along with Germany, to declare war immediately upon the opening of hostilities in the Pacific, he acquiesced willingly, almost gaily. It seemed to matter not at all that, under the terms of the pact, Italy was bound to assist Japan only in the event of an attack upon her by another power. On December 7, the Japanese attacked Pearl Harbor; and, on December 11, Italy, in company with Germany, declared war on the United States.

In Russia, the Nazi advance had, at first, gone as planned. But, with the onset of winter, the Germans, unprepared for the unrelenting cold, had been halted. On December 6, they were subjected to counteroffensive attacks which would probably have resulted in a general retreat if it had not been for Hitler's almost hysterical insistence that his generals fight to the last soldier rather than surrender a foot of ground. Mussolini, far from being alarmed, gloated quietly at the reverses of his ally. "The failure of the German troops cheers him," Ciano observed. But, as 1941 closed, there were other reverses, closer to home; and these the Duce did not find encouraging. On November 18, as the Axis forces in Africa, under Rommel, were preparing to resume their attack on Egypt, a fierce battle at Tobruk had cost the Germans over thirty thousand men. In view of these losses and of the critical state of his supplies, Rommel was compelled to order a general retreat, and it was rumored in Rome that the whole of Libya was at the point of being abandoned to the Allies.

By the beginning of 1942, troubles at home began to match those abroad. There was constant friction between the Axis partners, with Mussolini complaining of Hitler's stupidity in attacking the Soviet Union and the Germans blaming the Italians for their worsening military position. There were "incidents" between Italian civilians and the German soldiery who were increasingly infesting the country and behaving as though they had conquered Italy. And, more seriously, the Italian public was becoming more restless and more openly critical of the government as one military disaster followed another. Mussolini reacted by ordering mass arrests of anti-Fascists, and by expelling from the government such Fascist officeholders whom he regarded as tainted with defeatism. But still the tide rose, and even Ciano was heard to voice violent criticism of both the Fascist party and of Mussolini himself, while other members of Mussolini's cabinet did not hesitate to speak of the necessity for a separate peace with the Allies. Mussolini attempted to rally the nation once more by a series of speeches in the provinces, but the obvious hopelessness of the military situation and increasing economic hardship neutralized his efforts. Upon his return to Rome, Mussolini confessed that "I no longer have any doubt concerning lack of discipline, sabotage, and passive resistance all the way down the line." Berlin, of course, was alarmed at the prospect of Italy's disintegration, and Marshal Goering was sent to Rome so as to attempt to infuse some enthusiasm into the Italians. His visit, however, served only to strengthen the Italians in their dislike and contempt for their allies. He left Rome, Ciano sniffed, wearing "an enormous sable coat, something between what motorists wore in 1906 and what a high-class whore wears to the opera today."

For a while, early in the summer of 1942, the star of the Axis seemed again in the ascendancy over the Mediterranean. In May, Rommel again went on the offensive in Africa. Late in June, Tobruk fell to him, along with an enormous supply of gasoline—of which he was in critical need—and of other materiel. With his logistical problems temporarily solved, Rommel announced his intention of moving into Egypt. Mussolini was ecstatic. He did not doubt for a moment that the German commander's military genius would overcome any obstacles on the road to Suez; and he was determined that, in this instance at least, Italy, the Italian troops under Rommel's command, and he himself, would extract every possible drop of glory from the conquest of Egypt. So certain was he of the outcome of the battle for Egypt that, on June 29, he arrived in Africa fully prepared to ride into Cairo at the head of the victorious Axis troops—only to find that Rommel had been halted at El Alamein. For three weeks he wandered disconsolately in the deserts of Libya, inspecting troops and installations and generally making a nuisance of himself to the Germans. He returned to Rome on July 21, tired, ill, utterly discouraged, and abysmally pessimistic about the future. His attitude was more than justified by events. On October 23, the Allied forces, under Bernard Montgomery, fell upon the Italian and German troops at El Alamein and, two weeks later, the entire Axis front collapsed. On November 7, the Allies landed in Morocco and Algeria. It was a mortal blow to whatever hope remained for Italy. The morale of the army was, in the words of the chief of Italian military intelligence, now "sensationally low." And Mussolini himself recorded later the effect of the landings upon the country: ". . . the moral impact of the American landings in Algiers were immediate and profound. . . . The country began to feel the strain. So long as only the English were in the Mediterranean, Italy, with Germany's aid, could hope to hold the line, though at the cost of ever greater sacrifices. The appearance of America, however, panicked the weaker spirits and increased by many millions the already great number of people who listened to enemy radio broadcasts." Despite his contempt for the "weaker spirits," Mussolini must have been as aware as the ordinary Italian citizen of the real significance of the American landings in North Africa: Italy would now become the logical target for the next Allied offensive against the Axis. So certain did this seem that, only a month after the landings, the Vatican made its first attempt to have Rome declared an open city so as to save it from possible bombardment by the Allies. The attempt failed, however, because, although Mussolini was willing enough to remove himself and Italian military targets from the City, the Germans refused to do so with their own troops and materiel.

The Allied successes in Africa, and the increasingly rapid deterioration of the German position in Russia, combined with a growing number of Allied air raids on Italian towns and cities and the almost intolerable shortage of foodstuffs and commodities, exacerbated the war weariness of Italy at large. There was open talk, and underground literature, on the necessity of ridding Italy of the Fascists and discarding the fatal German alliance. The whole country wanted only one thing: peace, and that at any price and by any means. It was rumored everywhere that Marshal Count Ugo Cavallero, Italy's most prestigious military figure, was preparing to succeed Mussolini, and that various *coups* were being organized by Giuseppe Bottai and Dino Grandi, both old-line Fascists and members of Mussolini's cabinet. The spirit of the country, and the fact of the conspiracies, were duly reported to Mussolini; but, like a man who has abandoned himself to his fate, the Duce did nothing. At this point, he knew, only a resounding military success could rouse the country from its defeatism. When news came, however, it was not of victory. Instead, on May 13, the Italian and German forces in Africa surrendered to the Allies.

This fresh disaster gave courage to the forces in Italy that were now determined to pull down the Fascist regime, and Mussolini with it. The King was already holding secret meetings with politicians from the pre-Fascist years, although he decided not to intervene unless some new military event rendered the situation still more critical. On June 4, he told Dino Grandi: "The moment will come. Allow your King to choose it. In the meantime, help me to obtain the constitutional means." Victor Emmanuel's procrastinations were based on sound reasoning. If Italy suddenly and unilaterally withdrew from the war, then she could expect Germany to fall upon her with all the fury of an ally betrayed. Moreover, the King felt it necessary to observe the constitutional niceties in this crisis, and he was unwilling to act until or unless a vote, either in the Chamber or in the Grand Council, gave him a pretext for doing so.

On July 9, the Allies landed in Sicily, and they were greeted as liberators by the war-weary inhabitants. Italian troops surrendered happily, and only the stubborn resistance of the Germans slowed the advance of the invaders. By July 12, Rome was informing its ambassadors that "we cannot hold out any longer in Sicily." And on July 14, General Vittorio Ambrosio, Chief of the Army Staff, advised Mussolini that Sicily must be regarded as lost, and that the Duce must now consider "whether it would not be the proper moment to spare the country further sorrow and ruin by anticipating the end of the struggle, since the final result will undoubtedly be worse in one or more years than now." The Duce's response was to meet with Hitler at Feltre, near Venice, on July 18. The purpose of the conference, it was hoped by the members of Mussolini's government, was for Mussolini to describe Italy's condition forcefully to Hitler and to persuade the latter to allow Italy to withdraw from the war. The meeting, however, turned into a virtual monologue by the German dictator, who spent hours haranguing his Italian colleague on the inevitability of an Axis victory. Mussolini could not find the courage to confess that Italy was unable to continue the struggle. After the conference, the Duce explained to his staff that "I had no need to approach the Fuehrer in the way that you wished. This time, he has promised faithfully to send us all the assistance we ask for; but of course our requests must be reasonable and not astronomical."

The fall of Sicily, the imminence of an Allied invasion of the Italian mainland, and the fiasco at Feltre, all convinced the King that the time to act had come. With his consent, Dino Grandi prepared a draft motion which was to be presented at the forthcoming meeting of the Fascist Grand Council according to which the existing organs of government—the Council itself, the Parliament, the cabinet and the Corporations—were to be reestablished in their constitutional functions, and the King was to assume command of the armed forces. The draft was shown to Mussolini himself (Grandi was careful to avoid any move which might be construed as a conspiracy against the existing government), who dismissed it curtly as "inadmissible and contemptible." On July 22, two days before the scheduled meeting of the Grand Council, Grandi visited Mussolini in a final attempt to persuade him voluntarily to divest himself of his dictatorial powers and to allow the people of Italy freely to express their will. According to Grandi, Mussolini replied: "You would be right, and your solution of placing everything into the hands of the King would be correct, if the war were indeed lost. But the fact is that it is about to be won. In a few days, the Germans will launch a new weapon which will transform the situation. But we will discuss all this calmly at the session of the Grand Council on Saturday."

On that fateful Saturday, the plans of Grandi and his associates were complete. "We are about to do our duty" he notified the King. And the King, for his part, had it intimated to Marshal Pietro Badoglio, former Viceroy of Abyssinia and Chief of the General Staff, that Mussolini was about to be removed as head of government, and that Badoglio himself would be appointed to replace him. Only Mussolini in all Rome seemed unaware that he and Fascism were at the end of the road.

Shortly after five o'clock in the afternoon, Mussolini convened the Grand Council in the Palazzo Venezia. After a rambling speech by the Duce justifying the conduct of the war, Grandi made his motion and it was put to the vote. The results were nineteen members (including Ciano) in favor of the motion, and seven against it. After a moment of silence, Mussolini looked around at the men who had just voted to strip him of his powers and said quietly, "You have provoked the crisis of the regime. The session is closed." The members dispersed without knowing precisely what they had accomplished or what would be the outcome of their vote. Mussolini might choose to ignore the results of the meeting entirely, and even to arrest as traitors those who had voted for the motion.

For Grandi and the King, however, the meeting of the Grand Council was but the first step in the deposition of Mussolini. Victor Emmanuel now had the constitutional mandate that he required to replace Mussolini as head of the government. On the day following the meeting, Mussolini called upon the King and launched upon a long explanation of the reasons why he felt the action of the Council was not binding. Victor Emmanuel, however, interrupted him to say that, in this situation, and in view of the fact that Mussolini no longer commanded the loyalty and confidence of the country, he must ask for the Duce's resignation. When Mussolini attempted to argue, the King replied that "the solution could not have been otherwise," and that he had already appointed Marshal Badoglio to form a new government. There was nothing more to be said. The King accompanied the fallen Duce to the door, and there shook his hand, Mussolini recorded, "with great warmth." Then, as Mussolini emerged from the royal villa, he was met by two police officers who escorted him, a prisoner, to the *Carabinieri* barracks in Trastevere.

The news of Mussolini's fall and arrest and of Badoglio's appointment flashed like lightning throughout Italy. Everywhere, there were enthusiastic demonstrations, and crowds gathered outside the Quirinale to cheer the King. No one doubted that, with the end of Fascism, the war also would end. And even though the new prime minister declared that "the war continues," no one believed it. It was the general opinion—and indeed, it was a fact—that Badoglio intended to end the war as soon as possible, but that, in order to prevent a German take-over in Italy, he must await a favorable moment. Cautious approaches were made to the Allies in two neutral cities, Lisbon (on August 4) and Tangiers (August 5). The Italians, relying upon Allied propaganda to the effect that the fall of Mussolini would automatically change the British and American attitude toward Italy, believed that the Allies' resolve to accept only "unconditional surrender" would not apply to Italy. But they were quickly disillusioned. The Allied representatives made it clear that they would consider an Italian surrender only on their own terms—that is, unconditional surrender. On August 18, however, hope was held out by Roosevelt and Churchill that Italy might hope for some modification of her status if she chose to help in the war against Germany. The Italian government realized that there was no real choice; it must accept the Allied conditions, or face the ruin of the country. Making the most of a desperate situation, the Italian representatives attempted first to persuade the Allies to make a landing to the north of Rome so as to facilitate a rapid occupation of the entire peninsula and the protection of the royal family and the government from German retaliation. Finally, after much delay, they succeeded in extracting from General Dwight D. Eisenhower, Allied Commander in the Mediterranean, a guarantee that troops would be landed to the south of Rome—though the exact place of the landings was not specified for security reasons. An airborne division was to be parachuted into the City at the same time so as to defend it, in company with Italian troops, against the Germans, until troops were able to fight their way into Rome from the projected landing point to the south. The Italian government, with its back to the wall, accepted this compromise. On September 3, General Castellano signed the military articles of this armistice in the Sicilian town of Casibile, near Syracuse,* according to which hostilities were to cease immediately upon the

* This agreement is known as the "Short Armistice." Another document—the "Long Armistice"—stipulating the political, financial and economic conditions for the Allied occupation of Italy—was signed at Malta on September 29, by Prime Minister Badoglio.

surrender of the Italian armed forces, and an Anglo-American military government was to be established in Italian territory.

Such arrangements, if they had been carried out, might indeed have saved the day for Italy. But the projected airborne attack on Rome was deferred because the Italian troops in the City were insufficient to secure the necessary airfields against the Germans. Then Badoglio discovered that Eisenhower, by "an area to the south of Rome," had meant an area to the south of Naples. And this, of course, rendered the landings useless from the Italian point of view, for it left Rome, the King, and the government, at the mercy of the Germans. Alarmed at the prospect of Nazi vengeance, Badoglio now proposed that the announcement of the armistice be postponed until a new and more satisfactory plan could be worked out. Eisenhower refused peremptorily, and informed Badoglio that, unless Italy respected the terms already agreed upon, then the prime minister would have to face "the dissolution of your government and of your nation."

Badoglio had no alternative but to comply with Eisenhower's ultimatum. On September 3, the day on which the armistice was signed, Allied troops had landed on the boot of southern Italy and were rapidly advancing northward. If he delayed, he might lose, irretrievably, Italy's chance at least to end the war on the winning side. Badoglio therefore announced the signing of the armistice in a radio broadcast on September 8. A few hours after the announcement, the Germans moved into Rome in force, and the royal family, the government, and the military command fled to Brindisi in Apulia, beyond the reach of the Nazis. Within a few days, all Italy, except the southernmost parts, were in the hands of the Germans. The peninsula now would have to be recovered by force of arms—and at what cost in Allied and Italian lives and materiel only the future, and perhaps the Allied commanders who had engineered the situation, could tell.

The promised Allied landing "south of Rome" was made at Salerno, some forty miles below Naples, on September 9. The German troops there had had time to dig in, and heavy fighting ensued. After heavy losses, the British and American troops broke through the German encirclement, but by then the German troops to the south of Salerno had been able to withdraw to new positions toward the north, and one of the chief purposes of the landing—isolation of German units in the south of Italy—failed to be realized.

On October 1, Naples was liberated by Allied troops. Several days before that, however, the Neapolitans had risen against the Germans and conducted a house-to-house and street-to-street campaign against them. This period—the famous "five days of Naples"—marked the beginning of open Italian resistance, a movement intended, to a large extent, to symbolize not only the age-old contempt of the Latins for the Teutonic barbarians, but also the absolution of the Italian people from its Fascist sins.

Shortly after the liberation of Naples, the onset of winter put a halt to the Allied advance. The only offensive action undertaken before the spring of 1944 was a landing, on January 22, 1944, at Anzio—an operation which was contained by German units and which, under Allied naval protection, also remained static until spring. Now, Italy was cut into two parts. From the Garigliano River southward, the Allies were in control, with the government of King Victor Emmanuel and Marshal Badoglio functioning, token-style, in a few provinces in Apulia. The northern and central portions of the country, including Rome, were in the hands of the Germans. Within the jurisdiction of the latter, a new political phenomenon had made its appearance in the form of an "Italian Social Republic" (*Repubblica Sociale Italiana*). The chief of this new, German-sponsored puppet state was Benito Mussolini, who, on September 12, had been liberated by German parachutists from his place of detention on the Gran Sasso. Among the first acts of Mussolini's new government was the announcement that a new Fascist army would be formed to continue the war "until final victory," and that the "traitors" who had cooperated in the *coup* of July 25 would be punished. From its headquarters at Salò, Mussolini's new Fascist regime was able to live up to only one of its promises. On January 11, six of the members of the Grand Council who had voted against Mussolini, including the Duce's son-in-law and former Foreign Minister, Count Galeazzo Ciano, were executed by a firing squad. For the rest, the Salò Republic, as Mussolini's regime came to be called, remained a shadow government, wholly dominated by and subservient to German military and civil functionaries. Its very existence, however, and the limited loyalty which it commanded in the north, created the danger of civil war in opposition to the regime of Marshal Badoglio in the south. This danger was translated into reality when, on October 13, Badoglio's government declared war on Germany and Italy was recognized as a "co-belligerent nation" by the Allied authorities.* Henceforth, there were two Italys, one in the north and one in the south, each technically at war with the other.

* The only real advantage which accrued to the Italian people from this new status was the recognition by the Allies of Italy's right to choose its own form of government after the war. It was a right which, in any case, had already been recognized in the "Long Armistice," and which had been incorporated into the Atlantic Charter.

In the spring of 1944, the Allies launched a new offensive northward. On June 5, Rome was liberated. The City had been declared an "open city" in August of the previous year, and so had been relatively free from air attack, although this advantage had been more than compensated for by German brutality. Rome was also the center of organized resistance to the Germans, in which the C.L.N., or *Comitati di Liberazione Nazionale* (Committees of National Liberation) played the major role. In the south, the C.L.N.—which represented all political tendencies, from the extreme right to the extreme left—became the focus of political activity, while in the north and central parts of Italy it secretly organized a strong resistance movement against both the German occupiers and the neo-Fascist Salò Republic, especially in the Alban hills surrounding Rome. Following the fall of Rome, the Allied advance proceeded at an accelerated pace. In the first week of August, Florence was liberated with the strong, and perhaps decisive, aid of Italian resistance units which had, for the previous several months, been conducting guerrilla warfare from the mountains. By the end of September, however, the Allies ran up against the last line of German resistance, the so-called Gothic Line, which ran along the Apennines from the Tyrrhenian Sea to the Adriatic, between Bologna and Florence. And there the battle line remained during the winter of 1944–1945.

The events of the summer of 1944, and particularly the expulsion of the Germans from Rome, opened up new political vistas in Italy. In accordance with an agreement reached several months previously, King Victor Emmanuel now transferred his constitutional powers to Crown Prince Umberto, who was given the title of Lieutenant-General of the Realm. At the same time (June 5), Badoglio resigned, but was immediately recalled by Umberto. The prime minister, however, was unable to form a government because of the opposition of the C.L.N., who mistrusted Badoglio because of his early and long association with the Fascist regime. Umberto then turned to Ivanoe Bonomi, a pre-Fascist premier who had been president of the Rome Committee of National Liberation. Bonomi's cabinet, as might have been expected, was composed, with one exception, of C.L.N. members. The new government's first decree, on June 25, pledged the convocation of a Constituent Assembly at the termination of hostilities in Italy in order to give the country a new constitution. At the same time, it served notice on the royal family—who were fully aware of the C.L.N.'s basically anti-monarchical orientation—that its days were very likely numbered.

Bonomi's government was largely ineffectual; and, indeed, no one expected it to be otherwise. The government in Rome was controlled just as completely by the Allies as it had been by the Germans only a few weeks before, and Bonomi's activities were greatly circumscribed by that fact and by the limitations imposed by the armistice. Within that restrictive context, however, three things of importance were accomplished. First, the Italian government enlisted the support of the large Italo-American population of the United States in its behalf, and the response of the latter was so overwhelming and well organized—1944 was an election year in the United States—that, on October 26, the United States granted diplomatic recognition to the Bonomi government. Indeed, the American government, under pressure from influential citizens, was willing to grant full Allied status to Italy, but Great Britain, in the person of Mr. Churchill, was unmovable in its opposition to such recognition. Second, the Bonomi government, from its new bargaining position, was able to obtain a commitment in principle for the allocation of aid from UNRRA (United Nations Relief and Rehabilitation Administration).* Finally—and this was to be of considerable import for Italy's position among the Allies—Bonomi succeeded in securing the Allies' approval for Italy's greatly increased military participation in operations against Germany. As it happened, Bonomi's request for a greater role in operations came at an opportune time. Several major Allied units had been transferred from Italy to the Second Front, which had been opened on June 6, 1944, with Allied landings in Normandy, and Italian troops were now used to fill the gaps created by these transfers. By the fall of 1944, the newly equipped Italians—many of them experienced resistance men—had moved into position at the eastern end of the Gothic Line.

Despite these gains, Bonomi's government was short-lived. It fell at the end of November 1944, on the issues of the purge of former Fascists from public life and of the function of the C.L.N., and because of the resulting clash between the newly formed political parties of the Socialists and Actionists (backed by the Communists) on the one hand, and the Christian Democrats on the other. Bonomi himself, however, was asked by the Lieutenant-General of the Realm, Prince Umberto, to form a new government. The composition of his new cabinet resolved—at least until the end

* For the moment, this was only a speculative gain, since, because of scarcity of shipping, UNRRA had to postpone effective aid until after the cessation of hostilities. For the recovery of post-war Italy, however, it was of incalculable importance. From the beginning of 1946 to the middle of 1947, for example, Italy received aid from UNRRA amounting to almost half a billion dollars.

of the war—the growing dissension among factions of the C.L.N. from which all of the new parties had grown. These events have considerable importance, however, because they marked the first choosing of sides and the first confrontation between the left and the right of the post-Fascist era. The lines were drawn and the stage set for that interminable series of political crises which was to plague Italy for so many years following the war.

In the spring of 1945, the Allies made its first major attack on the strongly fortified Gothic Line. The offensive, though bitterly contested by the Germans, was successful, and on April 21 Bologna was liberated. The whole of the valley of the Po now lay open to the Allies, and it was only a matter of time until the Germans were once more pushed beyond the Alps. As the Allies continued their advance, Italian partisan forces rose up in all the major towns and cities and, in most cases, were in control before the actual arrival of the American and British forces. In the interim, the partisans—anti-Fascists to a man—frequently made use of their freedom of action to execute, by an act of summary if not commendable justice, such Fascist officials who had not had the wisdom to go into hiding. Among those who suffered this fate was Benito Mussolini and his mistress, Clara Petacci, whose devotion to the Duce had endured in defeat as it had in the days of glory. Mussolini and his retinue had been captured in attempting to flee to neutral Switzerland. They had been accorded a brief trial, and then executed on the spot, on April 28. Then their bodies were hanged, upside down, in a gasoline station in a Milanese square. According to all reports, Mussolini met his fate with courage and impressive calm. His pride allowed him to make only one request of his captors, that he be allowed to say good-by to Clara Petacci. And so ended in dignity a career in which dignity and pride had perhaps played too small, and vainglorious ambition too large a part.

The death of Mussolini, coinciding as it did with the final Allied offensive in Italy and the rising of the Italian partisans, marked the end of the war in the peninsula, and it anticipated by only a few months the collapse of Germany and the death, by his own hand, of Mussolini's erstwhile partner, friend and master, Adolf Hitler.

After years of brutal and disastrous conflict, Italy, at the hands of Benito Mussolini, had lost all and gained nothing. Her cities were in ruins, her crops destroyed, her youth dead or mutilated, and her people reduced to a level of economic privation and moral degradation unequaled in modern times. To those who survived him, the Duce left a single bequest: the interminable work of reconstruction. The ancient epitaph which Alan Bullock applied to Hitler is equally appropriate for Mussolini's grave:

Si monumentum requiris, circumspice.

"If you seek a monument to him, then look about you."

APPENDIX I
Chronological Tables of Popes and Emperors

YEAR OF ACCESSION A.D.	POPES	EMPERORS	YEAR OF ACCESSION A.D.
468	Simplicius	Romulus Augustulus	475
483	Felix III	Anastasius I*	491
492	Gelasius I		
496	Anastasius II		
498	Symmachus		
498	Laurentius**		
514	Hormisdas		
		Justin I	518
523	John I		
526	Felix IV		
		Justinian	527
530	Boniface II		
530	Dioscorus**		
532	John II		
535	Agapetus I		
536	Silverius		
537	Vigilius		
555	Pelagius I		
560	John III		
		Justin II	565
574	Benedict I		
578	Pelagius II	Tiberius II	578
590	Gregory I (the Great)		

* All the emperors between Romulus Augustulus and Charlemagne reigned at Constantinople.
** Anti-pope.

Italy: An Historical Survey

YEAR OF ACCESSION A.D.	POPES	EMPERORS	YEAR OF ACCESSION A.D.
		Phocas	602
604	Sabinianus		
607	Boniface III		
607	Boniface IV		
		Heraclius	610
615	Deusdedit		
618	Boniface V		
625	Honorius I		
638	Severinus		
640	John IV		
		Constantine III, Heracleonas, Constans II	641
642	Theodorus I		
649	Martin I		
654	Eugenius I		
657	Vitalianus		
		Constantine IV (Pogonatus)	668
672	Adeodatus		
676	Domnus I		
678	Agatho		
682	Leo II		
683?	Benedict II		
685	John V	Justinian II	685
685?	Conon		
687	Sergius I		
687	Paschal*		
687	Theodorus*		
		Leontius	694
		Tiberius Apsimar	697
701	John VI		
705	John VII	Justinian II (restored)	705
708	Sisinnius		
708	Constantine		
		Philippicus Bardanes	711
		Anastasius II	713
715	Gregory II		

* Anti-pope.

Chronological Tables of Popes and Emperors

YEAR OF ACCESSION A.D.	POPES	EMPERORS	YEAR OF ACCESSION A.D.
		Theodosius III	716
		Leo III (the Isaurian)	718
731	Gregory III		
741	Zacharias	Constantine V (Copronymus)	741
752	Stephen II		
752	Stephen III		
757	Paul I		
768	Stephen IV		
772	Adrian I		
		Leo IV	775
		Constantine VI	780
795	Leo III	Deposition of Constantine VI by the Empress Irene	797
		Charles I (the Great, or Charlemagne)	800
		Louis I (the Pious)*	814
816	Stephen IV	Lothair I*	817
817	Paschal I		
824	Eugenius		
827	Valentinus		
827	Gregory IV		
844	Sergius II		
847	Leo IV		
855	Benedict III	Louis II*	855
855	Anastasius**		
858	Nicholas I		
867	Adrian II		
872	John VIII	Charles II (the Bald)*	875
		Charles III (the Fat)*	881
882	Martin II		
884	Adrian III		
885	Stephen V		
891	Formosus	Guido (Italian)***	891
		Lambert (Italian)***	894
896	Boniface VI	Arnulf (German)	896

* Carolingian, or Carlovingian, line.
** Anti-pope.
*** Rival claimants.

YEAR OF ACCESSION A.D.	POPES	EMPERORS	YEAR OF ACCESSION A.D.
896	Stephen VI		
897	Romanus		
897	Theodore II		
898	John IX		
900	Benedict IV		
		Louis III (of Provence)	901
903	Leo V		
903	Christopher		
904	Sergius III		
911	Anastasius III		
913	Lando		
914	John X		
		Berengar (Italian)	915
928	Leo VI		
929	Stephen VII		
931	John XI		
936	Leo VII		
939	Stephen VIII		
941	Martin III		
946	Agapetus II		
955	John XII		
		Otto (the Great)*	962
964	Benedict V**		
965	John XIII		
972	Benedict VI		
		Otto II*	973
974	Boniface VII**		
974	Domnus II		
974	Benedict VII		
983	John XIV	Otto III*	983
985	John XV		
996	Gregory V		
996	John XVI**		
999	Silvester II		
		Henry II (of Bavaria)	1002
1003	John XVII		
1003	John XVIII		
1009	Sergius IV		

* Saxon line.
** Anti-pope.

Chronological Tables of Popes and Emperors

YEAR OF ACCESSION A.D.	POPES	EMPERORS	YEAR OF ACCESSION A.D.
1012	Benedict VIII		
1024	John XIX	Conrad II	1024
1033	Benedict IX		
		Henry III*	1039
1044	Silvester**		
1045?	Gregory VI		
1046	Clement II		
1048	Damasus II		
1048	Leo IX		
1054	Victor II		
		Henry IV*	1056
1057	Stephen IX		
1058	Benedict X		
1059	Nicholas II		
1061	Alexander II		
1073	Gregory VII (Hildebrand)		
1080	Clement**		
1086	Victor III		
1087	Urban II		
1099	Paschal II		
		Henry V*	1106
1118	Gelasius II		
1118	Gregory**		
1119	Calixtus II		
1121	Celestine**		
1124	Honorius II		
		Lothair II (the Saxon)	1125
1130	Innocent II		
1130	Anacletus**		
1138	Victor**	Conrad III***	1138
1143	Celestine II		
1144	Lucius II		
1145	Eugenius III		
		Frederick I (Barbarossa)****	1152
1153	Anastasius IV		

* Anti-pope.
** Franconian line.
*** Never crowned as emperor.
**** Hohenstaufen line.

YEAR OF ACCESSION A.D.	POPES	EMPERORS	YEAR OF ACCESSION A.D.
1154	Adrian IV		
1159	Alexander III		
1159	Victor*		
1164	Paschal*		
1168	Calixtus*		
1181	Lucius III		
1185	Urban III		
1187	Gregory VIII		
1187	Clement III		
		Henry VI**	1190
1191	Celestine III		
1198	Innocent III	Philip***	1198
		Otto IV of Brunswick	1198
		Frederick II**	1212
1216	Honorius III		
1227	Gregory IX		
1241	(vacancy)		
1243	Innocent IV		
		Conrad IV** *** and	1250
		William*** (rival claimants)	1250
1254	Alexander IV	Interregnum	1254
		Richard, Earl of Cornwall*** and Alfonso, King of Castile*** (rival claimants)	1257
1261	Urban IV		
1265	Clement IV		
1269	(vacancy)		
1271	Gregory X		
		Rudolf I (of Hapsburg)***	1272
1276	Innocent V		
1276	Adrian V		
1276	John XXI****		
1277	Nicholas III		

* Anti-pope.
** Hohenstaufen line.
*** Never crowned as emperor.
**** There was no Pope John XX.

Chronological Tables of Popes and Emperors

YEAR OF ACCESSION A.D.	POPES		EMPERORS	YEAR OF ACCESSION A.D.
1281	Martin IV			
1285	Honorius IV			
1289	Nicholas IV			
1292	(vacancy)		Adolf of Nassau*	1292
1294	Celestine V			
1294	Boniface VIII			
			Albert I (of Hapsburg)*	1298
1303	Benedict XI			
1305	Clement V	⎫		
			Henry VII (of Luxemburg)	1308
1314	(vacancy)		Louis IV (of Bavaria)	1314
1316	John XXII			
1334	Benedict XII	Avignon		
1342	Clement VI	papacy		
			Charles IV (of Luxemburg)	1347
1352	Innocent VI			
1362	Urban V			
1370	Gregory XI	⎭		
1378	Urban VI	⎫	Wenzel (of Luxemburg)*	1378
1378	Clement VII**			
1389	Boniface IX			
1394	Benedict**	Great Schism		
1406	Gregory XII***		Rupert, Count Palatine*	1400
1409	Alexander V***			
1410	John XXIII***	⎭	Sigismund (of Luxemburg)	1410
1417	Martin V			
1431	Eugene IV			
			Albert II (of Hapsburg)*	1438
1439	Felix V**			
			Frederick III	1440
1447	Nicholas V	⎫		
1455	Calixtus III			
1458	Pius II			
1464	Paul II	Popes of the Renaissance		
1471	Sixtus IV			
1484	Innocent VIII			
1493	Alexander VI		Maximilian I*	1486
1503	Pius III			
1503	Julius II			
1513	Leo X	⎭		

* Never crowned as emperor.   ** Anti-pope.   *** Rival claimants.

YEAR OF ACCESSION A.D.	POPES		EMPERORS	YEAR OF ACCESSION A.D.
			Charles V	1519
1522	Adrian VI			
1523	Clement VII			
1534	Paul III	⎫		
1550	Marcellus II	⎬ Council of Trent		
1555	Paul IV		Ferdinand I* **	1558
1559	Pius IV	⎭		
			Maximilian II	1564
1566	Pius V			
1572	Gregory XIII			
			Rudolf II	1576
1585	Sixtus V			
1590	Gregory XIV			
1591	Innocent IX			
1592	Clement VIII			
1605	Leo XI			
1605	Paul V			
			Matthias	1612
			Ferdinand II	1619
1621	Gregory XV			
1623	Urban VIII			
			Ferdinand III	1637
1644	Innocent X			
1655	Alexander VII			
			Leopold I	1658
1667	Clement IX			
1670	Clement X			
1676	Innocent XI			
1689	Alexander VIII			
1691	Innocent XII			
1700	Clement XI			
			Joseph I	1705
			Charles VI	1711
1720	Innocent XIII			
1724	Benedict XIII			
1740	Benedict XIV			

* Never crowned as emperor.
** After Charles V, none of the emperors were crowned at Rome. Ferdinand I and his successors took the title of Emperor-Elect.

Chronological Tables of Popes and Emperors

YEAR OF ACCESSION A.D.	POPES	EMPERORS	YEAR OF ACCESSION A.D.
		Charles VII	1742
		Francis I of Lorraine*	1745
1758	Clement XII		
		Joseph II	1765
1769	Clement XIII		
1775	Pius VI		
		Leopold II	1790
		Francis II	1792
1800	Pius VII		
		Extinction of the Holy Roman Empire by the abdication of Francis II**	1806
1823	Leo XII		
1829	Pius VIII		
1831	Gregory XVI		
1846	Pius IX		
1878	Leo XIII		
1903	Pius X		
1914	Benedict XV		
1922	Pius XI		
1939	Pius XII		

* Husband of Maria Theresa.
** Francis abdicated as Holy Roman Emperor, but took the title of Emperor of Austria.

APPENDIX II
Genealogy of the Medici

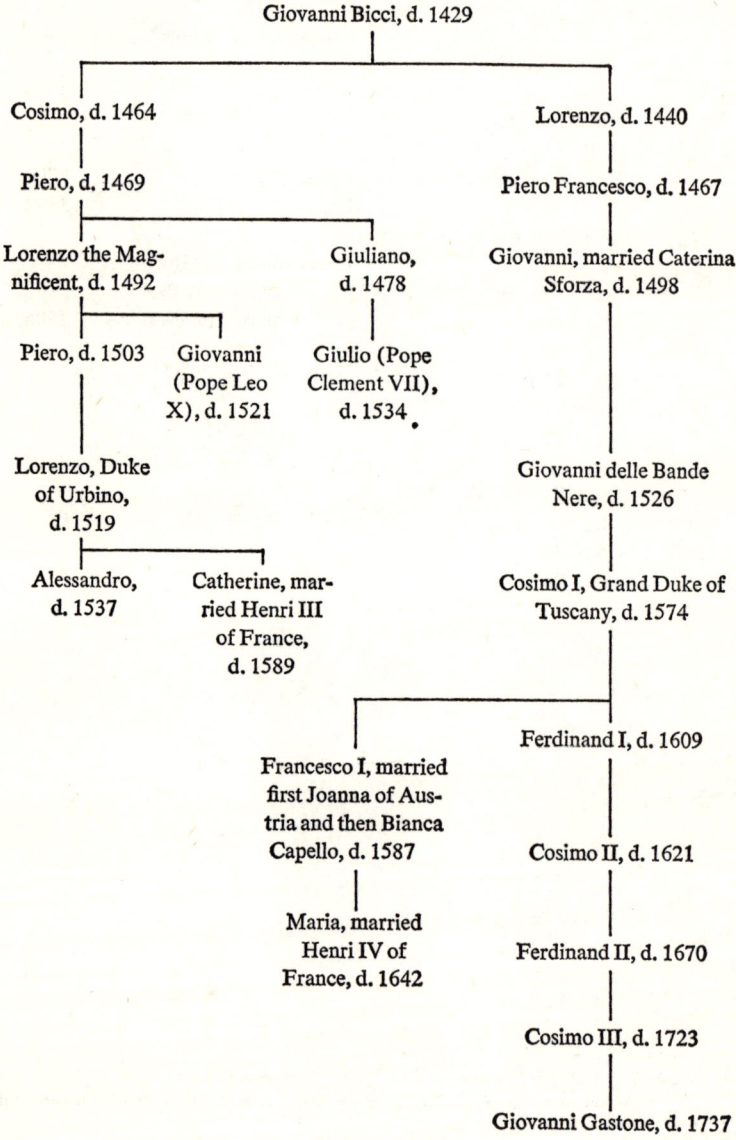

APPENDIX III
Skeleton Table of the Kings of the Two Sicilies*

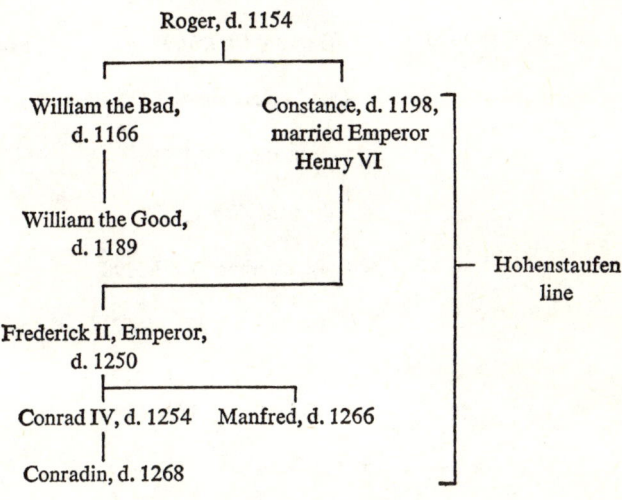

Naples	Kingdom of the Two Sicilies	Sicily
	Norman Conquest, latter half of eleventh century	
	Roger, d. 1154	
	William the Bad, d. 1166 — Constance, d. 1198, married Emperor Henry VI	
	William the Good, d. 1189	Hohenstaufen line
	Frederick II, Emperor, d. 1250	
	Conrad IV, d. 1254 Manfred, d. 1266	
	Conradin, d. 1268	
	French Conquest, 1266	
	Charles of Anjou 1266-1282	
House of Anjou 1266-1442		*Sicilian Vespers*, 1282 House of Aragon 1282-1442
	Alfonso of Aragon 1441-1458	
House of Aragon, illegitimate, 1458-1504		House of Aragon, legitimate, which, upon the marriage of Ferdinand of Aragon with Isabella of Castile, became House of Spain, 1458-1504

Naples	Kingdom of the Two Sicilies	Sicily
Spanish Conquest, 1504	Ferdinand the Catholic, 1504-1516	
	Charles V., Emperor, 1516-1556	
	Spanish Crown, 1556-1713	
Austria, 1713-1720	*Treaty of Utrecht,* 1713	Savoy, 1713-1720
	Quadruple Alliance, 1720	
	Austria, 1720-1738	
	Peace of Vienna, 1738	
	Spanish Bourbons, 1738-1798	
	French invasion, 1798-1802	
	Spanish Bourbons, 1802-1805	
	Joseph Bonaparte, 1806-1808	
	Joachim Murat, 1808-1815	
	Spanish Bourbons: Ferdinand I, 1815-1825	
	Francis I, 1825-1830	
	Ferdinand II, 1830-1859	
	Francis II, 1859-1860	

* When the kingdoms of Naples and Sicily are united, the names of the kings are placed in the center column; when separate, the names are placed in the side columns respectively.

APPENDIX IV
The Visconti and Sforza Houses of Milan

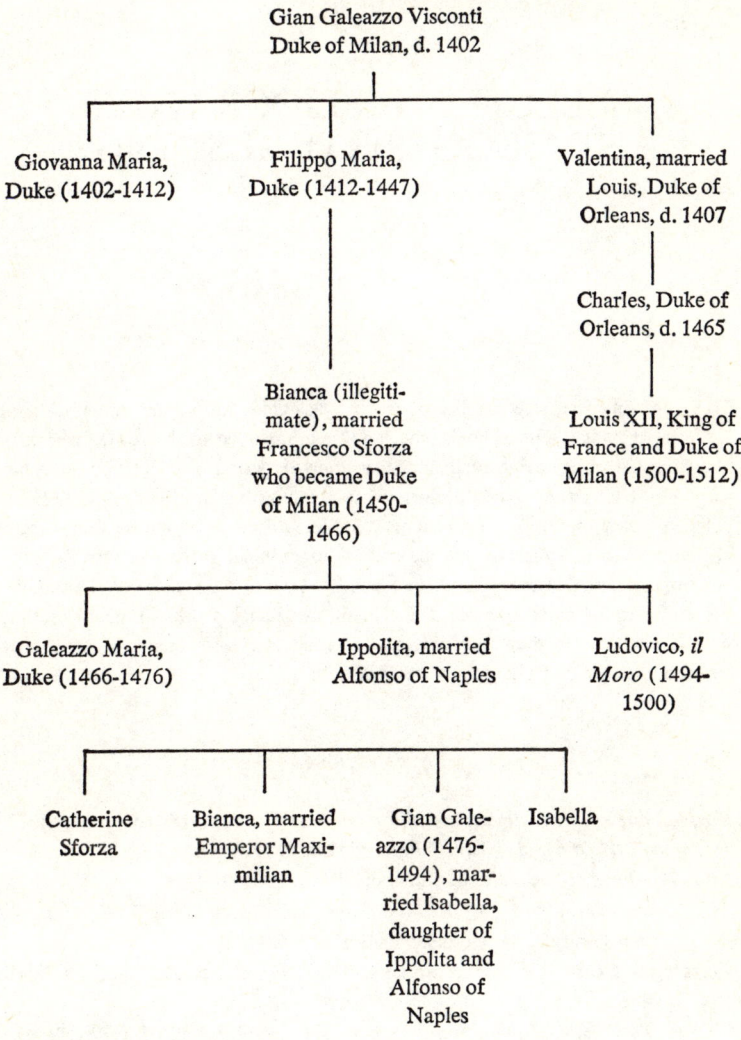

SELECTED BIBLIOGRAPHY AND SUGGESTED READINGS

The following is a selected list of works consulted during the preparation of UP FROM CAESAR, and of books specially recommended to the reader who may be interested in exploring further one or another period or event of Italian history. The list is neither comprehensive nor exhaustive in either respect, since, given the vast literature on all aspects of the subject, an immense tome would be required to give merely an adequate bibliographical guide. Because the present work is aimed at the general reader rather than at the student or the scholar, the author has limited himself to the mention of such works in English as are readily available to that audience, and of such works in languages other than English upon which he has leaned most heavily.

COLLECTIONS

Corpus Scriptorum Ecclesiasticorum Latinorum. Vienna, 1866–(continuing).
Documenti Diplomatici Italiani. Rome, 1952–*seq.*
Liber Pontificalis. 2 vols. Ed. L. Duchesne. Paris, 1884–1892.
Monumenta Germaniae Historica, inde ab a. 500 usque ad a. 1500. 120 vols. Ed. gen. Georg H. Pertz. Hanover-Berlin, 1826–1925.
Patrologiae Cursus Completus, Series Latina. 217 vols. Ed. J.-P. Migne. Paris, 1844–*seq.*
Regesta Pontificum Romanorum. Six vols. Ed. P. Jaffé, revised by W. Wattenbach, *et al.* Leipzig, 1885–1888.
Rerum Italicarum Scriptores. Ed. Ludovicus A. Muratori. Twenty-five vols. in folio. 1723–1750. (Rome, 1900–continuing).

Selected Bibliography and Suggested Readings 499

Sacrorum Conciliorum nova et amplissima collectio. Ed. Ioh. Dominicus Mansi. Fifty-three vols. Paris-Leipzig, 1901–1927.

CHAPTER I

The Fall of the Roman Empire and the Invasion of the Barbarians
(397–731 A.D.)

ACTON, JOHN E. E. D., First Baron Acton. *The History of Freedom and Other Essays.* Ed. J. N. Figgis and Reginald V. Laurence. 1909.
BARK, WILLIAM CARROLL. *Origins of the Medieval World.* New York, 1960.
BOETHIUS, ANICIUS MANLIUS SEVERINUS. *Philosophiae consolatio.* Ed. E. K. Rand and Hugh F. Stewart. 1918.
BOISSONADE, PROSPER. *Life and Work in Medieval Europe (Fifth to Fifteenth Centuries).* 1927.
BRÉHIER, LOUIS and RENÉ AIGRAIN. *Grégoire le grand, les états barbares et la conquête arabe (590–757).* Vol. V. of *Histoire de l'Eglise depuis les origines jusqu'à nos jours.* Paris, 1947.
BURY, J. B. *A History of the Later Roman Empire.* Two vols. 1923.
———. *The Invasion of Europe by the Barbarians.* 1928.
Cambridge Medieval History. Vols. 3–6. Cambridge, 1911–1936.
COCHRANE, CHARLES N. *Christianity and Classical Culture.* Oxford, 1940.
COURCELLE, PIERRE. *Histoire Littéraire des grandes invasions germaniques.* Paris, 1948.
DAWSON, CHRISTOPHER. *The Making of Europe.* 1932
DEANESLEY, MARGARET. *A History of Early Medieval Europe.* 1956.
DIEHL, CHARLES. *Byzance, Grandeur et décadence.* Paris, 1920.
———. *History of the Byzantine Empire.* Princeton, 1925.
DILL, SAMUEL. *Roman Society in the Last Century of the Western Empire.* 1899.
DUCKETT, ELEANOR SHIPLEY. *The Gateway to the Middle Ages.* Ann Arbor, 1938.
GIBBON, EDWARD. *The History of the Decline and Fall of the Roman Empire.* 5th ed. Ed. J. B. Bury. Six vols. 1923.
GUERDAN, RENÉ. *Byzantium.* 1956.
HUSSEY, J. M. *The Byzantine World.* 1957.
JENKINS, ROMILLY. *Byzantium: The Imperial Centuries.* 1966.
JEROME, ST. *Epistulae, Pars III.* Vol. LVI of *Corpus Scriptorum Ecclesiasticorum Latinorum,* ed. J. Hilberg. Vienna, 1918.
JONES, A. H. *The Later Roman Empire, 284–602.* Two vols. 1964.
LAISTNER, M. L. W. *Thought and Letters in Western Europe, A.D. 500 to 900.* new ed., 1957.

LOT, FERDINAND. *The End of the Ancient World and the Beginnings of the Middle Ages.* 1931.
———. *Les Invasions barbares et le peuplement de l'Europe.* Paris, 1937.
———. *Les invasions germaniques.* Paris, 1945.
LUZZATTO, GINO. *Storia Economica d'Italia.* Vol. I. Rome, 1949.
MARROU, HENRI-IRENEE. *The History of Education in Antiquity.* 1956.
MAZZARINO, SANTO. *The End of the Ancient World.* New York, 1966.
MURPHY, FRANCIS X. *Politics and the Early Christian.* New York, 1967.
RAND, E. K. *Founders of the Middle Ages.* Cambridge, Mass., 1928.
ROSTOVTZEFF, MICHAEL. *Social and Economic History of the Roman Empire.* Oxford, 1926.
SOUTHERN, R. W. *The Making of the Middle Ages.* 1959.
SPENGLER, O. *The Decline of the West.* 1926-29.
TOYNBEE, ARNOLD J. *A Study of History.* Twelve vols. 1962-1963.
VASILIEV, A. A. *History of the Byzantine Empire.* 1952.
WALBANK, F. W. *The Decline of the Roman Empire in the West.* 1946.
WALLACE-HADRILL, J. M. *The Barbarian West.* 1952.

CHAPTER II
The Emergence of Successors to Caesar (731–962)
and
CHAPTER III
Italy in the Middle Ages (962–1418)

ARTZ, F. *The Mind of the Middle Ages.* New York, 1953.
BLOCH, MARC. *Feudal Society.* Two vols. 1965.
BOASE, T. S. R. *Boniface VIII.* 1933.
BOISSONADE, P. *Le Travail dans l'Europe chrétienne au Moyen Age.* Paris, 1921.
BRYCE, JAMES. *The Holy Roman Empire.* 1904.
BULLOUGH, DONALD. *The Age of Charlemagne.* 1965.
Cambridge Medieval History. Seven vols. Cambridge, 1911–1936.
CANTOR, NORMAN F. *Medieval History.* 1963.
CHEYNEY, EDWARD P. *The Dawn of a New Era: 1250–1453.* 1936.
CROMBIE, A. C. *Augustine to Galileo,* 1952.
CURTIUS, ERNST R. *European Literature and the Latin Middle Ages.* 1953.
DAHMUS, JOSEPH. *A History of Medieval Civilization.* New York, 1964.
———. *Seven Medieval Kings.* New York, 1967.
DALY, L. J. *The Medieval University.* New York, 1961.
DANTE ALIGHIERI. *Il Canzoniere.* Ed. P. Fraticelli. Quarta Edizione. Florence, 1887.

———. *Il Convito* and *Le Epistole*. Ed. P. Fraticelli. Sesta Edizione. Florence, 1887.
———. *La Vita Nuova* and *I Trattati De Vulgari Eloquio, De Monarchia*. Ed. P. Fraticelli. Quinta Edizione. Florence, 1887.
———. *Divine Comedy*. Three vols. (Italian Text with English Translation and Comment by John D. Sinclair.) 1948.
DAWSON, CHRISTOPHER. *Medieval Essays*. 1953.
DEAUX, GEORGE. *The Black Death*. 1969.
DÉCARREAUX, J. *Les Moines et la Civilisation*. Paris, 1962.
DENZINGER, HENRICUS. *Enchiridion Symbolorum Definitionum et Declarationum de rebus fidei et morum*. 32nd ed. New York, 1953.
DE STEFANO, A. *La Cultura alle Corte de Federico II Imperatore*. Palermo, 1938.
FICHTENAU, HEINRICH. *The Carolingian Empire*. 1957.
FOLZ, R. *L'idée de l'Empire en Occident du 5ᵉ au 14ᵉ siècle*. Paris, 1953.
GANSHOF, F. L. *Feudalism*. 3rd ed., 1964.
HALLER, J. *Das Papsttum: Idee und Wirklichkeit*. Vols. II and III. Stuttgart, 1950–1953.
HASHAGEN, J. *Europa im Mittelalter*. Munich, 1951.
HASKINS, CHARLES HOMER. *The Normans in European History*. 1916.
———. *The Renaissance of the Twelfth Century*. Cambridge, Mass., 1927.
———. *Studies in the History of Medieval Science*. 1960.
———. *Studies in Medieval Culture*. 1958.
HEER, FRIEDRICH. *The Medieval World*. 1962.
HUIZINGA, J. *The Waning of the Middle Ages*. 1924.
JOHN OF SALISBURY. *The Letters of John of Salisbury*. Ed. W. J. Willor and H. E. Butler. Edinburgh, 1955.
KANTOROWICZ, ERNST. *Frederick the Second*. 1931.
LA BRIOLLE, P. DE. *Histoire de la Littérature Chrétienne*. Two vols. Paris, 1947.
LEA, HENRY C. *Studies in Church History*. Philadelphia, 1869.
———. *A History of the Inquisition of the Middle Ages*. Three vols. 1888.
———. *Superstition and Force*. Philadelphia, 1866.
LOPEZ, ROBERT S. *The Birth of Europe*. New York, 1966.
MUNDY, JOHN H. and PETER RIESENBERG. *The Medieval Town*. Princeton, 1958.
OTTO OF FREISING. *The Deeds of Frederick Barbarossa*. New York, 1953.
PAETOW, L. J. *A Guide to the Study of Mediaeval History*. London, 1931.
PIRENNE, HENRI. *Economic and Social History of Medieval Europe*. 1936.
———. *Medieval Cities*. Princeton, 1925.
———. *Mohammed and Charlemagne*. 1939.
POOLE, REGINALD LANE. *Illustrations of the History of Medieval Thought and Learning*. 2nd ed. 1920.
POWER, EILEEN. *Medieval People*. 1924.
PREVITÉ ORTON, C. W. *The Shorter Cambridge Medieval History*. Revised by P. Grierson. Cambridge, 1952.

PUTNAM, GEORGE H. *Books and Their Makers in the Middle Ages.* Two vols. New York, 1897–1898.
RASHDALL, H. *The Universities of Europe in the Middle Ages.* Three vols. Revised by F. Powicke and A. B. Emden. Oxford, 1936.
RUNCIMAN, STEVEN. *A History of the Crusades.* Three vols. New York, 1951-1954.
SALVATORELLI, L. *L'Italia communale dal s. xi alla metà del s. xiv.* Milan, 1940.
STADELMANN, R. *Vom Geist der Ausgehenden Mittelalters.* Halle, 1929.
TAYLOR, HENRY OSBORN. *The Classical Heritage of the Middle Ages.* Cambridge, Mass., 1901.
———. *The Medieval Mind.* 1925.
TELLENBACH, G. *Church, State and Christian Society at the Time of the Investiture Contest.* London, 1940.
THOMPSON, JAMES W. *Economic and Social History of the Middle Ages.* Two vols. 1928.
TOUT, T. F. *The Empire and the Papacy.* 4th ed. London, 1906.
TREECE, HENRY. *The Crusades.* 1962.
ULLMANN, W. *The Growth of Papal Government in the Middle Ages.* London, 1955.
VINCENT, MARVIN R. *The Age of Hildebrand.* Edinburgh, 1897.
VINOGRADOFF, PAUL. *Roman Law in Medieval Europe.* Edinburgh, 1909.
VON GRUNEBAUM, G. E. *Medieval Islam.* 2nd ed. Chicago, 1953.
WINSTON, RICHARD. *Charlemagne.* 1956.
ZEIGLER, PHILIP. *The Black Death.* New York, 1969.

CHAPTER IV

An Age of Renewal: The Renaissance (1400–1580)

ARIOSTO, LODOVICO. *Orlando Furioso.* Florence, n.d.
BALCARRES, LORD. *Evolution of Italian Sculpture.* 1909.
BARNES, HARRY ELMER. *An Intellectual and Cultural History of the Western World.* Three vols., 3rd ed. New York, 1965.
BELLONCI, MARIA. *The Life and Times of Lucrezia Borgia.* 1953.
BERENSON, BERNARD. *Florentine Painters of the Renaissance.* 1909.
———. *North Italian Painters of the Renaissance.* 1907.
BOCCACCIO, GIOVANNI. *Decameron.* 1934.
BRANDI, KARL. *Emperor Charles V.* 1939.
BRINTON, SELWYN. *The Gonzaga Lords of Mantua.* 1927.
BURCKHARDT, JACOB. *The Civilization of the Renaissance in Italy.* 1960.
CARTWRIGHT, JULIA. *Baldassare Castiglione.* 1908.

Selected Bibliography and Suggested Readings

CASTIGLIONE, B. *The Book of the Courtier.* 1956.
CELLINI, BENVENUTO. *Autobiography.* 1956.
CREIGHTON, MANDELL. *History of the Papacy during the Reformation.* Four vols. 1882.
CRUMP, C. H. and E. F. JACOB. *The Legacy of the Middle Ages.* Oxford, 1926.
DUHEM, P. *Etudes sur Léonardo de Vinci.* Three vols. Paris, 1906.
DURANT, WILL. *The Renaissance.* New York, 1953.
FERRARA, ORESTES. *The Borgia Pope: Alexander VI.* 1942.
FREUD, SIGMUND. *Leonardo da Vinci.* 1963.
GIONO, JEAN. *Le Désastre de Pavie.* Paris, 1963.
GUICCIARDINI, FRANCESCO. *History of Italy and History of Florence,* Chalfont St. Giles, 1966.
HEER, FRIEDRICH. *The Intellectual History of Europe.* 1966.
HOLT, ELIZABETH G. (Ed.) *A Documentary History of Art.* Two vols. New York, 1957.
JANELLE, PIERRE. *The Catholic Reformation.* Milwaukee, Wisc., 1949.
LANCIANI, RODOLFO. *The Golden Days of the Renaissance in Rome.* 1906.
LEONARDO DA VINCI. *Notebooks.* Ed. Edward McCurdy. 1938.
LUCAS, HENRY S. *The Renaissance and the Reformation.* 1934.
MACHIAVELLI, NICCOLO. *Discourses,* 1950.
Florentine History, 1909.
———. *The Prince.* 1960.
MATHER, F. J. *Western European Painting of the Renaissance.* New York, 1948.
MORLEY, J. *Machiavelli.* Oxford, 1897.
PASTOR, LUDWIG VON. *History of the Popes.* 1891.
PATER, WALTER. *The Renaissance.* 1877.
PREZZOLINI, GIUSEPPE. *Machiavelli.* 1928.
RANKE, LEOPOLD VON. *History of the Popes.* Three vols. 1878.
ROEDER, RALPH. *The Man of the Renaissance.* 1934.
RUSKIN, JOHN. *Stones of Venice.* Two vols. 1881.
SACERDOTE, GUSTAVO. *Cesare Borgia: La sua vita, la sua famiglia, i suoi tempi.* Milan, 1950.
SISMONDI, J. C. L. *History of the Italian Republics.* 1906.
STEINMANN, E. *Rom in der Renaissance, von Nicholas V bis auf Leo X.* Leipzig, 1908.
SYMONDS, J. A. *The Renaissance in Italy.* Six vols. 2nd ed. 1880.
TAYLOR, F. L. *The Art of War in Italy, 1494–1529.* Cambridge, 1921.
VASARI, GIORGIO. *Lives of the Most Eminent Painters, Sculptors, and Architects.* Four vols. 1897.
VILLARI, P. *Life and Times of Savonarola.* New York, 1888.
———. *Life and Times of Niccolo Machiavelli.* London, 1888.

CHAPTER V
Italy in the Modern World (1580–1814)

ALLEN, J. W. *A History of Political Thought in the Sixteenth Century.* 1928.
ANDRÉ, L. *Louis XIV et l'Europe.* Paris, 1950.
BARBAGALLO, C. *Riforme e Rivoluzione, 1699–1799.* Vol. 5 in *Storia Universale.* Turin, 1940.
BARNES, HARRY ELMER. *An Intellectual and Cultural History of the Western World.* Vol. II. 3rd ed. New York, 1965.
BEAUREGARD, COSTA DE. *Un homme d'autrefois.* Paris, 1891.
BEDARIDA, H. and PAUL HAZARD. *L'influence Francaise en Italie au XVIII siècle.* Paris, 1936.
BIANCHI, N. *Storia della monarchia piemontese dal 1773.* Four vols. Rome, 1877.
BONNAFFE, E. *Les arts et les moeurs d'autrefois: voyages et voyageurs de la Renaissance.* Paris, 1895.
BOURIENNE, M. DE. *Memoirs of Napoleon.* Four vols. 1836.
Cambridge Modern History. Vols. VII, VIII, IX. Cambridge, 1906–1909.
CLARK, G. N. *The Seventeenth Century.* 2nd ed. Oxford, 1947.
———. *War and Society in the Seventeenth Century.* London, 1958.
CROCE, BENEDETTO. *Storia del regno di Napoli.* Bari, 1925.
DANIEL-ROPS, H. *The Church in the Eighteenth Century.* 1964.
DE SANCTIS, FRANCESCO. *A History of Italian Literature.* Two vols. 1932.
DOWDEN, E. *Michel de Montaigne.* 1905.
FAURE, ELIE. *Napoléon.* Paris, 1924.
FERRARI, A. *L'Esplosione rivoluzionaria del Risorgimento, 1789–1815.* Milan, n.d.
FRANCHETTI, A. *Storia d'Italia dal 1789 al 1799.* Milan, 1907.
FRIEDERICH, C. J. *The Age of the Baroque, 1610–1660.* New York, 1952.
FUGIER, A. *La Révolution Francaise et l'Empire Napoléonien.* Paris, 1954.
HALL, A. R. *The Scientific Revolution, 1500–1800.* 1954.
HAUSER, D. *La Préponderance espagnole, 1559–1600.* Paris, 1935.
HAUTECOEUR, L. *Rome et la renaissance de l'antiquité à la fin du XVIIIe siècle.* Paris, 1912.
HAZARD, PAUL. *The European Mind: (1680-1715).* 1964.
———. *La Revolution francaise et les lettres Italiennes.* Paris, 1910.
HOLT, ELIZABETH G. *A Documentary History of Art.* Vol. II. New York, 1958.
KARPOVITCH, M. and A. USHER. *An Economic History of Europe since 1750.* New York, 1946.
LECKY, W. E. H. *History of European Morals.* London, 1869.
LEFEBVRE, GEORGES. *The French Revolution from Its Origins to 1793.* 1962.

LEGER, LOUIS. *The History of Austro-Hungary.* 1889.
LEMMI, F. *Le origini del Risorgimento Italiano, 1789–1815.* 2nd ed. Milan, 1924.
LUDWIG, EMIL. *Napoleon.* 1927.
MADELIN, LOUIS. *La Rome de Napoléon, 1809–1814.* Paris, 1906.
MAUGAIN, G. *L'Evolution intellectuelle en Italie de 1657 à 1750 environ.* Paris, 1909.
MELITO, MIOT DE. *Mémoires.* Paris, 1873.
MONTAIGNE, MICHEL EYQUEM DE. *Journal of Montaigne's Travels in Italy by Way of Switzerland and Germany in 1580 and 1581.* 1903.
NATALI, G. *Il Settecento.* Two vols. Milan, 1929.
NEUENBERG, MATTHIAS VON. *Quellenbuch zur Osterreichische Geschichte.* Two vols. Vienna, 1956.
OGG, DAVID. *Europe in the Seventeenth Century.* 7th ed. 1959.
ORSI, P. *L'Italia moderna.* 3rd ed. Milan, 1910.
ORTOLANI, G. *L'Italie au XVIIIe siècle.* Paris, 1929.
PINGAUD, A. *Bonaparte, président de la République italienne.* Paris, 1914.
PRATO, G. *La vita economica in Piemonte a mezzo il secolo xviii.* Turin, 1908.
ROTA, E. *Le origini del Risorgimento.* 2nd ed. Milan, 1950.
SAGNAC, P. *La fin de l'Ancien Regime.* 3rd ed. Paris, 1952.
SAVANT, JEAN. *Napoléon, raconté par les temoins de sa vie.* Paris, 1954.
SEDGWICK, HENRY D. *Short History of Italy.* 1906.
SEIGNOBOS, CHARLES. *Essai d'une histoire comparée des peuples de l'Europe.* Paris, 1938.
SHIPLEY, A. E. *The Revival of Science in the Seventeenth Century.* Princeton, 1914.
SIMIONI, ATTILIO. *Le origini del Risorgimento politico dell'Italia Meridionale.* Two vols. Rome, 1925.
SMITH, PRESERVED. *A History of Modern Culture: The Enlightenment, 1687–1776.* Two vols. 1930-1934.
SOREL, A. *L'Europe et la Révolution francaise.* Eight vols. Paris, 1904.
TIVARONI, G. *L'Italia prima della Rivoluzione francese, 1735–1789.* Turin, 1888.
WHITE, A. D. *A History of the Warfare of Science with Theology.* Two vols. 1955.
WILLIS, I. C. *Montaigne.* 1927.

CHAPTER VI
From Absolutism to Independence (1814–1870)

ACTON, HAROLD. *The Last Bourbons of Naples, 1825–1861.* 1961.
ARRIVABENE, COUNT CHARLES. *Italy Under Victor Emmanuel.* 1862.
AUBERT, R. *Le Pontificat de Pie IX, 1846–1878.* Paris, 1952.
ARTZ, F. B. *Reaction and Revolution, 1814–1832.* 1934.
BERTI, G. *I democratici e l'iniziativa meridionale nel Risorgimento.* Milan, 1962.
BIANCHI, NICOMEDE. *Storia documentata della diplomazia Europea in Italia dell'anno 1814 all'anno 1861.* Turin, 1865.
——. *Il Conte Camillo Cavour. Documenti editi ed inediti.* Turin, 1863.
BOURGEOIS, EMILE and E. CLERMONT. *Rome et Napoléon III, 1849–1870.* Paris, 1907.
BINCHY, DANIEL A. *Church and State in Fascist Italy.* 1941.
CASE, L. M. *Franco-Italian Relations 1860–1865: The Roman Question and the Convention of September.* Philadelphia, 1932.
CAVOUR, CAMILLO DI. *La Liberazione del Mezzogiorno e la formazione del Regno d'Italia.* Bologna, 1949–1954.
——. *Lettere edite ed inedite di Camillo Cavour.* Ed. Luigi Chiala. Turin, 1883–1887.
DE CESARE, RAFFAELE. *The Last Days of Papal Rome, 1850–1870.* 1909.
DELZELL, CHARLES F. (Ed.) *The Unification of Italy.* New York, 1965.
FARINI, LUIGI C. *The Roman State, 1815–1850.* 1851.
FERRERO, GUGLIELMO. *The Reconstruction of Europe.* New York, 1941.
GLADSTONE, W. E. *Two Letters to the Earl of Aberdeen on the State Prosecutions of the Neapolitan Government.* 1851.
GRAMSCI, ANTONIO. *Il Risorgimento.* Turin, 1949.
——. *Sul Risorgimento.* Ed. E. Fubini. Rome, 1959.
GREENFIELD, K. R. *Economics and Liberalism in the Risorgimento.* Baltimore, 1934.
HALES, E. E. Y. *Pio Nono.* 1954.
HERMAN, A. *Metternich.* 1932.
HOBSBAWM, E. J. *The Age of Revolution, 1789–1848.* 1962.
KING, BOLTON. *Mazzini.* 1902.
——. *A History of Italian Unity.* 1898.
MACK SMITH, DENIS. *Garibaldi:* 1957.
MATTER, PAUL. *Cavour et l'unité Italienne, 1856–1861.* Paris, 1927.
MAY, A. J. *The Age of Metternich, 1814–1848.* New York, 1933.
NICOLSON, H. *The Congress of Vienna.* 1946.
PALÉOLOGUE, MAURICE. *Cavour.* 1927.

PIERI, PIERO. *Storia militare del Risorgimento.* Turin, 1962.
ROBERTSON, PRISCILLA. *Revolutions of 1848: A Social History.* Princeton, 1952.
ROMEO, ROSARIO. *Il Risorgimento in Piemonte.* Turin, 1963.
SALVADORI, MASSIMO. *Cavour and the Unification of Italy.* New York, 1961.
SALVATORELLI, LUIGI. *Il pensiero politico italiano dal 1700 al 1870.* Turin, 1935.
SALVEMINI, GAETANO. *Scritti sul Risorgimento.* Ed. Piero Pieri and C. Pischedda. Milan, 1963.
STRAUS, H. A. *The Attitude of the Congress of Vienna to Nationalism in Germany, Italy, and Poland.* New York, 1950.
TAYLOR, A. J. P. *The Italian Problem in European Diplomacy, 1847–1849.* Manchester, 1934.
THOMPSON, J. M. *Louis Napoleon and the 2nd Empire.* Oxford, 1954.
THAYER, WILLIAM ROSCOE. *The Life and Times of Cavour.* 1911.
WEBSTER, C. K. *The Congress of Vienna, 1814–1815.* 1919.
WHYTE, ARTHUR JAMES. *The Political Life and Letters of Cavour, 1848–1861.* 1930.

CHAPTER VII
The New Italy (1870–1920)

ALBRECHT–CARRIÉ, RENÉ. *Italy at the Paris Peace Conference.* New York, 1938.
BEDESCHI, SANTE and RINO ALESSI. *Anni Giovanili di Mussolini.* Milan, 1938.
BEZANÇON, MARCEL. *Mussolini in der Schweiz.* Zurich, n.d.
BONOMI, IVANOE. *Dal socialismo al fascismo.* Rome, 1924.
CARDONA, L. *La Guerra alla Fronte Italiana.* Two vols. Rome, 1921.
CAROFIGLIO, MARIO F. *Vita di Mussolini e storia del fascismo.* Turin, 1950.
CARSTEN, F. L. *The Rise of Fascism.* 1967.
GIOLITTI, GIOVANNI. *Memoirs of My Life.* 1923.
HAYES, C. J. H. *The Historical Evolution of Modern Nationalism.* New York, 1931.
HENTZE, MARGOT. *Pre-Fascist Italy: The Rise and Fall of the Parliamentary Regime.* 1934.
HOLLIS, CHRISTOPHER. *Italy in Africa.* 1941.
JEMOLO, ARTURO C. *Chiesa e stato in Italia negli ultimi cento anni.* Rome, 1948.
KING, BOLTON and THOMAS OKEY. *Italy Today.* 1913.
MACARTNEY, MAXWELL H. and PAUL CREMONA. *Italy's Foreign and Colonial Policy, 1914–1937.* 1938.
MACMILLAN, HAROLD. *Winds of Change, 1914–1939.* 1966.
MEGARO, GAUDENS. *Mussolini in the Making.* 1938.
MUSSOLINI, BENITO. *The Political and Social Doctrine of Fascism.* 1933.
NOLTE, ERNEST. *Three Faces of Fascism.* Translated by Leila Vennewitz. 1965.

PREZZOLINI, GIUSEPPE. *Fascism.* 1926.
RAGIONIERI, ERNESTO. *Socialdemocrazia tedesca e socialisti italiani 1875–1895.* Milan, 1961.
ROSSATO, ARTURO. *Mussolini: colloquio intimo.* Milan, 1922.
SALANDRA, ANTONIO. *Italy and the Great War.* 1932.
SALOMONE, A. WILLIAM. *Italian Democracy in the Making: The Political Scene in the Giolittian Era 1900–1914.* n.d.
SALVATORELLI, LUIGI. *A Concise History of Italy.* New York, 1940.
SAN SEVERINO, B. Q. DI. *Mussolini as Revealed in His Political Speeches.* 1924.
SCHNEIDER, HERBERT. *Making the Fascist State.* New York, 1928.
SPRIGGE, CECIL J. S. *The Development of Modern Italy.* 1943.
STURZO, L. *Popolarismo e fascismo.* Turin, 1924.
WHYTE, A. J. *The Evolution of Modern Italy.* 1959.

CHAPTER VIII

The Age of Fascism: Benito Mussolini (1920–1945)

ALBRECHT–CARRIÉ, RENÉ. *Italy: From Napoleon to Mussolini.* New York, 1950.
BADOGLIO, PIETRO. *Italy in the Second World War.* 1948.
BONOMI, IVANOE. *Diario di un anno: 2 giungo 1943–10 giungo 1944.* Milan, 1947.
BULLOCK, ALAN. *Hitler: A Study in Tyranny.* 1952.
CAROFIGLIO, MARIO. *Vita di Mussolini e storia del fascismo.* Turin, 1950.
CAVALLERO, UGO. *Commando supremo: Diario 1940–1943.* Bologna, 1948.
CHABOD, FEDERICO. *A History of Italian Fascism.* 1963.
CHURCHILL, WINSTON S. *The Second World War.* Six vols. 1948-1954.
CIANO, GALEAZZO. *Ciano's Diary 1939-1943.* 1947.
———. *Europa verso la catastrofe.* Rome, 1948.
CLARK, W. MARK. *Calculated Risk.* 1951.
DEAKIN, F. WILLIAM. *The Brutal Friendship.* 1962.
DOMBROSKI, ROMAN. *Mussolini, Twilight and Fall.* 1956.
EDEN, ANTHONY. *The Memoirs of Anthony Eden.* 1960.
EISENHOWER, DWIGHT D. *Crusade in Europe.* 1948.
FERMI, LAURA. *Mussolini.* 1961.
FINER, HERMAN. *Mussolini's Italy.* 1935.
GARRATT, GEOFFREY T. *Mussolini's Roman Empire.* 1938.
GOEBBELS, JOSEPH. *The Goebbels Diaries: 1942–1943.* Edited and translated with an introduction by Louis P. Lochner. 1948.
HITLER, ADOLF and BENITO MUSSOLINI. *Lettere e documenti.* Milan, 1946.
HUGHES, H. STUART. *The United States and Italy.* (Rev. ed.) Cambridge, Mass., 1965.

Selected Bibliography and Suggested Readings

KIRKPATRICK, IVONE. *Mussolini: A Study in Power.* 1964.
KOGAN, NORMAN. *Italy and the Allies.* Cambridge, Mass., 1956.
MACK SMITH, D. *Italy: A Modern History.* Ann Arbor, 1959.
MACMILLAN, HAROLD. *Winds of Change, 1914–1939.* 1966.
———. *The Blast of War, 1939–1945.* 1967.
MAJDALANY, FRED. *The Fall of Fortress Europe.* 1969.
MAMMARELLA, GIUSEPPE. *Italy After Fascism.* Notre Dame, 1966.
MOSLEY, LEONARD. *On Borrowed Time: How World War II Began.* 1969.
MUSSOLINI, BENITO. *Memoirs, 1942–1943.* 1949.
NOGUÈRES, HENRI. *Munich: The Phoney Peace.* 1965.
PINI, GIORGIO and DUILIO SUSMEL. *Mussolini, l'uomo e l'opera.* Four vols. Florence, 1953.
RIBBENTROP, J. VON. *The Ribbentrop Memoirs.* 1954.
SALVATORELLI, L. and GIOVANNI MIRA. *Storia d'Italia nel periodo fascista.* Turin, 1961.
SARFATTI, MARGHERITA. *The Life of Mussolini.* 1925.
SCHMIDT, PAUL. *Hitler's Interpreter.* 1951.
SHIRER, WILLIAM L. *Berlin Diary.* 1941.
———. *The Rise and Fall of the Third Reich.* 1960.
TAMARO, ATTILIO. *Venti anni di storia, 1922–1943.* Three vols. Rome, 1953.
TAYLOR, A. J. P. *The Origins of the Second World War.* 1961.
WISKEMANN, ELIZABETH. *Italy.* 1947.
———. *The Rome-Berlin Axis: A History of the Relations between Hitler and Mussolini.* 1949.

INDEX

Abelard, Peter, 232
Abruzzi, the, 127. *See also* specific cities
Absolutism (*see also* Despotism); to independence from (1814–1870), 340 ff., 370–84; Mussolini and, 448
Abyssinia. *See* Ethiopia
Academy of Arcadia, 323
Achmed III, Sultan of Turkey, 313
Acre, 139, 159
Actionists, 482
Addis Ababa, 455
Adelaide, Otto I and, 100–1
Adoration of the Shepherds (Ghirlandaio), 250
Adrian I, Pope, 64, 65–72, 73, 74
Adrian II, Pope, 87, 91
Adrian IV, Pope, 129–33
Adriatic Sea, 420, 421–22
Aëtius, 16–17
Africa, 393, 397, 399, 406 (*see also* specific locations); Mussolini and, 407–9, 419, 420, 423, 454–55, 466, 467, 468, 469, 470, 471–72, 473–75; Roman Empire and, 10, 20, 44; World War II landings in, 474–75
Agadir incident, 408–9
Agapitus II, Pope, 100–1
Agiluf, King of the Lombards, 36
Agnellus, Bishop of Ravenna, 61
Agnes of Meran, 147–48
Agordat, 397

Agriculture, 377, 387, 389, 392, 396, 397
Aistulf, King of the Lombards, 58, 62
Alamein. *See* El Alamein
Alani, the, 11
Alaric, 10–14
Albania, 460–61
Alberic (Roman ruler), 92
Alberti, Leon Battista, 283–84
Albert of Cologne, 241
Albigensian heresies, 150
Albion, King of the Lombards, 35
Albizzi, Maso degli, 229
Alcuin, and Charlemagne, 72, 76–77, 232
Alemanni, the, 32
Alessandria, 364
Alessi, Galeazzo, 293
Alexander I, Tsar of Russia, 341
Alexander III, Pope, 133–35, 139
Alexander IV, Pope, 167, 168
Alexander VI (Rodrigo Borgia) Pope, 258, 259, 263, 264–67, 284
Alexandria, Egypt, 125
Alexius III, Emperor, 139
Alfieri, Vittorio, 331
Alfonso (of Aragon), King of Naples, 226, 251, 261
Algeria (Algiers), 474–75
Allah, 49
Allies, World War I, 411–24 *passim*, 432, 434, 435, 443. *See also* specific countries

Index

Allies, World War II, 467, 471, 474, 478–83. *See also* specific countries
Altinum, 16
Amadeus, King of Spain, 390
Amalfi, 93, 110, 111, 123, 124
Amati of Cremona, 325
Ambassadors, Conference of (1923), 445
Ambrose, St., 18
Ambrosio, Vittorio, 476
America(ns). *See* United States
Ammanati, Bartolommeo, 293
Anagni, 178, 221–22
Anarchists-Socialists, 391, 395–96, 425, 427–28
Anastasius I, Emperor, 25
Ancona, 330, 347
Ancona, March of, 162–63
Anfuso, Filippo, 466
Angelico, Fra (Fra Giovanni; Guido di Pietro), 235, 239–40, 241, 250
Angevin (Anjou) dynasty, 169–70, 172, 173, 174, 182, 186–87, 200, 208, 226, 256, 261. *See also* specific individuals by name
Anjou, House of. *See* Angevin (Anjou) dynasty; specific individuals by name
Anschluss, 457
Anthemius, Emperor, 18
Anti-Comintern Pact, 457
Antiquity, revival of interest in, 209–12, 230 ff., 241 ff.
Anzio, World War II landing at, 480
Aosta, Duke of, 468–69
Apulia, 99, 110, 111, 123, 130, 135, 138, 144, 165, 167, 386, 480
Aquila, 127
Aquileia, 12, 16
Aquinas, Thomas. *See* Thomas Aquinas, St.
Aquitaine, 84
Arabia, 48–49, 123. *See also* Arabs; specific people, places, religions
Arabs, 37, 156. *See also* Arabia; specific people, places, religions
Arachis, Duke of Benevento, 70–71
Aragon (Aragonese), 148, 150, 173–74, 187, 208, 226, 261–62. *See also* specific individuals
Arcadians, 323
Arcadius, 9, 10
Architecture (architects), 202–3, 231–38,

248, 272, 276–79, 283–84, 287, 292–94, 295, 298, 322
Argiropulo, John, 284
Arian Christians, 7, 17, 23, 29–31, 39, 44, 47
Ariditi, 423, 437
Ariosto, Lodovico, 273–74, 294, 324
Aristides, statue in Vatican Library of, 304
Aristotle, 231, 235, 242
Armenia, 49, 148
Arnold of Brescia, 127, 128
Arnolfo di Cambio, 202–3, 236
Arno of Salzburg, 73
Arnulf, King of Germany, 91, 98, 100
Arsenal of Venice, 227
Art(s), 200–4, 233–53, 272–86, 287, 292 ff., 298, 318–26, 348. *See also* Architecture; Literature; Music; Painting; Sculpture; specific artists, works
Asia Minor, 36
Aspromonte, Battle of, 379
Assisi, 228
Asti, 135
Astronomy, 312, 319–20
Athalaric, 31
Athanarich, 8
Athaulf, 14–15
Athens, 10
Atlantic Charter, 480
Attila, 15–16, 19
Attolico, Bernardo, 462–63
Augsburg, 118–19
Augustine, St., 247, 250
Austria, 181, 253, 255, 288, 291, 310, 313, 314–15, 318, 394 (*see also* Austro-Hungarian Empire; Hapsburgs; specific events, individuals, locations); Hitler and, 453–54, 457, 460; Italian independence and, 340–47, 348, 351, 352 ff., 359–69, 370 ff., 378, 379, 380–84, 385, 386, 390, 391, 392, 393; Italian nationalism and, 407; and Italy (Mussolini), World War II, 453–54, 457, 460; and Italy, Napoleonic era, 327 ff., 333 ff., 335 ff., 338 ff., 340–47 ff.; and Italy, World War I, 410–424 *passim;* and war with France, 366–69, 370 ff.
Austrian Succession, War of, 313, 314

Austro-Hungarian Empire, 410–13, 421. See also Austria; Hungary
Authari, King of the Lombards, 35–36
Autocrat of the Romans, title of, 37
Automobile industry, founding of, 403
Avanguardia Socialista (Socialist newspaper), 428
Avantil (Socialist newspaper), 398, 410, 429, 430–31, 432
Avars, the, 34–35, 37
Aversa, 110–11
Avignon, popes and papacy in, 179–80, 182, 184, 187, 218–19, 220, 222, 223, 225, 226
Avitus, 18
Axis, Italo-German, 454 ff., 468 ff., 476–84
Azeglio, Massimo d', 350, 352, 360, 361, 362, 363, 385
Azzo, 114

Babylonian Captivity of the Church (Avignon popes), 179–80, 182, 184, 187, 218–19, 220, 225; end of, 219
Bacon, Francis, 312, 320
Bacon, Roger, 232
Badoglio, Marshal Pietro, 455, 477–78, 479, 480, 481
Bakunin, M. A., 395–96, 425
Balbo, Italo, 438, 440, 441
Baldwin, Count of Flanders, 149
Balearic Islands, 123
Balkans, 419, 460–70, 471. See also specific countries
Bandieri brothers, 350
Banditti (brigands), 301, 307, 310, 316, 321
Banking industry, rise of, 188, 190–91
"Bank Scandal" (Bank of Rome), 395
Barbarossa (Frederick I), Emperor, 122–23, 127–36
Barbarians (*see also* specific events, individuals, locations, people); and founding of Italian kingdom, 9–53, 54 ff.; invasion of Roman Empire by, 1 ff.; invasions in Renaissance era (1494–1537) by, 253–71, 286 ff.; map of kingdoms of, 2–3; new invasions (mid-ninth century) by, 97–99
Barberini family, 317, 318
Bardia, 470

Bari, 110
Baronius, Cardinal, 90 n.
Baroque period, 292 ff., 298, 321 ff.
Barozzi, Giacomo. See Vignola
Barrès, Maurice, 407
Barsanti clubs, 391, 394
Basileus, title of, 37–38, 78, 79
Basilicata, 386
Battisti, Cesare, 428
"Battle of the Grain," 452
Bava-Beccaris, General, 400, 401
Bavaria, 71, 84, 100
Beauharnais, Eugene de, 338
Beccaria, Cesare, 327
Belfagor arcidiavolo (Machiavelli), 272
Belgium, 56
Belisarius, 31–32
Bellarmine, St. Robert, 90 n.
Bellegarde, Marshal, 338
Bellini, censorship of his opera *I Puritani,* 348
Benedict V, Pope, 104–5
Benedict XIII (Schismatic Pope), 224–25
Benedict XIV, Pope, 331
Benedict XV, Pope, 434
Benedictines, 42
Benedict of Nursia, St., 41–42, 46, 48
Beneš, Eduard, 458
Benevento (Beneventum), 35, 36, 68, 70–71, 91, 93, 99, 105, 110, 111, 169
Beneventum. See Benevento (Beneventum)
Bentinck, Lord William, 338
Berchet, Giovanni, 347
Berengar of Frivli, Emperor, 98, 101, 103, 104
Bergamo, 16, 126, 227
Bernhard (grandson of Charlemagne), King of Italy, 83
Bernini, Giovanni Lorenzo, 321–22
Berthier, General, 334
Berthold of Hohenburg, 167
Besancon, Diet of (1157), 130–31, 133
Bianchi, Michele, 433, 441
Birth of Venus (Botticelli), 249, 250
Bishops, 126, 151; appointment of, 106–8, 112–21, 126, 147
Bismarck, Otto von, 281, 405, 412
Bismarckianism, 405, 412
Bisticci, Vespasiano da, 235
Black Plague, 213
Black Shirts, 437–39, 440, 442, 445

Index

Blandrate, Count, 132
Boboli Gardens, 293
Boccaccio, Giovanni, 201, 213, 231, 233; *Decameron* by, 213, 231, 266
Boëthius, 30
Bohemia, 102, 109, 140, 148, 223–24, 459
Boiardo, Matteo, 273
Bologna, 127, 132, 134, 161, 191, 200, 207–8, 209, 228; described by Montaigne, 301; and independence, 348; language, 201; liberated, World War II, 483; Napoleonic era, 330, 333; University of, 198, 200, 209, 330
Bologna school of painting, 322
Bonapartes. *See* Joseph Bonaparte; Napoleon Bonaparte; Napoleon III
Boniface, St., 57
Boniface VIII, Pope, 171–79, 180, 181, 232
Bonifazio Veronese di Pitati, 296
Bonifica Integrale, 452
Bonomi, Ivanoe, 431, 439, 440, 481–82
Book of the Courtier (Castiglione), 273
Bordone, Paris, 296
Borgia, Caesare, 265, 266, 267, 276
Borgia, Lucrezia, 265, 267
Borgia, Rodrigo. *See* Alexander VI (Rodrigo Borgia), Pope
Borgias, 258, 259, 265–67. *See also* specific individuals by name
Boselli, Paolo, 415, 418
Botticelli, Sandro, 249–50
Bourbon, Charles, Duke of, 270, 271
Bourbons, French, 310, 334, 336, 340 ff., 345, 374. *See also* specific individuals, events, locations
Bourbons, Spanish, 314, 315, 330–31, 332, 334–35, 341, 358, 359, 387. *See also* specific events, individuals, locations
Bracciolini, Poggio, 243
Bramante (Donato d' Agnolo) of Urbino, 274, 276–77, 278, 279, 283, 284, 285
Bread (and circuses), Roman, 6, 8, 33
Brenner Line, World War I, 423
Brescia, 32, 126, 127, 131, 161, 183, 206, 207, 227, 333, 355, 379
Brindisi, 157, 158
Bronzino (Agnolo di Cosimo), 294
Brunelleschi, Filippo, 235–37, 238, 293
Bruni, Leonardo, 242–43

Bruno, Giordano, 318–19
Bryce, James, 78
Bulgaria, 148
Bullock, Alan, 484
Bülow, General Karl von, 417, 418
Buol, Count, 363–64, 365, 368
Burghers, city-republics, 191–92, 204 ff.
Bury, J. B., 17 n.
Byzantine architecture, 202
Byzantine civilization, 202, 203, 232, 233, 241–42
Byzantine Empire (Byzantium), 36–53, 54, 56 ff., 69 ff., 72, 73, 76, 78 ff., 83, 93, 97, 110, 120, 130, 149. *See also* Byzantine civilization; Constantinople, Greece; specific events, individuals, locations
Byzantine painting, 203

Cacciaguida, 199
Cadorna, General Luigi, 413–15, 416, 417, 418
Cairoli, Benedette, 390, 391, 392
Calabria, 170, 350, 386
Cambrai, League of, 261
Cambrai, Treaty of (1529), 286
Campanella, Tommaso, 318
Campo Formio, Treaty of, 333, 334
Canossa, 119
Canute, King of Denmark, 148
Caporetto, Battle of, 417, 418, 419, 421, 434
Cappello, Bianca, 302
Capua, 71, 99, 105, 110, 111, 128
Caracci, Agostino, 244, 322
Caracci, Annibale, 244, 322
Caracci, Lodovico, 244, 322
Caracciolo, Admiral, 336
Caravaggio, Michelangelo da, 294, 322
Carbonari, 345–46, 349, 350
Cardinals, Sacred College of, 109, 173, 185, 220–25, 351
Carolingian Empire, 58, 63 ff., 93. *See also* Franks; specific individuals, locations
Carrara family, 207, 210, 227
Carrion-Nisas, M., 334
Carthage, 15
Casibile, Sicily, 478
Cassiodorus, 27
Castellano, General Giuseppe, 478
Castelli, pleads for Galileo, 319

Castiglione, Baldassarre, 272–73, 294
Cateau-Cambrésis, Treaty of (1559), 286, 289, 302
Catena (robber), hanging of, 307
Catherine of Siena, St., 219, 222
Catholic Reformation. *See* La Counter-Reformation
Cavallero, Marshal Count Ugo, 475
Cavour (battleship), 470
Cavour, Camillo Benso, Count di, 353, 360–69, 370, 372–76, 377, 378–79, 383, 388; and "Great Ministry," 361 ff.
Celestine III, Pope, 137, 138, 139, 147
Celestine IV, Pope, 163
Celestine V, Pope, 172
Celibacy of the clergy, 106
Cellini, Benvenuto, 294
Center (Moderates), political party, 400
Central Powers, World War I, 411–24 *passim*, 432. *See also* specific countries
Centuriae Magdeburgenses, 90 n.
Chamberlain, Neville, 458, 459, 460, 462, 465
Chamber of Deputies (*see also* Parliament); abolished (1938), 450
Chamber of Fasces and Corporations, 450
Charlemagne (Charles I the Great), Emperor, 58, 63–84, 85–86, 94, 96, 99; coronation at St. Peter's of, 77–78; death of, 83–84; "Donation" of, 67 ff., 71, 73; map of empire of, 55; and "Translation of the Empire," 78–80
Charles (Charles of Durazzo), King of Naples, successor to Joanna I, 226
Charles, Count of Anjou, King of Naples, 168–70, 173, 186–87, 203
Charles, Count of Valois, 174
Charles II (the Bald), King of France, 84, 85, 87
Charles III (Bourbon), King of Naples, 330–31
Charles V, Emperor, 256, 260, 269–71, 287, 289, 290
Charles VIII, King of France, 256, 257, 265
Charles Albert, Prince of Carignan, King of Naples and Sicily, 347, 352, 353–54, 355, 356–57, 360
Charles Felix, King of Naples and Sicily, 347, 352
Charles Martel, King of the Franks, 52, 57
Cherasco, Treaty of, 333
Chigi family, 318
Childebert II, King, 35–36, 37
Childeric III, King, 58
Chioggia, War of (1378–1381), 227
Christ. *See* Jesus Christ
Christian Democrats, political party, 482
Christianity, 37, 40 ff., 81 (*see also* Bishops; Church and State; Churches; Clergy; Jesus Christ; Monasticism; Papacy; Religion; specific aspects, denominations, individuals); and fall of Rome, 1 n., 7, 11, 12, 16, 22 ff.; Gregory I and, 41, 42–47; Renaissance era, 230, 243–44, 247, 249–50; and revival of faith (13th and 14th centuries), 196–97
Church and State, separation of, 376, 380, 382–83; Mussolini and, 450–51
Churches, architecture, painting, and sculpture, 201–4. *See also* specific churches, locations
Churchill, Winston, 467, 478, 482
Cialdini, General Enrico, 379
Ciano, Count Galeazzo, 455–56, 458, 460, 461, 462–64, 465–66, 467, 468, 471, 472, 473; executed, 480
Cicero, 231, 242, 243
Cimabue, 203
Cinquecento, 286–97, 298 ff.; end of, 298 ff., 318 ff.
Circuses, Roman, 6, 8, 33
Cisalpine Republic, 333, 336
Cispadane Republic, 333
City-republics (cities; city-states) (*see also* specific cities, kingdoms, republics); economy, 190 ff.; government in, 188–90 ff., 204 ff., 255 ff.; Middle Ages, 183 ff., 186 ff.; physical structure of, 187–88; Renaissance era, 232 ff.; revival of faith in, 197; rise of, 122–39; trade (commerce), 190–95; warfare between, 191–93, 197, 214 ff., 226
Civitas Solis (Campanella), 318
Clarendon, Lord, 363
Classics, revival of interest in, 209–12; Renaissance era, 230 ff., 241 ff.

Index

Classic style (architecture), 293–94
Claudian (historian), 10
Clemenceau, Georges, 421
Clement III, Pope, 137, 140
Clement III (Guibert of Ravenna), anti-Pope, 120
Clement IV, Pope, 168–69, 170
Clement V, Pope, 179, 182, 184, 185
Clement VI, Pope, 211
Clement VII (Giulio de' Medici), Pope, 268, 269–71, 282, 289
Clement VII (Schismatic Pope), 222–23, 224
Clement XII, Pope, 331
Cleph, King of the Lombards, 35
Clergy, 41, 44, 86, 91–92, 94–99, 222 ff. (*see also* Bishops; Cardinals; Christianity; Monasticism; Papacy; Religion; specific aspects, individuals, locations, Orders, etc.); and Italian independence, 348; Napoleonic era, 327, 330; reforms, 106–21
C.L.N. (Committees of National Liberation), 481, 482, 483
Clothilde, Princess, 367, 368
Clovis, 35, 57
Cluny, reforms at, 106, 108
College of Cardinals. *See* Cardinals, Sacred College of
Colleone (Verrocchio), 249, 295
Colonialism (colonial imperialism), 392, 393–94, 395, 397, 398, 399, 402, 405–6; map of Italian Empire (1939), 444; Mussolini and, 407–9, 419 ff., 445–46, 452, 454 ff.
Colonna, Sciarra, 178
Colonna family, 173, 176, 178, 185, 205, 209, 225. *See also* individual members by name
Columbanus, 44
Commedia dell'arte, 324–25
Commerce (trade), 230, 409 (*see also* Economics; Guilds; Industry; Trade); rise of cities and, 122 ff., 389
Commines, Philippe de, 260
Communism, 457. *See also* Communists; Marxism; Soviet Union
Communists (Communist Party), 436, 438, 482. *See also* Communism; Marxism
Como, 126, 128

Concordat (1929), 451
Concordia, 16
Concubinage, 96, 113
Condottieri, 215, 216, 218
Confederation of Italian States, 344, 351, 367 ff., 372 ff. *See also* Italy, Kingdom of
Conference of Ambassadors (1923), 445
Confraternities, religious, 305–6
Conrad, Marshal, 414–15, 418
Conrad IV, Emperor, 164–65, 166–67
Conradin, King of Germany, 167, 170
Consolations of Philosophy (Boëthius), 30
Constance (of Sicily), Queen, 136, 137, 138, 141, 165
Constance: Ecumenical Council (1414), 224–25; Peace (Treaty) of, (1183), 135–36, 183
Constans I, Emperor, 46
Constantine I (the Great), Emperor, 22, 45, 56, 59–62, 224; "Donation of," 59–62, 63, 68, 78, 89
Constantine VI, Emperor, 79
Constantine Copronymus, Emperor, 56
Constantinople, 5, 8, 10, 18, 19–20, 21 ff., 30–53, 54, 56, 78 ff., 124, 139, 149 (*see also* Byzantine Empire); final collapse of (1453), 242; Sixth Ecumenical Council (681), 46, 47
Constantius, 15
Constitution(s), 333, 338, 344, 345–47, 352–53, 354, 374, 380; (1770), 344; (1848), 360; Mussolini and, 447 ff.
Consuls, city-states, 189
Conti family, 157. *See also* individual members by name
Convention of September (1864), 380, 381
Convent Law (1866), 389
Convents, 96. *See also* Monasticism
Corinthian style architecture, 294
Corporate State concept, Mussolini and, 449–50
Corradini, Enrico, 406
Corriere della Sera (periodical), 422
Corsica, 36, 41, 68, 138, 391, 466
Cortenuova, Battle of, 161
Council of Thirteen, 184, 185
Counter-Reformation (Catholic Reformation), 289–92, 296, 311, 316–18

Creda, 417
Crema, 126, 132, 197
Cremona, 12, 113, 126, 131, 138, 161–62, 168, 183, 197, 325, 326; Diet at (1226), 156
Crete, 312, 471
Crime, 321. See also Banditti; Morality; Robbery
Crimean War, 362–63, 364, 365
Crispi, Francesco, 373, 374, 394, 398; as Premier, 390, 393, 395–97, 402, 406, 426
Critica Sociale (Socialist newspaper), 396, 398
Croce, Benedetto, 405, 406
Crusades (crusaders), 136, 139, 141, 148–49, 150, 154, 156–61, 174
Curia, Roman (papal), 179, 184, 225, 263, 266, 271, 375, 376, 379
Cusa, Nicholas Cardinal, 60 n.
Custoza, Battle of, 354
Cyrenaica, 429
Czechoslovakia, 458–59, 460, 462

Daladier, Edouard, 459
Dalmatia, 312, 313, 407, 420, 421–22, 423, 435, 436, 472
Damascus, 49
D'Annunzio, Gabriele, 406, 413, 423, 437, 446
Dante Alighieri, 172, 188, 199, 204, 266; and Boniface VIII, 172, 175, 181–82; *De Monarchia*, 181, 186; *Divine Comedy*, 180, 181, 200–1, 202; described by Villani, 180–81; and Frederick II, 155, 165, 181; and Henry VII, 183–84, 186; and Petrarch, 210; and use of vernacular, 201, 245
Dante Alighieri (society), 407
Danzig, 461–63
David (Michelangelo), 280
David (Verrocchio), 248–49
De Bono, Emilio, 441, 454
Decameron (Boccaccio), 213, 231, 266
Decretals, false, 89–90, 119
Della Rocca, General, 366
Della Villa, Montaigne in, 308
Del Vaga, Perino, 278
Democracy, 204–5, 208, 234
De Monarchia (Dante), 181, 186
Denmark, 102, 148, 172

Depretis, Agostino, 390, 391–92, 393, 394
Desiderius, Bishop of Vienne, 46
Desiderius, King of the Lombards, 39, 62–68, 70
Despotism (despots), 204–9, 216 ff., 226, 227, 234, 255 ff., 333 ff., 348 ff. (see also specific countries, individuals, people, places); independence from (1814–1870), 340 ff., 370–84
De Stefani, Alberto, 443
De Vecchi, Cesare Maria, 441, 442
Devil (Satan; evil); 41, 45, 50, 79, 97
Dialogue (Galileo), 319–20
Dialogues (Gregory I), 45
Diaz, Armando, 418–19
Dido (opera), 326
Diocletian, Emperor, 5
Disease(s), 212–14
Divine Comedy (Dante), 180, 181, 200–1, 202
Dolfuss, Engelbert, 453
Dominic, St., 141, 197
Dominican Order, 152, 197, 290
Donatello, Donato, 235, 236, 237, 238, 243, 248
Donation of Charlemagne, 67 ff., 71, 73
Donation of Constantine, 59–62, 63, 68, 78, 89, 129 n.
Donation of Pepin, 59 ff., 67
Dossi, Dosso, 294
Drama (plays), 324–25, 331, 350
Durant, Will, 45

Ebbo, Archbishop of Rheims, 86
Ecclesiastical offices, sale of, 222
Ecclesiastical reforms, 106–21. See also Clergy; Counter-Reformation; Reforms; specific aspects, individuals
Economics (economy; finances); 20–21 (see also Commerce; Industry; Taxes; Trade; specific aspects); fall of Rome and, 5–7, 9, 18; Italian independence and problems of, 376–77, 378, 386–89, 392–93, 394–96, 397, 398, 403–4, 409; Mussolini and, 449–50, 452, 455; World War I and rise of fascism, 435–36
Ecumenical Council (Constance, 1414), 224–25
Ecumenical Councils, Law of Guarantees and guarantee of, 383

Index

Edmund, Prince of England, 167, 168
Education (learning; schools), 94–95, 151, 155, 197–99, 209 ff., 349, 376, 377, 380 (*see also* Literacy; Intellectual developments; Philosophy); compulsory, 392; Mussolini and, 449, 451
Edward I, King of England, 175–76
Egypt, 36, 49, 159, 469, 473, 474. See also specific places, e.g. Alexandria, Egypt
Einhard, on Charles I, 66, 78, 83–84, 94
Eisenhower, Dwight D., 478–79
El Alamein, Battle of, 474
Eleanora of Toledo (wife of Cosimo I de' Medici), 287
Elections (*see also* Suffrage); Mussolini and, 444–45, 448
Electoral Reform Bill (1923), 444–45
El-Kamil, Sultan of Egypt, 159
Emo, Angelo, 313
Emperors, 79–80 (*see also* specific emperors, events, individuals, locations); Charlemagne and revival of title, 78; and fall of Roman Empire, 5, 9, 18, 28 ff., 37 ff., 44 ff., 47, 54 ff.; Holy Roman Empire (and papacy), 86, 101 ff., 262 ff., 286 ff. (*see also* specific emperors, events, locations, popes); popes and crowning of, 86
Empresses, rule by, 79–80
Encyclopaedistes (*philosophes*), 326, 327, 331
England. *See* Great Britain
Enzio (son of Frederick II), 165
Epiphanius of Cyprus, 50
Epirus, 10
Erasmus (Desiderius) of Rotterdam, 271, 286
Eric, King of Denmark, 172
Eritrea, 399, 470, 471
Essay on Crimes and Punishments (Beccaria), 327
Essays (Montaigne), 309
Este, Ercole d', 251
Este family, 207, 251, 273–74, 287
Ethiopia, 393, 397, 398, 399, 402, 454–55, 456, 470, 471
Etruscan Republic, 334
Eudocia, 18
Eudoxia, Empress, 17, 18
Eugenius IV, Pope, 283

Euripides, 242
"Exceptional Provisions," 400
Excommunication(s), 118 ff., 146, 147, 156 ff., 162, 167, 174, 175, 176, 178. *See also* specific individuals and popes

Facta, Luigi, 440, 441–42
Faliero, Marino, 227
False decretals, 89–90, 119
Farnese, Alexander Cardinal, 266. See also Paul III, Pope
Farnese, Giulia, 266, 284
Farnese family, 266, 287, 292–93. See also individual members by name
Fasci de Azione Revoluzionaria, 413, 426, 433, 436
Fasci di Combattimento, 436
Fascism, 407, 412–13, 425–52, 459–84; *il Duce* and (1922–1939), 442–59 (*see also* Mussolini, Benito); inauguration of Fascist Party, 436 ff.; rise and triumph of (1920–22), 425–42; World War II and end of (1939–1945), 459–84
Federigo da Montefeltro, Duke of Urbino, 251
Felitheus, 24
Feltre, Hitler and Mussolini meeting at, 476
Ferdinand I, King of Naples and Sicily (the Two Sicilies), 334–35, 336, 338, 342, 343, 344, 345–46, 348
Ferdinand I ("the Cruel"), King of Naples, 261
Ferdinand II, King of Naples, 251, 261
Ferdinand II ("Bomba") King of Two Sicilies, 352, 354, 355, 358, 373
Ferdinand III, Grand Duke of Tuscany, 341, 344
Ferdinand VII, King of Spain, 345
Fermo, 114, 115
Ferrara, 168, 207, 251–52, 271, 273–74, 287, 300–1, 333
Ficino, Marsilio, 242, 246, 247, 279
Fiesco, Sinobaldo Cardinal (Pope Innocent IV), 163–64, 166, 167
Fiesole, 127; abbey, 235, 236, 248; library, 252
Fiesole, Mino da, 248
Filarete, Antonio, 238
Filiberto, Emanuele, 287–88

Finzi, Aldo, 447
Fiume, 421-22, 423, 436, 437, 445-46
Flagellants, 196-97, 206, 310
Florence (city-republic), 127, 152, 169, 174, 183-84, 186, 187, 188, 189, 190-91, 193, 195, 200, 201, 207, 208, 210, 215, 226, 228, 229, 256, 271; architecture and sculpture, 203-4, 234 ff., 248 ff., 279 ff., 294, 321; Baptistery, 237-38; Cathedral (dome), 236-37; Council (1439), 242; democracy, 205, 208, 229, 259; Henry VII and, 182, 183-84; and independence, 347, 380, 382; language, 201; Laurentian Library, 287; liberated, World War II, 481; literary humanism, 242 ff.; loss of liberty of, 257-60; Medici and, 229, 233 ff., 244, 257, 259-60, 272 ff., 287, 302 (*see also* specific individuals by name); Montaigne in, 302; plague in, 213; Platonic Academy, 242, 246, 247; Renaissance, 233 ff., 244 ff., 272 ff., 287, 290, 296-97, 321; Savonarola, 257-59; Uffizi, 287, 293; University of, 246
Foreign affairs, Italian independence and problems of, 389 ff. *See also* specific aspects, individuals, wars, etc.
Forlì, 425, 428, 429, 431
Formosus, Pope, 91, 98, 100
Foro Ecclesiastico (Church Court), 361
Foscari, Francesco, 227
Foscolo, Ugo, 347
Fossombroni, Count Vittorio, 344
Fourteen Points, Woodrow Wilson and World War I, 419-20, 421, 422-23; Point IX, 420
France, 56, 84-85, 87, 88, 93, 102, 133, 140, 141, 147-49, 150, 160, 163, 168, 291, 302, 387, 388, 389, 390, 391, 392 (*see also* specific events, individuals, locations); and invasions of Italy, 253, 255, 257, 261, 264-65, 269, 286-88, 302, 310, 311, 313, 314, 315, 318; and Italian independence, 355-57, 358 ff., 361-69, 370 ff., 378, 379-81, 382, 383, 390; and Italian nationalism, 408-9; and Italy, Napoleonic era, 326-39, 340 ff.; Mussolini and, 432, 452-59, 460, 461, 464-68; and papacy, 171-80, 182, 184, 187, 218-19, 220, 222; and war with Austria, 366-69, 270 ff.; and World War I, 411-13, 416, 418, 419, 420-24; and World War II, 460, 465-66, 467-68
Francis I, Emperor (of Austria), 343
Francis I, King of France, 256, 269, 276, 286, 287
Francis II, King of Two Sicilies, 373, 374, 375
Francis IV (Austrian archduke), 341, 343
Franciscan Order, 152, 264
Francis of Assisi, St., 141, 243
Franco, Francisco, 455-56, 460, 469
Franconia, 84, 100
Franco-Prussian War, 382, 383
Frankfurt, Council of (794), 72
Franks, the, 20, 32, 35-36, 37, 48, 52, 56 ff., 93, 98
Franz Joseph, Emperor of Austria, 364, 370, 372, 390, 391; assassinated, 410
Frederick, King of Sicily, 174
Frederick, Prince of Aragon, 187
Frederick I (Barbarossa), Emperor, 122-23, 127-36
Frederick II, Emperor, 138, 141, 144, 146, 147, 152-66, 171, 177, 199, 200, 205
Freemasonry, 331-32, 338
French language, 201
French Revolution, 332
Frescoes, 204, 239, 250, 251, 277-78

Gaeta, 110, 123, 134
Gaiseric, 15, 17, 18, 20
Galileo Galilei, 312, 317, 319-20
Gallia Placidia, 13, 14-15, 16
Gandia, Duke of, 266
Gardens, Vignola and making of, 292-93
Garibaldi, Giuseppe, 356-57, 365, 367, 369, 373-74, 377, 378, 379, 381
Gascony, 175
Gasparri, Cardinal, 451
Gaul, 14, 15, 18, 20, 58
Gelasius, Pope, 18
Genoa, 93, 112, 123-24, 137, 138, 168, 174, 187, 190, 192-93, 194, 197, 202, 207-8, 287; architecture, 293; and independence, 365; Napoleonic era, 332, 333, 335, 341; plague in, 213; and Venice, 226-29

Index

Gentile, Giovanni, 449
Gepids, 34
Germanic (Teutonic) tribes, 7 ff., 20 ff., 35. *See also* specific people, places
Germany, 56, 80, 84, 85, 88, 91, 93, 98, 100 ff., 181–86, 218, 223–24, 268, 269–71, 388, 390, 391, 392, 393, 394, 403 (*see also* Germanic (Teutonic) tribes; Holy Roman Empire; specific events, individuals, locations); Hitler and National Socialism (World War II), 452–84 *passim;* and Italian independence, 370, 381, 385; Italian nationalism and, 407, 408–9; Mussolini and, 452–84 *passim;* Napoleonic era, 344; World War I, 411–13, 415–16, 417, 418, 420–24
Ghibellines, 139, 144–46, 152–70, 173, 181–86, 187 ff., 197, 206, 209, 217, 301
Ghiberti, Lorenzo, 237–38, 248
Ghirlandaio, Domenico, 250, 279
Gibbon, Edward, 1 n., 9, 12
Gioberti, Vincenzo, 350–51
Giolitti, Giovanni, 394–95, 400, 402–5, 407, 408–10, 412, 415, 423, 429, 438
Giorgione, 296
Giostra, La (Politan), 246
Giotto, 203–4, 236, 239, 240
Giulay, General, 370, 372
Gladstone, William, 358
Glycerius, Emperor, 18
Goebbels, Joseph Paul, 462
Goering, Hermann, 465, 474
Goethe, Johann Wolfgang von, 293, 320, 321
Goldoni, Carlo, 323–24, 325
Gonzaga, Cardinal, 305
Gonzaga family, 207, 305
Gothic architecture, 202, 231, 236, 237
Gothic Line (World War II), 481, 482, 483
Goths, 8, 9 ff., 13–15, 18, 24 ff., 29–32, 38, 41
Gozzoli, Benozzo, 235, 250
Granada, 290
Grand Council of Fascism, 448, 476–77, 480
Grandella, Battle of, 169
Grandi, Dino, 438, 475, 476–77
Graziani, Marshal Rodolfo, 469, 470

Great Britain, 110, 129 n., 140, 148, 150, 159, 175–76, 223, 387, 388, 389, 391, 393; and Italian independence, 358, 359, 361, 362–63, 364, 365–66, 368, 369, 370, 374; and Italian nationalism, 408; and Italy, Napoleonic era, 335, 336, 338, 341; Mussolini and, 452–59, 460, 461, 464 ff.; and World War I, 411–12, 415–16, 418, 419, 420–24; and World War II, 460, 465 ff., 479–80, 482
Great Council, Venice, 194–95
Great Schism (1378), 220–25
Greece (Greek Empire), 10, 36–37 ff., 42, 52–53, 79 ff., 93, 105, 110, 139 (*see also* Byzantine Empire; Greece (modern); Greek Church; Greek language); revival of interest in classical heritage of, 209–12, 231 ff., 241 ff.
Greece (modern), Mussolini and, 445, 466, 469–70, 471
Greek Church, 52, 53, 79 ff., 139. *See also* Byzantine Empire; Constantinople; Greece (Greek Empire); specific events, individuals
Greek language, 4, 36, 56, 241 ff.
Gregorovius, Ferdinand, 33–34
Gregory I (the Great), Pope, 31, 41, 42–46, 47, 48, 50, 57, 67
Gregory II, Pope, 51–52, 54–56
Gregory III, Pope, 52
Gregory VII (Hildebrand), Pope, 108–21
Gregory IX, Pope, 157–63
Gregory X, Pope, 197
Gregory XI, Pope, 219–20, 224 n.
Gregory XII, Pope, 224
Gregory XIII, Pope, 303, 309
Gregory XV, Pope, 317
Gregory XVI, Pope, 351
Gregory, St. (of Nyssa), 37
Grimoald (son of Arachis, Duke of Benevento), 71
Grossi, Tomasso, 350
Guarantees, Law of, 380–83
Guelfs (Guelphs), 139, 144–46, 150, 152–70, 173, 181–86, 187 ff., 197, 206, 217, 218, 301, 351
Guilbert, Archbishop of Ravenna (anti-Pope Clement III), 120
Guicciardini, Francesco, 253, 294

Guidi, Rachele (wife of Mussolini), 433, 450
Guidi, Tommaso ("Masaccio"), 238–39
Guido, Duke of Tuscany, 92
Guilds, 93–94, 188, 190, 198, 204, 229, 230, 236
Guinicelli, Guido, 200
Guiscard, Robert (Norman prince), 111, 120
Guiscard, Roger, Count of Sicily, 111

Hadrian IV, Pope, 269
Haile Selassie, Emperor of Abyssinia, 455, 471
Hakon, King of Norway, 164
Hapsburgs, 128, 181, 255, 256, 310, 315, 327 ff., 332 ff., 359, 363 ff., 386. See also specific individuals, locations
Hawkwood, John, 215
Haynau, General, 355
Haywood, R. M., 4 n.
Henry, Count of Anjou, 133
Henry, Landgrave of Thuringia, 164
Henry II, King, 129 n.
Henry III, Emperor, 109
Henry III, King of England, 150, 159, 167
Henry IV, Emperor, 109, 114–21, 177
Henry IV, King of France, 311
Henry VI, Emperor, 136–39, 141, 144
Henry (VII), King of Germany (King of the Romans), 156, 161
Henry VII (Henry of Luxemburg), Emperor, 181–86, 206
Henry of Castile, 170
Heraclius, Emperor, 38, 46
Heresies (heretics), 38, 225, 232, 290, 309, 311, 316, 317, 318, 326. See also Excommunication(s); specific heresies, individuals, popes
Heruli, the, 18–19
Hildebrand (Pope Gregory VII), 108–21
History (historians), writing of, 320. See also specific individuals by name, e.g. Huizinga, Johan
History of Florence (Bruni), 243
History of the Popes (Pastor), 222
Hitler, Adolf, 452 ff., 484; death of, 483
Hoare, Sir Samuel, 454
Hohenstaufen dynasty, 122 ff. (see also specific individuals, locations); end of, 166–70, 171

Holland, 56
Holy Office, 290
Holy Roman Empire, 7–8, 21 ff., 28 ff., 256, 269 ff., 290 ff. (see also specific events, individuals, locations, popes, rulers); Charlemagne and, 78 ff.; clash with Catholic Church (Middle Ages), 100 ff.; collapse and last days of, 170 ff., 180 ff.; Otto and founding of, 102 ff.
Holy Rule, monastic, 42, 106
Homer, 246
Homilies (Gregory I), 45
Honorius, Emperor, 9–10, 11–12, 13, 14, 15
Honorius I, Pope, 46, 47
Honorius III, Pope, 152, 156–57
Horace, 242
House, Colonel Edward M., 420
Huguenots, 305
Huizinga, Johan, 96–97
Humanism (humanists), 210, 231 ff., 242 ff., 252 ff., 283
Humanities, 235, 251
Humbert I, King of Italy, 391, 393, 395, 401; assassination of, 401–2
Humbert (I) of the White Hand, Count of Savoy, 195
Huneric (Vandal king), 18
Hungary, 102, 109, 140, 148. See also Austro-Hungarian Empire; Magyars
Huns, 8, 9, 15–17, 31
Huntington, Ellsworth, 1 n.
Huss, John, 223–24, 225, 232

Iceland, 140
Iconoclastic Epoch (Iconoclasts), 49–53, 54 ff., 70, 72
Iconodules, 50–53
Idea Nazionale (newspaper), 406
Ignatius (of Loyola), St., 289
Ildico, 16
Illiteracy. See Literacy (illiteracy)
Illyria (Illyricum), 34, 36, 313
Illyricum. See Illyria
I mille, 373–74
Imperialism, 405–6 407 ff., 419 ff., 445–46, 454 ff. See also Colonialism (colonial imperialism)
Imperial Rome (Nillson), 4 n.
In Coena Domini (papal bull), 310–11

Index

Independence (independence movements), 338–39, 340 ff., 370–84
Index Librorum Prohibitorum, 290, 320
India, 317
Indulgences, 175, 222, 285
Industry (industrialization), 377, 387, 395–96, 401, 403, 406. *See also* Commerce; Trade
Ingeborg of Denmark, 147–48
Innocent I, Pope, 12
Innocent III, Pope, 139–51, 152, 154, 156, 157, 171, 232, 289; General Council (Lateran) of, 150–51
Innocent IV, Pope, 163–64, 166, 167
Innocent VIII, Pope, 264, 276, 284
Innocent X, 317–18
Inquisition, 289–90, 298, 316, 319–20, 327
Intellectual developments (*see also* Art(s); Education; History; Literature) papacy and, 283–86; philosophy, 318–20; Renaissance, 197–99, 209–12, 230 ff., 244 ff., 262, 263, 296, 298
Investiture of bishops, controversy over, 106–8, 112–21, 126, 147
Ionian Islands, 313
Ireland, 129 n., 140
Irene, Empress, 70, 73, 76, 79–80
Irredentists, 391, 392, 394, 395, 412, 413, 428, 435, 437
Isabelle I, Queen of Castile, 261
Isaurians, 31, 50, 52
Isidore of Seville, St., 89
Islam, 312–13. *See also* Crusades; Mohammed; Moslems; specific locations, people
Isonzo River front, World War I, 414–15, 416, 417, 418
Istria, 68, 391, 407
Italia del Popolo, L' (newspaper), 366
Italian language, 201, 245, 288
Italian Renaissance, 230 ff.; end of, 286–97
Italian Republic (former Cisalpine Republic, Napoleonic era), 336
Italians (people), ninth-century, 93–99
"Italian Social Republic" (1944), 480
Italy, Kingdom of (April 15, 1860), 373–84, 385 ff.; map of, 371; opening years (1871–1920) of, 385 ff.

Italy, Kingdom of (*Regno d'Italia*), Napoleonic era, 336, 337, 338

Jaffa, 123, 125
Japan, 457, 473
Jerome, St., 12, 13
Jerome of Prague, 225
Jerusalem, 49, 76, 141, 156, 159
Jesuits (Society of Jesus), 289, 293, 298, 305, 316, 317, 330, 352
Jesus Christ, 22, 23–24, 28, 37. *See also* Christianity
Jews, 44, 50, 213, 304, 415, 453
Jibuti, port of, 468
Joachim I (Joachim Murat), King of Naples, 336–37, 338, 340, 341–42
Joanna I, Queen of Naples, 208, 226
John, Bishop of Philadelphia, 47
John, King of England, 148, 150, 159
John, King of Ethiopia, 393
John, Prince of Bulgaria, 148
John I, Pope, 30–31
John VIII, Pope, 91
John X, Pope, 92
John XII (Octavian), Pope, 92, 101–4
John XIII, Pope, 105
John XXIII (Pisan Pope), 224
John of Antioch, 25
John of Bologna, 294, 301
John Zimisces, Emperor, 105
Jordanes (historian), 14, 15
Joseph II, Emperor, 327
Joseph Bonaparte, King of Naples (and Spain), 336–37
Juan (John), Don, of Austria, 288
Jubilee ("Holy Year") (1300), 174–75, 180
Julius II (Giuliano della Rovere), Pope, 263, 267–68, 276, 277, 280–81, 284–85, 292
Julius III, Pope, 283
Julius Nepos, Emperor, 18, 19–20
Justin I, Emperor, 29
Justin II, Emperor, 34–35
Justinian, Emperor, 29, 30, 31–32, 33–34, 38

Kassala, capture of, 397
Koran, 50

Labriola, Arturo, 429
La Farina, Guiseppe, 365, 367

La Marmora, General Alfonso, 367, 380–81
Landini, Taddeo, 294
Lando, Michele di, 229
Land reclamation, Mussolini and, 452
Landucci, Luca, 257–58
Language(s): French, 201; Greek, 4, 36, 56 (*see also* Classics); Italian dialects, 201; "Italian language" (Tuscan), 201, 245, 288, 295; Latin, 4, 36, 56, 95, 201, 235, 241 ff., 245, 246, 247, 288 (*see also* Classics); Roman Empire, 4, 36, 56
Lanza, Giovanni, 388
Laocoön, 285
Last Judgment (Michelangelo), 282–83
Last Supper (Leonardo da Vinci), 275
Lateran Council, Innocent III and, 150–51
Lateran Treaty (1929), 451
Latin language, 4, 36, 56, 95, 201, 235, 241 ff., 246, 247, 288. See also Classics
Latin literature. *See* Classics; Literature
Latins (people), 21 ff., 38 ff., 47–53, 54 ff., 81, 95
Laurentian Collection (Library), Florence, 242
Lausanne, Peace of (October, 1912), 409
Laval, Pierre, 454
Law of Guarantees, 382–83
Laws (legislation), 54, 102, 132, 151, 155, 377, 378, 384 (*see also* Constitution(s); specific aspects); church (ecclesiastical), 89–90; Roman, 27, 28; study of, 198, 209–10
League of Nations, 422, 454
Leagues, 253, 256 (*see also* specific leagues, locations); rise of cities and, 126 ff.
Left (Left Center), political party, 377–78, 390, 391, 400–1, 483
Legnano, Battle of, 135
Leo, King of Armenia, 148
Leo I, Emperor, 18
Leo I, Pope, 16, 17, 23
Leo III (Leo the Isaurian), Emperor, 50–52
Leo III, Pope, 72–79, 81, 82, 85, 86
Leo IV, Emperor, 70
Leo VIII, anti-Pope, 104–5

Leo IX, Pope, 108, 111
Leo X (Giovanni de' Medici), 260, 285, 288; and art (Age of Leo X), 252, 253, 268–69, 272, 277, 278, 281–82; death of, 282
Leo XIII, Pope, 391, 399, 450
Leonardo da Vinci, 239, 255, 274–76, 277, 278, 279
Leonard of Pisa, 155
Leopardi, Alessandro, 295
Leopardi, Giacomo, 347–48
Leopold (Leopold I) Emperor, 312
Leopold I, Grand Duke of Tuscany, 327–30
Leopold II, Grand Duke of Tuscany, 351, 353, 355
Lepanto, Battle of (1571), 288
Letters to the Earl of Aberdeen (Gladstone), 358
Levant, the, 123, 193, 194, 226
Liberal Democrats, political party, 438
Liberalism (liberals), 357 ff., 373, 379, 380, 383, 390, 402, 404–5, 407, 410, 427, 428, 437
Liber Pastoralis Curae, 44
Liber Pontificalis, 75
Libraries, 235, 242, 251, 252
Libya, 407–9, 411, 412, 420, 423, 429, 469, 470, 473, 474
Ligurian Republic, 333, 386
Ligurians, 333, 386
Lippi, Filippino, 241, 250–51
Lippi, Filippo, 240–41, 250
Literacy (illiteracy), 387, 405
Literature: Baroque period, 323–25; Renaissance era, 200–1, 210, 211, 231 ff., 235, 241–48, 272–74, 294–95, 298; and Italian independence, 331, 347–48, 350–51
Liutprand, on Pope John XII, 92, 103–4
Lives of Painters (Vasari), 293. *See also* Vasari, Giorgio
Livy, 251
Lloyd George, David, 421
Lodi, 126, 128, 134
Lombardi family, 295
Lombards, 34 ff., 47 ff., 52, 54, 57, 58 ff., 65, 68–69, 82, 93 (*see also* Lombardy); Germany and, 101, 102, 105, 110, 112
Lombard style architecture, 202

Index

Lombardy, 36, 65, 68–69, 82, 112, 123–39, 144, 162, 165 ff., 168, 183, 206, 228 (see also Lombards; specific cities); French invasions, 253, 255, 257, 261; and Italian independence, 352, 353 ff., 359, 364, 368, 369, 370 ff., 386; Napoleonic era, 352, 353 ff., 359, 364, 368, 369, 370 ff., 386; plague in, 213
Lombardy (ship), 373
London, Treaty of (1915), 413, 420, 421, 422, 433, 435
"Long Armistice" (World War II), 478 n., 480 n.
Loraine, Sir Percy, 462
Loreto, 308
Lorraine, 100
Lorraine, Duke of, 314
Lorsch Annals, 75
Lothair, Emperor, 84, 85, 87
Lothair, King of Lotharingia, 87–88
Lothair dei Segni. See Innocent III, Pope
Lotharingia, 85, 87
Lotta de Classe, La (newspaper), 428, 429
Lotto, Lorenzo, 296
Louis (the Sluggard), Emperor, 84
Louis I (the Pious), Emperor, 83, 84, 85, 86
Louis II (Louis the German), Emperor, 84, 85, 87
Louis XII, King of France, 256, 261
Louis XIV, King of France, 313, 332
Lucca, 191–92, 207, 287, 341
Lucera, 153, 154, 161, 167
Ludolph of Swabia, 101
Luini of Milan (artist), 294
Luna, Pedro de (Benedict XIII), 224–25 n.
Lunéville, Treaty of, 336
Luther, Martin, and Lutherans, 269, 286, 288–92
Luzzatti, Luigi, 407
Lyons, Council of (1245), 164

Machiavelli, Niccolò, 265, 272, 294, 324
Mack, General, 335
Magenta, Battle of, 370, 372
Magna Carta, 150
Magna Moralia (Gregory I), 45
Magyars (Hungarians) invasions by, 99. See also Hungary

Maiano, Benedetto da, 248
Maiano, Giuliano da, 248
Majorian, Emperor, 18
Malatesta family, 207, 209
Malmesbury, Lord, 368
Malta, 391
Mandragola (Machiavelli), 272
Manfred, King of Sicily, 166–70
Manicheans, 38
Manin, Daniele, 353, 357, 365
Mantua, 127, 168, 207, 287
Manzoni, Alessandro, 347
Marcian, Emperor, 16
Marengo, Battle of, 336
Margarito, Admiral, 137
Maria (wife of Honorius), 9
Maria Carolina, Queen of Naples, 335, 336
Maria Theresa, Empress, 313, 315, 327
Marie Louise (Bourbon), Duchess of Lucca, 341
Marie Louise (of Austria), French Empress and Duchess of Parma, 341, 370
Marignano, Battle of, 256
Maritime commerce, 190, 192–95, 227–28, 260
Mark, St., 124
Marozia (mother of Pope John XI, wife of Guido, Duke of Tuscany), 92, 101
Marriage of clergy, 106, 113, 114
Martin I, Pope, 46–47
Martin V, Pope, 224 n., 225, 262
Marxism, 405, 428. See also Communism
Masaccio (Tommaso Guidi), 238–39
Masonic Lodges, 331–32, 338
Massimi, Domenico, 271
Massowa, 393
Mathilda, Countess of Tuscany, 112, 119, 127, 144
Matteotti, Giacomo, Mussolini and murder of, 446–47, 448
Maurice, Emperor, 35, 37, 45
Maurras, Charles, 407
Maximilian, Archduke (Hapsburg), 364
Maximilian, Emperor, 261
Maximus, Petronius, 16–17, 18
Mazzini, Giuseppe, 348–49, 350, 355, 356, 357, 359, 365, 366, 377
Medici, Alessandro de', 260

Medici, Cosimo de' (1389–1464), 238, 239, 240–41, 242, 244, 245, 246, 248, 252, 284
Medici, Cosimo I de' (1537–1574), Grand Duke of Tuscany, 260, 287, 293, 302, 314
Medici, Francesco I de', Grand Duke of Tuscany, 302
Medici, Giovanni de', 233–34, 236
Medici, Giovanni de' (Pope Leo X), 252, 253, 260, 268–69, 272, 277, 278, 281–82, 285, 288
Medici, Giuliano de' (the Younger), 282
Medici, Lorenzo de' (Duke of Urbino), 282
Medici, Lorenzo de' ("the Magnificent"), 244–51, 252, 257, 259, 260, 273, 275, 279, 281, 284
Medici, Piero de', 233–34, 236
Medici, Salvestro de', 229
Medici family, 229, 233 ff., 244 ff., 257, 259–60, 268, 272 ff., 287, 314. *See also* specific individuals by name
Mediterranean Sea (and area), 47, 260, 336, 341, 377, 408, 452, 456, 466, 467, 470, 471, 472, 474–75, 478
Menabrea, General, 388, 390
Menelik II, King of Ethiopia, 393, 397
Mentana, Battle of, 381
Mercenary soldiers, 214–16
Merovingians, 35, 57–58
Mesopotamia, 49
Messina, 154, 354, 374
Metastasio, 326
Metternich, Prince Clemens Lothar Wenzel von, 340–45, 346, 347, 351, 352, 387
Metz, 15
Mexico, 317
Michael I, Emperor, 80
Michelangelo Buonarroti, 238, 246, 248, 260, 274, 276, 277, 278, 279–83, 284, 285, 294; poetry of, 274
Michelozzo di Bartolommeo (Michelozzi di Bartolommeo), 234–35, 237
Middlesex, Duke of, 331
Milan, 112–13, 114–15, 125, 126–27, 128 ff., 138, 152, 161–62, 168, 183, 187, 188, 197, 207–8, 226, 228–29, 251, 261; and Austria, 315, 364; Bread Riots, 426; "Five Days," 353; Flagellants, 196; and independence, 352, 353–54, 364, 370; invasions of, 11, 16, 255–57, 313–14; Napoleonic era, 327, 332, 333, 334; riots and massacres, 352, 400, 426; Sforzas, 251–52, 255–57; Socialist Congress (1910), 429; social life, 321; and Spain, 256–57, 286, 313–14; Tobacco Riots, 352; Visconti family, 207, 216–18, 228–29, 256
Milazzo, 374
Military conscription, Napoleonic era, 337
Mille, i, 373–74
Minghetti, Marco, 388, 390
"Minimum Program" (Socialist Program, 1895), 399
Modena, 271, 287, 330, 333, 341, 343; and independence, 348, 354, 357, 370, 372–73
Mohammed (Mohammedans), 37, 48–49, 76, 97. *See also* Crusades; Islam; Moslems; specific locations, people, places
Molotov, Vyacheslav, 471
Mona Lisa (Leonardo da Vinci), 275
Monasticism (monasteries, monks), 41–42, 43, 44, 72, 93, 94, 95, 96, 97, 327, 389; reforms, 106–21, 151
Monferrat, 127
Monferrat, Marquis of, 149
Monophysites, 38, 46–47, 48
Montaigne, Michel de, 299–310, 311, 320, 321
Monte Cassino, 42, 95
Montenegro, 421
Monteverdi, Claudio, 325
Montgomery, Lord Bernard, 474
Moral and Civil Primacy of the Italians, The (Gioberti), 350–51
Morality (immorality), 96–99, 266–67, 271, 307–8, 386. *See also* Crime; Robbery; specific aspects, individuals, locations
Moravia, 102, 459
Morea, 312, 313
Morgante Maggiore, Il, 246
Morocco, 408, 474
Moses (Michelangelo), 281
Moslems, 47, 50–51, 97, 139, 160. *See also* Crusades; Islam; Mohammed; specific people, places
Munich Conference, 459

Index

Murat, Joachim (Joachim I), King of Naples, 336–37, 338, 340, 341–42
Music, 324–25. *See also* Opera
Musical instruments, 324–25
Mussolini, Benito, 407, 410, 412–13, 425–84; birth and background of, 425 ff.; epitaph, 484; edits *Avanti!*, 431–32; edits *Popolo d'Italia*, 432, 433–34, 436, 437; and Hitler and Germany, 452 ff.; as *il Duce*, 446 ff.; imprisoned, 430; last days; arrest and death of, 475–84 loss of popularity and opposition to, 470, 473 ff.; in Parliament, 438, 448; as Premier, 442 ff.; and World War I, 432–36; and World War II, 405 ff.
Mussolini, Edvige, 434
Myth of Rome's Fall, The (Haywood), 4·n.

Naples, 54, 91, 93, 110, 111, 123, 127, 136, 137–38, 141, 151 ff., 163, 167, 170, 173, 174, 182, 185–86, 187, 205, 208–9, 226, 228, 261–62 (*see also* Sicily; Two Sicilies); Fascist convention (1922), 441–42; "five days of," 480; invasions of, 31–32, 36, 255–56, 261–62; and Italian independence, 345–46, 347, 350, 352 ff., 358 ff., 370 ff., 374, 386, 387, 390; Napoleonic era, 330–31, 332, 334–37, 338, 340 ff.; opera, 325; plague in, 213; social life, 321; Spain and, 261, 286, 290, 315, 330, 352 ff., 358; University of, 155; World War II, 479–80
Napoleon, Prince ("Plon-Plon"), 367, 368
Napoleon Bonaparte (Napoleon I), Emperor of France, 332–39, 340, 341–42
Napoleon III (Louis-Napoleon Bonaparte), Emperor, 355–56, 361, 362, 363–64, 365, 366–69, 370, 372 ff., 379–80, 384; defeat and downfall of, 382
Napoleonic era (1789–1815), 326–39, 340 ff.
Narses the Eunuch, 32, 35
Nationalism (1896–1915), 405–13 (*see also* Imperialism); World War I and, 419–24

Nationalist Party, 411–12, 413, 435, 437, 438
National Italian Committee, 359
National Italian Society, 365, 367
National Socialism (Nazis), Fascism (Mussolini) and, 452 ff.
Nativity (Botticelli), 250
Naturalism in painting, 322–23
Nelson, Lord Horatio, 336
Neo-Guelphs, 351
Nepos, Julius, Emperor, 18, 19–20
Nestorians, 23, 38
Newspapers, 398, 406 (*see also* specific newspapers by name); Mussolini and censorship of, 448
Niccoli, Niccolò de', 242, 243
Niccolini, Giovan Battista, 350
Nice, 367, 373, 391, 466, 468
Nicaea, Council of (787), 72
Nicephorus, Emperor, 80
Nicholas I, Pope, 86–91
Nicholas II, Pope, 109
Nicholas III, Pope, 173
Nicholas V, Pope, 252–53, 262, 263
Nillson, Martin P., 4 n.
Nitti, Francesco, 406, 423, 435, 438
Normandy, 110 (*see also* Normans); World War II landings, 482
Normans, 110 ff., 120 ff., 127, 128, 135 ff., 154
North Africa, 407–9, 419, 468, 470, 474–75. *See also* specific locations
Novara, 126; Battle of, 347, 355, 360, 363, 370
Nugent, General, 338–39

Oberdank (Oberdank clubs), 391, 394
Odescalchi family, 318
Odoacer, 19–20, 21, 24–25, 30, 32
Olybrius, Emperor, 18
Olympius (chancellor), and Stilicho, 11
On the Vernacular Tongue (Dante), 201
Opera, 325, 326, 348
Orange, Prince of, 271
Orestes, 19
Orfeo (Politan), 246
Oriani, Alfredo, 406
Orlando, Vittorio, 415, 418, 420–23, 435
Orlando Furioso (Boiardo), 273–74
Orlando Innamorato (Ariosto), 273
Orosius, 14

Orsini, attempt on Napoleon III's life by, 366–67
Orsini, Cardinal, 220
Orsini family, 152, 179, 185, 205, 209. See also specific members by name
Ostrogoths (East Goths), 11, 24–32
Otto I, Emperor, 100–6
Otto II, Emperor, 105–6
Otto IV, Emperor, 144–47
Otto of Freising, 127
Ottoman (Turkish) Empire, 407, 408, 409. See also Turkey
Oudinot, General, 357
Oviglio, Aldo, 443
OVRA (secret police), 448

Pacelli, Francesco, 451
Pacelli, Eugenio (Pope Pius XII), 22 n., 451
Pact of Rome (1924), 446
Pact of Steel (Italy-Germany, May, 1939), 461–62, 463, 467
Padua, 16, 113, 127, 134, 168, 206, 207, 227, 228, 229, 300, 301
Painting (painters), 203–4, 237, 238–41, 249–52, 272, 274–76, 282–84, 294, 295–96, 322–23. See also specific artists and their works
Palazzo Riccardi, 234
Palazzo Vecchio, 248, 249, 258
Palermo, 138, 155, 373
Palestine, 36, 156, 174, 175. See also Crusades; specific locations
Palladio (Andrea) and Palladian style, 293, 295
Palma Vecchio, 296
Palmerston, Lord, 358, 366
Pandulph, 105
Panem et circenses, 6, 8, 33
Pannonia, 24–25
Panther (German cruiser), 408
Papacy (popes), 292, 310 ff., 321 (*see also* Papal States; Roman Catholic Church; Rome; Vatican; specific events, individuals, locations, popes); as an Italian institution, 292; authority of, 4, 33, 88–90, 140–51, 381–82; Avignon popes ("Babylonian Captivity"), 179–80, 182, 184, 187, 218–19 ff., 225 (*see also* specific popes); Charlemagne and (*see* Charlemagne); founding of papal monarchy, 59 ff. (*see also* Papal States; specific individuals, locations, popes); Great Schism (1378), 200–25, and Holy Roman Empire, 100 ff., 180 ff. (*see also* Holy Roman Empire; specific emperors, locations, popes); and Italian independence, 359, 379–83, 389; and land acquisition, 59 ff., 144 f. (*see also* Papal States; specific locations, popes); Lombards and, 34 ff., 47 ff., 52, 54, 57, 58 ff.; medieval, collapse of, 170–80; morality, 266–67 (*see also* specific aspects, popes); Mussolini and, 450–51; Napoleonic era, 330 ff.; papal infallibility, 381–82; reforms (Reformation), 288–92, 311, 316 ff. (*see also* Counter-Reformation; Reforms; specific aspects, popes); Renaissance era, 252–53, 258, 259–60, 261, 262–86, 292 ff. (*see also* specific popes); Roman Empire era, 22–24, 28–53 *passim*, 54–99 *passim*
Papal infallibility, Pius IX and doctrine of, 381–82
Papal States (States of the Church), 145 n., 147, 152, 163, 172, 209, 219, 228, 261–71, 287, 292, 301, 316 ff., 320 (*see also* Papacy; specific locations, popes); and Italian independence, 348, 350, 359, 367, 368, 372–73, 374, 375, 381–83, 389; Napoleonic era, 300–31, 334, 336, 337, 341, 342, 343
Papini, Giovanni, 406
Parentucelli, Tommaso (Pope Nicholas V), 252–53, 262, 263
Pareto, Vilfredo, 427
Paris, Congress of (1856), 363, 364
Paris, Treaty of, 341
Paris, University of, 198, 222
Paris Peace Conference, World War I, 420–24
Parliament, 377–78, 391, 393, 394–98 *passim*, 400, 402–7 *passim*, 409, 411; first (1861), 374, 376, 377–78, 385; Mussolini and, 437, 438–39, 440–41, 442 ff., 446 ff., 450, 475–76; and World War I, 413, 415, 418, 423, 434, 436

Index

Parma, 162, 206, 271, 287, 315, 330, 341, 354, 359, 363, 367, 370, 372–73
Parthenopean Republic, 335
Partito Popolare (Catholic party), 437, 438
Party of Action, 378, 379
Paschal I, Pope, 86
Paschal III, anti-Pope, 133, 134
Pastor, Ludwig, 222–23
Patarini, 113
Patriarchs of Constantinople, 22
Patrician, office and title of, 19–20, 25, 59, 69
Paul, St., 22, 23
Paul I, Pope, 62–63
Paul II, Pope, 284
Paul III, Pope (Alexander Farnese), 282, 283, 287, 290
Paul IV, Pope, 283, 291
Paul V, Pope, 311, 312, 317
Paul VI, Pope, 22 n.
Pavia, 16, 58, 65, 68, 101, 102, 113, 125, 126, 129, 131, 134, 135, 152, 197, 228; Certosa of, 252
Pavia, Battle of (1525), 256, 286
Pavia, University of, 218
Pax Romana, 4
Pearl Harbor, 473
Pedro, King of Aragon, 173–74, 187
Pelagius II, Pope, 43
Pellico, Silvio, *Le Mie Prigioni* by, 350
Pelloux, General, 400–1
Penni, Gianfrancesco, 278
People's Banks, 404
Pepin I, King of Aquitaine, 84
Pepin (III) le Bref ("the Short"), King of the Franks, 57–59, 63, 64; Donation of, 59–64
Pepin of Italy (son of Charlemagne), 83
Persia(ns), 37, 49
Perugia, 73, 196, 207, 228, 277
Perugino, 277, 279
Petacci, Clara, 483
Pétain, Henri-Philippe, 468
Peter, King of Aragon, 148, 150
Peter, St., 22–23, 43, 89–90; tomb of, 73, 77–78, 92 (*see also* St. Peter's, Rome)
Petrarch, Francesco, 201, 209–11, 213–14, 215–16, 219, 232, 233, 241, 266
Petronius Maximus, 16–17, 18
Philip (Hohenstaufen), Emperor, 144–45
Philip (II) Augustus, King of France, 147–48
Philip IV ("the Fair"), King of France, 175–79, 182
Philip of Hess, Prince, 457
Philosophes, 326, 327, 331
Philosophy (philosophers), 318–20, 405–6, 407. *See also* Intellectual developments; specific individuals, philosophies
Piacenza, 113, 271, 292, 370, 372
Piave, Battle of, 417–18, 421
Piccolomini (highwayman), 301
Piccolomini, Enea Sylvius (Pope Pius II), 284
Pico della Mirandola, 246–47, 251, 279
Piedmont, 126, 183, 195, 286, 287, 288, 315–16; and Italian independence, 346–47, 348, 349, 351–52, 353 ff., 358 ff., 368 ff., 370 ff., 378, 387, 392; Napoleonic era, 326, 332, 333, 336, 341, 343, 344; and Sardinia, 315–16; system of government, 378, 387, 401
Piedmont (ship), 373
Pier della Vigna, 165
Pietà (Michelangelo), 279–80
Pietro, Guido di (Fra Angelico), 235, 239–40, 241, 250
Pilgrimages, 174–75
Pilo, Rosalino, 373
Pinturicchio, 284
Piombo, Sebastiano del, 296
Pisa, 93, 112, 123, 124, 127, 137, 138, 144, 149, 152, 170, 174, 186, 187, 190, 192–93, 206, 207–8, 228, 229; Baptistery, 201–2; Duomo ("leaning tower"), 202; and Genoa, 202; sculpture, 201–2
Pisa, Council of (1409), 223
Pisa, University of, 246, 330
Pisani, Vettor, 227
Pisano, Giovanni, 202, 203
Pisano, Niccolo, 201–2, 203, 209
Pitti Palace, Florence, 236, 293
Pius II, Pope, 284
Pius IV, Pope, 283
Pius V, Pope, 291
Pius VII, Pope, 341, 342, 343, 344
Pius IX ("Pio Nono"), Pope, 351, 353, 354–55, 359, 363, 367, 372, 373, 374, 375–76, 379, 380, 381–83, 389,

Pius IX, Pope (cont'd)
450; death of, 391; and Law of Guarantees, 383
Pius XI, Pope, 450–51, 459
Pius XII (Eugenio Pacelli), Pope, 22 n., 451
Placentia, 18
Placidia, 18
Plague(s), 212–14, 216, 218
Plato (Platonism), 242, 243, 247, 249, 274
Platonic Academy, 242, 246, 247
Plays (playwriting). See Drama (plays)
Pletho, Gemistus, 242
Plombières, 367, 370
Podestàs, office of, 132–33, 134, 135–36, 189–90, 204
Poerio, Baron Carlo, 358
Poetry (poets), 210, 241, 245, 246, 273–74, 308–9, 323–24, 347–48, 406
Poggio (Bracciolini, Poggio), 243
Poland, 102, 110, 148, 314, 461–65, 466
Polish Succession, War of, 314
Politan (Angelo Poliziano), 244, 246, 247, 251, 279
Pollaiuolo, Antonio, 248
Pollentia, 11
Pontine Marshes, draining of, 452
Pontorma (Iacopo Carrucci), 294
Popolo, Il (Socialist newspaper), 428
Popolo d'Italia (Socialist newspaper), 412, 432, 433–34, 436, 437
Population growth, Middle Ages, 192
Pordenone, Giovanni Antonio da, 296
Portugal, 148
Preachers (preaching), 197, 224, 257 ff., 304–5. See also specific individuals
Press and communications (see also Newspapers); Mussolini and censorship of, 448, 449
Prince, The (Machiavelli), 272
Procopius, 27
Prosper of Aquitaine, 32
Protestantism (Protestant Reformation), 269, 286, 288–92, 296, 298, 317–18
Prussia, 341, 368, 369, 370, 381, 382, 389, 405, 412. See also Germany
Pseudo-Isidoran Decretals, 89–90
Pulci, Luigi, 246

Quadi, 11
Quanta cura (encyclical), 380
Quintilian, Institutiones of, 243

Radagaisus, 11
Radetzky, Marshal, 353–55, 357, 359
Radicals, 398, 409, 411, 412. See also Communists; Left; Socialism
Railroads (railway system), 377, 387, 388, 390, 398, 399, 404; strikes, 403, 409, 430, 437
Rapallo, Treaty of, 423, 445
Raphael (Raffaelo Sanzio), 274, 276, 277–79, 283, 284, 322
Raspe, Henry, Landgrave of Thuringia, 164
Rattazzi, Urbano, 361, 372, 376, 379, 390
Ravenna, 10, 11, 16, 25, 27, 31, 33, 36, 52, 58, 127, 163, 202, 207, 271, 301; Exarchate of, 36, 38, 43, 44, 52, 59, 64, 68, 69
Reconquest, wars of the, 32, 33, 41
Reformation, Protestant, 269, 288–92, 296, 298, 317–18
Reforms (reformation), 106–21, 141 ff., 150–51 (see also Counter-Reformation; Protestantism; Reformation, Protestant; specific aspects, individuals, locations); Great Schism and, 223–25; Italian independence and, 351 ff., 359 ff., 380, 385 ff., 397 ff., 402 ff., 404 ff.; Mussolini and, 428, 444–45, 448, 449 ff.; Napoleonic era, 327 ff., 338, 341, 344 ff.; religious, 106–21, 141 ff., 150–51, 223–25, 252, 257 ff., 262 ff., 268, 269, 288–92, 316–18 (see also specific aspects, popes); Renaissance era, 252, 257 ff., 262 ff., 268, 269, 288–92, 316–18
Reggio, 271, 333
Reggio Emilia, Socialist Congress (1912), 430
Regiomontano (mathematician), 284
Regionalism, 377–78, 387–88; lessening of, 392–93
Regula Sancta, 42
Religion, 7 ff., 24–31 ff., 48 ff., 196–97 (see also Christianity; Jews; Mohammed; Moslems; Roman Catholic Church; Papacy; specific aspects, churches, denominations); at end of Cinquecento, 298, 299, 303, 304–6, 316–18; Byzantine emphasis on, 37–

Index

Religion (cont'd)
53; reforms, 106–21, 141 ff., 150–51, 223–25, 252, 257 ff., 262 ff., 268, 269, 288–92, 316–18; Renaissance era, 230, 243–44

Renaissance, the (1400–1580), 230 ff. (see also Art(s); Literature; Painting, specific individuals, locations); Barbarian invasions (1494–1537), 253–71; Early (1400–1464), 233–44; end of, 286–97, 298 ff.; Florentine (1464–1492), 244–53; High (1499–1521), 272–86, 292 ff.; papacy and, 252 ff., 262 ff., 292 ff. (see also specific popes); transition from Middle Ages to, 195–220 ff.

Reni, Guido, *Aurora* painting by, 322

Republicans (republicanism), 259–60, 262, 287, 333 ff., 358 ff., 370 ff., 390, 391, 394, 395, 398, 410, 430–31, 437, 438

Rerum Novarum (encyclical), 399

Revolution (revolutionary movements), 331 ff., 348 ff., 357 ff., 370 ff., 373 ff., 395–96, 399–400, 428 (see also specific aspects, individuals, movements, parties); Mussolini and, 435 ff.

Reynolds, Sir Joshua, 322

Rheims, 86

Rhodes, 49

Riario, Raffaello Cardinal, 279

Ribbentrop, Joachim von, 460, 461, 463, 464, 471, 472

Riccardi Palazzo, 234

Richard, Count of Segni, 141–44

Ricimer, 18, 19

Rienzo, Cola di, 210–12

Right (Right Center), party of the, 377, 388, 390, 391, 394, 400–1, 402, 410, 483

Rimini, 207

Risacoli, Baron Bettino, 376, 379, 388

Risorgimento, 326 ff., 360 ff., 401

Risorgimento, Il (newspaper), 352, 360

Rivo Alto, 124

Robbery, 191, 301, 307, 321. See also Banditti

Robbia, Luca della, 238

Robert, King of Naples, 185, 186, 208

Robert (Guiscard), Prince, 111, 120

Robert of Geneva, Cardinal (Clement VII, anti-Pope), 222–23

Roger I (Guiscard), Count of Sicily, 111, 138

Roger II (Guiscard), King of Sicily, 111

Romagna, 144, 161, 261, 264, 370, 372–73, 410, 425

Roman Catholic Church, 7–8, 21 ff., 39 ff., 59 ff. (see also Christianity; Church; Papacy; Papal States; Rome; specific events, individuals, locations); and Constantinople (Byzantine), 30 ff. (see also Byzantine Empire; Constantinople); and Holy Roman Empire, 100 ff. (see also Holy Roman Empire); and Italian independence, 375–76, 379–84, 390, 396; Napoleonic era, 327; nationalism and, 406; Reformation, 288 ff., 296 (see also Counter-Reformation); Renaissance era, 230, 232–33

Roman Empire, 1 ff. (see also Holy Roman Empire; Rome; specific aspects, individuals, locations); Eastern, 6, 8, 9–16, 18, 21, 22, 78 ff. (see also Byzantine Empire; Constantinople); fall of, 1 ff.; invasion by barbarians, 1 ff.; revival of interest in classical heritage of, 209–12, 221 ff., 241 ff.; Western, 9 ff., 78 ff., 85 ff.

Romanesque style architecture, 202, 236, 237, 293

Romano, Alberic da, 161, 168

Romano, Eccelin da, 161, 168, 205

Romano, Giulio, 294

Roman Republic (Napoleonic era), 334

Roman Republic (1849), 355–57

Rome (the City), 4–5, 8, 10, 11, 12–16 ff., 22 ff., 25, 27, 32, 316, 321 (see also Papacy; Roman Catholic Church); Alaric and surrender of, 12–14; anarchy (end of ninth century), 90–99; Attila and, 16; becomes capital of Italy, 382; Charlemagne and, 58, 63–84, 85–86; Charles V and sack of (1527), 270–71, 282, 286; Frederick I and, 127, 134; Frederick II and, 163; Germany and, 101 ff.,

Rome (cont'd)
269–71; Gesù church, 293; Goths and, 31–32; and independence, 354–57, 359, 374, 375–76, 378–80, 381, 382–84; Jubilee (1300), 174–75, 180; Justinian and, 32; Lombards and Franks and, 36 ff., 58–59, 64 ff.; Montaigne's description of, 303–8, 309; Moslem attack on, 97; Mussolini and march on, 440–42; Napoleonic era, 330 ff., 334, 335, 341, 342, 343, 344, 345; papacy returns to, 218–19 ff.; Palatine Hill, Farnese Gardens, 293; plague in, 213, 270; plight in fourteenth century, 184–86, 187; Renaissance era, 252–53, 266 ff., 276–86, 288 ff.; and rise of cities, 127 ff.; sacked by Normans, 120–21; St. Peter's (see St. Peter's); Theodoric and, 32; Vandals and, 17 ff.; World War II, 478, 479, 481–82

Rommel, Field Marshal Erwin, 472, 473, 474
Romuald (son of Arachis, Duke of Benevento), 70–71
Romulus Augustulus, 1–4, 19, 78
Roncaglio, Diet of, 132–33
Roosevelt, Franklin D., 467, 478
Rospigliosi family, 318
Rossellino, Antonio, 248
Rossellino, Bernardo, 284
Rossetti, Gabriele, 347
Rossi, Pellegrino, 354
Rostovtzeff, M. I., 4 n., 7
Rothrude (daughter of Charlemagne), 70
Rovere, Francesco della. See Sixtus IV, Pope
Rovere, Giuliano della. See Julius II, Pope
Rovigo, 300
Rudini, Marquis di, 394, 397–400
Rudolph, Archduke of Austria, King of Germany, 181
Rudolph, Duke of Swabia, King of Germany, 117, 120
Ruffo, Cardinal, 336
Rugii (Rugians), 18–19, 24
Rumania, 380, 469
Russia. See Soviet Union

Sacred College of Cardinals. See Cardinals, Sacred College of
Sadowa, Battle of, 381
St. John Lateran (Basilica, Rome), 184, 185–86
St. Mark's, Venice, 124
St. Paul's, Rome, 97
St. Peter's, Rome, 43, 48, 66, 67, 73, 75–76, 77–78, 97, 103–4, 185, 277; Basilica, 29, 77–78, 276–77, 283, 284, 451
Salandra, Antonio, 410, 411, 413, 415, 433, 442
Salerno, 71, 93, 99, 110, 111, 123; University of (medicine), 155, 198; World War II landing, 479
Salò Republic, 480, 481
Sangallo, Francesco da, 285
Sangallo, Giuliano da, 248, 284, 285
Sangro, Duke di, 331
San Lorenzo Church, Florence, 236, 281, 282
San Marco, convent of, Florence, 235
San Martino, Battle of, 372
Sansovino, Jacopo Tatti, 293, 295
Sant' Angelo Castel, 271
Saracco, P., 401, 402
Saracens, 37, 97, 110, 111, 154, 161, 167, 169, 232, 233
Saracenic civilization, 232, 233
Sardinia, 36, 41, 138, 315–16, 346, 372, 373, 403
Sarfatti, Margherita, 427
Sarpi, Fra Paolo, 311–12
Sarus, 13
Savonarola, Girolamo, 247, 249, 257–59, 268
Savoy, County of, 195
Savoy, Duchy and Dukes of, 127, 195, 287–88, 315, 401, 402; and independence, 350, 367, 373; and Sardinia, 315–16; and Sicily, 314; and Spain, 287–88, 314, 315
Savoy, House of, 195, 441
Saxons, 114, 117–18
Saxony, 84, 100
Scaglieri, Can Grande, 205–6
Scaglieri, Mastino, 206–7
Scaglieri family, 205–7, 210, 227
Scarlatti, Alessandro, 325
Scarlatti, Domenico, 325

Index

Schisms: (717–867), 49 ff.; (1378), 220–25
Scholasticism, 198 n., 230, 231, 242, 318
Schools (*see also* Education), 94–95; clerical, 94–95
Schuschnigg (Austrian Chancellor), 457
Science(s), 244, 318, 319–20
Scienza nuova (Vico), 320
Sciri, 18–19
Scot, Michael, 155
Sculpture (sculptors), 201–4, 235, 237–38, 248–49, 272, 279–82, 283–84, 294, 295, 298
Secret societies, 338, 345
Sedan, Battle of, 382
Seeck, Otto, 1 n.
Senate, Roman, 12, 16, 17, 18, 19, 20, 25, 28, 34, 90–91, 170, 211
Seneca, 231, 235
Serbia, 410–11, 421
Sergius III, Pope, 92
Severus, Emperor, 18
Sforza, Alessandro, 251
Sforza, Count, 423
Sforza, Francesco, 251–52, 255, 275
Sforza, Galeazzo Maria, 255
Sforza, Lodovico ("the Moor"), 255–56, 276
Sforza family, 251–52, 255–56, 264, 275. *See also* specific members by name
Shipping trade, 190, 192–95, 227–28, 260
"Short Armistice" (World War II), 478 n.
Siccardi Laws, 361
Sicilian Vespers (1283), 174, 187
Sicily, 14, 24, 25, 31–32, 36, 41, 49, 69, 97, 111, 129, 130, 136–39, 141–47, 148, 150, 153 ff., 166–70, 173–74, 186–87, 200, 205, 208–9, 226, 228, 255, 261–62, 403 (*see also* Two Sicilies); and independence, 352, 355, 374, 379, 387, 390, 392; Napoleonic era, 331, 336, 342; revolts by peasants in, 395–96, 399; Savoy and, 314; Spain and, 286, 314; World War II, 476
Sidi Barrani, 469, 470
Siena, 152, 187, 228, 287, 302; architecture, 202; plague in, 213; University of, 330
Siena, Roland, Cardinal of, 131, 133
Sigismund, Emperor, 223–24, 225 n.
Silvester I, Pope, 59–61
Silvester II, Pope, 284
Simony, 106–7, 109, 112–21
Sinkhovitch, V. G., 1 n.
Sistine Chapel, 250, 278, 284; Michelangelo and, 280–81, 282; Raphael's tapestries in, 278
Sixtus IV, Pope, 250, 263–64, 265, 266, 284
Sixtus V, Pope, 316
Slaves (slavery), 93; Roman Empire, 5, 7, 12, 13, 16
Sobieski, John, King of Poland, 312
Social and Economic History of the Roman Empire (Rostovtzeff), 4 n.
Socialism (Socialists), 390, 391, 394, 395–96, 398 ff., 405, 410, 411, 412–13, 415 (*see also* Socialist Party); Mussolini and, 425 ff., 445
Socialist Congress (1912), 429
Socialist Party, 429–40, 445, 446–47, 482. *See also* Socialism (Socialists)
Social life, 199–200, 273, 308–10, 320–21. *See also* Art(s); Crime; Morality; specific aspects
Society of Jesus. *See* Jesuits (Society of Jesus)
Socrates, 247
Soddu, Ubaldo, 470
Sodoma of Siena, 294
Soldiers, mercenary, 214–16
Solferino, 372
Somaliland, 423, 454, 469, 470, 471
Sonnino, Sidney, 403–4, 407, 412, 415, 421, 423
South America, 317
Soviet Union, 335, 337, 341, 362, 368, 380, 464; Germany and, 457, 464, 465, 466, 469, 471, 472, 473, 475; Mussolini and, 471, 472, 473; Revolution (1917), 434; and Spanish Civil War, 456; World War I, 411, 414, 416; World War II, 465, 466, 469, 471, 472, 473, 475
"Spagnoletto, Lo" (Ribera), 322–23
Spain, 15, 20, 44, 47, 58, 80, 97, 163, 226, 253, 255, 256–57, 261, 286, 289–90, 291, 292, 310, 313, 314, 315, 318, 390 (*see also* specific individuals); invasions of Italy by, 253, 255, 256–57, 261, 286, 289–90,

Spain (cont'd)
    292; and Italian independence, 355, 358–59; and Italy, Napoleonic era, 330, 334, 336, 341, 345; Mussolini and Civil War in, 455–56, 460
Spalatro, Council of (925), 96
Spanish Succession, War of, 313, 314
Speyer, 118
Spezzia, 364
Spoleto (Spoletum), 35, 36, 43, 45, 65, 68, 69–70, 73, 74, 91, 93, 127, 144; Frederick II and, 162–63; Gregory VII and, 114, 115
Squadre (Black Shirts), 437–39, 440, 442
Stablo, Abbot of, 74
Staroselo, 417
States of the Church. *See* Papal States
Stephen II, Pope, 58–59, 64
Stephen IV, Pope, 86
Stephen VI, Pope, 91–92
Stephen IX, Pope, 109
Stilicho, 9–10, 11, 12
Storie Fiorentine (Machiavelli), 272
Stradivarius, 326
Strasbourg Oaths, 84
Strozzi Palace, 248
Sudan, 397
Sudetenland, 458–59
Suffrage, 390, 392, 399, 409. *See also* Elections
Summa Theologica (Aquinas), 201
Superstition(s), 40–41, 96, 296, 298, 386
Susa, 135
Swabia, 84, 100
Switzerland, 391, 403
Syllabus (1864), 380, 382
Syracuse, 154
Syria, 36, 49, 123

Tagliamento River line, World War I, 417
Talleyrand, Prince, 340 ff.
Taranto, 470
Tancred, Count of Lecce, 137, 138, 141
Tannucci, and reforms in Naples, 330–31
Tasso, Torquato, 273, 294–95
Taxes (taxation), 5–6, 27, 32, 33, 52, 82, 155, 175–76, 191, 212, 228, 311, 312; Italian independence and, 377, 389, 390, 392, 394, 395, 397, 409; Napoleonic era, 327, 330, 339; Mussolini and, 445; Spain in Italy and, 286–87; World War I and, 436

Terra cotta sculpture, 238
Teutberga (wife of Lothair, King of Lotharingia), 87–88
Teutonic tribes. *See* Germanic (Teutonic) tribes
Thegan (biographer), 86
Theodatus, 31
Theodoric, King of the Ostrogoths, 24–31, 32
Theodosius I, 9, 10
Theophanes (chronicler), 77–78
Theophano (wife of Otto II), 105
Theophylact, 92
Thirty Years' War, 317–18
Thomas Aquinas, St., 1 n., 198–99, 201, 231, 235, 241, 304
Thomism, 198 n., 230, 231. *See also* Scholasticism
Thrace, 36
Tibaldeschi, Cardinal, 221
Tiberius, Emperor, 35
Ticino, 391
Ticinum (Pavia), 39
Tiepolo, defeat at Cortenuova of, 161
Tiepolo, Giovanni Batista, 323
Tintoretto (Iacopo Robusti), 296
Tirana, Albania, fall of, 460
Titian, 296
Tittoni, Tommaso, 423
Tobacco Riots, Milan, 352
Tobruk, 470
Toledo, Padre, 305
Tolentino, battle of, 342
Tortona, 128–29, 132
Totila, 31–32
Toulouse, 14
Toward the Understanding of Jesus (Sinkhovitch), 1 n.
Trade, 93–94, 112, 122 ff., 188, 190–95, 199, 227–28, 230, 260, 296, 343. *See also* Commerce; Industry
Transformism, 403
"Translation of the Empire," 78–80
Transpadane Republic, 333
Transubstantiation, doctrine of, 222
Trentino (Trent), 394, 407, 412, 413, 419, 420, 428. *See also* Trent, Council of
Trent, Council of (1545), 290–91, 312, 316
Treves (editor, *Avanti!*), 430
Treviso, 127, 134

Index

Tribur, 118
Trier, 15
Trieste, 391, 394, 412, 415, 416, 419, 420
Tripartite Pact, 473
Triple Alliance, 392, 393, 394, 395, 407, 411–12, 413
Tripolitania, 429–30
Tunis (Tunisia), 392, 468
Turin, 126–27, 195, 288, 332, 341, 342–43, 346, 347; capital at, 378, 379, 380, 390; and independence, 353, 354, 360, 370, 390
Turkey, 260, 263, 288, 310, 312–13, 362, 407, 408, 409, 421, 429
Tuscan language, 245, 295; as "Italian language", 201, 295
Tuscany, 71, 91, 92, 93, 112, 119, 123, 127, 144, 145, 146, 152, 161, 168, 169, 170, 184, 190, 200, 314 (*see also* specific cities); architecture, 202; Austria and, 314; and independence, 351, 353 ff., 359, 370, 372 ff., 377, 381; language, 201; Medici and, 235, 314; Montaigne on, 301–2; Napoleonic era, 327–30, 334, 336, 341, 344; painting, 203; plague in, 213; Renaissance era, 235, 237; school of sculpture, 202
Tusculum, 137
Two Sicilies, Kingdom of, 136–39, 141–47, 150, 151 ff., 166–70, 172, 173–74, 186–87, 208–9, 226 (*see also* Naples; Sicily); and independence, 345–46, 348, 352, 354, 355, 360 ff., 373 ff., 377 ff., 387; Napoleonic era, 331, 335, 342, 344; Spain and, 261–62, 331, 345–46
Tyrol, 391

Uccello, Paolo, 238
Udo of Treves, 117–18
Ugolino, Cardinal, 157
Umberto I, King, 481, 482
Umbria, 161, 184 (*see also* specific cities); league of cities of, 184
Unam sanctam (papal bull, 1302), 177
Unions, labor, 396, 439; *fasci*, 396
United States: World War I, 416, 419–24; World War II, 467, 473, 474–75, 478–82
Universities, 197–99, 231, 233, 241, 330

UNRRA (United Nations Relief and Rehabilitation Administration), 482
Urban IV, Pope, 168
Urban VI (Schismatic Pope), 221–22, 224 n.
Urban VIII, Pope, 317, 319–20
Urbino, 251, 273, 274, 287
Utrecht and Rastadt, Treaties of, 314
Uzzano, Niccolo da, 229

Valens, 9
Valentinian III, 15, 16–17
Valla, Laurentius, 60 n.
Valla, Lorenzo, 283
Valona, 420
Vandals, 9, 11, 15 ff., 25
Vasari, Giorgio, 287, 293; on Renaissance artists, 235–36, 238, 239, 240, 241, 249, 251, 277, 280, 282, 283, 284, 293
Vatican (*see also* Papacy); Lateran Treaty (1929), 450–51; Library, 252–53, 271, 284, 304; papacy and Renaissance art, 283–84
Vecchio Palazzio, Florence, 248, 249, 258
Venetia, 35, 52, 68, 72 (*see also* Venice); and independence, 353, 364, 370, 372, 386; Napoleonic era, 336, 341, 343
Venetian school of painting, 323
Venice, 36, 52, 93, 112, 123, 124, 125, 134, 148–49, 168, 174, 187, 188, 190, 193–95, 207, 208, 210, 226, 227, 271, 298, 321; architecture, 293, 295; Arsenal (fleet), 227–28; art, 295, 296, 323; barbarian invasions, 260–61; Council of Ten, 312; decline of, 310–13; Doge, 330; and Genoa, 226–29; government, 193–95, 227, 330; Great Council, 194–95, 312, 330; and independence, 353, 354, 357, 374, 375, 378, 379, 380–81; Montaigne in, 299, 300, 309; Napoleonic era, 330, 333, 336, 343; and papacy, 310–11, 312; social life, 321; trade (commerce), 190, 193–95, 227–28, 260; and Turkey, 288, 310, 312–13; warfare, 226–29, 260–61, 310, 312–13
Venice, Peace of, 135
Vercelli, Bishop of, 96
Verdun, Treaty of, 84–85

Verona, 16, 32, 65, 127, 134, 161, 170, 205–7, 227, 228, 229, 261, 299; and independence, 372
Veronese, Paolo, 296
Veronica, St., veil of, 305
Verrocchio (Andrea de Michele Cione), 248–49, 275, 295
Vicenza, 16, 127, 134, 161, 206, 299
Vico, Giambattista, 320
Victor II, Pope, 109
Victor IV, anti-Pope, 133
Victor Amadeus III, King, 326–27
Victor Emmanuel I, King, 341, 342, 343, 344–45, 346–47
Victor Emmanuel II, King, 355, 360, 361, 362, 364, 366, 367, 369, 370, 372–75, 376, 379–80, 381, 384, 385, 388, 390; death of, 391, given title of King of Italy, 375
Victor Emmanuel III, King, 402, 403, 409, 434, 440, 442, 443, 451, 459, 460–61, 462, 475–78, 479, 480; transfers power to Prince Umberto, 481
Victoria, Queen, 369
Vienna, Congress of (1814), 411
Vienna, Peace of, 314–15
Vignola (Giacomo Barozzi), 292–93
Villafranca, 372
Villani, Giovanni, 172, 180–81, 200
Vincent Ferrer, St., 222
Violin making, 325–26
Virgil, 231, 235, 242, 243; *Aeneid*, 13–14
Virgin of the Rocks (Leonardo da Vinci), 275–76
Visconti, Bernabo, 217–18
Visconti, Galeazzo II, 218, 228–29
Visconti, Gian Galeazzo II, 218, 229
Visconti, Giovanni, 216
Visconti family, 207–8, 210, 216–18, 228–29. *See also* specific members by name
Visigoths (West Goths), 14, 18, 20, 24
Visit of the Magi (Gozzoli), 250

Viterbo, 159, 163, 168
Vittorio Veneto, Battle of, 419, 421

Walter, Count of Brienne, 141
Walter of Brienne ("Duke of Athens"), 229
Wal-Wal, 454
Werner (mercenary soldier), 215
Westphalia, Treaty of (1648), 317–18
William, Count of Holland, 164–65, 166, 170
William, King (son of Tancred, Count of Lecce), 138
William I, Emperor of Germany, 390
William of Nogaret, 178
William the Conqueror (William I), 120, 129–30
Wilson, Woodrow, 419–23, 435, 436; Manifesto to the Italian People by, 422–23
Wipa (German writer, ninth century), 94
Wood trade, 190
World War I, 410–24; Mussolini and, 432–36
World War II, 465–83
Worms, Council of (1076), 115
Worms, Diet at (1520), 269
Wotton, Sir Henry, 312
Wyclif, John, 223, 232

Young Fascists (clubs), 449
Young Italy, 349–50
Yugoslavia, 421–22, 423–24, 445, 469, 471

Zacharias, Pope, 58
Zanardelli, Giuseppe, 402
Zara, 149
Zeno, Carlo, 227
Zeno, Emperor, 19, 24, 25
Zimisces, John, Emperor, 105
Zog, King of Albania, 460
Zosimus, 9